MODELING AND OPTIMIZATION OF PARALLEL AND DISTRIBUTED EMBEDDED SYSTEMS

MODELING AND OPTIMIZATION OF PARALLEL AND DISTRIBUTED EMBEDDED SYSTEMS

Arslan Munir

University of Nevada, Reno, USA

Ann Gordon-Ross

University of Florida, Gainesville, USA

Sanjay Ranka

University of Florida, Gainesville, USA

IEEE PRESS

This edition first published 2016

© 2016 John Wiley & Sons Ltd

Registered office
John Wiley & Sons Ltd, The Atrium, Southern Gate, Chichester, West Sussex, PO19 8SQ, United Kingdom

For details of our global editorial offices, for customer services and for information about how to apply for permission to reuse the copyright material in this book please see our website at www.wiley.com.

Library of Congress Cataloging-in-Publication Data applied for.

ISBN: 9781119086413

A catalogue record for this book is available from the British Library.

Cover Image: PaulPaladin, Plus69/Getty

Set in 10/12pt, TimesLTStd by SPi Global, Chennai, India.
Printed and bound in Singapore by Markono Print Media Pte Ltd

1   2016

To our families

Contents

Part II   MODELING

Preface

Advancements in silicon technology, micro-electro-mechanical systems (MEMS), wireless communications, computer networking, and digital electronics have led to the proliferation of embedded systems in a plethora of application domains (e.g., industrial and home automation, automotive, space, medical, and defense). To meet the diverse application requirements of these application domains, novel trends have emerged in embedded systems. One such trend is networking single-unit embedded systems to form a multiple-unit embedded system, also referred to as a *distributed embedded system*. Given the collective computing capabilities of the single-unit embedded systems, the distributed embedded system enables more sophisticated applications of greater value as compared to an isolated single-unit embedded system. An emerging trend is to connect these distributed embedded systems via a wireless network instead of a bulky, wired networking infrastructure. Another emerging trend in embedded systems is to leverage multicore/manycore architectures to meet the continuously increasing performance demands of many application domains (e.g., medical imaging, mobile signal processing). Both single-unit and distributed embedded systems can leverage multicore architectures for attaining high performance and energy efficiency. Since processing is done in parallel with multicore-based embedded systems, these systems are being termed as *parallel embedded systems*. The burgeoning of multicore architectures in embedded systems induces parallel computing into the embedded domain, which was previously used predominantly in the supercomputing domain only. In some applications, parallel embedded systems are networked together to form *parallel and distributed embedded systems*. For both parallel and distributed embedded systems, modeling and optimization at various design levels (e.g., verification, simulation, analysis) are of paramount significance. Considering the short time-to-market for many embedded systems, often embedded system designers resort to modeling approaches for the evaluation of design alternatives in terms of performance, power, reliability, and/or scalability.

About This Book

Embedded computers have advanced well beyond the early days of 8-bit microcontrollers. Contemporary embedded computers are organized into multiprocessors that execute millions of lines of code in real time and at very low power levels. This book targets *parallel and distributed embedded systems*, which have been enabled by technological advances in silicon technology, MEMS, wireless communications, computer networking, and digital electronics.

These parallel and distributed embedded systems have applications in various domains, such as military and defense, medical, automotive, and unmanned autonomous vehicles.

This book discusses parallel and distributed embedded systems with a main focus on three *design metrics*:

- Performance
- Power
- Dependability

Often design metrics have conflicting resource requirements, and the interplay between these design metrics presents interesting research challenges.

The emphasis of this book is on modeling and optimization of emerging parallel and distributed embedded systems with respect to these design metrics.[1] To illustrate the modeling and optimization of distributed embedded systems, we present our work on modeling and optimization of embedded sensor nodes in embedded wireless sensor networks (EWSNs). This book discusses optimization strategies employed in EWSNs at different design levels to meet application requirements, such as lifetime, throughput, and reliability. To illustrate modeling in distributed embedded systems, we discuss an application metrics estimation model that estimates high-level application metrics (e.g., lifetime, throughput) from low-level sensor node tunable parameters (e.g., processor voltage and frequency) and the sensor node's hardware internals (e.g., transceiver voltage, transceiver receive current). We discuss Markov Decision Process (MDP) for dynamic optimization of embedded sensor nodes in EWSNs to more closely adhere to application requirements. MDP is suitable for the dynamic optimization of the embedded sensor nodes because of MDP's inherent ability to perform dynamic decision making.

To enable in situ autonomous EWSN dynamic optimizations, we examine an online EWSN optimization methodology that extends static design time *parameter tuning*. Parameter tuning is the process of determining appropriate *parameter values* (e.g., processor voltage, processor frequency, sensing frequency) that meet application requirements. Static tuning optimizes an EWSN at deployment time and remains fixed for the EWSN's lifetime. Whereas static optimizations are suitable for stable/predictable applications, static optimizations are inflexible and do not adapt to changing application requirements and environmental stimuli. Our proposed methodology is advantageous over static design time parameter tuning because our methodology enables the embedded sensor node to automatically adapt to actual changing environmental stimuli, resulting in closer adherence to application requirements. Since many application designers are nonexperts (e.g., agriculturist, biologists) and lack sufficient expertise for parameter tuning, autonomous parameter tuning methodologies may alleviate many of these design challenges. Our methodology is more amenable to nonexpert application designers and requires no application designer effort after initial EWSN deployment. We develop lightweight (low computational and memory resources) online algorithms for the optimization methodology. These lightweight algorithms are crucial for embedded sensor nodes considering limited processing, storage, and energy resources of embedded sensor nodes in distributed EWSNs. We further discuss modeling and analysis of fault detection and fault tolerance (FT) in EWSNs.

---

[1] Major portion of this book stems from the Ph.D. dissertation of Dr. Arslan Munir at the University of Florida, Gainesville, USA.

This book elaborates on various high-performance and energy-efficient techniques at the architecture, middleware, and software levels for parallel multicore-based embedded systems. To elucidate the modeling of parallel embedded systems, this book discusses in detail our proposed queueing theoretic approach for modeling the performance of multicore embedded systems. This modeling technique enables quick and inexpensive architectural evaluation in terms of both design time and resources as compared to developing and/or using existing multicore simulators and running benchmarks on these simulators. Based on a preliminary evaluation using our model, architecture designers can run targeted benchmarks to further verify the performance characteristics of selected multicore architectures (i.e., our queueing theory-based model facilitates early design space pruning).

The book elucidates performance aspects of parallel multicore-based embedded systems by performance analysis of contemporary multicore embedded architectures: symmetric multiprocessors (SMPs) and tiled multicore architectures (TMAs). We compare the performance of SMPs and TMAs based on a parallelized information fusion application, a Gaussian elimination, and embarrassingly parallel benchmarks. We provide a quantitative comparison of these two architectures based on the calculations of various device metrics (e.g., computational density (CD), CD per watt (CD/W), internal memory bandwidth (IMB), and external memory bandwidth (EMB)). Although a quantitative comparison provides a high-level evaluation of the computational capabilities of the architectures, our work provides deeper insights based on parallelized benchmark-driven evaluation.

To illustrate parallel and distributed embedded systems with a unifying example, we discuss an architecture for heterogeneous hierarchical multicore embedded wireless sensor networks (MCEWSNs). We elaborate several compute-intensive tasks, such as information fusion, encryption, network coding, and software-defined radio, which will benefit in particular from the increased computation power offered by multicore embedded sensor nodes. We characterize and discuss various application domains for MCEWSNs. The book concludes with the research challenges and future research directions for parallel and distributed embedded systems.

Highlights

This book focuses on modeling, analysis, and optimization of parallel and distributed embedded systems. To illustrate the modeling and optimization of distributed embedded systems, we focus on modeling and optimization of distributed EWSNs. Specifically, we target dynamic optimization methodologies based on the sensor node tunable parameter value settings for EWSNs. We elaborate additional modeling issues in parallel embedded systems, which have come into existence owing to the burgeoning multicore/manycore revolution, by our performance modeling of multicore parallel embedded systems.

The highlights of this book include the following:

Overview of Parallel and Distributed Embedded Systems

The book gives an overview of parallel and distributed embedded systems and narrates the application of these embedded systems in various application domains.

Multicore-Based EWSNs—An Example of Parallel and Distributed Embedded Systems:
We deliberate on the feasibility and application of multicore parallel architectures as processing units in distributed embedded sensor nodes. We propose a MCEWSN architecture based on multicore embedded sensor nodes, which serves as an example of parallel and distributed embedded systems. Furthermore, we summarize the multicore initiative in EWSNs by academia and industry.

Modeling of Parallel and Distributed Embedded Systems

The book includes various chapters illustrating modeling of parallel and distributed embedded systems.

Application Metrics Estimation Model: The book discusses an application metrics estimation model that estimates high-level application metrics (e.g., lifetime, throughput) from low-level embedded sensor node tunable parameters and the embedded sensor node's hardware internals (e.g., processor voltage and frequency). Our dynamic optimization methodologies for embedded sensor nodes leverage this estimation model while comparing different operating states for optimization purposes.

Modeling and Analysis of Fault Detection and Fault Tolerance: The book illustrates the modeling of reliable embedded systems via modeling of fault detection and FT in EWSNs. We propose an FT sensor node model consisting of duplex sensors (i.e., one active sensor and one inactive spare sensor), which exploits the synergy of fault detection and FT.

Queueing Theoretic Modeling of Multicore-Based Parallel Embedded Architectures: The book proposes a queueing theory-based modeling technique for evaluating multicore parallel embedded architectures. The modeling technique would enable quick and inexpensive architectural evaluation in terms of both design time and resources as compared to developing and/or using existing multicore simulators and running benchmarks on these simulators.

Optimization of Parallel and Distributed Embedded Systems

The book includes various chapters illustrating optimizations of parallel and distributed embedded systems.

Optimization Approaches in Distributed Embedded Systems: The book discusses various optimization approaches in distributed embedded systems focusing on distributed EWSNs.

Performance and Energy Optimizations for Parallel Embedded Systems: We elaborate on performance and energy optimizations for parallel embedded systems. Although the literature discusses high-performance parallel computing for supercomputers, there exists little discussion on high-performance energy-efficient parallel embedded computing.

Dynamic Optimization Methodologies: We explore dynamic optimization methodologies for distributed embedded systems with EWSNs as an example. First, we propose an MDP-based dynamic optimization methodology for embedded sensor nodes. MDP is suitable for EWSN dynamic optimization because of MDP's inherent ability to perform dynamic decision making. We then present online algorithms for dynamic optimization of embedded sensor nodes in distributed EWSNs. Lightweight (low computational and memory resources) online algorithms for design space exploration are crucial for embedded sensor nodes considering the limited processing, storage, and energy resources of embedded sensor nodes. We discuss a lightweight dynamic optimization methodology for embedded sensor nodes that intelligently selects appropriate initial tunable parameter value settings by evaluating the application's unique requirements, the relative importance of these requirements with respect to each other, and the magnitude in which each parameter affects each requirement.

Analysis and Optimization of Parallel Embedded Systems: The book conducts a performance analysis of parallel embedded systems focusing on SMPs and TMAs—an architectural innovation in the multicore technology—based on parallelized benchmarks. We identify key architecture and software optimizations to attain high performance from parallel embedded systems focusing on TMAs. We discuss the performance optimizations on a single tile (processor core) as well as on parallel performance optimizations, such as application decomposition, cache locality, tile locality, memory balancing, and horizontal communication for TMAs. We elaborate on compiler-based optimizations that are applicable to TMAs, such as function inlining, loop unrolling, and feedback-based optimizations. We present a case study using optimized dense matrix multiplication algorithms for TMAs to experimentally demonstrate the performance and performance per watt optimizations on TMAs.

Intended Audience

The book is mainly aimed as a reference book for students and researchers in embedded systems. The book's main target audience consists of senior undergraduate students, graduate students, and researchers involved in embedded systems research. Some chapters of the book contain advanced material suitable for senior undergraduate students, graduate students, and researchers in computer engineering or computer science; however, the book also contains several introductory chapters that do not require any deep knowledge of embedded systems to follow the material. The book can be considered as a mix of introductory and advanced materials on embedded systems.

Organization of the Book

This book is organized into three parts:

- Overview
- Modeling
- Optimization

The "Overview" part provides an introduction to embedded systems, modeling, and optimization of parallel and distributed embedded systems. The "Modeling" and "Optimization" parts illustrate modeling and optimization issues, respectively, through EWSNs and multicore. Following is the description of the organization of the chapters into three parts of the book.

The "Overview" part consists of Chapters 1 and 2. Chapter 1 gives an overview of parallel and distributed embedded systems. Chapter 2 proposes an MCEWSN architecture based on multicore embedded sensor nodes. The MCEWSN architecture serves as an example for parallel and distributed embedded systems. The chapter then summarizes the multicore and parallel computing initiatives in EWSNs by academia and industry.

The "Modeling" part consists of Chapters 3–5. Chapter 3 presents an application metrics estimation model for distributed EWSN. Modeling and analysis of fault detection and fault tolerance in EWSNs are presented in Chapter 4. Chapter 5 discusses a novel, queueing theory-based modeling technique for evaluating multicore embedded architectures for parallel embedded systems.

The "Optimization" part consists of Chapters 6–12. Chapter 6 discusses various optimization approaches in distributed embedded systems focusing on distributed EWSNs. Various performance and energy optimizations for parallel multicore embedded systems are discussed in Chapter 7. The MDP-based dynamic optimization methodology for embedded sensor nodes in distributed EWSNs is presented in Chapter 8. Online algorithms for embedded sensor node's tunable parameter-based dynamic optimization are presented in Chapter 9. Chapter 10 presents a lightweight dynamic optimization methodology for embedded sensor nodes in distributed EWSNs. Chapter 11 evaluates performance of parallel embedded systems leveraging SMPs and TMAs based on parallelized benchmarks. Chapter 12 identifies key architecture and software optimizations to attain high performance from parallel embedded systems and illustrates these optimizations via a case study of dense matrix multiplication on TMAs. Finally, Chapter 13 concludes this book.

Acknowledgment

This work was supported in part by the National Science Foundation (CNS-0953447 and CNS-0905308). Any opinions, findings, and conclusions or recommendations expressed in this material are those of the authors and do not necessarily reflect the views of the National Science Foundation. This work was also supported in part by the US Department of Energy, National Nuclear Security Administration, and Advanced Simulation and Computing Program, as a Cooperative Agreement under the Predictive Science Academic Alliance Program, under Contract No. DE-NA0002378.

Part One

Overview

1

Introduction*

The word "embedded" literally means "within," so embedded systems are information processing systems *within* (embedded into) other systems. In other words, an embedded system is a system that uses a computer to perform a specific task but are neither used nor perceived as a computer. Essentially, an embedded system is virtually any computing system other than a desktop or a server computer. Embedded systems have links to physical components/systems, which distinguishes them from traditional desktop and server computing [1]. Embedded systems possess a large number of common characteristics such as real-time constraints, dependability, and power/energy efficiency.

Embedded systems can be classified based on functionality as transformational, reactive, or interactive [2]. *Transformational* embedded systems take input data and transform the data into output data. *Reactive* embedded systems react continuously to their environment at the speed of the environment, whereas *interactive* embedded systems react with their environment at their own speed.

Embedded systems can be classified based on orchestration/architecture as *single-unit* or *multi-unit/distributed* and/or *parallel* embedded systems. Single-unit embedded systems refer to embedded systems that possess computational capabilities and interact with the physical world via sensors and actuators, but are fabricated on a single chip and are enclosed in a single package. Multi-unit embedded systems, also referred to as *distributed embedded systems*, consist of a large number of physically distributed nodes that possess computation capabilities, interact with the physical world via a set of sensors and actuators, and communicate with each other via a wired or wireless network. An emerging trend is to connect these distributed embedded systems via a wireless network instead of a bulky, wired networking infrastructure. Cyber-physical systems (CPSs) and embedded wireless sensor networks (EWSNs) are typical examples of distributed embedded systems.

To meet the continuously increasing performance demands of many application domains (e.g., medical imaging, mobile signal processing), many embedded systems leverage multicore (manycore) architectures. Since processing is done in parallel in multicore-based embedded

*A portion of this chapter appeared in: Arslan Munir, Sanjay Ranka, and Ann Gordon-Ross, Modeling of Scalable Embedded Systems, CH 29 in *Scalable Computing and Communications: Theory and Practice*, Samee U. Khan, Lizhe Wang, and Albert Y. Zomaya (Eds.), ISBN: 978-1-1181-6265-1, John Wiley & Sons, pp. 629–657, January 2013.

systems, these embedded systems are often referred to as *parallel embedded systems*. Often parallel embedded systems are networked together to form *parallel and distributed embedded systems*. The burgeoning multicore revolution in computing industry is the main thrust behind the emergence of these parallel and distributed embedded systems. The multicore innovation in computer industry has induced parallel computing in embedded domain, which was previously used predominantly in supercomputing domain only. Parallel and distributed embedded systems have proliferated in a wide variety of application domains. These application domains include military, health, ecology, environment, industrial automation, transportation, control, and medical, to name a few.

Embedded systems often require specific quantifiable design goals, such as real-time constraints, performance, power/energy consumption, and cost. In order to design embedded computer systems to meet these quantifiable goals, designers realize that no one system is best for all embedded applications. Different requirements lead to different trade-offs between performance and power, hardware and software, and so on. Different implementations need to be created to meet the requirements of a family of applications. Solutions should be programmable enough to make the embedded design flexible and long-lived, but not provide unnecessary flexibility that would impede meeting the application requirements [3]. To meet various design goals, embedded systems design requires optimization of hardware and software. In particular, performance and power optimizations are required for many embedded applications. Embedded systems leverage various techniques to optimize and manage power in embedded systems. These techniques include, but are not limited to, power-aware high-level language compilers, dynamic power management policies, memory management schemes, and bus encoding techniques [4].

Embedded systems design is traditionally power-centric, but there has been a recent shift toward high-performance embedded computing (HPEC) due to the proliferation of compute-intensive embedded applications. For example, the signal processing for a 3G mobile handset requires 35–40 giga operations per second (GOPS) for a 14.4 Mbps channel and 210–290 GOPS for a 100 Mbps orthogonal frequency-division multiplexing (OFDM) channel. Considering the limited energy of a mobile handset battery, these performance levels must be met with a power dissipation budget of approximately 1 W, which translates to a performance efficiency of 25 mW/GOPS or 25 pJ/operation for the 3G receiver and 3–5 pJ/operation for the OFDM receiver [5, 6]. These demanding and competing power–performance requirements make modern embedded systems design challenging.

The high-performance energy-efficient embedded computing (HPEEC) domain addresses the unique design challenges of high-performance and low-power/energy embedded computing. The HPEEC domain can be termed as high-performance *green* computing; however, green may refer to a bigger notion of environmental impact. The high-performance and low-power design challenges are competing because high performance typically requires maximum processor speeds with enormous energy consumption, whereas low power typically requires nominal or low processor speeds that offer modest performance. HPEEC requires thorough consideration of the thermal design power (TDP) and processor frequency relationship while selecting an appropriate processor for an embedded application. For example, decreasing the processor frequency by a fraction of the maximum operating frequency (e.g., reducing from 3.16 to 3.0 GHz) can cause 10% performance degradation but can decrease power consumption by 30–40% [7]. To meet HPEEC power–performance requirements, embedded systems design has transitioned from a single-core paradigm to a multicore paradigm that favors multiple low-power cores running at low processor speeds rather than a single high-speed power-hungry core. The multicore embedded systems have integrated HPEEC and parallel computing into high-performance energy-efficient parallel embedded computing (HPEPEC) domain.

HPEPEC domain encompasses both single-unit and multi-unit distributed embedded systems. Chip multiprocessors (CMPs) provide a scalable HPEPEC platform as performance can be increased by increasing the number of cores as long as the increase in the number of cores offsets the clock frequency reduction by maintaining a given performance level with less power [8]. Multiprocessor systems-on-chip (MPSoCs), which are multiprocessor version of systems-on-chip (SoCs), are another alternative HPEPEC platform, which provide an unlimited combination of homogeneous and heterogeneous cores. Though both CMPs and MPSoCs are HPEPEC platforms, MPSoCs differ from CMPs in that MPSoCs provide custom architectures (including specialized instruction sets) tailored for meeting peculiar requirements of specific embedded applications (e.g., real-time, throughput-intensive, reliability-constrained). Both CMPs and MPSoCs rely on HPEPEC hardware/software techniques for delivering high performance per watt and meeting diverse application requirements.

Although HPEPEC enables more sophisticated embedded applications and meets better competing performance and energy requirements, HPEPEC further complicates embedded systems design. Embedded systems design is highly challenging as the interaction with the environment, timing of the operations, communication network, and peculiar application requirements that may need integration of on-chip hardwired and/or reconfigurable units have to be considered. Both hardware and software designs of embedded systems are complex, for example, current automotive embedded systems contain more than 100 million lines of code. Multicore—a crucial enabler for HPEPEC—while providing performance and energy benefits further aggravates design challenges of embedded systems. While industry focuses on increasing the number of on-chip processor cores to meet customer performance demands, this increasing number of cores has led to an exponential increase in design complexity. Embedded system designers face the new challenge of optimal layout of these processor cores along with the memory subsystem (caches and main memory) to satisfy power, area, and stringent real-time constraints. The short *time-to-market* (time from product conception to market release) of embedded systems further exacerbates design challenges.

Modeling of embedded systems helps the designers to cope with increasingly complex design challenges. Modeling of embedded systems helps in reducing the time-to-market by enabling fast application-to-device mapping, early proof of concept (POC), and system verification. Original equipment manufacturers (OEMs) increasingly adopt model-based design methodologies for improving the quality and reuse of hardware/software components. A model-based design allows development of control and dataflow applications in a graphical language familiar to control engineers and domain experts. Moreover, a model-based design enables components' definition at a higher level of abstraction that permits modularity and reusability. Furthermore, a model-based design allows verification of system behavior using simulation. However, different models provide different levels of abstraction for the system under design (SUD). To ensure timely completion of embedded systems design with sufficient confidence in the product's market release, design engineers have to make trade-offs between the abstraction level of a model and the accuracy a model can attain.

The remainder of this chapter is organized as follows. Section 1.1 elaborates on several embedded system application domains. Various characteristics of embedded system applications are discussed in Section 1.2. Section 1.3 discusses the main components of a typical embedded system's hardware and software. Section 1.4 elaborates modeling, modeling objectives, and various modeling paradigms. Section 1.5 provides an overview of optimization in embedded systems. Finally, Section 1.6 concludes this chapter.

1.1 Embedded Systems Applications

Embedded systems have applications in virtually all computing domains (except desktop computing) such as automobiles, medical, industry automation, home appliances (e.g., microwave ovens, toasters, washers/dryers), offices (e.g., printers, scanners), aircraft, space, military, and consumer electronics (e.g., smartphones, feature phones, portable media players, video games). In this section, we discuss some of these applications in detail.

1.1.1 Cyber-Physical Systems

A CPS is an emerging application domain of multi-unit/networked embedded systems. The CPS term emphasizes the link to physical quantities such as time, energy, and space. Although CPSs are embedded systems, the new terminology has been proposed by researchers to distinguish CPSs from simple microcontroller-based embedded systems. CPSs have become a hot topic for research in recent years and the difference between CPSs and embedded systems is not elucidated in many texts. We aim at making the distinction clear: *every CPS is an embedded system but not every embedded system is a CPS.* For instance, different distributed control functions in automobiles are examples of CPSs, and hence embedded systems (automotive CPSs are often also referred as automotive embedded systems). However, most of consumer electronic devices, such as mobile phones, personal digital assistants (PDAs), digital cameras, printers, and smart cards, are embedded systems but not CPSs.

CPSs enable monitoring and control of physical systems via a network (e.g., Internet, intranet, or wireless cellular network). CPSs are hybrid systems that include both continuous and discrete dynamics. Modeling of CPSs must use hybrid models that represent both continuous and discrete dynamics and should incorporate timing and concurrency. Communication between single-unit embedded devices/subsystems performing distributed computation in CPSs presents challenges due to uncertainty in temporal behavior (e.g., jitter in latency), message ordering because of dynamic routing of data, and data error rates. CPS applications include process control, networked building control systems (e.g., lighting, air-conditioning), telemedicine, and smart structures.

1.1.2 Space

Embedded systems are prevalent in space and aerospace systems where safety, reliability, and real-time requirements are critical. For example, a fly-by-wire aircraft with a 50-year production cycle requires an aircraft manufacturer to purchase, all at once, a 50-year supply of the microprocessors that will run the embedded software. All of these microprocessors must be manufactured from the same production line from the same mask to ensure that the validated real-time performance is maintained. Consequently, aerospace systems are unable to benefit from the technological improvements in this 50-year period without repeating the software validation and certification, which is very expensive. Hence, for aerospace applications, efficiency is of less relative importance as compared to predictability and safety, which is difficult to ensure without freezing the design at the physical level [9].

Embedded systems are used in satellites and space shuttles. For example, small-scale satellites in low earth orbit (LEO) use embedded systems for earth imaging and detection of ionospheric phenomenon that influences radio wave propagation (the ionosphere is produced by the ionization of atmospheric neutrals by ultraviolet radiation from the Sun and resides above the surface of earth stretching from a height of 50 km to more than 1000 km) [10]. Embedded systems enable unmanned and autonomous satellite platforms for space missions. For example, the dependable multiprocessor (DM), commissioned by NASA's New Millennium Program for future space missions, is an embedded system leveraging multicore processors and field-programmable gate array (FPGA)-based coprocessors [11].

1.1.3 Medical

Embedded systems are widely used in medical equipment where a product life cycle of 7 years is a prerequisite (i.e., processors used in medical equipment must be available for at least 7 years of operation) [12]. High-performance embedded systems are used in medical imaging devices (e.g., magnetic resonance imaging (MRI), computed tomography (CT), digital X-ray, and ultrasound) to provide high-quality images, which can accurately diagnose and determine treatment for a variety of patients' conditions. Filtering noisy input data and producing high-resolution images at high data processing rates require tremendous computing power (e.g., video imaging applications often require data processing at rates of 30 images/s or more). Using multicore embedded systems helps in efficient processing of these high-resolution medical images, whereas hardware coprocessors such as graphics processing units (GPUs) and FPGAs take parallel computing on these images to the next step. These coprocessors offload and accelerate some of the processing tasks that the processor would normally handle.

Some medical applications require real-time imaging to provide feedback while performing procedures such as positioning a stent or other devices inside a patient's heart. Some imaging applications require multiple modalities (e.g., CT, MRI, ultrasound) to provide optimal images as no single technique is optimal for imaging all types of tissues. In these applications, embedded systems combine images from each modality into a composite image that provides more information than the images from each individual modality separately [13].

Embedded systems are used in cardiovascular monitoring applications to treat high-risk patients while undergoing major surgery or cardiology procedures. Hemodynamic monitors in cardiovascular embedded systems measure a range of data related to a patient's heart and blood circulation on a beat-by-beat basis. These systems monitor the arterial blood pressure waveform along with the corresponding beat durations, which determines the amount of blood pumped out with each individual beat and heart rate.

Embedded systems have made telemedicine a reality enabling remote patient examination. Telemedicine virtually eliminates the distance between remote patients and urban practitioners by using real-time audio and video with one camera at the patient's location and another with the treatment specialist. Telemedicine requires standard-based platforms capable of integrating a myriad of medical devices via a standard input/output (I/O) connection such as Ethernet, Universal Serial Bus (USB), or video port. Vendors (e.g., Intel) supply embedded equipment for telemedicine that support real-time transmission of high-definition audio and video while simultaneously gathering data from the attached peripheral devices (e.g., heart monitor, CT scanner, thermometer, X-ray, and ultrasound machine) [14].

1.1.4 Automotive

Embedded systems are heavily used in the automotive industry for measurement and control. Since these embedded systems are commonly known as electronic control units (ECUs), we use the term ECU to refer to any automotive embedded system. A state-of-the-art luxury car contains more than 70 ECUs for safety and comfort functions [15]. Typically, ECUs in automotive systems communicate with each other over controller area network (CAN) buses.

ECUs in automotives are partitioned into two major categories: (1) ECUs for controlling mechanical parts and (2) ECUs for handling information systems and/ entertainment. The first category includes chassis control, automotive body control (interior air-conditioning, dashboard, power windows, etc.), power-train control (engine, transmission, emissions, etc.), and active safety control. The second category includes office computing, information management, navigation, external communication, and entertainment [16]. Each category has unique requirements for computation speed, scalability, and reliability.

ECUs responsible for power-train control, motor management, gear control, suspension control, airbag release, and antilocking brakes implement closed-loop control functions as well as reactive functions with hard real-time constraints and communicate over a class C CAN-bus (typically 1 Mbps). ECUs responsible for power-train have stringent real-time and computing power constraints requiring an activation period of a few milliseconds at high engine speeds. Typical power-train ECUs use 32-bit microcontrollers running at a few hundreds of megahertzs, whereas the remainder of the real-time subsystems use 16-bit microcontrollers running at less than 1 MHz. Multicore ECUs are envisioned as the next-generation solution for automotive applications with intense computing and high reliability requirements.

The body electronics ECUs, which serve the comfort functions (e.g., air-conditioning, power window, seat control, and parking assistance), are mainly reactive systems with only a few closed-loop control functions and have soft real-time requirements. For example, driver and passengers issue supervisory commands to initiate power window movement by pressing the appropriate buttons. These buttons are connected to a microprocessor that translates the voltages corresponding to button up and down actions into messages that traverse over a network to the power window controller. The body electronics ECUs communicate via a class B CAN-bus typically operating at 100 kbps.

ECUs responsible for entertainment and office applications (e.g., video, sound, phone, and global positioning system (GPS)) are software-intensive with millions of lines of code and communicate via an optical data bus typically operating at 100 Mbps, which is the fastest bus in automotive applications. Various CAN buses and optical buses that connect different types of ECUs in automotive applications are in turn connected through a central gateway, which enables the communication of all ECUs.

For high-speed communication of large volumes of data traffic generated by $360°$ sensors positioned around the vehicles, the automotive industry is moving toward the FlexRay communication standard (a consortium that includes BMW, DaimlerChrysler, General Motors, Freescale, NXP, Bosch, and Volkswagen/Audi as core members) [16]. The current

CAN standard limits the communication speed to 500 kbps and imposes a protocol overhead of more than 40%, whereas FlexRay defines the communication speed at 10 Mbps with comparatively less overhead than the CAN. FlexRay offers enhanced reliability using a dual-channel bus specification. The dual-channel bus configuration can exploit physical redundancy and replicate safety-critical messages on both bus channels. The FlexRay standard affords better scalability for distributed ECUs as compared to CAN because of a time-triggered communication channel specification such that each node only needs to know the time slots for its outgoing and incoming communications. To promote high scalability, the node-assigned time slot schedule is distributed across the ECU nodes where each node stores its own time slot schedule in a local scheduling table.

1.2 Characteristics of Embedded Systems Applications

Different embedded applications have different characteristics. Although a complete characterization of embedded applications with respect to applications' characteristics is outside the scope of this chapter, following are some of the embedded application characteristics that are discussed in context of their associated embedded domains.

1.2.1 Throughput-Intensive

Throughput-intensive embedded applications are applications that require high processing throughput. Networking and multimedia applications, which constitute a large fraction of embedded applications [17], are typically throughput-intensive due to ever increasing quality of service (QoS) demands. An embedded system containing an embedded processor requires a network stack and network protocols to connect with other devices. Connecting an embedded device or a widget to a network enables remote device management including automatic application upgrades. On a large scale, networked embedded systems can enable HPEC for solving complex large problems traditionally handled only by supercomputers (e.g., climate research, weather forecasting, molecular modeling, physical simulations, and data mining). However, connecting hundreds to thousands of embedded systems for high-performance computing (HPC) requires sophisticated and scalable interconnection technologies (e.g., packet-switched, wireless interconnects). Examples of networking applications include server I/O devices, network infrastructure equipment, consumer electronics (mobile phones, media players), and various home appliances (e.g., home automation including networked TVs, VCRs, stereos, refrigerators). Multimedia applications, such as video streaming, require very high throughput of the order of several GOPS. A broadcast video with a specification of 30 frames/s with 720×480 pixels/frame requires approximately 400,000 blocks (group of pixels) to be processed per second. A telemedicine application requires processing of 5 million blocks/s [18].

1.2.2 Thermal-Constrained

An embedded application is *thermal-constrained* if an increase in temperature above a threshold could lead to incorrect results or even the embedded system failure. Depending on the target market, embedded applications typically operate above 45 °C (e.g., telecommunication embedded equipment temperature exceeds 55 °C) in contrast to traditional computer systems, which normally operate below 38 °C [19]. Meeting embedded application thermal constraints is challenging due to typically harsh and high-temperature operating environments. Limited space and energy budgets exacerbate these thermal challenges since active cooling systems (fans-based) are typically infeasible in most embedded systems, resulting in only passive and fanless thermal solutions.

1.2.3   Reliability-Constrained

Embedded systems with high *reliability* constraints are typically required to operate for many years without errors and/or must recover from errors since many reliability-constrained embedded systems are deployed in harsh environments where postdeployment removal and maintenance are infeasible. Hence, hardware and software for reliability-constrained embedded systems must be developed and tested more carefully than traditional computer systems. Safety-critical embedded systems (e.g., automotive airbags, space missions, aircraft flight controllers) have very high reliability requirements (e.g., the reliability requirement for a flight-control embedded system on a commercial airliner is 10^{-10} failures/h where a failure could lead to aircraft loss [20]).

1.2.4   Real-Time

In addition to correct functional operation, *real-time* embedded applications have additional stringent timing constraints, which impose real-time operational deadlines on the embedded system's response time. Although real-time operation does not strictly imply high performance, real-time embedded systems require high performance only to the point that the deadline is met, at which time high performance is no longer needed. Hence, real-time embedded systems require *predictable* high performance. Real-time operating systems (RTOSs) provide guarantees for meeting the stringent deadline requirements for embedded applications.

1.2.5   Parallel and Distributed

Parallel and *distributed* embedded applications leverage distributed embedded devices to cooperate and aggregate their functionalities or resources. Wireless sensor network (WSN) applications use sensor nodes to gather sensed information (statistics and data) and use distributed fault-detection algorithms. Mobile agent (autonomous software agent)-based distributed embedded applications allow the process state to be saved and transported to another new embedded system where the process resumes execution from the suspended point (e.g., virtual migration). Many embedded applications exhibit varying degrees (low to high levels) of *parallelism*, such as instruction-level parallelism (ILP) and thread-level parallelism (TLP). Innovative architectural and software HPEEC techniques are required to exploit an embedded application's available parallelism to achieve high performance with low power consumption.

1.3 Embedded Systems—Hardware and Software

An interesting characteristic of embedded systems design is *hardware/software codesign* (i.e., both hardware and software need to be considered together to find the right combination of hardware and software that would result in the most-efficient product meeting the requirement specifications). The mapping of application software to hardware must adhere to the design constraints (e.g., real-time deadlines) and objective functions (e.g., cost, energy consumption) (objective functions are discussed in detail in Section 1.4). In this section, we give an overview of embedded systems hardware and software as depicted in Fig. 1.1.

1.3.1 Embedded Systems Hardware

Embedded systems hardware is less standardized as compared to that for desktop computers. However, in many embedded systems, hardware is used within a loop where sensors gather information about the physical environment and generate continuous sequences of analog signals/values. Sample-and-hold circuits and analog-to-digital (A/D) converters digitize the analog signals. The digital signals are processed, and the results are displayed and/or used to control the physical environment via actuators. At the output, a digital-to-analog (D/A) conversion is generally required because many actuators are analog. In the following sections, we describe briefly the hardware components of a typical embedded system [1].

1.3.1.1 Sensors

Embedded systems contain a variety of sensors since there are sensors for virtually every physical quantity (e.g., weight, electric current, voltage, temperature, velocity, and acceleration). A sensor's construction can exploit a variety of physical effects including the law of induction (voltage generation in an electric field) and photoelectric effects. Recent advances in smart embedded systems design (e.g., WSNs, CPSs) can be attributed to the large variety of available sensors.

1.3.1.2 Sample-and-Hold Circuits and A/D Converters

Sample-and-hold circuits and A/D converters work in tandem to convert incoming analog signals from sensors into digital signals. Sample-and-hold circuits convert an analog signal from the continuous time domain to the discrete time domain. The circuit consists of a clocked transistor and a capacitor. The transistor functions similar to a switch where each time the switch is closed by the clocked signal, the capacitor is charged to the voltage $v(t)$ of the incoming voltage $e(t)$. The voltage $v(t)$ essentially remains the same even after opening the switch because of the charge stored in the capacitor until the switch closes again. Each of the voltage values stored in the capacitor are considered as an element of a discrete sequence of values generated from the continuous signal $e(t)$. The A/D converters map these voltage values to a discrete set of possible values afforded by the quantization process that converts these values to digits. There exists a variety of A/D converters with varying speed and precision characteristics.

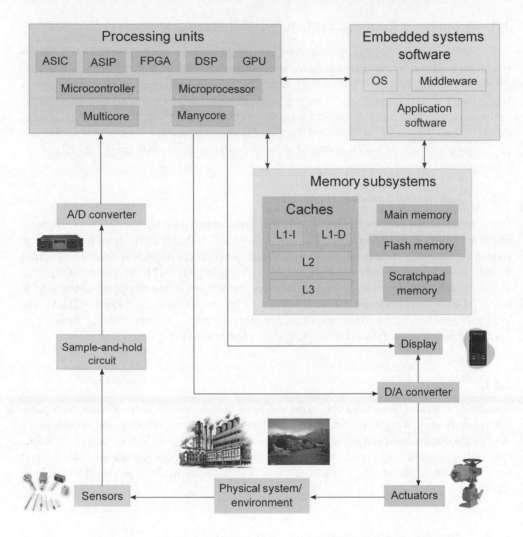

A/D converter: Analog-to-digital converter
D/A converter: Digital-to-analog converter
ASIC: Application-specific integrated circuit
ASIP: Application-specific instruction set processor
FPGA: Field programmable gate array
DSP: Digital signal processor

GPU: Graphics processing unit
OS: Operating system
L1-I: Level one instruction cache
L1-D: Level one data cache
L2: Level two cache
L3: Level three cache

Figure 1.1   Embedded systems hardware and software overview

1.3.1.3 Processing Units

The processing units in embedded systems process the digital signals output from the A/D converters. Energy efficiency is an important factor in the selection of processing units for embedded systems. We categorize processing units into three main types:

(1) *Application-Specific Integrated Circuits (ASICs):* ASICs implement an embedded application's algorithm in hardware. For a fixed process technology, ASICs provide the highest energy efficiency among available processing units at the cost of no flexibility (Fig. 1.1).
(2) *Processors:* Many embedded systems contain a general-purpose microprocessor and/or a microcontroller. These processors enable flexible programming but are much less energy efficient than ASICs. High-performance embedded applications leverage multicore/manycore processors, application domain-specific processors (e.g., digital signal processors (DSPs)), and application-specific instruction set processors (ASIPs) that can provide the required energy efficiency. GPUs are often used as coprocessors in imaging applications to accelerate and offload work from the general-purpose processors (Fig. 1.1).
(3) *Field-Programmable Gate Arrays (FPGAs):* Since ASICs are too expensive for low-volume applications and software-based processors can be too slow or energy inefficient, reconfigurable logic (of which FPGAs are the most prominent) can provide an energy-efficient solution. FPGAs can potentially deliver performance comparable to ASICs but offer reconfigurability using different, specialized configuration data that can be used to reconfigure the device's hardware functionality. FPGAs are mainly used for hardware acceleration of low-volume applications and rapid prototyping. FPGAs can be used for rapid system prototyping that emulates the same behavior as the final system and thus can be used for experimentation purposes.

1.3.1.4 Memory Subsystems

Embedded systems require memory subsystems to store code and data. Memory subsystems in embedded systems typically consist of on-chip caches and an off-chip main memory. Caches in embedded systems have different hierarchy: level one instruction cache (L1-I) for holding instructions, level one data cache for holding data (L1-D), level two unified (instruction/data) cache (L2), and recently level three cache (L3). Caches provide much faster access to code and data as compared to the main memory. However, caches are not suitable for real-time embedded systems because of limited predictability of hit rates and therefore access time. To offer better timing predictability for memory subsystems, many embedded systems especially real-time embedded systems use scratchpad memories. Scratchpad memories enable software-based control for temporary storage of calculations, data, and other work in progress instead of hardware-based control as in caches. For nonvolatile storage of code and data, embedded systems use Flash memory that can be electrically erased and reprogrammed. Examples of embedded systems using Flash memory include PDAs, digital audio and media players, digital cameras, mobile phones, video games, and medical equipment, and so on.

1.3.1.5 D/A Converters

As many of the output devices are analog, embedded systems leverage D/A converters to convert digital signals to analog signals. D/A converters typically use weighted resistors to generate a current proportional to the digital number. This current is transformed into a proportional voltage by using an operational amplifier.

1.3.1.6 Output Devices

Embedded systems' output devices include displays and electro-mechanical devices known as actuators. Actuators can directly impact the environment based on the processed and/or control information from embedded systems. Actuators are key elements in reactive and interactive embedded systems, especially CPSs.

1.3.2 Embedded Systems Software

Embedded systems software consists of an operating system (OS), a middleware, and an application software (Fig. 1.1). Embedded software has more stringent resource constraints (e.g., small memory footprint, small data word sizes) than traditional desktop software. In the following sections, we describe the main software components of embedded systems.

1.3.2.1 Operating System

Except for very simple embedded systems, most embedded systems require an operating system (OS) for scheduling, task switching, and I/O. Embedded operating systems (EOSs) differ from traditional desktop OSs because EOSs provide limited functionality but a high-level configurability in order to accommodate a wide variety of application requirements and hardware platform features. Many embedded system's applications (e.g., CPSs) are real-time and require support from a RTOS. An RTOS leverages deterministic scheduling policies and provides predictable timing behavior with guarantees on the upper bound of a task's execution time.

1.3.2.2 Middleware

Middleware is a software layer between the application software and the EOS. Middleware typically includes communication libraries (e.g., message passing interface (MPI), ilib API for Tilera [21]). We point out that real-time embedded systems require a real-time middleware.

1.3.2.3 Application Software

Embedded systems contain application software specific to an embedded application (e.g., a portable media player, a phone framework, a healthcare application, and an ambient condition monitoring application). Embedded applications leverage communication libraries provided by the middleware and EOS features. Application software development for embedded systems requires knowledge of the target hardware architecture as assembly language fragments are often embedded within the software code for hardware control or performance purposes. The software code is typically written in a high-level language, such as C, which promotes application software conformity to stringent resource constraints (e.g., limited memory footprint and small data word sizes).

Application software development for real-time applications must consider real-time issues, especially the worst-case execution time (WCET). The WCET is defined as the largest execution time of a program for any input and any initial execution state. We point out that the exact WCET can only be computed for certain programs and tasks such as programs without recursions, without while loops, and loops with a statically known iteration count [1]. Modern pipelined processor architectures with different types of hazards (e.g., data hazards, control hazards) and modern memory subsystems composed of different cache hierarchies with limited hit rate predictability make WCET determination further challenging. To offer better timing predictability for memory subsystems, many embedded systems (real-time embedded systems in particular) use scratchpad memories. Scratchpad memories enable software-based control for temporary storage of calculations, data, and other work in progress instead of hardware-based control as in caches. Since exact WCET determination is extremely difficult, designers typically specify upper bounds on the WCET.

1.4   Modeling—An Integral Part of the Embedded Systems Design Flow

Modeling stems from the concept of abstraction (i.e., defining a real-world object in a simplified form). Formally, a model is defined as [1]: "A model is a simplification of another entity, which can be a physical thing or another model. The model contains exactly those characteristics and properties of the modeled entity that are relevant for a given task. A model is minimal with respect to a task if it does not contain any other characteristics than those relevant for the task."

The design of embedded systems increasingly depends on a hierarchy of models. Models have been used for decades in computer science to provide abstractions. Since embedded systems have very complex functionality built on top of very sophisticated platforms, designers must use a series of models to successfully accomplish the system design. Early stages of the design process require simple models of reasonable accuracy; later design stages need more sophisticated and accurate models [3].

The key phases in the embedded systems design flow are as follows: requirement specifications, hardware/software (HW/SW) partitioning, preliminary design, detailed design, component implementation, component test/validation, code generation, system integration, system verification/evaluation, and production [15]. The first phase, requirement specifications, outlines the expected/desired behavior of the SUD, and *use cases* describe potential applications of the SUD. Young et al. [22] commented on the importance of requirement specifications: "A design without specifications cannot be right or wrong, it can only be surprising!". HW/SW partitioning partitions an application's functionality into a combination of interacting hardware and software. Efficient and effective HW/SW partitioning can enable a product to more closely meet the requirement specifications. The preliminary design is a high-level design with minimum functionality that enables designers to analyze the key characteristics/functionality of an SUD. The detailed design specifies the details that are absent from the preliminary design such as detailed models or drivers for a component. Since embedded systems are complex and are comprised of many components/subsystems, many embedded systems are designed and implemented component-wise, which adds component implementation and component testing/validation phases to the design flow. Component validation may involve simulation followed by a code generation phase that generates the appropriate code for the component. System integration is the process of integrating the design of the individual components/subsystem into the complete, functioning embedded system. Verification/evaluation is the process of verifying quantitative information of key objective functions/characteristics (e.g., execution time, reliability) of a certain (possibly partial) design. Once an embedded systems design has been verified, the SUD enters that production phase that produces/fabricates the SUD according to market requirements dictated by supply and demand economic model. Modeling is an integral part of the embedded systems design flow, which abstracts the SUD and is used throughout the design flow, from the requirement specifications' phase to the formal verification/evaluation phase.

Most of the errors encountered during embedded systems design are directly or indirectly related to incomplete, inconsistent, or even incorrect requirement specifications. Currently, the requirement specifications are mostly given in sentences of a natural language (e.g., English), which can be interpreted differently by the OEMs and the suppliers (e.g., Bosch, Siemens that provide embedded subsystems). To minimize the design errors, the embedded industry prefers to receive the requirement specifications in a modeling tool (e.g., graphical or language based). Modeling facilitates designers to deduce errors and quantitative aspects (e.g., reliability, lifetime) early in the design flow.

Once the SUD modeling is complete, the next phase is validation through simulation followed by code generation. Validation is the process of checking whether a design meets all of the constraints and performs as expected. Simulating embedded systems may require modeling the SUD, the operating environment, or both. Three terminologies are used in the literature depending on whether the SUD or the real environment or both are modeled: "Software-in-the-loop" refers to the simulation where both the SUD and the real environment are modeled for early system validation; "Rapid prototyping" refers to the simulation where the SUD is modeled and the real environment exists for early POC; and "Hardware-in-the-loop" refers to the simulation where the physical SUD exists and real environment is modeled for exhaustive characterization of the SUD.

Scalability in modeling/verification means that if a modeling/verification technique can be used to abstract/verify a specific small system/subsystem, the same technique can be used to abstract/verify large systems. In some scenarios, modeling/verification is scalable if the correctness of a large system can be inferred from a small verifiable modeled system. Reduction techniques such as partial order reduction and symmetry reduction address this scalability problem; however, this area requires further research.

1.4.1 Modeling Objectives

Embedded systems design requires characterization of several objectives, or design metrics, such as the average execution time and WCETs, code size, energy/power consumption, safety, reliability, temperature/thermal behavior, electromagnetic compatibility, cost, and weight. We point out that some of these objectives can be taken as design constraints since in many optimization problems, objectives can be replaced by constraints and vice versa. Considering multiple objectives is a unique characteristic of many embedded systems and can be accurately captured using mathematical models. A system or subsystem's mathematical model is a mathematical structure consisting of sets, definitions, functions, relations, logical predicates (true or false statements), formulas, and/or graphs. Many mathematical models for embedded

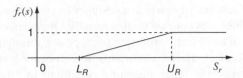

Figure 1.2   A linear objective function for reliability

systems use objective function(s) to characterize some or all of these objectives, which aids in early evaluation of embedded systems design by quantifying information for key objectives.

The objectives for an embedded system can be captured mathematically using linear, piecewise linear, or nonlinear functions. For example, a linear objective function for the reliability of an embedded system operating in a state s (Fig. 1.2) can be given as [23]

$$f_r(s) = \begin{cases} 1, & r \geq U_R \\ (r - L_R)/(U_R - L_R), & L_R < r < U_R \\ 0, & r \leq L_R \end{cases} \quad (1.1)$$

where r denotes the reliability offered in the current state s (denoted as s_r in Fig. 1.2), and the constant parameters L_R and U_R denote the minimum and maximum allowed/tolerated reliability, respectively. The reliability may be represented as a multiple of a base reliability unit equal to 0.1, which represents a 10% packet reception rate [24].

Embedded systems with multiple objectives can be characterized by using either multiple objective functions, each representing a particular design metric/objective, or a single objective function that uses a weighted average of multiple objectives. A single overall objective function can be formulated as

$$f(s) = \sum_{k=1}^{m} \omega_k f_k(s)$$

$$\text{s.t.} \quad s \in S$$

$$\omega_k \geq 0, \quad k = 1, 2, \ldots, m$$

$$\omega_k \leq 1, \quad k = 1, 2, \ldots, m$$

$$\sum_{k=1}^{m} \omega_k = 1 \quad (1.2)$$

where $f_k(s)$ and ω_k denote the objective function and weight factor for the Kth objective/design metric (weight factors signify the weightage/importance of objectives with respect to each other), respectively, given that there are m objectives. Individual objectives are characterized by their respective objective functions $f_k(s)$ (e.g., a linear objective function for reliability is given in Eq. (1.1) and depicted in Fig. 1.2).

A single objective function allows selection of a single design from the design space (the design space represents the set containing all potential designs); however, the assignments of weights for different objectives in the single objective function can be challenging using informal requirement specifications. Alternatively, the use of multiple, separate objective functions returns a set of designs from which a designer can select an appropriate design that meets the most critical objectives optimally/suboptimally. Often embedded systems modeling focuses on optimization of an objective function (e.g., power, throughput, reliability) subject to design constraints. Typical design constraints for embedded systems include safety, hard real-time requirements, and tough operating conditions in a harsh environment (e.g., aerospace) though some or all of these constraints can be added as objectives to the objective function in many optimization problems as described earlier.

1.4.2   Modeling Paradigms

Since embedded systems contain a large variety of abstraction levels, components, and aspects (e.g., hardware, software, functional, verification) that cannot be supported by one language or tool, designers rely on various modeling paradigms, each of which target a partial aspect of the complete design flow from requirement specifications to production. Each modeling paradigm describes the system from a different point of view, but none of the paradigms cover all aspects. We discuss some of the modeling paradigms used in embedded systems design in the following sections, each of which may use different tools to assist with modeling.

1.4.2.1   Differential Equations

Differential equations-based modeling can either use ordinary differential equations (ODEs) or partial differential equations (PDEs). ODEs (linear and nonlinear) are used to model systems or components characterized by quantities that are continuous in value and time, such as voltage and current in electrical systems, speed and force in mechanical systems, or temperature and heat flow in thermal systems [15]. ODE-based models typically describe analog electrical networks or the mechanical behavior of the complete system or component. ODEs are especially useful for studying feedback control systems that can make an unstable system into a stable one (feedback systems measure the error (i.e., difference between the actual and desired behavior) and use this error information to correct the behavior). We emphasize that ODEs work for smooth motion where linearity, time invariance, and continuity properties hold. Nonsmooth motion involving collisions requires hybrid models that are a mixture of continuous and discrete time models [25].

PDEs are used for modeling behavior in space and time, such as moving electrodes in electromagnetic fields and thermal behavior. Numerical solutions for PDEs are calculated by finite-element methods (FEMs) [25].

1.4.2.2   State Machines

State machines are used for modeling discrete dynamics and are especially suitable for reactive systems. Finite-state machines (FSMs) and state-charts are some of the popular examples of state machines. Communicating Finite-state machines (CFSMs) represent several FSMs communicating with each other. State-charts extend FSMs with a mechanism for describing hierarchy and concurrency. Hierarchy is incorporated using *super-states* and *sub-states*, where super-states are states that comprise other sub-states [1]. Concurrency in state-charts is modeled using *AND-states*. If a system containing a super-state S is always in all of the sub-states of S whenever the system is in S, then the super-state S is an *AND-super-state*.

1.4.2.3 Dataflow

Dataflow modeling identifies and models data movement in an information system. Dataflow modeling represents processes that transform data from one form to another, external entities that receive data from a system or send data into the system, data stores that hold data, and dataflow that indicates the routes over which the data can flow. A dataflow model is represented by a directed graph where the nodes/vertices, *actors*, represent computation (computation maps input data streams into output data streams) and the arcs represent communication channels. Synchronous dataflow (SDF) and Kahn process networks (KPNs) are common examples of dataflow models. The key characteristics of these dataflow models is that SDFs assume that all actors execute in a single clock cycle, whereas KPNs permit actors to execute with any finite delay [1].

1.4.2.4 Discrete Event-Based Modeling

Discrete event-based modeling is based on the notion of firing or executing a sequence of discrete events, which are stored in a queue and are sorted by the time at which these events should be processed. An event corresponding to the current time is removed from the queue, processed by performing the necessary actions, and new events may be enqueued based on the action's results [1]. If there is no event in the queue for the current time, the time advances. Hardware description languages (e.g., VHDL, Verilog) are typically based on discrete event modeling. SystemC, which is a system-level modeling language, is also based on discrete event modeling paradigm.

1.4.2.5 Stochastic Models

Numerous stochastic models exist, which mainly differ in the assumed distributions of the state residence times, to describe and analyze system performance and dependability. Analyzing the embedded system's performance in an early design phase can significantly reduce late-detected, and therefore cost-intensive, problems. Markov chains and queueing models are popular examples of stochastic models. The state residence times in Markov chains are typically assumed to have exponential distributions because exponential distributions lead to efficient numerical analysis, although other generalizations are also possible. Performance measures are obtained from Markov chains by determining steady-state and transient-state probabilities. Queueing models are used to model systems that can be associated with some notion of queues. Queueing models are stochastic models since these models represent the probability of finding a queueing system in a particular configuration or state.

Stochastic models can capture the complex interactions between an embedded system and its environment. Timeliness, concurrency, and interaction with the environment are primary characteristics of many embedded systems, and *nondeterminism* enables stochastic models to incorporate these characteristics. Specifically, nondeterminism is used for modeling unknown aspects of the environment or system. Markov decision processes (MDPs) are discrete stochastic dynamic programs, an extension of discrete time Markov chains, that exhibit nondeterminism. MDPs associate a reward with each state in the Markov chain.

1.4.2.6 Petri Nets

A Petri net is a mathematical language for describing distributed systems and is represented by a directed, bipartite graph. The key elements of Petri nets are conditions, events, and a flow relation. Conditions are either satisfied or not satisfied. The flow relation describes the conditions that must be met before an event can fire as well as prescribes the conditions that become true when after an event fires. Activity charts in unified modeling language (UML) are based on Petri nets [1].

1.4.3 Strategies for Integration of Modeling Paradigms

Describing different aspects and views of an entire embedded system, subsystem, or component over different development phases requires different modeling paradigms. However, sometimes partial descriptions of a system need to be integrated for simulation and code generation. Multiparadigm languages integrate different modeling paradigms. There are two types of multiparadigm modeling [15]:

(1) One model describing a system complements another model resulting in a model of the complete system.
(2) Two models give different views of the same system.

UML is an example of multiparadigm modeling, which is often used to describe software-intensive system components. UML enables the designer to verify a design before any hardware/software code is written/generated [26] and allows generation of the appropriate code for the embedded system using a set of rules. UML offers a structured and repeatable design: if there is a problem with the behavior of the application, then the model is changed accordingly; and if the problem lies in the performance of the code, then the rules are adjusted. Similarly, MATLAB's Simulink modeling environment integrates a continuous time and discrete time model of computation based on equation solvers, a discrete event model, and an FSM model.

Two strategies for the integration of heterogeneous modeling paradigms are [15] as follows:

(1) Integration of operations (analysis, synthesis) on models
(2) Integration of models themselves via model translation.

We briefly describe several different integration approaches that leverage these strategies in the following sections.

1.4.3.1 Cosimulation

Cosimulation permits simulation of partial models of a system in different tools and integrates the simulation process. Cosimulation depends on a central cosimulation engine, called a *simulation backplane*, that mediates between the distributed simulations run by the simulation engines of the participating computer-aided software engineering (CASE) tools. Cosimulation is useful and sufficient for model validation when simulation is the only purpose of model integration. In general, cosimulation is useful for the combination of a system model with a model of the system's environment since the system model is constructed completely in one tool and enters into the code generation phase, whereas the environment model is only used for simulation. Alternatively, cosimulation is insufficient if both of the models (the system and its environment model) are intended for code generation.

1.4.3.2 Code Integration

Many modeling tools have associated code generators, and code integration is the process of integrating the generated codes from multiple modeling tools. Code integration tools expedite the design process because in the absence of a code integration tool, subsystem codes generated by different tools have to be integrated manually.

1.4.3.3 Code Encapsulation

Code encapsulation is a feature offered by many CASE tools that permits code encapsulation of a subsystem model as a block box in the overall system model. Code encapsulation facilitates automated code integration as well as overall system simulation.

1.4.3.4 Model Encapsulation

In model encapsulation, an original subsystem model is encapsulated as an equivalent subsystem model in the modeling language of the enclosing system. Model encapsulation permits *coordinated code generation* in which the code generation for the enclosing system drives the code generator for the subsystem. The enclosing system tool can be regarded as a master tool and the encapsulated subsystem tool as a slave tool; therefore, model encapsulation requires the master tool to have knowledge of the slave tool.

1.4.3.5 Model Translation

In model translation, a subsystem model is translated syntactically and semantically to the language of the enclosing system. This translation results in a homogeneous overall system model so that one tool chain can be used for further processing of the complete system.

1.5 Optimization in Embedded Systems

General-purpose computing systems are designed to work well in a variety of contexts. Although embedded computing systems must be flexible, the embedded systems can often be tuned or optimized to a particular application. Consequently, some of the design precepts that are commonly adhered in the design of general-purpose computers do not hold for embedded computers. Given the huge number of embedded computers sold each year, many application areas make it worthwhile to spend the time to create a customized and optimized architecture.

Optimization techniques at different design levels (e.g., hardware and software, data link layer, routing, OS) assist designers in meeting application requirements. Embedded systems optimization techniques can be generally categorized as *static* or *dynamic*. Static optimizations optimize an embedded system at deployment time and remain fixed for the embedded system's lifetime. Static optimizations are suitable for stable/predictable applications, whereas they are inflexible and do not adapt to changing application requirements and environmental stimuli. Dynamic optimizations provide more flexibility by continuously optimizing an embedded system during runtime, providing better adaptation to changing application requirements and actual environmental stimuli.

Parallel and distributed embedded systems add more facets to optimization problem than traditional embedded systems as a growing number of distributed embedded systems leverage wireless communication to connect with different embedded devices. This wireless connectivity between distributed embedded systems requires optimization of radios (aka data transceivers) and various layers of Open Systems Interconnect (OSI) model of the International Standards Organization (ISO) implemented in these embedded systems. Embedded systems' radios carry digital information and are used to connect to networks. These networks may be specialized, as in cell phones, but increasingly radios are used as the physical layer in the Internet protocol systems [3]. The radios in these distributed wireless embedded systems must perform several tasks: demodulate the signal down to the baseband, detect the baseband signal to identify bits, and correct errors in the raw bit stream. Wireless data radios in these embedded systems may be built from combinations of analog, hardwired digital, configurable, and programmable components. Software-defined radios (SDRs) are also being used in some parallel and distributed embedded systems. A *software radio* is a radio that can be programmed; the term SDR is often used to mean either a purely or a partly programmable radio [3].

Although it may seem that embedded systems would be too simple to require the use of the OSI model, embedded systems increasingly implement multiple layers of the OSI model. Even relatively simple embedded systems provide physical, data link, network, and application services. An increasing number of embedded systems provide Internet service that requires implementing the full range of functions in the OSI model. The OSI model defines a seven-layer model for network services [3]:

(1) *Physical:* The electrical and physical connection
(2) *Data link:* Access and error control across a single link
(3) *Network:* Basic end-to-end service
(4) *Transport:* Connection-oriented services
(5) *Session:* Activity control, such as checkpointing
(6) *Presentation:* Data exchange formats
(7) *Application:* The interface between the application and the network.

The OSI model layers can be implemented in hardware and/or software in embedded systems depending on the embedded application requirements. Embedded systems are optimized for various application requirements and design metrics in almost all design phases. Embedded systems optimization benefits in particular from the following design phases:

• Modeling at different levels of abstraction
• Profiling and analysis revamp system requirements and software models into more specific requirements on the platform hardware architecture

- Design space exploration (whether exhaustive or some heuristic-based) evaluates hardware alternatives.

The design phases in embedded systems optimize various design metrics, such as performance, power, cost, and reliability. The remainder of this section focuses on optimization of these design metrics for embedded systems.

1.5.1 Optimization of Embedded Systems Design Metrics

An embedded application determines the basic *functional requirements*, such as input and output relationship. The embedded system designer must also determine the *nonfunctional requirements*, such as performance, power, cost, some of which are derived directly from the application and some from other factors, such as marketing. Design metrics are generally derived from application requirements. Often design metrics derived from nonfunctional requirements are equally important as those from functional requirements. An embedded systems applications may have many design metrics, such as performance, power, reliability, and quality. Some of these metrics can be accurately measured and predicted while others are less so.

Various optimization techniques at different levels (e.g., architecture, middleware, and software) can be used to enable an embedded platform to optimize various design metrics and meet the embedded application requirements. In the following, we elaborate the optimization of a few design metrics: performance, power, temperature, cost, design time, reliability, and quality.

1.5.1.1 Performance

Performance metric refers to some aspect of speed. Performance can be measured in many different ways: average performance versus worst-case or best-case performance, throughput versus latency, and peak versus sustained performance [3]. Chapter 7 of this book discusses various performance optimization techniques for embedded systems. For example, throughput-intensive applications can leverage architectural innovations (e.g., tiled multicore architectures, high-bandwidth interconnects), hardware-assisted middleware techniques (e.g., speculative approaches, dynamic voltage and frequency scaling (DVFS), hyperthreading), and software techniques (e.g., data forwarding, task scheduling, and task migration). Please refer to Chapter 7 of this book for a comprehensive discussion on performance optimization techniques.

1.5.1.2 Energy/Power

Energy and/or power consumption are critical metrics for many embedded systems. Energy consumption is particularly important for battery-operated embedded systems as reduced energy consumption leads to an increased battery life of the embedded system. Power consumption also affects heat generation. Less power consumption not only engenders less cooling costs but also enables sustainable long-term functioning without damaging the chip due to overheating. Energy/power optimization techniques for embedded systems include

DVFS, power gating, and clock gating. Please refer to Chapter 7 of this book for details on energy optimization techniques.

1.5.1.3 Temperature

Thermal-aware design has become a prominent aspect of microprocessor and SoC design due to the large thermal dissipation of modern chips. In very high-performance systems, heat may be difficult to dissipate even with fans and thermally controlled ambient environments. Many consumer devices avoid the use of cooling fans due to size constraints [3].

Heat transfer in integrated circuits relies on the thermal resistance and thermal capacitance of the chip, its package, and the associated heat sink. *Thermal resistance* is a heat property and a measurement of a temperature difference by which an object or material resists a heat flow. Absolute thermal resistance is the temperature difference across a structure when a unit of heat energy flows through the structure in unit time. *Thermal capacitance* is equal to the ratio of the heat added to (or subtracted from) an object to the resulting temperature change. Thermal models can be solved in the same manner as are electrical resistor–capacitor (RC) circuit models. The activity of the architectural units determines the amount of heat generated in each unit.

There exists various techniques to optimize temperature design metric, such as temperature-aware task scheduling [27], temperature-aware DVFS [28], thermal profile management [29], proactive scheduling for processor temperature [30], and reactive scheduling for processor temperature [31]. To illustrate optimization of temperature design metric, we summarize the approach in reactive scheduling for processor temperature in the following.

Wang and Bettati [31] developed a reactive scheduling algorithm while ensuring that the processor temperature remained below a threshold T_H. Let $S(t)$ represent the processor speed/frequency at time t. The processor power consumption is modeled as:

$$P(t) = KS^\alpha(t) \tag{1.3}$$

where K is a constant and $\alpha > 1$ (usually, it is assumed that $\alpha = 3$). The thermal properties of the system can be modeled as

$$a = \frac{K}{C_{th}} \tag{1.4}$$

$$b = \frac{1}{R_{th}C_{th}} \tag{1.5}$$

where b is a positive constant that represents the power dissipation rate. The *equilibrium speed* S_E is defined as the speed at which the processor stays at the threshold temperature T_H and is given as

$$S_E = \left(\frac{b}{a}T_H\right)^{1/\alpha} \tag{1.6}$$

According to reactive scheduling for processor temperature:

- When the processor has useful work to do and is at its threshold temperature, the processor clock speed is set to the S_E.

- When the processor has useful work to do and the temperature is below the threshold temperature, increase the processor speed (the processor speed can be increased up to the maximum available processor frequency/speed).

1.5.1.4 Cost

The monetary cost of a system is an important design metric. Cost can be measured in several ways. *Manufacturing cost* is determined by the cost of components and the manufacturing processes used. *Unit cost* is the monetary cost of manufacturing each copy of the system, excluding nonrecurring engineering (NRE) cost. *NRE cost* is the one-time monetary cost of designing the system. NRE cost is also known as *design cost*. Design cost is determined both by labor and by the equipment used to support the designers. The server farm and computer-aided design (CAD) tools needed to design a large chip cost several million dollars. *Lifetime cost* comprises of software and hardware maintenance and upgrades. The *total cost* of producing a certain number of units of an embedded design can be given as [32]

$$\text{Total cost} = \text{NRE cost} + (\text{unit cost} \times \text{number of units}) \tag{1.7}$$

The *per-product cost* can be given as [32]

$$\text{Per-product cost} = \frac{\text{total cost}}{\text{number of units}}$$

$$= \left(\frac{\text{NRE cost}}{\text{number of units}} \right) + \text{unit cost} \tag{1.8}$$

Let us consider an example for the illustration of different costs. Suppose NRE cost of designing an embedded system is $3000 and the unit cost is $100. If 20 units are produced for that embedded system, then total cost from Eq. (1.7) is as follows: total cost = $3000 + (20 × $100) = $3000 + $2000 = $5000. Per-product cost for that embedded system from Eq. (1.8) is as follows: per-product cost = $3000/20 + $100 = $150 + $100 = $250.

Many optimization problems deal with reducing the cost of an embedded systems design while meeting application requirements. In general, a cost minimization problem takes a form similar to the following equation:

$$\min \ f_c(x, y, z)$$

$$\text{s.t.} \quad x \leq a$$

$$y \leq b$$

$$z \leq c \tag{1.9}$$

where $f_c(x, y, z)$ represents the cost function to be minimized and is a function of parameters x, y, and z. The constraints of the optimization problem are also specified in Eq. (1.9) where a, b, and c denote some constants that restrict parameters x, y, and z, respectively.

1.5.1.5 Design Time

The time required to design a system is an important metric for many embedded systems. Design time is often constrained by *time-to-market*. Time-to-market is the time required to develop a system to the point that it can be released and sold to customers. If an embedded systems design takes too long to complete, the product may miss its intended market. Revenue for an embedded product depends on *market window*, which is the period during which the product would have highest sales. Delays can be costly in the delayed entry of an embedded product in the market window. For example, calculators must be ready for the back-to-school market each fall. Various modeling and CAD tools are used in embedded systems design to reduce the design time and meet the time-to-market constraints.

1.5.1.6 Reliability

Different embedded systems have different reliability requirements. In some consumer markets, customers do not expect to keep the product (e.g., mobile phone) for a long period. Automobiles, in contrast, must be designed to be safe and reliable. Dependability assimilation in safety-critical embedded systems (e.g., automobiles, aircrafts) is paramount because of product liability legislations, ISO standards, and increasing customer expectations. The product liability law holds responsible the manufacturers, distributors, suppliers, and retailers for the injuries caused by those products. According to the law, the manufacturer's product liability is excluded if a failure cannot be detected using the state-of-the-art science and technology at the time of product release.

Reliability techniques that help in designing a reliable embedded system include N-modular redundancy, watchdog timers, coding techniques (e.g., parity codes, checksum, cyclic codes), algorithm-based fault tolerance, acceptance tests, and checkpointing. Various reliability modeling methodologies also assist the designers in meeting reliability requirements of an embedded design.

1.5.1.7 Quality

Quality is a design metric that is often hard to quantify and measure. Quality or QoS is often considered as a performance measure. In some markets (e.g., few consumer devices), factors such as user interface design, availability of the connection, speed of data streaming, and processing may be associated with quality. In safety-critical systems, such as automobiles, QoS must be considered as a dependability or reliability measure that can impact the system's availability and safety. For example, if the end-to-end delay in a cyber-physical automotive system exceeds beyond a certain critical threshold, the driver can totally lose the control of his/her car.

1.5.2 *Multiobjective Optimization*

Embedded systems design must meet several different design objectives. The traditional operations research approach of defining a single objective function and possibly some minor objective functions, along with design constraints, may not befittingly capture an embedded system's requirements. Economist Vilfredo Pareto proposed a theory for multiobjective analysis known as *Pareto optimality*. The theory also delineates the method by which optimal solutions are assessed: an optimal solution cannot be improved without making some other part of the solution worse [3]. Optimization of embedded systems is often multiobjective, and the designer has to make trade-offs between different objectives depending on the criticality (weight factor) of an objective (Eq. (1.2)).

1.6 Chapter Summary

This chapter introduced parallel and distributed embedded systems. We elaborated on several embedded systems applications domains including CPSs, space, medical, and automotive. The chapter discussed various characteristics of embedded systems applications, such as throughput-intensive, thermal-constrained, reliability-constrained, real-time, and parallel and distributed. We elucidated the main components of a typical embedded system's hardware and software. We presented an overview of modeling, modeling objectives, and various modeling paradigms. Finally, we elaborated optimization of various design metrics, such as performance, energy/power, temperature, cost, design time, reliability, and quality, for embedded systems.

2

Multicore-Based EWSNs—An Example of Parallel and Distributed Embedded Systems*

Advancements in silicon technology, embedded systems, sensors, micro-electro-mechanical systems, and wireless communications have led to the emergence of embedded wireless sensor networks (EWSNs). EWSNs consist of sensor nodes with embedded sensors to sense data about a phenomenon, and these sensor nodes communicate with neighboring sensor nodes over wireless links. Many emerging EWSN applications (e.g., surveillance, volcano monitoring) require a plethora of sensors (e.g., acoustic, seismic, temperature, and, more recently, image sensors and/or smart cameras) embedded in the sensor nodes. Although traditional EWSNs equipped with scalar sensors (e.g., temperature, humidity) transmit most of the sensed information to a sink node (base station node), this *sense-transmit* paradigm is becoming infeasible for information-hungry applications equipped with a plethora of sensors, including image sensors and/or smart cameras.

Processing and transmission of the large amount of sensed data in emerging applications exceed the capabilities of traditional EWSNs. For example, consider a military EWSN deployed in a battlefield, which requires various sensors, such as imaging, acoustic, and electromagnetic sensors. This application presents various challenges for existing EWSNs since transmission of high-resolution images and video streams over bandwidth-limited wireless links from sensor nodes to the sink node is infeasible. Furthermore, meaningful processing of multimedia data (acoustic, image, and video in this example) in real time exceeds the capabilities of traditional EWSNs consisting of single-core embedded sensor nodes [33, 34] and requires more powerful embedded sensor nodes to realize this application.

*A portion of this chapter is copyrighted by IEEE. The definitive version appeared in: Arslan Munir, Ann Gordon-Ross, and Sanjay Ranka, Multi-core Embedded Wireless Sensor Networks: Architecture and Applications, *IEEE Transactions on Parallel and Distributed Systems (TPDS)*, vol. 25, no. 6, pp. 1553–1562, June 2014. URL http://ieeexplore.ieee.org/xpl/articleDetails.jsp?arnumber=6587244. ©[2014] IEEE. Reprinted with permission from IEEE as we are the authors of this work.

Since single-core EWSNs will soon be unable to meet the increasing requirements of information-rich applications (e.g., video sensor networks), next-generation sensor nodes must possess enhanced computation and communication capabilities. For example, the transmission rate for the first-generation MICA motes was 38.4 kbps, whereas the second-generation MICA motes (MICAz motes) can communicate at 250 kbps using IEEE 802.15.4 (ZigBee) [35]. Despite these advances in communication, limited wireless bandwidth from sensor nodes to the sink node makes timely transmission of multimedia data to the sink node infeasible. In traditional EWSNs, the communication energy dominates the computation energy. For example, an embedded sensor node produced by Rockwell Automation [36] expends 2000× more energy for transmitting a bit than that of executing a single instruction [37]. Similarly, transmitting a 15 frames per second (FPS) digital video stream over a wireless Bluetooth link takes 400 mW [38].

Fortunately, there exists a trade-off between transmission and computation in an EWSN, which is well suited for in-network processing for information-rich applications and allows transmission of only event descriptions (e.g., detection of a target of interest) to the sink node to conserve energy. Technological advancements in multicore architectures have made multicore processors a viable and cost-effective choice for increasing the computational ability of embedded sensor nodes. Multicore embedded sensor nodes can extract the desired information from the sensed data and communicate only this processed information, which reduces the data transmission volume to the sink node. By replacing a large percentage of communication with in-network computation, multicore embedded sensor nodes could realize large energy savings that would increase the sensor network's overall lifetime.

Multicore embedded sensor nodes enable energy savings over traditional single-core embedded sensor nodes in two ways. First, reducing the energy expended in communication by performing in situ computation of sensed data and transmitting only processed information. Second, a multicore embedded sensor node allows the computations to be split across multiple cores while running each core at a lower processor voltage and frequency, as compared to a single-core system, which results in energy savings. Utilizing a single-core embedded sensor node for information processing in information-rich applications requires the sensor node to run at a high processor voltage and frequency to meet the application's delay requirements, which increases the power dissipation of the processor. A multicore embedded sensor node reduces the number of memory accesses, clock speed, and instruction decoding, thereby enabling higher arithmetic performance at a lower power consumption as compared to a single-core processor [38].

Preliminary studies have demonstrated the energy efficiency of multicore embedded sensor nodes as compared to single-core embedded sensor nodes in an EWSN. For example, Dogan et al. [39] evaluated single-core and multicore architectures for biomedical signal processing in wireless body sensor networks (WBSNs) where both energy efficiency and real-time processing are crucial design objectives. Results revealed that the multicore architecture consumed 66% less power than the single-core architecture for high biosignal computation workloads (i.e., 50.1 mega operations per seconds (MOPS)), whereas the multicore architecture consumed 10.4% more power than that of the single-core architecture for relatively light computation workloads (i.e., 681 kilo operations per second (KOPS)).

This chapter's highlights are as follows:

- Proposal of a heterogeneous hierarchical multicore embedded wireless sensor networks (MCEWSN) and the associated multicore embedded sensor node architecture.

- Elaboration on several computation-intensive tasks performed by sensor networks that would especially benefit from multicore embedded sensor nodes.
- Characterization and discussion of various application domains for MCEWSNs.
- Discussion of several state-of-the-art multicore embedded sensor node prototypes developed in academia and industry.
- Research challenges and future research directions for MCEWSNs.

The remainder of this chapter is organized as follows. Section 2.1 proposes an MCEWSN architecture. Section 2.2 proposes a multicore embedded sensor node architecture for MCEWSNs. Section 2.3 elaborates on several compute-intensive tasks that motivated the emergence of MCEWSNs. Potential application domains amenable to MCEWSNs are discussed in Section 2.4. Section 2.5 discusses several prototypes of multicore embedded sensor nodes. Section 2.6 discusses the research challenges and future research directions for MCEWNS, and Section 2.7 concludes this chapter.

2.1 Multicore Embedded Wireless Sensor Network Architecture

Figure 2.1 depicts our proposed heterogeneous hierarchical MCEWSN architecture, which satisfies the increasing in-network computational requirements of emerging EWSN applications. The heterogeneity in the architecture subsumes the integration of numerous single-core embedded sensor nodes and several multicore embedded sensor nodes. We note that homogeneous hierarchical single-core EWSNs have been discussed in the literature for large EWSNs (EWSNs consisting of a large number of sensor nodes) [40, 41]. Our proposed architecture is hierarchical since the architecture comprises of various clusters (a group of embedded sensor nodes in communication range with each other) and a sink node. A hierarchical network is

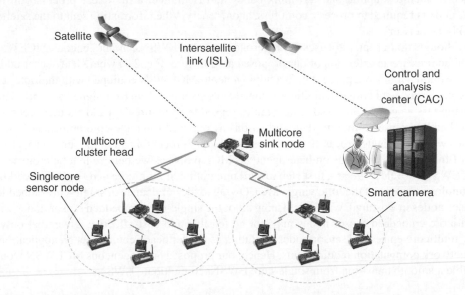

Figure 2.1   A heterogeneous multicore embedded wireless sensor network (MCEWSN) architecture

well suited for large EWSNs since small EWSNs, which consist of only a few sensor nodes, can send the sensed data directly to the base station or sink node.

Each cluster consists of several leaf sensor nodes and a cluster head. Leaf sensor nodes contain a single-core processor and are responsible for sensing, preprocessing sensed data, and transmitting sensed data to the cluster head nodes. Since leaf sensor nodes are not intended to perform complex processing of sensed data in our proposed architecture, a single-core processor sufficiently meets the computational requirements of leaf sensor nodes. Cluster head nodes consist of a multicore processor and are responsible for coalescing/fusing the data received from leaf sensor nodes for transmission to the sink node in an energy- and bandwidth-efficient manner. Our proposed architecture with multicore cluster heads is based on practical reasons since sending all the collected data from the cluster heads to the sink node is not feasible for bandwidth-limited EWSNs, which warrants complex processing and information fusion to be carried out at cluster head nodes, and only the concise processed information is transmitted to the sink node.

The sink node contains a multicore processor and is responsible for transforming high-level user queries from the control and analysis center (CAC) to network-specific directives, querying the MCEWSN for the desired information, and returning the requested information to the user/CAC. The sink node's multicore processor facilitates postprocessing of the information received from multiple cluster heads. The postprocessing at the sink node includes information fusion and event detection based on the aggregated data from all of the sensor nodes in the network. The CAC further analyzes the information received from the sink node and issues control commands and queries to the sink node.

MCEWSNs can be coupled with a satellite backbone network that provides long-haul communication from the sink node to the CAC since MCEWSNs are often deployed in remote areas with no wireless infrastructure, such as a cellular network infrastructure. The satellites in the satellite backbone network communicate with each other via intersatellite links (ISLs). Since a satellite's uplink and downlink bandwidth is limited, a multicore processor in the sink node is required to process, compress, and/or encrypt the information sent to the satellite backbone network.

Although this chapter focuses on heterogeneous MCEWSNs, homogeneous MCEWSN architectures are an extension of our proposed architecture (Fig. 2.1) where leaf sensor nodes also contain a multicore processor. In a homogeneous MCEWSN equipped with multiple sensors, each processor core in a multicore embedded sensor node can be assigned to process one sensing task (e.g., one processor core handles sensed temperature data and another processor core handles sensed humidity data and so on) as opposed to single-core embedded sensor nodes where the single processor core is responsible for processing all of the sensed data from all of the sensors. We focus on heterogeneous MCEWSNs as we believe that heterogeneous MCEWSNs would serve as a first step toward integration of multicore and sensor networking technology because of the following reason. Owing to the dominance of single-core embedded sensor nodes in existing EWSNs, replacing all of the single-core embedded sensor nodes with multicore embedded sensor nodes may not be feasible and cost effective, given that only a few multicore embedded sensor nodes operating as cluster heads could meet an application's in-network computation requirements. Hence, our proposed heterogeneous MCEWSN would enable a smooth transition from single-core EWSNs to multicore EWSNs.

2.2 Multicore Embedded Sensor Node Architecture

Figure 2.2 depicts the architecture of a multicore embedded sensor node in our MCEWSN. The multicore embedded sensor node consists of a sensing unit, a processing unit, a storage unit, a communication unit, a power unit, an optional actuator unit, and an optional location finding unit (optional units are represented by dotted lines in Fig. 2.2) [33].

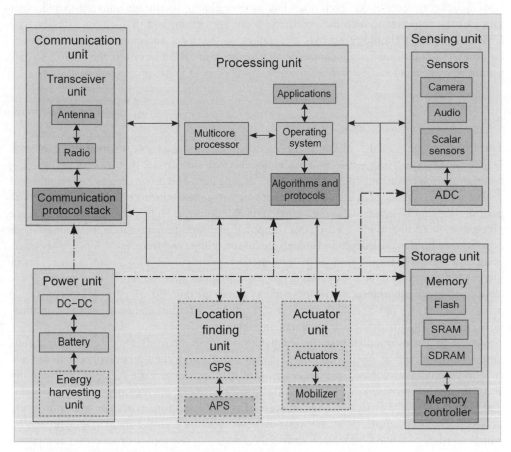

DC–DC: Direct current to direct current converter
SDRAM: Synchronous dynamic random-access memory
SRAM: Static random-access memory
ADC: Analog-to-digital converter
GPS: Global positioning system
APS: Ad hoc positioning system

—·—·—▶ Power wires
◀————▶ Peripheral interfaces

Figure 2.2 Multicore embedded sensor node architecture

2.2.1   Sensing Unit

The sensing unit senses the phenomenon of interest and is composed of two subunits: sensors (e.g., camera/image, audio, and scalar sensors such as temperature and pressure) and analog-to-digital converters (ADCs). Image sensors can either leverage traditional charge-coupled device (CCD) technology or complementary metal-oxide-semiconductor (CMOS) imaging technology. The CCD sensor accumulates the incident light energy as the charge accumulated on a pixel, which is then converted into an analog voltage signal. In CMOS imaging technology, each pixel has its own charge-to-voltage conversion and other processing components, such as amplifiers, noise correction, and digitization circuits. The CMOS imaging technology enables integration of the lens, an image sensor, and image compression and processing technology on a single chip. ADCs convert the analog signals produced by sensors to digital signals, which serve as input to the processing unit.

2.2.2   Processing Unit

The processing unit consists of a multicore processor and is responsible for controlling sensors, gathering and processing sensed data, executing the system software that coordinates sensing, communication tasks, and interfacing with the storage unit. The processing unit for traditional sensor nodes consists of a single-core processor for general-purpose applications, such as periodic sensing of scalar data (e.g., temperature, humidity). High-performance single-core processors would be infeasible to meet computational requirements since these single-core processors would require operation at high processor voltage and frequency. A processor operating at a high voltage and frequency consumes an enormous amount of power since power increases proportionally to the operating processor frequency and square of the operating processor voltage. Furthermore, even if these energy issues are ignored, a single high-performance processor core may not be able to meet the computational requirements of emerging applications, such as multimedia sensor networks, in real time.

Multicore processors distribute the computations across the available cores, which speeds up the computations as well as conserves energy by allowing each processor core to operate at a lower processor voltage and frequency. Multicore processors are suitable for streaming and complex, event-based monitoring applications, such as in smart camera sensor networks, that require data to be processed and compressed as well as require extraction of key information features. For example, the IC3D/Xetal single-instruction multiple-data (SIMD) processor, which consists of a linear processor array (LPA) with 320 reduced instruction set computers (RISC)/processors, is being used in smart camera sensor networks [42].

2.2.3   Storage Unit

The storage unit consists of the memory subsystem, which can be classified as *user memory* and *program memory*, and a memory controller, which coordinates memory accesses between different processor cores. The user memory stores sensed data when immediate data transmission is not possible due to hardware failures, environmental conditions, physical layer jamming, limited energy reserves, or when the data requires processing. The program memory is used for programming the embedded sensor node, and using Flash memory for the program memory provides persistent storage of application code and text segments. Static random-access memory (SRAM), which does not need periodic refreshing but is expensive in terms of area and power consumption, is used as dedicated processor memory. Synchronous dynamic random-access memory (SDRAM) is typically used as user memory. For example, the Imote2 embedded sensor node, which contains a Marvell PXA271 XScale processor operating between 13 and 416 MHz, has 256 kB SRAM, 32 MB Flash, and 32 MB SDRAM [43].

2.2.4   Communication Unit

The communication unit interfaces the embedded sensor node to the wireless network and consists of a transceiver unit (transceiver and antenna) and the communication unit software. The communication unit software mainly consists of the communication protocol stack and the physical layer software in the case of software-defined radio (SDR). The transceiver unit consists of either a wireless local area network (WLAN) card, such as an IEEE 802.11b compliant card, or an IEEE 802.15.4 compatible card, such as a Texas Instrument/Chipcon CC2420 chipset. The choice of a transceiver unit card depends on the application requirements such as desired range and allowable power. The maximum transmit power of IEEE 802.11b cards is higher in comparison to IEEE 802.15.4 cards, which results in a higher communication range but consumes more power. For example, the Intel PRO/Wireless 2011 card has a data rate of 11 Mbps and a typical transmit power of 18 dB m, but draws 300 and 170 mA for sending and receiving, respectively. The CC2420 802.15.4 radio has a maximum data rate of 250 kbps and a transmit power of 0 dB m, but draws 17.4 and 19.7 mA for sending and receiving, respectively.

2.2.5   Power Unit

The power unit supplies power to various components/units on the embedded sensor node and dictates the sensor node's lifetime. The power unit consists of a battery and a DC–DC converter. The DC–DC converter provides a constant supply voltage to the sensor node. The power unit may be augmented by an optional energy-harvesting unit that derives energy from external sources, such as solar cells. Although multicore embedded sensor nodes are more power efficient as compared to single-core embedded sensor nodes, energy-harvesting units in multicore cluster heads and the sink node would prolong the MCEWSN's lifetime. Energy-harvesting units are more suitable for cluster heads and the sink node as these nodes perform more computations as compared to the single-core leaf sensor nodes. Furthermore, incorporating energy-harvesting units in only a few embedded sensor nodes (i.e., cluster heads and sink nodes) would not substantially increase the cost of EWSN deployment. Without an energy-harvesting unit, MCEWSNs would only be suitable for applications with relatively small lifetime requirements.

2.2.6   Actuator Unit

The optional actuator unit consists of actuators (e.g., motors, servos, linear actuators, air muscles, muscle wire, camera pan tilt) and an optional mobilizer unit for sensor node mobility. Actuators enhance the sensing task by opening/closing a switch/relay to control functions, such as a camera or antenna orientation and repositioning sensors. Actuators, in contrast to sensors that only sense a phenomenon, typically affect the operating environment by opening a valve, emitting sound, or physically moving the sensor node.

2.2.7   Location Finding Unit

The optional location finding unit determines a sensor node's location. Depending on the application requirements and available resources, the location finding unit can either be global positioning system (GPS)-based unit or ad hoc positioning system (APS)-based unit. Although GPS is highly accurate, the GPS components are expensive and require direct line of sight between the sensor node and satellites. APS determines a sensor node's position with respect to defined *landmarks*, which may be other GPS-based sensor nodes [44]. A sensor node estimates the distance from itself to the landmark based on direct communication and the received communication signal strength. A sensor node that is two hops away from a landmark estimates its distance based on the distance estimate of a sensor node one hop away from a landmark via the message propagation. A sensor node with distance estimates to three or more landmarks can compute its own position via triangulation.

2.3   Compute-Intensive Tasks Motivating the Emergence of MCEWSNs

Many applications require embedded sensor nodes to perform various compute-intensive tasks that often exceeds the computing capability of traditional single-core sensor nodes. These tasks include information fusion, encryption, network coding, and SDR and motivate the emergence of MCEWSNs. In this section, we discuss these compute-intensive tasks requiring multicore support in an embedded sensor node.

2.3.1   Information Fusion

A critical processing task in EWSNs is information fusion, which can benefit from a multicore processor in an embedded sensor node. EWSNs produce a large amount of data that must be processed, delivered, and assessed according to application objectives. Since the transmission bandwidth is limited, information fusion condenses the sensed data and transmits only the selected fused information to the sink node. Additionally, the data received from neighboring sensor nodes is often redundant and highly correlated, which warrants fusing the sensed data. Formally, information fusion encompasses theory, techniques, and tools created and applied to exploit the synergy in the information acquired from multiple sources (sensors, databases, etc.) such that the resulting fused data/information is considered qualitatively or quantitatively better in terms of accuracy or robustness than the acquired data from any single data source [45]. Data aggregation is an instance of information fusion in which the data from various sources is aggregated using summarization functions (e.g., minimum, maximum, and average) that reduce the volume of data being manipulated. Information fusion can reduce the amount of data traffic, filter noisy measurements, and make predictions and inferences about a monitored entity.

Information fusion can be computationally expensive, especially for video sensing applications. Unlike scalar data, which can be combined using relatively simple mathematical manipulations such as average and summation, video data is vectorial and requires complex computations to fuse (e.g., edge detection, histogram formation, compression, filtering). Reducing transmission overhead via information fusion in video sensor networks requires a substantial increase in intermediate processing, which warrants the use of multicore cluster heads in MCEWSNs. Multicore cluster heads fuse data received from multiple sensor nodes to eliminate redundant transmission and provide fused information to the sink node with minimum data latency. Data latency is the sum of the delay involved in data transmission, routing, and information fusion/data aggregation [40]. Data latency is important in many applications, especially real-time applications, where freshness of data is an important factor. Multicore cluster heads can fuse data much faster than single-core sensor nodes, which justifies the use of multicore cluster heads in MCEWSNs with complex real-time computing requirements.

Omnibus Model for Information Fusion: The Omnibus model [46] guides information fusion for sensor-based devices. Figure 2.3 illustrates the Omnibus model with respect to our MCEWSN architecture, and we exemplify the model's usage by considering a surveillance application performing target tracking based on acoustic sensors [45]. The *Observe* stage, which can be carried out at single-core sensor nodes and/or multicore cluster heads, uses a filter (e.g., moving average filter) to reduce noise (*Signal Processing*) from acoustic sensor data provided by the embedded sensor nodes (*Sensing*). The *Orientate* stage, which is carried out at multicore cluster heads, uses the filtered acoustic data for range estimation (*Feature Extraction*) and estimates the target's location and trajectory (*Pattern Processing*). The *Decide* stage, which is carried out at multicore cluster heads and/or multicore sink nodes, classifies the sensed target (*Context Processing*) and determines whether the target represents a threat (*Decision Making*). If the target is a threat, the *Act* stage, which is carried out at the CAC, intercepts the target (*Control*) (e.g., with a missile) and activates available armaments (*Resource Tasking*).

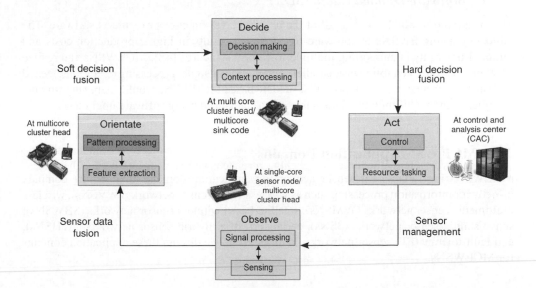

Figure 2.3   Omnibus sensor information fusion model for an MCEWSN architecture

2.3.2   Encryption

Security is an important issue in many sensor networking applications since sensors are deployed in open environments and are susceptible to malicious attacks. The sensed and/or aggregated data must be encrypted for secure transmission to the sink node. The two main practical issues involved in encryption are the size of the encrypted message and the encryption execution time. Privacy homomorphisms (PHs) are encryption functions suitable for MCEWSNs that allow a set of operations to be performed on encrypted data without knowing the decryption functions [40]. PHs use a positive integer $d \geq 2$ for computing the secret key for encryption such that the size of the encrypted data increases by a factor of d as compared to the original data. The security of the encrypted data increases with d as well as the execution time for encryption. For example, the execution time for encryption of one byte of data is 3481 clock cycles on a MICA2 mote when $d = 2$ and increases to 4277 clock cycles when $d = 4$. MICA2 motes cannot handle the computations for $d \geq 4$ [40], hence, applications requiring greater security require multicore sensor nodes and/or cluster heads to perform these computations.

2.3.3   Network Coding

Network coding is a coding technique to enhance network throughput in multinodal environments, such as EWSNs. Despite the effectiveness of network coding for EWSNs, excessive decoding cost associated with network coding hinders the technique's adoption in traditional EWSNs with constrained computing power [47]. Future MCEWSNs will enable adoption of sophisticated coding techniques, such as network coding to increase network throughput.

2.3.4   Software-Defined Radio (SDR)

SDR is a radio in which some or all of the physical layer functions execute as software. The radio in existing EWSNs is hardware-based, which results in higher production costs and minimal flexibility in supporting multiple waveform standards [48]. MCEWSNs can realize SDR-based radio by enabling fast, parallel computation of signal processing operations needed in SDR (e.g., fast Fourier transform (FFT)). SDR-based MCEWSNs would enable multimode, multiband, and multifunctional radios that can be enhanced using software upgrades.

2.4   MCEWSN Application Domains

MCEWSNs are suitable for sensor networking application domains that require complex in-network information processing such as wireless video sensor networks (WVSNs), wireless multimedia sensor networks (WMSNs), satellite-based wireless sensor networks (SBWSNs), space shuttle sensor networks (3SNs), aerial–terrestrial hybrid sensor networks (ATHSNs), and fault-tolerant (FT) sensor networks. In this section, we discuss these application domains for MCEWSNs.

2.4.1   Wireless Video Sensor Networks (WVSNs)

WVSNs are WSNs in which smart cameras and/or image sensors are embedded in the sensor nodes. WVSNs emulate the compound eye found in certain arthropods. Although WVSNs are a subset of WMSNs, we discuss WVSNs separately to emphasize the WVSNs' stand-alone existence. WVSNs are suitable for applications in areas such as homeland security, battlefield monitoring, and mining. For example, video sensors deployed at airports, borders, and harbors provide a level of continuous and accurate monitoring and protection that is otherwise unattainable. We discuss the application of multicore embedded sensor nodes both for image- and video-centric WVSNs.

In image-centric WVSNs, multiple image/camera sensors observe a scene from multiple directions and are able to describe objects in their true 3D appearance by overcoming occlusion problems. Low-cost imaging sensors are readily available, such as CCD and CMOS imaging sensors from Kodak, and the Cyclops camera from the University of California at Los Angeles (UCLA) designed as an add-on for MICA sensor nodes [38]. Image preprocessing involves convolutions and data-dependent operations using a limited neighborhood of pixels. The signal processing algorithms for image processing in WVSNs typically exhibit a high degree of parallelism and are dominated by a few regular kernels (e.g., FFT) that are responsible for a large fraction of the execution time and energy consumption. Accelerating these kernels on multicore embedded sensor nodes would achieve significant speedup in execution time and reduction in energy consumption, and would help achieve real-time computational requirements for many applications in energy-constrained domains.

Video-centric WVSNs rely on multiple video streams from multiple embedded sensor nodes. Since sensor nodes can only serve low-resolution video streams given the sensor nodes' resource limitations, a single video stream alone does not contain enough information for vision analysis such as event detection and tracking; however, multiple sensor nodes can capture video streams from different angles and distances together providing enormous visual data [35]. Video encoders rely on intraframe compression techniques that reduce redundancy within one frame and interframe compression techniques (e.g., predictive coding) that exploit redundancy among subsequent frames [33]. Video coding techniques require complex algorithms that exceed the computing power of single-core embedded sensor nodes. The visual data from numerous sensor nodes can be combined to give high-resolution video streams; however, this processing requires multicore embedded sensor nodes and/or cluster heads.

2.4.2   Wireless Multimedia Sensor Networks (WMSNs)

A WMSN consists of wirelessly connected embedded sensor nodes that can retrieve multimedia content such as video and audio streams, still images, and scalar sensor data of the observed phenomenon. WMSNs target a large variety of distributed, wireless, streaming multimedia networking applications ranging from home surveillance to military and space applications. A multimedia sensor captures audio and image/video streams using an embedded microphone and a microcamera.

Various sensors in a WMSN coordinate closely to achieve application goals. For example, in a military application for target detection and tracking, acoustic and electromagnetic sensors can enable early detection of a target but may not provide adequate information about the target. Additional target details, such as type of vehicle, equipped armaments, and onboard personnel, are often required and gathering these details requires image sensors. Although the sensing ability in most sensors is isotropic and attenuates with distance, a distinct characteristic of video/image sensors is these sensors' directional sensing ranges. Recently, omnicameras have become available, which can provide complete coverage of the scene around a sensor node; however, applications are limited to close range scenarios to guarantee sufficient image resolution for moving objects [35]. To ensure full coverage of the sensor field, a set of directional cameras is required to capture enough information for activity detection. The image and video sensors' high sensing cost limits these sensors' continuous activation given constrained embedded sensor node resources. Hence, the image and video sensors in a WMSN require sophisticated control such that the image and video sensors are triggered only after a target is detected based on sensed data from other lower cost sensors, such as acoustic and electromagnetic.

Desirable WMSN characteristics include the ability to store, process in real time, correlate, and fuse multimedia data originating from heterogeneous sources [33]. Multimedia contents, especially video streams, require data rates that are orders of magnitude higher than those supported by traditional single-core embedded sensor nodes. To process multimedia data in real time and to reduce the wireless bandwidth demand, multicore embedded sensor nodes in the network are required. Multicore embedded sensor nodes facilitate in situ processing of voluminous information from various sensors, notifying the CAC only once an event is detected (e.g., target detection).

2.4.3   Satellite-Based Wireless Sensor Networks (SBWSN)

A SBWSN is a wireless communication sensing network composed of many satellites, each equipped with multifunctional sensors, long-range wireless communication modules, thrusters for attitude adjustment, and a computational unit (potentially multicore) to carry out processing of the sensed data. Traditional satellite missions are extremely expensive to design, build, launch, and operate, thereby motivating the aerospace industry to focus on distributed space missions, which would consist of multiple small, inexpensive, and distributed satellites coordinating to attain mission goals. SBWSNs would enable robust space missions by tolerating the failure of a single or a few satellites as compared to a large single satellite, where a single failure could compromise the success of a mission. SBWSNs can be used for a variety of missions, such as space weather monitoring, studying the impact of solar storms on Earth's magnetosphere and ionosphere, environmental monitoring (e.g., pollution, land, and ocean surface monitoring), and hazard prediction (e.g., flood and earthquake prediction).

Each SBWSN mission requires specific orbits and constellations to meet mission requirements, and GPS provides an essential tool for orbit determination and navigation. Typical constellations include string-of-pearls, flower constellation, and satellite cluster. In particular, the flower constellation provides stable orbit configurations, which are suitable for *microsatellite* (mass < 100 kg), *nanosatellite* (mass < 10 kg), and *picosatellite* (mass < 1 kg) missions. Important orbital factors to consider in SBWSN design are relative range (distance) and speed between satellites, the ISL access opportunity, and the ground-link access opportunity.

The access time is the time for two satellites to communicate with each other and depends on the distance between the satellites (range). Satellites in an SBWSN can be used as an interferometer, which correlates different images acquired from slightly different angles/view points in order to get better resolution and more meaningful insights.

All of the satellites in an SBWSN collaborate to sense the desired phenomenon, communicate over long distances through beam-forming over an ISL, and maintain the network topology through self-organized mobility [49]. Studies indicate that IEEE 802.11b (Wi-Fi) and IEEE 802.16 (WiMax) can be used for intersatellite communications (communication between satellites) and IEEE 802.15.4 (ZigBee) can be used for intrasatellite (communication between sensor nodes within a satellite) communications [50]. We point out that the IEEE 802.11b protocol requires modifications for use in an ISL where the distance between satellites is more than 1 km since the IEEE 802.11b standard normally supports a communication range within 300 m. The feasibility of wireless protocols for intersatellite communication depends on the range, power requirements, medium access control (MAC) features, and support for mobility. The intrasatellite protocols are mainly selected based on power since the range is small within a satellite. A low duty cycle and the ability to put the radio to sleep are desirable features for intrasatellite communication protocols. For example, the MICA2DOT mote, which requires 24 mW of active power and 3 μW of standby power, supplied by a 3 V 750 mA h battery cell can last for 27,780 h ≈ 3 years and 2 months, while operating at a duty cycle of 0.1% (supported by ZigBee) [51].

Since an individual satellite within an SBWSN may not have sufficient power to communicate with a ground station, a sink satellite in an SBWSN can communicate with a ground station, which is connected to the CAC. Ground communication in SBWSNs takes place in very-high- frequency (VHF) (30–300 MHz) and ultra-high- frequency (UHF) (300 MHz–3 GHz) bands. VHF frequencies pass through the ionosphere with effects, such as scintillation, fading, Faraday's rotation, and multipath effects during intense solar cycles due to the reflection of the VHF signals. UHF bands, in which both S- and L-bands lie, can suffer severe disruptions during a solar storm. For a formation of several SNAP-1 nanosatellites, the typical downlink data rate is 38.4 or 76.8 kbps maximum [51], which necessitates multicore embedded sensor nodes in SBWSNs to perform in situ processing so that only event descriptions are sent to the CAC.

2.4.4   Space Shuttle Sensor Networks (3SN)

A 3SN corresponds to a network of sensors aimed to monitor a space shuttle during preflight, ascent, on-orbit, and reentry phases. Battery-operated embedded wireless sensors can be easily bonded to the space shuttle's structure and enable real-time monitoring of temperature, triaxial vibration, strain, pressure, tilt, chemical, and ultrasound data. MCEWSNs would enable real-time monitoring of space vehicles not possible by ground-based sensing systems. For example, the Columbia space shuttle accident was caused by damage done when foam shielding dislodged from the external fuel tank during the shuttle's launch, which damaged the wing's leading edge panels [52]. The vehicle lacked onboard sensors that could have enabled ground personnel to determine the extent and location of the damage. Ground-based cameras captured images of the impact but were not able to reliably characterize the location and severity of the impact and resulting damage.

MCEWSNs for space shuttles, currently under development, would be used for space shuttle main engine (SSME) crack investigation, space shuttle environmental control life support system (ECLSS) oxygen and nitrogen flexhose analysis, and wing leading edge impact detection. Since the amount of data acquired during the 10-min ascent period is nearly 100 MB, the time to download all data, even for a single event, via the radio frequency (RF) link is prohibitively long. Hence, information fusion algorithms are required in 3SNs to minimize the quantity and increase the quality of the data being transmitted via the RF link. Furthermore, MCEWSNs would enable a 10× reduction in the installation costs for the shuttle as compared to the sensing systems based on traditional wired approaches [52].

2.4.5   Aerial–Terrestrial Hybrid Sensor Networks (ATHSNs)

ATHSNs, which consist of ground sensors and aerial sensors, integrate terrestrial sensor networks with aerial/space sensor networks. To connect remote terrestrial EWSNs to a CAC located far away in urban areas, ATHSNs can include a satellite backbone network. The satellite backbone network is widely available at remote locations and provides a reliable and broadband communication network [53, 54]. Various satellite communication choices are possible, such as WildBlue, HughesNet, and geostationary operational environmental satellite (GOES) system of National Aeronautics and Space Administration (NASA). However, a satellite's uplink and downlink bandwidth is limited and requires preprocessing and compression of sensed data, especially multimedia data such as image and video streams. Multicore embedded sensor nodes are suitable for ATHSNs, and are capable of carrying out the processing and compression of high-quality image and video streams for transmission to and from a satellite backbone network.

Aerial networks in ATHSNs may consist of unmanned aerial vehicles (UAVs) and satellites. For example, consider an ATHSN in which UAVs contain embedded image and video sensors such that only the image scenes that are of significant interest from a military strategy perspective are sensed in greater detail. The working of ATHSNs consisting of UAVs and satellites can be described concisely in the following seven steps [53]. (1) Ground sensors detect the presence of a hostile target in the monitored field and store events in memory. (2) The satellite periodically contacts multicore cluster heads in the terrestrial EWSN to download updates about the target's presence. (3) Satellites contact UAVs to acquire image data about the scene where the intrusion is detected. (4) UAVs gather image data through the embedded image sensors. (5) The embedded multicore sensors in UAVs process and compress the image data for transmission to the satellite backbone network in a bandwidth-efficient manner. (6) The satellite backbone network relays the processed information received from the UAVs to the CAC. (7) The satellite backbone network relays the commands (e.g., launching the UAVs' arsenals) from the CAC to the UAVs.

Ye et al. [54] have implemented an ATHSN prototype for an ecological study using temperature, humidity, photosynthetically active radiation (PAR), wind speed, and precipitation sensors. The prototype consists of a small satellite dish and a communication modem for integrating a terrestrial EWSN with the WildBlue satellite backbone network, which provides commercial service. The prototype uses Intel's Stargate processor as the sink node, which provides access control and manages the use of the satellite link.

The transformational satellite (TSAT) system is a future generation satellite system that is designed for military applications by NASA, the U.S. Department of Defense (DoD), and the Intelligence Community (IC) [53]. The TSAT system is a constellation of five satellites, placed in geostationary orbit, that constitute a high-bandwidth satellite backbone network, which allows terrestrial units to access optical and radar imagery from UAVs and satellites in real time. TSAT provides broadband, reliable, worldwide, and secure transmission of data. TSAT supports RF communication links with data rates up to 45 Mbps and laser communication links with data rates up to 10–100 Gbps [53].

2.4.6   Fault-Tolerant (FT) Sensor Networks

The sensor nodes in an EWSN are typically deployed in harsh and unattended environments, which makes fault tolerance (FT) an important consideration in EWSN design, particularly for space-based WSNs. For example, the temperature of aerospace vehicles varies from cryogenic to extremely high temperature, and pressure varies from vacuum to very high pressure. Additionally, shock and vibration levels during launch can cause component failures. Furthermore, high levels of ionizing radiation require electronics to be FT if not radiation-hardened (rad-hard). Multicore embedded sensors can provide hardware-based (e.g., triple modular redundancy (TMR) or self-checking pairs (SCP)) as well as software-based (e.g., algorithm-based fault tolerance (ABFT)) FT mechanisms for applications requiring high reliability. Computations, such as preprocessing and data fusion, can be replicated on multiple cores so that if radiation corrupts processing on one core, processing on other cores would still enable reliable computation of results.

2.5   Multicore Embedded Sensor Nodes

Several initiatives toward multicore embedded sensor nodes have been undertaken by academia and industry for various real-time applications. In this section, we describe several state-of-the-art multicore embedded sensor node prototypes.

2.5.1   InstraNode

InstraNode is a dual-core sensor node for real-time health monitoring of civil structures, such as highway bridges and skyscrapers. InstraNode is equipped with a 4000 mA h lithium-ion battery, three accelerometers, a gyroscope, and an IEEE 802.11b (Wi-Fi) card for communication with other nodes. One low-power processor core in InstraNode runs at 3 V and 4 MHz and is dedicated to sampling data from sensors, whereas the other faster, high-power processor core runs at 4.3 V and 40 MHz and is responsible for networking tasks, such as transmission/reception of data and execution of a routing algorithm. Furthermore, InstraNode possesses multimodal operation capabilities such as wired/wireless and battery-powered/AC-adaptor powered options. Experiments indicate that the InstraNode outperforms single-core sensor nodes in terms of power efficiency and network performance [55].

2.5.2   Mars Rover Prototype Mote

Etchison et al. [56] have proposed a high-performance EWSN for the Mars Rover, which consists of dual-core mobile sensor nodes and a wireless cluster consisting of multiple processors to process image data gathered from the sensor nodes and to make decisions based on gathered information. The prototype mote consists of a Micro ATX motherboard with Intel's dual-core Atom processor, 2 GB of random-access memory (RAM), and is powered by a 12 V/5 A DC power supply for lab testing. Each mote performs data acquisition, processing, and transmission.

2.5.3   Satellite-Based Sensor Node (SBSN)

Vladimirova et al. [57] have developed a system-on-chip (SoC) satellite-based sensor node (SBSN). The SBSN prototype contains a SPARC V8 LEON3 soft processor core, which allows configuration in an SMP architecture [58]. The LEON3 processor core runs software applications and interfaces with the upper layers of the communication stack using the IEEE 802.11 protocol. The SBSN prototype uses a number of intellectual property (IP) cores, such as a hardware-accelerated Wi-Fi MAC, a transceiver core, and a Java coprocessor. The Java coprocessor enables distributed computing and Internet protocol (IP)-based networking functions in SBWSNs. The intersatellite communication module (ISCM) in the SBSN prototype adheres to IEEE 802.11 and CubeSat design specifications. The ISCM supports ground communication links and ISLs at variable data rates and configurable waveforms to adapt to channel conditions. The ISCM incorporates S-band (2.4 GHz) and a 434/144 MHz radio frontend interfaced to a single reconfigurable modem. The ISCM uses a high-end AD9861 ADC/digital-to-analog converter (DAC) for the 2.4 GHz radio frontend for a Maxim 2830 radio and a low-end AD7731 for the 434/144 MHz frontend for an Alinco DJC-7E radio. Additionally, ISCM incorporates current and temperature sensors and a 16-bit microcontroller for housekeeping purposes.

2.5.4   Multi-CPU-Based Sensor Node Prototype

Ohara et al. [59] have developed a prototype for an embedded sensor node using three PIC18 central processing units (CPUs). The prototype is supplied by a configurable voltage stabilized power supply, but the same voltage is supplied to all CPUs. The prototype allowed each CPU's frequency to be statically changed by changing a corresponding ceramic resonator. Experiments revealed that the multi-CPU sensor node prototype consumed 76% less power as compared to a single-core sensor node for benchmarks that involved sampling, root mean square calculation, and preprocessing samples for transmission.

2.5.5   Smart Camera Mote

Kleihorst et al. [38] developed a smart camera mote, which consists of four basic components: color image sensors, an IC3D SIMD processor (a member of the Philips' Xetal family of SIMD processors) for low-level image processing, a general-purpose processor for intermediate and high-level processing and control, and a communication module. Both of the processors are coupled with a dual-port RAM that enables these processors to work in a shared workspace. The IC3D SIMD processor consists of a linear array of 320 RISC processors. The peak pixel performance of the IC3D processor is approximately 50 giga operations per second (GOPS). Despite high pixel performance, the IC3D processor is an inherently low-power processor, which makes the processor suitable for multicore embedded sensor nodes. The power consumption of the IC3D processor for typical applications, such as feature finding or face detection, is below 100 mW in active processing modes.

2.6   Research Challenges and Future Research Directions

Despite few initiatives toward MCEWSNs, the domain is still in its infancy and requires addressing some challenges to facilitate ubiquitous deployment of MCEWSNs. In this section, we discuss several research challenges and future research directions for MCEWSNs.

Application Parallelization: Parallelization of existing serial applications and algorithms can be challenging, considering the limited number of parallel programmers as compared to serial programmers. Parallel applications with limited scalability present challenges for efficient utilization of multicore and future manycore embedded sensor nodes. Furthermore, synchronization between different cores by the use of barriers and locks limits the attainable speedup from parallel applications. A poor speedup due to limited scalability as the number of cores increases can diminish the energy and performance benefits attained by parallelization of sensor applications. To minimize potential performance degradation for parallel applications with limited scalability, designers can restrict these applications to a limited number of cores while turning off remaining cores to save power or utilizing other cores by multiprogramming other sensor applications on those cores. Consequently, existing operating systems for embedded sensor nodes (e.g., TinyOS [60], MANTIS [61]) would require updating their schedulers for efficient scheduling of multiprogrammed workloads and would also require some middleware support (e.g., OpenMP) to support multithreading of parallel applications.

Signal Processing and Computer Vision: Advances in sensor technology have led to a dramatic increase in the amount of data sensed, which is fueled by both the reduced cost of sensors and increased deployment over a large class of applications. This sensed data deluge problem exacerbates for MCEWSNs and places immense stress on our ability to process, store, and obtain meaningful information from the data. The fundamental reason behind the data deluge problem comes from sensor designs that are based on the Nyquist sampling theorem [62], which has been the dogma in traditional signal processing. However, as we build sensors and sensing platforms with increasing capabilities (e.g., MCEWSNs involving hyper-spectral imaging), designs based on Nyquist sampling are prohibitively costly because of high-resolution sensors and extremely fast data processing requirements. The failure of Nyquist sampling lies in its inability to exploit redundant structures in signals. This redundancy and compressibility in signals forms the basis of Fourier and wavelet transforms. Research in sensing and processing systems that exploit the redundant structures in signals includes sparse models, union-of-subspace models, and low-dimensional manifold models. The data deluge problem in MCEWSNs can be addressed in three fundamental ways: (1) parsimonious signal representations that facilitate efficient processing of visual signals; (2) novel compressive and computational imaging systems for sensing of data; and (3) scalable algorithms for large-scale machine learning systems. These novel techniques to address the data deluge problem in MCEWSNs require further research.

Another related research avenue for MCEWSNs is compressive sensing for high-dimensional visual signals, which requires sensors with capabilities that go beyond sensing 2D images. Examples of these novel sensors include the Lytro camera for sensing light fields [63]; the Kinect system that provides scene depth [64]; and flexible camera-arrays that provide unique trade-offs in the spatial, temporal, and angular resolutions of the incident light. Design of novel models, sensors, and technologies is imperative to better characterize objects with complex visual properties.

Furthermore, distilling information from a large number of low-resolution video streams obtained from multiple video sensors requires novel algorithms since current computer vision and signal processing algorithms can only analyze a few high-resolution images.

Reconfigurability: Reconfigurability in MCEWSNs is an important research avenue that would allow the network to adapt to new requirements by integrating code upgrades (e.g., a more efficient algorithm for video compression may be discovered after deployment). Mobility and self-adaptability of embedded sensor nodes require further research to obtain the desired view of the sensor field (e.g., an image sensor facing downward toward the earth may not be desirable).

Energy Harvesting: Considering that the battery energy is the most critical resource constraint for sensor nodes in MCEWSNs, research and development in energy-efficient batteries and energy-harvesting systems would be beneficial for MCEWSNs.

Near-Threshold Computing (NTC): NTC refers to using a supply voltage (V_{DD}) that is close to a single transistor's threshold voltage V_t (generally V_{DD} is slightly above V_t in near-threshold operation, whereas V_{DD} is below V_t for sub-threshold operation). Lowering the supply voltage reduces power consumption and increases energy efficiency by lowering the energy consumed per operation. With the advent of MCEWSNs leveraging manycore chips, sub- or near-threshold designs become a natural fit for these highly parallel architectures. Considering the stringent power constraints of the manycore chips leveraged in MCEWSNs, sub- or near-threshold designs may be the only practical way to power up all of the cores in these chips [65]. Hence, NTC provides a promising solution for the *dark silicon* problem (transistor under utilization) in manycore architectures. However, widespread adoption of NTC in MCEWSNs for reduced power consumption requires addressing NTC challenges such as increased process, voltage, and temperature variations, sub-threshold leakage power, and soft error rates.

Heterogeneous Architectures: MCEWSNs would benefit from parallel computer architecture research. Specifically, a heterogeneous manycore architecture that could leverage both super-threshold computing and NTC to meet performance and energy requirements of sensing applications might provide a promising solution for MCEWSNs. The heterogeneous architecture can integrate super-threshold (nominal voltage) SMP cores and near-threshold SIMD cores [66]. Research indicates that a combination of NTC and parallel SIMD computations achieves excellent energy efficiency for easy-to-parallelize applications [67]. With this heterogeneous architecture, sensing applications' tasks with less parallelism can be scheduled to high-power SMP cores, whereas tasks with abundant parallelism will benefit from scheduling on low-power near-threshold SIMD cores. Hence, research in heterogeneous architectures would enable a single architecture to serve a broad range of sensing applications with varying degrees of parallelism.

Transistor Technology: With ongoing technology scaling, conventional planar CMOS devices suffer from increasing susceptibility to numerous variations, such as circuit performance, short channel effects, delay, or leakage. Research in novel transistor technologies that improve the energy efficiency, provide better resistance to process variation, and are amenable for nanoscale fabrication would benefit sensor nodes in MCEWSNs. One of the promising transistor technologies for future process nodes (22 nm and below) is FinFET, in which the channel is a slab (fin) of undoped silicon perpendicular to the substrate [68]. The increased electrostatic control of the FinFET gate over the channel enables high on-current to off-current ratio, which improves carrier mobility, and is promising for near-threshold low-power designs. Other advantages of FinFET over planar CMOS include reduced random dopant fluctuations, lower parasitic junction capacitance, suppression of short channel effects, leakage currents, and parametric variations. However, the widespread transition to FinFET requires further research in prediction models for performance, energy, and process variation for this transistor technology as well as a complete overhaul of the current fabrication process.

2.7 Chapter Summary

In this chapter, we proposed an architecture for heterogeneous hierarchical MCEWSNs. Compute-intensive tasks, such as information fusion, encryption, network coding, and SDR, will benefit in particular from the increased computational power offered by multicore embedded sensor nodes. Many wireless sensor networking application domains, such as WVSNs, WMSNs, satellite-based sensor networks, 3SNs, ATHSNs, and fault-tolerant sensor networks, can benefit from MCEWSNs. Perceiving the potential benefits of MCEWSNs, several initiatives have been undertaken in both academia and industry to develop multicore embedded sensor nodes, such as InstraNode, SBSNs, and smart camera motes. We further highlighted the research challenges and future research avenues for MCEWSNs. Specifically, MCEWSNs would benefit from advancements in application parallelization, signal processing, computer vision, reconfigurability, energy harvesting, NTC, heterogeneous architectures, and transistor technology.

Part Two

Modeling

3

An Application Metrics Estimation Model for Embedded Wireless Sensor Networks*

Advancements in semiconductor technology, as predicted by Moore's law, have enabled high transistor density in a small chip area resulting in the miniaturization of embedded systems (e.g., sensor nodes). Wireless sensor networks (WSNs) are envisioned as ubiquitous computing systems, which are proliferating in many application domains (e.g., defense, health care, surveillance systems) each with varying application requirements that can be defined by high-level *application metrics* (e.g., lifetime, reliability). However, the diversity of WSN application domains makes it difficult for commercial off-the-shelf (COTS) sensor nodes to meet these application requirements.

Since COTS sensor nodes are mass-produced to optimize cost, many COTS sensor nodes possess tunable parameters (e.g., processor voltage and frequency, sensing frequency), whose values can be *tuned* for application specialization [69]. The WSN application designers (those who design, manage, or deploy the WSN for an application) are typically biologists, teachers, farmers, and household consumers that are experts within their application domain, but have limited technical expertise. Given the large design space and operating constraints, determining appropriate parameter values (operating state) can be a daunting and/or time-consuming task for nonexpert application managers. Typically, sensor node vendors assign initial generic tunable parameter value settings; however, no one tunable parameter value setting is appropriate for all applications. To assist the WSN managers with parameter tuning to best fit the application requirements, an automated parameter tuning process is required.

*A portion of this chapter is copyrighted by Elsevier. The definitive version appeared in: Arslan Munir, Ann Gordon-Ross, Susan Lysecky, and Roman Lysecky, A Lightweight Dynamic Optimization Methodology and Application Metrics Estimation Model for Wireless Sensor Networks, *Elsevier Sustainable Computing: Informatics and Systems*, vol. 3, no. 2, pp. 94–108, June 2013. URL http://www.sciencedirect.com/science/article/pii/S2210537913000048. ©[2013] Elsevier. The work is reproduced under automatic permission granted by Elsevier as we are the authors of this work.

Modeling and Optimization of Parallel and Distributed Embedded Systems, First Edition.
Arslan Munir, Ann Gordon-Ross and Sanjay Ranka.
© 2016 John Wiley & Sons, Ltd. Published 2016 by John Wiley & Sons, Ltd.

Application metrics estimation for distributed EWSNs is still in infancy. Only a few lifetime estimation model exists for distributed EWSNs [70–72]; however, these models either do not consider low-level sensor node tunable parameters or only consider a few low-level sensor node tunable parameters. Furthermore, existing models for distributed EWSNs focus mainly on networking issues in distributed EWSNs as opposed to embedded issues (e.g., processor, transceiver, sensors) in an embedded sensor node. Moreover, the literature does not discuss application metrics estimation model for other application metrics apart from lifetime such as throughput and reliability.

In this chapter, we propose an *application metrics estimation model* that estimates high-level application metrics from low-level sensor node tunable parameters and the sensor node's hardware internals (e.g., transceiver voltage, transceiver receive current). Dynamic optimization methodologies for distributed EWSNs (discussed in Part three of this book) leverage this estimation model while comparing different operating states for optimization purposes.

Application metrics estimation modeling has a broad impact on EWSN design and deployment. Our application metrics estimation model provides a first step toward high-level metrics estimation from sensor node tunable parameters and hardware internals. The estimation model establishes a relationship between sensor node operating state and high-level metrics. Since application managers typically focus on high-level metrics and are generally unaware of low-level sensor node internals, this model provides an interface between the application manager and the sensor node internals. Additionally, our model can potentially spark further research in application metrics estimation for EWSNs.

This chapter's highlights are as follows:

- Proposal of an *application metrics estimation model* that estimates high-level application metrics (lifetime, throughput, and reliability) from low-level sensor node tunable parameters and the sensor node's hardware internals (e.g., transceiver voltage, transceiver receive current).
- Examples demonstrating the estimation process of application metrics using the proposed model.

The remainder of this chapter is organized as follows. Section 3.1 describes our application metrics estimation model that is leveraged by various dynamic optimization methodologies for distributed EWSNs. Experimental results are presented in Section 3.2. Finally, Section 3.3 concludes this chapter.

3.1 Application Metrics Estimation Model

This section presents our application metrics estimation model, which is leveraged by our dynamic optimization methodology. This estimation model estimates high-level application metrics (lifetime, throughput, reliability) from low-level tunable parameters and sensor node hardware internals. The use of hardware internals is appropriate for application metrics modeling as similar approaches have been used in the literature especially for lifetime estimation [70–72]. Based on tunable parameter value settings corresponding to an operating state and hardware specific values, the application metrics estimation model determines the corresponding values for high-level application metrics. These high-level application metric values are then used in their respective objective functions to determine the objective function values corresponding to an operating state (e.g., lifetime estimation model determines s_l (lifetime offered by state s), which is then used in the lifetime objective function to determine the lifetime objective function value). This section presents a complete description of our application metrics estimation model, including a review of our previous application metrics estimation model [73] and additional details.

3.1.1   Lifetime Estimation

A sensor node's *lifetime* is defined as the time duration between sensor node deployment and sensor node failure due to a wide variety of reasons (e.g., battery depletion, hardware/software fault, environmental damage, external destruction). Lifetime estimation models typically consider battery depletion as the cause of sensor node failure [74]. Since sensor nodes can be deployed in remote and hostile environments, manual battery replacement after deployment is often impractical. A sensor node reaches the failed or *dead* state once the entire battery energy is depleted. The critical factors that determine a sensor node's lifetime are battery energy and energy consumption during operation.

The sensor node lifetime in days $\mathcal{L}_s$ can be estimated as

$$\mathcal{L}_s = \frac{E_b}{E_c \times 24} \tag{3.1}$$

where E_b denotes the sensor node's battery energy in joules and E_c denotes the sensor node's energy consumption per hour. The battery energy in milliwatt hour E_b' can be given by

$$E_b' = V_b \cdot C_b \quad \text{(mWh)} \tag{3.2}$$

where V_b denotes battery voltage in volts and C_b denotes battery capacity, typically specified in milliampere hour. Since $1\,\text{J} = 1\,\text{W s}$, E_b can be calculated as

$$E_b = E_b' \times \frac{3600}{1000} \quad \text{(J)} \tag{3.3}$$

The sensors in the sensor node gather information about the physical environment and generate continuous sequences of analog signals/values. Sample-and-hold circuits and analog-to-digital (A/D) converters digitize these analog signals. This digital information is processed by a processor, and the results are communicated to other sensor nodes or a base station node (sink node) via a transmitter. The *sensing energy* is the energy consumed by the sensor node due to sensing events. The *processing energy* is the energy consumed by the processor to process the sensed data (e.g., calculating the average of the sensor values over a time interval or the difference between the most recent sensor values and the previously sensed values). The *communication energy* is the energy consumed due to communication with other sensor nodes or the sink node. For example, sensor nodes send packets containing the sensed/processed data information to other sensor nodes and the sink node, which consumes communication energy.

We model E_c as the sum of the processing energy, communication energy, and sensing energy, that is,

$$E_c = E_{\text{sen}} + E_{\text{proc}} + E_{\text{com}} \quad \text{(J)} \tag{3.4}$$

where E_{sen}, E_{proc}, and E_{com} denote the sensing energy per hour, processing energy per hour, and communication energy per hour, respectively.

The sensing (sampling) frequency and the number of sensors attached to the sensor board (e.g., the MTS400 sensor board [75] has Sensirion SHT1x temperature, and humidity sensors [76]) are the main contributors to the total sensing energy. Our model considers energy conservation by allowing sensors to switch to a low power, idle mode while not sensing. E_{sen} is given by

$$E_{sen} = E_{sen}^m + E_{sen}^i \tag{3.5}$$

where E_{sen}^m denotes the sensing measurement energy per hour and E_{sen}^i denotes the sensing idle energy per hour. E_{sen}^m can be calculated as

$$E_{sen}^m = N_s \cdot V_s \cdot I_s^m \cdot t_s^m \times 3600 \tag{3.6}$$

where N_s denotes the number of sensing measurements per second, V_s denotes the sensing board voltage, I_s^m denotes the sensing measurement current, and t_s^m denotes the sensing measurement time. N_s can be calculated as

$$N_s = N_r \cdot F_s \tag{3.7}$$

where N_r denotes the number of sensors on the sensing board and F_s denotes the sensing frequency. E_{sen}^i is given by

$$E_{sen}^i = V_s \cdot I_s \cdot t_s^i \times 3600 \tag{3.8}$$

where I_s denotes the sensing sleep current and t_s^i denotes the sensing idle time. t_s^i is given by

$$t_s^i = 1 - t_s^m \tag{3.9}$$

We assume that the sensor node's processor operates in two modes: active mode and idle mode [77]. The processor operates in active mode while processing the sensed data and switches to the idle mode for energy conservation when not processing. The processing energy is the sum of the processor's energy consumption while operating in the active and the idle modes. We point out that although we only consider active and idle modes, a processor operating in additional sleep modes (e.g., power-down, power-save, and standby) can also be incorporated in our model. E_{proc} is given by

$$E_{proc} = E_{proc}^a + E_{proc}^i \tag{3.10}$$

where E_{proc}^a and E_{proc}^i denote the processor's energy consumption per hour in the active and idle modes, respectively. E_{proc}^a is given by

$$E_{proc}^a = V_p \cdot I_p^a \cdot t^a \tag{3.11}$$

where V_p denotes the processor voltage, I_p^a denotes the processor active mode current, and t^a denotes the time spent by the processor in the active mode. t^a can be estimated as

$$t^a = \frac{N_I}{F_p} \tag{3.12}$$

where N_I denotes the average number of processor instructions to process one sensing measurement and F_p denotes the processor frequency. N_I can be estimated as

$$N_I = N^b \cdot R_{sen}^b \tag{3.13}$$

where N^b denotes the average number of processor instructions to process 1 bit and R_{sen}^b denotes the sensing resolution bits (number of bits required for storing one sensing measurement).

E_{proc}^i is given by

$$E_{proc}^i = V_p \cdot I_p^i \cdot t^i \tag{3.14}$$

where I_p^i denotes the processor idle mode current and t^i denotes the time spent by the processor in the idle mode. Since the processor switches to the idle mode when not processing sensing measurements, t_i can be given as

$$t^i = 1 - t^a \tag{3.15}$$

The transceiver (radio) is the main contributor to the total communication energy consumption. The transceiver transmits/receives data packets and switches to the idle mode for energy conservation when there are no more packets to transmit/receive. The number of packets transmitted (received) and the packets' transmission (receive) interval dictate the communication energy. The communication energy is the sum of the transmission, receive, and idle energies for the sensor node's transceiver, that is,

$$E_{com} = E_{trans}^{tx} + E_{trans}^{rx} + E_{trans}^i \tag{3.16}$$

where E_{trans}^{tx}, E_{trans}^{rx}, and E_{trans}^i denote the transceiver's transmission energy per hour, receive energy per hour, and idle energy per hour, respectively. E_{trans}^{tx} is given by

$$E_{trans}^{tx} = N_{pkt}^{tx} \cdot E_{tx}^{pkt} \tag{3.17}$$

where N_{pkt}^{tx} denotes the number of packets transmitted per hour and E_{tx}^{pkt} denotes the transmission energy per packet. N_{pkt}^{tx} can be calculated as

$$N_{pkt}^{tx} = \frac{3600}{P_{ti}} \tag{3.18}$$

where P_{ti} denotes the packet transmission interval in seconds (1 h = 3600 s). E_{tx}^{pkt} is given as

$$E_{tx}^{pkt} = V_t \cdot I_t \cdot t_{tx}^{pkt} \tag{3.19}$$

where V_t denotes the transceiver voltage, I_t denotes the transceiver current, and t_{tx}^{pkt} denotes the time to transmit one packet. t_{tx}^{pkt} is given by

$$t_{tx}^{pkt} = P_s \times \frac{8}{R_{tx}} \tag{3.20}$$

where P_s denotes the packet size in bytes and R_{tx} denotes the transceiver data rate (in bits per second).

The transceiver's receive energy per hour E_{trans}^{rx} can be calculated using a similar procedure as E_{trans}^{tx}. E_{trans}^{rx} is given by:

$$E_{trans}^{rx} = N_{pkt}^{rx} \cdot E_{rx}^{pkt} \tag{3.21}$$

where N_{pkt}^{rx} denotes the number of packets received per hour and E_{rx}^{pkt} denotes the receive energy per packet. N_{pkt}^{rx} can be calculated as

$$N_{pkt}^{rx} = \frac{3600}{P_{ri}} \tag{3.22}$$

where P_{ri} denotes the packet receive interval in seconds. P_{ri} can be calculated as

$$P_{ri} = \frac{P_{ti}}{n_s} \tag{3.23}$$

where n_s denotes the number of neighboring sensor nodes. E_{rx}^{pkt} is given as

$$E_{rx}^{pkt} = V_t \cdot I_t^{rx} \cdot t_{rx}^{pkt} \tag{3.24}$$

where I_t^{rx} denotes the transceiver's receive current and t_{rx}^{pkt} denotes the time to receive one packet. Since the packet size is the same, the time to receive a packet is equal to the time to transmit the packet, that is, $t_{rx}^{pkt} = t_{tx}^{pkt}$.

E_{trans}^i can be calculated as

$$E_{trans}^i = V_t \cdot I_t^s \cdot t_{tx}^i \tag{3.25}$$

where I_t^s denotes the transceiver's sleep current and t_{tx}^i denotes the transceiver's idle time per hour. t_{tx}^i can be calculated as

$$t_{tx}^i = 3600 - \left(N_{pkt}^{tx} \cdot t_{tx}^{pkt} \right) - \left(N_{pkt}^{rx} \cdot t_{rx}^{pkt} \right) \tag{3.26}$$

3.1.2　Throughput Estimation

Throughput is defined as the amount of work processed by a system in a given unit of time. Defining throughput semantics for sensor nodes is challenging because three main components contribute to the throughput, sensing, processing, and communication (transmission), and these throughput components can have different significance for different applications. Since these throughput components are related, one possible interpretation is to take the throughput of the lowest throughput component as the *effective throughput*. However, the effective throughput may not be a suitable metric for a designer who is interested in throughputs associated with all three components.

In our model, we define the *aggregate throughput* as the combination of the sensor node's sensing, processing, and transmission rates to observe/monitor a phenomenon (measured in bits per second). The aggregate throughput can be considered as the weighted sum of the constituent throughputs. Our aggregate throughput model can be used for the effective throughput estimation by assigning a weight factor of 1 to the slowest of the three components and assigning a weight factor of 0 to the others. Since aggregate throughput modeling allows flexibility and can be adapted to varying needs of a WSN designer, we focus on modeling of the aggregate throughput. We model aggregate throughput as

$$R = \omega_s R_{sen} + \omega_p R_{proc} + \omega_c R_{com} \quad : \quad \omega_s + \omega_p + \omega_c = 1 \tag{3.27}$$

where R_{sen}, R_{proc}, and R_{com} denote the sensing, processing, and communication throughputs, respectively, and ω_s, ω_p, and ω_c denote the associated weight factors.

The sensing throughput, which is the throughput due to sensing activity, depends on the sensing frequency and sensing resolution bits per sensing measurement. R_{sen} is given by

$$R_{sen} = F_s \cdot R_{sen}^b \qquad (3.28)$$

where F_s denotes the sensing frequency.

The processing throughput, which is the processor's throughput while processing sensed measurements, depends on the processor frequency and the average number of instructions required to process the sensing measurement. R_{proc} is given by

$$R_{proc} = \frac{F_p}{N^b} \qquad (3.29)$$

The communication throughput, which measures the number of packets transferred successfully over the wireless channel, depends on the packet size and the time to transfer one packet. R_{com} is given by

$$R_{com} = P_s^{eff} \times \frac{8}{t_{tx}^{pkt}} \qquad (3.30)$$

where P_s^{eff} denotes the effective packet size excluding the packet header overhead (i.e., $P_s^{eff} = P_s - P_h$, where P_h denotes the packet header size).

3.1.3   Reliability Estimation

The reliability metric measures the number of packets transferred reliably (i.e., error-free packet transmission) over the wireless channel. Accurate reliability estimation is challenging due to dynamic changes in the network topology, number of neighboring sensor nodes, wireless channel fading, sensor network traffic, packet size, and so on. The two main factors that affect reliability are transceiver's transmission power P_{tx} and receiver sensitivity. For example, the AT86RF230 transceiver [78] has a receiver sensitivity of -101 dB m with a corresponding packet error rate (PER) $\leq 1\%$ for an additive white Gaussian noise (AWGN) channel with a physical service data unit (PSDU) equal to 20 bytes. Reliability can be estimated using Friis free space transmission equation [79] for different P_{tx} values, distance between transmitting and receiving sensor nodes, and assumptions on fading model parameters (e.g., shadowing fading model). Different reliability values can be assigned corresponding to different P_{tx} values such that the higher P_{tx} values give higher reliability; however, more accurate reliability estimation requires using profiling statistics for the number of packets transmitted and the number of packets received. These profiling statistics increase the estimation accuracy of the PER and, therefore, reliability.

3.1.4   Models Validation

Our models provide good accuracy in estimating application metrics since our models accommodate many sensor node hardware internals such as the battery voltage, battery capacity, sensing board voltage, sensing sleep current, sensing idle time, and sensing resolution bits and so on. Our models are also highly flexible since our models permit calculations for particular network settings such as the number of neighboring sensor nodes and different types of sensors with different hardware characteristics (e.g., sensing resolution bits, sensing measurement time, sensing measurement current).

Since our models provide a first step toward modeling application metrics, our models' accuracy cannot be completely verified against other models because there are no similar/related application metrics estimation models. The existing models for lifetime estimation take different parameters and have different assumptions, thus an exact comparison is not feasible; however, we observe that our lifetime model yields result in a similar range as other models [70–72]. We also compare the lifetime estimation from our model with an experimental study on WSN lifetimes [74]. This comparison verifies conformity of our lifetime model with real measurements. For example, with a sensor node battery capacity of 2500 mA h, experiments indicate a sensor node lifetime ranging from 72 to 95 h for a 100% duty cycle for different battery brands (e.g., Ansmann, Panasonic Industrial, Varta High Energy, Panasonic Extreme Power) [74]. Using our model with a duty cycle of 36% on average for the sensing, processing, and communication, we calculated that a lifetime of $95/0.36 = 264$ h ≈ 11 days can be attained. Similarly, for a duty cycle of 0.25% on average for the sensing, communication, and processing, the lifetime can be calculated as $95/0.0025 = 38,000$ hrs ≈ 1583 days (e.g., lifetime calculations using our model is given in Section 3.2.2.1).

The relative comparison of our models with existing models and real measurements provide insights into the accuracy of our models; however, more accurate models can be constructed following our modeling approach by considering additional parameters and more detailed hardware models for sensor nodes.

3.2 Experimental Results

In this section, we describe the experimental setup and results obtained from our application metrics estimation model.

3.2.1 Experimental Setup

Our experimental setup is based on the Crossbow IRIS mote platform [80] with a battery capacity of 2000 mA h using two AA alkaline batteries. The IRIS mote platform integrates an Atmel ATmega1281 microcontroller [77], an MTS400 sensor board [75] with Sensirion SHT1x temperature and humidity sensors [76], and an Atmel AT86RF230 low-power 2.4- GHz transceiver [78]. Table 3.1 shows the hardware-specific values of the sensor node, corresponding to the IRIS mote platform, which are used by the application metrics estimation model [76–78, 80].

We analyze six tunable parameters: processor voltage V_p, processor frequency F_p, sensing frequency F_s, packet size P_s, packet transmission interval P_{ti}, and transceiver's transmission power P_{tx}. In order to explore the fidelity of our methodology across small and large design spaces, we consider two design space cardinalities (number of states in the design space): $|S| = 729$ and $|S| = 31,104$. The tunable parameters for $|S| = 729$ are as follows: $V_p = \{2.7, 3.3, 4\}$ (V), $F_p = \{4, 6, 8\}$(MHz) [77], $F_s = \{1, 2, 3\}$ (samples/s) [76], $P_s = \{41, 56, 64\}$ (bytes), $P_{ti} = \{60, 300, 600\}$ (s), and $P_{tx} = \{-17, -3, 1\}$ (dB m) [78]. The tunable parameters

Table 3.1   Crossbow IRIS mote platform hardware specifications

Notation	Description	Value
V_b	Battery voltage	3.6 V
C_b	Battery capacity	2000 mA h
N_b	Processing instructions per bit	5
R_{sen}^b	Sensing resolution bits	24
V_t	Transceiver voltage	3 V
R_{tx}	Transceiver data rate	250 kbps
I_t^{rx}	Transceiver receive current	15.5 mA
I_t^s	Transceiver sleep current	20 nA
V_s	Sensing board voltage	3 V
I_s^m	Sensing measurement current	550 μA
t_s^m	Sensing measurement time	55 ms
I_s	Sensing sleep current	0.3 μA

for $|S| = 31,104$ are as follows: $V_p = \{1.8,\ 2.7,\ 3.3,\ 4,\ 4.5,\ 5\}$ (volts), $F_p = \{2,\ 4,\ 6,\ 8,\ 12,\ 16\}$ (MHz) [77], $F_s = \{0.2, 0.5, 1, 2, 3, 4\}$ (samples per second) [76], $P_s = \{32, 41, 56, 64, 100,\ 127\}$ (bytes), $P_{\text{ti}} = \{10,\ 30,\ 60,\ 300,\ 600,\ 1200\}$ (seconds), and $P_{\text{tx}} = \{-17,\ -3,\ 1,\ 3\}$ (dB m) [78]. All state-space tuples are feasible for $|S| = 729$, whereas $|S| = 31,104$ contains 7779 infeasible state-space tuples because all V_p and F_p pairs are not feasible.

Although we analyzed our application metrics estimation model for the IRIS motes platform and two design spaces, our application metrics estimation model is equally applicable to any platform, application domain, and design space. Our application metrics estimation model accommodates several sensor node hardware internals, which are hardware platform-specific and can be obtained from the platform's datasheets. Since the appropriate values can be substituted for any given platform, our model can be used with any hardware platform.

3.2.2   Results

In this section, we present example application metrics calculations using our application metrics estimation model.

Since the objective function values corresponding to different states depends on the estimation of high-level application metrics, we present example calculations to exemplify this estimation process using our application metrics estimation model (Section 3.1) and the IRIS mote platform hardware specifications (Table 3.1). We consider the example state $s_y = (V_{p_y}, F_{p_y}, F_{s_y}, P_{s_y}, P_{\text{ti}_y}, P_{\text{tx}_y}) = (2.7, 4, 1, 41, 60, -17)$.

3.2.2.1   Lifetime

First, we calculate the lifetime corresponding to s_y. Using Eq. (3.2), the battery energy is $E_b' = 3.6 \times 2000 = 7200$ mW h, which is $E_b = 7200 \times 3600/1000 = 25,920$ J from Eq. (3.3). The lifetime metric calculation requires calculation of processing, communication, and sensing energy.

For the processing energy per hour, Eqs. (3.12 and 3.13) give $N_I = 5 \times 24 = 120$ and $t^a = 120/(4 \times 10^6) = 30$ μs, respectively. The processor's active mode energy consumption per hour from Eq. (3.11) is $E^a_{proc} = 2.7 \times 2.5 \times 10^{-3} \times 30 \times 10^{-6} = 0.2025$ μJ where $I^a_p = 2.5$ mA corresponding to $(V_{p_y}, F_{p_y}) = (2.7, 4)$ [77]. Using Eq. (3.15) gives $t^i = 1 - 30 \times 10^{-6}$ s $= 999.97$ ms. The processor's idle mode energy consumption per hour from Eq. (3.14) is $E^i_{proc} = 2.7 \times 0.65 \times 10^{-3} \times 999.97 \times 10^{-3} = 1.755$ mJ where $I^i_p = 0.65$ mA corresponding to $(V_{p_y}, F_{p_y}) = (2.7, 4)$ [77]. The processor energy consumption per hour from Eq. (3.10) is $E_{proc} = 0.2025 \times 10^{-6} + 1.755 \times 10^{-3} = 1.7552$ mJ.

For the communication energy per hour, Eqs. (3.18 and 3.20) give $N^{tx}_{pkt} = 3600/60 = 60$ and $t^{pkt}_{tx} = 41 \times 8/(250 \times 10^3) = 1.312$ ms, respectively. Equation (3.19) gives $E^{pkt}_{tx} = 3 \times 9.5 \times 10^{-3} \times 1.312 \times 10^{-3} = 37.392$ μJ. The transceiver's transmission energy per hour from Eq. (3.17) is $E^{tx}_{trans} = 60 \times 37.392 \times 10^{-6} = 2.244$ mJ. Equation (3.23) gives $P_{ri} = 60/2 = 30$ where we assume $n_s = 2$; however, our model is valid for any number of neighboring sensor nodes. Equations (3.22 and 3.24) give $N^{rx}_{pkt} = 3600/30 = 120$ and $E^{pkt}_{rx} = 3 \times 15.5 \times 10^{-3} \times 1.312 \times 10^{-3} = 61.01$ μJ, respectively. The transceiver's receive energy per hour from Eq. (3.21) is $E^{rx}_{trans} = 120 \times 61.01 \times 10^{-6} = 7.3212$ mJ. Equation (3.26) gives $t^i_{tx} = 3600 - (60 \times 1.312 \times 10^{-3}) - (120 \times 1.312 \times 10^{-3}) = 3599.764$ s. The transceiver's idle energy per hour from Eq. (3.25) is $E^i_{trans} = 3 \times 20 \times 10^{-9} \times 3599.764 = 0.216$ mJ. Equation (3.16) gives communication energy per hour $E_{com} = 2.244 + 7.3212 + 0.216 = 9.7812$ mJ.

We calculate sensing energy per hour using Eq. (3.5). Equation (3.7) gives $N_s = 2 \times 1 = 2$ (since MTS400 sensor board [75] has Sensirion SHT1x temperature and humidity sensors [76]). Equation (3.6) gives $E^m_{sen} = 2 \times 3 \times 550 \times 10^{-6} \times 55 \times 10^{-3} \times 3600 = 0.6534$ J. Using Eqs. (3.8 and 3.9) gives $t^i_s = 1 - 55 \times 10^{-3} = 0.945$ s and $E^i_{sen} = 3 \times 0.3 \times 10^{-6} \times 0.945 \times 3600 = 3.062$ mJ, respectively. Equation (3.5) gives $E_{sen} = 0.6534 + 3.062 \times 10^{-3} = 0.6565$ J.

After calculating processing, communication, and sensing energy, we calculate the energy consumption per hour from Eq. (3.4) as $E_c = 1.7552 \times 10^{-3} + 9.7812 \times 10^{-3} + 0.6565 = 0.668$ J. Equation (3.1) gives $\mathcal{L}_s = 25,920/(0.668 \times 24) = 1616.77$ days.

3.2.2.2 Throughput

For the throughput application metric, Eqs. (3.28)–(3.30) give $R_{sen} = 1 \times 24 = 24$ bps, $R_{proc} = 4 \times 10^6/5 = 800$ kbps, and $R_{com} = 21 \times 8/(1.312 \times 10^{-3}) = 128.049$ kbps, respectively ($P^{eff}_s = 41 - 21 = 20$ where we assume $P_h = 21$ bytes). Equation (3.27) gives $R = (0.4)(24) + (0.4)(800 \times 10^3) + (0.2)(128.049 \times 10^3) = 345.62$ kbps where we assume ω_s, ω_p, and ω_c equal to 0.4, 0.4, and 0.2, respectively.

3.2.2.3 Reliability

We estimate the reliability corresponding to $P_{tx} = -17$ dB m to be 0.7 (Section 3.1.3); however, an accurate reliability value can only be obtained using profiling statistics for the number of packets transmitted and number of packets lost.

Similarly, the lifetime, throughput, and reliability for state $s_y = (V_{p_y}, F_{p_y}, F_{s_y}, P_{s_y}, P_{ti_y}, P_{tx_y}) =$ (5, 16, 4, 127, 10, 3) can be calculated as 10.6 days, 1321.77 kbps, and 0.9999, respectively.

These calculations reveal that the tunable parameter value settings for a sensor node can have a profound impact on the application metrics. For example, the lifetime of a sensor node in our two examples varied from 10.6 to 1616.8 days for different tunable parameter value settings. Hence, our proposed tunable parameter value settings technique and application metrics estimation model can help WSN designers to find appropriate tunable parameter value settings to conserve the sensor node's energy and to enhance the sensor node's lifetime after satisfying other application requirements such as throughput and reliability.

3.3 Chapter Summary

In this chapter, we proposed an application metric estimation model to estimate high-level metrics (lifetime, throughput, and reliability) from embedded sensor node's parameters. This estimation model assisted dynamic optimization methodologies for operating states' comparisons. Our application metrics estimation model provided a prototype model for application metric estimation.

Future work includes enhancing our application metrics estimation model for additional application metrics (e.g., security, delay). We plan to further validate our application metrics estimation model by comparing the statistics obtained from actual embedded sensor nodes operation in a distributed EWSN.

4

Modeling and Analysis of Fault Detection and Fault Tolerance in Embedded Wireless Sensor Networks*

Wireless sensor networks (WSNs) consist of spatially distributed autonomous sensor nodes that collaborate with each other to perform an application task. A *sensor node* comprises a sensing unit (a *sensing unit* contains sensors such as temperature and humidity sensors), a processing unit, a storage unit, a communication unit, a power unit, an actuator unit, and an optional location finding unit [44].

Figure 4.1 shows the WSN architecture that we consider in this chapter [81–83]. The sensor nodes distributed in the *sensor field* gather information (sensed data or statistics) about an observed phenomenon (e.g., environment, target) using attached sensors. A group of sensor nodes, located geographically close to each other, is called a *WSN cluster*. Each WSN cluster has one *cluster head* (WSN cluster formation, and cluster head determination/maintenance is beyond the scope of this chapter). Sensed data within a WSN cluster is collected by the cluster head and is relayed to a *sink node* (or base station) via the sensor nodes' ad hoc network. The sink node transmits the received information back to the *WSN designer* and/or *WSN manager* via a gateway node connected to a computer network. The WSN designer is responsible for designing the WSN for a particular application to meet application requirements such as lifetime, reliability, and throughput. After WSN design and deployment, the WSN manager manages WSN operations, such as data analysis, monitoring alive and dead sensor nodes, and alarm conditions (e.g., forest fire, volcano eruption).

*A portion of this chapter is copyrighted by ACM. The definitive version appeared in: Arslan Munir, Joseph Antoon, and Ann Gordon-Ross, Modeling and Analysis of Fault Detection and Fault Tolerance in Wireless Sensor Networks, *ACM Transactions on Embedded Computing Systems (TECS)*, vol. 14, no. 1, January 2015. URL http://dl.acm.org/citation.cfm?id=2680538. ©[2015] ACM, Inc. The work is reproduced/reprinted by permission granted by ACM as we are the authors of this work.

Modeling and Optimization of Parallel and Distributed Embedded Systems, First Edition.
Arslan Munir, Ann Gordon-Ross and Sanjay Ranka.
© 2016 John Wiley & Sons, Ltd. Published 2016 by John Wiley & Sons, Ltd.

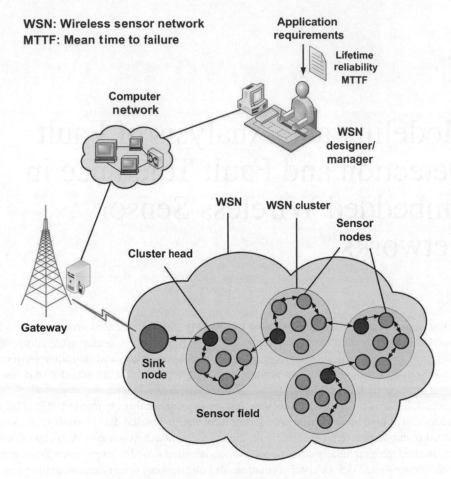

Figure 4.1　Wireless sensor network architecture

WSN research and design have gained significance in recent years because of the increasing proliferation of WSNs in a wide variety of application domains. These application domains include, but are not limited to, mission-critical (e.g., security, defense, space, satellite) or safety-related (e.g., health care, active volcano monitoring) systems. The utility of WSNs for safety-related systems can be illustrated by a volcano monitoring example. Studying active volcanoes typically requires sensor arrays to collect seismic and infrasonic (low-frequency acoustic) signals. Distributed sensor nodes in a WSN provide a correlated spatial distribution of seismic and infrasonic events that greatly facilitate scientific studies of wave propagation phenomena and volcanic source mechanisms [84]. The analytics of seismic and infrasonic data obtained by a WSN can help the scientists in better prediction of volcanic events, such as volcanic eruption and earthquakes. Although WSNs can benefit numerous applications, the realization of WSNs for an application requires addressing various design challenges.

A crucial challenge in WSN design is to meet varying application requirements (e.g., lifetime, throughput, reliability), given the limited energy, computation, and storage available on sensor nodes. Sensor nodes are often deployed in hostile environments, such as forests, the ocean floor [85], animal habitats [86], and active volcanoes [84], that further exacerbates the design challenge of meeting application requirements. Unattended and/or hostile deployment environments make sensor nodes more susceptible to failures than other systems [84], and manual inspection of sensor nodes after deployment can be impractical. Although faults can occur in any of the sensor node components, sensors and actuators have significantly higher fault rates than other semiconductor-based systems. For example, NASA aborted the launch of space shuttle Discovery [87] because of a sensor failure in the shuttle's external tank [88]. Sensor failure can occur due to deployment impact, accidents (animal, vehicular), fire, extreme weather, or aging [89]. Failed sensor nodes may result in sensor network partitioning (i.e., sensor nodes become isolated and are disconnected from the sensor network), reduced WSN availability, and WSN failure. In order to meet application requirements in the presence of sensor failures, incorporation of fault detection and fault tolerance (FT) mechanisms in WSNs is imperative.

While traditional reliability models can be readily applied to FT systems, faults do not always result in failure. Transient, malicious errors occur due to noise, voltage levels, and broken components. Therefore, it is imperative to model the ability for fault detection to provide coverage against such faults to protect mission-critical data. Fault detection includes distributed fault detection (DFD) algorithms that identify faulty sensor readings to diagnose a faulty sensor. DFD algorithms do not incur additional transmission cost as they use existing network traffic to identify sensor failures. The *accuracy* of a fault detection algorithm signifies the algorithm's ability to accurately identify faults. We analyze and study two well-cited fault detection algorithms and compare their performance under realistic conditions. We have implemented and simulated the DFD algorithms incorporating the protocol stack and a realistic WSN topology as opposed to only algorithm simulation that was done in most previous works [90, 91].

Although fault detection helps in isolating faulty sensors, FT incorporation in WSNs is imperative to reliably accomplish application tasks. A prominent FT technique is to add redundant hardware and/or software [92]. Stringent design constraints (e.g., power, cost) differentiate WSNs from other systems, and consequently the added redundancy for FT must justify the additional cost. Since sensors (e.g., temperature, light, motion) attached to sensor nodes have comparatively higher fault rates than other components (e.g., processor, transceiver) [88, 93, 94], sensor redundancy would be the most effective to enhance FT capability of sensor nodes. Fortunately, sensors are cheap and adding redundant spare sensors would add little to the individual sensor node's cost.

Although FT is a well-studied research field [95–100], fault diagnosis and FT for WSNs are relatively unstudied. Varying FT requirements across different applications increase the complexity of fault detection and FT for WSNs. For instance, mission-critical applications have relatively high reliability requirements as compared to non-mission-critical applications such as ambient conditions monitoring. To the best of our knowledge, there exists no sensor node model to provide better reliability for mission-critical applications. Since applications are typically designed to operate reliably for a certain period of time (i.e., lifetime requirement), *FT metrics* such as reliability and mean time to failure (MTTF) need to be considered in WSN design. WSN designers require a model to estimate FT metrics and determine necessary redundancy during design time. Unfortunately, the literature provides no rigorous mathematical model that provides insights into WSN reliability and MTTF. Previous works study fault detection and FT in isolation, and their synergistic relationship has not been investigated in the context of WSNs.

This chapter's highlights are as follows:

- Fault diagnosis in WSNs through various fault detection algorithms.
- Simulation of fault detection algorithms using ns−2 to determine the algorithms' accuracy and false alarm rates. ns−2 is a discrete event simulator that provides support for the simulation of networks and routing protocols over wired and wireless networks [101]. We further analyze the effectiveness of fault detection algorithms under conditions modeled from the real-world data.
- Proposal of an FT sensor node model consisting of duplex sensors (i.e., one active sensor and one inactive spare sensor) that exploits the synergy of fault detection and FT. Although our model can be extended for sensors with N-modular redundancy (NMR) [92], we suggest duplex sensor nodes to minimize the additional cost.
- Characterization of FT parameters, such as coverage factor, by exploiting the synergy between fault detection and FT.
- Proposal of hierarchical Markov models to characterize WSN reliability and MTTF. For the first time, we delineate reliability and MTTF hierarchically at the sensor node, WSN cluster, and WSN levels (Fig. 4.1).
- Determination of iso-MTTF (isoreliability) for WSN clusters.[1] We define iso-MTTF (isoreliability) as how many redundant sensor nodes a non-fault tolerance (NFT) WSN cluster requires over an FT WSN cluster to achieve an equal MTTF (reliability).
- Research challenges and future research directions for the design and deployment of reliable and trustworthy WSNs.

In our duplex sensor model, we assume that the redundant sensor is in a cold standby mode, which ideally consumes no power. Although we focus on sensor failures within the sensor node in this study due to higher sensor failure rates as compared to other sensor node components [88, 93], our model can be extended to include failures for other components within the sensor node such as the processor and transceiver. Our FT WSN modeling serves as a first step toward FT WSN modeling and can potentially facilitate further research in FT WSN modeling and evaluation.

Our Markov models are comprehensive and characterize sensor nodes, WSN clusters, and overall WSN reliability and MTTF. The proposed Markov modeling enables WSN designers to investigate the effects of different types of FT sensor nodes (e.g., duplex, NMR), number of WSN clusters, and the number of sensor nodes in the cluster on the FT of the overall WSN. Our hierarchical WSN Markov models enable designers to select an efficient WSN topology to better meet application requirements.

The remainder of this chapter is organized as follows. Section 4.1 gives a review of related work. Section 4.2 elaborates on fault diagnosis in WSNs. Section 4.3 discusses two fault detection algorithms to elucidate the fault diagnosis mechanism in WSNs. Section 4.4 describes our Markov models for characterizing WSN reliability and MTTF. Implementation and simulation of fault detection algorithms using ns−2 are presented in Section 4.5. Numerical results from our Markov modeling are presented in Section 4.6. Section 4.7 highlights research challenges

---

[1] The term "iso" is a combining form of the Greek word "isos" meaning "equal."

and future research directions for the design and deployment of reliable and trustworthy WSNs. Finally, Section 4.8 concludes the chapter.

4.1 Related Work

Despite fault detection and FT being well-studied research fields [95, 98, 100], little work exists in WSN fault detection and FT. This section summarizes some of the previous works in the literature related to fault detection and FT.

4.1.1 Fault Detection

Jiang [102] proposed a DFD scheme that detected faulty sensor nodes by exchanging data and mutually testing neighboring nodes. Jian-Liang et al. [103] proposed a weighted median fault detection scheme that used spatial correlations among the sensor measurements (e.g., temperature, humidity). Lee and Choi [104] presented a DFD algorithm that identified faulty sensor nodes based on comparisons between neighboring sensor nodes' data. The DFD algorithm used time redundancy to tolerate transient faults in sensing and communication. Khilar and Mahapatra [105] proposed a probabilistic approach to diagnose intermittent WSN faults. The simulation results indicated that the DFD algorithm's accuracy increased as the number of diagnostic rounds increased where neighboring sensor nodes exchanged measurements in each round.

Ding et al. [91] proposed algorithms for faulty sensor identification and FT event boundary detection. The algorithms considered that both the faulty sensors and normal sensors in an event region could generate abnormal readings (readings that deviate from a typical application-specific range). Krishnamachari and Iyengar [106] proposed a distributed Bayesian algorithm for sensor fault detection and correction. The algorithm considered that measurement errors due to faulty equipment are likely to be uncorrelated. Wu et al. [107] presented a fault detection scheme in which the fusion center (the node that aggregated data from different nodes) attempted to identify faulty sensor nodes through temporal sequences of received local decisions using a majority voting technique. Lo et al. [108] presented a distributed, reference-free fault detection algorithm based on local pairwise verification between sensor nodes monitoring the same physical phenomenon. The authors observed that a linear relationship existed between the outputs of a pair of sensor nodes that could be exploited to detect faulty sensor nodes. Since the fault detection was done pairwise, the algorithm was able to conserve energy. Results revealed that the proposed algorithm could achieve a detection accuracy of 84% and a false alarm rate of 0.04%.

Miao et al. [109] proposed agnostic diagnosis for detecting silent failures (i.e., failures with unknown types and symptoms). The proposed detection technique exploited the fact that a sensor node's metrics (e.g., radio on-time, number of packets transmitted in a time interval) exhibited certain correlation patterns, violation of which indicated potential silent failures. The detection accuracy of the proposed scheme was close to 100% for small WSNs, whereas the detection accuracy decreased sharply and false alarm rate increased as the WSN size increased. The proposed technique required a sink node to collect data from all the sensor nodes in the WSN, which resulted in rapid energy depletion of the sink node and sensor nodes near the sink node. Furthermore, the fault detection latency of the proposed scheme was high due to its centralized nature.

There exists some work related to anomaly detection in WSNs. Bhargava and Raghuvanshi [110] proposed a method for anomaly detection in WSNs based on S-transform (an extension of continuous wavelet transform). The S-transform extracted the features from sensor nodes' data set, which were used for training of support vector machine (SVM). The SVM was then used for the classification of normal and anomalous data. Results revealed that the proposed scheme's accuracy for data classification ranged from 78% to 94%. Salem et al. [111] proposed an anomaly detection algorithm for medical WSNs. The proposed algorithm first classified instances of sensed patient attributes as normal and abnormal. The algorithm then used regression prediction to discern between a faulty sensor reading and a patient entering into a critical state. The results demonstrated the algorithm's ability to achieve a relatively low false alarm rate ($\sim$1%) and a good detection accuracy (the attained accuracy was not specified) for the medical WSN application.

4.1.2   Fault Tolerance

In work related to FT for WSNs, Koushanfar et al. [94] proposed an FT scheme that provided backup for one type of sensor using another type of sensor, but they did not propose any FT model. Clouqueur et al. [112] presented algorithms for collaborative target detection in the presence of faulty sensors. Chiang et al. [113] designed system-level test interfaces for remote testing, repair, and software upgrade for sensor nodes. The authors evaluated the proposed test interfaces on Texas Instrument's MSP430 microcontroller-based sensor nodes. Experimental results revealed that the test interfaces with double, triple, and quadruple redundancies increased the WSN's availability.

Krasniewski et al. [114] proposed a protocol to diagnose and mask arbitrary sensor node failures in an event-driven WSN. The protocol considered a clustered WSN with rotating cluster heads. The protocol assigned each sensor node a *trust index* to indicate the sensor node's track record in reporting past events correctly. The cluster head analyzed the event reports using the trust index and made event decisions. The authors simulated the protocol using ns$-$2 and observed that the protocol was able to detect events correctly even if more than 50% of the sensor nodes were compromised. Sun et al. [115] introduced a trust mechanism to evaluate the trustworthiness of a sensor node and the sensor node's data. The authors defined *memory depth* to characterize the temporal correlation and *aggregation bandwidth* to characterize spatial correlation. A sensor node used memory depth to calculate self-trustworthiness of the sensor node's data based on stored historical/past data and the current data. When a sensor node reported its sensed data to the aggregator, the aggregator's trustworthiness to the reported result depended both on the trustworthiness of the sensor node reporting data and the trustworthiness of the sensor node to its sensed data. Subsequently, each aggregator reported the aggregated result and the aggregator's self-trust opinion to the upper layer aggregator progressively, and so on until the aggregated result reached the sink node. Results demonstrated the effectiveness of the proposed mechanism for continuous media streaming and discrete data in wireless multimedia sensor networks (WMSNs).

There exists some work on providing FT in WSNs by deploying relay nodes and considering *connectivity* as an FT metric. Relay nodes communicate with sensor nodes, other relay nodes, and sink nodes to prolong WSN lifetime. Zhang et al. [116] developed approximation algorithms for determining a minimum number of relay nodes along with the relay nodes' placement to achieve certain connectivity requirements. Han et al. [117] considered the problem of deploying relay nodes to provide FT in heterogeneous WSNs where sensor nodes had different transmission radii. They developed approximation algorithms for *full* and *partial* FT relay node placement. Full FT relay node placement deployed a minimum number of relay nodes to establish disjoint paths between every sensor and/or relay node pair, whereas partial FT relay node placement only considered sensor node pairs. Baldi et al. [118] evaluated gossip algorithms, which are distributed algorithms that distribute computational burden across all nodes and considered connectivity as an FT metric.

Sen et al. [119] introduced *region-based connectivity*: an FT metric defined as the minimum number of nodes within a region whose failure would disconnect the network. Alwan and Agarwal [120] provided a survey of FT routing techniques in WSNs. Souza [121] presented a framework for failure management in WSNs, focusing on fault diagnosis and recovery techniques. The presented FT framework mitigated the failure propagation in a business (enterprise) environment by implementing different FT techniques.

4.1.3 WSN Reliability Modeling

There exists some work on FT WSN modeling. Cai et al. [122] presented a reliability model to prolong the network lifetime and availability based on connectivity and coverage constraints. Zhu and Papavassiliou [123] presented a model that characterized sensor connectivity and investigated the trade-offs among sensor node connectivity, power consumption, and data rate. They also discussed the impact of sensor connectivity on system reliability. Vasar et al. [124] presented Markov models for WSN reliability analysis. They presented a reliability comparison for various numbers of dcfcctive components' replacements with hot-standby redundant components. Xing and Michel [125] presented WSN reliability and security modeling in an integrated manner. Their modeling technique differentiated two types of WSN failures: security failures due to malicious intrusions and traditional failures due to malfunctioning components.

Moustapha and Selmic [88] used recurrent neural networks to model sensor node dynamics for sensor fault detection. Their network model corresponded to the WSN topology such that the recurrent neural network input was taken from the modeled sensor node and neighboring sensor nodes. Kannan and Iyengar [126] developed a game-theoretic model of reliable length- and energy-constrained routing in WSNs. They showed that optimal length-constrained paths could be computed in polynomial time in a distributed manner using geographic routing. Mukhopadhyay et al. [127] presented a method that used sensor data properties to enable reliable data collection. The method consisted of predictive models based on temporal correlation in sensor data. They demonstrated that their method could handle multiple sources of errors simultaneously and could correct transient errors arising in sensor node hardware and wireless communication channels.

Although DFD algorithms were proposed in the literature for detecting sensor faults, the fault detection was not leveraged to provide FT. There exists work in the literature regarding FT in WSNs [94, 116, 117, 119, 122]; however, FT metrics such as reliability and MTTF were not investigated rigorously in the context of WSNs. Specifically, reliability and MTTF were not considered hierarchically at the sensor node, WSN cluster, and WSN level. This hierarchical characterization of FT metrics facilitates a WSN designer to determine an appropriate WSN topology (i.e., number of clusters and sensor nodes with required FT capability in each cluster).

4.2 Fault Diagnosis in WSNs

The sensor nodes in WSNs are often deployed in unattended and possibly hostile environments that make sensor nodes susceptible to failures. Faults in sensor nodes can occur at various levels, such as processing unit, transceiver, storage unit, power unit, sensors, and actuators. Since faults are inevitable, it is imperative to determine faulty and fault-free sensor nodes in the WSN. Traditional fault diagnosis techniques that are developed for multiprocessor systems are not directly applicable to WSNs due to the sensor nodes' stringent resource constraints. This section describes sensor faults and then elaborates on fault diagnosis in WSNs.

4.2.1 Sensor Faults

The faults in sensor nodes include permanent faults where a node becomes dead and Byzantine faults where the node behaves arbitrarily or maliciously. Figure 4.2 shows an example of Byzantine faults where sensor nodes A–E are equipped with temperature sensors and process the measured reading to give temperature in Fahrenheit. The sensor nodes send the sensor node's sensed temperature readings to other neighboring nodes. The temperature sensor in the sensor node D behaves maliciously and sends inconsistent and arbitrary temperature values to other nodes (60, 100, 150, and 10 to A, B, C, and E, respectively). The rest of the sensor nodes send consistent values to other neighboring nodes. As a consequence, nonfaulty sensor nodes obtain different global information about the temperature in the region and may conclude on a false value of the overall temperature of the region. The fault detection algorithm needs to be robust to such inconsistent behavior that can jeopardize the collaboration in the WSN [112].

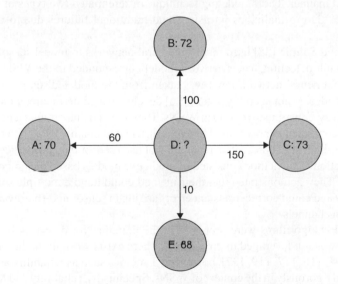

Figure 4.2   Byzantine faulty behavior in WSNs

Several efforts have been made to classify malicious sensor behavior [93, 128]. While different sensor fault taxonomies have been proposed, three particular behaviors are targeted by DFD methods. The *outlier faults* occur when a sensor signal spikes in value (Fig. 4.3(a)) and can be detected by comparing sensor readings to previous readings or neighboring sensor nodes' readings. The *stuck-at faults* occur when the output remains at a constant level (Fig. 4.3(b)). The *noisy faults* occur when the signal-to-noise ratio of the sensor's output is low, resulting in random data (Fig. 4.3(c)). An effective fault detection algorithm must be able to identify the broadest possible range of malicious output while minimizing fault positives. Because the broad range of sensor failures result in a mixed detection rate for different algorithms, accurate simulation is important for studying sensor failures [93].

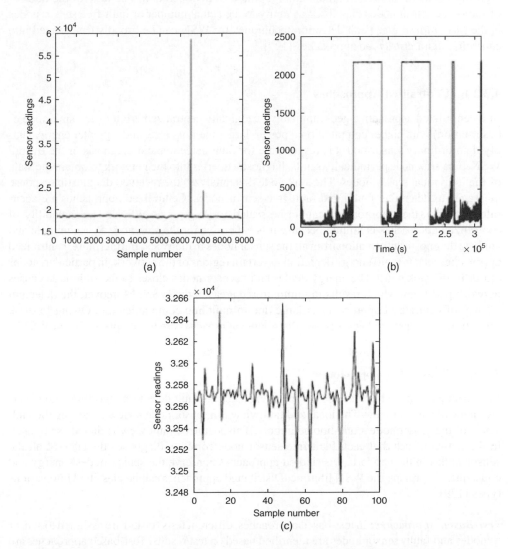

Figure 4.3 Various types of sensor faults [93]: (a) outlier faults; (b) stuck-at faults; (c) noisy faults

4.2.2   Taxonomy for Fault Diagnosis Techniques

A *fault diagnosis system* is a monitoring system that detects faulty sensor nodes and their location in the WSN. Fault diagnosis techniques are classified based on the nature of tests, correlation between sensor readings, and characteristics of sensor nodes [129]. The key component of a fault diagnosis system is a *fault detection algorithm*, and the key terminology includes correctness, latency, detection accuracy, and false alarm rate. A fault diagnosis is *correct* if no fault-free sensor nodes are mistakenly diagnosed as faulty. *Latency* is defined as the time elapsed since the appearance of the fault to the isolation of the faulty sensor node. *Detection accuracy* is defined as the ratio of the number of faulty sensor nodes detected to the actual number of faulty sensor nodes in the network. The accuracy of the fault detection algorithm is a crucial factor in maintaining reliable WSN operation. The ratio of the number of fault-free sensor nodes diagnosed as faulty to the actual number of fault-free sensor nodes is the *false alarm rate*. Fault detection techniques for WSN can be broadly categorized into *centralized* and *distributed* approaches [129].

4.2.2.1   Centralized Approaches

In a centralized approach, a geographically or logically centralized arbiter (i.e., sink node or base station) with higher computational power, larger memory size, and a greater energy supply than ordinary sensor nodes is responsible for fault detection and diagnosis of the overall WSN. The sink node periodically sends diagnostic queries into the network to obtain the state of the individual sensor nodes. The sink node then analyzes the received diagnostic response messages to determine faulty and fault-free sensor nodes. Centralized approaches are accurate; however, these approaches cannot be scaled for large-scale WSNs. The scalability of centralized approaches is limited because it is expensive for the sink node to accumulate and analyze diagnostic information from all the sensor nodes in the WSN. Furthermore, centralized approaches lead to rapid energy depletion in certain regions of the network, in particular, nodes closer to the sink node. The energy depletion in sensor nodes closer to the sink node causes network partitions, which results in unmonitored areas in the WSN. Moreover, the detection latency of centralized approaches is large due to multihop communication. Owing to these limitations of centralized approaches, distributed approaches are highly preferable in WSNs.

4.2.2.2   Distributed Approaches

In distributed approaches, each sensor node executes the fault detection algorithm and generates a localized fault view. The localized fault view is a sensor node's view regarding the fault states of the sensor node's one hop neighbors. This localized fault view is then disseminated in the network such that each fault-free sensor node correctly diagnoses the state of all the sensor nodes in the network. Distributed approaches conserve the sensor nodes' energy and consequently prolong the WSN lifetime. Distributed approaches can be classified into various types [129]:

Test-Based Approaches: In test-based approaches, different tests (tasks) are assigned to sensor nodes and faulty sensor nodes are identified based on test results. Test-based approaches are further classified into *invalidation-based* and *comparison-based* approaches.

In *invalidation-based* approaches, every sensor node tests a set of sensor nodes. Each sensor node then passes the test results to other sensor nodes based on which a consensus is made on the faulty sensor nodes. Each sensor node must be tested by at least t one-hop neighbors to achieve a t-diagnosability. The greater the t, the greater the message overhead. In most of invalidation-based approaches, the number of faulty sensor nodes that can be detected is upper bounded by t. The detection accuracy of these approaches is close to 100% and the false alarm rate is close to zero; however, the detection latency exhibited by most of these approaches is high.

In *comparison-based* approaches, different tests (tasks) are assigned to a pair of sensor nodes and the results of these tasks are compared. The agreement and disagreement between these results form the basis for diagnosing faulty sensor nodes. Comparison-based approaches have comparatively less message and time complexity overhead than the invalidation-based approaches.

Neighbor Coordination Approaches: In neighbor coordination approaches, one-hop neighbors coordinate with each other to determine whether or not to disregard their own sensor readings based on the neighboring sensors readings or on the weights based on physical distances from the event and trustworthiness of the sensor node's measurements. Neighbor coordination approaches are further categorized into *majority voting* and *weighted majority voting* approaches.

Majority voting approaches exploit the fact that the faulty measurements are uncorrelated while nonfaulty measurements are spatially correlated. For example, assume that a sensor node s_i is a neighbor of s_j, and r_i and r_j are the readings for s_i and s_j, respectively. Sensor readings r_i and r_j are similar when $|r_i - r_j| < \delta$ where δ is application dependent and typically a small number. Majority voting techniques can provide good detection accuracy and low false alarm rates. However, majority voting techniques are *topology* dependent as the effectiveness of these approaches depends on the node degree in the WSN.

Weighted majority voting approaches weigh the sensing measurements based on properties such as physical distance from the event and trustworthiness of the measurements. Unlike simple majority voting, these weighted measurements are used to decide the state of a sensor node (i.e., faulty or nonfaulty) in a WSN. Weighted majority voting approaches are computationally more expensive than simple majority voting approaches. Weighted majority voting approaches are also topology dependent such as simple majority voting approaches (i.e., majority voting approaches accuracy degrades drastically in sparse networks).

Hierarchical Detection: In hierarchical detection, a spanning tree with the sink node as the root node is constructed that spans all fault-free sensor nodes in the WSN. This spanning tree is then used to determine faults at each level of the tree. The fault results are disseminated across the spanning tree such that each node in the network correctly diagnoses the fault states of all the sensor nodes in the WSN. The detection latency in a hierarchical detection approach is high because the diagnosis process is started either by the sink node or the leaf nodes and requires multihop communication of diagnostic messages. Furthermore, similar to the centralized approach, the hierarchical detection approach leads to rapid energy depletion in certain regions of the WSN, in particular, in sensor nodes close to the sink.

Node Self-Detection: In sensor node self-detection, the sensor node detects its own status (faulty or nonfaulty) with the help of additional hardware incorporated in the sensor node. Since the sensor node self-detection approach requires additional hardware, the approach increases hardware complexity, weight, and energy consumption.

Clustering-Based Approaches: Clustering-based approaches divide the overall WSN into clusters, which are groups of sensor nodes located geographically close to each other. Each cluster head executes a fault detection algorithm in the cluster head's group using a centralized or distributed approach. Clustering-based diagnostic approaches are communication-efficient; however, the cluster head requires more energy for leading the diagnostic process.

Watchdog Approaches: In watchdog approaches, a sensor node monitors whether the sensor node's packets are forwarded by the sensor node's one-hop neighbor by overhearing the communication channel. If a sensor node's neighboring node does not forward a packet within a certain time, the neighboring node is viewed as misbehaving. When the misbehaving rate exceeds a threshold, the misbehaving node is diagnosed as faulty. The source node then sends packets along other routes avoiding the diagnosed faulty node.

Probabilistic Approaches: Probabilistic approaches exploit the fact that sensor failure probability for different sensor nodes is not identical in a time interval that is not infinitesimally small. Probabilistic approaches normally leverage Bayesian or other statistical methods for fault diagnosis.

Event-Driven Diagnosis: In event-based WSNs as opposed to data-driven or query-driven WSNs, sensor nodes only report events of interest to the sink node in a timely manner. Fault diagnosis in event-driven WSNs requires special consideration for fault-event disambiguation since an event also causes abnormal data to be sensed by the sensor nodes that could be interpreted as a faulty measurement. Event detection approaches work effectively in dense networks with relatively low fault probability of sensor nodes. Most of the event detection approaches fail in distinguishing between events and faults if faults are located at the event boundary.

4.3   Distributed Fault Detection Algorithms

DFD algorithms are those in which each sensor node executes a fault detection algorithm to diagnose the status of the sensor node's neighboring sensor nodes and to obtain a localized fault view (Section 4.2.2.2). The localized fault view is then shared with neighboring sensor nodes to reach a consensus on faulty sensor nodes. We analyze different fault detection algorithms [90, 91, 102, 103, 106]; however, we present two fault detection algorithms for explaining the fault detection algorithms' functionalities:

4.3.1   Fault Detection Algorithm 1: The Chen Algorithm

The first algorithm, which we refer to as the Chen algorithm [90], relies on simple majority counts to determine faults. The approach is practical because sensor nodes have limited computing ability; hence, lightweight calculations are preferred over intensive calculations. Each sensor node $S_i \in S$ can exist in four states: good (GD), faulty (FT), likely good (LG), or likely faulty (LF). A sensor node in likely states is unsure if the sensor node is faulty and uses the neighbors' states of sensor nodes to finalize the sensor node's decision. The algorithm's implementation complexity is low and the probability of correct diagnosis is high.

Algorithm 1: The Chen algorithm [90] for WSN fault detection.

Input: Sensors S_i with measurements
Output: Tendency of good and faulty sensors

Step 1: For each sensor node S_i, compute the bit vector $C_i\{S\}$, where a 1 means S_i and S_j are consistent;
Let $S_{ij}(t) = |S_i(t) - S_j(t)|$;
$C_i\{S_j\} = 1$ if $S_{ij}(t) > \theta_1$ and $|S_{ij}(t) - S_{ij}(t+1)| > \theta_2$;

Step 2: Calculate the tendency of each sensor:
$T_i = $ Likely Good (LG) if $\sum C_i > \frac{N_S}{2}$, else Likely Faulty (LF) where N_s is the number of neighboring sensor nodes;

Step 3: Determine if the sensor node is good:
$T_i = $ Good (GD) if $N_C - \overline{N_C} > \frac{N_S}{2}$;
where N_C and $\overline{N_C}$ denote the number of consistent and inconsistent neighbors respectively;

Step 4: If a node is not sure, find Good or Faulty neighbors (set N). For each sensor:
if $S_i \in \{$LG, LF$\}$, then for each $N_j \in N$:
$T_i = $ GD if $(T_j = $ GD and $C_i\{N_j\} = 1)$ or $(T_j = $ FT and $C_i\{N_j\} = 0)$;
$T_i = $ FT if $(T_j = $ FT and $C_i\{N_j\} = 1)$ or $(T_j = $ GD and $C_i\{N_j\} = 0)$;
Repeat until all sensor nodes have a state of Good (GD) or Faulty (FT);

Table 4.1 lists the notations used in the Chen algorithm [90]. The neighboring sensor nodes in a WSN are those that are within the transmission range of each other. Each sensor node sends the sensor node's sensed values to the sensor node's neighboring sensor nodes. A sensor S_i generates test result c_{ij} based on the sensor node's neighbor S_j's measurements using variables d_{ij}, $\Delta d_{ij}^{\Delta t_l}$, and threshold values θ_1 and θ_2. The sensors S_i and S_j are both good or both faulty if $c_{ij} = 0$; however, the sensor nodes have a different good or faulty status if $c_{ij} = 1$. Each sensor

Table 4.1 Summary of notations used in the DFD algorithms

Notation	Description
S	Set of all the sensors involved in the DFD algorithm
$N(S_i)$	Set of neighbors of sensor node S_i
x_i	Measurement of S_i
d_{ij}^t	Measurement difference between S_i and S_j at time t (i.e., $d_{ij}^t = x_i^t - x_j^t$)
Δt_l	Measurement time difference, $t_{l+1} - t_l$
$\Delta d_{ij}^{\Delta t_l}$	Measurement difference between S_i and S_j from time t_l to t_{l+1} (i.e., $\Delta d_{ij}^{\Delta t_l} = d_{ij}^{t_{l+1}} - d_{ij}^{t_l}$)
c_{ij}	Test between S_i and S_j, $c_{ij} \in \{0, 1\}$, $c_{ij} = c_{ji}$
θ_1 and θ_2	Two predefined thresholds
T_i	Tendency value of a sensor: $T_i \in \{$LG, LF, GD, FT$\}$

node sends the sensor node's tendency values (i.e., estimated state) to all the sensor node's neighboring sensor nodes. The test values from neighboring sensors determine the tendency value of sensors to be LG or LF, and the number of LG sensors with the same results determines whether the sensors are GD or FT. Precisely, $\forall \; S_j \in N(S_i)$ and $T_j = LG$, $\sum(1 - c_{ij}) - \sum c_{ij} = \sum(1 - 2c_{ij})$ must be greater than or equal to $\lceil |N(S_i)/2| \rceil$ for S_i to be identified as good. The algorithm diagnoses a good sensor S_i as GD in the first round if the sensor node has less than $k/4$ bad neighbors. The Chen algorithm's important steps are depicted in Algorithm 1.

4.3.2 Fault Detection Algorithm 2: The Ding Algorithm

The second algorithm, which we refer to as the Ding algorithm [91], is a WSN fault detection algorithm with a low computational overhead. The results indicate that the algorithm can identify faulty sensors with relatively high accuracy even when the sensor failure probability is as high as 20%. The Ding algorithm's important steps are shown in Algorithm 2.

Algorithm 2: The Ding algorithm [91] for WSN fault detection.

Input: Sensors S_i with measurements
Output: Set of faulty sensors $\mathcal{F}$

Step 1: Identify the neighboring sensor nodes of sensor node S_i. For each sensor node S_i perform Steps 2 - 4;

Step 2: Compute d_i for each sensor node S_i using Eq. (4.1);

Step 3: Compute y_i for each sensor node S_i using Eq. (4.4);

Step 4: If $|y_i| \geq \theta$, assign S_i to $\mathcal{F}$, otherwise treat S_i as a normal sensor;

The algorithm compares the sensor node S_i's reading with the sensor node's k neighbors $S_{i1}, S_{i2}, \cdots, S_{ik}$ with measurements $x_1^{(i)}, x_2^{(i)}, \cdots, x_k^{(i)}$. The comparison is done by comparing x_i with median med_i of $\{x_1^{(i)}, x_2^{(i)}, \cdots, x_k^{(i)}\}$, that is,

$$d_i = x_i - \text{med}_i \tag{4.1}$$

If there are n sensors in total, the algorithm computes $d_i \; \forall \; n$ (i.e., $D = \{d_1, d_2, \cdots, d_i, \cdots, d_n\}$). The mean $\hat{\mu}$ of D is given by Ding et al. [91]:

$$\hat{\mu} = \frac{1}{n} \sum_{i=1}^{n} d_i \tag{4.2}$$

The standard deviation $\hat{\sigma}$ of D is given as [91]:

$$\hat{\sigma} = \sqrt{\frac{1}{n-1} \sum_{i=1}^{n} (d_i - \hat{\mu})^2} \tag{4.3}$$

Standardizing the dataset D yields $Y = \{y_1, y_2, \cdots, y_i, \cdots, y_n\}$, that is:

$$y_1 = \frac{d_1 - \hat{\mu}}{\hat{\sigma}}$$

$$y_2 = \frac{d_2 - \hat{\mu}}{\hat{\sigma}}$$

$$\vdots$$

$$y_i = \frac{d_i - \hat{\mu}}{\hat{\sigma}}$$

$$\vdots$$

$$y_n = \frac{d_n - \hat{\mu}}{\hat{\sigma}} \tag{4.4}$$

If $|y_i| \geq \theta$, then the Ding algorithm detects S_i as faulty where $\theta > 1$ is a predefined threshold value. Mathematically, $S_i \in \mathcal{F}$ if $|y_i| \geq \theta$ where $\mathcal{F}$ denotes the set of sensors claimed as faulty.

Section 4.5 discusses the implementation and effectiveness, in particular the detection accuracy, which is used implicitly in our Markov model as the coverage factor c, of these fault detection algorithms.

4.4 Fault-Tolerant Markov Models

In this section, we present our Markov models for FT WSNs. Our Markov models are comprehensive and encompass hierarchically the sensor node, WSN cluster, and WSN levels (Fig. 4.1). We adopt a bottom-up paradigm in our modeling by first developing a sensor node model and determining the model's reliability and MTTF [130]. The sensor node MTTF gives the average sensor node failure rate, which is utilized in the WSN cluster model. The WSN cluster model gives the WSN cluster reliability and MTTF, which determines the WSN cluster average failure rate. The WSN cluster average failure rate is then utilized in the WSN model to determine the WSN reliability and MTTF. Our bottom-up approach enables WSN reliability and MTTF characterization by leveraging sensor node and WSN cluster models. We note that some WSN architectures do not employ cluster-based hierarchy due to the additional energy cost associated with cluster formation and cluster head election. However, our modeling approach is equally applicable for WSN architectures without a cluster-based hierarchy by assuming that the WSN is composed of just one cluster where the cluster head is the sink node. For clarity, Table 4.2 summarizes important notations used in our Markov models.

4.4.1 Fault-Tolerance Parameters

Fault tolerance in WSNs is highly dependent on fault diagnosis in WSNs (Section 4.2). In this section, we characterize the FT parameters by exploiting the synergy between fault detection and FT in WSNs. The FT parameters leveraged in our Markov model are the *coverage factor* and *sensor failure rate*.

Table 4.2   Summary of notations used in our Markov models

Notation	Description
n	Total number of sensors in a WSN
c	Coverage factor
p	Cumulative sensor failure probability
λ_s	Sensor failure rate
t_s	Time over which sensor failure rate is specified
$P_i(t)$	Probability of being in state i at time t
$R_{s_d}(t)$	Reliability of FT (duplex) sensor node
MTTF_{s_d}	Mean time to failure of an FT sensor node
k	Average number of neighbor sensor nodes
$\lambda_{s_d}(k)$	FT sensor node failure rate with k neighbors
$R_c(t)$	WSN cluster reliability
$\lambda_c(n)$	WSN cluster failure rate with n sensor nodes
N	Number of clusters in the WSN
$R_{wsn}(t)$	Wsn reliability

4.4.1.1   Coverage Factor

The coverage factor c is defined as the probability that the faulty active sensor is correctly diagnosed, disconnected, and replaced by a good inactive spare sensor. The c estimation is critical in an FT WSN model and can be determined by

$$c = c_k - c_c \tag{4.5}$$

where c_k denotes the accuracy of the fault detection algorithm in diagnosing faulty sensors and c_c denotes the probability of an unsuccessful replacement of the identified faulty sensor with the good spare sensor. c_c depends on the sensor switching circuitry and is usually a constant, whereas c_k's estimation is challenging as different fault detection algorithms have different accuracies. We analyze different fault detection algorithms [91, 102, 103, 106] and observe that the accuracy of a fault detection algorithm depends on the average number of sensor node neighbors k and the cumulative probability of sensor failure p. We model $c_k : c_k \leq 1$ with the empirical relation:

$$c_k = \frac{k \times (1-p)}{k^{(k/M(p))^{1/M(p)}} + (1 - k/M(p))^k} \tag{4.6}$$

where $M(p)$ is a function of p and denotes an adjustment parameter that may correspond loosely to the desired average number of neighboring sensor nodes required to achieve a good fault detection accuracy for a given p. We have derived Eq. (4.6) by experimenting with the relationship between the fault detection algorithms' parameters (i.e., the average number of sensor node neighbors), sensor failure probability, and the fault detection algorithms' accuracy. We point out that Eq. (4.6) provides a good estimate of c_k in general for any fault detection algorithm, whereas exact c_k for a particular fault detection algorithm can be derived from the algorithm's mathematical model. Equation (4.6) approximates the relationship between a fault detection algorithm's parameters to obtain the fault detection algorithm's accuracy (in case the accuracy is unknown). In practice, a fault detection algorithm's accuracy should be determined accurately by the algorithm's designer that would alleviate the need of using an approximation (as in Eq. (4.6)). To clarify further, we point out that our Markov models are independent of c_k's determination methodology and are equally applicable to any c_k value.

4.4.1.2 Sensor Failure Rate

The sensor failure rate can be represented by exponential distribution with a failure rate of λ_s over the period t_s [131]. The exponential distribution, which has a property of constant failure rate, is a good model for the long, flat intrinsic failure portion of the *bathtub curve*. The exponential distribution is applicable to a variety of practical situations since many embedded components and systems spend most of their lifetimes in the flat portion of the bathtub curve. Furthermore, any failure rate curve can be approximated by piecewise exponential distribution segments patched together. Each exponential distribution segment in the overall approximation specifies a constant failure rate over a small time unit (e.g., daily, weekly, or monthly) that is the average of the failure rates during the respective time duration. The constant failure rate assignment for each exponential distribution segment is justifiable as many natural phenomena have a constant failure rate (or occurrence rate) property (e.g., the arrival rate of cosmic ray alpha particles). The failure rate curve approximation by piecewise exponential distributions is analogous to a curve approximation by piecewise straight line segments.

The exponential model works well for the interarrival times where the total number of events in a given time period is given by the Poisson distribution. When these events trigger failures, the exponential lifetime distribution model naturally applies [132]. The cumulative distribution function (CDF) for the sensors with exponentially distributed failure rate is

$$F_s(t_s; \lambda_s) = p = 1 - \exp(-\lambda_s t_s) \tag{4.7}$$

where p denotes the cumulative probability of sensor failure (for simplicity) and t_s signifies the time over which p is specified. Solving Eq. (4.7) for λ_s gives

$$\lambda_s = -\frac{1}{t_s} \ln(1 - p) \tag{4.8}$$

4.4.2 Fault-Tolerant Sensor Node Model

As a base case, we describe an NFT sensor node Markov model (Fig. 4.4) containing one sensor (temperature sensor in this case, but the sensor type is arbitrary). The NFT sensor node model consists of two states: state 1 (good state) and state 0 (failed state). The NFT sensor node

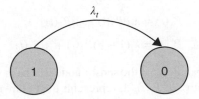

Figure 4.4   A non-FT (NFT) sensor node Markov model

fails when the node transitions from state 1 to state 0 due to a sensor failure. The differential equations describing the NFT sensor node Markov model are

$$P_1'(t) = -\lambda_t P_1(t)$$

$$P_0'(t) = \lambda_t P_1(t) \tag{4.9}$$

where $P_i(t)$ denotes the probability that the sensor node will be in state i at time t, and $P_i'(t)$ represents the first-order derivative of $P_i(t)$. λ_t represents the failure rate of an active temperature sensor.

Solving Eq. (4.9) with the initial conditions $P_1(0) = 1$ and $P_0(0) = 0$ yields

$$P_1(t) = e^{-\lambda_t t}$$

$$P_0(t) = 1 - e^{-\lambda_t t} \tag{4.10}$$

The reliability of the NFT sensor node is

$$R_s(t) = 1 - P_0(t) = P_1(t) = e^{-\lambda_t t} \tag{4.11}$$

The MTTF of the NFT sensor node is

$$\text{MTTF}_s = \int_0^\infty R_s(t) \, dt = \frac{1}{\lambda_t} \tag{4.12}$$

The average failure rate of the NFT sensor node is

$$\lambda_s = \frac{1}{\text{MTTF}_s} = \lambda_t \tag{4.13}$$

Since sensors have comparatively higher fault rates than other components [88, 93, 94], we propose an FT duplex sensor node model consisting of one active sensor and one inactive spare sensor. Using TMR [92] for FT is a possible scenario, but we consider a duplex sensor node model to minimize the additional cost as the additive cost of spare sensors can be prohibitive for large WSNs. In addition, a duplex model limits the increase in sensor node size. We point out that our modeling methodology can be extended to sensor nodes with NMR.

In our duplex sensor node, the inactive sensor becomes active only once the active sensor is declared faulty by the fault detection algorithm. We refer to our duplex sensor node as an FT sensor node, whose Markov model is depicted in Fig 4.5. The states in the Markov model represent the number of good sensors. The differential equations describing the FT sensor node Markov model are

$$P_2'(t) = -\lambda_t P_2(t)$$
$$P_1'(t) = \lambda_t c P_2(t) - \lambda_t P_1(t)$$
$$P_0'(t) = \lambda_t (1 - c) P_2(t) + \lambda_t P_1(t) \tag{4.14}$$

where $P_i(t)$ denotes the probability that the sensor node will be in state i at time t and $P_i'(t)$ represents the first-order derivative of $P_i(t)$. λ_t represents the failure rate of an active temperature sensor and $c\lambda_t$ is the rate at which recoverable failure occurs. The probability that the sensor

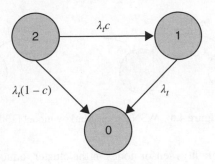

Figure 4.5   FT sensor node Markov model [130]

failure cannot be recovered is $(1 - c)$ and the rate at which unrecoverable failure occurs is $(1 - c)\lambda_t$.

Solving Eq. (4.14) with the initial conditions $P_2(0) = 1$, $P_1(0) = 0$, and $P_0(0) = 0$ yields

$$P_2(t) = e^{-\lambda_t t}$$

$$P_1(t) = c\lambda_t t e^{-\lambda_t t}$$

$$P_0(t) = 1 - P_1(t) - P_2(t) \tag{4.15}$$

The reliability of the FT sensor node is

$$R_{s_d}(t) = 1 - P_0(t) = P_2(t) + P_1(t) = e^{-\lambda_t t} + c\lambda_t t e^{-\lambda_t t} \tag{4.16}$$

where subscript d in $R_{s_d}(t)$ stands for duplex. The MTTF of the FT sensor node is

$$\text{MTTF}_{s_d} = \int_0^\infty R_{s_d}(t)\, dt = \frac{1}{\lambda_t} + \frac{c}{\lambda_t} \tag{4.17}$$

The average failure rate of the FT sensor node depends on k (since the fault detection algorithm's accuracy depends on k (Section 4.4.1)):

$$\lambda_{s_d(k)} = \frac{1}{\text{MTTF}_{s_d(k)}} \tag{4.18}$$

where $\lambda_{s_d(k)}$ and $\text{MTTF}_{s_d(k)}$ denote the failure rate and MTTF of an FT sensor node with k neighbors.

4.4.3   Fault-Tolerant WSN Cluster Model

A typical WSN consists of many clusters (Fig. 4.1), and we assume for our model that all nodes in a cluster are neighbors to each other (could be one-hop or two-hop neighbors depending on the topology). We note that our model does not impose any specific topology on a sensor network cluster. If the average number of nodes in a cluster is n, then the average number of neighboring nodes per sensor node is $k = n - 1$. Figure 4.6 depicts our Markov model for a WSN cluster. We assume that a cluster fails (i.e., fails to perform its assigned application task)

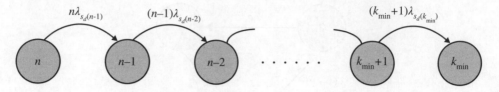

Figure 4.6   WSN cluster Markov model [130]

if the number of alive (nonfaulty) sensor nodes in the cluster reduces to k_{min}. The differential equations describing the WSN cluster Markov model are

$$P'_n(t) = -n\lambda_{s_d(n-1)}P_n(t)$$

$$P'_{n-1}(t) = n\lambda_{s_d(n-1)}P_n(t) - (n-1)\lambda_{s_d(n-2)}P_{n-1}(t)$$

$$\vdots$$

$$P'_{k_{min}}(t) = (k_{min} + 1)\lambda_{s_d(k_{min})}P_{k_{min}+1}(t) \tag{4.19}$$

where $\lambda_{s_d(n-1)}$, $\lambda_{s_d(n-2)}$, and $\lambda_{s_d(k_{min})}$ represent the FT (duplex) sensor node failure rate (Eq. (4.18)) when the average number of neighboring sensor nodes are $n-1$, $n-2$, and k_{min}, respectively. For mathematical tractability and closed-form solution, we analyze a special (simple) case when $n = k_{min} + 2$, which reduces the Markov model to three states (Fig. 4.7). The differential equations describing the WSN cluster Markov model when $n = k_{min} + 2$ are

$$P'_{k_{min}+2}(t) = -(k_{min} + 2)\lambda_{s_d(k_{min}+1)}P_{k_{min}+2}(t)$$

$$P'_{k_{min}+1}(t) = (k_{min} + 2)\lambda_{s_d(k_{min}+1)}P_{k_{min}+2}(t) - (k_{min} + 1)\lambda_{s_d(k_{min})}P_{k_{min}+1}(t)$$

$$P'_{k_{min}}(t) = (k_{min} + 1)\lambda_{s_d(k_{min})}P_{k_{min}+1}(t) \tag{4.20}$$

Solving Eq. (4.20) with the initial conditions $P_{k_{min}+2}(0) = 1$, $P_{k_{min}+1}(0) = 0$, and $P_{k_{min}}(0) = 0$ yields

$$P_{k_{min}+2}(t) = e^{-(k_m+2)\lambda_{s_d(k_m+1)}t}$$

$$P_{k_{min}+1}(t) = \frac{(k_m + 2)\lambda_{s_d(k_m+1)}e^{-(k_m+2)\lambda_{s_d(k_m+1)}t}}{(k_m + 1)\lambda_{s_d(k_m)} - (k_m + 2)\lambda_{s_d(k_m+1)}} + \frac{(k_m + 2)\lambda_{s_d(k_m+1)}e^{-(k_m+1)\lambda_{s_d(k_m)}t}}{(k_m + 2)\lambda_{s_d(k_m+1)} - (k_m + 1)\lambda_{s_d(k_m)}}$$

$$P_{k_{min}}(t) = 1 - P_{k_{min}+1}(t) - P_{k_{min}+2}(t) \tag{4.21}$$

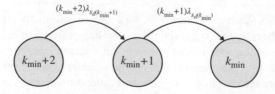

Figure 4.7   WSN cluster Markov model with three states [130]

where k_{min} denotes k_m in Eq. (4.21) for conciseness. The reliability of the WSN cluster is

$$R_c(t) = 1 - P_{k_{min}}(t)$$

$$= e^{-(k_{min}+2)\lambda_{s_d(k_{min}+1)}t} + \frac{(k_{min}+2)\lambda_{s_d(k_{min}+1)}e^{-(k_{min}+2)\lambda_{s_d(k_{min}+1)}t}}{(k_{min}+1)\lambda_{s_d(k_{min})} - (k_{min}+2)\lambda_{s_d(k_{min}+1)}}$$

$$+ \frac{(k_{min}+2)\lambda_{s_d(k_{min}+1)}e^{-(k_{min}+1)\lambda_{s_d(k_{min})}t}}{(k_{min}+2)\lambda_{s_d(k_{min}+1)} - (k_{min}+1)\lambda_{s_d(k_{min})}} \tag{4.22}$$

The MTTF of the WSN cluster is

$$\text{MTTF}_c = \int_0^\infty R_c(t)\,dt = \frac{1}{(k_m+2)\lambda_{s_d(k_m+1)}} + \frac{1}{(k_m+1)\lambda_{s_d(k_m)} - (k_m+2)\lambda_{s_d(k_m+1)}}$$

$$+ \frac{(k_m+2)\lambda_{s_d(k_m+1)}}{(k_m+2)(k_m+2)\lambda_{s_d(k_m)}\lambda_{s_d(k_m+1)} - (k_m+1)^2\lambda_{s_d(k_m)}^2} \tag{4.23}$$

where k_{min} denotes k_m in Eq. (4.23) for conciseness. The average failure rate of the cluster $\lambda_{c(n)}$ depends on the average number of nodes in the cluster n at deployment time:

$$\lambda_{c(n)} = \frac{1}{\text{MTTF}_{c(n)}} \tag{4.24}$$

where $\text{MTTF}_{c(n)}$ denotes the MTTF of a WSN cluster of n sensor nodes.

4.4.4 Fault-Tolerant WSN Model

A typical WSN consists of $N = n_s/n$ clusters where n_s denotes the total number of sensor nodes in the WSN and n denotes the average number of nodes in a cluster. Figure 4.8 depicts our WSN Markov model. We assume that the WSN fails to perform the WSN's assigned task when the number of alive clusters reduces to N_{min}. The differential equations describing the WSN Markov model are

$$P'_N(t) = -N\lambda_{c(n)}$$

$$P'_{N-1}(t) = N\lambda_{c(n)}P_N(t) - (N-1)\lambda_{c(n)}P_{N-1}(t)$$

$$\vdots$$

$$P'_{N_{min}}(t) = (N_{min}+1)\lambda_{c(n)}P_{N_{min}+1}(t) \tag{4.25}$$

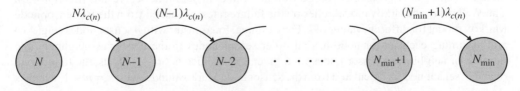

Figure 4.8 WSN Markov model [130]

where $\lambda_{c(n)}$ represents the average cluster failure rate (Eq. (4.24)) when the cluster contains n sensor nodes at deployment time. For mathematical tractability, we analyze a special (simple) case when $N = N_{min} + 2$, which reduces the Markov model to three states. The differential equations describing the WSN Markov model when $N = N_{min} + 2$ are

$$P'_{N_{min}+2}(t) = -(N_{min} + 2)\lambda_{c(n)}P_{N_{min}+2}(t)$$

$$P'_{N_{min}+1}(t) = (N_{min} + 2)\lambda_{c(n)}P_{N_{min}+2}(t) - (N_{min} + 1)\lambda_{c(n)}P_{N_{min}+1}(t)$$

$$P'_{N_{min}}(t) = (N_{min} + 1)\lambda_{c(n)}P_{N_{min}+1}(t) \tag{4.26}$$

Solving Eq. (4.26) with the initial conditions $P_{N_{min}+2}(0) = 1$, $P_{N_{min}+1}(0) = 0$, and $P_{N_{min}}(0) = 0$ yields

$$P_{N_{min}+2}(t) = e^{-(N_{min}+2)\lambda_{c(n)}t}$$

$$P_{N_{min}+1}(t) = (N_{min} + 2)\lambda_{c(n)}\left[e^{-(N_{min}+1)\lambda_{c(n)}t} - e^{-(N_{min}+2)\lambda_{c(n)}t}\right]$$

$$P_{N_{min}}(t) = 1 - P_{N_{min}+1}(t) - P_{N_{min}+2}(t) \tag{4.27}$$

The WSN reliability is

$$R_{wsn}(t) = 1 - P_{N_{min}}(t)$$

$$= e^{-(N_{min}+2)\lambda_{c(n)}t} + (N_{min} + 2)\lambda_{c(n)}\left[e^{-(N_{min}+1)\lambda_{c(n)}t} - e^{-(N_{min}+2)\lambda_{c(n)}t}\right] \tag{4.28}$$

The WSN MTTF when $N = N_{min} + 2$ is

$$\text{MTTF}_{wsn} = \int_0^\infty R_{wsn}(t)\,dt$$

$$= \frac{1}{(N_{min} + 2)\lambda_{c(n)}} + \frac{N_{min} + 2}{N_{min} + 1} - 1 \tag{4.29}$$

Discussion: Our hierarchical Markov modeling exploits the relationship between failure rates at the sensor component, sensor node, WSN cluster, and WSN levels. Markov modeling of sensor nodes (Section 4.4.2) takes the failure rate of the sensor node's components λ_t (e.g., temperature sensor) as input and then derives the failure rate of the sensor node λ_s (for simplicity, the failure rate of one component is considered for illustration; however, the failure rates of different components can be considered or combined into a single representative failure rate).

For an FT sensor node model (e.g., duplex sensor node or triple modular redundant sensor node), the average failure rate of the FT sensor node implicitly depends on k since the fault detection algorithm's accuracy depends on k (Sections 4.3 and 4.4.1.1). Hence, the failure rate of an FT sensor node is calculated for different k values in our numerical results (Section 4.6). The WSN cluster Markov model relies on the failure rates calculated from the FT sensor node Markov model for different values of k. For example, for a cluster with n sensor nodes (Fig. 4.6) and assuming each sensor node has all other sensor nodes in the cluster as neighbors, the number of neighboring sensor nodes for a given sensor node is $(n - 1)$. Thus, the failure rate of an FT sensor node is calculated from the sensor node Markov model with $k = n - 1$, which is then used in the WSN cluster Markov model (Fig. 4.6). When a sensor node fails, the remaining operational (healthy) neighboring nodes of a given sensor node in a cluster become $(n - 2)$; thus, the failure rate of an FT sensor node is calculated from the sensor node's Markov model with $k = n - 2$ and so on. The cluster becomes nonoperational when the number of operational sensor nodes in the cluster reaches a minimum k_{min} and consequently the overall failure rate of a WSN cluster with n sensor nodes is calculated for that k_{min}.

The WSN cluster failure rate with n sensor nodes obtained from the WSN cluster Markov model is then used in the WSN Markov model (Section 4.4.4). The WSN is assumed to be consisting of N clusters and WSN becomes nonoperational when the number of alive (operational) clusters reduces to N_{min}. The WSN Markov model is then used to calculate the MTTF and reliability of a given WSN using the cluster failure rate calculated from the WSN cluster Markov model.

4.5 Simulation of Distributed Fault Detection Algorithms

In this section, we discuss our implementation of two DFD algorithms: the Chen and Ding algorithms (Section 4.3). Our analysis is challenging since it is difficult to compare fault detection algorithms without a standard benchmark (Section 4.7.2). Since different DFD algorithms can use different fault models, a comparison between DFD algorithms can be made by observing the performance of the algorithms under similar fault models and similar topologies.

4.5.1 Using ns−2 to Simulate Faulty Sensors

In prior work, the Chen and Ding algorithms were simulated strictly algorithmically using simplified fault models that approximated a Poisson process. To compare these two models as realistically as possible, we use ns−2 [101], which is a widely used discrete event simulator for both wired and wireless networks, and a custom fault model. ns−2 allows us to see how these algorithms perform atop a detailed network stack over a wireless channel. We have leveraged ns−2 instead of ns−3 as ns−2 provides better support for WSN and mobile ad hoc network (MANET) protocols [133].

Wireless entities in ns−2 are called nodes and have modules called agents representing network layers stacked atop the nodes. Agents are typically used to generate application traffic, but we use agents as a fault detection unit in a sensor node (Fig. 4.9). The agent first receives scheduled, scripted commands to read values from a `SensorNodeData` module. The `SensorNodeData` module generates random sensor readings based on our implemented fault models.

After recording a data sample, the sensor node broadcasts the data as a packet and builds a record of each broadcasted packet that the sensor node receives from other sensor nodes. After a listening period, a separately scheduled event commands the detection agent to apply the two fault detection algorithms (i.e., the Ding and Chen algorithms). A fault tracker unit records statistics of detected and undetected errors. In the case of the Chen algorithm, each round of tendency broadcasting occurs in two-second intervals. The sensor readings are also broadcasted similarly in two-second intervals.

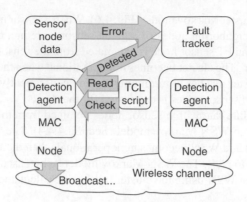

Figure 4.9   The ns−2-based simulation architecture

A duplex configuration was implemented for permanent errors. When a sensor node passes a threshold of detected errors, the sensor "fails" and is replaced by a spare sensor. For the simplified fault model, this replacement helps little because Poisson events are memoryless, and a sensor node with a new sensor and a sensor node with an old sensor will have the same error rate. However, for realistic data, constant errors are permanent and are repaired when the sensor is replaced. The realistic data usage also results in a penalty of false positives and causes more sensor nodes to be identified as faulty. The following sections describe our experiments with both simulated and real-world data.

4.5.2   *Experimental Setup for Simulated Data*

To compare the performance of each algorithm, it is useful to observe each algorithm using a simplified fault model; thus, we consider the scenario used by Chen et al. [90]. Each sensor records a uniformly random temperature between 70° and 75°. Errors occur as a Poisson process, with an arbitrary, scalable mean, and corrupt a single sensor on a single sensor node during the event. A corrupted sample is randomly distributed between 100° and 105°. We simulate each sensor node for 4 h and take samples every 30 s.

Fig. 4.10(a) and (b) depicts the detection performance of the Chen algorithm across different parameters and error rates. We observe that for the Chen algorithm, the error rate affects detection performance significantly; however, the θ value has a relatively minor impact. Fig. 4.11(a) and (b) depicts the detection performance of the Ding algorithm across different parameters and error rates. For the Ding algorithm, as θ is scaled, the number of false positives scales proportionally. For both algorithms, low error rates improve detection accuracy as low error rates make errors more distinguishable. In the simulated data scenario, the Chen algorithm performs better than the Ding algorithm in terms of the percentage of false positives, and the detection accuracy is relatively less dependent on θ. However, this simulated scenario is very specific and consistent, which may not always be the case.

4.5.3   *Experiments Using Real-World Data*

Since transient faults are manifested in different ways, a more realistic error model that closely follows a real-world scenario is desirable for analysis. For our real-world data case study,

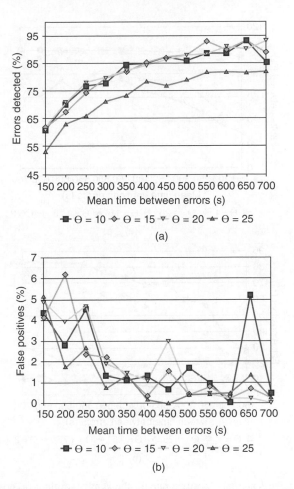

Figure 4.10 Effectiveness and false positive rate of the Chen algorithm: (a) error detection accuracy for the Chen algorithm; (b) false positive rate of Chen algorithm

we leverage publicly available sensor data from the Intel Berkeley Research Laboratory [134]. The data comes from an indoor sensor network deployment that measures temperature, humidity, and other metrics. Using temperature data from 53 sensor nodes, we have produced a variety of empirical observations on which we have based our simulation.

We note a few empirical observations from the Intel Berkeley data. One observation is that the real-world data includes noise. Noise in sensor readings is correlated with past values (autocorrelated) and can have high power levels for certain time periods. To measure the effect of noise on sensor data, we apply a denoising filter available in the MATLAB Wavelet toolkit to the Intel Berkeley data to approximate a reference "noise-free" signal. We measure the power level of noise in the data (Fig. 4.12) and record the values in a text file. We play back the recorded noise power level values during simulation, and multiply the noise values with simulated white Gaussian noise to imitate the bursty behavior of noisy faults.

Another observation from the Intel Berkeley data is that for nearly all sensor nodes, sensor samples level off as they approach their end-of-life, resulting in a "constant" fault. A histogram

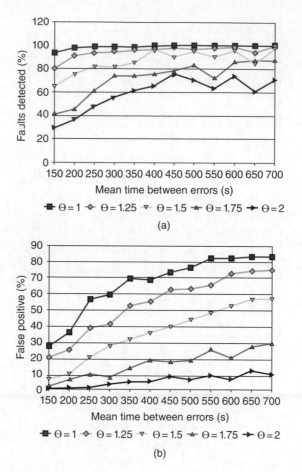

Figure 4.11 Effectiveness and false positive rate for the Ding algorithm: (a) error detection accuracy for the Ding algorithm; (b) false positive rate for the Ding algorithm

of the times at which this occurs (Fig. 4.13) reveals that the distribution of sensor node lifetimes fits well into a Student's t-distribution, which is supported by MATLAB's distribution fitting tools. For our experiments, we have recorded a set of several thousand random numbers fitting the Student's t-distribution. The sensor nodes then randomly select a value from the recorded t-distribution values to select a time for the fault occurrence.

Finally, we observe that voltage spikes are not frequent in the Intel Berkeley data set, occurring in only 6 out of 53 nodes. Because of the rare occurrence of voltage spikes, our simulations inject a spike once during the lifetime of each sensor node. The time of the spike occurrence is modeled using a uniform process. The base signal is a sine wave with a period of 2 h between 20 and 30 °C. To allow minor variations in temperature readings sensed by sensor nodes, the temperature values are treated as being generated from a radiating heat source. The nodes furthest from the center have a lower temperature proportional to the inverse of the distance squared as in the free space path loss model. The noise and spike errors are added to the signal, and the constant fault causes the signal to hang at the signal's last valid value during an error.

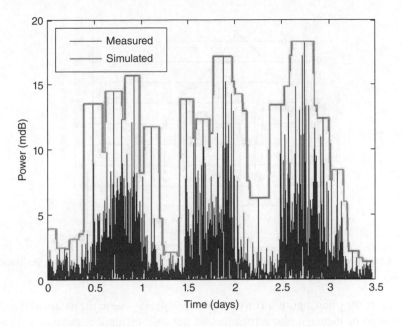

Figure 4.12   Noise power levels in the Intel Berkeley sample

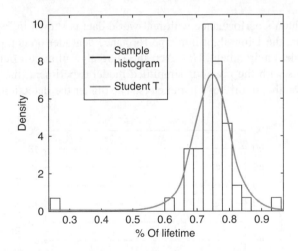

Figure 4.13   Distribution of constant error occurrences

A signal is considered erroneous if the variation is more than half a degree from the signal's true value. In our experiments, the faulty signals are never repaired unless faults accumulate, and ultimately the sensor is replaced if diagnosed as faulty.

Figure 4.14 shows the performance of the Chen algorithm for the real-world data. Despite detecting over 90% of the faults in the simplified model, the algorithm fails to perform well with the real-world data, detecting fewer than 50% of erroneous readings. The poor

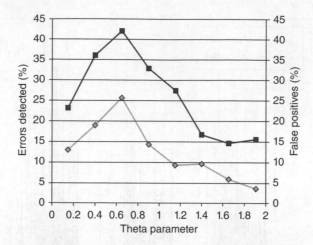

Figure 4.14   Error detection and false positive rate for the Chen algorithm using real-world data

performance of the Chen algorithm on the real-world data is due to the nature of the algorithm. For an error to be detected, the error must be not only disruptive, causing a node to have different values from the node's neighbors, but also transient and have a sharp transition boundary. Since noise events last for multiple samples, the Chen algorithm is not equipped to handle these errors.

The Ding algorithm's performance with real-world data is shown in Fig. 4.15. Similar to the Chen algorithm, the Ding algorithm's performance degrades as compared to the previous simplified model environment. However, the Ding algorithm still detects a majority of occurring faults. As with the previous simplified model experiment, the Ding algorithm is highly dependent on the algorithm's parameters. The higher the detection rate is, the higher

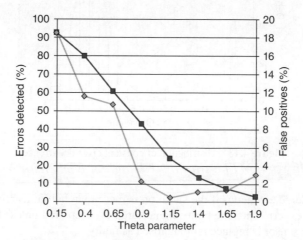

Figure 4.15   Error detection and false positive rate for the Ding algorithm using real-world data

the rate of false positives is for the Ding algorithm; however, the false positive rate remains low, peaking at 20%.

4.6 Numerical Results

In this section, we present reliability and MTTF results for our Markov models (Section 4.4) implemented in the SHARPE (Symbolic Hierarchical Automated Reliability and Performance Evaluator) Software Package [135, 136]. SHARPE provides MTTF results directly based on our models' implementations; however, SHARPE does not provide reliability results directly, but reliability results can be calculated from state probabilities. We present example reliability calculations as well as detailed reliability and MTTF results for an NFT as well as an FT sensor node, WSN cluster, and WSN using our bottom-up Markov modeling paradigm.

4.6.1 Experimental Setup

In this section, we describe our FT sensor node, WSN cluster, and WSN model implementation in the SHARPE Software Package [135, 136]. We also present a typical fault detection algorithm's accuracy for different cumulative sensor failure probability p values. Owing to SHARPE limitations that take only exponential polynomials, we assume our sensor failure rate to be exponentially distributed (Section 4.4.1.2).

SHARPE is a software tool for performance, reliability, and performability model specification and analysis. The SHARPE toolkit provides a specification language and solution methods for commonly used performance, reliability, and performability model types. Supported models of SHARPE include combinatorial models, state-space (e.g., Markov and semi-Markov reward models), and stochastic Petri nets. SHARPE allows computation of steady-state, transient, and interval measures. SHARPE allows output measures of a model to be used as parameters of other models to facilitate the hierarchical combination of different model types.

Our Markov model exploits the synergy of fault detection and fault tolerance for WSNs. Table 4.3 depicts c_k values estimated for a DFD algorithm using Eq. (4.6) for different p and k values. These estimated c_k values approximate the accuracy of the DFD algorithms proposed in [91, 102, 103, 106]. We note that any inaccuracy in the c_k estimation does not affect our calculations of results because these calculations leverage c_k values but are independent of whether these values reflect accurately a particular DFD algorithm's accuracy. We assume $c_c = 0$ in Eq. (4.5) (i.e., once a faulty sensor is identified, the faulty sensor is replaced by a good spare sensor perfectly), which gives $c = c_k$ in Eq. (4.5).

4.6.2 Reliability and MTTF for an NFT and an FT Sensor Node

In this section, we present the reliability and MTTF results for an NFT and an FT sensor node for the two cases: $c \neq 1$ and $c = 1$, when $k = 5$ and $p = 0.05$. The case $c \neq 1$ corresponds to a real-world fault detection algorithm (typical values are shown in Table 4.3), whereas the case $c = 1$ corresponds to an ideal fault detection algorithm, which detects faulty sensors perfectly for all p values. We calculate reliability at $t = 100$ days since we assume $t_s = 100$ days [137]

Table 4.3 Estimated values for a fault detection algorithm's accuracy

p	$M(p)$	k				
		5	6	7	10	15
0.05	25	0.979	1	1	1	1
0.1	50	0.858	0.895	0.921	0.957	0.96
0.2	56	0.755	0.717	0.81	0.845	0.851
0.3	65	0.652	0.679	0.699	0.732	0.742
0.4	66	0.558	0.5813	0.599	0.627	0.636
0.5	67	0.464	0.484	0.498	0.522	0.53
0.6	68	0.371	0.386	0.398	0.417	0.424
0.7	69	0.278	0.29	0.298	0.313	0.318
0.8	70	0.185	0.193	0.198	0.208	0.212
0.9	71	0.092	0.096	0.099	0.104	0.106
0.99	72	0.0092	0.00962	0.0099	0.0104	0.0106

in Eq. (4.8); however, we point out that reliability can be calculated for any other time value using our Markov models.

For an NFT sensor node reliability calculation, we require the sensor failure rate λ_t, which can be calculated using Eq. (4.8) (i.e., $\lambda_t = (-1/100)\ln(1 - 0.05) = 5.13 \times 10^{-4}$ failures/day). SHARPE gives $P_1(t) = e^{-5.13 \times 10^{-4}t}$ and sensor node reliability $R_s(t) = P_1(t)$. Evaluating $R_s(t)$ at $t = 100$ gives $R_s(t)|_{t=100} = 0.94999$.

For an FT sensor node when $c \neq 1$, different reliability results are obtained for different k because the fault detection algorithm's accuracy and coverage factor c depend on k. For $k = 5$, $c = 0.979$ (Table 4.3), SHARPE gives $P_2(t) = e^{-5.13 \times 10^{-4}t}$ and $P_1(t) = 5.0223 \times 10^{-4}te^{-5.13 \times 10^{-4}t}$. The reliability $R_s(t) = P_2(t) + P_1(t)$, which when evaluated at $t = 100$ gives $R_s(t)|_{t=100} = 0.99770$. For an FT sensor node when $c = 1$ for all k, p, SHARPE gives $P_2(t) = e^{-5.13 \times 10^{-4}t}$ and $P_1(t) = 5.13 \times 10^{-4}te^{-5.13 \times 10^{-4}t}$. Using Eq. (4.16), the reliability $R_s(t)|_{t=100} = 0.99872$.

Table 4.4 shows the reliability for an NFT and an FT sensor node evaluated at $t = 100$ days for k values of 5, 10, and 15. As expected, the results show that reliability decreases for both NFT and FT sensor nodes as p increases, and the reliability attained by an FT sensor node (both for $c \neq 1$ and $c = 1$) is always better than an NFT sensor node. For example, the percentage reliability improvement achieved by an FT sensor node with $c \neq 1, k = 15$ over an NFT sensor node is 18.98% when $p = 0.2$. However, an FT sensor node with $c = 1$ outperforms both an FT sensor node with $c \neq 1$ and an NFT sensor node for all p values. For example, the percentage improvement in reliability for an FT sensor node with $c = 1$ over an NFT sensor node is 69.09%, and the percentage improvements in reliability for an FT sensor node with $c = 1$ over an FT sensor node ($c \neq 1$) with k equal to 5, 10, and 15 are 28.11%, 24.32%, and 23.82%, respectively, for $p = 0.5$. The percentage improvement in reliability attained by an FT sensor node with $c = 1$ over an NFT sensor node is 230%, and the percentage improvements in reliability for an FT sensor node with $c = 1$ over an FT sensor node ($c \neq 1$) with k equal to 5, 10, and 15 are 172.36%, 166.31%, and 165.32%, respectively, for $p = 0.9$. These results reveal that the percentage improvement in reliability attained by an FT sensor node with $c = 1$

Table 4.4   Reliability for an NFT and an FT sensor node

Probability p	NFT k, c : N/A	FT $(k = 5, c \neq 1)$	FT $(k = 10, c \neq 1)$	FT $(k = 15, c \neq 1)$	FT $(c = 1)$
0.05	0.94999	0.99770	0.99872	0.99872	0.99872
0.1	0.89996	0.98135	0.99074	0.99102	0.99482
0.2	0.80011	0.93481	0.95088	0.95195	0.97853
0.3	0.69977	0.86265	0.88263	0.88513	0.94959
0.4	0.59989	0.77094	0.79209	0.79485	0.90643
0.5	0.5007	0.66086	0.68097	0.68374	0.84662
0.6	0.40012	0.53610	0.55295	0.55552	0.76663
0.7	0.30119	0.40167	0.41432	0.41612	0.66262
0.8	0.19989	0.25943	0.26683	0.26812	0.52171
0.9	0.10026	0.12148	0.12424	0.12470	0.33086
0.99	0.01005	0.01048	0.01053	0.01056	0.05628

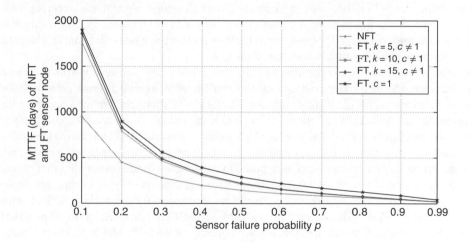

Figure 4.16   MTTF in days for an NFT and an FT sensor node [130]

increases as $p \rightarrow 1$ because for an FT sensor node with $c \neq 1$, c decreases as $p \rightarrow 1$ (Table 4.3). The sensor node reliability analysis reveals that a robust fault detection algorithm with $c \approx 1$ for all p and k values is necessary to attain good reliability for an FT sensor node.

Figure 4.16 depicts the MTTF for an NFT and an FT sensor node for k values of 5, 10, and 15 versus the sensor failure probability p when t_s in Eq. (4.7) is 100 days [91, 106]. The results show that the MTTF for an FT sensor node improves with increasing k. However, the MTTF shows negligible improvement when $k = 15$ over $k = 10$ as the fault detection algorithm's accuracy improvement gradient (slope) decreases for large k values.

Figure 4.16 also compares the MTTF for an FT sensor node when $c = 1 \ \forall k, p$. When $c \neq 1$ for existing fault detection algorithms, comparison with $c = 1$ provides insight into how the fault detection algorithm's accuracy affects the sensor node's MTTF. Figure 4.16 shows that the MTTF for an FT sensor node with $c = 1$ is always greater than an FT sensor node with $c \neq 1$.

Figure 4.16 shows that the MTTF for an NFT and an FT sensor node decreases as p increases; however, the FT sensor node maintains better MTTF than the NFT sensor node for all p values. This observation reveals that a sensor with a lower failure probability achieves better MTTF for both the NFT and FT sensor nodes. Figure 4.16 also shows that the MTTF for both the NFT and the FT sensor nodes approaches zero as p approaches 1 (i.e., MTTF $\rightarrow 0 \iff p \rightarrow 1$). This observation is intuitive because a faulty sensor (with $p = 1$) is unreliable and leads to a failed sensor node with zero MTTF and suggests that depending on the application's reliability and MTTF requirements, the faulty sensor should be replaced before p approaches 1.

Table 4.5 depicts the percentage MTTF improvement gained by an FT sensor node over an NFT sensor node for different values of p. We calculate the percentage improvement as % MTTF mprovement = $(MTTF_{FT} - MTTF_{NFT})/MTTF_{NFT} \times 100$. The table shows that the MTTF percentage improvement for an FT sensor node decreases as p increases when $c \neq 1$. The percentage MTTF improvement for an FT sensor node with $k = 5$ and $k = 10$ are 85.75% and 95.65%, respectively, for $p = 0.1$ and drops to 0.875% and 1.34%, respectively, for $p = 0.99$. This observation reveals that having more neighboring sensor nodes (a higher k value) improves MTTF because, in general, a fault detection algorithm's accuracy and c improve with increasing k. Table 4.5 also shows that the MTTF percentage improvement for an FT sensor node over an NFT sensor node is 100% on average when $c = 1$, thus highlighting the importance of a robust fault detection algorithm.

Model Validation: We compare the MTTF results for an NFT sensor node obtained using our Markov model with other existing models in the literature as well as practical sensor node implementations to provide insights into the accuracy of our models. We note that a detailed comparison and verification of our model with existing models is not possible because there are no similar/related models that leverage FT constructs. Jung et al. [71] modeled the lifetime of trigger-driven sensor nodes with different event arrival rates (trigger-driven sensor nodes perform processing based on events as opposed to duty-cycle-based sensor nodes that perform processing based on a duty cycle), which can be interpreted as sensing events that depend on the sensor node's sensing frequency. Results were obtained for three trigger-driven sensor node platforms: XSM, MICAz, and Telos. XSM and MICAz consisted of an ATmega128L 8-bit processor with a maximum processor frequency of 16 MHz and a maximum performance of 16 million instructions per second (MIPS). Telos consisted of a TI MSP430 16-bit

Table 4.5 Percentage MTTF improvement for an FT sensor node as compared to an NFT sensor node

Probability p	FT $(k = 5, c \neq 1)$	FT $(k = 10, c \neq 1)$	FT $(c = 1)$
0.1	85.75	95.65	100
0.2	75.61	84.63	100
0.3	65.14	72.99	100
0.5	46.25	52.49	100
0.7	27.62	31.23	100
0.9	9.37	10.52	100
0.99	0.875	1.34	100

processor with a maximum processor frequency of 8 MHz and a maximum performance of 16 MIPS. Results revealed that Telos, XSM, and MICAz delivered lifetimes of 1500, 1400, and 600 days, respectively, with an event arrival rate of 0.1 events/h, which dropped to 350, 100, and 0 days, respectively, with an event arrival rate of 100 events/h. The lifetime values for an NFT sensor node obtained from our Markov model ranges from 949 to 22 days for different sensor failure probabilities. Depending on the sensor node energy consumption, the lifetime model proposed in [70] estimated that the sensor node lifetime varied from 25 to 215 days. These comparisons indicate that our Markov model yields sensor node lifetime values in the range obtained from other existing models.

We also compare the NFT sensor node lifetime estimation from our model with an experimental study on sensor node lifetimes [74]. This comparison verifies conformity of our model with real measurements. For example, with a sensor node battery capacity of 2500 mA h, experiments indicate a sensor node lifetime ranging from 72 to 95 h for a 100% duty cycle for different battery brands (e.g., Ansmann, Panasonic Industrial, Varta High Energy, Panasonic Extreme Power) [74]. The sensor node lifetime for a duty cycle of 18% can be estimated as $95/0.18 = 528 \text{ h} \approx 22$ days and for a duty cycle of 0.42% as $95/0.0042 = 22{,}619 \text{ h} \approx 942$ days. This comparison reveals that our NFT sensor node lifetime model estimates lifetime values in the range obtained by experimental sensor node implementations.

4.6.3   Reliability and MTTF for an NFT and an FT WSN Cluster

In this section, we present the reliability and MTTF results for two WSN clusters that contain on average $n = k_{min} + 2$ and $n = k_{min} + 5$ sensor nodes at deployment time ($k_{min} = 4$). The selection of two different n values provides insight into how the size of the cluster affects reliability and MTTF (other n and k_{min} values depicted similar trends). The NFT WSN cluster consists of NFT sensor nodes and the FT WSN cluster consists of FT sensor nodes. For brevity, we present example WSN cluster reliability calculations for $n = k_{min} + 2$ ($k_{min} = 4$) and $p = 0.1$.

Leveraging our bottom-up approach model, the NFT WSN cluster uses the failure rate λ_s of an NFT sensor node. By using Eq. (4.8), $\lambda_t = 1.054 \times 10^{-3}$ failures/day. Since the coverage factor c does not appear in the reliability (and MTTF) calculation for an NFT sensor node, the failure rate $\lambda_s = \lambda_t = 1/\text{MTTF}_s = 1.054 \times 10^{-3}$ failures/day. In other words, for an NFT sensor node, $\lambda_{s(k_{min})} = \lambda_{s(k_{min}+1)}$, $\lambda_{s(k_{min})} = \lambda_{s(4)}$, and $\lambda_{s(k_{min})+1} = \lambda_{s(5)}$, which denote the sensor node failure rate when the average number of neighboring sensor nodes are 4 and 5, respectively. The NFT WSN cluster reliability calculation utilizes $\lambda_{s(4)}$ and $\lambda_{s(5)}$, which gives $P_{k_{min}+2}(t) = e^{-6.324 \times 10^{-3}t}$ and $P_{k_{min}+1}(t) = 6 \times e^{-5.27 \times 10^{-3}t} - 6 \times e^{-6.324 \times 10^{-3}t}$. The reliability $R_c(t) = P_{k_{min}+2}(t) + P_{k_{min}+1}(t)$, which when evaluated at $t = 100$ days gives $R_c(t)|_{t=100} = 0.88562$.

For an FT WSN cluster when $c \neq 1$, the reliability calculation requires $\lambda_{s_d(k_{min})}$ and $\lambda_{s_d(k_{min}+1)}$, which depends on k as the fault detection algorithm's accuracy and c depends on k, yielding different reliability results for different k_{min} values. Using Table 4.3 and Eq. (4.18), $\lambda_{s_d(k_{min})} = \lambda_{s_d(4)} = 1/\text{MTTF}_{s_d(4)} = 1/1.715 \times 10^3 = 5.83 \times 10^{-4}$ failures/day and $\lambda_{s_d(k_{min}+1)} = \lambda_{s_d(5)} = 1/\text{MTTF}_{s_d(5)} = 1/1.763 \times 10^3 = 5.67 \times 10^{-4}$ failures/day. SHARPE gives $P_{k_{min}+2}(t) = e^{-3.402 \times 10^{-3}t}$ and $P_{k_{min}+1}(t) = 6.9856 \times e^{-2.915 \times 10^{-3}t} - 6.9856 \times e^{-3.402 \times 10^{-3}t}$. The reliability of the FT WSN cluster is calculated as $R_c(t)|_{t=100} = 0.95969$.

Table 4.6 Reliability for an NFT and an FT WSN cluster when $n = k_{min} + 2$ ($k_{min} = 4$)

p	NFT	FT ($c \neq 1$)	FT ($c = 1$)
0.05	0.96720	0.99058	0.99098
0.1	0.88562	0.95969	0.96552
0.2	0.65567	0.84304	0.87474
0.3	0.41968	0.66438	0.74422
0.4	0.23309	0.45925	0.59388
0.5	0.10942	0.26595	0.43653
0.6	0.04098	0.11837	0.28732
0.7	0.01114	0.03548	0.16279
0.8	1.5957×10^{-3}	4.3470×10^{-3}	0.06723
0.9	5.5702×10^{-5}	1.4838×10^{-4}	0.01772
0.99	6.1056×10^{-10}	1.0057×10^{-9}	5.5702×10^{-5}

For an FT WSN cluster when $c = 1$, the reliability calculation does not depend on k, which gives $\lambda_{s_d(k_{min})} = \lambda_{s_d(4)} = 1/\text{MTTF}_{s_d(4)} = 1/1898 = 5.269 \times 10^{-4}$ failures/day and $\lambda_{s_d(k_{min}+1)} = \lambda_{s_d(5)} = 1/\text{MTTF}_{s_d(5)} = 1/1898 = 5.269 \times 10^{-4}$ failures/day. SHARPE gives $P_{k_{min}+2}(t) = e^{-3.1614 \times 10^{-3} t}$ and $P_{k_{min}+1}(t) = 6 \times e^{-2.6345 \times 10^{-3} t} - 6 \times e^{-3.1614 \times 10^{-3} t}$, from which we calculate $R_c(t)|_{t=100} = 0.96552$.

Table 4.6 shows the reliability for an NFT and an FT WSN cluster (for $c \neq 1$ and $c = 1$) evaluated at $t = 100$ days when $n = k_{min} + 2$ ($k_{min} = 4$). We observe similar trends as with sensor node reliability (Table 4.4) where the reliability of both NFT and FT WSN clusters decreases as p increases (i.e., reliability $R_c \to 0 \Longleftrightarrow p \to 1$) because decreased individual sensor node reliability decreases the overall WSN cluster reliability. Table 4.6 depicts that an FT WSN cluster with $c = 1$ outperforms an FT WSN cluster with $c \neq 1$ and an NFT WSN cluster for all p values. For example, the percentage improvement in reliability for an FT WSN cluster with $c = 1$ over an NFT WSN cluster and an FT WSN cluster with $c \neq 1$ is 77.33% and 12.02% for $p = 0.3$ and 601.12% and 142.73% for $p = 0.6$, respectively. These results show that the percentage improvement in reliability attained by an FT WSN cluster increases as p increases because a fault detection algorithm's accuracy and c decrease as p increases (Table 4.3). This trend is similar to the percentage improvement in reliability for an FT sensor node (Section 4.6.2). The results show that an FT WSN cluster always performs better than an NFT WSN cluster. For example, the percentage improvement in reliability for an FT WSN cluster with $c \neq 1$ over an NFT WSN cluster is 58.31% for $p = 0.3$.

Figure 4.17 depicts the MTTF for an NFT WSN cluster and an FT WSN cluster versus p when $k_{min} = 4$ for average cluster sizes of $n = k_{min} + 2$ and $n = k_{min} + 5$ sensor nodes, respectively, at deployment time. The figure reveals that the FT WSN cluster's MTTF is considerably greater than the NFT WSN cluster's MTTF for both cluster sizes. Figure 4.17 also compares the MTTF for an FT WSN cluster when $c = 1$ with $c \neq 1$ and shows that the MTTF for an FT WSN cluster with $c = 1$ is always better than an FT WSN cluster with $c \neq 1$. This observation again verifies the significance of a robust (ideal) fault detection algorithm, which can ideally provide c values close to 1 (i.e., $c \approx 1$ for all p values). We note that both an NFT and an FT WSN clusters with $n > k_{min}$ have redundant sensor nodes and can inherently tolerate $n - k_{min}$ sensor

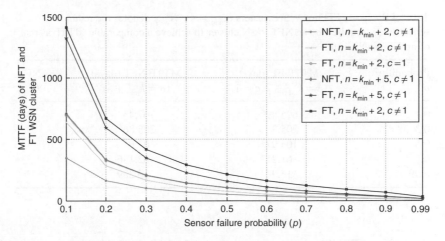

Figure 4.17 MTTF in days for an NFT WSN cluster and an FT WSN cluster with $k_{min} = 4$ [130]

node failures. The WSN cluster with $n = k_{min} + 5$ has more redundant sensor nodes than the WSN cluster with $n = k_{min} + 2$, resulting in a comparatively greater MTTF. Figure 4.17 shows that the MTTF for both an NFT and an FT WSN clusters approaches zero as p approaches 1 and further solidifies the necessity of low failure probability sensors to achieve better MTTF in WSN clusters. The MTTF variation for a WSN cluster with varying p is similar to the MTTF variation for a sensor node (Fig. 4.16) because a WSN cluster is composed of sensor nodes and reflects the MTTF variation of WSN cluster's constituent sensor nodes.

Table 4.7 shows the percentage MTTF improvement for an FT WSN cluster as compared to an NFT WSN cluster for cluster sizes of $n = k_{min} + 2$ and $n = k_{min} + 5$ sensor nodes. The percentage improvements are calculated separately for the two cluster sizes and we compare the MTTFs of clusters of the same size. We observe that the MTTF improvement for an FT cluster is slightly greater when $n = k_{min} + 5$ as compared to when $n = k_{min} + 2$; however, the MTTF improvement decreases with increasing p when $c \neq 1$. This observation reveals that a WSN cluster consisting of more sensor nodes can achieve better MTTF improvements when compared to a WSN cluster containing fewer sensor nodes. The MTTF percentage

Table 4.7 Percentage MTTF improvement for an FT WSN cluster as compared to an NFT WSN cluster ($k_{min} = 4$)

Probability p	FT ($n = k_{min} + 2, c \neq 1$)	FT ($n = k_{min} + 5, c \neq 1$)	FT ($n = k_{min} + 2, c = 1$)
0.1	83.04	87.55	100
0.2	73.84	77.24	100
0.3	63.58	66.51	100
0.5	44.97	47.22	100
0.7	26.4	28.71	100
0.9	9.81	9.57	100
0.99	2.26	2.47	100

Table 4.8 Iso-MTTF for WSN clusters ($k_{min} = 4$). $\mathfrak{R}^s_{NFT}$ denotes the redundant sensor nodes required by an NFT WSN cluster to achieve a comparable MTTF as that of an FT WSN cluster

Probability p	MTTF FT (days) $(n = k_{min} + 2, c = 1)$	MTTF NFT (days) $(n = k_{min} + 5)$	NFT $\mathfrak{R}^s_{NFT}$
0.1	695.89	707.43	3
0.3	205.3	208.86	3
0.5	105.97	107.6	3
0.7	61.213	62.136	3
0.99	15.942	16.209	3

improvement for an FT WSN cluster with $n = k_{min} + 2, c \neq 1$, is 83.04% for $p = 0.1$ and drops to 2.26% for $p = 0.99$. Similarly, the percentage MTTF improvement for an FT WSN cluster with $n = k_{min} + 5, c \neq 1$, is 87.55% for $p = 0.1$ and drops to 2.47% for $p = 0.99$. The percentage MTTF improvement for both cluster sizes is 100% on average when $c = 1$ (results are not shown for $n = k_{min} + 5$ when $c = 1$ in Table 4.7 for brevity). We observed that the MTTF percentage improvement for an FT WSN cluster with $n = k_{min} + 5$ over $n = k_{min} + 2$ is 103.35% on average. Intuitively, these results confirm that clusters with more redundant sensor nodes are more reliable and have a better MTTF than clusters with fewer redundant sensor nodes.

Since SHARPE provides information on MTTF directly from Markov models whereas reliability calculation requires manual substitution in state transition probabilities, we present iso-MTTF results for WSN clusters. Table 4.8 depicts the MTTFs for an FT WSN cluster and an NFT WSN cluster for p varying from 0.1 to 0.99 and when $k_{min} = 4$. Results indicate that an NFT WSN cluster requires three redundant NFT sensor nodes to achieve a comparable MTTF as that of an FT WSN cluster.

4.6.4   Reliability and MTTF for an NFT and an FT WSN

This section presents the reliability and MTTF results for an NFT WSN and an FT WSN containing $N = N_{min} + 2$ and $N = N_{min} + 5$ clusters at deployment time ($N_{min} = 0$). We consider WSNs containing different number of clusters to provide an insight into how the number of clusters affects WSN reliability and MTTF (other N and N_{min} values depicted similar trends). The FT WSN contains FT sensor nodes, and the NFT WSN contains NFT sensor nodes. We present example WSN reliability calculations for $N = N_{min} + 2$ ($N_{min} = 0$, i.e., each WSN fails when there are no more active clusters) and $p = 0.2$. We assume that both WSNs contain clusters with $n = k_{min} + 5$ ($k_{min} = 4$) $= 9$ sensor nodes on average with a cluster failure rate $\lambda_{c(9)}$.

The reliability calculation for an NFT WSN requires the NFT WSN cluster failure rate $\lambda_{c(9)}$, which can be calculated using Eq. (4.24) with $n = 9$ (i.e., $\lambda_{c(9)} = 1/MTTF_{c(9)} = 1/3.34 \times 10^2 = 2.99 \times 10^{-3}$ failures/day). Using $\lambda_{c(9)}$, SHARPE gives $P_{N_{min}+2}(t) = e^{-5.98 \times 10^{-3}t}$ and

Table 4.9   Reliability for an NFT WSN and an FT WSN when $N = N_{min} + 2 \ (N_{min} = 0)$

p	NFT	FT $(c \neq 1)$	FT $(c = 1)$
0.05	0.99557	0.99883	0.99885
0.1	0.98261	0.99474	0.99534
0.2	0.93321	0.97583	0.98084
0.3	0.85557	0.93775	0.95482
0.4	0.75408	0.87466	0.91611
0.5	0.63536	0.78202	0.86218
0.6	0.51166	0.65121	0.78948
0.7	0.36303	0.49093	0.69527
0.8	0.20933	0.30328	0.55494
0.9	0.08807	0.11792	0.39647
0.99	4.054×10^{-3}	4.952×10^{-3}	0.08807

$P_{N_{min}+1}(t) = 2 \times e^{-2.99 \times 10^{-3}t} - 2 \times e^{-5.98 \times 10^{-3}t}$. The WSN reliability $R_{wsn}(t) = P_{N_{min}+2}(t) + P_{N_{min}+1}(t)$ when evaluated at $t = 100$ days gives $R_{wsn}(t)|_{t=100} = 0.93321$.

For an FT WSN when $c \neq 1$, the reliability calculation requires the FT WSN cluster failure rate $\lambda_{c(9)}$ (for $c \neq 1$) (i.e., $\lambda_{c(9)} = 1/MTTF_{c(9)} = 1/5.92 \times 10^2 = 1.69 \times 10^{-3}$ failures/day). Using $\lambda_{c(9)}$, SHARPE gives $P_{N_{min}+2}(t) = e^{-3.38 \times 10^{-3}t}$, $P_{N_{min}+1}(t) = 2 \times e^{-1.69 \times 10^{-3}t} - 2 \times e^{-3.38 \times 10^{-3}t}$. The WSN reliability $R_{wsn}(t)|_{t=100} = 0.97583$.

For an FT WSN cluster when $c = 1$, the reliability calculation requires the FT WSN cluster failure rate $\lambda_{c(9)}$ (for $c = 1$) (i.e., $\lambda_{c(9)} = 1/MTTF_{c(9)} = 1/668.73 = 1.49 \times 10^{-3}$ failures/day). Using $\lambda_{c(9)}$, SHARPE gives $P_{N_{min}+2}(t) = P_2(t) = e^{-2.98 \times 10^{-3}t}$, $P_{N_{min}+1}(t) = P_1(t) = 2 \times e^{-1.49 \times 10^{-3}t} - 2 \times e^{-2.98 \times 10^{-3}t}$, which gives $R_{wsn}(t)|_{t=100} = 0.98084$.

Table 4.9 shows the reliability for an NFT WSN and an FT WSN evaluated at $t = 100$ days when $N = N_{min} + 2 \ (N_{min} = 0)$ for clusters with nine sensor nodes on average. We observe similar trends as with sensor node reliability (Table 4.4) and WSN cluster reliability (Table 4.6) where reliability for both an NFT WSN and an FT WSN decreases as p increases (i.e., reliability $R_{wsn} \to 0 \Longleftrightarrow p \to 1$) because a WSN contains clusters of sensor nodes and decreased individual sensor node reliability, with increasing p decreases both WSN cluster and WSN reliability. Table 4.9 shows that an FT WSN with $c = 1$ outperforms an FT WSN with $c \neq 1$ and an NFT WSN for all p values. For example, the percentage improvement in reliability for an FT WSN with $c = 1$ over an NFT WSN and an FT WSN with $c \neq 1$ is 5.1% and 0.51% for $p = 0.2$ and 350.18% and 236.22% for $p = 0.9$, respectively. These results show that the percentage improvement in reliability attained by an FT WSN increases as p increases because the fault detection algorithm's accuracy and c decreases as p increases (Table 4.3). This trend is similar to the percentage improvement in reliability for an FT sensor node (Section 4.6.2) and an FT WSN cluster (Section 4.6.3). The results show that an FT WSN always performs better than NFT WSN. For example, the percentage improvement in reliability for an FT WSN with $c \neq 1$ over an NFT WSN is 4.57% for $p = 0.2$.

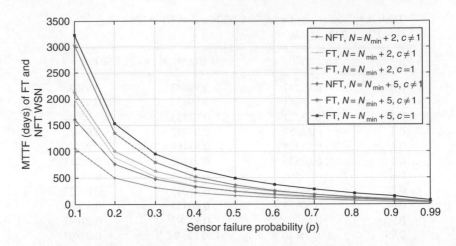

Figure 4.18 MTTF in days for an NFT WSN and an FT WSN with $N_{min} = 0$ [130]

Figure 4.18 depicts the MTTF for an NFT WSN and an FT WSN containing on average $N = N_{min} + 2$ and $N = N_{min} + 5$ clusters ($N_{min} = 0$) at deployment time. The figure reveals that an FT WSN improves the MTTF considerably over an NFT WSN for both number of clusters. Figure 4.18 also shows that the MTTF for an FT WSN when $c = 1$ is always greater than the MTTF for an FT WSN when $c \neq 1$. We observe that since the MTTF for an FT WSN drops nearly to that of an NFT WSN as $p \to 1$, building a more reliable FT WSN requires low failure probability sensors. This WSN MTTF variation with p follows similar trends as observed in WSN clusters (Fig. 4.17) and sensor nodes (Fig. 4.16). Similar MTTF variations for a WSN, WSN cluster, and a sensor node results from our bottom-up modeling approach (Section 4.4), where each hierarchical level captures the MTTF variation trends of lower levels. We observe that the MTTF for a WSN with $N = N_{min} + 5$ is always greater than the MTTF for a WSN with $N = N_{min} + 2$. This observation is intuitive because WSNs with $N = N_{min} + 5$ have more redundant WSN clusters (and sensor nodes) and can survive more cluster failures before reaching the failed state ($N = 0$) as compared to a WSN with $N = N_{min} + 2$.

We observe the percentage MTTF improvement for an FT WSN over an NFT WSN containing on average $N = N_{min} + 2$ and $N = N_{min} + 5$ clusters. We observe that the MTTF improvement for both number of clusters decreases with increasing p when $c \neq 1$ (similar trend as for a WSN cluster and for a sensor node). The MTTF percentage improvement for an FT WSN with $N = N_{min} + 2$, $c \neq 1$, is 87.56% for $p = 0.1$ and drops to 3.3% for $p = 0.99$. Similarly, the MTTF percentage improvement for an FT WSN with $N = N_{min} + 5$, $c \neq 1$, is 88.2% for $p = 0.1$ and drops to 3.26% for $p = 0.99$. We observe that the MTTF improvement for an FT WSN with $c = 1$ is 100% on average for all p values and is greater than an FT WSN with $c \neq 1$. The MTTF percentage improvement for an FT WSN with $N = N_{min} + 5$ over an FT WSN with $N = N_{min} + 2$ is 52.22% on average.

We also investigate iso-MTTF for WSNs. Table 4.10 depicts the MTTFs for an FT WSN and an NFT WSN for p varying from 0.1 to 0.99 and when $N_{min} = 0$. Results indicate that an NFT WSN requires nine redundant NFT WSN clusters to achieve a comparable MTTF as that of an FT WSN.

Table 4.10 Iso-MTTF for WSNs ($N_{min} = 0$). $\mathfrak{R}^c_{NFT}$ denotes the redundant WSN clusters required by an NFT WSN to achieve a comparable MTTF as that of an FT WSN

Probability p	MTTF FT (days) $(N = N_{min} + 2, c = 1)$	MTTF NFT (days) $(N = N_{min} + 11)$	NFT $\mathfrak{R}^c_{NFT}$
0.1	2121.6	2135.7	9
0.3	627.62	631.77	9
0.5	323.28	326.12	9
0.7	186.8	188.74	9
0.99	48.387	48.71	9

4.7 Research Challenges and Future Research Directions

WSNs are susceptible to a plethora of different fault types and external attacks after the WSN's deployment. Fault detection and tolerance in WSNs is paramount especially for safety-critical WSNs such as military target applications, biomedical applications (body sensor networks), and volcanic eruption detection systems. Although there has been research done in fault diagnosis and FT in WSNs, various issues remain to be addressed. This section highlights research challenges and future research directions for development and deployment of reliable and trustworthy WSNs.

4.7.1 Accurate Fault Detection

Our Markov modeling results in Section 4.6 reveal that the fault detection algorithm's accuracy plays a crucial role in realizing FT WSNs. An accuracy close or equal to 100% and a false alarm rate close or equal to 0% is desirable for fault detection algorithms. There is a need to develop novel fault detection algorithms and/or improve the existing fault detection algorithms with the objective of attaining ∼100% fault detection accuracy.

4.7.2 Benchmarks for Comparing Fault Detection Algorithms

There is a need to develop standard benchmarks for comparing different fault detection algorithms for various fault models and topologies. The development of these benchmarks would facilitate designers to select an appropriate fault detection algorithm for WSNs with given FT requirements.

4.7.3 Energy-Efficient Fault Detection and Tolerance

Since sensor nodes have stringent resource constraints, fault detection and FT approaches for WSNs need to be energy efficient. Although initiatives have been taken in developing DFD approaches to minimize energy overhead, the area requires further research. Moreover, FT techniques developed for WSNs need to be energy efficient. The impact of added redundancy in sensor nodes to provide FT not only has economic cost overhead but can also have power consumption overhead, which needs to be considered and minimized during the design. Energy efficiency in fault detection and tolerance can also be achieved by exploiting near-threshold computing (NTC) in sensor node design. NTC refers to using a supply voltage (V_{DD}) that is close to a single transistor's threshold voltage V_t (generally V_{DD} is slightly above V_t in near-threshold operation, whereas V_{DD} is below V_t for subthreshold operation). Lowering the supply voltage reduces power consumption and increases energy efficiency by lowering the energy consumed per operation. The widespread adoption of NTC in sensor node designs for reduced power consumption requires addressing NTC challenges such as increased process, voltage, and temperature variations, subthreshold leakage power, and soft error rates.

4.7.4   Machine-Learning-Inspired Fault Detection

Machine learning-based approaches can be leveraged to classify normal and anomalous data. Since sensor nodes are resource constrained, innovative approaches are required to extract features from the sensed data. The machine learning techniques for sensor nodes need to reduce the training data size for the classifier (e.g., SVM) based on extracted features. The goal of machine-learning-inspired fault detection is to classify normal and anomalous data in or near real time. There exist some initiatives in machine-learning-inspired fault detection [110]; however, further work is required in this domain for accurate and energy-efficient fault detection.

4.7.5   FT in Multimedia Sensor Networks

Fault detection and tolerance in WMSNs is a relatively new research field [115]. FT data aggregation in WMSNs is imperative to reduce the throughput of data transmission, energy conservation, accuracy of event detection, and alleviate the interference from compromised nodes. Another research challenge in WMSNs is to ensure the trustworthiness of aggregated results. Since multimedia data sensed by sensor nodes require compute-intensive processing, multicore-based design of sensor nodes could meet the performance, energy, and FT requirements of WMSNs. Accurate fault detection, FT, reliability, and security in WMSNs require further research endeavors.

4.7.6   Security

Security is critical for many WSNs, such as military target tracking and biomedical applications. Security aspects are crucial to consider in developing a reliable, robust, and trustworthy WSNs. Since sensor nodes use wireless communication, WSNs are susceptible to eavesdropping, message injection, replay, and other attacks. In many situations, an adversary is capable of deploying malicious nodes in the WSN or compromising some legitimate sensor nodes. Since the sink node is a gateway between a WSN and the outside world, compromising the sink node could render the entire WSN useless. Hence, security integration in sink nodes is imperative. The security integration objective in WSNs is to provide confidentiality, integrity, authenticity, and availability of all messages in the presence of adversaries. In a secure and reliable WSN, every eligible receiver should receive all messages intended for that receiver.

Furthermore, the receiver should be able to verify the integrity of each message as well as the identity of the sender.

Integration of security and privacy in sensor nodes is challenging because of the sensor nodes' resource constraints in terms of computation, communication, memory/storage, and energy supply. The security mechanisms for prevalent end-to-end systems (e.g., secure socket layer (SSL)) are not directly applicable to WSNs. In traditional end-to-end systems, it is neither necessary nor desirable for the contents of the message (except the message headers) to be available to the intermediate routers. On the contrary, in WSNs, the dominant traffic pattern is many-to-one (i.e., from sensor nodes to the sink node) [138]. Each intermediate sensor node in a WSN also needs access to message contents to perform in-network processing, such as data aggregation and data compression, to conserve energy. Security incorporation in WSNs has several aspects, some of which are discussed below.

Time Synchronization: Due to the collaborative nature of sensor nodes, secure time synchronization is important for various WSN operations, such as coordinated sensing tasks, sensor scheduling, target tracking, data aggregation, and time division multiple access (TDMA) medium access control. The network time protocol (NTP), which is used for synchronization in the Internet, cannot be directly used by WSNs due to a sensor node's constrained resources. Sometimes, synchronization protocols for WSNs have been proposed in the literature such as reference-broadcast synchronization (RBS) [139] and timing-sync protocol for sensor networks (TPSN) [140]; however, security is not considered in the design of these synchronization protocols.

Sensor Location Discovery: Sensor node location is important for many WSN applications, such as target tracking and environmental monitoring. The geographical routing protocols developed for WSNs also require sensor node location information to make routing decisions. Sensor location discovery protocols make use of special nodes known as beacon nodes, which are assumed to know their own location via global positioning system (GPS) or manual configuration. Nonbeacon nodes receive radio signals (reference signals) from beacon nodes. These reference signals contain the location of beacon nodes. The nonbeacon nodes then determine their own location based on features of the reference messages, such as using received signal strength indicator (RSSI). Without any protection, the adversary has the potential to mislead the location estimation at sensor nodes. For example, an attacker may provide incorrect location references by replaying the beacon signals intercepted in different locations. A more serious attack launched by an adversary could be compromising a beacon node and distributing malicious location references by manipulating the beacon signals (e.g., changing the signal strength if RSSI is used to estimate the distance). In the presence of such attacks, nonbeacon nodes will determine their location incorrectly. There are a few methods to counter these attacks and to increase the reliability and trustworthiness of WSN. For instance, voting-based location references use voting of different received location references from different beacon nodes; however, this technique would increase the cost of the WSN as the approach would require more beacon nodes equipped with GPS.

Secure Routing: An adversary can also impact routing within a WSN, which consequently degrades the reliability of the WSN. Secure routing protocols for MANETs or wired networks are not suitable for WSNs because these protocols are computationally expensive and are meant for routing between any pair of nodes and not for the many-to-one traffic pattern prevalent in WSNs.

Intrusion Detection: Most of the existing WSNs are designed without considering security and intrusion detection. WSNs are more prone to malicious intruders as compared to traditional wired networks due to an open medium, a low degree of physical security, the dynamic topology, and a limited power supply. Security vulnerabilities in WSNs can be alleviated using an intrusion detection system (IDS). Intrusion detection is a security technology that attempts to identify those who are trying to break into and misuse a system without authorization as well as those who have legitimate access to the system but are abusing their privileges [141]. By modeling the behavior of normal sensor node activities and operations, an IDS can identify potential intruders and maintain trustworthy operation of a WSN. IDSs are of two types: misuse-based detection and anomaly-based detection. A *misuse-based* IDS encodes known attack signatures and vulnerabilities and stores this information in a database. An alarm is generated by the IDS if a discrepancy exists between the current activities and stored signatures. A misuse-based IDS cannot detect novel attacks because of the lack of corresponding signatures. An *anomaly-based* IDS creates normal profiles of sensor node behavior and compares them with current activities. If a significant deviation in a sensor node's behavior is observed, the anomaly-based IDS raises an alarm. An anomaly-based IDS can detect unknown attacks; however, developing profiles of a sensor node's normal behavior is challenging.

4.7.7 WSN Design and Tuning for Reliability

WSNs are more susceptible to failure than wired networks due to a WSN's deployment in unattended and often hostile environments. The vulnerability of sensor nodes to failures and attacks from malicious intruders requires reliability and security incorporation in the design of sensor nodes and WSNs. For instance, in the case of failures of some sensor nodes or some sensor nodes being compromised by an adversary, a WSN should be able to detect these failures and then adapt accordingly to remain operational. For example, if a few nodes are diagnosed as misbehaving or failed, routing protocol should be able to adapt to the situation and find alternative routes. This adaptation may require some sensor nodes to increase their transmission energy to get their sensed information to healthy nodes. Furthermore, the frequency of packet transmission can be reduced in such situations to conserve energy of sensor nodes to compensate for the increased transmission energy. This tuning of sensor nodes and the WSN would maintain the reliable operation of WSN although at a reduced efficiency. Moreover, the WSN manager should be alarmed of the situation to take necessary actions to increase the efficiency of the WSN, including removal of identified malicious nodes and placement of new healthy sensor nodes in the WSN.

4.7.8 Novel WSN Architectures

To maintain reliable and secure operation of WSNs in the presence of failures and malicious intruders, innovative WSN architectures are desired. For instance, a heterogeneous hierarchical multicore embedded wireless sensor network (MCEWSN) can better meet performance and reliability requirements of WSN [142]. The heterogeneity in the architecture subsumes the integration of numerous single-core embedded sensor nodes and several multicore embedded sensor nodes. A hierarchical architecture comprising of various clusters and a sink node is appropriate for large WSNs since in small WSNs, sensor nodes can send the sensed data directly to the sink node. Each cluster comprises several leaf sensor nodes and a cluster head. Leaf sensor nodes embed a single-core processor and are responsible for sensing, preprocessing, and transmitting the sensed data to the cluster head nodes. Cluster head nodes embed a multicore processor and are responsible for coalescing/fusing the data received from leaf sensor nodes for transmission to the sink node. Multicore embedded sensor nodes enable energy savings over conventional single-core embedded sensor nodes in two ways. First, multicore embedded sensor nodes reduce the energy expended in communication by performing in situ computation of sensed data and transmitting only processed information. Second, a multicore embedded sensor node permits the computations to be split across multiple cores while running each core at a lower processor voltage and frequency, as compared to a single-core system, which results in energy savings. Multicore cluster heads are also amenable for supervising a fault diagnosis algorithm within the cluster. Additionally, security primitives could be integrated in these multicore cluster heads to thwart attacks from malicious intruders or malicious sensor nodes.

4.8   Chapter Summary

This chapter provided a comprehensive research on modeling and analysis of fault detection and tolerance in WSNs. To elucidate fault detection in WSNs, we provided a taxonomy for fault diagnosis in WSNs. We simulated prominent fault detection algorithms using ns−2 to determine the algorithms' accuracies and false alarm rates. We further analyzed the effectiveness of fault detection algorithms under conditions modeled from real-world data. We proposed an FT duplex sensor node model based on the novel concept of determining the coverage factor using a sensor node's fault detection algorithm's accuracy. We developed comprehensive Markov models that hierarchically encompass sensor nodes, WSN clusters, and the overall WSN. Our Markov models characterized WSN reliability and MTTF for different sensor failure probabilities. Our models could assist WSN designers to better meet application requirements by determining the reliability and MTTF in the predeployment phase.

Our ns−2 simulation results of fault detection algorithms suggested that both the simulated and real-world data needed to be considered for rigorous evaluation of fault detection algorithms. Although some algorithms performed better than other algorithms on simulated data, these algorithms performed inferior to other algorithms on real-world data. We observed that the fault detection algorithm's accuracy played a crucial role in FT WSNs by comparing our results against a perfect fault detection algorithm ($c = 1$). The results indicated that the percentage improvement in reliability for an FT sensor node with $c = 1$ over an NFT sensor node is 230% and the percentage improvements in reliability for an FT sensor node with $c = 1$ over an FT sensor node ($c \neq 1$) with an average number of neighbors k equal to 5, 10, and 15 was 172.36%, 166.31%, and 165.32%, respectively, for $p = 0.9$. The percentage improvement in reliability for an FT WSN cluster with $c = 1$ over an NFT WSN cluster and an FT WSN cluster with $c \neq 1$ was 601.12% and 142.73%, respectively, for $p = 0.6$. The percentage improvement in reliability for an FT WSN with $c = 1$ over an NFT WSN and an FT WSN with $c \neq 1$ was 350.18% and 236.22%, respectively, for $p = 0.9$.

Results indicated that our FT model could provide on average a 100% MTTF improvement with a perfect fault detection algorithm, whereas the MTTF improvement varied from

95.95% to 1.34% due to a fault detection algorithm's typical poor performance at high sensor failure rates. We also observed that the redundancy in WSNs plays an important role in improving WSN reliability and MTTF. Results revealed that just three redundant sensor nodes in a WSN cluster resulted in an MTTF improvement of 103.35% on average. Similarly, redundancy in WSN clusters contributes to the reliability and MTTF improvement, and the results indicated that three redundant WSN clusters could improve the MTTF by 52.22% on average. The iso-MTTF results indicated that an NFT WSN cluster required three redundant sensor nodes to attain a comparable MTTF as that of an FT WSN cluster. Iso-MTTF results further indicated that an NFT WSN required nine redundant WSN clusters to achieve a comparable MTTF as that of an FT WSN.

5

A Queueing Theoretic Approach for Performance Evaluation of Low-Power Multicore-Based Parallel Embedded Systems*

With Moore's law supplying billions of transistors on-chip, embedded systems are undergoing a paradigm shift from single core to multicore to exploit this high transistor density for high performance. This paradigm shift has led to the emergence of diverse multicore embedded systems in a plethora of application domains (e.g., high-performance computing, dependable computing, mobile computing). Many modern embedded systems integrate multiple cores (whether homogeneous or heterogeneous) on-chip to satisfy computing demand while maintaining design constraints (e.g., energy, power, performance). For example, a 3G mobile handset's signal processing requires 35–40 giga operations per second (GOPS). Considering the limited energy of a mobile handset battery, these performance levels must be met with a power dissipation budget of approximately 1 W, which translates to a performance efficiency of 25 mW/GOPS or 25 pJ/operation for the 3G receiver [143]. These demanding and competing power-performance requirements make modern embedded system design challenging.

Increasing customer expectations/demands for embedded system functionality has led to an exponential increase in design complexity. While industry focuses on increasing the number of on-chip processor cores to meet customer performance demands, embedded system designers face the new challenge of optimal layout of these processor cores along with the memory subsystem (caches and main memory (MM)) to satisfy power, area, and stringent real-time

---

*A portion of this chapter is copyrighted by Elsevier. The definitive version appeared in: Arslan Munir, Ann Gordon-Ross, Sanjay Ranka, and Farinaz Koushanfar, A Queueing Theoretic Approach for Performance Evaluation of Low-Power Multi-core Embedded Systems, *Elsevier Journal of Parallel and Distributed Computing (JPDC)*, vol. 74, no. 1, pp. 1872–1890, January 2014. URL http://www.sciencedirect.com/science/article/pii/S0743731513001299. ©[2014] Elsevier. The work is reproduced under automatic permission granted by Elsevier as we are the authors of this work.

---

constraints. The short *time-to-market* (time from product conception to market release) of embedded systems further exacerbates design challenges. Architectural modeling of embedded systems helps in reducing the time-to-market by enabling fast application-to-device mapping since identifying an appropriate architecture for a set of target applications significantly reduces the design time of an embedded system. To ensure timely completion of an embedded system's design with sufficient confidence in the product's market release, design engineers must make tradeoffs between the abstraction level of the system's architecture model and the attainable accuracy.

Modern multicore embedded systems allow processor cores to share hardware structures, such as last-level caches (LLCs) (e.g., level two (L2) or level three (L3) cache), memory controllers, and interconnection networks [144]. Since the LLC's configuration (e.g., size, line size, associativity) and the layout of the processor cores (on-chip location) have a significant impact on a multicore embedded system's performance and energy, our work focuses on the performance and energy characterization of embedded architectures based on different LLC configurations and layout of the processor cores. Although there is a general consensus on using private level one (L1) instruction (L1-I) and data (L1-D) caches in embedded systems, there has been no dominant architectural paradigm for private or shared LLCs. Since many embedded systems contain an L2 cache as the LLC, we focus on the L2 cache; however, our study can easily be extended for L3 caches and beyond as LLCs.

Since multicore benchmark simulation requires significant simulation time and resources, a lightweight modeling technique for multicore architecture evaluation is crucial [145]. Furthermore, simulation-driven architectural evaluation is based on specific benchmarks and consequently only provides performance information for programs similar to the benchmarks. A well-devised modeling technique can model diverse workloads, thus enabling performance evaluation for workloads with any computing requirements. Previous work presents various multicore system models; however, these models become increasingly complex with varying degrees of cache sharing [146]. Many of the previous models assumed that sharing among processor cores occurred at either the main memory level or the processor cores, all shared the same cache hierarchy; however, multicore embedded systems can have an L2 cache shared by a subset of cores (e.g., Intel's six-core Dunnington processor has L2 caches shared by two processor cores). We leverage for the first time, to the best of our knowledge, the queueing network theory as an alternative approach for modeling multicore embedded systems for performance analysis (though queueing network models have been studied in the context of traditional computer systems [135]). Our queueing network model approach allows modeling the layout of processor cores (processor cores can be either homogeneous or heterogeneous) with caches of different capacities and configurations at different cache levels. Our modeling technique only requires a high-level workload characterization of an application (i.e., whether the application is processor-bound (requiring high processing resources), memory-bound (requiring a large number of memory accesses), or mixed).

Our main contributions in this chapter are as follows:

- We present a novel, queueing theory-based modeling technique for evaluating multicore embedded architectures that do not require architectural-level benchmark simulation. This modeling technique enables quick and inexpensive architectural evaluation, with respect to design time and resources, as compared to developing and/or using existing multicore simulators and running benchmarks on these simulators. Based on a preliminary evaluation

using our models, architectural designers can run targeted benchmarks to further verify the performance characteristics of selected multicore architectures (i.e., our queueing theory-based models facilitate early design space pruning).
- Our queueing theoretic approach enables architectural evaluation for synthetic workloads with any computing requirements characterized probabilistically. We also propose a method to quantify computing requirements of real benchmarks probabilistically. Hence, our modeling technique can provide performance evaluation for workloads with any computing requirements as opposed to simulation-driven architectural evaluation that can only provide performance results for specific benchmarks.
- Our queueing theoretic modeling approach can be used for performance per watt and performance per unit area characterizations of multicore embedded architectures, with varying number of processor cores and cache configurations, to provide a comparative analysis. For performance per watt and performance per unit area computations, we calculate chip area and power consumption for different multicore embedded architectures with a varying number of processor cores and cache configurations.

We point out that although queueing theory has been used in the literature for performance analysis of multidisk and pipelined systems [135, 147, 148], we for the first time, to the best of our knowledge, apply queueing theory-based modeling and performance analysis techniques to multicore embedded systems. Furthermore, we for the first time develop a methodology to synthesize workloads/benchmarks on our queueing theoretic multicore models based on probabilities that are assigned according to workload characteristics (e.g., processor-bound, memory-bound, or mixed) and cache miss rates. We verify our queueing theoretic modeling approach by running SPLASH-2 multithreaded benchmarks on the SuperESCalar (SESC) simulator. Results reveal that our queueing theoretic model qualitatively evaluates multicore architectures accurately with an average difference of 5.6% as compared to the architectures' evaluations from the SESC simulator. The SESC simulation results validate our queueing theoretic modeling approach as a quick and inexpensive architectural evaluation method.

Our queueing theoretic approach can be leveraged for *early design space pruning* by eliminating infeasible architectures in very early design stages, which reduces the number of lengthy architectural evaluations when running targeted benchmarks in later design stages. Specifically, our approach focuses on the qualitative comparison of architectures in the early design stage and not the quantitative comparison of architectures for different benchmarks. Our model is designed to operate using *synthetic workloads* that a designer can categorize for an expected behavior, such as process- or memory-bound workloads, along with an estimate of the expected cache miss rates. The synthetic workloads preclude the need to obtain benchmark-specific statistics from an architecture-level simulator. Furthermore, the cache miss rates are estimates, and thus are not required to be the exact miss rates for any specific benchmark. Our discussion in Section 5.3.2 regarding statistics obtained from an architecture-level simulator only explains how a real workload can be represented with our queueing theoretic model and is not required for synthetic workloads.

Our investigation of performance and energy for different cache miss rates and workloads is significant because cache miss rates and workloads can significantly impact the performance and energy of an embedded architecture. Furthermore, cache miss rates also give an indication of the degree of cache contention between different threads' working sets. Our performance, power, and performance per watt results indicate that multicore embedded architectures that leverage shared LLCs are scalable and provide the best LLC performance per watt. However, shared LLC architectures may introduce main memory response time and throughput bottlenecks for high cache miss rates. The architectures that leverage a hybrid of private and shared LLCs are scalable and alleviate main memory bottlenecks at the expense of reduced performance per watt. The architectures with private LLCs exhibit less scalability but do not introduce main memory bottlenecks at the expense of reduced performance per watt.

The remainder of this chapter is organized as follows. Section 5.1 gives a review of related work. Section 5.2 illustrates queueing network modeling of multicore embedded architecture. Validation of queueing network models is presented in Section 5.3. Section 5.4 provides insights obtained from our queueing theoretic models regarding performance, performance per watt, and performance per unit area for different multicore embedded architectures. Finally, Section 5.5 concludes the chapter.

5.1 Related Work

Several previous works investigated analytical modeling techniques for performance evaluation. Sorin et al. [149] developed an analytical model for evaluating shared memory systems with processors that aggressively exploited instruction-level parallelism (ILP). The application's ILP and interaction with the memory subsystem were characterized by the model's input parameters. İpek et al. [150] used predictive modeling based on artificial neural networks to efficiently explore architectural design spaces. Simulation of sampled points in the design space helped the model to generate functions that described the relationship between design parameters, which were then used to estimate performance for other points in the design space. Chandra et al. [151] investigated performance models that predicted the impact of cache sharing on coscheduled threads for chip multiprocessors (CMPs). The authors observed that cache contention could significantly increase a thread's cache miss rate depending on the coscheduled threads' memory requirements. Chen and Aamodt [152] proposed an analytical model for predicting the impact of cache contention on cache miss rates for multiprogrammed workloads running on multithreaded manycore architectures.

Queueing theory has been used in the literature for the performance analysis of computer networks and other computer systems. Samari and Schneider [153] used queueing theory for the analysis of distributed computer networks. The authors proposed a correction factor in the analytical model and compared these results with the analytical model without this correction factor [154] and with simulation results to verify the correctness of the proposed model. Mainkar and Trivedi [155] used queueing theory-based models for performance evaluation of computer systems with a central processing unit (CPU) and disk drives. Willick and Eager [156] used queueing theory to model packet-switched multistage interconnection networks. The analytical model permitted general interconnection network topologies (including arbitrary switch sizes) and arbitrary memory reference patterns. Our work differs from the previous work on queueing theory-based models for computer systems in that our work applies queueing theory for performance evaluation of multicore embedded systems with different cache subsystems, which have not been investigated using queueing theory. Furthermore, our work introduces a novel way of representing workloads with different computing requirements probabilistically in a queueing theory-based model.

Characterization of workloads for analytical models has been explored in the literature. Nussbaum and Smith [157] developed an analytical performance model for superscalar processors based on statistical simulation. The model depended on detailed simulation to gather statistical information that was used to generate a synthetic instruction trace that was then fed as input to the model along with cache miss rate and branch prediction statistics. Karkhanis and Smith [158] developed an analytical performance model for superscalar processors. The model used trace-derived data dependence information, data and instruction cache miss rates, and branch miss-prediction rates as input. Wunderlich et al. [159] proposed a framework for statistical sampling that enabled sampling of a minimal subset of a benchmark's instruction execution stream to estimate the performance of the complete benchmark. Our work differs from previous work on workload characterization for analytical models in that we characterize workloads probabilistically, which provides an alternative to statistical sampling.

Previous work presents evaluation and modeling techniques for multicore embedded architectures for different applications with varying workload characteristics. Savage and Zubair [146] proposed a unified memory hierarchy model for multicore architectures that captured varying degrees of cache sharing at different cache levels. However, the model was only applicable to straight-line computations that could be represented by directed acyclic graphs (DAGs) (e.g., matrix multiplication, fast Fourier transform (FFT)). Our queueing theoretic models are virtually applicable to any type of workload with any computing requirements. Fedorova et al. [144] studied contention-aware task scheduling for multicore architectures with shared resources (caches, memory controllers, and interconnection networks). The authors modeled the contention-aware task scheduler and investigated the scheduler's impact on the application performance for multicore architectures. In contrast to these prior works, our queueing theoretic models permit a wide range of scheduling disciplines based on workload requirements (e.g., first-come-first-served (FCFS), priority, round robin (RR)).

Some previous works investigated performance and energy aspects for multicore systems. Kumar et al. [160] studied power, throughput, and response time metrics for heterogeneous CMPs. The authors observed that heterogeneous CMPs could improve energy per instruction by 4–6× and throughput by 63% over an equivalent-area homogeneous CMP because of closer adaptation to the resource requirements of different application phases. The authors used a multicore simulator for performance analysis; however, our queueing theoretic models can be used as a quick and inexpensive alternative for investigating performance aspects of heterogeneous CMPs. Sabry et al. [161] investigated performance, energy, and area tradeoffs for private and shared L2 caches for multicore embedded systems. The authors proposed a SystemC-based platform that could model private, shared, and hybrid L2 cache architectures. A hybrid L2 cache architecture contains several private L2 caches, each containing only private data, and a unified shared L2 cache that stores only shared data. However, the SystemC-based model required integration with other simulators, such as MPARM, to obtain performance results. Our queueing theoretic models do not require integration with other multicore simulators to obtain performance results and serve as an independent comparative performance analysis approach for multicore architecture evaluation.

Benítez et al. [162] proposed an adaptive L2 cache architecture that adapted to fit the code and data during runtime using partial cache array shutdown. The adaptive cache could be configured in four modes that prioritized instructions per cycle (IPC), processor power dissipation, processor energy consumption, or processor power^2 × delay product. Experiments revealed that CMPs with 2 MB of private adaptive L2 cache provided 14.2%, 44.3%, 18.1%, and 29.4% improvements in IPC, power dissipation, energy consumption, and power^2 × delay, respectively, over a 4 MB shared L2 cache. Our work does not consider adaptive private caches but compares private, shared, and hybrid caches on an equal area basis to provide a fair comparison between different LLCs.

There exists work in the literature related to memory subsystem latency and throughput analysis. Ruggiero [163] investigated cache latency (at all cache levels), memory latency, cache bandwidth/throughput (at all cache levels), and memory bandwidth for multicore embedded systems using LMBench, an open-source benchmark suite, on Intel processors. Our models enable measurement of cache latency and throughput of modeled architectures in an early design phase when fabricated architectures are not available.

Although there exist previous works on performance evaluation, our work is novel because we for the first time develop queueing network models for various multicore embedded architectures. Some previous works present benchmark-driven evaluation for specific embedded architectures; however, multicore embedded architecture evaluation considering different workload characteristics, cache configurations (private, shared, or hybrid), and miss rates with comparative analysis has not been addressed.

5.2 Queueing Network Modeling of Multicore Embedded Architectures

Although queueing networks are widely used in computer networks, the interpretation of queueing network terminology for multicore embedded architectures is a prerequisite for queueing theory-based modeling. Furthermore, because of the diversity of queueing network models, the specific approach taken to model multicore embedded architectures is the most critical aspect of queueing theory-based modeling. Finally, the queueing theory-based model relies on some assumptions under which the model is a valid representation of the multicore embedded architectures. This section discusses the queueing network terminology in the context of multicore embedded architectures, our modeling approach, and the underlying simplifying assumptions.

5.2.1   Queueing Network Terminology

A *queueing network* consists of *service centers* (e.g., processor core, L1-I cache, L1-D cache, L2 cache, and main memory (MM)) and *customers* (e.g., jobs/tasks). A service center consists of one or more queues to hold jobs waiting for service. We use the term *jobs* instead of *tasks* (decomposed workload resulting from parallelizing a job) to be consistent with general queueing network terminology. Our modeling approach is broadly applicable to *multiprogrammed workloads* where multiple jobs run on the multicore embedded architecture as well as for *parallelized applications/jobs* that run different *tasks* on the multicore architectures. Arriving jobs enter the service center's queue, and a *scheduling/queueing discipline* (e.g., FCFS, priority, round-robin (RR), processor sharing (PS)) selects the next job to be served when a service center becomes idle. The queueing discipline is *preemptive* if an arriving higher priority job can suspend the service/execution of a lower priority job, otherwise the queueing discipline is *nonpreemptive*. FCFS is a nonpreemptive queueing discipline that serves the waiting jobs in the order in which the jobs enter the queue. Priority-based queueing disciplines can be preemptive or nonpreemptive and serve the jobs based on an assigned job priority. In the RR queueing discipline, a job receives a service time quantum (slot). If the job does not complete during the service time quantum, the job is placed at the end of the queue to resume during a subsequent service time quantum. In the PS queueing discipline, all jobs at a service center are serviced simultaneously (and hence there is no queue) with the service center's speed equally divided across all of the jobs. After being serviced, a job either moves to another service center or leaves the network.

A queueing network is *open* if jobs arrive from an external source, spend time in the network, and then depart. A queueing network is *closed* if there is no external source and no departures (i.e., a fixed number of jobs circulate indefinitely among the service centers). A queueing network is a *single-chain* queueing network if all jobs possess the same characteristics (e.g., arrival rates, required service rates, and routing probabilities for various service centers) and are serviced by the same service centers in the same order. If different jobs can belong to different chains, the network is a *multichain* queueing network. An important class of queueing networks is *product-form* where the joint probability of the queue sizes in the network is a product of the probabilities for the individual service center's queue sizes.

The queueing network performance metrics include response time, throughput, and utilization. The *response time* is the amount of time a job spends at the service center including the queueing delay (the amount of time a job waits in the queue) and the service time. The service time of a job depends on the amount of work (e.g., number of instructions) needed by that job. The *throughput* is defined as the number of jobs served per unit of time. In our multicore embedded architecture context, throughput measures the number of instructions/data (bits) processed by the architectural element (processor, cache, MM) per second. *Utilization* measures the fraction of time that a service center (processor, cache, MM) is busy. Little's law governs the relationship between the number of jobs in the queueing network N and response time tr (i.e., $N = \kappa \cdot tr$ where κ denotes the average arrival rate of jobs admitted to the queueing network [164]).

5.2.2 Modeling Approach

We consider the closed product-form queueing network for modeling multicore embedded architectures because the closed product-form queueing network enables unequivocal modeling of workloads. A typical embedded system executes a fixed number of jobs (e.g., a mobile phone has only a few applications to run, such as instant messaging, audio coding/decoding, calculator, and graphics interface). We point out that additional applications can be added/updated in an embedded system (e.g., a smartphone) over time; however, these additional applications can be represented as synthetic workloads in our queueing theoretic model. Furthermore, closed product-form queueing networks assume that a job leaving the network is replaced instantaneously by a statistically identical new job [135]. Table 5.1 describes the multicore embedded architectures that we evaluate in this chapter. We focus on embedded architectures ranging from 2 (2P) to 4 (4P) processor cores to reflect current architectures [165]; however, our model is applicable to any number of cores. Our modeled embedded architectures contain processor cores, L1-I and L1-D private caches, L2 caches (private or shared), and MM (embedded systems are typically equipped with DRAM/NAND/NOR Flash memory [166, 167]).

We consider a closed product-form queueing network with I service centers where each service center $i \in I$ has a service rate μ_i. Let p_{ij} be the probability of a job leaving service

Table 5.1 Multicore embedded architectures with varying processor cores and cache configurations

Architecture	Description
2P-2L1ID-2L2-1M	Multicore embedded architecture with two processor cores, private L1-I/D caches, private L2 caches, and a shared M
2P-2L1ID-1L2-1M	Multicore embedded architecture with two processor cores, private L1-I/D caches, a shared L2 cache, and a shared M
4P-4L1ID-4L2-1M	Multicore embedded architecture with four processor cores, private L1-I/D caches, private L2 caches, and a shared M
4P-4L1ID-1L2-1M	Multicore embedded architecture with four processor cores, private L1-I/D caches, a shared L2 cache, and a shared M
4P-4L1ID-2L2-1M	Multicore embedded architecture with four processor cores, private L1-I/D caches, 2 shared L2 caches, and a shared M

(P denotes the processor core, M the main memory, and the integer constants in front of P, L1ID (L1 instruction and data cache), L2, and M denotes the number of these architectural components in the embedded architecture)

center i and entering another service center j. The relative visit count ϑ_j to service center j is

$$\vartheta_j = \sum_{i=1}^{I} \vartheta_i p_{ij} \tag{5.1}$$

The performance metrics (e.g., throughput, response time) for a closed product-form queueing network can be calculated using a *mean value analysis* (MVA) iterative algorithm [168]. The basis of MVA is a theorem stating that when a job arrives at a service center in a closed network with N jobs, the distribution of the number of jobs already queued is the same as the steady-state distribution of $N - 1$ jobs in the queue [169]. Solving Eq. (5.1) using MVA recursively gives the following performance metric values: the mean response time $r_i(k)$ at service center i (k denotes the number of jobs in the network), the mean network response time $R(k)$, the mean queueing network throughput $T(k)$, the mean throughput of jobs $\lambda_i(k)$ at service center i, and the mean queue length $l_i(k)$ at service center i when there are k jobs in the network. The initial recursive conditions are $k = 0$ such that $r_i(0) = R(0) = T(0) = t_i(0) = l_i(0) = 0$. The values for these performance metrics can be calculated for k jobs based on the computed values for $k - 1$ jobs as [135]:

$$r_i(k) = \frac{1}{\mu_i}(1 + l_i(k-1)) \tag{5.2}$$

$$R(k) = \sum_{i=1}^{I} \vartheta_i \cdot r_i(k) \tag{5.3}$$

$$T(k) = \frac{k}{R(k)} \tag{5.4}$$

$$\lambda_i(k) = \vartheta_i \cdot T(k) \tag{5.5}$$

$$l_i(k) = \lambda_i(k) \cdot r_i(k) \tag{5.6}$$

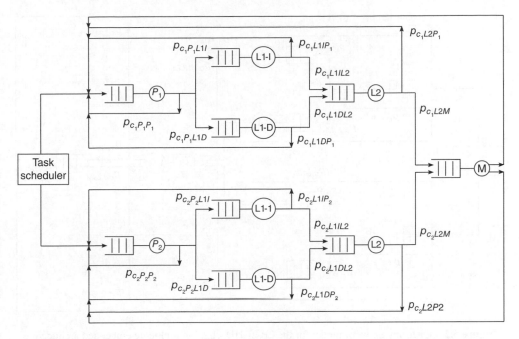

Figure 5.1   Queueing network model for the 2P-2L1ID-2L2-1M multicore embedded architecture

To explain our modeling approach for multicore embedded architectures, we describe a sample queueing model for the 2P-2L1ID-2L2-1M architecture in detail (other architecture models follow a similar explanation). Figure 5.1 depicts the queueing network model for 2P-2L1ID-2L2-1M. The *task scheduler* schedules the tasks/jobs on the two processor cores P_1 and P_2. We assume that the task scheduler is contention-aware and schedules tasks with minimal or no contention on cores sharing LLCs [144]. The queueing network consists of two chains: chain 1 corresponds to processor core P_1 and chain 2 corresponds to processor core P_2. The jobs serviced by P_1 either reenter P_1 with probability $p_{c_1P_1P_1}$ (c_1 in the subscript denotes chain 1) or enter the L1-I cache with probability $p_{c_1P_1L1I}$ or the L1-D cache with probability $p_{c_1P_1L1D}$. The job arrival probabilities into the service centers (processor core, L1-I, L1-D, L2, or MM) depend on the workload characteristics (i.e., processor-bound, memory-bound, or mixed). The data from the L1-I cache and the L1-D cache returns to P_1 with probabilities $p_{c_1L1IP_1}$ and $p_{c_1L1DP_1}$, respectively, after L1-I and L1-D cache hits. The requests from the L1-I cache and the L1-D cache are directed to the L2 cache with probabilities p_{c_1L1IL2} and p_{c_1L1DL2}, respectively, after L1-I and L1-D cache misses. The probability of requests entering P_1 or the L2 cache from the L1-I and L1-D caches depends on the miss rates of the L1-I and L1-D caches. After an L2 cache hit, the requested data is transferred to P_1 with probability $p_{c_1L2P_1}$ or enters MM with probability p_{c_1L2M} after an L2 cache miss. The requests from MM always return to P_1 with probability $p_{c_1MP_1} = 1$. The queueing network chain and the path for chain 2 corresponding to P_2 follow the same pattern as chain 1 corresponding to P_1. For example, requests from the L2 cache in chain 2 either return to P_2 with probability $p_{c_2L2P_2}$ after an L2 cache hit or enter MM with probability p_{c_2L2M} after an L2 cache miss (c_2 in the subscript denotes chain 2).

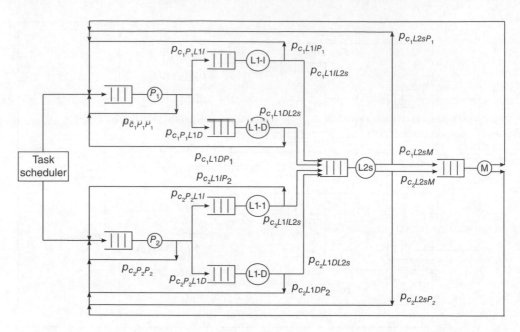

Figure 5.2   Queueing network model for the 2P-2L1ID-1L2-1M multicore embedded architecture

To further elaborate on our modeling approach, Fig. 5.2 depicts the queueing model for 2P-2L1ID-1L2-1M, which is similar to the model for 2P-2L1ID-2L2-1M (Fig. 5.1), except that this queueing model contains a shared L2 cache (L2s denotes the shared L2 cache in Fig. 5.2) for the two processor cores P_1 and P_2 instead of private L2 caches. The queueing network consists of two chains: chain 1 corresponds to processor core P_1 and chain 2 corresponds to processor core P_2. The requests from the L1-I cache and the L1-D cache for chain 1 go to the shared L2 cache (L2s) with probability $p_{c_1L1IL2s}$ and $p_{c_1L1DL2s}$, respectively, on L1-I and L1-D cache misses. The requested data is transferred from the L2 cache to P_1 with probability $p_{c_1L2sP_1}$ on an L2 cache hit whereas the data request goes to MM with probability p_{c_1L2sM} on an L2 cache miss. The requests from the L1-I cache and the L1-D cache for chain 2 go to the shared L2 cache (L2s) with probability $p_{c_2L1IL2s}$ and $p_{c_2L1DL2s}$, respectively, on L1-I and L1-D cache misses. The requested data from the L2 cache is transferred to P_2 with probability $p_{c_2L2sP_2}$ on an L2 cache hit, whereas the data request goes to MM with probability p_{c_2L2sM} on an L2 cache miss.

The assignment of the probabilities in our queueing network models to represent a synthetic workload (or to emulate a real workload) on a multicore architecture is critical to our modeling approach and the fidelity of our evaluations. Our models can be leveraged for studying workloads based on an overall workload behavior, where processor-to-processor probability p_{PP} and processor-to-memory probability p_{PM} remain uniform throughout the workload, or for a more detailed study of workloads with different phases, where a different p_{PP} and p_{PM} would be assigned for each phase. These probabilities can be determined based on processor and memory statistics for a given workload using one of the two methods: actual statistics for real workloads can be gathered using a functional simulator if these statistics are not available from prior research; or synthetic workloads can be leveraged wherein the designer would assign these statistics based on the expected workload behavior. For our models, p_{PP} can be estimated as

$$p_{PP} = O_P/O_T \tag{5.7}$$

where O_P and O_T denote the number of processor operations and total operations (processor and memory) in a benchmark, respectively. Processor operations refer to arithmetic and logic unit (ALU) micro-operations, such as add and subtract, and memory operations refer to micro-operations involving memory accesses, such as load and store. For floating point benchmarks, O_P can be assumed to be equal to the number of floating point operations. O_T can be estimated as

$$O_T = O_P + O_M \tag{5.8}$$

where O_M denotes the number of memory operations, which is the sum of the total read and total write operations. p_{PM} can be estimated as

$$p_{PM} = 1 - p_{PP} \tag{5.9}$$

The probability of requests going from the processor core P_i in chain i to the L1-I and L1-D caches can be estimated from the L1-I and L1-D cache access ratios (defined later), which requires the number of L1-I and L1-D accesses. The number of L1-I accesses can be calculated as (assuming there is no self-modifying code):

$$\text{L1-I accesses} = \text{L1-I read misses} + \text{L1-I read hits} \tag{5.10}$$

The number of L1-D accesses can be calculated as

$$\text{L1-D accesses} = \text{L1-D read misses} + \text{L1-D read hits}$$
$$+ \text{L1-D write misses} + \text{L1-D write hits} \tag{5.11}$$

Total number of L1 cache accesses can be calculated as

$$\text{Total L1 accesses} = \text{L1-D accesses} + \text{L1-I accesses} \tag{5.12}$$

The L1-I access ratio can be calculated as

$$\text{L1-I access ratio} = \frac{\text{L1-I accesses}}{\text{Total L1 accesses}} \tag{5.13}$$

The L1-D access ratio can be calculated as

$$\text{L1-D access ratio} = 1 - \text{L1-I access ratio} \tag{5.14}$$

The probability of requests going from the processor core P_i in chain i to the L1-I cache $p_{c_i P_i L1I}$ can be calculated as

$$p_{c_i P_i L1I} = p_{PM} \times \text{L1-I access ratio} \tag{5.15}$$

Similarly, the probability of requests going from the processor core P_i in chain i to the L1-D cache $p_{c_i P_i L1D}$ can be calculated as

$$p_{c_i P_i L1D} = p_{PM} \times \text{L1-D access ratio} \tag{5.16}$$

The probabilities of requests going from the L1-I and L1-D caches to the L2 cache and from the L2 cache to MM can be calculated directly from the cache miss rate statistics and are omitted for brevity.

We exemplify the assignment of probabilities for our queueing network models using the 2P-2L1ID-2L2-1M multicore architecture for memory-bound workloads given the following statistics: $p_{PP} = 0.1$; $p_{PM} = 0.9$ assuming that the L1-I, L1-D, and L2 cache miss rates are 25%, 50%, and 30%, respectively; and L1-I and L1-D access ratios are 0.8 and 0.2, respectively. The probabilities are set as: $p_{c_1 P_1 P_1} = 0.1$, $p_{c_1 P_1 L1I} = 0.72$, $p_{c_1 P_1 L1D} = 0.18$, $p_{c_1 L1I P_1} = 0.75$, $p_{c_1 L1DP_1} = 0.5$, $p_{c_1 L1IL2} = 0.25$, $p_{c_1 L1DL2} = 0.5$, $p_{c_1 L2P_1} = 0.7$, $p_{c_1 L2M} = 0.3$, $p_{c_1 MP_1} = 1$ (different probabilities can be assigned for processor-bound or mixed workloads).

Our queueing theoretic models determine performance metrics of component-level architectural elements (e.g., processor cores, L1-I, L1-D); however, embedded system designers are often also interested in system-wide performance metrics. For example, system-wide response time of an architecture is an important metric for real-time embedded applications. Our queueing theoretic models enable calculations of system-wide performance metrics. Based on our queueing theoretic models, we can calculate the system-wide response time $\bar{R}$ of a multicore embedded architecture as

$$
\begin{aligned}
\bar{R} = \max_{\forall i=1,\dots,N_P} & ((p_{c_i P_i P_i} \times r_{P_i}) \\
& + (p_{c_i P_i L1I} \times r_{iL1I}) \\
& + (p_{c_i P_i L1D} \times r_{iL1D}) \\
& + ((p_{c_i L1IL2} + p_{c_i L1DL2}) \times r_{iL2}) \\
& + (p_{c_i L2M} \times r_M))
\end{aligned}
\tag{5.17}
$$

where N_P denotes the total number of processor cores in the multicore embedded architecture. r_{P_i}, r_{iL1I}, r_{iL1D}, r_{iL2}, and r_M denote the response times for processor core P_i, L1-I, L1-D, and L2 corresponding to chain i and MM, respectively. $p_{c_i P_i P_i}$ denotes the probability of requests looping back from processor core P_i to processor core P_i in the queueing network chain i (the total number of chains in the queueing network is equal to N_P). $p_{c_i P_i L1I}$ and $p_{c_i P_i L1D}$ denote the probability of requests going from processor core P_i in chain i to the L1-I cache and the L1-D cache, respectively. $p_{c_i L1IL2}$ and $p_{c_i L1DL2}$ denote the probability of requests going from the L1-I cache and the L1-D cache in chain i to the L2 cache, respectively. $p_{c_i L2M}$ denotes the probability of requests going from the L2 cache in chain i to MM. We point out that Eq. (5.17) is an extension of Eq. (5.3) for a multichain queueing network and also simplifies the calculation by using probabilities between architectural elements directly instead of relative visit counts as in Eq. (5.3). Since processor cores in a multicore embedded architecture operate in parallel, the effective response time of a multicore architecture is the maximum response time out of all of the chains in the queueing network operating in parallel, as given in Eq. (5.17). In the context of queueing networks for parallel computing, the overall response time is determined by the slowest chain since the other chains must wait idle for the slowest chain to complete (load balancing deals with making the processor cores' response times close to each other to minimize the idle waiting). The response time of a single chain in the queueing network is the sum of the processing times of the architectural elements in a chain (e.g., processor core, L1-I, L1-D, L2, and MM) multiplied by the associated service probabilities of these architectural elements. System-wide throughput can be given similar to Eq. (5.17).

Our queueing network modeling provides a faster alternative for performance evaluation of multicore architectures as compared to running complete benchmarks on multicore simulators (and/or trace simulators) though at the expense of accuracy. Our queueing network models require simulating only a subset of the benchmark's instructions (specified implicitly by the service rates of the architectural components, such as processor cores and caches) that are necessary to reach a steady state/equilibrium in the queueing network with the workload behavioral characteristics captured by the processor-to-processor and processor-to-memory probabilities (as shown in Fig. 5.1). Since the service centers (processors, caches, memory) have been modeled explicitly in our queueing theoretic models, the effect of these service centers on the overall system performance is captured by our model [156].

5.2.3 Assumptions

Our queueing theoretic models make some simplifying assumptions, which do not affect the general applicability of our approach. Our queueing network models assume cycle-level assignments of tokens (service time slices) for a given workload/job such that in each cycle, the tokens receive service from a particular service center with a given probability. For example, a job leaving the processor core either returns to the processor core's queue to wait for another time slice or goes to either the L1-I or L1-D cache for an instruction or data fetch, respectively [135]. Completed jobs are replaced immediately by a statistically identical job, an assumption for closed product-form queueing networks, which holds true for embedded systems [135]. Our queueing network modeling approach can be extended to instruction-level tokens if desired (although not required) for a given workload where an instruction can go to multiple service centers simultaneously (e.g., an instruction going to the L1-I and L1-D caches simultaneously to obtain the instruction opcodes and data, respectively). For these cases, a compound service center can be added to our queueing network model (e.g., L1-I + L1-D) that represents multiple service centers. The probability of a job going to a compound service center would be the sum of the probabilities of the individual service centers represented by that compound service center.

Our models are well suited for multiprogrammed workloads that are common in embedded systems; however, our approach is also applicable to multithreaded workloads with some simplifying assumptions. We assume that sizes of the LLCs are large enough to hold the working sets of the executing threads, which alleviate performance problems, such as suboptimal throughput arising due to cache thrashing and thread starvation [151]. We assume that appropriate inter-thread cache partitioning schemes alleviate performance issues due to cache sharing and is not the focus of our model. Furthermore, since cache contention impacts cache miss rates, our model allows specification of appropriate cache miss rates for investigating the impact of workloads with cache contention. For example, workloads that are likely to cause cache contention can be assigned higher cache miss rates in our models to incorporate the cache contention effects. Additionally, shared LLCs and MM in our queueing network model account for the contention of resources between processor cores and/or executing threads [135].

Although our current models do not explicitly model critical sections and coherence in multithreaded programs as stated in our modeling assumptions, our models can capture critical sections in a workload. We point out that a critical section is a piece of code that accesses a shared resource (e.g., a data structure) that must not be concurrently accessed by more than one thread of execution. Since critical sections are effectively serialized, the response time of the workload containing critical sections will increase depending on the number of critical sections and the number of instructions in each critical section. Hence, additional time for executing critical sections can be calculated by the number of critical sections and the number of instructions in each critical section and then added to the response time of the workload. The coherence is implicitly modeled in our queueing theory models since coherence issues will cause coherence misses and these misses can be incorporated into our cache miss rate specifications for a workload as our models enable specification of any cache miss rates for our synthesized workloads.

We note that even though some of these assumptions may violate practical scenarios, such violations would not significantly impact the insights obtained from our queueing theoretic models because our models measure performance trends and focus on the *relative* performance of architectures for different benchmarks rather than the absolute performance.

5.3 Queueing Network Model Validation

In this section, we validate our queueing network models to assure that our models' results conform with expected queueing theoretic results. We further validate our queueing network models with a multicore simulator running multithreaded benchmarks. We also calculate the speedups attained by our queueing network models as compared to a multicore simulator for architectural performance evaluation.

5.3.1   Theoretical Validation

We analyzed our queueing network models for different cache miss rates and workloads and find that the model's simulation results conform with expected queueing theoretical results. For example, Fig. 5.3 depicts the response time for mixed workloads ($p_{PP} = 0.5$, $p_{PM} = 0.5$) for 2P-2L1ID-1L2-1M as the number of jobs/tasks N varies. The figure shows that as N increases, the response time for the processor core, L1-I, L1-D, L2, and MM increases for all of the cache miss rates. We point out that cache miss rates could increase as N increases due to inter-task address conflicts and increasing cache pressure (increased number of working sets in the cache), but we assume that the cache sizes are sufficiently large enough so that capacity misses remain the same for the considered number of jobs. We present the average response time individually for the processor cores and for the L1-I, L1-D, and L2 caches. For smaller L1-I, L1-D, and L2 cache miss rates, the response time of the processor core increases drastically as N increases because most of the time jobs are serviced by the processor core, whereas for larger L1-I, L1-D, and L2 cache miss rates, the response time of the MM increases drastically because of a large number of MM accesses. These results along with our other observed results conform with the expected queueing theoretical results and validate our queueing network models for multicore architectures.

5.3.2   Validation with a Multicore Simulator

We further validate our queueing theoretic approach for modeling multicore architectures using multithreaded benchmarks executing on a multicore simulator. We choose

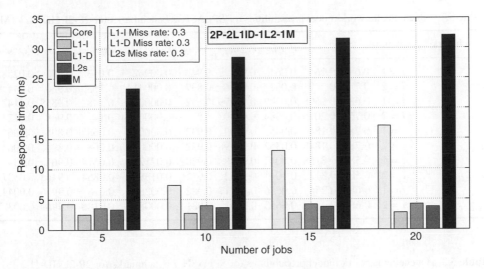

Figure 5.3   Queueing network model validation of the response time in ms for mixed workloads for 2P-2L1ID-1L2-1M for a varying number of jobs N

kernels/applications from the SPLASH-2 benchmark suite, which represent a range of computations in the scientific, engineering, and graphics domains. Our selected kernels/applications from the SPLASH-2 benchmark suite include FFT, LU decomposition, Radix, Raytrace, and Water-spatial [170]. We briefly describe our selected kernels/applications from the SPLASH-2 benchmark suite:

Fast Fourier transform: The FFT kernel is a complex 1D algorithm for FFT calculation, which is optimized to minimize interprocess communication. The kernel's time and memory requirement growth rates are $\mathcal{O}(N^{1.5} \log N)$ and $\mathcal{O}(N)$, respectively.

LU decomposition: The LU kernel factors a dense matrix into the product of a lower triangular and an upper triangular matrix using a blocking algorithm that exploits temporal locality on submatrix elements. We obtain results using the noncontiguous version of LU in the SPLASH-2 suite as the noncontiguous version exhibits better performance on CMPs [171], which is the focus of our study. The kernel's time and memory requirement growth rates are $\mathcal{O}(N^3)$ and $\mathcal{O}(N)$, respectively.

Radix: The integer Radix sort kernel implements an iterative noncomparison-based sorting algorithm for integers. The kernel's time and memory requirement growth rates are both $\mathcal{O}(N)$.

Raytrace: The Raytrace application renders a 3D scene using ray tracing. The kernel's time and memory requirement growth rates for this application is unpredictable [145].

Water-spatial: This application evaluates forces that occur over time in a system of water molecules. The application's time and memory requirement growth rates are both $\mathcal{O}(N)$.

Tables 5.2 and 5.3 depict the queueing network model probabilities for SPLASH-2 benchmarks for 2P-2L1ID-2L2-1M and 2P-2L1ID-1L2-1M, respectively (Section 5.2.2). These probabilities are obtained using Eqs. (5.7)–(5.16) where the statistics required by these equations are acquired from an architecture-level simulator (SESC in this case) for an accurate representation of the benchmarks in our queueing network model. From our

Table 5.2   Queueing network model probabilities for SPLASH-2 benchmarks for 2P-2L1ID-2L2-1M

Benchmark	Chain i	$P_{c_iP_iP_i}$	$P_{c_iP_iL1I}$	$P_{c_iP_iL1D}$	$P_{c_iL1IP_i}$	$P_{c_iL1DP_i}$	P_{c_iL1IL2}	P_{c_iL1DL2}	$P_{c_iL2P_i}$	P_{c_iL2M}
	i = 1	0.68	0.26	0.06	0.99	0.947	0.00962	0.053	0.97	0.0258
FFT	i = 2	0.7	0.249	0.051	0.9996	0.837	0.000414	0.163	0.956	0.044
	i = 1	0.68	0.2598	0.0602	0.99979	0.852	0.00021	0.148	0.9858	0.0142
LU	i = 2	0.76	0.2016	0.0384	0.9999	0.87	0.0000314	0.13	0.988	0.012
	i = 1	0.781	0.184	0.035	0.9999	0.932	0.000051	0.068	0.894	0.106
Radix	i = 2	0.78	0.1848	0.0352	0.99998	0.932	0.0000151	0.068	0.894	0.106
	i = 1	0.58	0.3158	0.1042	0.9788	0.9382	0.0212	0.0618	0.961	0.039
Raytrace	i = 2	0.584	0.312	0.104	0.9862	0.9146	0.0138	0.0854	0.9463	0.0537
	i = 1	0.68	0.2544	0.0656	0.99717	0.982	0.00283	0.018	0.9956	0.00442
Water-spatial	i = 2	0.68	0.2547	0.0653	0.9991	0.9814	0.000882	0.0186	0.9969	0.00307

Table 5.3   Queueing network model probabilities for SPLASH-2 benchmarks for 2P-2L1ID-1L2-1M

Benchmark	Chain i	$P_{c_iP_iP_i}$	$P_{c_iP_iL1I}$	$P_{c_iP_iL1D}$	$P_{c_iL1IP_i}$	$P_{c_iL1DP_i}$	P_{c_iL1IL2}	P_{c_iL1DL2}	$P_{c_iL2P_i}$	P_{c_iL2M}
FFT	i = 1	0.68	0.26	0.06	0.9905	0.947	0.0095	0.053	0.982	0.018
	i = 2	0.7	0.249	0.051	0.9996	0.84	0.0004	0.16	0.982	0.018
LU	i = 1	0.68	0.2624	0.0576	0.9998	0.9655	0.000166	0.0345	0.9987	0.0013
	i = 2	0.76	0.202	0.036	0.9999	0.86	0.000011	0.14	0.9987	0.0013
Radix	i = 1	0.781	0.184	0.035	0.99996	0.9331	0.000036	0.0669	0.888	0.112
	i = 2	0.78	0.1848	0.0352	0.999998	0.9335	0.0000022	0.0665	0.888	0.112
Raytrace	i = 1	0.582	0.314	0.1037	0.9791	0.752	0.0209	0.248	0.9881	0.0119
	i = 2	0.584	0.312	0.104	0.9867	0.9285	0.0133	0.0715	0.9881	0.0119
Water-spatial	i = 1	0.679	0.256	0.0655	0.9972	0.9821	0.00283	0.0179	0.99819	0.00181
	i = 2	0.679	0.2558	0.0652	0.99915	0.9814	0.000854	0.0186	0.99819	0.00181

probabilistic characterization of the workloads, FFT, LU, Radix, and Water-spatial can be classified as processor-bound workloads and Raytrace can be classified as a mixed workload. We reemphasize that this statistics gathering is only required for accurate representation of real benchmarks and is not required for synthetic workloads.

We simulate the architectures in Table 5.1 using SESC [172]. To accurately capture our modeled architectures with SESC, our queueing theoretic models use the same processor and cache parameters (e.g., processor operating frequency, cache sizes, and associativity) for the architectures as specified in the SESC configuration files. We consider single-issue processors with five pipeline stages and a 45 nm process technology. The execution times for the benchmarks on SESC are calculated from the number of cycles required to execute those benchmarks (i.e., execution time = (number of cycles) × (cycle time)). For example, FFT requires 964,057 cycles to execute on 4P-4L1ID-4L2-1M at 16.8 MHz (59.524 ns), which gives an execution time of 57.38 ms.

To verify that the insights obtained from our queueing theoretic models regarding architectural evaluation are the same as those obtained from a multicore simulator, we compare the execution time results for the FFT, LU (noncontiguous), Raytrace, Radix (an example for

Table 5.4 Execution time comparison of the SPLASH-2 benchmarks on SESC for multicore architectures

Architecture	FFT (ms)	LU (ms)	Radix (s)	Raytrace (s)	Water-spatial (s)
2P-2L1ID-2L2-1M	65.06	518.52	4.24	26.32	24.47
2P-2L1ID-1L2-1M	60.23	480.85	4.16	23.5	24.22
4P-4L1ID-4L2-1M	57.38	362.13	2.24	17.84	13.06
4P-4L1ID-1L2-1M	52.77	336.54	2.19	15.91	14.08
4P-4L1ID-2L2-1M	52.81	337.3	2.38	16.52	14.16

memory-bound workloads), and Water-spatial (an example for mixed workloads) benchmarks on SESC and our queueing theoretic models (the benchmarks are represented probabilistically for our queueing theoretic models (as shown in Tables 5.2 and 5.3 for the dual-core architectures). System-wide response time is obtained from our queueing theoretic models for these benchmarks using Eq. (5.17). We compare the execution time trends for the FFT, LU, Raytrace, Water-spatial, and Radix benchmarks on SESC and the modeled benchmarks for our queueing theoretic models using the SHARPE modeling tool/simulator [135].

Table 5.4 summarizes the performance (execution time) results on SESC for the FFT, LU (noncontiguous), Radix, Raytrace, and Water-spatial benchmarks for both the two-core and four-core processor architectures. The results from SESC and our queueing theoretic models provide similar insights and show that the multicore architectures with shared LLCs provide better performance than the architectures with private and hybrid LLCs for these benchmarks. Furthermore, architectures with hybrid LLCs exhibit superior performance than the architectures with private LLCs. Since our queueing theoretic models provide relative performance measures for different architectures and benchmarks by simulating a minimum number of the benchmarks' representative instructions, the results show a difference in the absolute execution times obtained from SESC and our queueing theoretic models. Furthermore, execution time of the benchmarks on SESC depends on the input sizes for the benchmarks and varies for different input sizes but normally retains similar trends across different architectures. Our queuing theoretic models capture the performance trends, which are important for the relative comparison of different architectures, and these trends match the performance trends obtained from SESC.

In a high-level qualitative comparison of architectures, designers are typically interested in relative performance measures for various benchmarks on the evaluated architectures. To verify that our queueing network models can capture the differences in execution times for various benchmarks, Table 5.5 summarizes the evaluation results comparing different dual-core architectures (2P-2L1ID-2L2-1M and 2P-2L1ID-1L2-1M) on SESC and our queueing theoretic model. Results indicate that our queueing theoretic model qualitatively evaluates the two architectures accurately with an average difference of 5.6% as compared to the SESC simulator evaluation of the architectures. We observed similar architectural evaluation trends for four-core architectures and omit these details for brevity.

The SESC simulation results on multithreaded benchmarks verify the results and insights obtained from our queueing theoretic models for mixed and processor-bound workloads (Section 5.4.3). From the probabilistic characterization of the SPLASH-2 benchmarks, we ascertain that it is difficult to find benchmarks in a benchmark suite that cover the entire

Table 5.5 Dual-core architecture evaluation (T_y/T_z) on SESC and QT (our queueing theoretic model) based on the SPLASH-2 benchmarks

Evaluation	FFT	LU	Radix	Raytrace	Water-spatial
SESC	1.08×	1.08×	0.935×	1.166×	1.01×
QT	1.16×	1.13×	0.99×	1.07×	1.02×
% Difference	7.4	4.63	5.88	8.97	0.99

T_y and T_z denote the time to execute a benchmark on architecture y = 2P-2L1ID-2L2-1M and z = 2P-2L1ID-1L2-1M, respectively. For each benchmark, architectural evaluation results are reported as (T_y/T_z): time ratio of executing the benchmark on the two architectures (y and z)

range of processor-to-processor and processor-to-memory probabilities (e.g., p_{PP} ranging from 0.05 for some benchmarks to 0.95 for others). The lack of computationally diverse benchmarks in terms of processor and memory requirements in a benchmark suite makes our queueing theoretic modeling approach an attractive solution for rigorous architectural evaluation because our modeling approach enables architectural evaluation via synthetic benchmarks with virtually any computing requirements characterized probabilistically.

5.3.3 Speedup

To verify that our queueing theoretic modeling approach provides a quick architectural evaluation as compared to executing benchmarks on a multicore simulator, we compare the execution time required to evaluate multicore embedded architectures on SESC to our queueing theoretic model's execution time. The execution times for the SPLASH-2 benchmarks on SESC were measured using the Linux `time` command on an Intel Xeon E5430 processor running at 2.66 GHz. The execution times for our queueing theoretic models were measured using the Linux `time` command on an AMD Opteron 246 processor running at 2 GHz, and these results were scaled to 2.66 GHz to provide a fair comparison. The SHARPE execution time was measured on the AMD Opteron processor due to site-specific server installations [173]. The results reveal that our queueing theoretic models require 1.92 and 8.33 ms on average for multicore embedded architectures with two and four processor cores, respectively. We note that the execution times of our queueing theoretic models do not include the time taken to obtain processor, memory, and cache statistics (either from any prior work in the literature or running benchmarks on a multicore simulator or a functional simulator if these statistics are not available in any prior work) as the time to gather these statistics can vary for different benchmarks and depend on the existing work in the literature and available functional simulators for different benchmarks. Table 5.6 depicts the average execution time for the SPLASH-2 benchmarks on SESC for multicore embedded architectures with two and four processor cores and the ratio of the SESC execution times compared to our queueing theoretic models' execution times. Results reveal that our queuing theoretic models can provide architectural evaluation results 482,995× faster as compared to executing benchmarks on SESC. Therefore, our queueing theoretic modeling approach can be used for quick architectural evaluation for multicore embedded systems for virtually any set of workloads.

Table 5.6 Execution time and speedup comparison of our queueing theoretic models versus SESC. $T_Y^{x\text{-core}}$ denotes the execution time required for simulating an x-core architecture using Y where $Y = \{$SESC, QT$\}$ (QT denotes our queueing theoretic model)

Benchmark	$T_{\text{SESC}}^{2\text{-core}}$ (s)	$T_{\text{SESC}}^{2\text{-core}}/T_{\text{QT}}^{2\text{-core}}$	$T_{\text{SESC}}^{4\text{-core}}$ {(s)}	$T_{\text{SESC}}^{4\text{-core}}/T_{\text{QT}}^{4\text{-core}}$
FFT	1.7	885	1.4	168
LU	21	10,938	26.1	3,133
Radix	72.1	37,552	77.3	9,280
Raytrace	772.7	402,448	780.3	93,673
Water-spatial	927.35	482,995	998.4	119,856

5.4 Queueing Theoretic Model Insights

In this section, we present insights obtained from our queueing theoretic models regarding performance, performance per watt, and performance per unit area for the five different multi-core embedded architectures depicted in Table 5.1. Furthermore, we verify the insights/trends for various workloads with diffcrent computational requirements that cannot be captured by a subset of benchmarks in a benchmark's suite and corroborate these results with our presented trends (for brevity, we present a subset of the results; however, our analysis and derived conclusions are based on our complete set of experimental results).

5.4.1 Model Setup

We consider the ARM7TDMI processor core, which is a 32-bit low-power processor with 32-bit instruction and data bus widths [174, 175]. We consider the following cache parameters [176]: *cache sizes* of 8, 8, and 64 KB for the L1-I, L1-D, and L2 caches, respectively; *associativities* of direct-mapped, two-way, and two-way for the L1-I, L1-D, and L2 caches, respectively; and *block (line) sizes* of 64, 16, and 64 B for the L1-I, L1-D, and L2 caches, respectively. We assume a 32 MB MM for all architectures, which is typical for mobile embedded systems (e.g., Sharp Zaurus SL-5600 personal digital assistant (PDA)) [177]. To provide a fair comparison between architectures, we ensure that the total L2 cache size for the shared L2 cache architectures and the private L2 cache architectures is equal. Furthermore, the shared bus bandwidth for the shared LLC (L2 in our experiments) architectures is n times the bandwidth of the private LLC architectures, where n is the number of cores sharing an LLC cache.

We implement our queueing network models of the multicore embedded architectures using the SHARPE modeling tool/simulator [135]. Figure 5.4 depicts the flow chart for our queueing network model setup in SHARPE. To set up our queueing network model simulation in SHARPE, we first specify the probabilities for a synthesized workload for a given multicore architecture (Section 5.2). For example, for 2P-2L1ID-2L2-1M for memory-bound workloads (processor-to-processor probability $p_{\text{PP}} = 0.1$, processor-to-memory probability $p_{\text{PM}} = 0.9$) assuming that the L1-I, L1-D, and L2 cache miss rates are 25%, 50%, and 30%, respectively, and L1-I and L1-D access ratios are 0.8 and 0.2, respectively, the probabilities are set as: $p_{c_1 P_1 P_1} = 0.1, p_{c_1 P_1 L1I} = 0.72, p_{c_1 P_1 L1D} = 0.18, p_{c_1 L1I P_1} = 0.75, p_{c_1 L1D P_1} = 0.5, p_{c_1 L1I L2} = 0.25, p_{c_1 L1D L2} = 0.5, p_{c_1 L2 P_1} = 0.7, p_{c_1 L2M} = 0.3, p_{c_1 MP_1} = 1$ (different probabilities can be

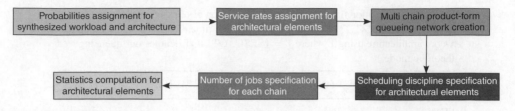

Figure 5.4   Flow chart for our queueing network model setup in SHARPE

assigned for processor-bound or mixed workloads). The code snippet for assigning these probabilities in SHARPE for the two chains is as follows:

```
bind
pr1P1P1 0.1
pr1P1L1I 0.72
pr1L1IP1 0.75
pr1L1IL2 0.25
pr1P1L1D 0.18
pr1L1DP1 0.5
pr1L1DL2 0.5
pr1L2P1 0.7
pr1L2M 0.3

pr2P2P2 0.1
pr2P2L1I 0.72
pr2L1IP2 0.75
pr2L1IL2 0.25
pr2P2L1D 0.18
pr2L1DP2 0.5
pr2L1DL2 0.5
pr2L2P2 0.7
pr2L2M 0.7
```

We then calculate the service rates for the service centers used in our multicore queueing models. We assume that the processor core delivers 15 MIPS at 16.8 MHz [174] (cycle time $= 1/(16.8 \times 10^6) = 59.524$ ns), which for 32-bit instructions corresponds to a service rate of 480 Mbps. We assume L1-I, L1-D, and L2 caches and MM access latencies of 2, 2, 10, and 100 cycles, respectively [174, 178]. With an L1-I cache line size of 64 B, an access latency of 2 cycles, and a 32-bit (4 B) bus, transferring 64 B requires $64/4 = 16$ cycles, which results in a total L1-I time (cycles) = access time + transfer time $= 2 + 16 = 18$ cycles, with a corresponding L1-I service rate $= (64 \times 8)/(18 \times 59.524 \times 10^{-9}) = 477.86$ Mbps. With an L1-D cache line size of 16 B, the transfer time $= 16/4 = 4$ cycles, and the total L1-D time $= 2 + 4 = 6$ cycles, with a corresponding L1-D service rate $= (16 \times 8)/(6 \times 59.524 \times 10^{-9}) = 358.4$ Mbps. With an L2 cache line size of 64 B, the transfer time $= 64/4 = 16$ cycles, which gives the total L2 time $= 10 + 16 = 26$ cycles, with a corresponding L2 service rate $= (64 \times 8)/(26 \times 59.524 \times 10^{-9}) = 330.83$ Mbps. With an MM line size of 64 B, the transfer time $= 64/4 = 16$ cycles, which gives a total MM time $= 100 + 16 = 116$ cycles, with a corresponding service rate $= (64 \times 8)/(116 \times 59.524 \times 10^{-9}) = 74.15$ Mbps. We assume that each individual job/task requires processing 1 Mb of instruction and data, which is implicit in our queueing models via service rate specifications (ensures steady-state/equilibrium behavior of the queueing network for our simulated workloads). The code snippet for assigning the service rates for the architectural elements (processor cores, caches, and MM) in Mbps in SHARPE is as follows:

```
P1rate 480
P2rate 480
L1Irate 477.86
L1Drate 358.4
L2rate 330.83
// Main memory service rate for chain 1
sMrate1 74.15
// Main memory service rate for chain 2
sMrate2 74.15
```

After service rate assignments for the architectural elements, we create a multichain product-form queueing network that outlines the architectural elements in each chain along with the associated transition probabilities between the architectural elements. We specify the architectural elements in each chain of the multichain product-form queueing network with associated transition probabilities between the architectural elements. The queueing network performs calculations for a given number of jobs NumJobs. The code snippet for creating a multichain product-form queueing network in SHARPE is as follows:

```
mpfqn embarch1(NumJobs)

chain 1
P1 1L1I pr1P1L1I
1L1I 1L2 pr1L1IL2
1L1I P1 pr1L1IP1
P1 1L1D pr1P1L1D
1L1D 1L2 pr1L1DL2
1L1D P1 pr1L1DP1
1L2 P1 pr1L2P1
1L2 M pr1L2M
M P1 1
end

chain 2
P2 2L1I pr2P2L1I
2L1I 2L2 pr2L1IL2
2L1I P2 pr2L1IP2
P2 2L1D pr2P2L1D
2L1D 2L2 pr2L1DL2
2L1D P2 pr2L1DP2
2L2 P2 pr2L2P2
2L2 M pr2L2M
M P2 1
end

end
```

Next, we specify appropriate scheduling disciplines for the architectural elements (Section 5.2), such as FCFS scheduling for the processor core, L1-I, L1-D, and L2, and PS for MM. The scheduling discipline is specified for the architectural elements along with the associated service rates for these elements. The code snippet for specifying the scheduling disciplines for the architectural elements in SHARPE is as follows:

```
P1 fcfs P1rate
end
P2 fcfs P2rate
end

1L1I fcfs L1Irate
end
1L1D fcfs L1Drate
end
2L1I fcfs L1Irate
end
2L1D fcfs L1Drate
end
1L2 fcfs L2rate
end
2L2 fcfs L2rate
end

M ps
1 sMrate1
2 sMrate2
end
```

We specify the number of jobs for each chain in the queueing network depending on the workloads (parallelized tasks in a workload or multiprogrammed workloads). To simulate a particular (single) benchmark in SHARPE, we set the number of jobs equal to 1 in our queueing network models. For a balanced workload, the number of jobs should be divided equally between the two chains. The code snippet for specifying the number of jobs for each chain in SHARPE is as follows:

```
1 NumJobs/2
2 NumJobs/2
end
```

Finally, we compute statistics (e.g., queue length, throughput, utilization, response time) from the queueing network models for a given number of jobs for the architectural elements. The SHARPE code snippet below calculates these statistics for the processor core in chain 1. The code loops through the number of jobs varying from 5 to 20, incrementing by five jobs in each iteration.

```
loop NumJobs,5,20,5
    expr mqlength(embarch1,P1;NumJobs)
    expr mtput(embarch1,P1;NumJobs)
```

```
    expr mutil(embarch1,P1;NumJobs)
    expr mrtime(embarch1,P1;NumJobs)
end
```

5.4.2   The Effects of Cache Miss Rates on Performance

In this section, we present results describing the effects of different L1-I, L1-D, and L2 cache miss rates on the architecture response time and throughput performance metrics for mixed, processor-bound, and memory-bound workloads. Considering the effects of different cache miss rates is an important aspect of performance evaluation of multicore embedded architectures with shared resources because cache miss rates give an indication whether the threads (corresponding to tasks) are likely to experience cache contention. Threads with higher LLC miss rates are more likely to have large working sets since each miss results in the allocation of a new cache line. These working sets may suffer from contention because threads may repeatedly evict the other threads' data (i.e., *cache thrashing*) [144]. We obtained results for cache miss rates of 0.0001, 0.05, and 0.2 up to 0.5, 0.7, and 0.7 for the L1-I, L1-D, and L2 caches, respectively. These cache miss rate ranges represent typical multicore embedded systems for a wide diversity of workloads [179–181].

Figure 5.5 depicts the effects of cache miss rate on the response time for mixed workloads ($p_{PP} = 0.5, p_{PM} = 0.5$) for 2P-2L1ID-2L2-1M as the number of jobs N varies. We observe that MM response time increases by 314% as miss rates for the L1-I, L1-D, and L2 caches increase from 0.0001, 0.05, and 0.2, to 0.5, 0.7, and 0.7, respectively, when $N = 5$. This response time increase is explained by the fact that as the cache miss rate increases, the number of accesses to MM increases, which increases the queue length and MM utilization, which causes an increase in the MM response time. The L1-I and L1-D response times decrease by 14% and 18%, respectively, as the miss rates for the L1-I and L1-D caches increase from 0.0001 and 0.05 to 0.5 and 0.7, respectively, when $N = 5$. This decrease in response time occurs because increased miss rates decrease the L1-I and L1-D queue lengths and utilizations. The L2 cache response time increases by 12% as the miss rates for the L1-I and L1-D caches increase from 0.0001 and 0.05 to 0.5 and 0.7, respectively, when $N = 5$ (even though the L2 cache miss rate also increases from 0.2 to 0.7, but increased L1-I and L1-D miss rates effectively increase the number of L2 cache references, which increases the L2 cache queue length and utilization and thus L2 cache response time).

We observed that for mixed workloads ($p_{PP} = 0.5$, $p_{PM} = 0.5$), the response times for the processor core, L1-I, L1-D, and MM for 2P-2L1ID-1L2-1M are very close to the response times for 2P-2L1ID-2L2-1M; however, the L2 response time presents interesting differences. The L2 response time for 2P-2L1ID-1L2-1M is 22.3% less than the L2 response time for 2P-2L1ID-2L2-1M when the L1-I, L1-D, and L2 cache miss rates are 0.0001, 0.05, and 0.2, respectively, and $N = 5$ (similar percentage differences were observed for other values of N), whereas the L2 response time for 2P-2L1ID-1L2-1M is only 6.5% less than the L2 response time when the L1-I, L1-D, and L2 cache miss rates are 0.5, 0.7, and 0.7, respectively. This result shows that the shared L2 cache (of comparable area as the sum of the private L2 caches) performs better than the private L2 caches in terms of response time for small cache miss rates; however, the performance improvement decreases as the cache miss rate increases. Similar trends were observed for processor-bound ($p_{PP} = 0.9, p_{PM} = 0.1$) and memory-bound workloads ($p_{PP} = 0.1, p_{PM} = 0.9$).

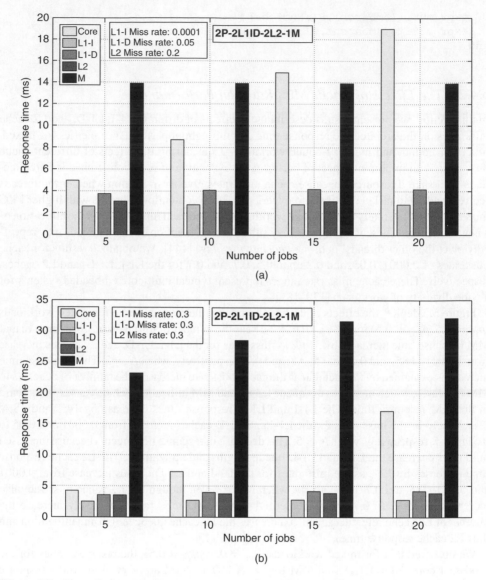

Figure 5.5 The effects of cache miss rate on response time (ms) for mixed workloads for 2P-2L1ID-2L2-1M for a varying number of jobs N: (a) relatively low cache miss rates; (b) relatively high cache miss rates

For mixed workloads, the response times for the processor core, L1-I, L1-D, and MM for 4P-4L1ID-1L2-1M are 1.2×, 1×, 1.1×, and 2.4× greater than the corresponding architectural elements for 4P-4L1ID-4L2-1M, whereas the L2 response time for 4P-4L1ID-1L2-1M is 1.1× less than the L2 response time for 4P-4L1ID-4L2-1M when the L1-I, L1-D, and L2 cache miss rates are 0.5, 0.7, and 0.7, respectively, and $N = 5$. This observation, in conjunction with our other experiments' results, reveals that the architectures with private LLCs provide improved response time for processor cores and L1 caches as compared to the architectures with shared LLCs; however, the response time of the LLC alone can be slightly better for architectures with shared LLCs because of the larger effective size for each core. The results also indicate that the MM response time could become a bottleneck for architectures with shared LLCs, especially when the cache miss rates become high. Another interesting observation is that shared LLCs could lead to increased response time for processor cores as compared to the private LLCs because of stalling or idle waiting of processor cores for bottlenecks caused by MM. Similar trends were observed for processor- and memory-bound workloads.

For mixed workloads, the L2 response time for 4P-4L1ID-2L2-1M is 1.2× less than 4P-4L1ID-4L2-1M and 1.1× greater than 4P-4L1ID-1L2-1M when the L1-I, L1-D, and L2 cache miss rates are 0.0001, 0.05, and 0.2, respectively, and $N = 5$. MM response time for 4P-4L1ID-2L2-1M is 2.3× less than 4P-4L1ID-1L2-1M, whereas MM response time for 4P-4L1ID-2L2-1M and 4P-4L1ID-4L2-1M is the same when the L1-I, L1-D, and L2 cache miss rates are 0.5, 0.7, and 0.7, respectively, and $N = 5$. The response times for the processor core and L1-I/D are comparable for the three architectures (4P-4L1ID-4L2-1M, 4P-4L1ID-2L2-1M, and 4P-4L1ID-1L2-1M). These results, in conjunction with our other experiments' results, show that having LLCs shared by fewer cores (e.g., the L2 cache shared by two cores in our considered architecture) do not introduce MM as a response time bottleneck, whereas the MM becomes the bottleneck as more cores share the LLCs, especially for large cache miss rates. Similar trends were observed for processor- and memory-bound workloads.

We observe the effects of cache miss rates on throughput for various multicore embedded architectures. For mixed workloads, the throughput for the processor core, L1-I, L1-D, and MM for 2P-2L1ID-1L2-1M is very close to the throughput for 2P-2L1ID-2L2-1M; however, L2 throughput for 2P-2L1ID-1L2-1M is 100% greater on average than the L2 throughput for 2P-2L1ID-2L2-1M for different miss rates for the L1-I, L1-D, and L2 and $N = 5$. However, the combined throughput of the two private L2 caches in 2P-2L1ID-2L2-1M is comparable to the L2 throughput for 2P-2L1ID-1L2-1M. This shows that the shared and private L2 caches provide comparable net throughputs for the two architectures. The throughput for the processor core, L1-I, L1-D, and L2 for 4P-4L1ID-4L2-1M is 2.1× less on average than the corresponding 2P-2L1ID-2L2-1M architectural elements, whereas the throughput for the processor core, L1-I, L1-D, and L2 for the two architectures is the same when the miss rates for the L1-I, L1-D, and L2 caches are 0.5, 0.7, and 0.7, respectively, and $N = 5$. This indicates that the throughput for the individual architectural elements (except MM since it is shared for both the architectures) decreases for the architecture with more cores since the workload remains the same. The throughput for the processor core, L1-I, L1-D, L2, and MM for 4P-4L1ID-2L2-1M is 1.5×, 1.5×, 1.5×, 2.5×, and 1.3× less than the throughput for the corresponding 4P-4L1ID-1L2-1M architectural elements when the miss rates for the L1-I, L1-D, and L2 caches are 0.0001, 0.05, and 0.2, respectively, and $N = 5$. These observations reveal that changing the L2 cache from private to shared can also impact the throughput for other architectural elements because of the interactions between these elements.

We evaluate the effects of cache miss rates on throughput for processor-bound workloads ($p_{PP} = 0.9$, $p_{PM} = 0.1$) for 2P-2L1ID-2L2-1M as N varies. Results reveal that there is no appreciable increase in processor core throughput as N increases from 5 to 20 because the processors continue to operate at utilization close to 1 when the L1-I, L1-D, and L2 cache miss rates are 0.3, 0.3, and 0.3, respectively (similar trends were observed for other cache miss rates). The MM throughput increases by 4.67% (4.67% − 1.64% = 3.03% greater than the mixed workloads) as N increases from 5 to 20 when L1-I, L1-D, and L2 cache miss rates are 0.5, 0.7, and 0.7, respectively. In this case, the MM percentage throughput increase is greater for processor-bound workloads as compared to mixed workloads because the MM is underutilized for processor-bound workloads (e.g., utilization of 0.519 for processor-bound workloads as compared to the utilization of 0.985 for mixed workloads when $N = 5$). However, the MM absolute throughput for processor-bound workloads is less than the mixed workloads (e.g., an MM throughput of 38.5 Mbps for processor-bound workloads as compared to an MM throughput of 73 Mbps for mixed workloads when $N = 5$). For processor-bound workloads, the throughput for the processor core, L1-I, L1-D, and MM for 2P-2L1ID-1L2-1M is similar to the throughput for 2P-2L1ID-2L2-1M; however, the L2 throughput for 2P-2L1ID-1L2-1M is 100% greater than the L2 throughput for 2P-2L1ID-2L2-1M for all cache miss rates on average and $N = 5$. Similar trends were observed for memory-bound and mixed workloads for architectures with two or four cores with private and shared LLCs (these throughput trends would continue as the number of cores increases).

5.4.3 The Effects of Workloads on Performance

In this section, we present results describing the effects of different workloads on the response time and throughput performance metrics when the L1-I, L1-D, and L2 cache miss rates are held constant. We discuss the effects of varying the *computing requirements* of these workloads. The computing requirement of a workload signifies the workload's demand for processor resources, which depends on the percentage of arithmetic, logic, and control instructions in the workload relative to the load and store instructions. The computing requirements of the workloads are captured by p_{PP} and p_{PM} in our models.

The results show that the response time for the processor core, L1-I, and L1-D for 2P-2L1ID-1L2-1M is very close (within 7%) to 2P-2L1ID-2L2-1M as the computing requirements of the processor-bound workload vary. However, 2P-2L1ID-1L2-1M provides a 21.5% improvement in L2 response time and a 12.3% improvement in MM response time as compared to 2P-2L1ID-2L2-1M when $p_{PP} = 0.7$ and a 23.6% improvement in L2 response time and a 1.4% improvement in MM response time when $p_{PP} = 0.95$ and $N = 5$. 4P-4L1ID-2L2-1M provides a 22.3% improvement in L2 response time and a 13% improvement in MM response time over 4P-4L1ID-4L2-1M when $p_{PP} = 0.7$ and $N = 5$. 4P-4L1ID-2L2-1M provides a 22.3% improvement in L2 response time and a 3% improvement in MM response time as compared to 4P-4L1ID-4L2-1M when $p_{PP} = 0.95$ because a larger p_{PP} results in fewer MM references. 4P-4L1ID-1L2-1M provides a 7.4% improvement in L2 response time with a 5.2% degradation in MM response time as compared to 4P-4L1ID-2L2-1M when $p_{PP} = 0.7$ and $N = 5$. 4P-4L1ID-1L2-1M provides a 12.4% improvement in L2 response time with no degradation in MM response time over 4P-4L1ID-2L2-1M when $p_{PP} = 0.95$ and $N = 5$. These results indicate that shared LLCs provide more improvement in L2 response time as compared to hybrid and private LLCs for more compute-intensive processor-bound workloads. However, the hybrid LLCs provide better MM response time than shared LLCs for more compute-intensive processor-bound workloads. These results suggest that hybrid LLCs may be more suitable than shared LLCs in terms of scalability and overall response time for comparatively less compute-intensive processor-bound workloads.

Response time and throughput results reveal that memory subsystems for an architecture with private, shared, or hybrid LLCs have a profound impact on the response time of the architecture and throughputs for the L2 and MM with relatively little impact on throughput for the processor cores, L1-I, and L1-D.

Figure 5.6 depicts the effects of varying computing requirements for processor-bound workloads on response time for 2P-2L1ID-2L2-1M as N varies where the L1-I, L1-D, and L2 cache miss rates are 0.01, 0.13, and 0.3, respectively. The figure depicts that as N increases, the response time for the processor core, L1-I, L1-D, L2, and MM increases for all values of p_{PP} and p_{PM}. The figure shows that as p_{PP} increases, the response time of the processor increases, whereas the response times of L1-I, L1-D, L2, and MM show negligible effects due to the processor-bound nature of the workloads. For example, the processor response time increases by 19.8% as p_{PP} increases from 0.7 to 0.95 when $N = 5$. The response times of L1-I, L1-D, L2, and MM decrease by 10.8%, 14.2%, 2.2%, and 15.2%, respectively, as p_{PP} increases from 0.7 to 0.95 when $N = 5$ because an increase in p_{PP} results in a decrease in memory requests, which decreases the response time for the caches and MM.

For memory-bound workloads, 2P-2L1ID-1L2-1M provides a 16.7% improvement in L2 response time and a 31.5% improvement in MM response time as compared to 2P-2L1ID-2L2-1M when $p_{PM} = 0.95$ and $N = 5$. 2P-2L1ID-1L2-1M provides an 18.2% improvement in L2 response time and a 25.8% improvement in MM response time over 2P-2L1ID-2L2-1M when $p_{PM} = 0.7$ and $N = 5$. 4P-4L1ID-2L2-1M provides a 19.8% improvement in L2 response time and a 20.2% improvement in MM response time on average over 4P-4L1ID-4L2-1M for both $p_{PM} = 0.95$ and $p_{PM} = 0.7$ and $N = 5$. 4P-4L1ID-1L2-1M provides a 2.4% improvement in L2 response time with a 15% degradation in MM response time as compared to 4P-4L1ID-2L2-1M when $p_{PM} = 0.95$ and $N = 5$. 4P-4L1ID-1L2-1M provides no improvement in L2 response time, with an 11.5% degradation in MM response time as compared to 4P-4L1ID-2L2-1M when $p_{PM} = 0.7$ and $N = 5$. These results indicate that shared LLCs provide a larger improvement in L2 and MM response time as compared to private LLCs for memory-bound workloads. Furthermore, hybrid LLCs are more amenable in terms of response time as compared to shared and private LLCs for memory-bound workloads. Similar trends were observed for mixed workloads for architectures with two or four cores containing private, shared, or hybrid LLCs.

We observe the effects of varying computing requirements for processor-bound workloads on throughput for 2P-2L1ID-2L2-1M as N varies. As N increases, the throughputs for the processor core, L1-I, L1-D, L2, and MM increase for all values of p_{PP} and p_{PM}. Furthermore, as p_{PP} increases, the throughput of the processor core increases, whereas the throughputs of L1-I, L1-D, L2, and MM decrease because of relatively fewer memory requests. For memory-bound workloads, L1-I and L1-D throughputs for 2P-2L1ID-2L2-1M and 2P-2L1ID-1L2-1M are comparable; however, 2P-2L1ID-1L2-1M improves the L2 throughput by 106.5% and 111% (due to larger combined L2 cache), whereas the MM throughput decreases by 126% and 121.2% when p_{PM} is 0.7 and 0.95, respectively. For memory-bound workloads, 2P-2L1ID-1L2-1M provides a 5.3% and 3.4% improvement in processor core throughput over 2P-2L1ID-2L2-1M when $p_{PM} = 0.95$ and $p_{PM} = 0.7$, respectively, and $N = 5$. For processor-bound workloads, the processor core throughputs for

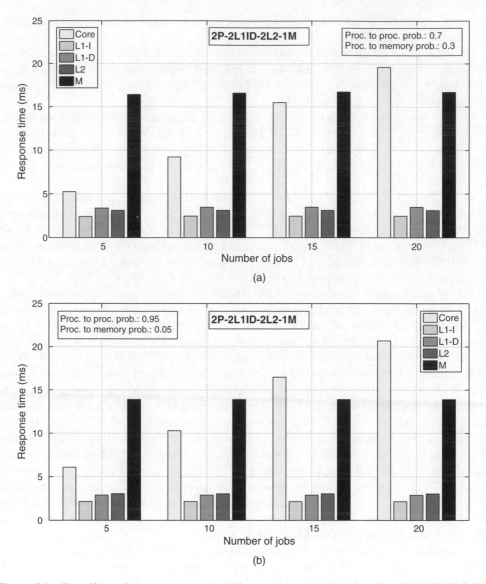

Figure 5.6 The effects of processor-bound workloads on response time (ms) for 2P-2L1ID-2L2-1M for a varying number of jobs N for cache miss rates: L1-I = 0.01, L1-D = 0.13, and L2 = 0.3: (a) processor-bound workloads (processor-to-processor probability $p_{PP} - 0.7$); (b) processor bound workloads (processor-to-processor probability $p_{PP} = 0.95$)

2P-2L1ID-2L2-1M and 2P-2L1ID-1L2-1M are comparable. Similar trends were observed for the architectures with four cores containing private, shared, or hybrid LLCs since the processor cores operate close to saturation (at high utilization) for processor-bound workloads, and memory stalls due to memory subsystem response time have a negligible effect on the processor core performance as memory accesses are completely overlapped with computation.

5.4.4   Performance per Watt and Performance per Unit Area Computations

In this section, we compute performance per watt and performance per unit area for the multicore embedded architectures using our queueing theoretic models. The performance per unit area is an important metric for embedded systems where the entire system is constrained to a limited space; however, performance per unit area is less important for desktop and supercomputing. Our performance per watt and performance per unit area computations assist in relative comparisons between different multicore embedded architectures. For these computations, we first need to calculate area and worst-case (peak) power consumption for different multicore embedded architectures, which we obtain using CACTI 6.5 [182], International Technology Roadmap for Semiconductors (ITRS) specifications [183], and datasheets for multicore embedded architectures.

Tables 5.7 and 5.8 show the area and peak power consumption for the processor cores, L1-I, L1-D, L2, and MM for two-core and four-core embedded architectures, respectively, assuming a 45 nm process. The core areas are calculated using Moore's law and the ITRS specifications [183] (i.e., the chip area required for the same number of transistors reduces by approximately $1/2\times$ every technology node (process) generation). For example, ARM7TDMI core area is $0.26\,mm^2$ at 130 nm process [184], the core area at 45 nm process (after three technology node generations, i.e., 130, 90, 65, and 45 nm) is approximately $(1/2)^3 \times 0.26 = 0.0325\,mm^2$.

To illustrate our area and power calculation procedure that can be combined with the results obtained from our queuing theoretic models to obtain performance per unit area and performance per watt, we provide example area and power calculations for 2P-2L1ID-2L2-1M.

Table 5.7   Area and power consumption of architectural elements for two-core embedded architectures

Element	2P-2L1ID-2L2-1M		2P-2L1ID-1L2-1M	
	Area (mm^2)	Power (mW)	Area (mm^2)	Power (mW)
Core	0.065	2.016	0.065	2.016
L1-I	0.11	135.44	0.11	135.44
L1-D	0.0998	79.76	0.0998	79.76
L2	0.578	307.68	0.5075	253.283
MM	34.22	3174.12	34.22	3174.12

Table 5.8   Area and power consumption of architectural elements for four-core embedded architectures

Element	4P-4L1ID-4L2-1M		4P-4L1ID-1L2-1M		4P-4L1ID-2L2-1M	
	Area (mm^2)	Power (mW)	Area (mm^2)	Power (mW)	Area (mm^2)	Power (mW)
Core	0.13	4.032	0.13	4.032	0.13	4.032
L1-I	0.2212	270.88	0.2212	270.88	0.2212	270.88
L1-D	0.1996	159.52	0.1996	159.52	0.1996	159.52
L2	1.1556	615.36	0.9366	354.04	1.015	506.8
MM	34.22	3174.12	34.22	3174.12	34.22	3174.12

The area calculations for 2P-2L1ID-2L2-1M are as follows: total processor core area $=$ $2 \times 0.0325 = 0.065\,\text{mm}^2$; total L1-I cache area $= 2 \times (0.281878 \times 0.19619) = 2 \times 0.0553$ $= 0.11\,\text{mm}^2$ (CACTI provides cache height $\times$ width for individual caches (e.g., $0.281878 \times$ 0.19619 for the L1-I cache)); total L1-D cache area $= 2 \times (0.209723 \times 0.23785) = 2 \times 0.0499$ $= 0.0998\,\text{mm}^2$; total L2 cache area $= 2 \times (0.45166 \times 0.639594) = 2 \times 0.2889 = 0.578\,\text{mm}^2$; and total MM area $= 8.38777 \times 4.08034 = 34.22\,\text{mm}^2$. The power consumption of the caches and MM is the sum of the dynamic power and the leakage power. Since CACTI gives dynamic energy and access time, dynamic power is calculated as the ratio of the dynamic energy to the access time. For example, for the L1-I cache, the dynamic power $= 0.020362\,(\text{nJ})/0.358448\,(\text{ns}) = 56.8\,\text{mW}$ and the leakage power $= 10.9229\,\text{mW}$, which gives the L1-I power consumption $= 56.8 + 10.9229 = 67.72\,\text{mW}$. For the MM dynamic power calculation, we calculate the average dynamic energy per read and write access $= (1.27955 + 1.26155)/2 = 1.27055\,\text{mJ}$, which gives the dynamic power $= 1.27055\,(\text{nJ})/5.45309\,(\text{ns}) = 233\,\text{mW}$. The total power consumption for the MM $= 233 + 2941.12 = 3174.12\,\text{mW}$ ($2941.12\,\text{mW}$ is the leakage power for the MM). The power consumption calculations for 2P-2L1ID-2L2-1M are as follows: total processor core power consumption $= 2 \times 1.008 = 2.016\,\text{mW}$; total L1-I cache power consumption $= 2 \times 67.72 = 135.44\,\text{mW}$; total L1-D cache power consumption $= 2 \times 39.88 = 79.76\,\text{mW}$; and total L2 cache power consumption $= 2 \times 153.84 = 307.68\,\text{mW}$.

The area and power results for multicore embedded architectures show that the MM consumes the most area and power consumption followed by L2, L1-I, L1-D, and the processor core. We observe that the shared L2 caches for 2P-2L1ID-1L2-1M and 4P-4L1ID-1L2-1M require 14% and 24% less area and consume 21.5% and 74% less power as compared to the private L2 caches for 2P-2L1ID-2L2-1M and 4P-4L1ID-4L2-1M, respectively. The hybrid L2 caches for 4P-4L1ID-2L2-1M require 14% less area and consume 21.4% less power as compared to the private L2 caches for 4P-4L1ID-4L2-1M, whereas the shared L2 cache for 4P-4L1ID-1L2-1M requires 8.7% less area and consumes 43% less power as compared to the hybrid L2 caches for 4P-4L1ID-2L2-1M. These results indicate that the power efficiency of shared LLCs improves as the number of cores increases.

Table 5.9 shows the area and peak power consumption for different multicore embedded architectures. Table 5.9 does not include the MM area and power consumption, which allows the results to isolate the area and peak power consumption of the processor cores and caches. This MM isolation from Table 5.9 enables deeper insights and a fair comparison for the embedded architectures since we assume an off-chip MM that has the same size and characteristics for all evaluated architectures. To illustrate the area and power calculations for multicore embedded architectures, we provide area and power consumption calculations for 2P-2L1ID-2L2-1M as an example. We point out that these area and power consumption calculations use constituent area and power consumption calculations for the architectural elements in a multicore embedded architecture. For 2P-2L1ID-2L2-1M, the total cache area $= 0.11 + 0.0998 + 0.578 - 0.7878\,\text{mm}^2$, which gives an overall area (excluding the MM) $= 0.065 + 0.7878 = 0.8528\,\text{mm}^2$ ($0.065\,\text{mm}^2$ is the area for the processor cores as calculated earlier). For 2P-2L1ID-2L2-1M, the total cache power consumption $= 135.44$ $+ 79.76 + 307.68 = 522.88\,\text{mW}$, which gives an overall power consumption (excluding the MM) $= 2.016 + 522.88 = 524.896\,\text{mW}$ ($2.016\,\text{mW}$ is the power consumption for the processor cores).

Table 5.9 Area and power consumption for multicore architectures

Architecture	Area (mm^2)	Power (mW)
2P-2L1ID-2L2-1M	0.8528	524.896
2P-2L1ID-1L2-1M	0.7823	470.5
4P-4L1ID-4L2-1M	1.7064	1049.79
4P-4L1ID-1L2-1M	1.4874	788.472
4P-4L1ID-2L2-1M	1.5658	941.232

The overall area and power consumption results for different multicore embedded architectures (Table 5.9) show that 2P-2L1ID-2L2-1M requires 8.3% more on-chip area and consumes 10.4% more power as compared to 2P-2L1ID-1L2-1M. 4P-4L1ID-4L2-1M requires 8.2% and 12.8% more on-chip area and consumes 10.3% and 24.9% more power as compared to 4P-4L1ID-2L2-1M and 4P-4L1ID-1L2-1M, respectively. These results reveal that the architectures with shared LLCs become more area and power efficient as compared to the architectures with private or hybrid LLCs as the number of cores in the architecture increases.

We discuss performance per watt and performance per unit area results for multicore embedded architectures assuming 64-bit floating point operations. We observe that the performance per watt and performance per unit area delivered by the processor cores and the L1-I and L1-D caches for these architectures are very close (within 7%); however, the L2 cache presents interesting results. Although the MM performance per watt for these architectures also differs, this difference does not provide meaningful insights for the following two reasons: (1) the MM is typically off-chip and the performance per watt is more critical for on-chip architectural components than for the off-chip components; and (2) if more requests are satisfied by the LLC, then fewer requests are deferred to the MM, which decreases the MM throughput and hence the performance per watt. Therefore, we mainly focus on the performance per watt and performance per unit area calculations for the LLCs for our studied architectures.

We calculate performance per watt results for memory-bound workloads when the L1-I, L1-D, and L2 cache miss rates are 0.01, 0.13, and 0.3, respectively. The performance per watt values for the L2 caches are 2.42 and 3.1 MFLOPS/W, and the performance per watt for the MM is 0.164 and 0.074 MFLOPS/W for 2P-2L1ID-2L2-1M and 2P-2L1ID-1L2-1M, respectively, when $p_{PM} = 0.95$ and $N = 5$. Our performance per watt calculations for 2P-2L1ID-2L2-1M incorporate the aggregate throughput for the L2 cache, which is the sum of the throughputs for the two private L2 caches in 2P-2L1ID-2L2-1M. The performance per watt for the L2 caches drops to 2.02 and 2.53 MFLOPS/W, whereas the performance per watt for the MM drops to 0.137 and 0.06 MFLOPS/W for 2P-2L1ID-2L2-1M and 2P-2L1ID-1L2-1M, respectively, when $p_{PM} = 0.7$ and $N = 5$. The performance per watt values for the L2 caches are 2.21, 4.77, and 3.08 MFLOPS/W for 4P-4L1ID-4L2-1M, 4P-4L1ID-1L2-1M, and 4P-4L1ID-2L2-1M, respectively, when $p_{PM} = 0.95$ and $N = 10$. We observe similar trends for mixed workloads and processor-bound workloads but with comparatively lower performance per watt for the LLC caches because these workloads have comparatively lower p_{PM} as compared to memory-bound workloads. The performance per watt for caches drops as p_{PM} decreases because fewer requests are directed to the LLC caches for a low p_{PM}, which decreases the throughput and hence the performance per watt. These results indicate that architectures with shared LLCs provide the highest LLC performance per watt followed by architectures with hybrid LLCs and private LLCs. The difference in performance per watt for these multicore architectures is mainly due to the difference in the LLC power consumption as there is a relatively small difference in the throughput delivered by these architectures for the same workloads with identical cache miss rates.

Based on our experimental results for different cache miss rates and workloads, we determine the peak performance per watt for the LLCs for our studied multicore embedded architectures. The peak performance per watt values for the L2 caches are 11.8 and 14.3 MFLOPS/W for 2P-2L1ID-2L2-1M and 2P-2L1ID-1L2-1M, respectively, when the L1-I, L1-D, and L2 cache miss rates are all equal to 0.3, $p_{PM} = 0.9$, and $N = 20$. The peak performance per watt values for the L2 caches are 7.6, 9.2, and 13.8 MFLOPS/W for 4P-4L1ID-4L2-1M, 4P-4L1ID-2L2-1M, and 4P-4L1ID-1L2-1M, respectively, when the L1-I, L1-D, and L2 cache miss rates are all equal to 0.2, $p_{PM} = 0.9$, and $N = 20$. Results reveal that these architectures deliver peak LLC performance per watt for workloads with mid-range cache miss rates (e.g., miss rates of 0.2 or 0.3) because at higher cache miss rates, a larger number of requests are directed toward the LLCs, which causes the LLCs' utilization to be close to one, which results in an increased response time and decreased throughput.

To investigate the effects of cache miss rates on the performance per watt of the LLCs, we calculate the performance per watt for memory-bound workloads ($p_{PM} = 0.9$) at high cache miss rates: L1-I = 0.5, L1-D = 0.7, and L2 = 0.7, and when $N = 10$. The performance per watt values for the L2 caches are 5.4 and 6.55 MFLOPS/W for 2P-2L1ID-2L2-1M and 2P-2L1ID-1L2-1M, respectively, whereas the performance per watt values are 2.7, 3.28, and 4.69 MFLOPS/W for 4P-4L1ID-4L2-1M, 4P-4L1ID-2L2-1M, and 4P-4L1ID-2L2-1M, respectively. Results reveal that at high cache miss rates, the performance per watt of the LLCs increases because relatively more requests are directed to the LLCs at higher cache miss rates than lower cache miss rates, which increases the throughput, and hence the performance per watt.

We calculate performance per unit area results for memory-bound workloads when the L1-I, L1-D, and L2 cache miss rates are 0.01, 0.13, and 0.3, respectively. The performance per unit area values for the L2 caches are 1.29 and 1.54 MFLOPS/mm^2, and the performance per unit area values for the MM are 15.25 and 6.9 KFLOPS/mm^2 for 2P-2L1ID-2L2-1M and 2P-2L1ID-1L2-1M, respectively, when $p_{PM} = 0.95$ and $N = 5$. The performance per unit area values for the L2 caches drop to 1.08 and 1.26 MFLOPS/mm^2, whereas the performance per unit area values for the MM drop to 12.68 and 5.6 KFLOPS/mm^2 for 2P-2L1ID-2L2-1M and 2P-2L1ID-1L2-1M, respectively, when $p_{PM} = 0.7$ and $N = 5$. The performance per unit area values for the L2 caches are 1.18, 1.8, and 1.54 MFLOPS/mm^2 for 4P-4L1ID-4L2-1M, 4P-4L1ID-1L2-1M, and 4P-4L1ID-2L2-1M, respectively, when $p_{PM} = 0.95$ and $N = 10$. We observe similar trends for performance per unit area for mixed and processor-bound workloads as for the performance per watt trends explained earlier. These results indicate that architectures with shared LLCs provide the highest LLC performance per unit area followed by architectures with hybrid LLCs and private LLCs. The difference in performance per unit area for these multicore architectures is mainly due to the difference in the LLC throughput as we ensure that the total LLC area occupied by a multicore embedded architecture with a given number of cores remains close enough (a minor difference in the occupied area of the LLCs occurs for different multicore embedded architectures due to practical implementation and fabrication constraints as determined by CACTI) to provide a fair comparison.

Based on our queuing theoretic models' results and area calculations, we determine the peak performance per unit area for the LLCs for our studied multicore embedded architectures. The peak performance per unit area values for the L2 caches are 6.27 and 7.14 MFLOPS/mm^2 for 2P-2L1ID-2L2-1M and 2P-2L1ID-1L2-1M, respectively, when the L1-I, L1-D, and L2 cache miss rates are all equal to 0.3, $p_{PM} = 0.9$, and $N = 20$. The peak performance per unit area values for the L2 caches are 4.04, 4.6, and 5.22 MFLOPS/mm^2 for 4P-4L1ID-4L2-1M, 4P-4L1ID-2L2-1M, and 4P-4L1ID-1L2-1M, respectively, when the L1-I, L1-D, and L2 cache miss rates are all equal to 0.2, $p_{PM} = 0.9$, and $N = 20$. Other results for peak performance per unit area reveal similar trends as for the peak performance per watt trends and therefore omit these discussions for brevity.

5.5   Chapter Summary

In this chapter, we developed closed product-form queueing network models for performance evaluation of multicore embedded architectures for different workload characteristics. The simulation results for the SPLASH-2 benchmarks executing on the SESC simulator (an architecture-level cycle-accurate simulator) verified the architectural evaluation insights obtained from our queueing theoretic models. Results revealed that our queueing theoretic model qualitatively evaluated multicore architectures accurately with an average difference of 5.6% as compared to the architectures' evaluations from the SESC simulator. The performance evaluation results indicated that the architectures with shared LLCs provided better cache response time and MFLOPS/W than the private LLCs for all cache miss rates especially as the number of cores increases. The results also revealed the disadvantage of shared LLCs indicating that the shared LLCs are more likely to cause a main memory response time bottleneck for larger cache miss rates as compared to the private LLCs. The memory bottleneck caused by shared LLCs may lead to increased response time for processor cores because of stalling or idle waiting. However, results indicated that the main memory bottleneck created by shared LLCs can be mitigated by using a hybrid of private and shared LLCs (i.e., sharing LLCs by a fewer number of cores) though hybrid LLCs consume more power than the shared LLCs and deliver comparatively less MFLOPS/W. The performance per watt and performance per unit area results for the multicore embedded architectures revealed that the multicore architectures with shared LLCs become more area and power efficient as compared to the architectures with private LLCs as the number of processor cores in the architecture increases.

Part Three

Optimization

6

Optimization Approaches in Distributed Embedded Wireless Sensor Networks*

Embedded wireless sensor networks (EWSNs) are distributed embedded systems consisting of embedded sensor nodes with attached sensors to sense data about a phenomenon and communicate with neighboring sensor nodes over wireless links (we refer to wireless sensor networks (WSNs) as EWSNs since sensor nodes are embedded in the physical environment/system). Due to advancements in silicon technology, micro-electro-mechanical systems (MEMS), wireless communications, computer networking, and digital electronics, distributed EWSNs have been proliferating in a wide variety of application domains. These application domains include military, health, ecology, environment, industrial automation, civil engineering, and medical, to name a few. This wide application diversity combined with complex embedded sensor node architectures, functionality requirements, and highly constrained and harsh operating environments makes EWSN design very challenging.

One critical EWSN design challenge involves meeting *application requirements* such as lifetime, reliability, throughput, and delay (responsiveness) for a myriad of application domains. Furthermore, EWSN applications tend to have competing requirements, which exacerbate design challenges. For example, a high-priority security/defense system may have both high responsiveness and long lifetime requirements. The mechanisms needed for high responsiveness typically drain battery life quickly, thus making long lifetime difficult to achieve given limited energy reserves.

Commercial off-the-shelf (COTS) embedded sensor nodes have difficulty in meeting application requirements because of the generic design traits necessary for wide application diversity. COTS sensor nodes are mass-produced to optimize cost and are not specialized for any

*A portion of this chapter appeared in: Arslan Munir and Ann Gordon-Ross, Optimization Approaches in Wireless Sensor Networks, CH 13 in *Sustainable Wireless Sensor Networks*, Winston Seah and Yen Kheng Tan (Eds.), ISBN: 978-953-307-297-5, INTECH (Open Access Publisher), pp. 313–338, December 2010.

Table 6.1   EWSN optimizations at different design levels

Design level	Optimizations
Architecture level	Bridging, sensor web, tunneling
Component level	Parameter-tuning (e.g., processor voltage and frequency, sensing frequency)
Data link-level	Load balancing and throughput, power/energy
Network level	Query dissemination, data aggregation, real-time, network topology, resource adaptive, dynamic network reprogramming
Operating system level	Event-driven, dynamic power management, fault-tolerance

particular application. Fortunately, COTS sensor nodes contain *tunable parameters* (e.g., processor voltage and frequency, sensing frequency) whose values can be specialized to meet application requirements. However, optimizing these tunable parameters is left to the application designer.

Optimization techniques at different design levels (e.g., sensor node hardware and software, data link layer, routing, operating system (OS)) assist designers in meeting application requirements. EWSN optimization techniques can be generally categorized as *static* or *dynamic*. Static optimizations optimize an EWSN at deployment time and remain fixed for the EWSN's lifetime. These optimizations are suitable for stable/predictable applications, whereas they are inflexible and do not adapt to the changing application requirements and environmental stimuli. Dynamic optimizations provide more flexibility by continuously optimizing an EWSN/embedded sensor node during runtime, providing better adaptation to changing application requirements and actual environmental stimuli.

This chapter introduces distributed EWSNs from an optimization perspective and explores optimization strategies employed in EWSNs at different design levels to meet application requirements as summarized in Table 6.1. We present a typical WSN architecture and architectural-level optimizations in Section 6.1. We describe sensor node component-level optimizations and tunable parameters in Section 6.2. Next, we discuss data link-level medium access control (MAC) optimizations and network-level routing optimizations in Sections 6.3 and 6.4, respectively, and OS-level optimizations in Section 6.5. After presenting these optimization techniques, we focus on dynamic optimizations for WSNs. There exists much previous work on dynamic optimizations (e.g., [185–188]), but most previous work targets the processor or cache subsystem in computing systems. WSN dynamic optimizations present additional challenges because of a unique design space, stringent design constraints, and varying operating environments. We discuss the current state of the art in dynamic optimization techniques in Section 6.6. Finally, Section 6.7 concludes the chapter.

6.1   Architecture-Level Optimizations

Figure 6.1 shows an integrated EWSN architecture (i.e., an EWSN integrated with external networks). Embedded sensor nodes are distributed in a *sensor field* to observe a phenomenon of interest (i.e., environment, vehicle, object). Embedded sensor nodes in the sensor field form an ad hoc wireless network and transmit the sensed information (data or statistics) gathered

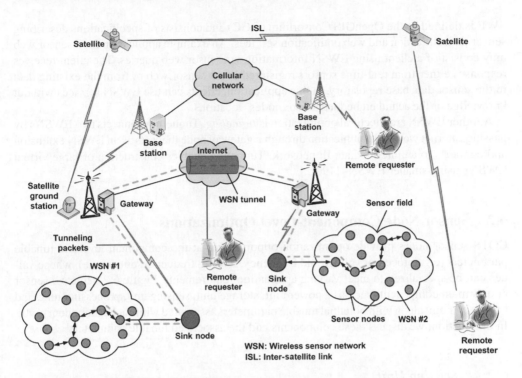

Figure 6.1   Embedded wireless sensor network architecture

via attached sensors about the observed phenomenon to a base station or *sink node*. The sink node relays the collected data to the remote requester (user) via an arbitrary computer communication network such as a gateway and the associated communication network. Since different applications require different communication network infrastructures to efficiently transfer sensed data, EWSN designers can optimize the communication architecture by determining the appropriate topology (number and distribution of embedded sensor nodes within the EWSN) and the communication infrastructure (e.g., gateway nodes) to meet the application's requirements.

An infrastructure-level optimization called *bridging* facilitates the transfer of sensed data to remote requesters residing at different locations by connecting the EWSN to external networks such as Internet, cellular, and satellite networks. Bridging can be accomplished by overlaying a sensor network with portions of the IP network where gateway nodes encapsulate sensor node packets with transmission control protocol or user datagram protocol/Internet protocol (TCP/IP or UDP/IP).

Since embedded sensor nodes can be integrated with the Internet via bridging, this EWSN–Internet integration can be exploited to form a *sensor web*. In a sensor web, embedded sensor nodes form a web view where data repositories, sensors, and image devices are discoverable, accessible, and controllable via the World Wide Web (WWW). The sensor web can use service-oriented architectures (SoAs) or sensor web enablement (SWE) standards [189]. SoAs leverage extensible markup language (XML) and simple object access protocol (SOAP) standards to describe, discover, and invoke services from heterogeneous platforms.

SWE is defined by the OpenGIS Consortium (OGC) and consists of specifications describing sensor data collection and web notification services. An example application for a sensor web may consist of a client using EWSN information via sensor web queries. The client receives responses either from real-time sensors registered in the sensor web or from the existing data in the sensor data base repository. In this application, clients can use EWSN services without knowledge of the actual embedded sensor nodes' locations.

Another EWSN architectural optimization is *tunneling*. Tunneling connects two EWSNs by passing Internet work communication through a gateway node that acts as an EWSN extension and connects to an intermediate IP network. Tunneling enables construction of large virtual EWSNs using smaller EWSNs [190].

6.2   Sensor Node Component-Level Optimizations

COTS sensor nodes provide optimization opportunities at the component level via tunable parameters (e.g., processor voltage and frequency, sensing frequency, duty cycle), whose values can be specialized to meet varying application requirements. Figure 6.2 depicts a sensor node's main components such as a power unit, storage unit, sensing unit, processing unit, and transceiver unit along with potential tunable parameters associated with each component [190]. In this section, we discuss these components and the associated tunable parameters.

6.2.1   Sensing Unit

The sensing unit senses the phenomenon of interest using sensors and an analog-to-digital converter (ADC). The sensing unit can contain a variety of sensors depending upon an EWSN application since there are sensors for virtually every physical quantity (e.g., weight, electric current, voltage, temperature, velocity, and acceleration). A sensor's construction can exploit a variety of physical effects including the law of induction (voltage generation in an electric field) and photoelectric effects. Recent advances in EWSNs can be attributed to the large variety of available sensors. ADCs convert the analog signals produced by sensors to digital signals, which serve as input to the processing unit.

The sensing unit's tunable parameters can control power consumption by changing the sensing frequency and the speed-resolution product of the ADC. Sensing frequency can be tuned to provide constant sensing, periodic sensing, and/or sporadic sensing. In constant sensing, sensors sense continuously and sensing frequency is limited only by the sensor hardware's design capabilities. Periodic sensing consumes less power than constant sensing because periodic sensing is duty cycle based where the sensor node takes readings after every T seconds. Sporadic sensing consumes less power than periodic sensing because sporadic sensing is typically event-triggered by either external (e.g., environment) or internal (e.g., OS-based or hardware-based) interrupts. The speed-resolution product of the ADC can be tuned to provide high speed-resolution with higher power consumption (e.g., seismic sensors use 24-bit converters with a conversion rate on the order of thousands of samples per second) or low speed-resolution with lower power consumption.

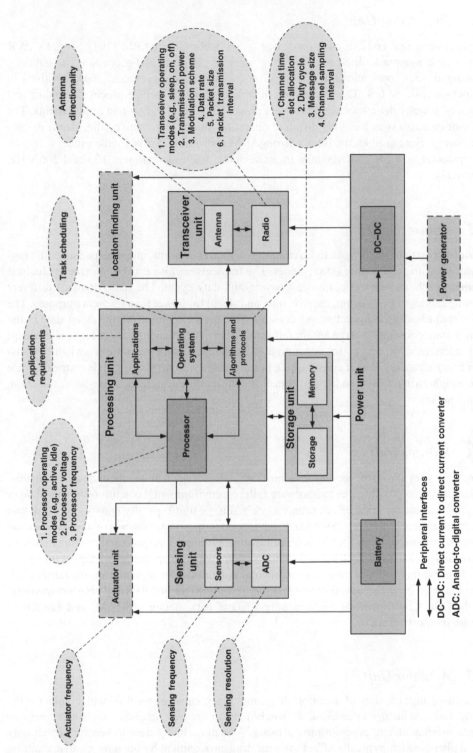

Figure 6.2 Embedded sensor node architecture with tunable parameters

6.2.2 Processing Unit

The processing unit consists of a processor (e.g., Intel's StrongARM [191], Atmel's AVR [192]) whose main tasks include controlling sensors, gathering and processing sensed data, executing EWSN applications, and managing communication protocols and algorithms in conjunction with the OS. The processor's tunable parameters include processor voltage and frequency, which can be specialized to meet power budget and throughput requirements. The processor can also switch among different operating modes (e.g., active, idle, sleep) to conserve energy. For example, the Intel's StrongARM consumes 75 mW in idle mode, 0.16 mW in sleep mode, and 240 and 400 mW in active mode while operating at 133 and 206 MHz, respectively.

6.2.3 Transceiver Unit

The transceiver unit consists of a radio (transceiver) and an antenna, and is responsible for communicating with neighboring sensor nodes. The transceiver unit's tunable parameters include modulation scheme, data rate, transmit power, and duty cycle. The radio contains different operating modes (e.g., transmit, receive, idle, and sleep) for power management purposes. The sleep state provides the lowest power consumption, but switching from the sleep state to the transmit state consumes a large amount of power. The power-saving modes (e.g., idle, sleep) are characterized by their power consumption and latency overhead (time to switch to transmit or receive modes). Power consumption in the transceiver unit also depends on the distance to the neighboring sensor nodes and transmission interferences (e.g., solar flare, radiation, channel noise).

6.2.4 Storage Unit

Sensor nodes contain a storage unit for temporary data storage when immediate data transmission is not always possible due to hardware failures, environmental conditions, physical layer jamming, and energy reserves. A sensor node's storage unit typically consists of Flash and static random access memory (SRAM). Flash is used for persistent storage of application code and text segments, whereas SRAM is for runtime data storage. One potential optimization uses an extremely low-frequency (ELF) Flash file system, which is specifically adapted for sensor node data logging and operating environmental conditions. Storage unit optimization challenges include power conservation and memory resources (limited data and program memory, e.g., the MICA2 sensor node contains only 4 KB of data memory (SRAM) and 128 KB of program memory (Flash)).

6.2.5 Actuator Unit

The actuator unit consists of actuators (e.g., mobilizer, camera pan tilt), which enhance the sensing task. Actuators open/close a switch/relay to control functions such as camera or antenna orientation and repositioning sensors. Actuators, in contrast to sensors which only sense a phenomenon, typically affect the operating environment by opening a valve, emitting sound, or physically moving the sensor node. The actuator unit's tunable parameter is actuator frequency, which can be adjusted according to application requirements.

6.2.6 Location Finding Unit

The location finding unit determines a sensor node's location. Depending on the application requirements and available resources, the location finding unit can be either global positioning system (GPS) based or ad hoc positioning system (APS) based. The GPS-based location finding unit is highly accurate, but has high monetary cost and requires direct line of sight between the sensor node and satellites. The APS-based location finding unit determines a sensor node's position with respect to *landmarks*. Landmarks are typically GPS-based position-aware sensor nodes, and landmark information is propagated in a multiple-hop manner. A sensor node in direct communication with a landmark estimates its distance from a landmark based on the received signal strength. A sensor node two hops away from a landmark estimates its distance from the landmark using message propagation of the distance estimate of the sensor node one hop away from the landmark. When a sensor node has distance estimates to three or more landmarks, the sensor node computes its own position as a centroid of the landmarks.

6.2.7 Power Unit

The power unit supplies power to a sensor node and determines a sensor node's lifetime. The power unit consists of a battery and a DC–DC converter. The electrode material and the diffusion rate of the electrolyte's active material affect the battery capacity. The DC–DC converter provides a constant supply voltage to the sensor node.

6.3 Data Link-Level Medium Access Control Optimizations

Data link-level MAC manages the shared wireless channel and establishes data communication links between embedded sensor nodes in an EWSN. Traditional MAC schemes emphasize high quality of service (QoS) [193] or bandwidth efficiency [194, 195]; however, EWSN platforms have different priorities [196], thus inhibiting the straightforward adoption of the existing MAC protocols [197]. For example, since EWSN lifetime is typically an important application requirement and batteries are not easily interchangeable/rechargeable, energy consumption is a primary design constraint for EWSNs. Similarly, since the network infrastructure is subject to change because of dying nodes, self-organization and failure recovery are important. To meet application requirements, EWSN designers tune MAC layer protocol parameters (e.g., channel access schedule, message size, duty cycle, and receiver power-off). This section discusses MAC protocols for EWSNs with reference to their tunable parameters and optimization objectives.

6.3.1 Load Balancing and Throughput Optimizations

MAC layer protocols can adjust wireless channel slot allocation to optimize throughput while maintaining the traffic load balance between sensor nodes. A *fairness* index measures load balancing or the uniformity of packets delivered to the sink node from all the senders. For the perfectly uniform case (ideal load balance), the fairness index is 1. MAC layer protocols that adjust channel slot allocation for load balancing and throughput optimizations include Traffic-Adaptive Medium Access (TRAMA) protocol [198], Berkeley Media Access Control (B-MAC) [199], and Zebra MAC (Z-MAC) [200].

TRAMA is a MAC protocol that adjusts channel time slot allocation to achieve load balancing while focusing on providing collision-free medium access. TRAMA divides the channel access into random and scheduled access periods and aims to increase the utilization of the scheduled access period using time division multiple access (TDMA). TRAMA calculates a message-digest algorithm 5 (MD5) hash for every one-hop and two-hop neighboring sensor nodes to determine a node's priority. Experiments comparing TRAMA with both contention-based protocols (IEEE 802.11 and sensor-MAC (S-MAC) [201]) and a scheduled-based protocol (node-activation multiple access (NAMA) [202]) revealed that TRAMA achieved higher throughput than contention-based protocols and a comparable throughput with NAMA [203].

B-MAC is a carrier sense MAC protocol for EWSNs. B-MAC adjusts the duty cycle and time slot allocation for throughput optimization and high channel utilization. B-MAC supports on-the-fly reconfiguration of the MAC backoff strategy for performance (e.g., throughput, latency, power conservation) optimization. Results from B-MAC and S-MAC implementations on TinyOS using MICA2 motes indicated that B-MAC outperformed S-MAC by $3.5 \times$ on average [199]. No sensor node was allocated more than 15% additional bandwidth as compared with other nodes, thus ensuring fairness (load balancing).

Z-MAC is a hybrid MAC protocol that combines the strengths of TDMA and carrier sense multiple access (CSMA) and offsets their weaknesses. Z-MAC allocates time slots at sensor node deployment time by using an efficient channel scheduling algorithm to optimize throughput, but this mechanism requires high initial overhead. A time slot's *owner* is the sensor node allocated to that time slot, and all other nodes are called *non-owners* of that time slot. Multiple owners are possible for a given time slot because Z-MAC allows any two sensor nodes beyond their two-hop neighborhoods to own the same time slot. Unlike TDMA, a sensor node may transmit during any time slot, but slot owners have a higher priority. Experimental results from Z-MAC implementation on both ns−2 and TinyOS/MICA2 indicated that Z-MAC performed better than B-MAC under medium-to-high contention, but exhibited worse performance than B-MAC under low contention (inherits from TDMA-based channel access). The fairness index of Z-MAC was between 0.7 and 1, whereas that of B-MAC was between 0.2 and 0.3 for a large number of senders [200].

6.3.2 Power/Energy Optimizations

MAC layer protocols can adapt their transceiver operating modes (e.g., sleep, on, and off) and duty cycle for reduced power and/or energy consumption. MAC layer protocols that adjust duty cycle for power/energy optimization include power aware multi-access with signaling (PAMAS) [190, 204], S-MAC [201], timeout-MAC (T-MAC) [205], and B-MAC.

PAMAS is a MAC layer protocol for EWSNs that adjusts the duty cycle to minimize radio on time and optimize power consumption. PAMAS uses separate data and control channels (the control channel manages the request to send/clear to send (RTS/CTS) signals or the receiver busy tone). If a sensor node receives an RTS message on the signaling channel while the sensor node is receiving a message on the data channel, then the sensor node responds with a busy tone on the signaling channel. This mechanism avoids collisions and results in energy savings. The PAMAS protocol powers off the receiver if either the transmit message queue is empty and the node's neighbor is transmitting or the transmit message queue is not empty but at least one neighbor is transmitting and one neighbor is receiving. EWSN simulations with 10–20 sensor nodes with 512-byte data packets, 32-byte RTS/CTS packets, and 64-byte busy tone signal packets revealed power savings between 10% and 70% [206]. PAMAS optimization challenges include implementation complexity and the associated area cost because the separate control channel requires a second transceiver and duplexer.

The S-MAC protocol tunes the duty cycle and message size for energy conservation. S-MAC minimizes wasted energy due to *frame* (packet) collisions (since collided frames must be retransmitted with additional energy cost), overhearing (a sensor node receiving/listening to a frame destined for another node), control frame overhead, and idle listening (channel monitoring to identify possible incoming messages destined for that node). S-MAC uses a periodic sleep and listen (sleep–sense) strategy defined by the duty cycle. S-MAC avoids frame collisions by using virtual sense (network allocation vector (NAV)-based) and physical carrier sense (receiver listening to the channel) similar to IEEE 802.11. S-MAC avoids overhearing by instructing interfering sensor nodes to switch to sleep mode after hearing an RTS or CTS packet [204]. Experiments conducted on Rene Motes [207] for a traffic load comprising of sent messages every 1–10 s revealed that an IEEE 802.11-based MAC consumed 2×–6× more energy than S-MAC [208].

T-MAC adjusts the duty cycle dynamically for power-efficient operation. T-MAC allows a variable sleep–sense duty cycle as opposed to the fixed duty cycle used in S-MAC (e.g., 10% sense and 90% sleep). The dynamic duty cycle further reduces the idle listening period. The sensor node switches to sleep mode when there is no activation event (e.g., data reception, timer expiration, communication activity sensing, or impending data reception knowledge through neighbors' RTS/CTS) for a predetermined period of time. Experimental results obtained from T-MAC protocol implementation on OMNeT++ [209] to model EYES sensor nodes [210] revealed that under homogeneous load (sensor nodes sent packets with 20- to 100-byte payloads to their neighbors at random), both T-MAC and S-MAC yielded 98% energy savings as compared to CSMA, whereas T-MAC outperformed S-MAC by 5× under variable load [203].

B-MAC adjusts the duty cycle for power conservation using channel assessment information. B-MAC duty cycles the radio through a periodic channel sampling mechanism known as low power listening (LPL). Each time a sensor node wakes up, the sensor node turns on the radio and checks for channel activity. If the sensor node detects activity, the sensor node powers up and stays awake for the time required to receive an incoming packet. If no packet is received, indicating inaccurate activity detection, a time out forces the sensor node to sleep mode. B-MAC requires an accurate clear channel assessment to achieve low power operation. Experimental results obtained from B-MAC and S-MAC implementations on TinyOS using MICA2 motes revealed that B-MAC power consumption was within 25% of S-MAC for low throughputs (below 45 bits/s), whereas B-MAC outperformed S-MAC by 60% for higher throughputs. Results indicated that B-MAC performed better than S-MAC for latencies under 6 s, whereas S-MAC yielded lower power consumption as latency approached 10 s [199].

6.4 Network-Level Data Dissemination and Routing Protocol Optimizations

One commonality across diverse EWSN application domains is the embedded sensor node's task to sense and collect data about a phenomenon and transmit the data to the sink node. To meet application requirements, this data dissemination requires energy-efficient routing protocols to establish communication paths between the embedded sensor nodes and the sink node. Typically, harsh operating environments coupled with stringent resource and energy constraints make data dissemination and routing challenging for EWSNs. Ideally, data dissemination and routing protocols should target energy efficiency, robustness, and scalability. To achieve these optimization objectives, routing protocols adjust transmission power, routing strategies, and leverage by either single-hop or multiple-hop routing. In this section, we discuss protocols, which optimize data dissemination and routing in EWSNs.

6.4.1   Query Dissemination Optimizations

Query dissemination (transmission of a sensed data query/request from a sink node to a sensor node) and data forwarding (transmission of sensed data from a sensor node to a sink node) require routing layer optimizations. Protocols that optimize query dissemination and data forwarding include Declarative Routing Protocol (DRP) [211], directed diffusion [212], GRAdient routing (GRAd) [213], GRAdient Broadcast (GRAB) [214], and energy aware routing (EAR) [203, 215].

DRP targets energy efficiency by exploiting in-network aggregation (multiple data items are aggregated as they are forwarded by sensor nodes). Figure 6.3 shows in-network data aggregation where sensor node I aggregates sensed data from source nodes A, B, and C; sensor node J aggregates sensed data from source nodes D and E; and sensor node K aggregates sensed data from source nodes F, G, and H. The sensor node L aggregates the sensed data from sensor nodes I, J, and K and transmits the aggregated data to the sink node. DRP uses reverse path

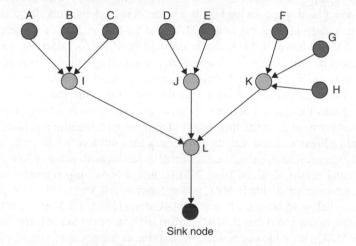

Sink node

Figure 6.3   Data aggregation

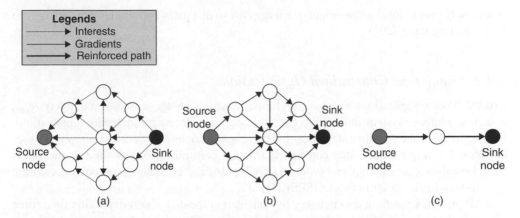

Figure 6.4 Directed diffusion: (a) interest propagation, (b) initial gradient setup, and (c) data delivery along the reinforced path

forwarding where data reports (packets containing sensed data in response to query) flow in the reverse direction of the query propagation to reach the sink.

Directed diffusion targets energy efficiency, scalability, and robustness under network dynamics using reverse path forwarding. Directed diffusion builds a shared mesh to deliver data from multiple sources to multiple sinks. The sink node disseminates the query, a process referred to as *interest propagation* (Fig. 6.4(a)). When a sensor node receives a query from a neighboring node, the sensor node sets up a vector called the *gradient* from itself to the neighboring node and directs future data flows on this gradient (Fig. 6.4(b)). The sink node receives an initial batch of data reports along multiple paths and uses a mechanism called *reinforcement* to select a path with the best forwarding quality (Fig. 6.4(c)). To handle network dynamics such as sensor node failures, each data source floods data reports periodically at lower rates to maintain alternate paths. Directed diffusion challenges include formation of initial gradients and wasted energy due to redundant data flows to maintain alternate paths.

GRAd optimizes data forwarding and uses cost-field based forwarding where the cost metric is based on the hop count (i.e., sensor nodes closer to the sink node have smaller costs and those farther away have higher costs). The sink node floods a REQUEST message, and the data source broadcasts the data report containing the requested information (information is based on the data sensed by the data source). The neighbors with smaller costs forward the report to the sink node. GRAd drawbacks include wasted energy due to redundant data report copies reaching the sink node.

GRAB optimizes data forwarding and uses cost-field based forwarding where the cost metric denotes the total energy required to send a packet to the sink node. GRAB was designed for harsh environments with high channel error rate and frequent sensor node failures. GRAB controls redundancy by controlling the width (number of routes from the source sensor node to the sink node) of the forwarding mesh but requires that sensor nodes make assumptions about the energy required to transmit a data report to a neighboring node.

EAR optimizes data forwarding and uses cost-field based forwarding where the cost metric denotes energy per neighbor. EAR optimization objectives are load balancing and energy conservation. EAR makes forwarding decisions probabilistically where the assigned probability is inversely proportional to the neighbor energy cost so that paths consuming more energy are used less frequently [203].

6.4.2   Real-Time Constrained Optimizations

Critical EWSN applications may have real-time requirements for sensed data delivery (e.g., a security/defense system monitoring enemy troops or a forest fire detection application). Failure to meet the real-time deadlines for these applications can have catastrophic consequences. Routing protocols that consider the timing constraints for real-time requirements include real-time architecture and protocol (RAP) [216] and a stateless protocol for real-time communication in sensor networks (SPEED) [217].

RAP provides real-time data delivery by considering the data report expiration time (time after which the data is of little or no use) and the remaining distance the data report needs to travel to reach the sink node. RAP calculates the desired velocity $v = d/t$ where d and t denote the destination distance and packet lifetime, respectively. The desired velocity is updated at each hop to reflect the data report's urgency. A sensor node uses multiple first-in-first-out (FIFO) queues where each queue accepts reports of velocities within a certain range and then schedules transmissions according to a report's degree of urgency [203].

SPEED provides real-time data delivery and uses an exponentially weighted moving average for delay calculation. Given a data report with velocity v, SPEED calculates the speed v_i of the report if the neighbor N_i is selected as the next hop and then selects a neighbor with $v_i > v$ to forward the report [203].

6.4.3   Network Topology Optimizations

Routing protocols can adjust radio transmission power to control network topology (based on routing paths). Low-Energy-Adaptive Clustering Hierarchy (LEACH) [218] optimizes the network topology for reduced energy consumption by adjusting the radio's transmission power. LEACH uses a hybrid single-hop and multiple-hop communication paradigm. The sensor nodes use multiple-hop communication to transmit data reports to a cluster head (LEACH determines the cluster head using a randomized distributed algorithm). The cluster head forwards data to the sink node using long-range radio transmission.

6.4.4   Resource-Adaptive Optimizations

Routing protocols can adapt routing activities in accordance with the available resources. Sensor Protocols for Information via Negotiation (SPIN) [219] optimizes performance efficiency by using data negotiation and resource adaptation. In data negotiation, sensor nodes associate metadata with nodes and exchange this metadata before actual data transmission begins. The sensor nodes interested in the data content, based on metadata, request the actual data. This data negotiation ensures that data is sent only to interested nodes. SPIN allows sensor nodes to adjust routing activities according to the available energy resources. At low-energy levels, sensor nodes reduce or eliminate certain activities (e.g., forwarding of metadata and data packets) [196].

6.5   Operating System-Level Optimizations

An embedded sensor node's OS presents optimization challenges because embedded sensor node operation falls between single-application devices that typically do not need an OS and general-purpose devices with resources to run traditional embedded OSs. An embedded sensor node's OS manages processor, radio, I/O buses, and Flash memory and provides hardware abstraction to application software, task coordination, power management, and networking services. In this section, we discuss several optimizations provided by existing OSs for embedded sensor nodes [196].

6.5.1   Event-Driven Optimizations

Embedded sensor nodes respond to events by controlling sensing and actuation activity. Since sensor nodes are event-driven, it is important to optimize the OS for event handling. EWSN OSs optimized for event handling include TinyOS [220] and PicOS [221].

TinyOS operates using an event-driven model (tasks are executed based on events). TinyOS is written in the nesC programming language and allows application software to access hardware directly. TinyOS's advantages include simple OS code, energy efficiency, and a small memory foot print. TinyOS challenges include introduced complexity in application development and porting of existing C code to TinyOS.

PicOS is an event-driven OS written in C and designed for limited memory microcontrollers. PicOS tasks are structured as a finite state machine (FSM) and state transitions are triggered by events. PicOS is effective for reactive applications whose primary role is to react to events. PicOS supports multitasking and has small memory requirements but is not suitable for real-time applications.

6.5.2   Dynamic Power Management

A sensor node's OS can control hardware components to optimize power consumption. Examples include Operating System-directed Power Management (OSPM) [222] and MagnetOS [223], each of which provide mechanisms for dynamic power management. OSPM offers greedy-based dynamic power management, which switches the sensor node to a sleep state when idle. Sleep states provide energy conservation; however, transition to sleep state has the overhead of storing the processor state and requires a finite amount of wake-up time. OSPM greedy-based adaptive sleep mechanism disadvantages include wake-up delay and potentially missing events during sleep time. MagnetOS provides two online power-aware algorithms and an adaptive mechanism for applications to effectively utilize the sensor node's resources.

6.5.3   Fault Tolerance

Since maintenance and repair of embedded sensor nodes is typically not feasible after deployment, embedded sensor nodes require fault-tolerant mechanisms for reliable operation. MANTIS [224] is a multithreaded OS that provides fault-tolerant isolation between applications by not allowing a blocking task to prevent the execution of other tasks. In the absence of fault-tolerant isolation, if one task executes a conditional loop whose logical condition is never satisfied, then that task will execute in an infinite loop blocking all other tasks. MANTIS facilitates simple application development and allows dynamic reprogramming to update the sensor node's binary code. MANTIS offers a multimodal prototyping environment for testing EWSN applications by providing a remote shell and command server to enable inspection of the sensor node's memory and status remotely. MANTIS challenges include context switch time, stack memory overhead (since each thread requires one stack), and high energy consumption.

6.6   Dynamic Optimizations

Dynamic optimizations enable in situ parameter tuning and empower the embedded sensor node to adapt to the changing application requirements and environmental stimuli throughout the embedded sensor node's lifetime. Dynamic optimizations are important because application requirements change over time and environmental stimuli/conditions may not be accurately predicted at design time. Although some OS, MAC layer, and routing optimizations discussed in prior sections of this chapter are dynamic in nature, in this section we present additional dynamic optimization techniques for EWSNs.

6.6.1   Dynamic Voltage and Frequency Scaling

Dynamic voltage and frequency scaling (DVFS) adjusts a sensor node's processor voltage and frequency to optimize energy consumption. DVFS trades off performance for reduced energy consumption by considering that the peak computation (instruction execution) rate is much higher than the application's average throughput requirement and that sensor nodes are based on CMOS logic, which has a voltage-dependent maximum operating frequency. Min et al. [225] demonstrated that a DVFS system containing a voltage scheduler running in tandem with the operating system's task scheduler resulted in a 60% reduction in energy consumption. Yuan and Qu [226] studied a DVFS system for sensor nodes that required the sensor nodes to insert additional information (e.g., packet length, expected processing time, and deadline) into the data packet's header. The receiving sensor node utilized this information to select an appropriate processor voltage and frequency to minimize the overall energy consumption.

6.6.2   Software-Based Dynamic Optimizations

Software can provide dynamic optimizations using techniques such as duty cycling, batching, hierarchy, and redundancy reduction. Software can control the *duty cycle* so that sensor nodes are powered in a cyclic manner to reduce the average power draw. In *batching*, multiple operations are buffered and then executed in a burst to reduce startup overhead cost. Software can arrange operations in a *hierarchy* based on energy consumption and then invoke low-energy operations before high-energy operations. Software can reduce *redundancy* by compression, data aggregation, and/or message suppression. Kogekar et al. [227] proposed an approach for software reconfiguration in EWSNs. The authors modeled the EWSN operation space (defined by the EWSN software components' models and application requirements) and defined reconfiguration as the process of switching from one point in the operation space to another.

6.6.3   Dynamic Network Reprogramming

Dynamic network reprogramming reprograms embedded sensor nodes to change/modify tasks by disseminating code in accordance with changing environmental stimuli. Since recollection and reprogramming are not a feasible option for most sensor nodes, dynamic network reprogramming enables the sensor nodes to perform different tasks. For example, an EWSN initially deployed for measuring relative humidity can measure temperature statistics after dynamic reprogramming. The MANTIS OS possesses the dynamic reprogramming ability (Section 6.5.3).

6.7   Chapter Summary

In this chapter, we discussed distributed EWSNs from an optimization perspective and explored optimization strategies employed in EWSNs at different design levels to meet application requirements. We discussed architectural-level optimizations in EWSNs, particulary tunneling and bridging, which could be exploited to form sensor web. We elaborated sensor node component-level optimizations that leveraged tunable parameters (e.g., processor voltage and frequency, sensing frequency, duty cycle, etc.), whose values could be specialized to meet varying application requirements. We presented data link-level MAC optimizations that exploited MAC layer protocol parameters (e.g., channel access schedule, message size, duty cycle, and receiver power-off). We illustrated network-level routing optimizations and routing protocols that adjusted transmission power and routing strategies for improving energy efficiency, robustness, and scalability. We illustrated OS-level optimizations of sensor nodes, such as power management and fault tolerance, via examples of state-of-the-art sensor node OSs. Finally, we described dynamic optimizations such as DVFS and dynamic network reprogramming.

7

High-Performance Energy-Efficient Multicore-Based Parallel Embedded Computing*

Embedded system design is traditionally power-centric, but there has been a recent shift toward high-performance embedded computing (HPEC) due to the proliferation of compute-intensive embedded applications. For example, the signal processing for a 3G mobile handset requires 35–40 giga operations per second (GOPS) for a 14.4 Mbps channel and 210–290 GOPS for a 100 Mbps orthogonal frequency-division multiplexing (OFDM) channel. Considering the limited energy of a mobile handset battery, these performance levels must be met with a power dissipation budget of approximately 1 W, which translates to a performance efficiency of 25 mW/GOPS or 25 pJ/operation for the 3G receiver and 3–5 pJ/operation for the OFDM receiver [5, 6]. These demanding and competing power–performance requirements make modern embedded system design challenging.

The high-performance energy-efficient embedded computing (HPEEC) domain addresses the unique design challenges of high-performance and low-power/energy embedded computing. The HPEEC domain can be termed as high-performance *green* computing; however, green may refer to a bigger notion of environmental impact. These design challenges are competing because high performance typically requires maximum processor speeds with enormous energy consumption, whereas low power typically requires nominal or low processor speeds that offer modest performance. HPEEC requires thorough consideration of the thermal design power (TDP) and processor frequency relationship while selecting an appropriate processor for an embedded application. For example, decreasing the processor frequency by a fraction of the maximum operating frequency (e.g., reducing from 3.16 to 3.0 GHz) can cause

---

*A portion of this chapter is copyrighted by IEEE. The definitive version appeared in: Arslan Munir, Sanjay Ranka, and Ann Gordon-Ross, High-Performance Energy-Efficient Multi-core Embedded Computing, *IEEE Transactions on Parallel and Distributed Systems (TPDS)*, vol. 23, no. 4, pp. 684–700, April 2012. URL http://ieeexplore.ieee.org/xpl/articleDetails.jsp?arnumber=5963659. ©[2012] IEEE. Reprinted with permission from IEEE as we are the authors of this work.

Modeling and Optimization of Parallel and Distributed Embedded Systems, First Edition.
Arslan Munir, Ann Gordon-Ross and Sanjay Ranka.
© 2016 John Wiley & Sons, Ltd. Published 2016 by John Wiley & Sons, Ltd.

10% performance degradation but can decrease power consumption by 30–40% [7]. To meet HPEEC power–performance requirements, embedded system design has transitioned from a single-core to a multicore paradigm that favors multiple low-power cores running at low processors speeds rather than a single high-speed power-hungry core.

Chip multiprocessors (CMPs) provide a scalable HPEEC platform as performance can be increased by increasing the number of cores as long as the increase in the number of cores offsets the clock frequency reduction by maintaining a given performance level with less power [8]. Multiprocessor systems-on-chip (MPSoCs), which are multiprocessor version of systems-on-chip (SoCs), are another alternative HPEEC platform, which provide an unlimited combination of homogeneous and heterogeneous cores. Although both CMPs and MPSoCs are HPEEC platforms, MPSoCs differ from CMPs in that MPSoCs provide custom architectures (including specialized instruction sets) tailored for meeting peculiar requirements of specific embedded applications (e.g., real-time, throughput-intensive, reliability-constrained). Both CMPs and MPSoCs rely on HPEEC hardware/software techniques for delivering high performance per watt and meeting diverse application requirements.

Although the literature discusses high-performance computing (HPC) for supercomputers [228–231], there exists little discussion on HPEEC [232]. In embedded systems, mostly high performance and energy efficiency are attained via multicore architectures, which induce parallel computing in embedded systems. The integration of HPEEC and parallel computing can be coined as high-performance energy-efficient parallel embedded computing (HPEPEC).

The distinction between HPC and parallel computing for supercomputers and HPEPEC is important because performance is the most significant metric for supercomputers with less emphasis given to energy efficiency, whereas energy efficiency is a primary concern for HPEPEC. For example, each of the 10 most powerful contemporary supercomputers has a peak power requirement of up to 10 MW, which is equivalent to the power needs of a city with a population of 40,000 [232, 233]. To acknowledge the increasing significance of energy-efficient computing, the Green500 list ranks supercomputers using the FLOPS per watt performance metric [234]. Table 7.1 lists the top 5 green supercomputers along with their top 500 supercomputer ranking. The table shows that the top performing supercomputers

Table 7.1   Top Green500 and Top500 supercomputers as of November 2014 [233, 234]

Supercomputer	Green500 rank	Top500 rank	Total cores	Power efficiency (MFLOPS/W)	Theoretical peak performance (TFLOPS)	Peak power (kW)
L-CSC (GSI Helmholtz Center, Germany)	1	168	10,976	5271.81	593.6	57.15
Suiren (High Energy Accelerator Research Organization/KEK, Japan)	2	369	262,784	4945.63	395.3	37.83
TSUBAME-KFC (GSIC Center, Tokyo Institute of Technology, Japan)	3	392	2992	4447.58	239.6	35.39
Storm1 (Cray Inc., USA)	4	361	3080	3962.73	259.4	44.54
Wilkes (Cambridge University, UK)	5	241	5120	3631.70	367.6	52.62

are not necessarily energy efficient [233, 234]. Table 7.1 indicates that most of the top green supercomputers consist of low-power embedded processor clusters aiming at achieving high performance per watt and high performance per unit area [235].

Figure 7.1 gives an overview of the HPEPEC domain, which spans architectural approaches to middleware and software approaches. In this chapter, we focus on high-performance and energy-efficient techniques that are applicable to embedded systems (CMPs, SoCs, or MPSoCs) to meet particular application requirements. Although the main focus of the chapter is on embedded systems, many of the energy and performance issues are equally applicable to supercomputers since state-of-the-art supercomputers leverage embedded processors/chips (e.g., Tianhe-2 supercomputer (rank 1 supercomputer as of November 2014 and located at National Supercomputer Center in Guangzhou, China) comprises 3,120,000 processor cores leveraging Intel Xeon E5-2692v2 12-core CMPs operating at 2.2 GHz [233]). However, we summarize several differences between supercomputing applications and embedded applications as follows:

(1) Supercomputing applications tend to be highly data parallel where the goal is to decompose a task with a large data set across many processing units where each subtask operates on a portion of the data set. On the other hand, embedded applications tend to consist of many tasks where each task is executed on a single processing unit and may have arrival and deadline constraints.
(2) Supercomputing applications tend to focus on leveraging a large number of processors, whereas the scale of embedded applications is generally much smaller.
(3) Supercomputing applications' main optimization objective is performance (although energy is increasingly becoming a very important secondary metric), while performance and energy are equally important objectives for embedded applications. Also, reliability and fault tolerance play a more important role in embedded applications as compared to supercomputing applications.

The HPEPEC domain benefits from architectural innovations in processor core layouts (e.g., heterogeneous CMP, tiled multicore architectures), memory design (e.g., transactional memory, cache partitioning), and interconnection networks (e.g., packet-switched, photonic, wireless). The HPEPEC platforms provide hardware support for functionalities that can be controlled by middleware such as dynamic voltage and frequency scaling (DVFS), hyper-threading, helper threading, energy monitoring and management, dynamic thermal management (DTM), and various power-gating techniques. The HPEPEC domain benefits from software approaches such as task scheduling, task migration, and load balancing. Many of the HPEPEC techniques at different levels (e.g., architectural, middleware, and software) are complementary in nature and work in conjunction with one another to meet better application requirements. To the best of our knowledge, this is the first work targeting HPEPEC that provides a comprehensive classification of various HPEPEC techniques in relation to meeting diverse embedded application requirements.

The remainder of this chapter is organized as follows. Various characteristics of embedded system applications are discussed in Section 7.1. Section 7.2 presents novel architectural approaches to increase performance and reduce energy consumption in parallel embedded systems. Section 7.3 discusses hardware-assisted middleware techniques for performance and energy optimization of parallel embedded systems. Section 7.4 describes software approaches

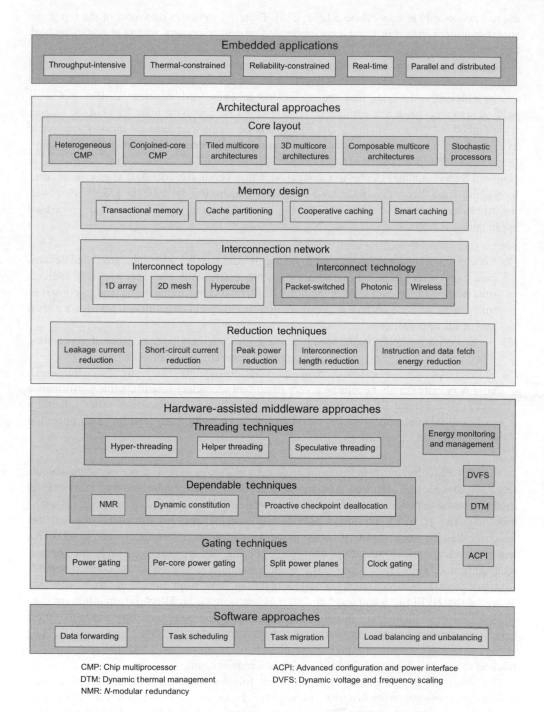

Figure 7.1 High-performance energy-efficient parallel embedded computing (HPEPEC) domain

for improving performance and power efficiency of a parallel embedded platform. Section 7.5 presents some prominent multicore-based parallel processors and emphasizes on their HPEEC features. Section 7.6 highlights research challenges and future research directions for HPEPEC. Finally, Section 7.7 concludes the chapter.

7.1 Characteristics of Embedded Systems Applications

The proliferation of embedded systems in various domains (e.g., consumer electronics, automotive, industrial automation, networking, medical, defense, space) due to technological advancements has given rise to a plethora of embedded applications. Thus, embedded systems require HPEEC hardware/software techniques to meet the ever increasing processing demands of the embedded applications. Since economic pressures have a large influence on embedded system development, many embedded applications require embedded systems to be reliable and robust, easy to use, able to connect with other devices, and low cost. Since many embedded application requirements are competing, trade-offs must be made between these requirements, such as size versus flexibility, robustness versus richness of functionality, and power consumption versus performance. Therefore, embedded system vendors market domain-specific platforms that are specialized for a particular domain and offer appropriate trade-offs to better meet that domain's typical application requirements [17].

Different embedded applications have different characteristics. Although a complete characterization of embedded applications with respect to applications' characteristics is outside the scope of this paper, Fig. 7.2 provides a concise classification of embedded applications based on their characteristics. We discuss below some of these application characteristics in the context of their associated embedded domains.[1]

7.1.1 Throughput-Intensive

Throughput-intensive embedded applications are applications that require high processing throughput. Networking and multimedia applications, which constitute a large fraction of embedded applications [17], are typically throughput-intensive due to ever increasing quality of service (QoS) demands. An embedded system containing an embedded processor requires a network stack and network protocols to connect with other devices. Connecting an embedded device or a widget to a network enables remote device management including automatic application upgrades. On a large scale, networked embedded systems can enable HPEC for solving complex large problems traditionally handled only by supercomputers (e.g., climate research, weather forecasting, molecular modeling, physical simulations, and data mining). However, connecting hundreds to thousands of embedded systems for HPC requires sophisticated and scalable interconnection technologies (e.g., packet-switched, wireless interconnects). Examples of networking applications include server input/output (I/O) devices, network infrastructure equipment, consumer electronics (mobile phones, media players), and various home appliances (e.g., home automation including networked TVs, VCRs, stereos, refrigerators). Multimedia applications, such as video streaming, require very high throughput

---

[1]Portion of this section is reproduced here from Chapter 1 of this book for completeness.

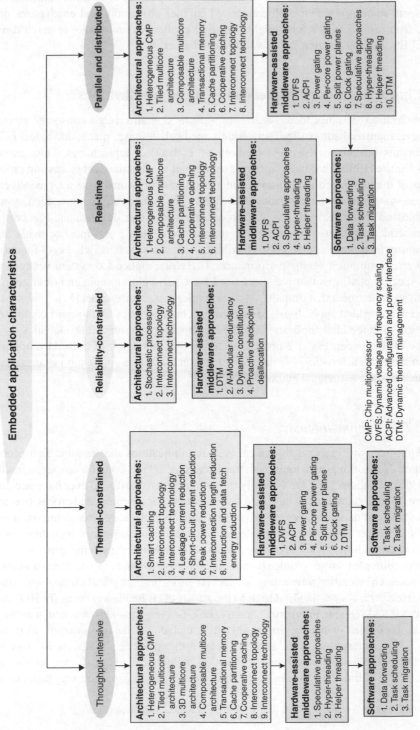

Figure 7.2 Classification of optimization techniques based on embedded application characteristics

of the order of several GOPS. A broadcast video with a specification of 30 frames/s with 720 × 480 pixels/frame requires approximately 400,000 blocks (group of pixels) to be processed per second. A telemedicine application requires processing of 5 million blocks/s [18].

7.1.2   Thermal-Constrained

An embedded application is *thermal-constrained* if an increase in temperature above a threshold could lead to incorrect results or even the embedded system failure. Depending on the target market, embedded applications typically operate above 45 °C (e.g., telecommunication embedded equipment temperature exceeds 55 °C) in contrast to traditional computer systems, which normally operate below 38 °C [19]. Meeting embedded application thermal constraints is challenging due to typically harsh and high-temperature operating environments. Limited space and energy budgets exacerbate these thermal challenges since active cooling systems (fans-based) are typically infeasible in most embedded systems, resulting in only passive and fanless thermal solutions.

7.1.3   Reliability-Constrained

Embedded systems with high *reliability* constraints are typically required to operate for many years without errors and/or must recover from errors since many reliability-constrained embedded systems are deployed in harsh environments where postdeployment removal and maintenance is infeasible. Hence, hardware and software for reliability-constrained embedded systems must be developed and tested more carefully than traditional computer systems. Safety-critical embedded systems (e.g., automotive airbags, space missions, aircraft flight controllers) have very high reliability requirements (e.g., the reliability requirement for a flight-control embedded system on a commercial airliner is 10^{-10} failures/h where a failure could lead to aircraft loss [20]).

7.1.4   Real-Time

In addition to correct functional operation, *real-time* embedded applications have additional stringent timing constraints, which impose real-time operational deadlines on the embedded system's response time. Although real-time operation does not strictly imply high performance, real-time embedded systems require high performance only to the point that the deadline is met, at which time high performance is no longer needed. Hence, real-time embedded systems require *predictable* high performance. Real-time operating systems (RTOSs) provide guarantees for meeting the stringent deadline requirements for embedded applications.

7.1.5   Parallel and Distributed

Parallel and *distributed* embedded applications leverage distributed embedded devices to cooperate and aggregate their functionalities or resources. Wireless sensor network (WSN) applications use sensor nodes to gather sensed information (statistics and data) and use distributed fault-detection algorithms. Mobile agent (autonomous software agent)-based distributed embedded applications allow the process state to be saved and transported to another new embedded system where the process resumes execution from the suspended point (e.g., virtual migration). Many embedded applications exhibit varying degrees (low to high levels) of *parallelism*, such as instruction-level parallelism (ILP) and thread-level parallelism (TLP). Innovative architectural and software HPEEC techniques are required to exploit an embedded application's available parallelism to achieve high performance with low power consumption.

Various HPEEC techniques at different levels (e.g., architecture, middleware, and software) can be used to enable an embedded platform to meet the embedded application requirements. Figure 7.2 classifies embedded application characteristics and the HPEEC techniques available at architecture, middleware, and software levels that can be leveraged by the embedded platforms executing these applications to meet the application requirements (we describe the details of these techniques in later sections of the paper). For example, throughput-intensive applications can leverage architectural innovations (e.g., tiled multicore architectures, high-bandwidth interconnects), hardware-assisted middleware techniques (e.g., speculative approaches, DVFS, hyper-threading), and software techniques (e.g., data forwarding, task scheduling, and task migration). We point out that HPEEC techniques are not orthogonal, and many of these techniques can be applied in conjunction with one another to more closely meet application requirements. Furthermore, HPEEC techniques that benefit one application requirement (e.g., reliability) may also benefit other application requirements (e.g., throughput, real-time deadlines). For example, the interconnection network not only determines the fault-tolerance characteristics of embedded systems but also affects the attainable throughput and response time.

7.2   Architectural Approaches

Novel HPEEC architectural approaches play a dominant role in meeting varying application requirements. These architectural approaches can be broadly categorized into four categories: core layout, memory design, interconnection networks, and reduction techniques. In this section, we describe these HPEEC architectural approaches.

7.2.1   Core Layout

In this section, we discuss various core layout techniques encompassing chip and processor design since high performance cannot be achieved only from semiconductor technology advancements. There exist various core layout considerations during chip and processor design such as whether to use homogeneous (cores of the same type) or heterogeneous cores (cores of varying types), whether to position the cores in a 2D or 3D layout on the chip, whether to design independent processor cores with switches that can turn on/off processor cores, or whether to have a reconfigurable integrated circuit that can be configured to form processor cores of different granularity. In this section, we describe a few core layout techniques including heterogeneous CMP, conjoined-core CMP, tiled multicore architectures, 3D multicore architectures, composable multicore architectures, multicomponent architectures, and stochastic processors. We also discuss the power/energy issues associated with these architectural approaches.

7.2.1.1 Heterogeneous CMP

Heterogeneous CMPs consist of multiple cores of varying size, performance, and complexity on a single die. Since the amount of ILP or TLP varies for different workloads, building a CMP with some large cores with high single-thread performance and some small cores with greater throughput per die area provides an attractive approach for chip design. Research indicates that the best heterogeneous CMPs contain cores customized to a subset of application characteristics (since no single core can be well suited for all embedded applications) resulting in *nonmonotonic* cores (i.e., cores cannot be strictly ordered in terms of performance or complexity for all the applications) [236]. To achieve high performance, applications are mapped to the heterogeneous cores such that the assigned core best meets an application's resource requirements. Heterogeneous CMPs can provide performance gains as high as 40% but at the expense of additional customization cost [237].

7.2.1.2 Conjoined-Core CMP

Conjoined-core CMPs are multiprocessors that allow topologically feasible resource sharing (e.g., floating-point units (FPUs), instruction, and data caches) between adjacent cores to reduce die area with minimal impact on performance and improve the overall computational efficiency. Since conjoined-core CMPs are topology oriented, the layout must be codesigned with the architecture, otherwise the architectural specifications for resource sharing may not be topologically possible or may incur higher communication costs. In general, the shared resources should be large enough so that the cost of the additional wiring required for sharing may not exceed the area benefits achieved by sharing. Static scheduling is the simplest way to organize resource sharing in conjoined-core CMPs where cores share resources in different nonoverlapping cycles (e.g., one core may use the shared resource during even cycles and the other core may use the shared resource during odd cycles, or one core may share the resource for the first five cycles and the other core for the next five cycles, and so on). Results indicate that conjoined-core CMPs can reduce area requirements by 50% and maintain performance within 9–12% of conventional cores without conjoining [238].

7.2.1.3 Tiled Multicore Architectures

Tiled multicore architectures exploit massive on-chip resources by combining each processor core with a switch to create a modular element called a *tile*, which can be replicated to create a multicore embedded system with any number of tiles. Tiled multicore architectures contain a high-performance interconnection network that constrains interconnection wire length to no longer than the tile width, and a switch (communication router) interconnects neighboring switches. Examples of tiled multicore architectures include the Raw processor, Intel's Tera-Scale research processor, Tilera TILE64, TILE*Pro*64, and TILE-Gx processor family [239].

7.2.1.4   3D Multicore Architectures

A 3D multicore architecture is an integrated circuit that orchestrates architectural units (e.g., processor cores and memories) across cores in a 3D layout. The architecture provides HPEEC by decreasing the interconnection lengths across the chip, which results in reduced communication latency. Research reveals that 3D multicore processors can achieve 47% performance gain and 20% power reduction on average over 2D multicore processors [240]. The 3D multicore architectures' disadvantages include high power density that exacerbates thermal challenges as well as increased interconnect capacitance due to electrical coupling between different layers [241].

7.2.1.5   Composable Multicore Architectures

The *composable* multicore architecture is an integrated circuit that allows the number of processors and each processor's granularity to be configured based on application requirements (i.e., large powerful processors for applications (tasks) with more ILP and small less powerful processors for tasks with more TLP). The architecture consists of an array of composable lightweight processors (CLPs) that can be aggregated to form large powerful processors to achieve high performance depending on the task granularity. Examples of composable multicore architectures include TRIPS and TFlex [239].

7.2.1.6   Stochastic Processors

Stochastic processors are processors used for fault-tolerant computing that are scalable with respect to performance requirements and power constraints while producing outputs that are *stochastically correct* in the worst case. Stochastic processors maintain scalability by exposing multiple functionally equivalent units to the application layer that differ in their architecture and exhibit different reliability levels. Applications select appropriate functional units for a program or program phase based on the program and/or program phase's reliability requirements. Stochastic processors can provide significant power reduction and throughput improvement especially for stochastic applications (applications with a priori knowledge of reliability requirements, such as multimedia applications, where computational errors are considered an additional noise source). Results indicate that stochastic processors can achieve 20–60% power savings in the motion estimation block of H.264 video encoding application [242].

7.2.2   Memory Design

The cache miss rate, fetch latency, and data transfer bandwidth are some of the main factors impacting the performance and energy consumption of embedded systems. The memory subsystem encompasses the main memory and cache hierarchy and must take into consideration issues such as consistency, sharing, contention, size, and power dissipation. In this section, we discuss HPEEC memory design techniques, which include transactional memory, cache partitioning, cooperative caching, and smart caching.

7.2.2.1 Transactional Memory

Transactional memory incorporates the definition of a *transaction* (a sequence of instructions executed by a single process with the following properties: atomicity, consistency, and isolation) in parallel programming to achieve lock-free synchronization efficiency by coordinating concurrent threads. A computation within a transaction executes atomically and *commits* on successful completion, making the transaction's changes visible to other processes, or *aborts*, causing the transaction's changes to be discarded. A transaction ensures that concurrent reads and writes to shared data do not produce inconsistent or incorrect results. The isolation property of a transaction ensures that a transaction produces the same result as if no other transactions were running concurrently [243]. In transactional memories, regions of code in parallel programming can be defined as a transaction. Transactional memory benefits from hardware support that ranges from complete execution of transactions in hardware to hardware-accelerated software implementations of transactional memory [239].

7.2.2.2 Cache Partitioning

One of the major challenges in using multicore embedded systems for real-time applications is timing unpredictability due to core contention for on-chip shared resources (e.g., level two (L2) or level three (L3) caches, interconnect networks). Worst-case execution time (WCET) estimation techniques for single-core embedded systems are not directly applicable to multicore embedded systems because a task running on one core may evict useful L2 cache contents of another task running on another core. Cache partitioning is a cache space isolation technique that exclusively allocates different portions of shared caches to different cores to avoid cache contention for hard real-time tasks, thus ensuring a more predictable runtime. Cache partitioning-aware scheduling techniques allow each task to use a fixed number of cache partitions ensuring that a cache partition is occupied by at most one scheduled task at any time [244]. Cache partitioning can enhance performance by assigning larger portions of shared caches to cores with higher workloads as compared to the cores with lighter workloads.

7.2.2.3 Cooperative Caching

Cooperative caching is a hardware technique that creates a globally managed shared cache using the cooperation of private caches. Cooperative caching allows remote L2 caches to hold and serve data that would not fit in the local L2 cache of a core and, therefore, improves average access latency by minimizing off-chip accesses [245]. Cooperative caching provides three performance enhancing mechanisms: cooperative caching facilitates cache-to-cache transfers of unmodified data to minimize off-chip accesses, cooperative caching replaces replicated data blocks to make room for unique on-chip data blocks called *singlets*, and cooperative caching allows eviction of singlets from a local L2 cache to be placed in another L2 cache. Cooperative caching implementation requires placement of cooperation-related information in private caches and the extension of cache coherence protocols to support data migration across private caches for capacity sharing. Results indicate that for an eight-core CMP with 1 MB L2 cache per core, cooperative caching improves the performance of multithreaded commercial workloads by 5–11% and 4–38% as compared to shared L2 cache and private L2 caches, respectively [246].

7.2.2.4 Smart Caching

Smart caching focuses on energy-efficient computing and leverages cache set (way) prediction and low-power cache design techniques [18]. Instead of waiting for the tag array comparison, way prediction predicts the matching way prior to the cache access. Way prediction enables faster *average* cache access time and reduces power consumption because only the predicted way is accessed if the prediction is correct. However, if the prediction is incorrect, the remaining ways are accessed during the subsequent clock cycle(s), resulting in a longer cache access time and increased energy consumption as compared to a cache without way prediction. The *drowsy cache* is a low-power cache design technique that reduces leakage power by periodically setting the unused cache line's SRAM cells to a drowsy, low-power mode. A drowsy cache is advantageous over turning off cache lines completely because the drowsy mode preserves the cache line's data, whereas turning off the cache line loses the data. However, drowsy mode requires transitioning the drowsy cache line to a high-power mode before accessing cache line's data. Research reveals that 80–90% of cache lines can be put in drowsy mode with less than a 1% performance degradation and result in a cache static and dynamic energy reduction of 50–75% [247].

7.2.3 Interconnection Network

As the number of on-chip cores increases, a scalable and high-bandwidth interconnection network to connect on-chip resources becomes crucial. Interconnection networks can be *static* or *dynamic*. Static interconnection networks consist of point-to-point communication links between computing nodes and are also referred to as *direct* networks (e.g., bus, ring, hypercube). Dynamic interconnection networks consist of switches (routers) and links and are also referred to as *indirect* networks (e.g., packet-switched networks). This section discusses prominent interconnect topologies (e.g., bus, 2D mesh, hypercube) and interconnect technologies (e.g., packet-switched, photonic, wireless).

7.2.3.1 Interconnect Topology

One of the most critical interconnection network parameters is the network topology, which determines the on-chip network cost and performance. The number of hops that must be traversed by a message and the interconnection length are dictated by the interconnect topology. Therefore, the interconnect topology determines the communication latency and energy dissipation (since message traversal across links and through routers dissipates energy). Furthermore, the interconnect topology determines the number of alternate paths between computing nodes, which affects reliability (since messages can route around faulty paths) as well as the ability to evenly distribute network traffic across multiple paths, which affects the effective on-chip network bandwidth and performance. The interconnect topology cost is dictated by the *node degree* (the number of links at each computing node) and length of the interconnecting wires.

Examples of on-chip interconnection network topologies include buses (linear 1D array or ring), 2D mesh, and hypercube. In bus topology, the processor cores share a common bus for exchanging data. Buses are the most prevalent interconnect network in multicore embedded systems due to the bus's low cost and ease of implementation. Buses provide lower costs than other interconnect topologies because of a lower node degree: the node degree for a bus interconnect is 2, for a 2D mesh is 4, and for a hypercube is $\log p$ where p is the total number of computing nodes. However, buses do not scale well as the number of cores in the CMP increases. The 2D mesh interconnect topology provides short channel lengths and low router complexity; however, the 2D mesh diameter is proportional to the perimeter of the mesh, which can lead to energy inefficiency and high network latency (e.g., the diameter of 10×10 mesh is 18 hops) [248]. The hypercube topology is a special case of a d-dimensional mesh (a d-dimensional mesh has a node degree of $2d$) when $d = \log p$.

7.2.3.2   Packet-Switched Interconnect

Packet-switched interconnection networks replace buses and crossbar interconnects as scalability and high-bandwidth demand increase for multicore embedded systems. Packet-switched networks connect a router to each computing node, and routers are connected to each other via short-length interconnect wires. Packet-switched interconnection networks multiplex multiple packet flows over the interconnect wires to provide highly scalable bandwidth [239]. Tilera's TILE architectures leverage the packet-switched interconnection network.

7.2.3.3   Photonic Interconnect

As the number of on-chip cores in a CMP increases, *global on-chip communication* plays a prominent role in overall performance. While local interconnects scale with the number of transistors, the global wires do not because the global wires span across the entire chip to connect distant logic gates and the global wires' bandwidth requirements increase as the number of cores increases. A photonic interconnection network—consisting of a photonic source, optical modulators (rates exceed 12.5 Gbps), and symmetrical optical waveguides—can deliver higher bandwidth and lower latencies with considerably lower power consumption than an electronic signaling based interconnect network.

In photonic interconnects, once a photonic path is established using optical waveguides, data can be transmitted end-to-end without repeaters, regenerators, or buffers as opposed to the electronic interconnects that require buffering, regeneration, and retransmission of messages multiple times from source to destination [249]. The photonic interconnection network is divided into zones each with a drop point such that the clock signal is optically routed to the drop point where the optical clock signal is converted to the electrical signal. Analysis reveals that power dissipation in an optical clock distribution is lower than an electrical clock distribution [241].

The photonic interconnection networks can benefit several classes of embedded applications, including real-time and throughput-intensive applications (especially applications with limited data reuse such as streaming applications). However, even though photonic interconnection networks provide many benefits, these networks have several drawbacks such as delays associated with the rise and fall times of optical emitters and detectors, losses in the optical waveguides, signal noise due to waveguides coupling, limited buffering, and signal processing [241].

7.2.3.4 Wireless Interconnect

Wireless interconnect is an emerging technology that promises to provide high bandwidth, low latency, and low-energy dissipation by eliminating lengthy wired interconnects. Carbon nanotubes are a good candidate for wireless antennas due to a carbon nanotube's high aspect ratio (virtually a 1D wire), high conductance (low losses), and high current-carrying capacity ($109 \, A/cm^2$, which is much higher than silver and copper) [241]. Wireless interconnect can deliver high bandwidth by providing multiple channels and using time-division, code-division, frequency-division, or some hybrid of these multiplexing techniques.

Experiments indicate that a wireless interconnect can reduce the communication latency by 20–45% as compared to a 2D-mesh interconnect while consuming a comparable amount of power [248]. A wireless interconnect's performance advantage increases as the number of on-chip cores increases. For example, a wireless interconnect can provide a performance gain of 217%, 279%, 600% over a 2D-mesh interconnect when the number of on-chip cores is equal to 128, 256, and 512, respectively [250].

7.2.4 Reduction Techniques

Due to an embedded system's constrained resources, embedded system architectural design must consider power dissipation reduction techniques. Power reduction techniques can be applied at various design levels: the *complementary metal-oxide-semiconductor (CMOS)-level* targets leakage and short-circuit current reduction, the *processor-level* targets instruction/data supply energy reduction as well as power-efficient management of other processor components (e.g., execution units, reorder buffers), and the *interconnection network-level* targets minimizing interconnection length using an appropriate network layout. In this section, we present several power reduction techniques including leakage current reduction, short-circuit current reduction, peak power reduction, and interconnection length reduction.

7.2.4.1 Leakage Current Reduction

As advances in the chip fabrication process reduces the feature size, the CMOS leakage current and the associated leakage power have increased. Leakage current reduction techniques include back biasing, silicon-on-insulator technologies, multithreshold MOS transistors, and power gating [18].

7.2.4.2 Short-Circuit Current Reduction

Short-circuit current flows in a CMOS gate when both nMOSFET and pMOSFET are on, which causes a large amount of current to flow through transistors and can result in increased power dissipation or even transistor burnout. The short-circuit effect is exacerbated as the clock period approaches the transistor switching period due to increasing clock frequencies.

The short-circuit current can be reduced using low-level design techniques that aim to reduce the time during which both nMOSFET and pMOSFET are on [18].

7.2.4.3 Peak Power Reduction

Peak power reduction not only increases power supply efficiency but also reduces packaging, cooling, and power supply cost as these costs are proportional to the peak power dissipation rather than the average power dissipation. *Adaptive processors* can reduce peak power by centrally managing architectural component configurations (e.g., instruction and data caches, integer and floating-point instruction queues, reorder buffers, load–store execution units, integer and floating-point registers, register renaming) to ensure that not of all these components are maximally configured simultaneously. Adaptive processors incur minimal performance loss and high peak power reduction by restricting maximum configuration to a single resource or a few resources (but not all) at a time. Research reveals that adaptive processors reduce peak power consumption by 25% with only a 5% performance degradation [251].

7.2.4.4 Interconnection Length Reduction

The interconnecting wire length increases as the number of on-chip devices increases, resulting in both increased power dissipation and delay. An energy-efficient design requires reduced interconnection wire lengths for high switching activity signals and use of placement and routing optimization algorithms for reduced delay and power consumption [18]. Chip design techniques (e.g., 3D multicore architectures) and various interconnect topologies (e.g., 2D mesh, hypercube) help in reducing interconnection wire lengths.

7.2.4.5 Instruction and Data Fetch Energy Reduction

Hardwired ASICs typically provide $50\times$ more efficient computing as compared to general-purpose programmable processors; however, architecture-level energy consumption analysis can help in energy-efficient design of programmable processors [5]. Previous work indicates that the programmable processors spend approximately 70% of the total energy consumption fetching instructions (42%) and data (28%) to the arithmetic units, whereas performing the arithmetic consumes a small fraction of the total energy (around 6%). Moreover, the instruction cache consumes the majority of the instruction fetch energy (67%) [5]. Research indicates that reducing instruction and data fetch energy can reduce the energy-efficiency gap between ASICs and programmable processors to $3\times$. Specifically, instruction fetch techniques that avoid accessing power-hungry caches are required for energy-efficient programmable processors (e.g., the Stanford efficient low-power microprocessor (ELM) fetches instructions from a set of distributed instruction registers rather than the cache) [5].

7.3 Hardware-Assisted Middleware Approaches

Various HPEEC techniques (Fig. 7.1) are implemented as middleware and/or part of an embedded OS to meet application requirements. The HPEEC middleware techniques are assisted and/or partly implemented in hardware to provide the requested functionalities (e.g., power gating support in hardware enables middleware to power gate processor cores). HPEEC hardware-assisted middleware techniques include DVFS, advanced configuration and power interface (ACPI), threading techniques (hyper-threading, helper threading, and speculative threading), energy monitoring and management, DTM, dependable high-performance energy-efficient embedded computing (DHPEEC) techniques (N-modular redundancy (NMR), dynamic constitution, and proactive checkpoint deallocation), and various low-power gating techniques (power gating, per-core power gating, split power planes, and clock gating).

7.3.1 Dynamic Voltage and Frequency Scaling

DVFS is a dynamic power management (DPM) technique in which the performance and power dissipation are regulated by adjusting the processor's voltage and frequency. The one-to-one correspondence between processor's voltage and frequency in CMOS circuits imposes a strict constraint on dynamic voltage scaling (DVS) techniques to ensure that the voltage adjustments do not violate application timing (deadline) constraints (especially for real-time applications). Multicore embedded systems leverage two DVFS techniques: *global DVFS* scales the voltages and frequencies of all the cores simultaneously and *local DVFS* scales the voltage and frequency on a per-core basis [18]. Experiments indicate that local DVFS can improve performance (throughput) by 2.5× on average and can provide an 18% higher throughput than global DVFS on average [252, 253].

DVFS-based optimizations can be employed for real-time applications to conform with tasks' deadlines in an energy-efficient manner. For example, if a task deadline is impending, DVFS can be adjusted to operate at the highest frequency to meet the task deadline whereas if the task deadline is not close, then DVFS can be adjusted to lower voltage and frequency settings to conserve energy while still meeting the task deadline.

Although DVFS is regarded as one of the most efficient energy-saving technique, the associated overhead of performing DVFS needs to be considered. DVFS requires a programmable DC–DC converter and a programmable clock generator (mostly phase lock loop (PLL) based) that incurs time and energy overhead whenever the processor changes its voltage and frequency setting. This overhead dictates the minimum duration of time that the target system should stay in a particular voltage–frequency state for the DVS to produce a positive energy gain [254].

7.3.2 Advanced Configuration and Power Interface

Although DPM techniques can be implemented in hardware as part of the electronic circuit, hardware implementation complicates the modification and reconfiguration of power management policies. The ACPI specification is a platform-independent software-based power management interface that attempts to unify existing DPM techniques (e.g., DVFS, power, and clock gating) and put these techniques under the OS control [255]. ACPI defines various states for an ACPI-compliant embedded system, but the processor power states (C-states) and the processor performance states (P-states) are most relevant to HPEEC. ACPI defines four C-states: C0 (the *operating state* where the processor executes instructions normally), C1 (the *halt state* where the processor stops executing instructions but can return to C0 instantaneously), C2 (the *stop-clock state* where the processor and cache maintain state but can take longer to return to C0), and C3 (the *sleep state* where the processor goes to sleep, does not maintain the processor and cache state, and takes longest as compared to other C-states to return to C0). ACPI defines n P-states (P1, P2, ... , Pn) where $n \leq 16$, corresponding to the processor C0 state. Each P-state designates a specific DVFS setting such that P0 is the highest performance state while P1 to Pn are successively lower performance states. ACPI specification is implemented in various manufactured chips (e.g., Intel names P-states as SpeedStep while AMD as Cool"n"Quiet).

7.3.3   Gating Techniques

To enable low-power operation and meet an application's constrained energy budget, various hardware-supported low-power gating techniques can be controlled by the middleware. These gating techniques can switch off a component's supply voltage or clock signal to save power during otherwise idle periods. In this section, we discuss gating techniques such as power gating, per-core power gating, split power planes, and clock gating.

7.3.3.1   Power Gating

Power gating is a power management technique that reduces leakage power by switching off the supply voltage to idle logic elements after detecting no activity for a certain period of time. Power gating can be applied to idle functional units, cores, and cache banks [18].

7.3.3.2   Per-Core Power Gating

Per-core power gating is a fine-grained power gating technique that individually switches off idle cores. In conjunction with DVFS, per-core power gating provides more flexibility in optimizing performance and power dissipation of multicore processors running applications with varying degrees of parallelism. Per-core power gating increases single-thread performance on a single active core by increasing the active core's supply voltage while power gating the other idle cores, which provides additional power- and thermal-headroom for the active core. Experiments indicate that per-core power gating in conjunction with DVFS can increase the throughput of a multicore processor (with 16 cores) by 16% on average for different workloads exhibiting a range of parallelism while maintaining the power and thermal constraints [256].

7.3.3.3   Split Power Planes

Split power planes is a low-power technique that allows different power planes to coexist on the same chip and minimizes both static and dynamic power dissipation by removing power from idle portions of the chip. Each power plane has separate pins, a separate (or isolated) power supply, and independent power distribution routing. For example, Freescale's MPC8536E PowerQUICC III processor has two power planes: one plane for the processor core (e500) and L2 cache arrays, and a second plane for the remainder of the chip's components [257].

7.3.3.4   Clock Gating

Clock gating is a low-power technique that allows gating off the clock signal to registers, latches, clock regenerators, or entire subsystems (e.g., cache banks). Clock gating can yield significant power savings by gating off the functional units (e.g., adders, multipliers, and shifters) not required by the currently executing instruction, as determined by the instruction decode unit. Clock gating can also be applied internally for each functional unit to further reduce power consumption by disabling the functional unit's upper bits for small operand values that do not require the functional unit's full-bit width. The granularity at which clock gating can be applied is limited by the overhead associated with the clock to enable signal generation [18].

7.3.4   Threading Techniques

Different threading techniques target high performance either by enabling a single processor to execute multiple threads or by speculatively executing multiple threads. Prominent high-performance threading techniques include hyper-threading, helper threading, and speculative threading. We point out that helper threading and speculative threading are performance-centric and may lead to increased power consumption in case of misspeculation where speculative processing needs to be discarded. Therefore, helper and speculative threading should be used with caution in energy-critical embedded systems. In the following section, we describe a brief description of these threading techniques.

7.3.4.1   Hyper-Threading

Hyper-threading leverages simultaneous multithreading to enable a single processor to appear as two logical processors and allows instructions from both of the logical processors to execute simultaneously on the shared resources [245]. Hyper-threading enables the OS to schedule multiple threads to the processor so that different threads can use the idle execution units. The architecture state, consisting of general-purpose registers, interrupt controller registers, control registers, and some machine state registers, is duplicated for each logical processor. However, hyper-threading does not offer the same performance as a multiprocessor with two physical processors.

7.3.4.2   Helper Threading

Helper threading leverages special execution modes to provide faster execution by reducing cache miss rates and miss latency [245]. Helper threading accelerates performance of single-threaded applications using speculative pre-execution. This pre-execution is most beneficial for irregular applications where data prefetching is ineffective due to the difficulty in prediction of data addresses. The helper threads run ahead of the main thread and reduce cache miss rates and miss latencies by pre-executing regions of the code that are likely to incur many cache misses. Helper threading can be particularly useful for applications with multiple control paths where helper threads pre-execute all possible paths and prefetch the data references for all paths instead of waiting until the correct path is determined. Once the correct execution path is determined, all the helper threads executing incorrect paths are aborted.

7.3.4.3 Speculative Threading

Speculative threading approaches provide high performance by removing unnecessary serialization in programs. We discuss two speculative approaches: speculative multithreading and speculative synchronization.

Speculative multithreading divides a sequential program into multiple contiguous program segments called tasks and execute these tasks in parallel on multiple cores. The architecture provides hardware support for detecting dependencies in a sequential program and rolling back the program state on misspeculations. Speculative multithreaded architectures exploit high transistor density by having multiple cores and relieve programmers from parallel programming, as is required for conventional CMPs. Speculative multithreaded architectures provide instruction windows much larger than conventional uniprocessors by combining the instruction windows of multiple cores to exploit distant TLP as opposed to the nearby ILP exploited by conventional uniprocessors [239].

Speculative synchronization removes unnecessary serialization by applying thread-level speculation to parallel applications and preventing speculative threads from blocking at barriers, busy locks, and unset flags. Hardware monitors detect conflicting accesses and roll back the speculative threads to the synchronization point prior to the access violation. Speculative synchronization guarantees forward execution using a safe thread that ensures that the worst-case performance of the order of conventional synchronization (i.e., threads not using any speculation) when speculative threads fail to make progress.

7.3.5 Energy Monitoring and Management

Profiling the power consumption of various components (e.g., processor cores, caches) for different embedded applications at a fine granularity identifies how, when, and where power is consumed by the embedded system and the applications. Power profiling is important for energy-efficient HPEEC system design. Energy-monitoring software can monitor, track, and analyze performance and power consumption for different components at the function-level or block-level granularity. PowerPack is an energy-monitoring tool that uses a combination of hardware (e.g., sensors and digital meters) and software (e.g., drivers, benchmarks, and analysis tools). PowerPack profiles power and energy, as well as power dynamics, of DVFS in CMP-based cluster systems for different parallel applications at the component and code segment granularity [258].

Power management middleware dynamically adapts the application behavior in response to fluctuations in workload and power budget. PowerDial is a power management middleware that transforms static application configuration parameters into dynamic control variables stored in the address space of the executing application [259]. These control variables are accessible via a set of dynamic knobs to change the running application's configuration dynamically to trade-off computation accuracy (as far as the application's minimum accuracy requirements are satisfied) and resource requirements, which translates to power savings. Experiments indicate that PowerDial can reduce power consumption by 75%.

Green is a power management middleware that enables application programmers to exploit approximation opportunities to meet performance demands while meeting QoS guarantees [260]. Green provides a framework that enables application programmers to approximate expensive functions and loops. Green operates in two phases: the *calibration phase* and the *operation phase*. In the calibration phase, Green creates a QoS loss model for the approximated functions to quantify the approximation impact (loss in accuracy). The operational phase uses this QoS loss model to make approximation decisions based on programmer-specified QoS constraints. Experiments indicate that Green can improve the performance and energy consumption by 21% and 14%, respectively, with only a 0.27% QoS degradation.

7.3.6   Dynamic Thermal Management

Temperature has become an important constraint in HPEEC embedded systems because high temperature increases cooling costs, degrades reliability, and reduces performance. Furthermore, an embedded application's distinct and time-varying thermal profile necessitates DTM approaches. DTM for multicore embedded systems is more challenging than for the single-core embedded systems because a core's configuration, and workload has a significant impact on the temperature of neighboring cores due to lateral heat transfer between adjacent cores. The goal of DTM techniques is to maximize performance while keeping temperature below a defined threshold.

7.3.6.1   Temperature Determination for DTM

DTM requires efficient chip thermal profiling, which can be done using *sensor-based*, *thermal model-based*, or *performance counters-based* methods. Sensor-based methods leverage physical sensors to monitor the temperature in real time. DTM typically uses one of the two sensor placement techniques: *global sensor placement* monitors global chip hotspots and *local sensor placement* places sensors in each processor component to monitor local processor components. Thermal model-based methods use thermal models that exploit the duality between electrical and thermal phenomena by leveraging lumped-RC (resistor/capacitor) models. Thermal models can be either low level or high level. *Low-level thermal models* estimate temperature accurately and report the steady state as well as provide transient temperature estimation; however, these low-level thermal models are computationally expensive. *High-level thermal models* leverage a simplified lumped-RC model that can only estimate the steady-state temperature; however, these high-level thermal models are computationally less expensive than the low-level thermal models. Performance counters-based methods estimate the temperature of different on-chip functional units using temperature values read from specific processor counter registers. These counter readings can be used to estimate the access rate and timing information of various on-chip functional units.

7.3.6.2   Techniques Assisting DTM

DVFS is one of the major technique that helps DTM in maintaining a chip's thermal balance and alleviates a core's thermal emergency by reducing the core voltage and frequency. DVFS can be *global* or *local*. Global DVFS provides less control and efficiency as a single core's hotspot could result in unnecessary stalling or scaling of all the remaining cores. Local DVFS controls each core's voltage and frequency individually to alleviate thermal emergency of the affected cores; however, the local DVFS makes the design more complex. A *hybrid* local–global thermal management approach has the potential to provide better performance than local DVFS while maintaining the simplicity of global DVFS. The hybrid approach applies global DVFS across all the cores but specializes the architectural parameters (e.g., instruction window size, issue width, fetch throttling/gating) of each core locally. Research reveals that the hybrid approach achieves a 5% better throughput than the local DVFS [253]. Although DVFS can help DTM to maintain thermal balance, there exist other techniques to assist DTM. (For example, Zhou et al. [261] suggested that adjusting microarchitectural parameters such as instruction window size and issue width has relatively lower overhead than DVFS-based approaches.)

7.3.7 Dependable Techniques

To achieve performance efficiency while meeting an application's reliability requirements defines the DHPEEC domain, which ranges from redundancy techniques to dependable processor design. DHPEEC platforms are critical for space exploration, space science, and defense applications with ever increasing demands for high data bandwidth, processing capability, and reliability. We describe several hardware-assisted middleware techniques leveraged by DHPEEC including NMR, dynamic constitution, and proactive checkpoint deallocation.

7.3.7.1 *N*-Modular Redundancy

The process variation, technology scaling (deep submicron and nanoscale devices), and computational energy approaching thermal equilibrium leads to high error rates in CMPs, which necessitates redundancy to meet reliability requirements. Core-level NMR runs N program copies on N different cores and can meet high reliability goals for multicore processors. Each core performs the same computation, and the results are voted (compared) for consistency. Voting can either be time-based or event-based. Based on the voting result, program execution continues or rolls back to a checkpoint (a previously stored, valid architectural state). A multicore NMR framework can provide either *static* or *dynamic* redundancy. Static redundancy uses a set of statically configured cores, whereas dynamic redundancy assigns redundant cores during runtime based on the application's reliability requirements and environmental stimuli [262]. Static redundancy incurs high area requirement and power consumption due to the large number of cores required to meet an application's reliability requirements, whereas dynamic redundancy provides better performance, power, and reliability trade-offs.

The dependable multiprocessor (DM) is an example of a DHPEEC platform that leverages NMR. The DM design includes a fault-tolerant embedded message passing interface (FEMPI) (a lightweight fault-tolerant version of the message passing interface (MPI) standard) for providing fault tolerance to parallel embedded applications [11]. Furthermore, DM can leverage HPEC platforms such as the Tile*Pro*64 [173].

7.3.7.2 Dynamic Constitution

Dynamic constitution, an extension of dynamic redundancy, permits an arbitrary core on a chip to be a part of an NMR group, which increases dependability as compared to the static NMR configuration by scheduling around cores with permanent faults. For example, if an NMR group is statically constituted and the number of cores with permanent faults drops below the threshold to meet the application's reliability requirements, the remaining nonfaulty cores in the NMR group are rendered useless. Dynamic constitution can also be helpful in alleviating thermal constraints by preventing NMR hotspots [263].

7.3.7.3 Proactive Checkpoint Deallocation

Proactive checkpoint deallocation is a high-performance extension for NMR that permits cores participating in voting to continue execution instead of waiting on the voting logic results. After a voting logic decision, only the cores with correct results are allowed to continue further execution.

7.4 Software Approaches

The performance and power efficiency of an embedded platform not only depends on the built-in hardware techniques but also depends on the software's ability to effectively leverage the hardware support. Software-based HPEEC techniques assist DPM by signaling the hardware of the resource requirements of an application phase. Software approaches enable high performance by scheduling and migrating tasks statically or dynamically to meet application requirements. HPEEC software-based techniques include data forwarding, task scheduling, task migration, and load balancing.

7.4.1 Data Forwarding

Data forwarding benefits HPEEC by hiding memory latency, which is more challenging in multiprocessor systems as compared to uniprocessor systems because uniprocessor caches can hide memory latency by exploiting spatial and temporal locality, whereas coherent multiprocessors have sharing misses in addition to the nonsharing misses present in uniprocessor systems. In a shared memory architecture, processors that cache the same data address are referred as *sharing processors*. Data forwarding integrates fine-grained message passing capabilities in a shared memory architecture and hides the memory latency associated with sharing accesses by sending the data values to the sharing processors as soon as the data values are produced [264]. Data forwarding can be performed by the compiler where the compiler inserts *write and forward* assembly instructions in place of ordinary write instructions. Compiler-assisted data forwarding uses an extra register to indicate the processors that should receive the forwarded data. Another data forwarding technique referred as programmer-assisted data forwarding requires a programmer to insert a *poststore* operation that causes a copy of an updated data value to be sent to all the sharing processors. Experiments indicate that remote writes together with prefetching improve performance by 10–48% relative to the base system (no data forwarding and prefetching), whereas remote writes improve performance by 3–28% relative to the base system with prefetching [245].

7.4.2 Load Distribution

A multicore embedded system's performance is dictated by the workload distribution across the cores, which in turn dictates the execution time and power/thermal profile of each core.

Load distribution techniques focus on load balancing between the executing cores via task scheduling and task migration.

7.4.2.1 Task Scheduling

The task scheduling problem can be defined as determining an optimal assignment of tasks to cores that minimizes the power consumption while maintaining the chip temperature below the DTM enforced ceiling temperature with minimal or no performance degradation given the total energy budget. Task scheduling applies for both DPM and DTM and plays a pivotal role in extending battery life for portable embedded systems, alleviating thermal emergencies, and enabling long-term savings from reduced cooling costs. Task scheduling can be applied in conjunction with DVFS to meet real-time task deadlines as a higher processing speed results in faster task execution and shorter scheduling lengths, but at the expense of greater power consumption. Conversely, the decrease in processor frequency reduces power consumption but increases the scheduling length, which may increase the overall energy consumption. Since the task scheduling overhead increases as the number of cores increases, hardware-assisted task scheduling techniques are the focus of emerging research (e.g., thread scheduling in graphics processing units (GPUs) is hardware-assisted). Experiments indicate that hardware-assisted task scheduling can improve the scheduling time by 8.1% for CMPs [265].

7.4.2.2 Task Migration

In a multithreaded environment, threads periodically and/or aperiodically enter and leave cores. Thread migration is used both as a DPM and DTM technique that allows a scheduled thread to execute, preempt, or migrate to another core based on the thread's thermal and/or power profile. The OS or thread scheduler can dynamically migrate threads running on cores with limited resources to the cores with more resources as resources become available. Depending on the executing workloads, there can be a substantial temperature variation across cores on the same chip. Thread migration-based DTM periodically moves threads away from the hot cores to the cold cores based on this temperature differential to maintain the cores' thermal balance. A thread migration technique must take into account the overhead incurred due to thread migration communication costs and address space updates. Temperature determination techniques (e.g., performance counter-based, sensor-based) assist thread management techniques in making migration decisions.

Thread migration techniques can be characterized as *rotation-based*, *temperature-based*, or *power-based* [266]. The rotation-based technique migrates a thread from core (i) to core (($i + 1$)mod N) where N denotes the total number of processor cores. The temperature-based technique orders cores based on the cores' temperature", and the thread on core (i) is swapped with the thread on core ($N - i - 1$) (i.e., the thread on the hottest core is swapped with the thread on the coldest core, the thread on the second hottest core is swapped with the thread on the second coldest core, and so on). The power-based technique orders cores based on the cores' temperature in ascending order and orders threads based on the threads' power consumption in descending order. The power-based technique then schedules thread (i) to core (i) (e.g., the most power-hungry thread is scheduled to the coldest core).

Thread migration can be applied in conjunction with DVFS to enhance performance. Research indicates that thread migration alone can improve performance by 2× on average, whereas thread migration in conjunction with DVFS can improve performance by 2.6× on average [252].

7.4.2.3 Load Balancing and Unbalancing

Load balancing techniques distribute a workload equally across all the cores in a multicore embedded system. Load unbalancing can be caused by either *extrinsic* or *intrinsic* factors. Extrinsic factors are associated with the OS and hardware topology. For example, the OS can schedule daemon processes during the execution of a parallel application, and an asymmetric hardware topology can result in varying communication latencies for different processes. Intrinsic factors include imbalanced parallel algorithms, imbalanced data distribution, and changes in the input dataset. An unbalanced task assignment can lead to a performance degradation because cores executing light workloads may have to wait/stall for other cores executing heavier workloads to reach a synchronization point. Load balancing relies on efficient task scheduling techniques as well as balanced parallel algorithms. Cache partitioning can assist load balancing by assigning more cache partitions to the cores executing heavier workloads to decrease the cache miss rate and increase the core's execution speed, and thus reduce the stall time for the cores executing light workloads [267].

Although load balancing provides a mechanism to achieve high performance in embedded systems, load balancing may lead to high power consumption if not applied judiciously because load balancing focuses on utilizing all the cores even for a small number of tasks. A load unbalancing strategy that considers workload characteristics (i.e., *periodic* or *aperiodic*) can achieve better performance and lower power consumption as compared to a load balancing or a load unbalancing strategy that ignores workload characteristics. A workload-aware load unbalancing strategy assigns repeatedly executed periodic tasks to a minimum number of cores and distributes aperiodic tasks that are not likely to be executed repeatedly to a maximum number of cores. We point out that the critical performance metric for periodic tasks is deadline satisfaction rather than faster execution (a longer waiting time is not a problem as long as the deadline is met), whereas the critical performance metric for aperiodic tasks is response time rather than deadline satisfaction. The periodic tasks not distributed over all the cores leave more idle cores for scheduling aperiodic tasks, which shortens the response time of aperiodic tasks. Results on an ARM11 MPCore chip demonstrate that the workload-aware load unbalancing strategy reduces power consumption and the mean waiting time of aperiodic tasks by 26% and 82%, respectively, as compared to a load balancing strategy. The workload-aware load unbalancing strategy reduces the mean waiting time of aperiodic tasks by 92% with similar power efficiency as compared to a workload unaware load unbalancing strategy [268].

7.5 High-Performance Energy-Efficient Multicore Processors

Silicon and chip vendors have developed various high-performance multicore processors that leverage the various HPEEC techniques discussed in this chapter. Although providing an exhaustive list of all the prevalent high-performance multicore processors that can be used

Table 7.2 High-performance energy-efficient multicore processors

Processor	Cores	Speed	Power	Performance
ARM11 MPCore	1–4	620 MHz	600 mW	2600 DMIPS
ARM Cortex A-9 MPCore	1–4	800 MHz–2 GHz	250 mW per CPU	4000–10,000 DMIPS
MPC8572E PowerQUICC III	2	1.2–1.5 GHz	17.3 W at 1.5 GHz	6897 MIPS at 1.5 GHz
Tilera TILE*Pro*64	64 tiles	700–866 MHz	19–23 W at 700 MHz	443 GOPS
Tilera TILE-Gx	16/36/64/100 tiles	1–1.5 GHz	10–55 W	750 GOPS
AMD Opteron 6100	8/12	1.7–2.3 GHz	65–105 W	—
Intel Xeon Processor LV 5148	2	2.33 GHz	40 W	—
Intel Sandy Bridge	4	3.8 GHz	35–45 W	121.6 GFLOPS
AMD Phenom II X6 1090T	6	3.6 GHz	125 W	—
NVIDIA GeForce GTX 460	336 CUDA cores	1.3 GHz	160 W	748.8 GFLOPS
NVIDIA GeForce 9800 GX2	256 CUDA cores	1.5 GHz	197 W	1152 GFLOPS
NVIDIA GeForce GTX 295	480 CUDA cores	1.242 GHz	289 W	748.8 GFLOPS
NVIDIA Tesla C2050/C2070	448 CUDA cores	1.15 GHz	238 W	1.03 TFLOPS
AMD FireStream 9270	800 stream cores	750 MHz	160 W	1.2 TFLOPS
ATI Radeon HD 4870 X2	1600 stream cores	750 MHz	423 W	2.4 TFLOPS

in embedded applications is outside of the scope of this chapter, we discuss some prominent multicore processors (summarized in Table 7.2) and focus on their HPEEC features.

7.5.1 ARM11 MPCore

The ARM11 MPCore processor features configurable level one caches, a fully coherent data cache, 1.3 GB/s memory throughput from a single CPU, and vector floating-point coprocessors. The ARM11 MPCore processor provides energy efficiency via accurate branch and subroutine return prediction (reduces the number of incorrect instruction fetches and decode operations), physically addressed caches (reduces the number of cache flushes and refills), and power and clock gating to disable inputs to idle functional blocks [269].

The ARM11 MPCore supports adaptive shutdown of idle processors to yield dynamic power consumption of 0.49 mW/MHz at 130 nm process. The ARM Intelligent Energy Manager (IEM) can dynamically predict the application performance and performs DVFS to reduce power consumption to 0.3 mW/MHz [270].

7.5.2 ARM Cortex A-9 MPCore

The ARM Cortex A-9 MPCore is a multi-issue out-of-order superscalar pipelined multicore processor consisting of one to four Cortex-A9 processor cores grouped in a cluster and delivers a peak performance of 2.5 DMIPS/MHz [271]. The ARM Cortex A-9 MPCore features a snoop control unit (SCU) that ensures cache coherence within the Cortex-A9 processor cluster and a high-performance L2 cache controller that supports between 128K and 8M of L2 cache. The Cortex-A9 processor incorporates the ARM Thumb-2 technology that delivers the peak performance of traditional ARM code while providing up to a 30% instruction memory storage reduction. Each Cortex A-9 processor in the cluster can be in one of the following modes: *run mode* (the entire processor is clocked and powered-up), *standby mode* (the CPU clock is gated off and only the logic required to wake up the processor is active), *dormant mode* (everything except RAM arrays are powered off), and *shutdown* (everything is powered off) [272]. The ARM Cortex A-9 MPCore processor can support up to 14 power domains: 4 Cortex-A9 processor power domains (1 for each core); 4 Cortex-A9 processor data engines power domains (1 for each core); 4 power domains (1 for each of the Cortex-A9 processor caches and translation lookaside buffer (TLB) RAMs); 1 power domain for SCU duplicated tag RAMs; and 1 power domain for the remaining logic, private peripherals, and the SCU logic cells [272]. Typical ARM Cortex A-9 MPCore applications include high-performance networking and mobile communications.

7.5.3 MPC8572E PowerQUICC III

Freescale's PowerQUICC III integrated communications processor consist of two processor cores: enhanced peripherals, and a high-speed interconnect technology to match processor performance with I/O system throughput. The MPC8572E PowerQUICC III processor contains an application acceleration block that integrates four powerful engines: a table lookup unit (TLU) (performs complex table searches and header inspections), a pattern-matching engine (PME) (carriers out expression matching), a deflate engine (handles file decompression), and a security engine (accelerates cryptography-related operations) [273]. The processor uses DPM to minimize power consumption of idle blocks by putting idle blocks in one of the power saving modes (doze, nap, and sleep) [274]. Typical MPC8572E PowerQUICC III applications include multiservice routing and switching, unified threat management, firewall, and wireless infrastructure equipment (e.g., radio node controllers).

7.5.4 Tilera TILEPro64 and TILE-Gx

Tilera revolutionizes high-performance multicore embedded computing by leveraging a tiled multicore architecture (e.g., the TILE*Pro*64 and TILE-Gx processor family [275, 276]).

The TILE*Pro*64 and TILE-Gx processor family feature an 8×8 grid and an array of 16–100 tiles (cores), respectively, where each tile consists of a 32-bit very long instruction word (VLIW) processor, three deep pipelines delivering up to 3 instructions per cycle (IPC), integrated L1 and L2 cache, and a nonblocking switch that integrates the tile into a power-efficient interconnect mesh. The TILE*Pro*64 and TILE-Gx processors offer 5.6 and 32 MB of on-chip cache, respectively, and implement Tilera's dynamic distributed cache (DDC) technology that provides a 2× improvement on average in cache coherence performance over traditional cache technologies using a cache coherence protocol. Each tile can independently run a complete OS or multiple tiles can be grouped together to run a multiprocessing OS such as SMP Linux. The TILE*Pro*64 and TILE-Gx processor family employs DPM to put idle tiles into a low-power sleep mode. The TILE*Pro*64 and TILE-Gx family of processor can support a wide range of computing applications including advanced networking, wireless infrastructure, telecom, digital multimedia, and cloud computing.

7.5.5 AMD Opteron Processor

The AMD Opteron is a dual-core processor where each core has a private L2 cache but shares an on-chip memory controller. The AMD Opteron 6100 series platform consists of 8 or 12 core AMD Opteron processors. The AMD Opteron's *Cool'n'Quiet* technology switches cores to low-power states when a temperature threshold is reached [277].

7.5.6 Intel Xeon Processor

Intel leverages Hafnium Hi-K and metal gates in next-generation Xeon processors to achieve higher clock speeds and better performance per watt. The Xeon processors also implement *hyper-threading* and *wide dynamic execution* technologies for high performance. The wider execution pipelines enable each core to simultaneously fetch, dispatch, execute, and retire up to 4 IPC [278]. The Intel Xeon 5500 processor family features 15 power states and a fast transition between these power states ($< 2\,\mu s$) [7]. The Xeon processors are based on Intel Core 2 Duo microarchitecture where the two cores share a common L2 cache to provide faster inter-core communication. The shared L2 cache can be dynamically resized depending on individual core's needs. Intel's *deep power down* technology enables both cores and the L2 cache to be powered down when the processor is idle [279]. Intel's *dynamic power coordination* technology allows software-based DPM to alter each core's sleep state to trade-off between power dissipation and performance. The processor incorporates digital temperature sensors on each core to monitor thermal behavior using Intel's *advanced thermal manager* technology [165]. The dual-core Intel Xeon processor LV 5148—a low-power embedded processor—enables *micro-gating* of processor circuitry to disable the processor's inactive portions with finer granularity [280]. Typical applications for the Intel Xeon processor include medical imaging, gaming, industrial control and automation systems, mobile devices, military, and aerospace.

7.5.7 Intel Sandy Bridge Processor

The Sandy Bridge is Intel's second-generation quad-core processor that offers high sustained throughput for floating-point math, media processing applications, and data-parallel computation [281, 282]. The processors's floating-point unit supports the advanced vector extension (AVX) instruction set that allows vector processing of up to 256 bits in width. The processor leverages the hyper-threading technology that provides the OS with eight logical CPUs. Intel Sandy Bridge leverages Intel Turbo Boost Technology that allows processor cores and the built-in integrated graphics processor (IGP) to run faster than the base operating frequency if the processor is operating below power, current, and temperature specification limits [283]. The processor uses a ring-style interconnect between the cores offering a communication bandwidth up to 384 GB/s.

7.5.8   Graphics Processing Units

A GPU is a massively parallel processor capable of executing a large number of threads concurrently, and accelerates and offloads graphics rendering from the CPU. GPUs feature high memory bandwidth that is typically 10× faster than contemporary CPUs. NVIDIA and AMD/ATI are the two main GPU vendors. GPUs are suitable for high-definition (HD) videos, photos, 3D movies, high-resolution graphics, and gaming. Apart from high graphics performance, GPUs enable general-purpose computing on graphics processing units (GPGPU), which is a computing technique that leverages GPUs to perform compute-intensive operations traditionally handled by CPUs. GPGPUs are realized by adding programmable stages and higher precision arithmetic to the rendering pipelines, which enables stream processors to process nongraphics data. For example, NVIDIA Tesla personal supercomputer consisting of 3 or 4 T C1060 computing processors [284] offers up to 4 TFLOPS of compute capability with 4 GB of dedicated memory per GPU [285].

NVIDIA's PowerMizer technology—available on all NVIDIA GPUs—is a DPM technique that adapts the GPU to suit an application's requirements [286]. Digital watchdogs monitor GPU utilization and turn off idle processor engines. NVIDIA's Parallel DataCache technology accelerates algorithms, such as ray-tracing, physics solvers, and sparse matrix multiplication, where data addresses are not known a priori [287]. ATI's PowerPlay technology is a DPM solution that monitors GPU activity and adjusts GPU power between low, medium, and high states via DVFS based on workload characteristics. For example, PowerPlay puts the GPU in a low-power state when receiving and composing emails, and switches the GPU to a high-power state for compute-intensive gaming applications. PowerPlay incorporates on-chip sensors to monitor the GPU's temperature and triggers thermal actions accordingly. The PowerPlay technology is available on the ATI Radeon HD 3800 and 4800 series graphics processors, the ATI Mobility Radeon graphics processors, and the Radeon Express motherboard chipsets.

7.6   Challenges and Future Research Directions

HPEEC is an active and expanding research domain with applications ranging from consumer electronics to supercomputers. The introduction of HPEEC into supercomputing has boosted the significance of the HPEEC domain as power is becoming a concern for modern supercomputing considering the long-term operation and cooling costs. Modern supercomputers are a combination of custom design and embedded processors, such as Opteron, Xeon, and coprocessors such as NVIDIA Tesla general-purpose graphics processing units (GPGPUs), AMD graphics processing units (GPUs), and so on. For example, the Titan supercomputer (the world's second fastest supercomputer as of November 2014 and located at the DOE/SC/Oak Ridge National Laboratory, United States [233]) leverages AMD Opteron 6274 16-core processors as well as NVIDIA Tesla K20x GPGPUs. An increasing growth and expansion of HPEEC is envisioned in the foreseeable future as supercomputers rely more and more on HPEEC.

This chapter gives an overarching survey of HPEEC techniques that enable meeting diverse embedded application requirements. We discuss state-of-the-art multicore processors that leverage these HPEEC techniques. Despite remarkable advancements, the HPEEC domain still faces various arduous challenges, which require further research to leverage the full-scale benefits of HPEEC techniques. Although power is still a first-order constraint in HPEEC platforms, we discuss several additional challenges facing the HPEEC domain (summarized in Table 7.3) along with future research directions.

Heterogeneous CMPs provide performance efficiency, but present additional design challenges as design space increases considering various types of cores and the flexibility of changing each core's architectural parameters (e.g., issue width, instruction window size, fetch gating) for an arbitrary permutations of workloads. Furthermore, for a given die size, there exists a fundamental trade-off between the number and type of cores and appropriate cache sizes for these cores. Efficient distribution of available cache size across the cache hierarchies (private and shared) to provide high performance is challenging [236].

Synchronization between multiple threads running on multiple cores introduces performance challenges. Threads use semaphores or locks to control access to shared data, which degrades performance due to the busy waiting of threads. Furthermore, threads use synchronization barriers (a defined point in the code where all threads must reach before further execution), which decreases performance due to idle-waiting of faster threads for slower threads.

Although different threads can work independently on private data, shared memory becomes a bottleneck due to a large number of shared-data accesses to different cache partitions. Furthermore, threads can communicate via shared memory, which requires cache state transitions to transfer data between threads. Threads must stall until cache state transitions occur, as there

Table 7.3 High-performance energy-efficient embedded computing (HPEEC) challenges

Challenge	Description
Complex design space	Large design space due to various core types (homogeneous, heterogeneous) and each core's tunable parameters (e.g., instruction window size, issue width, fetch gating)
High on-chip bandwidth	Increased communication due to increasing number of cores requires high-bandwidth on-chip interconnects
Synchronization	Synchronization primitives (e.g., locks, barriers) results in programs serialization degrading performance
Shared memory bottleneck	Threads running on different cores make large number of accesses to various shared memory data partitions
Cache coherence	Heterogeneous cores with different cache line sizes require cache coherence protocols redesign and synchronization primitives (e.g., semaphores, locks) increase cache coherence traffic
Cache thrashing	Threads working concurrently evict each others data out of the shared cache to bring their own data

is likely insufficient speculative or out-of-order work available for these threads. Moreover, designing a common interface to the shared cache, clock distribution, and cache coherence provides additional design challenges [245].

Cache coherence is required to provide a consistent memory view in shared-memory multicore processors with various cache hierarchies. Embedded systems conventionally rely on software-managed cache coherency, which does not scale well with the number of cores and thereby necessitates hardware-assisted cache coherence. Hardware–software codesign of cache coherence protocol defines challenging trade-offs between performance, power, and time-to-market [288].

Cache thrashing—an additional HPEEC challenge—is a phenomenon where threads continually evict each other's working set from the cache, which increases the miss rate and latency for all threads. Although direct-mapped caches present an attractive choice for multicore embedded systems due to a direct-mapped cache's power efficiency as compared to associative caches, direct-mapped caches are more predisposed to thrashing as compared to set associative caches. Cache thrashing can be minimized by providing larger and more associative caches; however, these opportunities are constrained by strict power requirements for embedded systems. Victim caches employed alongside direct-mapped caches help to alleviating cache thrashing by providing associativity for localized cache conflict regions [289].

Various new avenues are emerging in HPEEC such as energy-efficient data centers, grid and cluster embedded computing, and DHPEEC. Various vendors are developing energy-efficient high-performance architectures for data centers by leveraging a huge volume of low-power mobile processors (e.g., SeaMicro's SM10000 servers family integrates 512 low-power X86 1.66 GHz, 64-bit, Intel Atom cores [290]). Advances are being made in grid and cluster embedded computing, for example, AMAX's ClusterMax SuperG GPGPU clusters consisting of NVIDIA Tesla 20-series GPU computing platforms feature 57,344 GPU cores and offer 131.84 TFLOPS of single precision performance and 65.92 TFLOPS of double precision performance [291]. Although grid embedded computing has revolutionized HPEEC, but it requires further investigation in the associated task scheduling policies because of the unique dynamics of grid embedded computing. Different heterogeneous embedded processors can be added to or removed from the grid dynamically, which requires intelligent dynamic task scheduling policies to map tasks to the best available computing nodes. The task scheduling policies must consider the impact of dynamic changes in available computing resources on time and energy requirements of tasks.

As the number of on-chip cores increases to satisfy performance demands, communicating data between these cores in an energy-efficient manner becomes challenging and requires scalable, high-bandwidth interconnection networks. Although wireless interconnects provide a power-efficient high-performance alternative to wired interconnects, associated research challenges include partitioning of wired and wireless interconnect domains, directional antenna design, and lightweight medium access control (MAC) protocols. Since many supercomputing applications leverage multiple manycore chips (CMOS technology and power dissipation limit restricts the number of processor cores on a single chip), design of high-bandwidth and low-power interconnection networks between these manycore chips is also an emerging research avenue. Although photonic network designs have been proposed in the literature as a prospective low-power and high-bandwidth solution to interconnect manycore CMPs [292, 293], the domain of scalable interconnection networks (interchip and intrachip) requires further research.

Dynamic optimization techniques that can autonomously adapt embedded systems according to changing application requirements and environmental stimuli present an interesting research avenue. The task scheduling techniques in real-time embedded systems are typically based on tasks' WCETs, which can produce slack time whenever a task finishes execution before the task's deadline. Therefore, dynamic task scheduling techniques that leverage this slack time information at runtime to reduce energy consumption are crucial for HPEEC systems and require further research.

To keep up with the Moore's law, innovative transistor technologies are needed that can permit high transistor density on-chip facilitating chip miniaturization while allowing operation at higher speeds with lower power consumption as compared to the contemporary CMOS transistor technology. Miniaturized embedded multicore processor/memory design and fabrication using new transistor technologies (e.g., multiple gate field-effect transistors (MuGFETs), Fin-FETs, Intel's tri-gate) are interesting HPEEC lithography research avenue [294].

Finally, advanced power monitoring and analysis tools are required for HPEEC platforms to monitor power at a fine granularity (i.e., the functional unit level in relation to an application's code segments) and profile architectural components with respect to power consumption for different code segments. Specifically, power measurement and analysis tools for GPUs are required, considering the proliferation of GPUs in the HPEEC domain [295].

7.7   Chapter Summary

This chapter gave an overarching survey of HPEPEC techniques that enable meeting diverse embedded application requirements. We presented novel architectural approaches in core layout (e.g., heterogeneous CMPs, tiled multicore architectures, 3D multicore architectures), memory design (e.g., cache partitioning, cooperative caching), interconnection networks (e.g., 2D mesh, hypercube), and reduction techniques (e.g., leakage current reduction, peak power reduction) to enhance performance and reduce energy consumption in parallel embedded systems. We discussed hardware-assisted middleware techniques, such as DVFS, ACPI, threading techniques (hyper-threading, helper threading, and speculative threading), DTM, and various low-power gating techniques, for the performance and energy optimization of parallel embedded systems. We described software approaches, such as task scheduling, task migration, and load balancing, for improving performance and power efficiency attainable from a parallel embedded platform. We presented some prominent multicore-based parallel processors and emphasized on their HPEEC features. Finally, we highlighted research challenges and future research directions for HPEPEC.

8

An MDP-Based Dynamic Optimization Methodology for Embedded Wireless Sensor Networks*

Embedded wireless sensor networks (EWSNs) are distributed systems consisting of spatially distributed autonomous sensor nodes that span diverse application domains. The EWSN application domains include security and defense systems, industrial monitoring, building automation, logistics, ecology, environment and ambient conditions monitoring, healthcare, home and office applications, vehicle tracking, and so on. However, this wide application diversity combined with increasing embedded sensor nodes complexity, functionality requirements, and highly constrained operating environments makes EWSN design very challenging.

One critical EWSN design challenge involves meeting *application requirements* such as reliability, lifetime, throughput, and delay (responsiveness) for a myriad of application domains. For example, a vineyard irrigation system may require less responsiveness to environmental stimuli (i.e., decreased irrigation during wet periods), but have a long lifetime requirement. On the other hand, in a disaster relief application, sensor nodes may require high responsiveness but have a short lifetime. Additional requirements may include high adaptability to rapid network changes as sensor nodes are destroyed. Meeting these application-specific requirements is critical to accomplishing the application's assigned function. Nevertheless, satisfying these demands in a scalable and cost-effective way is a challenging task.

Commercial off-the-shelf (COTS) embedded sensor nodes have difficulty meeting application requirements due to inherent manufacturing traits. In order to reduce manufacturing costs,

*A portion of this chapter is copyrighted by IEEE. The definitive version appeared in: Arslan Munir and Ann Gordon-Ross, An MDP-based Dynamic Optimization Methodology for Wireless Sensor Networks, *IEEE Transactions on Parallel and Distributed Systems (TPDS)*, vol. 23, no. 4, pp. 616–625, April 2012. URL http://ieeexplore.ieee .org/xpl/articleDetails.jsp?arnumber=5963653. ©[2012] IEEE. Reprinted with permission from IEEE as we are the authors of this work.

---

generic COTS embedded sensor nodes capable of implementing nearly any application are produced in large volumes and are not specialized to meet any specific application requirements. In order to meet application requirements, sensor nodes must possess tunable parameters. Fortunately, some COTS have *tunable parameters* such as processor voltage, processor frequency, sensing frequency, radio transmission power, and radio transmission frequency.

Embedded sensor node *parameter tuning* is the process of determining appropriate *parameter values*, which meet application requirements. However, determining such values presents several tuning challenges. First, *application managers* (the individuals responsible for EWSN deployment and management) typically lack sufficient technical expertise [297, 298], as many managers are nonexperts (i.e., biologists, teachers, structural engineers, agriculturists). In addition, parameter value tuning is still a cumbersome and time-consuming task even for expert application managers because of unpredictable EWSN environments and difficulty in creating accurate simulation environments. Second, selected parameter values may not be optimal (suboptimal). Given a highly configurable embedded sensor node with many tunable parameters and with many values for each tunable parameter, choosing the optimal combination is difficult. In addition, unanticipated changes in the sensor node's environment can alter optimal parameter values. For example, an embedded sensor node designed to monitor a short-lived volcanic eruption may need to operate for more months/years than expected if earthquakes alter magma flow.

To ease parameter value selection, *dynamic optimizations* enable embedded sensor nodes to dynamically tune their parameter values in situ according to application requirements and environmental stimuli. This dynamic tuning of parameters ensures that an EWSN performs the assigned task optimally, enabling the embedded sensor node to constantly conform to the changing environment. In addition, the application manager need not know embedded sensor node and/or dynamic optimization specifics, thus easing parameter tuning for nonexpert application managers.

Unfortunately, there exists little previous work on EWSN dynamic optimizations with respect to the related high-level application requirements to low-level embedded sensor node parameters. Moreover, changes in application requirements over time were not addressed in previous work. Hence, novel dynamic optimization methodologies that respond to changing application requirements and environmental stimuli are essential.

In this chapter, we propose an application-oriented dynamic tuning methodology for embedded sensor nodes in distributed EWSNs based on Markov decision process (MDP). Our MDP-based application-oriented tuning methodology performs dynamic voltage, frequency, and sensing (sampling) frequency scaling (DVFS2). MDP is an appropriate candidate for EWSN dynamic optimizations where dynamic decision making is a requirement in light of changing environmental stimuli and wireless channel condition. We focus on DVFS2 for several reasons. Traditional microprocessor-based systems use dynamic voltage and frequency scaling (DVFS) for energy optimizations. However, sensor nodes are distinct from traditional systems in that they have embedded sensors coupled with an embedded processor. Therefore, DVFS only provides a partial tuning methodology and does not consider sensing frequency. Sensing frequency tuning is essential for sensor nodes to meet application requirements because the sensed data delay (the delay between the sensor sensing the data and the data's reception by the application manager) depends on the sensor node sensing frequency as it influences the amount of processed and communicated data. Thus, DVFS2 provides enhanced optimization potential as compared to DVFS with respect to EWSNs.

Our main contributions in this chapter are as follows:

- We propose an MDP for dynamic optimization of embedded sensor nodes in EWSNs. MDP is suitable for embedded sensor nodes dynamic optimization because of MDP's inherent ability to perform dynamic decision making. This chapter presents a first step toward MDP-based dynamic optimization.
- Our MDP-based dynamic optimization methodology gives a policy that performs DVFS2 and specifies good quality solution for embedded sensor node parameter tuning for EWSN lifetime.
- Our MDP-based dynamic tuning methodology adapts to changing application requirements and environmental stimuli.
- We provide implementation guidelines for our proposed dynamic tuning methodology in embedded sensor nodes.

We compare our proposed MDP-based application-oriented dynamic tuning methodology with several fixed heuristics. The results show that our proposed methodology outperforms other heuristics for the given application requirements. The broader impacts of our research include facilitating EWSN designers (persons who design EWSNs for an application) to better meet application requirements by selecting suitable tunable parameter values for each sensor node. As this chapter presents a first step toward MDP-based dynamic optimization, our work can potentially spark further research in MDP-based optimizations for embedded sensor nodes in EWSNs.

The remainder of this chapter is organized as follows. A review of related work is given in Section 8.1. Section 8.2 provides an overview of MDP with respect to EWSNs and our proposed MDP-based application-oriented dynamic tuning methodology. Section 8.3 describes the formulation of our proposed methodology as an MDP. Section 8.4 provides implementation guidelines and our proposed methodology's computational complexity. Section 8.5 provides model extensions to our proposed policy. Numerical results are presented in Section 8.6. Section 8.7 concludes our study and outlines future research work directions.

8.1   Related Work

There is a lot of research in the area of dynamic optimizations [187–189, 299], but however, most previous work focuses on the processor or memory (cache) in computer systems. These endeavors can provide valuable insights into embedded sensor nodes' dynamic optimizations, whereas they are not directly applicable to embedded sensor nodes because of different design spaces, platform particulars, and embedded sensor nodes' tight design constraints.

Stevens-Navarro et al. [299] applied MDPs for vertical hands-off decisions in heterogeneous wireless networks. Although our work leverages the reward function idea from their work, our work, for the first time to the best of our knowledge, applies MDPs to dynamic optimizations of embedded sensor nodes in EWSNs.

Little previous work exists in the area of application-specific tuning and dynamic profiling in EWSNs. Sridharan and Lysecky [300] obtained accurate environmental stimuli by dynamically profiling the EWSN's operating environment; however, they did not propose any methodology to leverage these profiling statistics for optimizations. Tilak et al. [301] investigated infrastructure (referred to as sensor node characteristics, number of deployed sensors, and deployment strategy) trade-offs on application requirements. The application requirements considered were accuracy, latency, energy efficiency, fault tolerance, goodput (ratio of total number of packets received to the total number of packets sent), and scalability. However, the authors did not delineate the interdependence between low-level sensor node parameters and high-level application requirements. Kogekar et al. [227] proposed an approach for dynamic software reconfiguration in EWSNs using dynamically adaptive software. Their approach used tasks to detect environmental changes (event occurrences) and adapt the software to the new conditions. Their work did not consider embedded sensor node tunable parameters. Kadayif and Kandemir [302] proposed an automated strategy for data filtering to determine the amount of computation or data filtering to be done at the sensor nodes before transmitting data to the sink node. Unfortunately, the authors only studied the effects of data filtering tuning on energy consumption and did not consider other sensor node parameters and application requirements.

Some previous and current work investigates EWSN operation in changing application (mission) requirements and environmental stimuli. Marrón et al. [303] presented an adaptive cross-layer architecture *TinyCubus* for TinyOS-based sensor networks that allowed dynamic management of components (e.g., caching, aggregation, broadcast strategies) and reliable code distribution considering EWSN topology. *TinyCubus* considered optimization parameters (e.g., energy, communication latency, and bandwidth), application requirements (e.g., reliability), and system parameters (e.g., mobility). The system parameters selected the best set of components based on current application requirements and optimization parameters. Vecchio [304] discussed adaptability in EWSNs at three different levels: communication level (by tuning the communication scheme), application level (by software changes), and hardware level (by injecting new sensor nodes). The International Technology Alliance (ITA) in Network and Information Sciences, sponsored by the UK Ministry of Defense (MoD) and US Army Research Laboratory (ARL), investigates task reassignment and reconfiguration (including physical movement of sensor nodes or reprocessing of data) of already deployed sensor nodes in the sensor field in response to current or predicted future conditions to provide the expected sensed information at a sufficient quality [305]. However, ITA current projects, to the best of our knowledge, do not consider sensor node parameter tuning, and our MDP-based parameter tuning can optimize EWSN operation in changing application requirements.

Several papers explored DVFS for reduced energy consumption. Pillai and Shin [306] proposed real-time dynamic voltage scaling (RT-DVS) algorithms capable of modifying the operating systems' real-time scheduler and task management service for reduced energy consumption. Childers et al. [307] proposed a technique for adjusting supply voltage and frequency at runtime to conserve energy. Their technique monitored a program's instruction-level parallelism (ILP) and adjusted processor voltage and speed in response to the current ILP. Their proposed technique allowed users to specify performance constraints, which the hardware maintained while running at the lowest energy consumption.

Liu and Svensson [308] investigated reducing processor speed by varying the supply and threshold voltages for low power consumption in complementary metal-oxide-semiconductor (CMOS) very-large-scale integration (VLSI). Results showed that an optimized threshold voltage revealed an 8× power savings without any negative performance impacts. In addition, significantly greater energy savings could be achieved by reducing processor speed in tandem with threshold voltage. Burd et al. [309] presented a microprocessor system that dynamically varied its supply voltage and clock frequency to deliver high throughput during critical high-speed execution periods and extended battery life during low-speed execution periods. Results revealed that dynamic voltage scaling (DVS) could improve energy efficiency by 10× for battery-powered processor systems without sacrificing peak throughput.

Min et al. [225] demonstrated that DVS in a sensor node's processor reduced energy consumption. Their technique used a voltage scheduler, running in tandem with the operating system's task scheduler, to adjust voltage and frequency based on a priori knowledge of the predicted sensor node's workload. Yuan and Qu [226] studied a DVFS system for sensor nodes, which required sensor nodes sending data to insert additional information into a transmitted data message's header such as the packet length, expected processing time, and deadline. The receiving sensor node used this message information to select an appropriate processor voltage and frequency to minimize the overall energy consumption.

Some previous works in EWSN optimizations explored greedy and simulated annealing (SA)-based methods. Lysecky and Vahid [310] proposed an SA-based automated application-specific tuning of parameterized sensor-based embedded systems and found that automated tuning can improve EWSN operation by 40% on average. Verma [311] studied SA and particle swarm optimization (PSO) methods for automated application-specific tuning and observed that SA performed better than PSO because PSO often quickly converged to local minima. In prior work, Munir et al. [312] proposed greedy-based and simulated annealing (SA)-based algorithms for parameter tuning. Greedy- and SA-based algorithms are lightweight, whereas these algorithms do not ensure convergence to an optimal solution.

There exists previous work related to DVFS and several initiatives toward application-specific tuning were taken. Nevertheless, the literature presents no mechanisms to determine a dynamic tuning policy for sensor node parameters in accordance with changing application requirements. To the best of our knowledge, we propose the first methodology to address EWSN dynamic optimizations with the goal of meeting application requirements in a dynamic environment.

8.2   MDP-Based Tuning Overview

In this section, we present our MDP-based tuning methodology along with an MDP overview with respect to EWSNs [137].

8.2.1   MDP-Based Tuning Methodology for Embedded Wireless Sensor Networks

Figure 8.1 depicts the process diagram for our MDP-based application-oriented dynamic tuning methodology. Our methodology consists of three logical domains: the application characterization domain, the communication domain, and the sensor node tuning domain.

The *application characterization domain* refers to the EWSN application's characterization/specification. In this domain, the application manager defines various *application metrics* (e.g., tolerable power consumption, tolerable delay), which are calculated from (or based on) application requirements. The application manager also assigns *weight factors* to application metrics to signify the weightage or importance of each application metric. Weight factors provide application managers with an easy method to relate the relative importance of each application metric. The application manager defines an MDP *reward function*, which signifies

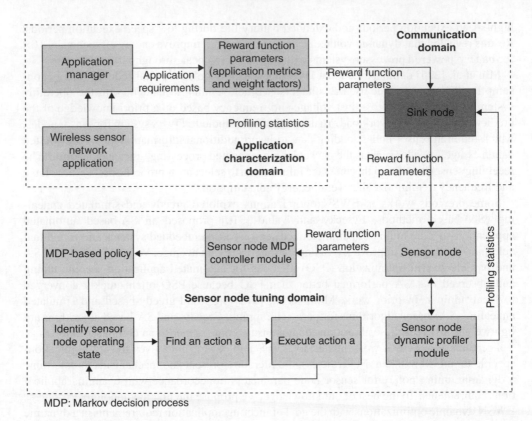

Figure 8.1 Process diagram for our MDP-based application-oriented dynamic tuning methodology for embedded wireless sensor networks

the overall reward (revenue) for given application requirements. The application metrics along with the associated weight factors represents the MDP *reward function parameters*.

The *communication domain* contains the sink node (which gathers statistics from the embedded sensor nodes) and encompasses the communication network between the application manager and the sensor nodes. The application manager transmits the MPD reward function parameters to the sink node via the communication domain. The sink node in turn relays reward function parameters to the embedded sensor nodes.

The *sensor node tuning domain* consists of embedded sensor nodes and performs sensor node tuning. Each sensor node contains an *MDP controller module*, which implements our MDP-based tuning methodology (summarized here and described in detail in Section 8.3). After an embedded sensor node receives reward function parameters from the sink node through the communication domain, the sensor node invokes the MDP controller module. The MDP controller module calculates the *MDP-based policy*. The MDP-based policy prescribes the sensor node *actions* to meet application requirements over the lifetime of the sensor node. An action prescribes the sensor node *state* (defined by processor voltage, processor frequency, and sensing frequency) to transition from the current state. The sensor node identifies its current operating state, determines an action "*a*" prescribed by the MDP-based policy (i.e., whether to continue operation in the current state or transition to another state), and subsequently executes action "*a*."

Our proposed MDP-based dynamic tuning methodology can adapt to changes in application requirements (since application requirements may change with time, for example, a defense system initially deployed to monitor enemy troop position for 4 months may later be required to monitor troop activity for an extended period of 6 months). Whenever application requirements change, the application manager updates the reward function (and/or associated parameters) to reflect the new application requirements. Upon receiving the updated reward function, the sensor node reinvokes MDP controller module and determines the new MDP-based policy to meet the new application requirements.

Our MDP-based application-oriented dynamic tuning methodology reacts to environmental stimuli via a *dynamic profiler module* in the sensor node tuning domain. The dynamic profiler module monitors environmental changes over time and captures unanticipated environmental situations not predictable at design time [300]. The dynamic profiler module may be connected to the sensor node and profiles the *profiling statistics* (e.g., wireless channel condition, number of packets dropped, packet size, radio transmission power) when triggered by the EWSN application. The dynamic profiler module informs the application manager of the profiled statistics via the communication domain. After receiving the profiling statistics, the application manager evaluates the statistics and possibly updates the reward function parameters. This reevaluation process may be automated, thus eliminating the need for continuous application manager input. Based on these received profiling statistics and updated reward function parameters, the sensor node MDP controller module determines whether application requirements are met or not met. If application requirements are not met, the MDP controller module reinvokes the MDP-based policy to determine a new operating state to better meet application requirements. This feedback process continues to ensure that the application requirements are met in the presence of changing environmental stimuli.

Algorithm 3 depicts our MDP-based dynamic tuning methodology in an algorithmic form, which applies to all embedded sensor nodes in the WSN (line 1) and spans the entire lifetime of the embedded sensor nodes (line 2). The algorithm determines an MDP-based policy π^* according to the application's initial requirements (captured by the MDP reward function parameters) at the time of EWSN deployment (lines 3 and 4). The algorithm determines a new MDP-based policy to adapt to the changing application requirements (lines 6 and 7). After determining π^*, the algorithm specifies the action a according to π^* for each embedded sensor node state s, given the total number of states S (lines 9–17).

8.2.2   MDP Overview with Respect to Embedded Wireless Sensor Networks

In this section, we define basic MDP terminology in the context of EWSNs and give an overview of our proposed MDP-based dynamic tuning policy formulation for embedded sensor nodes. MDPs, also known as stochastic dynamic programming, are used to model and solve dynamic decision-making problems. We use standard notations as defined in [313] for our MDP-based problem formulation. Table 8.1 presents a summary of key notations used in this chapter.

The basic elements of an MDP model are *decision epochs and periods*, *states*, *action sets*, *transition probabilities*, and *rewards*. An MDP is *Markovian* (memoryless) because the transition probabilities and rewards depend on the past only through the current state and the action

---

Algorithm 3: Algorithm for our MDP-based application-oriented dynamic tuning methodology for embedded wireless sensor networks.

Input: MDP Reward Function Parameters
Output: An MDP-based Optimal Policy Meeting Application Requirements

1 **foreach** *Embedded Sensor Node in Wireless Sensor Network* **do**
2   **while** *Embedded Sensor Node Alive* **do**
3   **if** *Initial Deployment of Embedded Wireless Sensor Network* **then**
4   Determine MDP-based policy π^* according to initial application requirements characterized by MDP reward function parameters
5   **end**
6   **if** *Embedded Wireless Sensor Network Application Requirements Change* **then**
7   Determine new MDP-based policy π^* according to new application requirements characterized by MDP reward function parameters
8   **end**
9   **foreach** *Embedded Sensor Node State $s \in S$* **do**
10   **while** *embedded sensor node in state i* **do**
11   **if** *action a suggests state different from i* **then**
12   switch to the state given by action a
13   **else**
14   continue operating in state i
15   **end**
16   **end**
17   **end**
18   **end**
19 **end**

Table 8.1 Summary of MDP notations

Notation	Description
s	Sensor node state
S	State space
N	Number of decision epochs
I	Number of sensor node state tuples
$r_t(s, a)$	Reward at time t given state s and action a
$a_{i,j}$	Action to transition from state i to state j
A_s	Allowable actions in state s
$p_t(j|s, a)$	Transition probability function
E_s^π	Expected reward of policy π with initial state s
λ	Discount factor
$v_N^\pi(s)$	Expected total reward
$v_N^\lambda(s)$	Expected total discounted reward
$v(s)$	Maximum expected total discounted reward
d^*	Optimal decision rule
d_t	Decision rule at time t
π^*	Optimal policy
π^{MDP}	MDP-based policy

selected by the decision maker in that state. The *decision epochs* refer to the points of time during a sensor node's lifetime at which the sensor node makes a decision. Specifically, a sensor node makes a decision regarding its operating state at these decision epochs (i.e., whether to continue operating at the current state (processor voltage, frequency, and sensing frequency) or transition to another state). We consider a discrete time process where time is divided into *periods* and a decision epoch corresponds to the beginning of a period. The set of decision epochs can be denoted as $T = \{1, 2, 3, \dots, N\}$, where $N \leq \infty$ and denotes the sensor node's lifetime (each individual time period in T can be denoted as time t). The *decision problem* is referred to as a *finite horizon* problem when the decision-making horizon N is finite and *infinite horizon* otherwise. In a finite horizon problem, the final decision is made at decision epoch $N - 1$; hence, the finite horizon problem is also known as the $N - 1$ period problem.

The system (a sensor node) operates in a particular *state* at each decision epoch, where S denotes the complete set of possible system states. States specify particular sensor node parameter values and each state represents a different combination of these values. An *action set* represents all allowable actions in all possible states. At each decision epoch, the sensor node decides whether to continue operating in the current state or to switch to another state. The sensor node state (in our problem) represents a tuple consisting of processor voltage (V_p), processor frequency (F_p), and sensing frequency (F_s). If the system is in state $s \in S$ at a decision epoch, the sensor node can choose an action a from the set of allowable actions A_s in state s. Thus, an action set can be written as $A = \bigcup_{s \in S} A_s$. We assume that S and A_s do not vary with time t [313].

When a sensor node selects action $a \in A_s$ in state s, the sensor node receives a *reward* $r_t(s, a)$ and the *transition probability distribution* $p_t(\cdot|s, a)$ determines the system state at the next decision epoch. The real-valued function $r_t(s, a)$ denotes the value of the reward received at time t in period t. The reward is referred to as income or cost depending on whether or not $r_t(s, a)$ is positive or negative, respectively. When the reward depends on the system state at the next decision epoch, we let $r_t(s, a, j)$ denote the value of the reward received at time t when the system state at decision epoch t is s. The sensor node selects action $a \in A_s$, and the system occupies the state j at decision epoch $t + 1$. The sensor node evaluates $r_t(s, a)$ using [313]

$$r_t(s, a) = \sum_{j \in S} r_t(s, a, j) p_t(j|s, a) \tag{8.1}$$

where the nonnegative function $p_t(j|s, a)$ is called a *transition probability function*. $p_t(j|s, a)$ denotes the probability that the system occupies state $j \in S$ at time $t + 1$ when the sensor node selects action $a \in A_s$ in state s at time t and usually $\sum_{j \in S} p_t(j|s, a) = 1$. Formally, an MDP is defined as the collection of objects $\{T, S, A_s, p_t(\cdot|s, a), r_t(s, a)\}$.

A *decision rule* prescribes an action in each state at a specified decision epoch. Our decision rule for sensor nodes is a function $d_t : S \rightarrow A_s$, which specifies the action at time t when the system is in state s for each $s \in S$, $d_t(s) \in A_s$. This decision rule is both *Markovian* and *deterministic*.

A *policy* specifies the decision rule for all decision epochs. In the case of sensor nodes, the policy prescribes action selection under any possible system state. A policy π is a sequence of decision rules, that is, $\pi = (d_1, d_2, d_3, \dots, d_{N-1})$ for $N \leq \infty$. A policy is *stationary* if $d_t = d \ \forall t \in T$, that is, for stationary policy $\pi = (d, d, d, \dots, d)$.

As a result of selecting and implementing a particular policy, the sensor node receives rewards at time periods $\{1, 2, 3, \dots, N\}$. The reward sequence is random because the rewards received in different periods are not known prior to policy implementation. The sensor node's optimization objective is to determine a policy that maximizes the corresponding random reward sequence.

8.3 Application-Specific Embedded Sensor Node Tuning Formulation as an MDP

In this section, we describe the formulation of our embedded sensor node application-specific DVFS2 tuning as an MDP. We formulate MDP-based policy constructs (i.e., state space, decision epochs, actions, state dynamics, policy, performance criterion, and reward function) for our system. We also introduce optimality equations and the policy iteration algorithm.

8.3.1 State Space

The state space for our MDP-based tuning methodology is a composite state space containing the Cartesian product of embedded sensor node tunable parameters' state spaces. We define the state space S as

$$S = S_1 \times S_2 \times \cdots \times S_M \; : \; |S| = I \tag{8.2}$$

where $\times$ denotes the Cartesian product, M is the total number of sensor node tunable parameters, S_k denotes the state space for tunable parameter k where $k \in \{1, 2, \ldots, M\}$, and $|S|$ denotes the state space S cardinality (the number of states in S).

The tunable parameter k's state space ($k \in \{1, 2, \ldots, M\}$) S_k consists of n values

$$S_k = \{s_{k_1}, s_{k_2}, s_{k_3}, \ldots, s_{k_n}\} \; : \; |S_k| = n \tag{8.3}$$

where $|S_k|$ denotes the tunable parameter k's state space cardinality (the number of tunable values in S_k). S is a set of n-tuples where each n-tuple represents a sensor node state s. Each state s_i is an n-tuple, that is, $s_i = (v_1, v_2, \ldots, v_M) \; : \; v_k \in S_k$. Note that some n-tuples in S may not be feasible (e.g., all processor voltage and frequency pairs are not feasible) and can be regarded as *do not care* tuples.

Each embedded sensor node state has an associated power consumption, throughput, and delay. The power, throughput, and delay for state s_i are denoted by p_i, t_i, and d_i, respectively. Since different sensor nodes may have different embedded processors and attached sensors, each node may have node-specific power consumption, throughput, and delay information for each state.

8.3.2 Decision Epochs and Actions

Embedded sensor nodes make decisions at decision epochs, which occur after fixed time periods. The sequence of decision epochs is represented as

$$T = \{1, 2, 3, \ldots, N\}, \quad N \leq \infty \tag{8.4}$$

where the random variable N corresponds to the embedded sensor node's lifetime.

At each decision epoch, a sensor node's *action* determines the next state to transition to the given current state. The sensor node action in state $i \in S$ is defined as

$$A_i = \{a_{i,j}\} \in \{0, 1\} \tag{8.5}$$

where $a_{i,j}$ denotes the action taken at time t that causes the sensor node to transition to state j at time $t + 1$ from the current state i. A *policy* determines whether an action is taken or not. If $a_{i,j} = 1$, the action is taken and if $a_{i,j} = 0$, the action is not taken. For a given state $i \in S$, a selected action cannot result in a transition to a state that is not in S. The action space can be defined as

$$A = \{a = [a_{i,j}] : \{a_{i,j}\} \in \{0, 1\},$$

$$i = \{1, 2, 3, \ldots, I\}, j = \{1, 2, 3, \ldots, I\}\} \tag{8.6}$$

8.3.3   State Dynamics

The state dynamics of the system can be delineated by the state transition probabilities of the embedded Markov chain. We formulate our sensor node policy as a deterministic dynamic program (DDP) because the choice of an action determines the subsequent state with certainty. Our sensor node DDP policy formulation uses a *transfer function* to specify the next state. A transfer function defines a mapping $\tau_t(s, a)$ from $S \times A_s \rightarrow S$, which specifies the system state at time $t + 1$ when the sensor node selects action $a \in A_s$ in state s at time t. To formulate our DDP as an MDP, we define the *transition probability function* as

$$p_t(j|s, a) = \begin{cases} 1 & \text{if } \tau_t(s, a) = j \\ 0 & \text{if } \tau_t(s, a) \neq j \end{cases} \tag{8.7}$$

8.3.4   Policy and Performance Criterion

For each given state $s \in S$, a sensor node selects an action $a \in A_s$ according to a policy $\pi \in \Pi$ where Π is a set of admissible policies defined as

$$\Pi = \{\pi : S \rightarrow A_s | d_t(s) \in A_s, \forall s \in S\} \tag{8.8}$$

A *performance criterion* compares the performance of different policies. The sensor node selects an action prescribed by a policy based on the sensor node's current state. If the random variable X_t denotes the state at decision epoch t and the random variable Y_t denotes the action selected at decision epoch t, then for the deterministic case, $Y_t = d_t(X_t)$.

As a result of selecting an action, the sensor node receives a reward $r(X_t, Y_t)$ at time t. The *expected total reward* denotes the expected total reward over the decision-making horizon given a specific policy. Let $v^\pi(s)$ denote the expected total reward over the decision-making horizon when the horizon length N is a random variable, the system is in state s at the first decision epoch, and policy π is used [300, 314]

$$v^\pi(s) = E_s^\pi \left[E_N \left\{ \sum_{t=1}^{N} r(X_t, Y_t) \right\} \right] \tag{8.9}$$

where E_s^π represents the expected reward with respect to policy π and the initial state s (the system state at the time of the expected reward calculation), and E_N denotes the expected reward with respect to the probability distribution of the random variable N. We can write Eq. (8.9) as [313]

$$v^\pi(s) = E_s^\pi \left\{ \sum_{t=1}^\infty \lambda^{t-1} r(X_t, Y_t) \right\} \tag{8.10}$$

which gives the *expected total discounted reward*. We assume that the random variable N is geometrically distributed with parameter λ, and hence the distribution *mean* is $1/(1-\lambda)$ [299]. The parameter λ can be interpreted as a *discount factor*, which measures the present value of one unit of reward received for one period in the future. Thus, $v^\pi(s)$ represents the expected total present value of the reward (income) stream obtained using policy π [313]. Our objective is to find a policy that maximizes the expected total discounted reward, that is, a policy π^* is *optimal* if

$$v^{\pi^*}(s) \geq v^\pi(s), \forall \pi \in \Pi \tag{8.11}$$

8.3.5   Reward Function

The reward function captures application metrics and sensor node characteristics. Our reward function characterization considers the power consumption (which affects the sensor node's lifetime), throughput, and delay application metrics. We define the reward function $f(s,a)$, given the current sensor node state s and the sensor node's selected action a as

$$f(s,a) = \omega_p f_p(s,a) + \omega_t f_t(s,a) + \omega_d f_d(s,a) \tag{8.12}$$

where $f_p(s,a)$ denotes the power reward function; $f_t(s,a)$ denotes the throughput reward function; $f_d(s,a)$ denotes the delay reward function; and ω_p, ω_t, and ω_d represent the *weight factors* for power, throughput, and delay, respectively. The weight factors' constraints are given as $\sum_m \omega_m = 1$ where $m = \{p,t,d\}$ such that $0 \leq \omega_p \leq 1, 0 \leq \omega_t \leq 1$, and $0 \leq \omega_d \leq 1$. The weight factors are selected based on the relative importance of application metrics with respect to each other, for example, a habitat monitoring application taking camera images of the habitat requires a minimum image resolution to provide meaningful analysis that necessitates a minimum throughput, and therefore throughput can be assigned a higher weight factor than the power metric for this application.

We define linear reward functions for application metrics because an application metric reward (objective function) typically varies linearly, or piecewise linearly, between the minimum and the maximum allowed values of the metric [300, 311]. However, a nonlinear characterization of reward functions is also possible and depends on the particular application. We point out that our methodology works for any characterization of reward function. The reward function characterization only defines the reward obtained from operating in a given state. Our MDP-based policy determines the reward by selecting an optimal/suboptimal operating state, given the sensor node design space and application requirements for any reward function characterization. We consider linear reward functions as a typical example from the space of possible reward functions (e.g., piecewise linear, nonlinear) to illustrate our MDP-based policy. We define the power reward function (Fig. 8.2(a)) in Eq. (8.12) as

$$f_p(s,a) = \begin{cases} 1, & 0 < p_a \leq l_r \\ (U_P - p_a)/(U_P - L_P), & L_P < p_a < U_P \\ 0, & p_a \geq U_P \end{cases} \tag{8.13}$$

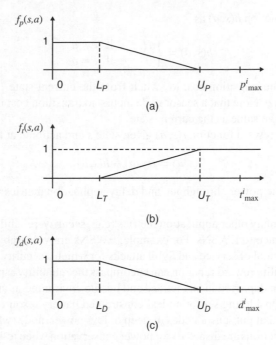

Figure 8.2 Reward functions: (a) power reward function $f_p(s, a)$; (b) throughput reward function $f_t(s, a)$; (c) delay reward function $f_d(s, a)$

where p_a denotes the power consumption of the current state given action a taken at time t, and the constant parameters L_P and U_P denote the minimum and maximum allowed/tolerated sensor node power consumption, respectively.

We define the throughput reward function (Fig. 8.2(b)) in Eq. (8.12) as

$$f_t(s, a) = \begin{cases} 1, & t_a \geq U_T \\ (t_a - L_T)/(U_T - L_T), & L_T < t_a < U_T \\ 0, & t_a \leq L_T \end{cases} \tag{8.14}$$

where t_a denotes the throughput of the current state given action a taken at time t and the constant parameters L_T and U_T denote the minimum and maximum allowed/tolerated throughput, respectively.

We define the delay reward function (Fig. 8.2(c)) in Eq. (8.12) as

$$f_d(s, a) = \begin{cases} 1, & 0 < d_a \leq L_D \\ (U_D - d_a)/(U_D - L_D), & L_D < d_a < U_D \\ 0, & d_a \geq U_D \end{cases} \tag{8.15}$$

where d_a denotes the delay in the current state and the constant parameters L_D and U_D denote the minimum and maximum allowed/tolerated delay, respectively.

State transitioning incurs a cost associated with switching parameter values from the current state to the next state (typically in the form of power and/or execution overhead). We define the transition cost function $h(s, a)$ as

$$h(s, a) = \begin{cases} H_{i,a} & \text{if } i \neq a \\ 0 & \text{if } i = a \end{cases} \tag{8.16}$$

where $H_{i,a}$ denotes the transition cost to switch from the current state i to the next state as determined by action a. Note that a sensor node incurs no transition cost if action a prescribes that the next state is the same as the current state.

Hence, the overall reward function $r(s, a)$ given state s and action a at time t is

$$r(s, a) = f(s, a) - h(s, a) \tag{8.17}$$

which accounts for the power, throughput, and delay application metrics as well as state transition cost.

We point out that many other application metrics (e.g., security, reliability, and lifetime) are of immense significance to EWSNs. For example, EWSNs are vulnerable to security attacks such as distributed denial of service and Sybil attacks for which a security reward function can be included. A reliability reward function can encompass the reliability aspect of EWSNs since sensor nodes are often deployed in unattended and hostile environments and are susceptible to failures. Similarly, considering sensor nodes' constrained battery resources, power optimization techniques exist that put sensor nodes in sleep or low-power mode (where communication and/or processing functions are disabled) for power conservation when less activity is observed in the sensed region as determined by previously sensed data. These power optimizations can be captured by a lifetime reward function. These additional metrics incorporation in our model is the focus of our future work.

8.3.6 Optimality Equation

The optimality equation, also known as Bellman's equation, for expected total discounted reward criterion is given as [313]

$$v(s) = \max_{a \in A_s} \left\{ r(s, a) + \sum_{j \in S} \lambda p(j|s, a)v(j) \right\} \tag{8.18}$$

where $v(s)$ denotes the maximum expected total discounted reward. The following are the salient properties of the optimality equation: the optimality equation has a unique solution; an optimal policy exists in given conditions on states, actions, rewards, and transition probabilities; the value of the discounted MDP satisfies the optimality equation; and the optimality equation characterizes stationary policies.

The solution of Eq. (8.18) gives the maximum expected total discounted reward $v(s)$ and the MDP-based policy π^{MDP}, which gives the maximum $v(s)$. π^{MDP} prescribes the action a from action set A_s, given the current state s for all $s \in S$. There are several methods to solve the optimality equation (8.18) such as value iteration, policy iteration, and linear programming; however, in this work, we use the policy iteration algorithm.

8.3.7   Policy Iteration Algorithm

The policy iteration algorithm can be described in four steps:

(1) Set $l = 0$ and choose any arbitrary decision rule $d_0 \in D$ where D is a set of all possible decision rules.
(2) *Policy evaluation*—Obtain $v^l(s) \ \forall \ s \in S$ by solving the equations:

$$v^l(s) = r(s, a) + \lambda \sum_{j \in S} p(j|s, a)v^l(j) \tag{8.19}$$

(3) *Policy improvement*—Select $d_{l+1} \ \forall \ s \in S$ to satisfy the equations:

$$d_{l+1}(s) \in \arg\max_{a \in A_s} \left\{ r(s, a) + \lambda \sum_{j \in S} p(j|s, a)v^l(j) \right\} \tag{8.20}$$

   and setting $d_{l+1} = d_l$ if possible.
(4) If $d_{l+1} = d_l$, stop and set $d^* = d_l$ where d^* denotes the optimal decision rule. If $d_{l+1} \neq d_l$, set $l = l + 1$ and go to step 2.

Step 2 is referred to as policy evaluation because, by solving Eq. (8.19), we obtain the expected total discounted reward for decision rule d_l. Step 3 is referred to as policy improvement because this step selects a v^l-improving decision rule. In step 4, $d_{l+1} = d_l$ quells cycling because a decision rule is not necessarily unique.

8.4   Implementation Guidelines and Complexity

In this section, we describe the implementation guidelines and computational complexity for our proposed MDP-based policy. The implementation guidelines describe the mapping of MDP specifications (e.g., state space, reward function) in our problem formulation (Section 8.3) to actual sensor node hardware. The computational complexity focuses on the convergence of the policy iteration algorithm and the data memory analysis for our MDP-based dynamic tuning methodology. The prototype implementation of our MDP-based tuning methodology on hardware sensor platforms is the focus of our future work.

8.4.1   Implementation Guidelines

In order to implement our MDP-based policy, particular values must be initially defined. The reward function Eq. (8.17) uses the power, throughput, and delay values offered in an embedded sensor node state s_i (Section 8.3.1). An application manager specifies the minimum and maximum power, throughput, and delay values required by Eq. (8.13)–(8.15), respectively, and the power, throughput, and delay weight factors required in Eq. (8.12) according to application specifications.

A sensor node's embedded processor defines the transition cost $H_{i,a}$ as required in Eq. (8.16), which is dependent on a particular processor's power management and switching techniques. Processors have a set of available voltage and frequency pairs, which defines the V_p and F_p values, respectively, in a sensor node state tuple (Section 8.3.1). Embedded sensors can operate at different defined sensing rates, which define the F_s value in a sensor node state tuple (Section 8.3.1). The embedded processor and sensor characteristics determine the value of I, which characterizes the state space in Eq. (8.2) (i.e., the number of allowable processor voltage, processor frequency, and sensing frequency values determine the total number of sensor node operating states, and thus the value of I).

The sensor nodes perform parameter tuning decisions at decision epochs (Section 8.2.2). The decision epochs can be guided by the dynamic profiler module to adapt to the environmental stimuli. For instance, for a target-tracking application and a fast-moving target, the decision epoch period should be small to better capture the fast-moving target. On the other hand, for stationary or slow-moving targets, decision epoch period should be large to conserve battery energy. However, since the exact decision epoch period is application specific, the period should be adjusted to control the sensor node's lifetime.

Both the MDP controller module (which implements the policy iteration algorithm to calculate the MDP-based policy π^{MDP}) and the dynamic profiler module (Section 8.2.1) can either be implemented as software running on a sensor node's embedded processor or custom hardware for faster execution.

One of the drawbacks for MDP-based policy is that computational and storage overhead increases as the number of states increases. Therefore, EWSN designer would like to restrict the embedded sensor states (e.g., 2, 4, or 16) to reduce the computational and storage overhead. If state restriction is not a viable option, the EWSN configuration could be augmented with a back-end base station node to run our MDP-based optimization, and the sensor node operating states would be communicated to the sensor nodes. This communication of operating state information to sensor nodes by the base station node would not consume enough power resources, given that this state information is transmitted periodically and/or aperiodically after some minimum duration determined by the agility of the environmental stimuli (e.g., more frequent communication would be required for a rapidly changing environmental stimuli as opposed to a slow changing environmental stimuli). This EWSN configuration could also consider *global optimizations*, which are optimizations that take into account sensor node interactions and dependencies and is a focus of our future work. We point out that global optimization storage and processing overhead increases rapidly as the number of sensor nodes in EWSN increases.

8.4.2 Computational Complexity

Since sensor nodes have limited energy reserves and processing resources, it is critical to analyze our proposed MDP-based policy's computational complexity, which is related to the convergence of the policy iteration algorithm. Since our problem formulation (Section 8.3) consists of finite states and actions, Puterman [313] proves a theorem that establishes the convergence of the policy iteration algorithm for finite states and actions in a finite number of iterations. Another important computational complexity factor is the algorithm's convergence rate. Puterman [313] shows that for a finite number of states and actions, the policy iteration algorithm converges to the optimal/suboptimal value function at least quadratically fast. Empirical observations suggest that the policy iteration algorithm can converge in $\mathcal{O}(\ln |S|)$

iterations where each iteration takes $\mathcal{O}(|S|^3)$ time (for policy evaluation); however, no proof yet exists to verify these empirical observations [314]. Based on these empirical observations for convergence, policy iteration algorithm can converge in four iterations for $|S| = 64$.

8.4.3   Data Memory Analysis

We performed data memory analysis using the 8-bit Atmel ATmega128L microprocessor [192] in XSM sensor nodes [315]. The Atmel ATmega128L microprocessor contains 128 KB of on-chip in-system reprogrammable Flash memory for program storage, 4 KB of internal SRAM data memory, and up to 64 KB of external SRAM data memory. Integer and floating-point data types require 2 and 4 B of storage, respectively. Our data memory analysis considers all storage requirements for our MDP-based dynamic tuning formulation (Section 8.3) including state space, action space, state dynamics (transition probability matrix), Bellman's equation (8.18), MDP reward function calculation (reward matrix), and policy iteration algorithm. We estimate data memory size for three sensor node configurations:

- 4 sensor node states with 4 allowable actions in each state (16 actions in the action space) (Fig. 8.4);
- 8 sensor node states with 8 allowable actions in each state (64 actions in the action space);
- 16 sensor node states with 16 allowable actions in each state (256 actions in the action space).

Data memory analysis revealed that 4, 8, and 16 sensor node state configurations required approximately 1.55, 14.8, and 178.55 KB, respectively. Thus, currently available sensor node platforms contain enough memory resources to implement our MDP-based dynamic tuning methodology with 16 sensor node states or fewer. However, the memory requirements increase rapidly as the number of states increases due to the transition probability matrix and reward matrix specifications. Therefore, depending on the available memory resources, an application developer could restrict the number of states accordingly or otherwise would have to resort to doing computations on the back-end base station as outlined in Section 8.4 to conserve power and storage.

8.5   Model Extensions

Our proposed MDP-based dynamic tuning methodology for EWSNs is highly adaptive to different EWSN characteristics and particulars, including additional sensor node tunable parameters (e.g., radio transmission power) and application metrics (e.g., reliability). Furthermore, our problem formulation can be extended to form MDP-based stochastic dynamic programs. Our current MDP-based dynamic optimization methodology provides a basis for MDP-based stochastic dynamic optimization that would react to the changing environmental stimuli and wireless channel conditions to autonomously switch to an appropriate operating state. This stochastic dynamic optimization would provide a major incentive to use an MDP-based policy (because of the capability of MDP to formulate stochastic dynamic programs) as opposed to using lightweight heuristic policies (e.g., greedy or simulated annealing based) for parameter tuning that can determine appropriate operating state out of a large state space without requiring large computational and memory resources [316].

To exemplify additional tuning parameters, we consider a sensor node's transceiver (radio) transmission power. The extended state space can be written as

$$S = V_p \times F_p \times F_s \times P_{tx} \tag{8.21}$$

where P_{tx} denotes the state space for a sensor node's radio transmission power.

We define the sensor node's radio transmission power state space P_{tx} as

$$P_{tx} = \{P_{tx_1}, P_{tx_2}, P_{tx_3}, \dots, P_{tx_m}\} \; : \; |P_{tx}| = m \tag{8.22}$$

where $P_{tx_i} \in P_{tx} \; \forall \, i \in \{1, 2, 3, \dots, m\}$ denotes a radio transmission power, m denotes the number of radio transmission power values, and $|P_{tx}| = m$ denotes the radio transmission power state space cardinality.

To exemplify the inclusion of additional application metrics, we consider reliability, which measures the reliability of sensed data, such as the total number of sensed data packets received at the sink node without error in an arbitrary time window. The reliability can be interpreted as the packet reception rate, which is the complement of the packet error rate (PER) [24]. The factors that affect reliability include wireless channel condition, network topology, traffic patterns, and the physical phenomenon that triggered the sensor node communication activity [24]. In general, the wireless channel condition has the most affect on the reliability metric because sensed data packets may experience different error rates depending on the channel condition. A sensor node may maintain application-specified reliability in different wireless channel conditions by tuning/changing the error correcting codes, modulation schemes, and/or transmission power. The dynamic profiler module in our proposed tuning methodology helps estimating the reliability metric at runtime by profiling the number of packet transmissions from each sensor node and the number of packet receptions at the sink node.

The sensor node's reliability can be added to the reward function and the extended reward function can be written as

$$f(s, a) = \omega_p f_p(s, a) + \omega_t f_t(s, a)$$
$$+ \omega_d f_d(s, a) + \omega_r f_r(s, a) \tag{8.23}$$

where $f_r(s, a)$ denotes the reliability reward function, ω_r represents the weight factor for reliability, and the remainder of the terms in Eq. (8.23) has the same meaning as in Eq. (8.12). The weight factors' constraints are given as $\sum_m \omega_m = 1$ where $m = \{p, t, d, r\}$ such that $0 \leq \omega_p \leq 1$, $0 \leq \omega_t \leq 1$, $0 \leq \omega_d \leq 1$, and $0 \leq \omega_r \leq 1$.

The reliability reward function (Fig. 8.3(a)) in Eq. (8.23) can be defined as

$$f_r(s, a) = \begin{cases} 1, & r_a \geq U_R \\ (r_a - L_R)/(U_R - L_R), & L_R < r_a < U_R \\ 0, & r_a \leq L_R \end{cases} \tag{8.24}$$

where r_a denotes the reliability offered in the current state given action a taken at time t and the constant parameters L_R and U_R denote the minimum and maximum allowed/tolerated reliability, respectively. The reliability may be represented as a multiple of a base reliability unit equal to 0.1, which represents a 10% packet reception rate [24].

The reward function capturing an application's metrics can be defined according to particular application requirements, and may vary quadratically (Fig. 8.3(b)) instead of linearly

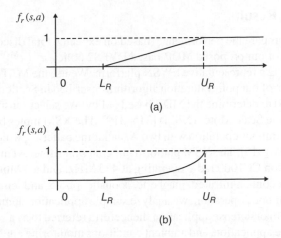

Figure 8.3   Reliability reward functions: (a) linear variation; (b) quadratic variation

(as defined earlier) over the minimum and maximum allowed parameter values and can be expressed as

$$f_r(s, a) = \begin{cases} 1, & r_a \geq U_R \\ (r_a - L_R)^2/(U_R - L_R)^2, & L_R < t_a < U_R \\ 0, & r_a \leq L_R \end{cases} \quad (8.25)$$

Thus, our proposed MDP-based dynamic tuning methodology works with any reward function formulation.

Currently, our problem formulation considers a DDP with fixed states and state transition probabilities equal to 1 (Section 8.3.3); however, our formulation can be extended to form stochastic dynamic programs with different state transition probabilities [317]. One potential extension could include environmental stimuli and wireless channel condition in the state space. The environmental stimuli and wireless channel condition vary with time and have a different probability of being in a certain state at a given point in time. For instance, considering the wireless channel condition along with the sensor node state, the state space vector $s(t)$ can be given as

$$s(t) = [s_s(t), s_c(t)]$$

$$= [s_{s,1}(t), s_{s,2}(t), \dots, s_{s,I}(t),$$

$$s_{c,1}(t), s_{c,2}(t), \dots, s_{c,J}(t)] \quad (8.26)$$

where $s_s(t)$ and $s_c(t)$ represent sensor state and wireless channel state at time t assuming that there are I total sensor states and J total wireless channel states. The state dynamics could be given by $p_t(j|t, s, a)$, which denotes the probability that the system occupies state j in t time units given s and a. If the wireless channel condition does not change state with time, then $p_t(j|t, s, a) = 1 \ \forall \ t$ thus forming a DDP. The determination of $p_t(j|t, s, a)$ requires probabilistic modeling of wireless channel condition over time and is the focus of our future work.

8.6 Numerical Results

In this section, we compare the performance (based on expected total discounted reward criterion (Section 8.3.6)) of our proposed MDP-based DVFS2 policy π^* (π^{MDP}) with several fixed heuristic policies using a representative EWSN platform. We use the MATLAB MDP tool box [318] implementation of our policy iteration algorithm described in Section 8.3.7 to solve Bellman's equation (8.18) to determine the MDP-based policy. We select sensor node state parameters based on eXtreme Scale Motes (XSM) [315, 319]. The XSM motes have an average lifetime of 1000 h of continuous operation with two AA alkaline batteries, which can deliver 6 W h or an average of 6 mW [315]. The XSM platform integrates an Atmel ATmega128L microcontroller [192], a Chipcon CC1000 radio operating at 433 MHz, and a 4 Mbit serial Flash memory. The XSM motes contain infrared, magnetic, acoustic, photo, and temperature sensors.

To represent sensor node operation, we analyze sample application domains that represent a typical security system or defense application (henceforth referred to as a *security/defense system*) [137], healthcare application, and ambient conditions monitoring application. For brevity, we select a single sample EWSN platform configuration and several application domains, but we point out that our proposed MDP model and methodology works equally well for any other EWSN platform and application.

For each application domain, we evaluate the effects of different discount factors, different state transition costs, and different application metric weight factors on the expected total discounted reward for our MDP-based policy and several fixed heuristic policies (Section 8.6.1). The magnitude of difference in the total expected discounted reward for different policies is important as it provides relative comparisons between the different policies.

8.6.1 Fixed Heuristic Policies for Performance Comparisons

Due to the infancy of EWSN dynamic optimizations, there exist no dynamic sensor node tuning methods for comparison with our MDP-based policy. Therefore, we compare to several fixed heuristic policies (heuristic policies have been shown to be a viable comparison method [299]). To provide a consistent comparison, fixed heuristic policies use the same reward function and the associated parameter settings as that of our MDP-based policy. We consider the following four fixed heuristic policies:

- A fixed heuristic policy π^{POW} that always selects the state with the lowest power consumption.
- A fixed heuristic policy π^{THP} that always selects the state with the highest throughput.
- A fixed heuristic policy π^{EQU} that spends an equal amount of time in each of the available states.
- A fixed heuristic policy π^{PRF} that spends an unequal amount of time in each of the available states based on a specified preference for each state. For example, given a system with four possible states, the π^{PRF} policy may spend 40% of time in the first state, 20% of time in the second state, 10% of time in the third state, and 30% of time in the fourth state.

8.6.2 MDP Specifications

We compare different policies using the *expected total discounted reward* performance criterion (Section 8.3.6). The state transition probability for each sensor node state is given by Eq. (8.7). The sensor node's lifetime and the time between decision epochs are subjective and may be assigned by an application manager according to application requirements. A sensor node's *mean lifetime* is given by $1/(1 - \lambda)$ *time units*, which is the time between successive decision epochs (which we assume to be 1 h). For instance for $\lambda = 0.999$, the sensor node's mean lifetime is $1/(1 - 0.999) = 1000\,h \approx 42\,days$.

For our numerical results, we consider a sensor node capable of operating in four different states (i.e., $I = 4$ in Eq. (8.2)). Figure 8.4 shows the symbolic representation of our MDP model with four sensor node states. Each state has a set of allowed actions prescribing transitions to available states. For each allowed action a in a state, there is a $\{r_a, p_a\}$ pair where r_a specifies the immediate reward obtained by taking action a and p_a denotes the probability of taking action a.

Table 8.2 summarizes state parameter values for each of the four states s_1–s_4. We define each state using a $[V_p, F_p, F_s]$ tuple where V_p is specified in volts, F_p in MHz, and F_s in kHz. For instance, state one s_1 is defined as $[2.7, 2, 2]$, which corresponds to a processor voltage of

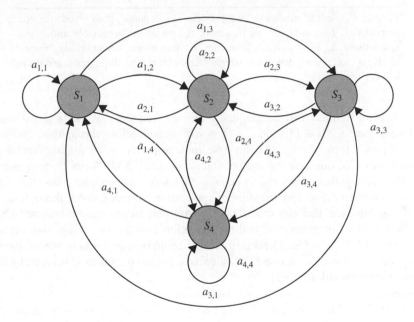

Figure 8.4   Symbolic representation of our MDP model with four sensor node states

Table 8.2   Parameters for wireless sensor node state $s_i = [V_p, F_p, F_s]$ (V_p is specified in volts, F_p in MHz, and F_s in kHz)

Notation	$s_1 = [2.7, 2, 2]$ (units)	$s_2 = [3, 4, 4]$ (units)	$s_3 = [4, 6, 6]$ (units)	$s_4 = [5.5, 8, 8]$ (units)
p_i	10	15	30	55
t_i	4	8	12	16
d_i	26	14	8	6

Parameters are specified as a multiple of a base unit where one power unit is equal to 1 mW, one throughput unit is equal to 0.5 MIPS, and one delay unit is equal to 50 ms. Parameter values are based on the XSM mote (p_i, t_i, and d_i denote the power consumption, throughput, and delay, respectively, in state s_i)

Table 8.3 Minimum L and maximum U reward function parameter values and application metric weight factors for a security/defense system, health care, and ambient conditions monitoring application

Notation	Security/defense	Health care	Ambient monitoring
L_P	12 units	8 units	5 units
U_P	35 units	20 units	32 units
L_T	6 units	3 units	2 units
U_T	12 units	9 units	8 units
L_D	7 units	8 units	12 units
U_D	16 units	20 units	40 units
ω_p	0.45	0.5	0.65
ω_t	0.2	0.3	0.15
ω_d	0.35	0.2	0.2

L_P and U_P denote minimum and maximum acceptable power consumption, respectively; L_T and U_T denote minimum and maximum acceptable throughput, respectively; L_D and U_D denote minimum and maximum acceptable delay, respectively; ω_p, ω_t, and ω_d denote the weight factors for power, throughput, and delay, respectively.

2.7 V, a processor frequency of 2 MHz, and a sensing frequency of 2 kHz (2000 samples/s). We represent state $s_i \ \forall \ i \in \{1, 2, 3, \dots, I\}$ power consumption, throughput, and delay as multiples of power, throughput, and delay base units, respectively. We assume one base power unit is equal to 1 mW, one base throughput unit is equal to 0.5 MIPS (millions of instructions per second), and one base delay unit is equal to 50 ms. We assign base units such that these units provide a convenient representation of application metrics (power, throughput, delay). We point out, however, that any other feasible base unit values can be assigned [299]. We assume, without loss of generality, that the transition cost for switching from one state to another is $H_{i,a} = 0.1$ if $i \neq a$. The transition cost could be a function of power, throughput, and delay, but we assume a constant transition cost for simplicity as it is typically constant for different state transitions [192].

Our selection of the state parameter values in Table 8.2 corresponds to XSM mote specifications [193, 316]. The XSM mote's Atmel ATmega128L microprocessor has an operating voltage range of 2.7–5.5 V and a processor frequency range of 0–8 MHz. The ATmega128L throughput varies with processor frequency at 1 MIPS/MHz, thus allowing an application manager to optimize power consumption versus processing speed [192]. Our chosen sensing frequency also corresponds with standard sensor node specifications. The Honeywell HMC1002 magnetometer sensor [320] consumes on average 15 mW of power and can be sampled in 0.1 ms on the Atmel ATmega128L microprocessor, which results in a maximum sampling frequency of approximately 10 kHz (10,000 samples/s). The acoustic sensor embedded in the XSM mote has a maximum sensing frequency of approximately 8.192 kHz [315]. Although the power consumption in a state depends not only on the processor voltage and frequency but also on the processor utilization, which also depends on sensing frequency, we report the average power consumption values in a state as derived from the data sheets [193, 322].

Table 8.3 summarizes the minimum L and maximum U reward function parameter values for application metrics (power, throughput, and delay) and the associated weight factors for a security/defense system, health care, and ambient conditions monitoring application. Our selected reward function parameter values represent typical application requirements [81]. We describe later the relative importance of these application metrics with respect to our considered applications.

Although power is a primary concern for all EWSN applications and tolerable power consumption values are specified based on the desired EWSN lifetime considering limited battery resources of sensor nodes. However, a relative importance in power for different applications can be delineated mainly by the infeasibility of sensor node's battery replacement due to hostile environments. For example, sensor nodes in a war zone for a security/defense application and an active volcano monitoring application make battery replacement almost impractical. For a healthcare application with sensors attached to a patient to monitor physiological data (e.g., heart rate, glucose level), sensor node's battery may be replaced though power is constrained because excessive heat dissipation could adversely affect a patient's health. Similarly, delay can be an important factor for security/defense in case of enemy target tracking and health care for a patient in intensive health conditions, whereas delay may be relatively less important for a humidity monitoring application. A data-sensitive security/defense system may require a comparatively large minimum throughput in order to obtain a sufficient number of sensed data samples for meaningful analysis. Although relative importance and minimum and maximum values of these application metrics can vary widely with an application domain and between application domains, we pick our parameter values (Table 8.3) for demonstration purposes to provide an insight into our optimization methodology.

We point out that all of our considered application metrics specifically throughput depends on the traffic pattern. EWSN throughput is a complex function of the number of nodes, traffic volume and patterns, and the parameters of the medium access technique. As the number of nodes and traffic volume increases, contention-based medium access methods result in an increased number of packet collisions, which waste energy without transmitting useful data. This contention and packet collision results in saturation, which decreases the effective throughput and increases the delay sharply. We briefly outline the variance in EWSN traffic patterns for our considered applications. The security/defense application would have infrequent bursts of heavy traffic (e.g., when an enemy target appears within the sensor nodes' sensing range), healthcare applications would have a steady flow of medium-to-high traffic, and ambient conditions monitoring applications would have a steady flow of low-to-medium traffic except for emergencies (e.g., volcano eruption). Although modeling of application metrics with respect to traffic patterns would result in a better characterization of these metric values at particular instants/times in WSN, these metric values can still be bounded by a lower minimum value and an upper maximum value as captured by our reward functions (Section 8.3.5).

Given the reward function, sensor node state parameters corresponding to XSM mote, and transition probabilities, our MATLAB MDP tool box [318] implementation of policy iteration algorithm solves Bellman's equation (8.18) to determine the MDP-based policy and determines the expected total discounted reward (Eq. (8.10)).

8.6.3   Results for a Security/Defense System Application

8.6.3.1   The Effects of Different Discount Factors on the Expected Total Discounted Reward

Table 8.4 and Fig. 8.5 depict the effects of different discount factors λ on the heuristic policies and π^{MDP} for a security/defense system when the state transition cost $H_{i,j}$ is held constant

Table 8.4 The effects of different discount factors λ for a security/defense system

Discount factor λ	Sensor lifetime (h)	π^{MDP}	π^{POW}	π^{THP}	π^{EQU}	π^{PRF}
0.94	16.67	10.0006	7.5111	9.0778	7.2692	7.5586
0.95	20	12.0302	9.0111	10.9111	8.723	9.0687
0.96	25	15.0747	11.2611	13.6611	10.9038	11.3339
0.97	33.33	20.1489	15.0111	18.2445	14.5383	15.1091
0.98	50	30.2972	22.5111	27.4111	21.8075	22.6596
0.99	100	60.7422	45.0111	54.9111	43.6150	45.3111
0.999	1000	608.7522	450.0111	549.9111	436.15	453.0381
0.9999	10,000	6.0889×10^3	4.5×10^3	5.5×10^3	4.4×10^3	4.5×10^3
0.99999	100,000	6.1×10^4	4.5×10^4	5.5×10^4	4.4×10^4	4.5×10^4

$H_{i,j} = 0.1$ if $i \neq j$, $\omega_p = 0.45$, $\omega_t = 0.2$, $\omega_d = 0.35$

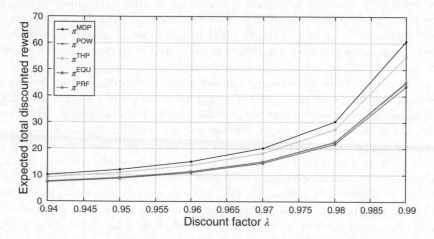

Figure 8.5 The effects of different discount factors on the expected total discounted reward for a security/defense system. $H_{i,j} = 0.1$ if $i \neq j$, $\omega_p = 0.45$, $\omega_t = 0.2$, $\omega_d = 0.35$

at 0.1 for $i \neq j$, and $\omega_p, \omega_t,$ and ω_d are equal to 0.45, 0.2, and 0.35, respectively. Since we assume the time between successive decision epochs to be 1 h, the range of λ from 0.94 to 0.99999 corresponds to a range of average sensor node lifetime from 16.67 to 100,000 h ≈ 4167 days ≈ 11.4 years. Table 8.4 and Fig. 8.5 show that π^{MDP} results in the highest expected total discounted reward for all values of λ and corresponding average sensor node lifetimes.

Figure 8.6 shows the percentage improvement in expected total discounted reward for π^{MDP} for a security/defense system as compared to the fixed heuristic policies. The percentage improvement is calculated as $[(R^{\text{MDP}} - R^X)/R^{\text{MDP}}] \times 100$ where R^{MDP} denotes the expected total discounted reward for π^{MDP} and R^X denotes the expected total discounted reward for the X fixed heuristic policy where $X = \{\text{POW, THP, EQU, PRF}\}$. For instance, when the average sensor node lifetime is 1000 h ($\lambda = 0.999$), π^{MDP} results in a 26.08%, 9.67%, 28.35%, and 25.58% increase in expected total discounted reward compared to π^{POW}, π^{THP}, π^{EQU}, and

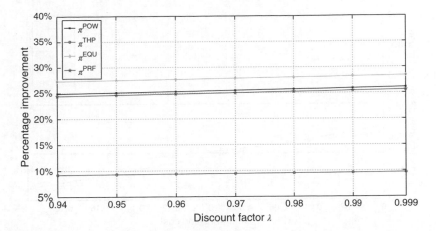

Figure 8.6 Percentage improvement in expected total discounted reward for π^{MDP} for a security/defense system as compared to the fixed heuristic policies. $H_{i,j} = 0.1$ if $i \neq j$, $\omega_p = 0.45$, $\omega_t = 0.2, \omega_d = 0.35$

π^{PRF}, respectively. Figure 8.6 also depicts that π^{MDP} shows increased savings as the average sensor node lifetime increases due to an increase in the number of decision epochs and thus prolonged operation of sensor nodes in optimal/suboptimal states as prescribed by π^{MDP}. On average over all discount factors λ, π^{MDP} results in a 25.57%, 9.48%, 27.91%, and 25.1% increase in expected total discounted reward compared to π^{POW}, π^{THP}, π^{EQU}, and π^{PRF}, respectively.

8.6.3.2 The Effects of Different State Transition Costs on the Expected Total Discounted Reward

Figure 8.7 depicts the effects of different state transition costs on the expected total discounted reward for a security/defense system with a fixed average sensor node lifetime of 1000 h ($\lambda = 0.999$) and ω_p, ω_t, and ω_d equal to 0.45, 0.2, and 0.35, respectively. Figure 8.7 shows that π^{MDP} results in the highest expected total discounted reward for all transition cost values.

Figure 8.7 also shows that the expected total discounted reward for π^{MDP} is relatively unaffected by state transition cost. This relatively constant behavior can be explained by the fact that our MDP policy does not perform many state transitions. Relatively few state transitions to reach the optimal/suboptimal state according to the specified application metrics may be advantageous for some application managers who consider the number of state transitions prescribed by a policy as a secondary evaluation criteria [299]. π^{MDP} performs state transitions primarily at sensor node deployment or whenever a new MDP-based policy is determined as the result of changes in application requirements.

We further analyze the effects of different state transition costs on the fixed heuristic policies, which consistently result in a lower expected total discounted reward as compared to π^{MDP}. The expected total discounted rewards for π^{POW} and π^{THP} are relatively unaffected by state transition cost. The explanation for this behavior is that these heuristics perform state

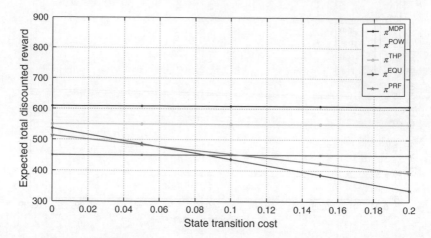

Figure 8.7 The effects of different state transition costs on the expected total discounted reward for a security/defense system. $\lambda = 0.999, \omega_p = 0.45, \omega_t = 0.2, \omega_d = 0.35$

transitions only at initial sensor node deployment when the sensor node transitions to the lowest power state and the highest throughput state, respectively, and remain in these states for the entire sensor node's lifetime. On the other hand, state transition cost has the largest affect on the expected total discounted reward for π^{EQU} due to high state transition rates because the policy spends an equal amount of time in all states. Similarly, high switching costs have a large affect on the expected total discounted reward for π^{PRF} (although less severely than π^{EQU}) because π^{PRF} spends a certain percentage of time in each available state (Section 8.6.1), thus requiring comparatively fewer transitions than π^{EQU}.

8.6.3.3 The Effects of Different Reward Function Weight Factors on the Expected Total Discounted Reward

Figure 8.8 shows the effects of different reward function weight factors on the expected total discounted reward for a security/defense system when the average sensor node lifetime is 1000 h ($\lambda = 0.999$) and the state transition cost $H_{i,j}$ is held constant at 0.1 for $i \neq j$. We explore various weight factors that are appropriate for different security/defense system specifics, that is, $(\omega_p, \omega_t, \omega_d) = \{(0.35, 0.1, 0.55), (0.45, 0.2, 0.35), (0.5, 0.3, 0.2), (0.55, 0.35, 0.1)\}$. Figure 8.8 reveals that π^{MDP} results in the highest expected total discounted reward for all weight factor variations.

8.6.4 Results for a Healthcare Application

8.6.4.1 The Effects of Different Discount Factors on the Expected Total Discounted Reward

Figure 8.9 depicts the effects of different discount factors λ for a healthcare application when the state transition cost $H_{i,j}$ is held constant at 0.1 for $i \neq j$, and $\omega_p, \omega_t,$ and ω_d are equal to

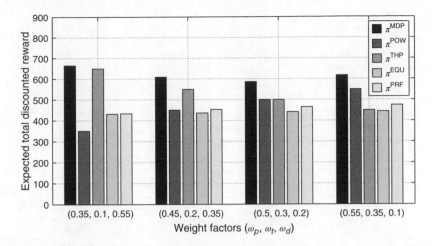

Figure 8.8 The effects of different reward function weight factors on the expected total discounted reward for a security/defense system. $\lambda = 0.999$, $H_{i,j} = 0.1$ if $i \neq j$

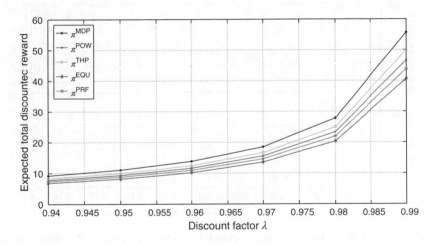

Figure 8.9 The effects of different discount factors on the expected total discounted reward for a healthcare application. $H_{i,j} = 0.1$ if $i \neq j$, $\omega_p = 0.5$, $\omega_t = 0.3$, $\omega_d = 0.2$

0.5, 0.3, and 0.2, respectively. Figure 8.9 shows that π^{MDP} results in the highest expected total discounted reward for all values of λ and the corresponding average sensor node lifetimes as compared to other fixed heuristic policies.

Figure 8.10 shows the percentage improvement in expected total discounted reward for π^{MDP} for a healthcare application as compared to the fixed heuristic policies. For instance, when the average sensor node lifetime is 1000 h ($\lambda = 0.999$), π^{MDP} results in a 16.39%, 10.43%, 27.22%, and 21.47% increase in expected total discounted reward compared to π^{POW}, π^{THP}, π^{EQU}, and π^{PRF}, respectively. On average over all discount factors λ, π^{MDP}

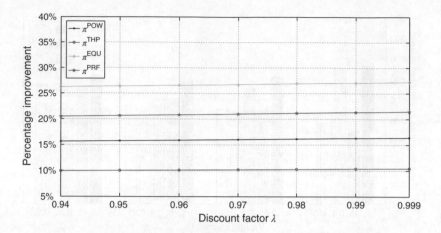

Figure 8.10   Percentage improvement in expected total discounted reward for π^{MDP} for a healthcare application as compared to the fixed heuristic policies. $H_{i,j} = 0.1$ if $i \neq j$, $\omega_p = 0.5, \omega_t = 0.3, \omega_d = 0.2$

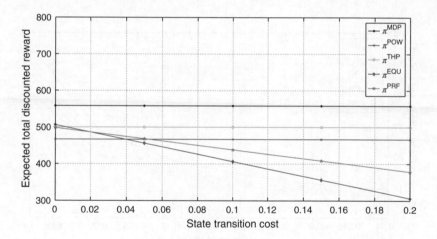

Figure 8.11   The effects of different state transition costs on the expected total discounted reward for a healthcare application. $\lambda = 0.999$, $\omega_p = 0.5, \omega_t = 0.3, \omega_d = 0.2$

results in a 16.07%, 10.23%, 26.8%, and 21.04% increase in expected total discounted reward compared to π^{POW}, π^{THP}, π^{EQU}, and π^{PRF}, respectively.

8.6.4.2   The Effects of Different State Transition Costs on the Expected Total Discounted Reward

Figure 8.11 shows the effects of different state transition costs on the expected total discounted reward for a healthcare application with a fixed average sensor node lifetime of 1000 h

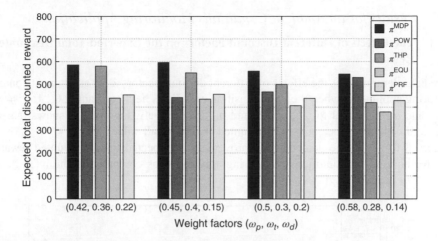

Figure 8.12   The effects of different reward function weight factors on the expected total discounted reward for a healthcare application. $\lambda = 0.999$, $H_{i,j} = 0.1$ if $i \neq j$

($\lambda = 0.999$) and ω_p, ω_t, and ω_d equal to 0.5, 0.3, and 0.2, respectively. Figure 8.11 shows that π^{MDP} results in the highest expected total discounted reward for all transition cost values. The fixed heuristic policies consistently result in a lower expected total discounted reward as compared to π^{MDP}. Comparison of Figs. 8.7 and 8.11 reveals that a security/defense system and a healthcare application have similar trends with respect to different state transition costs on the expected total discounted reward.

8.6.4.3   The Effects of Different Reward Function Weight Factors on the Expected Total Discounted Reward

Figure 8.12 depicts the effects of different reward function weight factors on the expected total discounted reward for a healthcare application when the average sensor node lifetime is 1000 h ($\lambda = 0.999$) and the state transition cost H_{ij} is kept constant at 0.1 for $i \neq j$. We explore various weight factors that are appropriate for different healthcare application specifics (i.e., $(\omega_p, \omega_t, \omega_d) = \{(0.42, 0.36, 0.22), (0.45, 0.4, 0.15), (0.5, 0.3, 0.2), (0.58, 0.28, 0.14)\}$). Figure 8.12 shows that π^{MDP} results in the highest expected total discounted reward for all weight factor variations.

Figures 8.8 and 8.12 show that the expected total discounted reward of π^{POW} gradually increases as the power weight factor increases and eventually exceeds that of π^{THP} for a security/defense system and a healthcare application, respectively. However, close observation reveals that the expected total discounted reward of π^{POW} for a security/defense system is affected more sharply than a healthcare application because of the more stringent constraint on maximum acceptable power for a healthcare application (Table 8.3). Figures 8.8 and 8.12 show that π^{PRF} tends to perform better than π^{EQU} with increasing power weight factors because π^{PRF} spends a greater percentage of time in low power states.

8.6.5   Results for an Ambient Conditions Monitoring Application

8.6.5.1   The Effects of Different Discount Factors on the Expected Total Discounted Reward

Figure 8.13 demonstrates the effects of different discount factors λ for an ambient conditions monitoring application when the state transition cost $H_{i,j}$ is held constant at 0.1 for $i \neq j$, and ω_p, ω_t, and ω_d are equal to 0.65, 0.15, and 0.2, respectively. Figure 8.13 shows that π^{MDP} results in the highest expected total discounted reward for all values of λ.

Figure 8.14 shows the percentage improvement in expected total discounted reward for π^{MDP} for an ambient conditions monitoring application as compared to the fixed heuristic

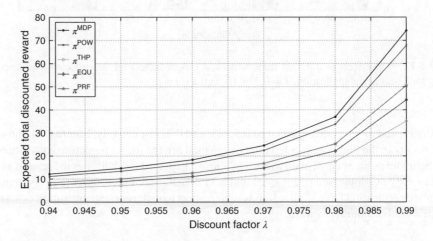

Figure 8.13   The effects of different discount factors on the expected total discounted reward for an ambient conditions monitoring application. $H_{i,j} = 0.1$ if $i \neq j$, $\omega_p = 0.65$, $\omega_t = 0.15$, $\omega_d = 0.2$

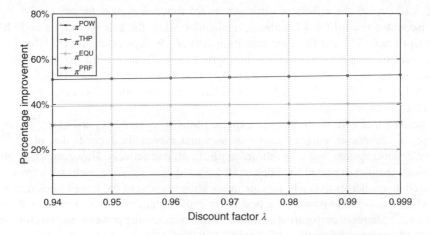

Figure 8.14   Percentage improvement in expected total discounted reward for π^{MDP} for an ambient conditions monitoring application as compared to the fixed heuristic policies. $H_{i,j} = 0.1$ if $i \neq j$, $\omega_p = 0.65$, $\omega_t = 0.15$, $\omega_d = 0.2$

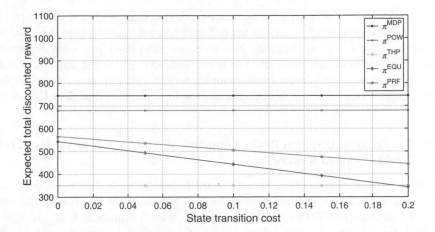

Figure 8.15   The effects of different state transition costs on the expected total discounted reward for an ambient conditions monitoring application. $\lambda = 0.999, \omega_p = 0.65, \omega_t = 0.15, \omega_d = 0.2$

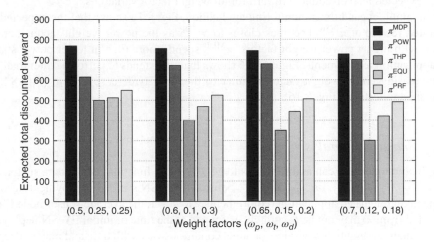

Figure 8.16   The effects of different reward function weight factors on the expected total discounted reward for an ambient conditions monitoring application. $\lambda = 0.999, H_{i,j} = 0.1$ if $i \neq j$

policies. For instance, when the average sensor node lifetime is 1000h ($\lambda = 0.999$), π^{MDP} results in a 8.77%, 52.99%, 40.49%, and 32.11% increase in expected total discounted reward as compared to $\pi^{POW}, \pi^{THP}, \pi^{EQU}$, and π^{PRF}, respectively. On average over all discount factors λ, π^{MDP} results in a 8.63%, 52.13%, 39.92%, and 31.59% increase in expected total discounted reward as compared to $\pi^{POW}, \pi^{THP}, \pi^{EQU}$, and π^{PRF}, respectively.

8.6.5.2   The Effects of Different State Transition Costs on the Expected Total Discounted Reward

Figure 8.15 depicts the effects of different state transition costs on the expected total discounted reward for an ambient conditions monitoring application with a fixed average sensor node lifetime of 1000 h ($\lambda = 0.999$) and ω_p, ω_t, and ω_d equal to 0.65, 0.15, and 0.2, respectively. Figure 8.15 reveals that π^{MDP} results in the highest expected total discounted reward for all transition cost values. The fixed heuristic policies consistently result in a lower expected total discounted reward as compared to π^{MDP}. Figure 8.15 reveals that the ambient conditions monitoring application has similar trends with respect to different state transition costs as compared to the security/defense system (Fig. 8.7) and healthcare applications (Fig. 8.7).

8.6.5.3　The Effects of Different Reward Function Weight Factors on the Expected Total Discounted Reward

Figure 8.16 shows the effects of different reward function weight factors on the expected total discounted reward for an ambient conditions monitoring application when the average sensor node lifetime is 1000 h ($\lambda = 0.999$) and the state transition cost $H_{i,j}$ is held constant at 0.1 for $i \neq j$. We explore various weight factors that are appropriate for different ambient conditions monitoring application specifics (i.e., $(\omega_p, \omega_t, \omega_d) = \{(0.5, 0.25, 0.25),$ $(0.6, 0.1, 0.3), (0.65, 0.15, 0.2), (0.7, 0.12, 0.18)\}$). Figure 8.16 reveals that π^{MDP} results in the highest expected total discounted reward for all weight factor variations.

For an ambient conditions monitoring application, Fig. 8.16 shows that the expected total discounted reward of π^{POW} becomes closer to π^{MDP} as the power weight factor increases, because with higher power weight factors, π^{MDP} spends more time in lower power states to meet application requirements. Figure 8.16 shows that π^{PRF} tends to perform better than π^{EQU} with increasing power weight factors similar to the security/defense system (Fig. 8.8) and healthcare applications (Fig. 8.16).

8.6.6　Sensitivity Analysis

An application manager can assign values to MDP reward function parameters, such as $H_{i,a}$, L_P, U_P, L_T, U_T, L_D, U_D, ω_p, ω_t, and ω_d, before an EWSN's initial deployment according to projected/anticipated application requirements. However, the average sensor node lifetime (calculated from λ) may not be accurately estimated at the time of initial EWSN deployment, as environmental stimuli and wireless channel conditions vary with time and may not be accurately anticipated. The sensor node's lifetime depends on sensor node activity (both processing and communication), which varies with the changing environmental stimuli and wireless channel conditions. *Sensitivity analysis* analyzes the effects of changes in average sensor node lifetime after initial deployment on the expected total discounted reward. Thus, if the actual lifetime is different than the estimated lifetime, what is the loss in total expected discounted reward if the actual lifetime had been accurately predicted at deployment.

EWSN sensitivity analysis can be carried out with the following steps [299]:

(1) Determine the expected total discounted reward given the actual average sensor node lifetime $l = 1/(1 - \lambda)$, referred to as the *Optimal Reward R_o*.
(2) Let $\hat{l}$ denote the estimated average sensor node lifetime, and δl denote the percentage change from the actual average sensor node lifetime (i.e., $\hat{l} = (1 + \delta l)l$). $\hat{l}$ results in a

suboptimal policy with a corresponding suboptimal total expected discounted reward, referred to as *Suboptimal Reward* R_{so}.

(3) The *Reward Ratio* r is the ratio of the suboptimal reward to the optimal reward (i.e., $r = R_{so}/R_o$), which indicates suboptimal expected total discounted reward variation with the average sensor node lifetime estimation inaccuracy.

It can be shown that the reward ratio varies from $(0, 2]$ as δl varies from $(-100\%, 100\%]$. The reward ratio's ideal value is 1, which occurs when the average sensor node lifetime is accurately estimated/predicted ($\hat{l} = l$ corresponding to $\delta l = 0$). Sensitivity analysis revealed that our MDP-based policy is sensitive to accurate determination of parameters, especially average lifetime, because inaccurate average sensor node lifetime results in a suboptimal expected total discounted reward. The dynamic profiler module (Fig. 8.1) measures/profiles the remaining battery energy (lifetime) and sends this information to the application manager along with other profiled statistics (Section 8.2.1), which helps in accurate estimation of λ. Estimating λ using the dynamic profiler's feedback ensures that the estimated average sensor node lifetime differs only slightly from the actual average sensor node lifetime, and thus helps in maintaining a reward ratio close to 1.

8.6.7   Number of Iterations for Convergence

The policy iteration algorithm determines π^{MDP} and the corresponding expected total discounted reward on the order of $O(\ln(|S|))$, where S is the total number of states. In our numerical results with four sensor node states, the policy iteration algorithm converges in two iterations on average.

8.7   Chapter Summary

In this chapter, we presented an application-oriented dynamic tuning methodology for embedded sensor nodes in distributed EWSNs based on MDPs. Our MDP-based policy tuned embedded sensor node processor voltage, frequency, and sensing frequency in accordance with application requirements over the lifetime of a sensor node. Our proposed methodology was adaptive and dynamically determined the new MDP-based policy whenever application requirements change (which may be in accordance with changing environmental stimuli). We compared our MDP-based policy with four fixed heuristic policies and concluded that our proposed MDP-based policy outperformed each heuristic policy for all sensor node lifetimes, state transition costs, and application metric weight factors. We provided the implementation guidelines of our proposed policy in embedded sensor nodes. We proved that our proposed policy had fast convergence rate, computationally inexpensive, and thus could be considered for implementation in sensor nodes with limited processing resources.

Extension of this work includes enhancing our MDP model to incorporate additional high-level application metrics (e.g., security, reliability, energy, lifetime) as well as additional embedded sensor node tunable parameters (such as radio transmission power, radio transmission frequency). Furthermore, incorporation of wireless channel condition in the MDP state space, thus formulating a stochastic dynamic program that enables sensor node tuning in accordance with changing wireless channel condition, will be an interesting research. Sensor node tuning automation can be enhanced using profiling statistics by architecting mechanisms that enable the sensor node to automatically react to environmental stimuli without the need for an application manager's feedback. Extension of our MDP-based dynamic optimization methodology for performing *global optimization* (i.e., selection of sensor node tunable parameter settings to ensure that application requirements are met for EWSN as a whole where different sensor nodes collaborate with each other in optimal/suboptimal tunable parameter settings determination) will be an interesting research problem to explore.

9

Online Algorithms for Dynamic Optimization of Embedded Wireless Sensor Networks*

An embedded wireless sensor network (EWSN) typically consists of a set of spatially distributed embedded sensor nodes that wirelessly communicate with each other to collectively accomplish an application-specific task. Due to technological advancements in wireless communications and embedded systems, there exists a plethora of EWSN applications, including security/defense systems, industrial automation, health care, and logistics.

Given the wide range of EWSN applications, an application designer is left with the challenging task of designing an EWSN while taking into consideration *application requirements* (lifetime, throughput, reliability, etc.). Moreover, these application requirements are affected by environmental stimuli (e.g., poor wireless channel conditions may necessitate increased transmission power) and can change over time as operational situations evolve (e.g., unexpected winds fuel a dying forest fire). Since commercial off-the-shelf (COTS) embedded sensor nodes have limited resources (i.e., battery lifetime, processing power), delicate design and trade-off considerations are necessary to meet often competing application requirements (e.g., high processing requirements with long lifetime requirements).

In order to meet a wide range of application requirements, COTS embedded sensor nodes are generically designed, but however, *tunable parameters* (e.g., processor voltage, processor frequency, sensing frequency, radio transmission power, packet size) enable the embedded sensor node to *tune* operation to meet application requirements. Nevertheless, application designers are left with the task of *parameter tuning* during EWSN design time. Parameter tuning is the process of assigning appropriate values for sensor node tunable parameters in

*A portion of this chapter is copyrighted by IEEE. The definitive version appeared in: Arslan Munir, Ann Gordon-Ross, Susan Lysecky, and Roman Lysecky, Online Algorithms for Wireless Sensor Networks Dynamic Optimization, in *Proc. of IEEE Consumer Communications and Networking Conference (CCNC)*, Las Vegas, Nevada, January 2012. URL http://ieeexplore.ieee.org/xpl/articleDetails.jsp?arnumber=6181082. ©[2012] IEEE. Reprinted with permission from IEEE as we are the authors of this work.

order to meet application requirements. Parameter tuning involves several challenges such as optimal parameter value selection given large design spaces, consideration for competing application requirements and tunable parameters, difficulties in creating accurate simulation environments, slow simulation times, and so on. In addition, design time static determination of these parameters leaves the embedded sensor node with little or no flexibility to adapt to the actual operating environment. Furthermore, many application designers are nonexperts (e.g., agriculturist, biologists) and lack sufficient expertise for parameter tuning. Therefore, autonomous parameter tuning methodologies may alleviate many of these design challenges.

Dynamic optimizations enable autonomous embedded sensor node parameter tuning using special hardware/software algorithms to determine parameter values in situ according to application requirements and changing environmental stimuli. Dynamic optimizations require minimal application designer effort and enable application designers to specify only high-level application requirements without the knowledge of parameter specifics. Nevertheless, dynamic optimizations rely on fast and lightweight online optimization algorithms for in situ parameter tuning.

The dynamic profiling and optimization project aspires at alleviating the complexities associated with sensor-based system design through the use of dynamic profiling methods capable of observing application-level behavior and dynamic optimization to tune the underlying platform accordingly [321]. The dynamic profiling and optimization project has evaluated dynamic profiling methods for observing application-level behavior by gathering profiling statistics, but dynamic optimization methods still need exploration. In our previous work [137], we proposed a Markov decision process (MDP)-based methodology to prescribe optimal/suboptimal sensor node operation to meet application requirements and adapt to changing environmental stimuli. However, the MDP-based policy was not autonomous because the methodology required the application designer to orchestrate MDP-based policy reevaluation whenever application requirements and environmental stimuli changed. In addition, since policy reevaluation was computationally and memory expensive, this process was done offline on a powerful desktop machine.

To enable in situ autonomous EWSN dynamic optimizations, we propose an online EWSN optimization methodology that extends static design time parameter tuning [310]. Our methodology is advantageous over static design time parameter tuning because our methodology enables the embedded sensor node to automatically adapt to actual changing environmental stimuli, resulting in closer adherence to application requirements. Furthermore, our methodology is more amenable to nonexpert application designers and requires no application designer effort after initial EWSN deployment. Lightweight (low computational and memory resources) online algorithms are crucial for embedded sensor nodes considering limited processing, storage, and energy resources of embedded sensor nodes in distributed EWSNs. Our online lightweight optimization algorithms impart fast design space exploration to yield an optimal or near-optimal parameter value selection.

The remainder of this chapter is organized as follows. A review of related work is given in Section 9.1. Section 9.2 provides an overview of dynamic optimization methodology and also presents online lightweight optimization algorithms/heuristics for our dynamic optimization methodology. Experimental results for online optimization algorithms are presented in Section 9.3. Finally, Section 9.4 concludes the chapter.

9.1 Related Work

There exists much research in the area of dynamic optimizations [185–188], but however, most previous work focuses on the processor or memory (cache) in computer systems. These endeavors can provide valuable insights into EWSN dynamic optimizations, whereas they are not directly applicable to EWSNs due to different design spaces, platform particulars, and a sensor node's tight design constraints.

In the area of EWSN dynamic profiling and optimizations, Sridharan and Lysecky [300] obtained accurate environmental stimuli by dynamically profiling the EWSN's operating environment, but however, did not propose any methodology to leverage these profiling statistics for optimizations. In our previous work [137], we proposed an automated MDP-based methodology to prescribe optimal sensor node operation to meet application requirements and adapt to changing environmental stimuli. Kogekar et al. [227] proposed an approach for dynamic software reconfiguration in EWSNs using dynamically adaptive software, which used tasks to detect environmental changes (event occurrences) and adapt the software to the new conditions. Their work did not consider sensor node tunable parameters.

Several papers explored dynamic voltage and frequency scaling (DVFS) for reduced energy consumption in EWSNs. Min et al. [225] demonstrated that dynamic processor voltage scaling reduced energy consumption by 60%. Similarly, Yuan and Qu [226] studied a DVFS system that used additional transmitted data packet information to select appropriate processor voltage and frequency values. Although DVFS provides a mechanism for dynamic optimizations, considering additional sensor node tunable parameters increases the design space and the sensor node's ability to meet application requirements. To the best of our knowledge, our work is the first to explore an extensive sensor node design space.

Some previous works in EWSN optimizations explore greedy and simulated annealing (SA)-based methods, but these previous works did not analyze execution time and memory requirements. Huber et al. [322] maximized the amount of data gathered using a distributed greedy scheduling algorithm that aimed at determining an optimal sensing schedule, which consisted of a time sequence of scheduled sensor node measurements. In prior work, Lysecky and Vahid [310] proposed an SA-based automated application-specific tuning of parameterized sensor-based embedded systems and found that automated tuning can improve EWSN operation by 40% on average. Verma [311] studied SA and particle swarm optimization (PSO) methods for automated application-specific tuning and observed that SA performed better than PSO because PSO often quickly converged to local minima.

Although previous works in EWSN optimizations explore greedy and SA-based methods, these previous works did not analyze execution time and memory requirements. Furthermore, the previous works did not investigate greedy and SA algorithms as online algorithms for dynamic optimizations. Prior work [310, 311] considered a limited design space with a few sensor node tunable parameters. To address the deficiencies in previous work, we analyze greedy and SA algorithms as online algorithms for performing dynamic optimizations considering a large design space containing many tunable parameters and values. This fine-grained design space enables embedded sensor nodes to more closely meet application requirements, but exacerbates optimization challenges considering an embedded sensor node's constrained memory and computational resources.

9.2   Dynamic Optimization Methodology

In this section, we give an overview of our dynamic optimization methodology. We also formulate the state space, objective function, and online lightweight optimization algorithms/ heuristics for our dynamic optimization methodology.

9.2.1   Methodology Overview

Figure 9.1 depicts our dynamic optimization methodology. The application designer specifies application requirements using high-level application metrics (e.g., lifetime, throughput, reliability), associated minimum and maximum desired/acceptable values, and associated *weight factors* that specify the importance of each high-level metric with respect to each other.

The shaded box in Fig. 9.1 depicts the overall operational flow, orchestrated by the *dynamic optimization controller*, at each sensor node. The dynamic optimization controller receives application requirements and invokes the *dynamic optimization module*. The dynamic optimization module determines the sensor node's operating *state* (tunable parameter value settings) using an online optimization algorithm. The sensor node will operate in that state until a state change is necessary. State changes occur to react to changing environmental stimuli using the *dynamic profiler module* and *profiling statistics processing module*.

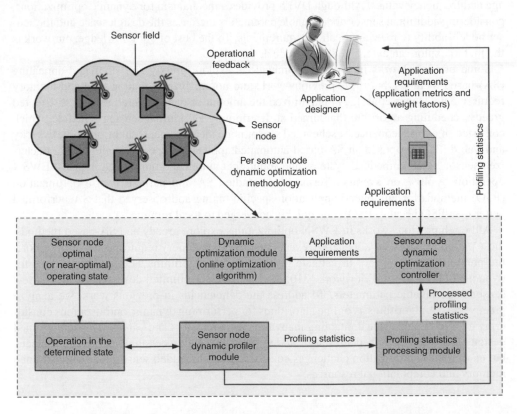

Figure 9.1   Dynamic optimization methodology for distributed EWSNs

The dynamic profiler module records profiling statistics (e.g., wireless channel condition, number of dropped packets, packet size, radio transmission power), and the profiling statistics processing module performs any necessary data processing. The dynamic optimization controller evaluates the processed profiling statistics to determine if the current operating state meets the application requirements. If the application requirements are not met, the dynamic optimization controller reinvokes the dynamic optimization module to determine a new operating state. This feedback process continues to ensure the selection of an appropriate operating state to best meet the application requirements. Currently, our online algorithms do not directly consider these profiling statistics, but that incorporation is the focus of our future work.

9.2.2   State Space

The state space S for our dynamic optimization methodology is defined as

$$S = S_1 \times S_2 \times \ldots \times S_N \tag{9.1}$$

where N denotes the number of tunable parameters, S_i denotes the state space for tunable parameter $i, \forall\, i \in \{1, 2, \ldots, N\}$, and $\times$ denotes the Cartesian product. Each tunable parameter's state space S_i consists of n values

$$S_i = \{s_{i_1}, s_{i_2}, s_{i_3}, \ldots, s_{i_n}\} \quad : \quad |S_i| = n \tag{9.2}$$

where $|S_i|$ denotes the tunable parameter i's state space cardinality (the number of tunable values in S_i). S is a set of n-tuples where each n-tuple represents a sensor node state s. Note that some n-tuples in S may not be feasible (e.g., all processor voltage and frequency pairs are not feasible) and can be regarded as *do not care* tuples.

9.2.3   Objective Function

The embedded sensor node dynamic optimization problem can be formulated as

$$\max\ \ f(s)$$
$$\text{s.t.}\ \ \ s \in S \tag{9.3}$$

where $f(s)$ represents the objective function and captures application requirements and can be given as

$$f(s) = \sum_{k=1}^{m} \omega_k f_k(s)$$
$$\text{s.t.}\ \ \ s \in S$$
$$\omega_k \geq 0, k = 1, 2, \ldots, m$$
$$\omega_k \leq 1, k = 1, 2, \ldots, m$$
$$\sum_{k=1}^{m} \omega_k = 1 \tag{9.4}$$

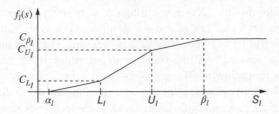

Figure 9.2   Lifetime objective function $f_l(s)$

where $f_k(s)$ and ω_k denote the objective function and weight factor for the kth application metric, respectively, given that there are m application metrics. Our objective function characterization considers lifetime, throughput, and reliability (i.e., $m = 3$) (additional application metrics can be included) and is given as

$$f(s) = \omega_l f_l(s) + \omega_t f_t(s) + \omega_r f_r(s) \tag{9.5}$$

where $f_l(s), f_t(s)$, and $f_r(s)$ denote the lifetime, throughput, and reliability objective functions, respectively, and ω_l, ω_t, and ω_r denote the weight factors for lifetime, throughput, and reliability, respectively.

We consider piecewise linear objective functions for lifetime, throughput, and reliability [310, 311]. We define the lifetime objective function (Fig. 9.2) in Eq. (9.5) as

$$f_l(s) = \begin{cases} 1, & s_l \geq \beta_l \\ C_{U_l} + \dfrac{(C_{\beta_l} - C_{U_l})(s_l - U_l)}{(\beta_l - U_l)}, & U_l \leq s_l < \beta_l \\ C_{L_l} + \dfrac{(C_{U_l} - C_{L_l})(s_l - L_l)}{(U_l - L_l)}, & L_l \leq s_l < U_l \\ C_{L_l} \cdot \dfrac{(s_l - \alpha_l)}{(L_l - \alpha_l)}, & \alpha_l \leq s_l < L_l \\ 0, & s_l < \alpha_l \end{cases} \tag{9.6}$$

where s_l denotes the lifetime offered by state s, the constant parameters L_l and U_l denote the desired minimum and maximum lifetime, and the constant parameters α_l and β_l denote the acceptable minimum and maximum lifetime. Using both desirable and acceptable values enable the application designer to specify the reward (gain) for operating in either a desired range or an acceptable range, where the reward gradient (slope) in the desired range would be greater than the reward gradient in the acceptable range, but however, there would be no reward for operating outside of the acceptable range. The constant parameters C_{L_l}, C_{U_l}, and C_{β_l} in Eq. (9.6) denote the lifetime objective function value at L_l, U_l, and β_l, respectively. The throughput and reliability objective functions can be defined similar to Eq. (9.6).

9.2.4   Online Optimization Algorithms

In this section, we present our online optimization algorithms/heuristics for dynamic optimizations. We focus on two main online optimization algorithms, a greedy and an SA based.

9.2.4.1 Greedy Algorithm

Algorithm 4: Greedy algorithm for embedded sensor node dynamic optimization.

Input: $f(s)$, N, n
Output: Sensor node state that maximizes $f(s)$ and the corresponding $f(s)$ value
1 $\mu \leftarrow$ initial tunable parameter values ;
2 *objBestSol* $\leftarrow$ solution from state μ ;
3 **foreach** *Embedded Sensor Node Tunable Parameter* **do**
4   **for** $i \leftarrow 1$ **to** n **do**
5   *objSolTemp* $\leftarrow$ current state β solution ;
6   **if** *objSolTemp* > *objBestSol* **then**
7   *objBestSol* $\leftarrow$ *objSolTemp* ;
8              $\mu \leftarrow \beta$;
9   **else**
10   break ;
11   **end**
12   **end**
13   select the next tunable parameter ;
14 **end**
15 **return** μ, *objBestSol*

Algorithm 4 depicts our greedy algorithm, which takes as input the objective function $f(s)$ (Eq. (9.5)), the number of embedded sensor node tunable parameters N, and each tunable parameter's design space cardinality n (the algorithm assumes the same state space cardinality for all tunable parameters for notational simplicity). The algorithm sets the initial state μ with initial tunable parameter values (line 1) and the best solution objective function value *objBestSol* to the value obtained from the initial state μ (line 2). The algorithm explores each parameter in turn, starting from the last parameter (with state space S_N in Eq. (9.1)), while holding all other parameters fixed according to μ. For each parameter values (explored in ascending order) denoted as current state β, the algorithm computes the objective function value *objSolTemp* (lines 4 and 5). If the current state results in an improvement in the objective function value (line 6), *objSolTemp* and μ are updated to the new best state (lines 6–8). This process continues until there is no objective function value improvement (*objSolTemp* < *objBestSol*), at which point that parameter value is fixed (lines 9–11) and the next parameter is explored (e.g., S_{N-1} is explored after S_N (Eq. (9.1))). After exploring all parameters (lines 3–14), the algorithm returns the best state μ and μ's objective function value *objBestSol* (line 15).

In the greedy algorithm, the exploration order of the tunable parameters and parameter values (i.e., ascending or descending) can be governed by high-level metric weight factors to produce higher quality results and/or explore fewer states. For example, parameters with the greatest effect on a high-level metric with a high weight factor could be explored first. Currently, our greedy algorithm explores tunable parameter values in an ascending order, considering a generic EWSN application assuming all weight factors to be equal (i.e., $\omega_l = \omega_t = \omega_r$ in Eq. (9.5)). However, our future work will explore specializing parameter exploration with respect to high-level metrics and weight factors.

Algorithm 5: Simulated annealing algorithm for embedded sensor node dynamic optimization.

Input: $f(s)$, N, n, T_0, α, c_0, t_0
Output: Sensor node state that maximizes $f(s)$ and the corresponding $f(s)$ value

1   $c, t, q \leftarrow 0$;
2   $\mu \leftarrow \mathtt{rand}()\,\%N$;
3   $T_q \leftarrow T_0$;
4   *objSolInit* $\leftarrow$ solution from state μ ;
5   *objSolTemp* $\leftarrow$ *objSolInit* ;
6   *objBestSol* $\leftarrow$ *objSolInit* ;
7   $q \leftarrow q + 1$;
8   **while** $t < t_0$ **do**
9   **while** $c < c_0$ **do**
10   **if** $\mathtt{rand}() > \mathtt{RAND\_MAX}/2$ **then**
11          $\beta \leftarrow |(\mu + \mathtt{rand}()\,\%N)|\%N$;
12   **else**
13          $\beta \leftarrow |(\mu - \mathtt{rand}()\,\%N)|\%N$;
14   **end**
15   *objSolNew* $\leftarrow$ new state β solution ;
16   **if** *objSolNew* > *bestSol* **then**
17   *objBestSol* $\leftarrow$ *objSolNew* ;
18          $\zeta \leftarrow \beta$;
19   **end**
20   **if** *objSolNew* > *objSolTemp* **then**
21          $P \leftarrow 1$;
22   **else**
23          $P \leftarrow exp((objSolNew - objSolTemp)/T_q)$;
24   **end**
25        $rP \leftarrow \mathtt{rand}()/\mathtt{RAND\_MAX}$;
26   **if** $P > rP$ **then**
27   *objSolTemp* $\leftarrow$ *objSolNew* ;
28          $\zeta \leftarrow \beta$;
29   **end**
30        $q \leftarrow q + 1$;
31        $c \leftarrow c + 1$;
32   **end**
33      $T_q \leftarrow \alpha \cdot T_q$;
34      $t \leftarrow t + 1$;
35      $c \leftarrow 0$;
36 **end**
37 **return** ζ, *objBestSol*

9.2.4.2 Simulated Annealing Algorithm

Algorithm 5 depicts our SA algorithm, which takes as input the objective function $f(s)$ (Eq. (9.5)), the number of sensor node tunable parameters N, each tunable parameter's design space cardinality n, the SA initial temperature T_0, the cooling schedule scale factor α (which determines the annealing schedule), the number of trials c_0 performed at each temperature t_i, and the total number of temperature reductions t_0. The algorithm performs the following initializations (lines 1–6): the number of trials c at a given temperature t_i, the number of temperature reductions t, and the number of states explored q are initialized to zero (line 1); the initial values for all tunable parameters μ where $|\mu| = N$ are set pseudorandomly (line 2) [323]; the current annealing temperature T_q is initialized to T_0 (line 3); the initial state μ's objective function value is assigned to the variable *objSolInit* (line 4); the current state objective function value *objSolTemp* and the best state objective function value *objBestSol* are initialized to *objSolInit* (lines 5 and 6).

The algorithm begins the state exploration by first incrementing the number of states explored q from 0 to 1 (line 7). For each *trial* (lines 10–31), the algorithm explores new neighboring states β where $|\beta| = N$ pseudorandomly (lines 10–14) in search of a better solution and calculates the resulting objective function value *objSolNew* (line 15). If the new state β offers a higher objective function value as compared to the previous *objBestSol*, the new state becomes the best solution (lines 16–19), otherwise the algorithm determines the *acceptance probability* P of the new state being selected as the current state using the Metropolis–Hastings random walk algorithm (lines 20–29) [324]. At high temperatures, the Metropolis–Hastings algorithm accepts all moves (random walk) while at low temperatures, the Metropolis–Hastings algorithm performs stochastic hill-climbing (the acceptance probability depends on the difference between the objective function and the annealing temperature). At the end of each trial, the annealing temperature is decreased exponentially (line 33), and the process continues until $t \rightarrow t_0$ (lines 8–36). After all trials have completed, the algorithm returns the current best state ζ and the resulting objective function value *objBestSol* (line 37).

The selection of the SA algorithm's parameters is critical in determining a good quality solution for embedded sensor node parameter tuning. Specifically, the selection of the T_0 value is important because an inappropriate T_0 value may yield lower quality solutions. We propose to set T_0 equal to the maximal objective function difference between any two neighboring states (i.e., $T_0 = \max|\Delta f(s)|$ where $\Delta f(s)$ denotes the objective function difference between any two neighboring states). This proposition is an extension of T_0 selection based on the maximal energy difference between neighboring states [324, 325]. However, it is not possible to estimate $\max|\Delta f(s)|$ between two neighboring states because SA explores the design space pseudorandomly. We propose an approximation $T_0 \approx |\max|f(s)| - \min|f(s)||$ where $\min|f(s)|$ and $\max|f(s)|$ denote the minimum and maximum objective function values in the design space, respectively. The exhaustive search algorithm can be used to find $\min|f(s)|$ and $\max|f(s)|$ by minimizing and maximizing the objective function, respectively.

9.3 Experimental Results

In this section, we describe our experimental setup and experimental results for greedy and SA algorithms for different application domains. These results evaluate the greedy and SA algorithms in terms of solution quality and the percentage of state space explored. We also present data memory, execution time, and energy results to provide insights into the complexity and energy requirements of our online algorithms.

9.3.1 Experimental Setup

Our experiments are based on the Crossbow IRIS motes [80] that operate using two AA alkaline batteries with a battery capacity of 2000 mA h. This platform integrates an Atmel

ATmega1281 microcontroller [77], an Atmel AT86RF230 low-power 2.4-GHz transceiver [78], and a MTS400 sensor board [75] with Sensirion SHT1x humidity and temperature sensors [76]. In order to investigate the fidelity of our online algorithms across small and large design spaces, we consider two design space cardinalities (number of states in the design space) $|S| = 729$ and $|S| = 31,104$. The state space $|S| = 729$ results from six tunable parameters with three tunable values each: processor voltage $V_p = \{2.7, 3.3, 4\}$ (V), processor frequency $F_p = \{4, 6, 8\}$ (MHz) [77], sensing frequency $F_s = \{1, 2, 3\}$ (samples/s) [76], packet transmission interval $P_{ti} = \{60, 300, 600\}$ (s), packet size $P_s = \{41, 56, 64\}$ (B), and transceiver transmission power $P_{tx} = \{-17, -3, 1\}$ (dBm) [78]. The tunable parameters for $|S| = 31,104$ are $V_p = \{1.8, 2.7, 3.3, 4, 4.5, 5\}$ (V), $F_p = \{2, 4, 6, 8, 12, 16\}$ (MHz) [77], $F_s = \{0.2, 0.5, 1, 2, 3, 4\}$ (samples/s) [76], $P_s = \{32, 41, 56, 64, 100, 127\}$ (B), $P_{ti} = \{10, 30, 60, 300, 600, 1200\}$ (s), and $P_{tx} = \{-17, -3, 1, 3\}$ (dBm) [78]. All state space tuples are feasible for $|S| = 729$, whereas $|S| = 31,104$ contains 7779 infeasible state space tuples (e.g., all V_p and F_p pairs are not feasible).

We analyze three sample application domains: a security/defense system, a healthcare application, and an ambient conditions monitoring application. To model each application domain, we assign application-specific values for the desirable minimum L, desirable maximum U, acceptable minimum α, and acceptable maximum β objective function parameter values for application metrics and the associated weight factors. We specify the objective function parameters as a multiple of a base unit where one lifetime unit is equal to 5 days, one throughput unit is equal to 20 kbps, and one reliability unit is equal to 0.05 (percentage of error-free packet transmissions). We assign application metric values for an application considering the application's typical requirements [137]. For example, a healthcare application with a sensor implanted into a patient to monitor physiological data (e.g., heart rate, glucose level) may have a longer lifetime requirement because frequent battery replacement may be difficult. Table 9.1

Table 9.1 Desirable minimum L, desirable maximum U, acceptable minimum α, and acceptable maximum β objective function parameter values for a security/defense system, health care, and an ambient conditions monitoring application

Notation	Security/defense (units)	Health care (units)	Ambient monitoring (units)
L_l	8	12	6
U_l	30	32	40
α_l	1	2	3
β_l	36	40	60
L_t	20	19	15
U_t	34	36	29
α_t	0.5	0.4	0.05
β_t	45	47	35
L_r	14	12	11
U_r	19.8	17	16
α_r	10	8	6
β_r	20	20	20

One lifetime unit = 5 days, one throughput unit = 20 kbps, one reliability unit = 0.05.

depicts the application requirements in terms of objective function parameter values for the three application domains.

The lifetime, throughput, and reliability objective function values corresponding to the desirable minimum and maximum parameter values are 0.1 and 0.9, respectively, and the objective function values corresponding to the acceptable minimum and maximum parameter values are 0 and 1, respectively.

For brevity, we selected a single sample EWSN platform configuration and three application domains, but we point out that our dynamic optimization methodology and online optimization algorithms are equally applicable to any EWSN platform and application.

9.3.2   Results

We implemented our greedy and SA-based online optimization algorithms in C++ and evaluated the algorithms in terms of the percentage of the design space explored, the quality (objective function value) of each algorithm's determined best state as compared to the optimal state determined using an exhaustive search, and the total execution time. We also performed data memory and energy analysis to analyze scalability for different design space sizes.

Figure 9.3 shows the objective function value normalized to the optimal solution for the SA and greedy algorithms versus the number of states explored for a security/defense system for $|S| = 729$ where $\omega_l = 0.25$, $\omega_t = 0.35$, and $\omega_r = 0.4$. The SA parameters are calculated as outlined in Section 9.2.4.2 (e.g., $T_0 = |\max|f(s)| - \min|f(s)|| = |0.7737 - 0.1321| = 0.6416$ and $\alpha = 0.8$ [324]). Figure 9.3 shows that the greedy and SA algorithms converged to a steady state solution after exploring 11 and 400 states, respectively. These convergence results show that the greedy algorithm converged to the final solution faster than the SA algorithm, exploring only 1.51% of the design space, whereas the SA algorithm explored 54.87% of the design

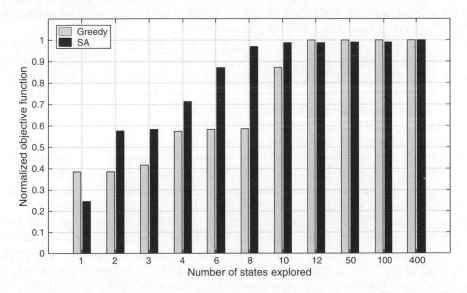

Figure 9.3   Objective function value normalized to the optimal solution for a varying number of states explored for the greedy and simulated annealing algorithms for a security/defense system where $\omega_l = 0.25$, $\omega_t = 0.35$, $\omega_r = 0.4$, $|S| = 729$

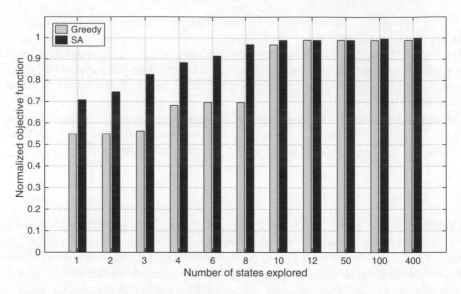

Figure 9.4   Objective function value normalized to the optimal solution for a varying number of states explored for the greedy and simulated annealing algorithms for a healthcare application where $\omega_l = 0.25$, $\omega_t = 0.35$, $\omega_r = 0.4$, $|S| = 729$

space. The figure reveals that the average growth rate for increasing the solution quality was faster in the initial iterations than in the later iterations. Figure 9.3 shows an average growth rate of approximately 22.96% and 52.56% for the initial iterations for the greedy and SA algorithms, respectively, and decreased to 12.8% and 0.00322% for the later iterations of the greedy and SA algorithms, respectively. Both the algorithms converged to the optimal solution as was obtained from an exhaustive search of the design space.

Figure 9.4 shows the objective function value normalized to the optimal solution for the SA and greedy algorithms versus the number of states explored for a healthcare application for $|S| = 729$ where $\omega_l = 0.25$, $\omega_t = 0.35$, and $\omega_r = 0.4$. The SA parameters are $T_0 = |0.7472 - 0.2254| = 0.5218$ and $\alpha = 0.8$ [324]. Figure 9.4 shows that the greedy and SA algorithms converged to a steady-state solution after exploring 11 states (1.51% of the design space) and 400 states (54.87% of the design space), respectively. The SA algorithm converged to the optimal solution after exploring 400 states, whereas the greedy algorithm's solution quality after exploring 11 states was within 0.027% of the optimal solution. Figure 9.4 shows an average growth rate of approximately 11.76% and 5.22% for the initial iterations for the greedy and SA algorithms, respectively, and decreased by 2.27% and 0.001% for the later iterations of the greedy and SA algorithms, respectively.

Figure 9.5 shows the objective function value normalized to the optimal solution for the SA and greedy algorithms versus the number of states explored for an ambient condition monitoring application for $|S| = 31, 104$ where $\omega_l = 0.6$, $\omega_t = 0.25$, $\omega_r = 0.15$. The SA parameters are $T_0 = |0.8191 - 0.2163| = 0.6028$ and $\alpha = 0.8$ [324]. Figure 9.5 shows that the greedy and SA algorithms converged to a steady-state solution after exploring 9 states (0.029% of the design space) and 400 states (1.29% of the design space), respectively (this represents a similar trend as for the security/defense and health-care applications). The greedy and SA algorithms' solutions after exploring 9 and 400 states are within 6.6% and 0.5% of the optimal solution,

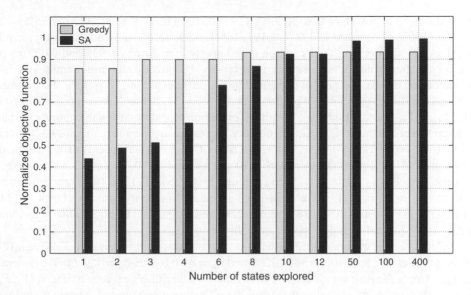

Figure 9.5   Objective function value normalized to the optimal solution for a varying number of states explored for the greedy and simulated annealing algorithms for an ambient conditions monitoring application where $\omega_l = 0.6$, $\omega_t = 0.25$, $\omega_r = 0.15$, $|S| = 31,104$

respectively. Figure 9.5 shows an average growth rate of approximately 5.02% and 8.16% for the initial iterations for the greedy and SA algorithms, respectively, and 0.11% and 0.0017% for the later iterations of the greedy and SA algorithms, respectively.

The results also provide insights into the convergence rates and reveal that even though the design space cardinality increases by 43×(from 729 to 31,104), the greedy and SA algorithms still explore only a small percentage of the design space and result in high-quality solutions. The results indicate that the SA algorithm converges to the optimal (or near optimal) solution slowly; however, the SA algorithm can result in a desired solution quality by controlling the allowable number of states explored. The results reveal that for tightly constrained runtimes, the greedy algorithm can provide better results than the SA algorithm (e.g., when exploration of only 6 states (0.82% of S) or less is allowed); however, the SA algorithm requires longer runtimes to achieve a near-optimal solutions (e.g., the greedy algorithm obtained a solution within 8.3% of the optimal solution on average after exploring 1.37% of design space, whereas the SA algorithm obtained a solution within 0.237% of the optimal solution on average after exploring 54.87% of design space for $|S| = 729$).

To verify that our algorithms are lightweight, we analyzed the execution time, energy consumption, and data memory requirements. We measured the execution time (averaged over 10,000 runs to smooth any discrepancies due to operating system overheads) for both algorithms on an Intel Xeon CPU running at 2.66 GHz [326] using the Linux/Unix `time` command [327]. We scaled these runtimes to the Atmel ATmega1281 microcontroller [77] running at 8 MHz. This scaling does not provide exact absolute runtimes for the Atmel processor, whereas the comparison of these values provides valuable insights. For each SA run, we initialized the pseudorandom number generator with a different seed using `srand()` [328]. We observe that the greedy algorithm explores 1 (0.14% of the design space S), 4 (0.55% of S), and 10 (1.37% of S) states in 0.366, 0.732, and 0.964 ms, respectively (the greedy algorithm converged after

10 iterations). The SA algorithm explores 1, 4, 10, 100 (13.72% of S), 421 (57.75% of S), and 729 (100% of S) states in 1.097, 1.197, 1.297, 3.39, 11.34, and 18.19 ms, respectively, for $|S| = 729$. On average, the execution time linearly increases by 0.039 and 0.023 ms per state for the greedy and SA algorithms, respectively. The greedy algorithm requires 34.54% less execution time on average as compared to SA (after exploring 10 states). We measured the greedy and SA algorithms' execution time for $|S| = 31, 104$ and observed similar results as for $|S| = 729$ because both the algorithms' execution time depends on the number of states explored and not on the design space cardinality. The exhaustive search requires 29.526 ms and 2.765 s for $|S| = 729$ and $|S| = 31, 104$, respectively. Compared with an exhaustive search, the greedy and SA algorithms (after exploring 10 states) requires 30.63×and 22.76×less execution time, respectively, for $|S| = 729$, and requires 2868.26×and 2131.84×less execution time, respectively, for $|S| = 31, 104$. We verified our execution time analysis using clock() [328] and observed similar trends. These execution time results indicate that our online algorithms' efficacy increases as the design space cardinality increases.

We calculated the energy consumption of our algorithms E_{algo} for an Atmel ATmega1281 microcontroller [77] operating at $V_p = 2.7$ V and $F_p = 8$ MHz as $E_{algo} = V_p \cdot I_p^a \cdot T_{exe}$ where I_p^a and T_{exe} denote the processor's active current and the algorithm's execution time at (V_p, F_p), respectively (we observed similar trends for other processor voltage and frequency settings). Our calculations indicate that the greedy algorithm requires 5.237, 10.475, and 13.795 µJ to explore 1, 4, and 10 states, respectively, whereas the SA algorithm requires 15.698, 17.129, 18.56, 48.51, 162.28, and 260.3 µJ for exploring 1, 4, 10, 100, 421, and 729 states, respectively, both for $|S| = 729$ and $|S| = 31, 104$. The exhaustive search requires 0.422 and 39.567 mJ for $|S| = 729$ and $|S| = 31, 104$, respectively. The SA algorithm requires 34.54% more energy as compared to the greedy algorithm for exploring 10 states, whereas both the algorithms are highly energy efficient as compared to exhaustive search.

Figure 9.6 depicts low data memory requirements for both algorithms for design space cardinalities of 8, 81, 729, and 46,656. We observe that the greedy algorithm requires 452, 520, 562,

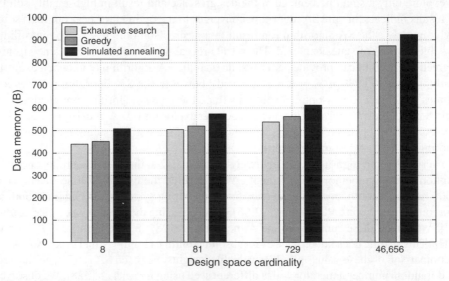

Figure 9.6 Data memory requirements for exhaustive search, greedy, and simulated annealing algorithms for design space cardinalities of 8, 81, 729, and 46,656

and 874 B, whereas the SA algorithm requires 508, 574, 612, and 924 B of storage for design space cardinalities of 8, 81, 729, and 46,656, respectively. The data memory analysis shows that the SA algorithm has comparatively larger memory requirements (9.35% on average for analyzed design space cardinalities) than the greedy algorithm. The data memory requirements for both the algorithms increase linearly as the number of tunable parameters and tunable values (and thus the design space) increases. We point out that the data memory requirements for the exhaustive search is comparable to the greedy algorithm because the exhaustive search simply evaluates the objective function value for each state in the design space. However, the exhaustive search yields a high penalty in execution time because of complete design space evaluation. The figure reveals that our algorithms scale well with increased design space cardinality, and thus our proposed algorithms are appropriate for sensor nodes with a large number of tunable parameters and parameter values.

9.4   Chapter Summary

In this chapter, we proposed a dynamic optimization methodology using greedy and SA online optimization algorithms for distributed EWSNs. Compared to previous work, our methodology considered an extensive embedded sensor node design space, which allowed embedded sensor nodes to more closely meet application requirements. Results revealed that our online algorithms were lightweight, required little computational, memory, and energy resources and thus were amenable for the implementation on sensor nodes with tight resource and energy constraints. Furthermore, our online algorithms could perform in situ parameter tuning to adapt to changing environmental stimuli to meet application requirements.

10

A Lightweight Dynamic Optimization Methodology for Embedded Wireless Sensor Networks*

Advancements in semiconductor technology, as predicted by Moore's law, have enabled high transistor density in a small chip area resulting in the miniaturization of embedded systems (e.g., embedded sensor nodes). Embedded wireless sensor networks (EWSNs) are envisioned as distributed computing systems, which are proliferating in many application domains (e.g., defense, health care, surveillance systems), each with varying application requirements that can be defined by high-level *application metrics* (e.g., lifetime, reliability). However, the diversity of EWSN application domains makes it difficult for commercial off-the-shelf (COTS) embedded sensor nodes to meet these application requirements.

Since COTS embedded sensor nodes are mass-produced to optimize cost, many COTS embedded sensor nodes possess tunable parameters (e.g., processor voltage and frequency, sensing frequency), whose values can be *tuned* for application specialization [69]. The EWSN application designers (those who design, manage, or deploy the EWSN for an application) are typically biologists, teachers, farmers, and household consumers that are experts within their application domain, but have limited technical expertise. Given the large design space and operating constraints, determining appropriate parameter values (operating state) can be a daunting and/or time-consuming task for nonexpert application managers. Typically, embedded sensor node vendors assign initial generic tunable parameter value settings;

*A portion of this chapter is copyrighted by Elsevier. The definitive version appeared in: Arslan Munir, Ann Gordon-Ross, Susan Lysecky, and Roman Lysecky, A Lightweight Dynamic Optimization Methodology and Application Metrics Estimation Model for Wireless Sensor Networks, *Elsevier Sustainable Computing: Informatics and Systems*, vol. 3, no. 2, pp. 94–108, June 2013. URL http://www.sciencedirect.com/science/article/pii/S2210 537913000048. ©[2013] Elsevier. The work is reproduced under automatic permission granted by Elsevier as we are the authors of this work.

Modeling and Optimization of Parallel and Distributed Embedded Systems, First Edition.
Arslan Munir, Ann Gordon-Ross and Sanjay Ranka.
© 2016 John Wiley & Sons, Ltd. Published 2016 by John Wiley & Sons, Ltd.

however, no one tunable parameter value setting is appropriate for all applications. To assist the EWSN managers with parameter tuning to best fit the application requirements, an automated parameter tuning process is required.

Parameter optimization is the process of assigning appropriate (optimal or near-optimal) tunable parameter value settings to meet application requirements. Parameter optimizations can be static or dynamic. *Static optimizations* assign parameter values at deployment, and these values remain fixed for the lifetime of the sensor node. One of the challenges associated with static optimizations is accurately determining the tunable parameter value settings using environmental stimuli prediction/simulation. Furthermore, static optimizations are not appropriate for applications with varying environmental stimuli. Alternatively, *dynamic optimizations* assign (and reassign/change) parameter values during runtime enabling the sensor node to adapt to changing environmental stimuli, and thus more accurately meet application requirements.

EWSN dynamic optimizations present additional challenges as compared to traditional processor or memory (cache) dynamic optimizations because sensor nodes have more tunable parameters and a larger design space. The dynamic profiling and optimization (DPOP) project aims to address these challenges and complexities associated with sensor-based system design through the use of automated optimization methods [321]. The DPOP project has gathered dynamic profiling statistics from a sensor-based system; however, the parameter optimization process has not been addressed.

In this chapter, we investigate parameter optimization using dynamic profiling data already collected from the platform. We analyze several dynamic optimization methods and evaluate algorithms that provide a good operating state without significantly depleting the battery energy. We explore a large design space with many tunable parameters and values, which provide a fine-grained design space, enabling embedded sensor nodes to more closely meet application requirements as compared to smaller, more course-grained design spaces. Gordon-Ross et al. [329] showed that finer-grained design spaces contain interesting design alternatives and result in increased benefits in the cache subsystem (though similar trends follow for other subsystems). However, the large design space exacerbates optimization challenges, taking into consideration an embedded sensor node's constrained memory and computational resources. Considering the embedded sensor node's limited battery life, energy-efficient computing is always of paramount significance. Therefore, optimization algorithms that conserve energy by minimizing design space exploration to find a good operating state are critical, especially for large design spaces and highly constrained systems. Additionally, rapidly changing application requirements and environmental stimuli coupled with limited battery reserves necessitates a highly responsive and low overhead methodology.

Our main contributions in this chapter are as follows:

- We propose a lightweight dynamic optimization methodology that intelligently selects appropriate initial tunable parameter value settings by evaluating application requirements, the relative importance of these requirements with respect to each other, and the magnitude in which each parameter effects each requirement. This *one-shot* operating state obtained from appropriate initial parameter value settings provides a high-quality operating state with minimal design space exploration for highly constrained applications. Results reveal that the one-shot operating state is within 8% of the optimal operating state averaged over several different application domains and design spaces.

- We present a dynamic optimization methodology to iteratively improve the one-shot operating state to provide an optimal or near-optimal operating state for less constrained applications. Our dynamic optimization methodology combines the initial tunable parameter value settings with an intelligent exploration ordering of tunable parameter values and an exploration arrangement of tunable parameters (since some parameters are more critical for an application than others and thus should be explored first [330] (e.g., the transmission power parameter may be more critical for a lifetime-sensitive application than for processor voltage)).

- We architect a lightweight online greedy algorithm that leverages intelligent parameter arrangement to iteratively explore the design space, resulting in an operating state within 2% of the optimal operating state while exploring only 0.04% of the design space.

This work has a broad impact on EWSN design and deployment. Our work enables nonexpert application managers to leverage our dynamic optimization methodology to automatically tailor the embedded sensor node tunable parameters to best meet the application requirements with little design time effort. Our proposed methodology is suitable for all EWSN applications ranging from highly constrained to highly flexible applications. The one-shot operating state provides a good operating state for highly constrained applications, whereas greedy exploration of the parameters provides improvement over the one-shot operating state to determine a high-quality operating state for less constrained applications. Our initial parameter value settings, parameter arrangement, and exploration ordering techniques are also applicable to other systems or application domains (e.g., cache tuning) with different application requirements and different tunable parameters.

The remainder of this chapter is organized as follows. Section 10.1 overviews the related work. Section 10.2 presents our dynamic optimization methodology along with the state space and objective function formulation. We describe our dynamic optimization methodology's steps and algorithms in Section 10.3. Experimental results are presented in Section 10.4. Finally, Section 10.5 concludes the chapter.

10.1   Related Work

There exists much research in the area of dynamic optimizations [186–188, 330], but most previous work targets the processor or memory (cache) in computer systems. There exists little previous work on EWSN dynamic optimization, which presents more challenges given a unique design space, design constraints, platform particulars, and external influences from the EWSN's operating environment.

In the area of DPOP, Sridharan and Lysecky [300] dynamically profiled an EWSN's operating environment to gather profiling statistics; however, they did not describe a methodology to leverage these profiling statistics for dynamic optimization. Shenoy et al. [331] investigated profiling methods for dynamically monitoring sensor-based platforms with respect to network traffic and energy consumption, but did not explore dynamic optimizations. In prior work, Munir and Gordon-Ross [23, 69] proposed a Markov decision process (MDP)-based methodology for optimal sensor node parameter tuning to meet application requirements as a first step toward EWSN dynamic optimization. The MDP-based methodology required high computational and memory resources for large design spaces and needed a high-performance base station node (sink node) to compute the optimal operating state for large design spaces. The operating states determined at the base station were then communicated to the other sensor nodes. The high resource requirements made the MDP-based methodology infeasible for autonomous dynamic optimization for large design spaces given the constrained resources of individual sensor nodes. Kogekar et al. [227] proposed dynamic software reconfiguration to adapt software to new operating conditions; however, their work did not consider sensor node tunable parameters and application requirements. Verma [311] investigated simulated annealing (SA) and particle swarm optimization (PSO)-based parameter tuning for EWSNs and observed that SA performed better than PSO because PSO often quickly converged to local minima. Although there exists work on optimization of EWSNs, our work uses multi-objective optimization and fine-grained design space to find optimal (or near-optimal) sensor node operating states that meet application requirements.

One of the prominent dynamic optimization techniques for reducing energy consumption is dynamic voltage and frequency scaling (DVFS). Several previous works explored DVFS in EWSNs. Min et al. [225] utilized a voltage scheduler, running in tandem with the operating system's task scheduler, to perform DVFS based on an a priori prediction of the sensor node's workload and resulted in a 60% reduction in energy consumption. Similarly, Yuan and Qu [226] used additional transmitted data packet information to select appropriate processor voltage and frequency values. Although DVFS is a method for dynamic optimization, DVFS considers only two sensor node tunable parameters (processor voltage and frequency). In this chapter, we expand the embedded sensor node parameter tuning space, which provides a finer-grained design space, enabling embedded sensor nodes to more closely meet application requirements.

Some dynamic optimization work utilized dynamic power management for energy conservation in EWSNs. Wang et al. [332] proposed a strategy for optimizing mobile sensor node placement to meet coverage and energy requirements. Their strategy utilized dynamic power management to optimize the sensor nodes' sleep state transitions for energy conservation. Ning and Cassandras [333] presented a link layer dynamic optimization approach for energy conservation in EWSNs by minimizing the idle listening time. Their approach utilized traffic statistics to optimally control the receiver sleep interval. In our work, we incorporate energy conservation by switching the sensors, processors, and transceivers to low power, idle modes when these components are not actively sensing, processing, and communicating, respectively.

Although there exists work on EWSN optimizations, dynamic optimization requires further research. Specifically, there is a need for lightweight dynamic optimization methodologies for sensor node parameter tuning considering a sensor node's limited energy and storage. Furthermore, sensor node tunable parameter arrangement and exploration order require further investigation. Our work provides contribution to the dynamic optimization of EWSNs by proposing a lightweight dynamic optimization methodology for EWSNs in addition to a sensor node's tunable parameter arrangement and exploration order techniques.

10.2   Dynamic Optimization Methodology

In this section, we give an overview of our dynamic optimization methodology along with the state space and objective function formulation for the methodology.

10.2.1   Overview

Figure 10.1 depicts our dynamic optimization methodology for distributed EWSNs. EWSN designers evaluate application requirements and capture these requirements as high-level

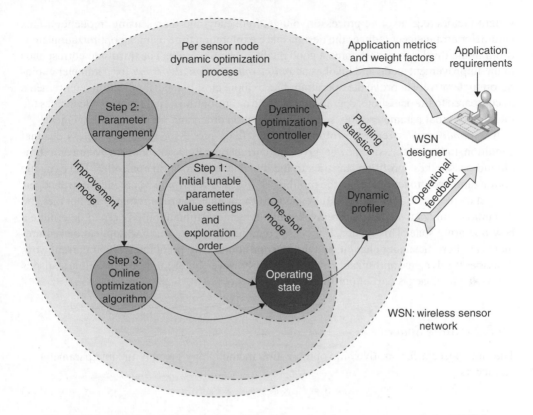

Figure 10.1   A lightweight dynamic optimization methodology per sensor node for EWSNs

application metrics (e.g., lifetime, throughput, reliability) and associated *weight factors*. The weight factors signify the weightage/importance of application metrics with respect to each other. The sensor nodes use application metrics and weight factors to determine an appropriate operating state (tunable parameter value settings) by leveraging an application metrics estimation model. The application metrics estimation model (elaborated in Chapter 3) estimates high-level application metrics from low-level sensor node parameters and sensor node hardware-specific internals.

Figure 10.1 shows the per sensor node dynamic optimization process (encompassed by the dashed circle), which is orchestrated by the *dynamic optimization controller*. The process consists of two operating modes: the *one-shot mode* wherein the sensor node operating state is directly determined by initial parameter value settings and the *improvement mode* wherein the operating state is iteratively improved using an online optimization algorithm. The dynamic optimization process consists of three steps. In the first step corresponding to the one-shot mode, the dynamic optimization controller intelligently determines the initial parameter value settings (operating state) and exploration order (ascending or descending), which is critical in reducing the number of states explored in the third step. In the one-shot mode, the dynamic optimization process is complete and the sensor node transitions directly to the operating state specified by the initial parameter value settings. The second step corresponds to the improvement mode, which determines the parameter arrangement based on application metric weight factors (e.g., explore processor voltage, frequency, and then sensing frequency). This parameter arrangement reduces the design space exploration time using an optimization algorithm in the third step to determine a good quality operating state. The third step corresponds to the improvement mode and invokes an *online optimization algorithm* for parameter exploration to iteratively improve the operating state to more closely meet application requirements as compared to the one-shot's operating state. The online optimization algorithm leverages the intelligent initial parameter value settings, exploration order, and parameter arrangement.

A *dynamic profiler* records profiling statistics (e.g., processor voltage, wireless channel condition, radio transmission power) given the current operating state and environmental stimuli and passes these profiling statistics to the dynamic optimization controller. The dynamic optimization controller processes the profiling statistics to determine whether the current operating state meets the application requirements. If the application requirements are not met, the dynamic optimization controller reinvokes the dynamic optimization process to determine a new operating state. This feedback process continues to ensure that the application requirements are best met under changing environmental stimuli. We point out that our current work describes the dynamic optimization methodology; however, incorporation of profiling statistics to provide feedback is part of our future work.

10.2.2 State Space

The state space S for our dynamic optimization methodology given N tunable parameters is defined as

$$S = P_1 \times P_2 \times \cdots \times P_N \tag{10.1}$$

where P_i denotes the state space for tunable parameter i, $\forall\, i \in \{1, 2, \cdots, N\}$ and $\times$ denotes the Cartesian product. Each tunable parameter's state space P_i consists of n values

$$P_i = \{p_{i_1}, p_{i_2}, p_{i_3}, \cdots, p_{i_n}\} \;:\; |P_i| = n \tag{10.2}$$

where $|P_i|$ denotes the tunable parameter i's state space cardinality (the number of tunable values in P_i). S is a set of n-tuples formed by taking one tunable parameter value from each tunable parameter. A single n-tuple $s \in S$ is given as

$$s = (p_{1_y}, p_{2_y}, \cdots, p_{N_y}) \;:\; p_{i_y} \in P_i, \quad \forall\, i \in \{1, 2, \cdots, N\}, y \in \{1, 2, \cdots, n\} \tag{10.3}$$

Each n-tuple represents a sensor note operating state. We point out that some n-tuples in S may not be feasible (such as invalid combinations of processor voltage and frequency) and can be regarded as *do not care* tuples.

10.2.3 Optimization Objection Function

The sensor node dynamic optimization problem can be formulated as

$$\max f(s)$$

$$\text{s.t.} \;\; s \in S \tag{10.4}$$

where $f(s)$ represents the objective function and captures application metrics and weight factors and is given as

$$f(s) = \sum_{k=1}^{m} \omega_k f_k(s)$$

$$\text{s.t. } s \in S$$

$$\omega_k \geq 0, \quad k = 1, 2, \ldots, m$$

$$\omega_k \leq 1, \quad k = 1, 2, \ldots, m$$

$$\sum_{k=1}^{m} \omega_k = 1 \qquad (10.5)$$

where $f_k(s)$ and ω_k denote the objective function and weight factor for the kth application metric, respectively, given that there are m application metrics.

For our dynamic optimization methodology, we consider three application metrics ($m = 3$): lifetime, throughput, and reliability, whose objective functions are represented by $f_l(s)$, $f_t(s)$, and $f_r(s)$, respectively. We define $f_l(s)$ (Fig. 10.2) using the piecewise linear function

$$f_l(s) = \begin{cases} 1, & s_l \geq \beta_l \\ C_{U_l} + \frac{(C_{\beta_l} - C_{U_l})(s_l - U_l)}{(\beta_l - U_l)}, & U_l \leq s_l < \beta_l \\ C_{L_l} + \frac{(C_{U_l} - C_{L_l})(s_l - L_l)}{(U_l - L_l)}, & L_l \leq s_l < U_l \\ C_{L_l} \cdot \frac{(s_l - \alpha_l)}{(L_l - \alpha_l)}, & \alpha_l \leq s_l < L_l \\ 0, & s_l < \alpha_l \end{cases} \qquad (10.6)$$

where s_l denotes the lifetime offered by state s, the constant parameters L_l and U_l denote the *desired* minimum and maximum lifetime, and the constant parameters α_l and β_l denote the *acceptable* minimum and maximum lifetime. The piecewise linear objective function provides EWSN designers with a flexible application requirement specification, as it allows both desirable and acceptable ranges [310]. The objective function reward gradient (slope) would be greater in the desired range than the acceptable range; however, there would be no reward/gain for operating outside the acceptable range. The constant parameters C_{L_l}, C_{U_l}, and C_{β_l} in Eq. (10.6) denote the $f_l(s)$ value at L_l, U_l, and β_l, respectively (constant parameters are assigned by the EWSN designer based on the minimum and maximum acceptable/desired values of application metrics). The $f_t(s)$ and $f_r(s)$ can be defined similar to Eq. (10.6).

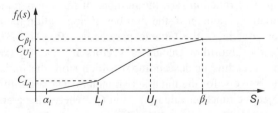

Figure 10.2   Lifetime objective function $f_l(s)$

The objective function characterization enables the reward/gain calculation from operating in a given state based on the high-level metric values offered by the state. Although different characterization of objective functions results in different reward values from different states, our dynamic optimization methodology selects a high-quality operating state from the design space to maximize the given objective function value. We consider piecewise linear objective functions as a typical example from the possible objective functions (e.g., linear, piecewise linear, nonlinear) to illustrate our dynamic optimization methodology, though other characterizations of objective functions work equally well for our methodology.

10.3 Algorithms for Dynamic Optimization Methodology

In this section, we describe our dynamic optimization methodology's three steps (Fig. 10.1) and associated algorithms.

10.3.1 Initial Tunable Parameter Value Settings and Exploration Order

The first step of our dynamic optimization methodology determines initial tunable parameter value settings and exploration order (ascending or descending). These initial tunable parameter value settings results in a high-quality operating state in *one-shot*, hence the name *one-shot mode* (Fig. 10.1). The algorithm calculates the application metric objective function values for the first and last values in the set of tunable values for each tunable parameter while other tunable parameters are set to an arbitrary initial setting (either first or last value). We point out that the tunable values for a tunable parameter can be arranged in an ascending order (e.g., for processor voltage $V_p = \{2.7, 3.3, 4\}$ (V)). This objective function values calculation determines the effectiveness of setting a particular tunable parameter value in meeting the desired objective (e.g., lifetime). The tunable parameter setting that gives a higher objective function value is selected as the initial parameter value for that tunable parameter. The exploration order for that tunable parameter is set to descending if the last value in the set of tunable values (e.g., $V_p = 4$ in our previous example) gives a higher objective function value or ascending otherwise. This exploration order selection helps in reducing design space exploration for a greedy-based optimization algorithm (step 3), which stops exploring a tunable parameter as soon as a tunable parameter setting gives a lower objective function value than the initial setting. This initial parameter value setting and exploration order determination procedure are then repeated for all other tunable parameters and application metrics.

Algorithm 6 describes our technique to determine initial tunable parameter value settings and exploration order (first step of our dynamic optimization methodology). The algorithm takes as input the objective function $f(s)$, the number of tunable parameters N, the number of values for each tunable parameter n, the number of application metrics m, and $\mathbf{P}$ where $\mathbf{P}$ represents a vector containing the tunable parameters, $\mathbf{P} = \{P_1, P_2, \cdots, P_N\}$. For each application metric k, the algorithm calculates vectors $\mathbf{P_0^k}$ and $\mathbf{P_d^k}$ (where d denotes the exploration direction (ascending or descending)), which store the initial value settings and exploration order, respectively, for the tunable parameters. The algorithm determines the kth application metric objective function values $f_{p_{i_1}}^k$ and $f_{p_{i_n}}^k$ where the parameter being explored P_i is assigned its first p_{i_1} and last p_{i_n} tunable values, respectively, and the rest of the tunable parameters $P_j, \forall j \neq i$ are assigned initial values (lines 3 and 4). $\delta f_{P_i}^k$ stores the difference

---

Algorithm 6: Initial tunable parameter value settings and exploration order algorithm.

Input: $f(s)$, N, n, m, **P**
Output: Initial tunable parameter value settings and exploration order

1 **for** $k \leftarrow 1$ **to** m **do**
2   **for** $P_i \leftarrow P_1$ **to** P_N **do**
3         $f^k_{p_{i_1}} \leftarrow k^{\text{th}}$ metric objective function value when parameter setting is
          $\{P_i = p_{i_1}, P_j = P_{j_0}, \forall i \neq j\}$;
4         $f^k_{p_{i_n}} \leftarrow k^{\text{th}}$ metric objective function value when parameter setting is
          $\{P_i = p_{i_n}, P_j = P_{j_0}, \forall i \neq j\}$;
5         $\delta f^k_{P_i} \leftarrow f^k_{p_{i_n}} - f^k_{p_{i_1}}$;
6   **if** $\delta f^k_{P_i} \geq 0$ **then**
7   explore P_i in descending order ;
8            $P^k_d[i] \leftarrow$ descending ;
9            $P^k_0[i] \leftarrow p^k_{i_n}$;
10   **else**
11   explore P_i in ascending order ;
12           $P^k_d[i] \leftarrow$ ascending ;
13           $P^k_0[i] \leftarrow p^k_{i_1}$;
14   **end**
15   **end**
16 **end**
    return P^k_d, P^k_0, $\forall k \in \{1, \dots, m\}$

---

between $f^k_{p_{i_n}}$ and $f^k_{p_{i_1}}$. If $\delta f^k_{P_i} \geq 0$, p_{i_n} results in a greater (or equal when $\delta f^k_{P_i} = 0$) objective function value as compared to p_{i_1} for parameter P_i (i.e., the objective function value decreases as the parameter value decreases). Therefore, to reduce the number of states explored while considering that the greedy algorithm (Section 10.3.3) stops exploring a tunable parameter if a tunable parameter's value yields a comparatively lower objective function value, P_i's exploration order must be descending (lines 6–8). The algorithm assigns p_{i_n} as the initial value of P_i for the kth application metric (line 9). If $\delta f^k_{P_i} < 0$, the algorithm assigns the exploration order as ascending for P_i and p_{i_1} as the initial value setting of P_i (lines 11–13). This $\delta f^k_{P_i}$ calculation procedure is repeated for all m application metrics and all N tunable parameters (lines 1–16).

10.3.2 Parameter Arrangement

Depending on the application metric weight factors, some parameters are more critical to meeting application requirements than other parameters. For example, sensing frequency is a critical parameter for applications with a high responsiveness weight factor, and therefore, sensing frequency should be explored first. In this section, we describe a technique for parameter arrangement such that parameters are explored in an order characterized by the parameters' impact on application metrics based on relative weight factors. This parameter arrangement technique (step 2) is part of the *improvement mode*, which is suitable for relatively less constrained applications that would benefit from a higher quality operating state than the one-shot mode's operating state (Fig. 10.1).

The parameter arrangement step determines an arrangement for the tunable parameters corresponding to each application metric, which dictates the order in which the parameters will be explored. This arrangement is based on the difference between the application metric's objective function values corresponding to the first and last values of the tunable parameters, which is calculated in step 1 (i.e., the tunable parameter that gives the highest difference in an application metric's objective function values is the first parameter in the arrangement vector for that application metric). For an arrangement that considers all application metrics, the tunable parameters' order is set in accordance with application metrics' weight factors such that the tunable parameters having a greater effect on application metrics with higher weight factors are situated before parameters having a lesser affect on application metrics with lower weight factors in the arrangement. We point out that the effect of the tunable parameters on an application metric is determined from the objective function value calculations as described in step 1. The arrangement that considers all application metrics selects the first few tunable parameters corresponding to each application metric, starting from the application metric with the highest weight factor such that no parameters are repeated in the final intelligent parameter arrangement. For example, if processor voltage is among the first few tunable parameters corresponding to two application metrics, then the processor voltage setting corresponding to the application metric with the greater weight factor is selected, whereas the processor voltage setting corresponding to the application metric with the lower weight factor is ignored in the final intelligent parameter arrangement. Step 3 (online optimization algorithm) uses this intelligent parameter arrangement for further design space exploration. The mathematical details of the parameter arrangement step are as follows.

Our parameter arrangement technique is based on calculations performed in Algorithm 6. We define

$$\nabla \mathbf{f_P} = \{\nabla f_P^1, \nabla f_P^2, \cdots, \nabla f_P^m\} \tag{10.7}$$

where $\nabla \mathbf{f_P}$ is a vector containing $\nabla f_P^k, \forall\, k \in \{1, 2, \cdots, m\}$ arranged in descending order by their respective values and is given as

$$\nabla \mathbf{f_P^k} = \{\delta f_{P_1}^k, \delta f_{P_2}^k, \cdots, \delta f_{P_N}^k\} : |\delta f_{P_i}^k| \geq |\delta f_{P_{i+1}}^k|, \quad \forall\, i \in \{1, 2, \cdots, N-1\} \tag{10.8}$$

The tunable parameter arrangement vector $\mathbf{P^k}$ corresponding to $\nabla \mathbf{f_P^k}$ (one-to-one correspondence) is given by

$$\mathbf{P^k} = \{P_1^k, P_2^k, \cdots, P_N^k\}, \quad \forall\, k \in \{1, 2, \cdots, m\} \tag{10.9}$$

An intelligent parameter arrangement $\hat{\mathbf{P}}$ must consider all application metrics' weight factors with higher importance given to the higher weight factors, that is,

$$\hat{\mathbf{P}} = \{P_1^1, \cdots, P_{l_1}^1, P_1^2, \cdots, P_{l_2}^2, P_1^3, \cdots, P_{l_3}^3, \cdots, P_1^m, \cdots, P_{l_m}^m\} \tag{10.10}$$

where l_k denotes the number of tunable parameters taken from $P^k, \forall\, k \in \{1, 2, \cdots, m\}$ such that $\sum_{k=1}^{m} l_k = N$. Our technique allows taking more tunable parameters from parameter arrangement vectors corresponding to higher weight factor application metrics: $l_k \geq l_{k+1}, \forall\, k \in \{1, 2, \cdots, m-1\}$. In Eq. (10.10), l_1 tunable parameters are taken from vector P^1, then l_2 from vector P^2, and so on to l_m from vector P^m such that

$\{P_1^k, \cdots, P_{l_k}^k\} \cap \{P_1^{k-1}, \cdots, P_{l_{k-1}}^{k-1}\} = \emptyset, \forall k \in \{2, 3, \cdots, m\}$. In other words, we select those tunable parameters from parameter arrangement vectors corresponding to the lower weight factors that are not already selected from parameter arrangement vectors corresponding to the higher weight factors (i.e., $\widehat{P}$ comprises of disjoint or nonoverlapping tunable parameters corresponding to each application metric).

In the situation where weight factor ω_1 is much greater than all other weight factors, an intelligent parameter arrangement $\widetilde{P}$ would correspond to the parameter arrangement for the application metric with weight factor ω_1

$$\widetilde{P} = P^1 = \{P_1^1, P_2^1, \cdots, P_N^1\} \iff \omega_1 \gg \omega_q, \quad \forall q \in \{2, 3, \cdots, m\} \tag{10.11}$$

The initial parameter value vector $\widehat{P}_0$ and the exploration order (ascending or descending) vector $\widehat{P}_d$ corresponding to $\widehat{P}$ (Eq. (10.10)) can be determined from $\widehat{P}$ (Eq. (10.10)), P_d^k, and $P_0^k, \forall k \in \{1, \cdots, m\}$ (Algorithm 6) by examining the tunable parameter from $\widehat{P}$ and determining the tunable parameter's initial value setting from P_0^k and exploration order from P_d^k.

10.3.3 Online Optimization Algorithm

Step 3 of our dynamic optimization methodology, which also belongs to the *improvement mode*, iteratively improves the one-shot operating state. This step leverages information from steps 1 and 2 and uses a greedy optimization algorithm for tunable parameters exploration in an effort to determine a better operating state than the one obtained from step 1 (Section 10.3.1). The greedy algorithm explores the tunable parameters in the order determined in step 2. The greedy algorithm stops exploring a tunable parameter as soon as a tunable parameter setting yields a lower objective function value as compared to the previous tunable parameter setting for that tunable parameter, and hence named as *greedy*. This greedy approach helps in reducing design space exploration to determine an operating state. Although we propose a greedy algorithm for design space exploration, any other algorithm can be used in step 3.

Algorithm 7 depicts our online greedy optimization algorithm, which leverages the initial parameter value settings (Section 10.3.1), parameter value exploration order (Section 10.3.1), and parameter arrangement (Section 10.3.2). The algorithm takes as input the objective function $f(s)$, the number of tunable parameters N, the number of values for each tunable parameter n, the intelligent tunable parameter arrangement vector $\widehat{P}$, the tunable parameters' initial value vector $\widehat{P}_0$, and the tunable parameter's exploration order (ascending or descending) vector $\widehat{P}_d$. The algorithm initializes state κ from $\widehat{P}_0$ (line 1) and f_{best} with κ's objective function value (line 2). The algorithm explores each parameter in $\widehat{P}_i$ where $\widehat{P}_i \in \widehat{P}$ (Eq. (10.10)) in ascending or descending order as given by $\widehat{P}_d$ (lines 3 and 4). For each tunable parameter $\widehat{P}_i$ (line 5), the algorithm assigns f_{temp} the objective function value from the current state ζ (line 6). The current state $\zeta \in S$ denotes tunable parameter value settings and can be written as

$$\zeta = \{P_i = p_{i_x}\} \cup \{P_j, \forall j \neq i\}, \ i, j \in \{1, 2, \cdots, N\} \tag{10.12}$$

where $p_{i_x} : x \in \{1, 2, \cdots, n\}$ denotes the parameter value corresponding to the tunable parameter P_i being explored and set $P_j, \forall j \neq i$ denotes the parameter value settings other than the current tunable parameter P_i being explored and is given by

$$P_j = \begin{cases} P_{j0}, & \text{if } P_j \text{ not explored before}, \quad \forall j \neq i \\ P_{jb}, & \text{if } P_j \text{ explored before}, \quad \forall j \neq i \end{cases} \tag{10.13}$$

Algorithm 7: Online greedy optimization algorithm for tunable parameters exploration.

Input: $f(s)$, N, n, $\widehat{P}$, $\widehat{P}_0$, $\widehat{P}_d$
Output: Sensor node state that maximizes $f(s)$ and the corresponding $f(s)$ value
1   $\kappa \leftarrow$ initial tunable parameter value settings from $\widehat{P}_0$;
2   $f_{best} \leftarrow$ solution from initial parameter settings κ ;
3   **for** $\widehat{P}_i \leftarrow \widehat{P}_1$ to $\widehat{P}_N$ **do**
4   explore $\widehat{P}_i$ in ascending or descending order as suggested by $\widehat{P}_d$;
5   **foreach** $\widehat{P}_i = \{\hat{p}_{i_1}, \hat{p}_{i_2}, \dots, \hat{p}_{i_n}\}$ **do**
6         $f_{temp} \leftarrow$ current state ζ solution ;
7   **if** $f_{temp} > f_{best}$ **then**
8            $f_{best} \leftarrow f_{temp}$;
9            $\xi \leftarrow \zeta$;
10   **else**
11   break ;
12   **end**
13   **end**
14 **end**
    return ξ, f_{best}

---

where P_{j0} denotes the initial value of the parameter as given by $\widehat{P}_0$ and P_{jb} denotes the best found value of P_j after exploring P_j (lines 5–13 of Algorithm 7).

If $f_{temp} > f_{best}$ (the objection function value increases), f_{temp} is assigned to f_{best} and the state ζ is assigned to state ξ (lines 7–9). If $f_{temp} \leq f_{best}$, the algorithm stops exploring the current parameter $\widehat{P}_i$ and starts exploring the next tunable parameter (lines 10–12). The algorithm returns the best found objective function value f_{best} and the state ξ corresponding to f_{best}.

10.3.4 Computational Complexity

The computational complexity for our dynamic optimization methodology is $\mathcal{O}(Nm \log N + Nn)$, which is comprised of the intelligent initial parameter value settings and exploration ordering (Algorithm 6) $\mathcal{O}(Nm)$, parameter arrangement $\mathcal{O}(Nm \log N)$ (sorting ∇f_P^k (Eq. (10.8)) contributes the $N \log N$ factor) (Section 10.3.2), and the online optimization algorithm for parameter exploration (Algorithm 7) $\mathcal{O}(Nn)$. Assuming that the number of tunable parameters N is larger than the number of parameter's tunable values n, the computational complexity of our methodology can be given as $\mathcal{O}(Nm \log N)$. This complexity reveals that our proposed methodology is lightweight and is thus feasible for implementation on sensor nodes with tight resource constraints.

10.4 Experimental Results

In this section, we describe the experimental setup and results for three application domains: security/defense, health care, and ambient conditions monitoring. The results include the percentage improvements attained by our initial tunable parameter settings (one-shot operating

Table 10.1 Crossbow IRIS mote platform hardware specifications

Notation	Description	Value
V_b	Battery voltage	3.6 V
C_b	Battery capacity	2000 mA h
N_b	Processing instructions per bit	5
R^b_{sen}	Sensing resolution bits	24
V_t	Transceiver voltage	3 V
R_{tx}	Transceiver data rate	250 kbps
I^{rx}_t	Transceiver receive current	15.5 mA
I^s_t	Transceiver sleep current	20 nA
V_s	Sensing board voltage	3 V
I^m_s	Sensing measurement current	550 μA
t^m_s	Sensing measurement time	55 ms
I_s	Sensing sleep current	0.3 μA

state) over other alternative initial value settings, and a comparison of our greedy algorithm (which leverages intelligent initial parameter settings, exploration order, and parameter arrangement) for design space exploration with other variants of a greedy algorithm and SA. This section also presents an execution time and data memory analysis to verify the complexity of our dynamic optimization methodology.

10.4.1 Experimental Setup

Our experimental setup is based on the Crossbow IRIS mote platform [80] with a battery capacity of 2000 mA h using two AA alkaline batteries. The IRIS mote platform integrates an Atmel ATmega1281 microcontroller [77], an MTS400 sensor board [75] with Sensirion SHT1x temperature and humidity sensors [76], and an Atmel AT86RF230 low-power 2.4-GHz transceiver [78]. Table 10.1 shows the sensor node hardware-specific values, corresponding to the IRIS mote platform, which are used by the application metrics estimation model [76–78, 80].

We analyze six tunable parameters: processor voltage V_p, processor frequency F_p, sensing frequency F_s, packet size P_s, packet transmission interval P_{ti}, and transceiver transmission power P_{tx}. In order to explore the fidelity of our methodology across small and large design spaces, we consider two design space cardinalities (number of states in the design space): $|S| = 729$ and $|S| = 31,104$. The tunable parameters for $|S| = 729$ are $V_p = \{2.7, 3.3, 4\}$ (V), $F_p = \{4, 6, 8\}$ (MHz) [77], $F_s = \{1, 2, 3\}$ (samples/s) [76], $P_s = \{41, 56, 64\}$ (B), $P_{ti} = \{60, 300, 600\}$ (s), and $P_{tx} = \{-17, -3, 1\}$ (dB m) [78]. The tunable parameters for $|S| = 31,104$ are $V_p = \{1.8, 2.7, 3.3, 4, 4.5, 5\}$ (V), $F_p = \{2, 4, 6, 8, 12, 16\}$ (MHz) [77], $F_s = \{0.2, 0.5, 1, 2, 3, 4\}$ (samples/s) [76], $P_s = \{32, 41, 56, 64, 100, 127\}$ (B), $P_{ti} = \{10, 30, 60, 300, 600, 1200\}$ (s), and $P_{tx} = \{-17, -3, 1, 3\}$ (dB m) [78]. All state space tuples are feasible for $|S| = 729$, whereas $|S| = 31,104$ contains 7779 infeasible state space tuples because all V_p and F_p pairs are not feasible.

In order to evaluate the robustness of our methodology across different applications with varying application metric weight factors, we model three sample application domains: a

Table 10.2 Desirable minimum L, desirable maximum U, acceptable minimum α, and acceptable maximum β objective function parameter values for a security/defense (defense) system, health care, and an ambient conditions monitoring application

Notation	Defense (units)	Health care (units)	Ambient monitoring (units)
L_l	8	12	6
U_l	30	32	40
α_l	1	2	3
β_l	36	40	60
L_t	20	19	15
U_t	34	36	29
α_t	0.5	0.4	0.05
β_t	45	47	35
L_r	14	12	11
U_r	19.8	17	16
α_r	10	8	6
β_r	20	20	20

One lifetime unit = 5 days, one throughput unit = 20 kbps, one reliability unit = 0.05

security/defense system, a healthcare application, and an ambient conditions monitoring application. We assign application-specific values for the desirable minimum L, desirable maximum U, acceptable minimum α, and acceptable maximum β objective function parameter values for application metrics (Section 10.2.3) as shown in Table 10.2. We specify the objective function parameters as a multiple of base units for lifetime, throughput, and reliability. We assume one lifetime unit is equal to 5 days, one throughput unit is equal to 20 kbps, and one reliability unit is equal to 0.05 (percentage of error-free packet transmissions).

In order to evaluate our one-shot dynamic optimization solution quality, we compare the solution from the one-shot initial parameter settings $\widehat{\mathbf{P}_0}$ with the solutions obtained from the following four potential initial parameter value settings (although any feasible n-tuple $s \in S$ can be taken as the initial parameter settings):

- $\mathcal{I}_1$ assigns the first parameter value for each tunable parameter, that is, $\mathcal{I}_1 = p_{i_1}, \forall i \in \{1, 2, \cdots, N\}$.
- $\mathcal{I}_2$ assigns the last parameter value for each tunable parameter, that is, $\mathcal{I}_2 = p_{i_n}, \forall i \in \{1, 2, \cdots, N\}$.
- $\mathcal{I}_3$ assigns the middle parameter value for each tunable parameter, that is, $\mathcal{I}_3 = \lfloor p_{i_n}/2 \rfloor, \forall i \in \{1, 2, \cdots, N\}$.
- $\mathcal{I}_4$ assigns a random value for each tunable parameter, that is, $\mathcal{I}_4 = p_{i_q} : q = \text{rand}() \% n, \forall i \in \{1, 2, \cdots, N\}$ where $\text{rand}()$ denotes a function to generate a random/pseudorandom integer and $\%$ denotes the modulus operator.

Although we analyzed our methodology for the IRIS motes platform, three application domains, and two design spaces, our algorithms are equally applicable to any platform, application domain, and design space. Since the constant assignments for the minimum and maximum desirable values and weight factors are application dependent and designer specified, appropriate assignments can be made for any application given the application's specific requirements. Finally, since the number of tunable parameters and the parameters' possible/allowed tunable values dictates the size of the design space, we evaluate both large and small design spaces but any sized design space could be evaluated by varying the number of tunable parameters and associated values.

10.4.2 Results

In this section, we present results for percentage improvements attained by our dynamic optimization methodology over other optimization methodologies. We implemented our dynamic optimization methodology in C++. To evaluate the effectiveness of our one-shot solution, we compare the one-shot solution's results with four alternative initial parameter arrangements (Section 10.4.1). We normalize the objective function values corresponding to the operating states attained by our dynamic optimization methodology with respect to the optimal solution obtained using an exhaustive search. We compare the relative complexity of our one-shot dynamic optimization methodology with two other dynamic optimization methodologies, which leverage greedy- and SA-based algorithms for design space exploration [316]. Although for brevity we present results for only a subset of the initial parameter value settings, application domains, and design spaces, we observed that results for extensive application domains, design spaces, and initial parameter settings revealed similar trends.

10.4.2.1 Percentage Improvements of One-Shot Over Other Initial Parameter Settings

Table 10.3 depicts the percentage improvements attained by the one-shot parameter settings $\widehat{P_0}$ over other parameter settings for different application domains and weight factors. We point out that different weight factors could result in different percentage improvements; however, we observed similar trends for other weight factors. Table 10.3 shows that one-shot initial parameter settings can result in as high as 155% improvement as compared to other initial value settings. We observe that some arbitrary settings may give a comparable or even a better solution for a particular application domain, application metric weight factors, and design space

Table 10.3 Percentage improvements attained by one-shot $(\widehat{P_0})$ over other initial parameter settings for $|S| = 729$ and $|S| = 31, 104$

–	$|S| = 729$				$|S| = 31, 104$			
Application domain	I_1 (%)	I_2 (%)	I_3 (%)	I_4 (%)	I_1 (%)	I_2 (%)	I_3 (%)	I_4 (%)
Security/defense	155	10	57	29	148	0.3	10	92
Health care	78	7	31	11	73	0.3	10	45
Ambient conditions monitoring	52	6	20	7	15	−7	−12	18

cardinality, but that arbitrary setting would not scale to other application domains, application metric weight factors, and design space cardinalities. For example, $\mathcal{I}_3$ obtains a 12% better quality solution than $\widehat{\mathbf{P}_0}$ for the ambient conditions monitoring application for $|S| = 31,104$, but yields a 10% lower quality solution for the security/defense and healthcare applications for $|S| = 31,104$, and a 57%, 31%, and 20% lower quality solution than $\widehat{\mathbf{P}_0}$ for the security/defense, health care, and ambient conditions monitoring applications, respectively, for $|S| = 729$. The percentage improvement attained by $\widehat{\mathbf{P}_0}$ over all application domains and design spaces is 33% on average. Our one-shot methodology is the first approach (to the best of our knowledge) to intelligent initial tunable parameter value settings for sensor nodes to provide a good quality operating state, as arbitrary initial parameter value settings typically result in a poor operating state. Results reveal that on average $\widehat{\mathbf{P}_0}$ gives a solution within 8% of the optimal solution obtained from exhaustive search.

The percentage improvement attained by $\widehat{\mathbf{P}_0}$ over all application domains and design spaces is 33% on average. Our one-shot methodology is the first approach (to the best of our knowledge) to intelligent initial tunable parameter value settings for sensor nodes to provide a good quality operating state, as arbitrary initial parameter value settings typically result in a poor operating state. Results reveal that on average $\widehat{\mathbf{P}_0}$ gives a solution within 8% of the optimal solution obtained from an exhaustive search [73].

10.4.2.2 Comparison of One-Shot with Greedy Variants and SA-Based Dynamic Optimization Methodologies

In order to investigate the effectiveness of our one-shot methodology, we compare the one-shot solution's quality (indicated by the attained objective function value) with two other dynamic optimization methodologies, which leverage SA-based and greedy-based (denoted by $\mathrm{GD}^{\mathrm{asc}}$ where asc stands for ascending order of parameter exploration) exploration of design space. We assign initial parameter value settings for greedy- and SA-based methodologies as $\mathcal{I}_1$ and $\mathcal{I}_4$, respectively. Note that, for brevity, we present results for $\mathcal{I}_1$ and $\mathcal{I}_4$; however, other initial parameter settings such as $\mathcal{I}_2$ and $\mathcal{I}_3$ would yield similar trends when combined with greedy-based and SA-based design space exploration.

Figure 10.3 shows the objective function value normalized to the optimal solution (obtained from exhaustive search) versus the number of states explored for the one-shot, $\mathrm{GD}^{\mathrm{asc}}$, and SA algorithms for a security/defense system for $|S| = 729$. The one-shot solution is within 1.8% of the optimal solution obtained from exhaustive search. The figure shows that $\mathrm{GD}^{\mathrm{asc}}$ and SA explore 11 states (1.51% of the design space) and 10 states (1.37% of the design space), respectively, to attain an equivalent or better quality solution than the one-shot solution. Although greedy- and SA-based methodologies explore few states to reach a comparable solution as that of our one-shot methodology, the one-shot methodology is suitable when design space exploration is not an option due to an extremely large design space and/or extremely stringent computational, memory, and timing constraints. These results indicate that other arbitrary initial value settings (e.g., $\mathcal{I}_1$, $\mathcal{I}_4$) do not provide a good quality operating state and necessitate design space exploration by online algorithms (e.g., greedy) to provide a good quality operating state. We point out that if the greedy- and SA-based methodologies leverage our one-shot initial tunable parameter value settings $\mathcal{I}$, further improvements over the one-shot solution can produce a very good quality (optimal or near-optimal) operating state [316].

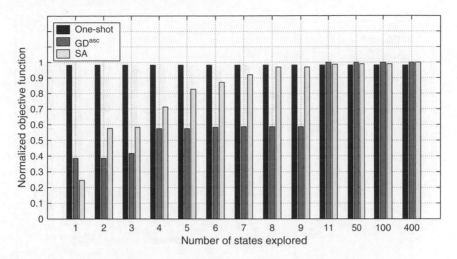

Figure 10.3   Objective function value normalized to the optimal solution for a varying number of states explored for one-shot, greedy, and SA algorithms for a security/defense system where $\omega_l = 0.25$, $\omega_t = 0.35$, $\omega_r = 0.4$, and $|S| = 729$

Figure 10.4 shows the objective function value normalized to the optimal solution versus the number of states explored for a security/defense system for $|S| = 31,104$. The one-shot solution is within 8.6% of the optimal solution. The figure shows that GD^{asc} converges to a lower quality solution than the one-shot solution after exploring 9 states (0.029% of the design space) and SA explores 8 states (0.026% of the design space) to yield a better quality solution than the one-shot solution. These results reveal that the greedy exploration of parameters may not necessarily attain a better quality solution than our one-shot solution.

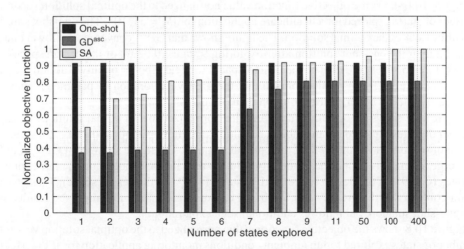

Figure 10.4   Objective function value normalized to the optimal solution for a varying number of states explored for one-shot, greedy, and SA algorithms for a security/defense system where $\omega_l = 0.25$, $\omega_t = 0.35$, $\omega_r = 0.4$, and $|S| = 31,104$

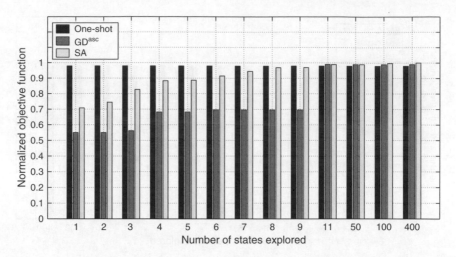

Figure 10.5   Objective function value normalized to the optimal solution for a varying number of states explored for one-shot, greedy, and SA algorithms for a healthcare application where $\omega_l = 0.25$, $\omega_t = 0.35$, $\omega_r = 0.4$, and $|S| = 729$

Figure 10.5 shows the objective function value normalized to the optimal solution versus the number of states explored for a healthcare application for $|S| = 729$. The one-shot solution is within 2.1% of the optimal solution. The figure shows that GD^{asc} converges to an almost equal quality solution as compared to the one-shot solution after exploring 11 states (1.5% of the design space) and SA explores 10 states (1.4% of the design space) to yield an almost equal quality solution as compared to the one-shot solution. These results indicate that further exploration of the design space is required to find an equivalent quality solution as compared to one-shot if the intelligent initial value settings leveraged by one-shot is not used.

Figure 10.6 shows the objective function value normalized to the optimal solution versus the number of states explored for a healthcare application for $|S| = 31,104$. The one-shot solution is within 1.6% of the optimal solution. The figure shows that GD^{asc} converges to a lower quality solution than the one-shot solution after exploring 9 states (0.029% of the design space) and SA explores 6 states (0.019% of the design space) to yield a better quality solution than the one-shot solution. These results confirm that the greedy exploration of parameters may not necessarily attain a better quality solution than our one-shot solution.

Figure 10.7 shows the objective function value normalized to the optimal solution versus the number of states explored for an ambient conditions monitoring application for $|S| = 729$. The one-shot solution is within 7.7% of the optimal solution. The figure shows that GD^{asc} and SA converge to an equivalent or better quality solution than the one-shot solution after exploring 4 states (0.549% of the design space) and 10 states (1.37% of the design space). These results again confirm that the greedy- and SA-based exploration can provide improved results over the one-shot solution, but requires additional state exploration.

Figure 10.8 shows the objective function value normalized to the optimal solution versus the number of states explored for an ambient conditions monitoring application for $|S| = 31,104$. The one-shot solution is within 24.7% of the optimal solution. The figure shows that both GD^{asc}

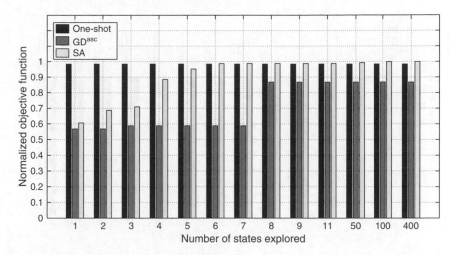

Figure 10.6 Objective function value normalized to the optimal solution for a varying number of states explored for one-shot, greedy, and SA algorithms for a healthcare application where $\omega_l = 0.25$, $\omega_t = 0.35$, $\omega_r = 0.4$, and $|S| = 31, 104$

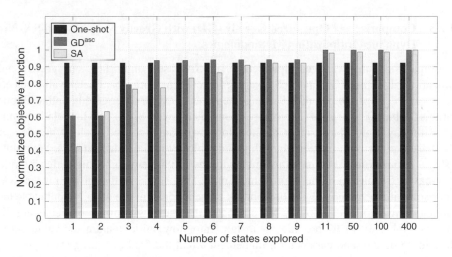

Figure 10.7 Objective function value normalized to the optimal solution for a varying number of states explored for one-shot, greedy, and SA algorithms for an ambient conditions monitoring application where $\omega_l = 0.4$, $\omega_t = 0.5$, $\omega_r = 0.1$, and $|S| = 729$

and SA converge to an equivalent or better quality solution than the one-shot solution after exploring 3 states (0.01% of the design space). These results indicate that both greedy and SA can give good quality solutions after exploring a very small percentage of the design space and both greedy-based and SA-based methods enable lightweight dynamic optimizations [316]. The results also indicate that the one-shot solution provides a good quality solution when further design space exploration is not possible due to resource constraints.

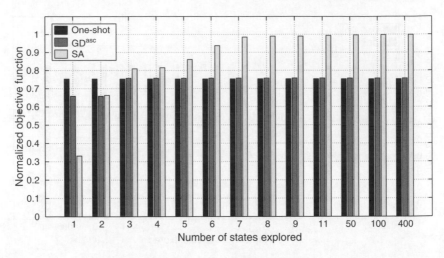

Figure 10.8   Objective function value normalized to the optimal solution for a varying number of states explored for one-shot, greedy, and SA algorithms for an ambient conditions monitoring application where $\omega_l = 0.4$, $\omega_t = 0.5$, $\omega_r = 0.1$, and $|S| = 31,104$

10.4.2.3   Comparison of Optimized Greedy (GD) with Greedy Variants and SA-Based Dynamic Optimization Methodologies

For comparison purposes, we implemented an SA-based algorithm, our greedy online optimization algorithm (GD) (which leverages intelligent initial parameter value selection, exploration ordering, and parameter arrangement), and several other greedy online algorithm variations (Table 10.4) in C++. We compare our results with SA to provide relative comparisons of our dynamic optimization methodology with another methodology that leverages an SA-based online optimization algorithm and arbitrary initial value settings. We point out that step 3 of our dynamic optimization methodology can use any lightweight algorithm (e.g., greedy-based, SA-based) in the improvement mode (Fig. 10.1). Although we present SA for comparison with the greedy algorithm, both of these algorithms are equally applicable to our dynamic optimization methodology. We compare GD results with different greedy algorithm variations (Table 10.4) to provide an insight into how initial parameter value settings, exploration ordering, and parameter arrangement affect the final operating state quality. We normalize the objective function value (corresponding to the operating state) attained by the algorithms with respect to the optimal solution (objective function value corresponding to the optimal operating state) obtained from an exhaustive search.

Figure 10.9 shows the objective function values normalized to the optimal solution for SA and greedy algorithms versus the number of states explored for a security/defense system for $|S| = 729$. Results indicate that GD^{ascA}, GD^{ascB}, GD^{ascC}, GD^{desD}, GD^{desE}, GD^{desF}, and GD converge to a steady-state solution (objective function value corresponding to the operating state) after exploring 11, 10, 11, 10, 10, 9, and 8 states, respectively. We point out that we do not plot the results for each iteration and greedy algorithm variations for brevity; however, we obtained the results for all iterations and greedy algorithm variations. These convergence results show that GD converges to a final operating state slightly faster than other greedy algorithms, exploring only 1.1% of the design space. GD^{ascA} and GD^{ascB} converge to almost equal

Table 10.4   Greedy algorithms with different parameter
arrangements and exploration orders

Notation	Description
GD	Greedy algorithm with parameter exploration order $\hat{\mathbf{P}}_{\mathbf{d}}$ and arrangement $\hat{\mathbf{P}}$
GD^{ascA}	Explores parameter values in ascending order with arrangement $\mathcal{A} = \{V_p, F_p, F_s, P_s, P_{ti}, P_{tx}\}$
GD^{ascB}	Explores parameter values in ascending order with arrangement $\mathcal{B} = \{P_{tx}, P_{ti}, P_s, F_s, F_p, V_p\}$
GD^{ascC}	Explores parameter values in ascending order with arrangement $\mathcal{C} = \{F_s, P_{ti}, P_{tx}, V_p, F_p, P_s\}$
GD^{desD}	Explores parameter values in descending order with arrangement $\mathcal{D} = \{V_p, F_p, F_s, P_s, P_{ti}, P_{tx}\}$
GD^{desE}	Explores parameter values in descending order with arrangement $\mathcal{E} = \{P_{tx}, P_{ti}, P_s, F_s, F_p, V_p\}$
GD^{desF}	Explores parameter values in descending order with arrangement $\mathcal{F} = \{P_s, F_p, V_p, P_{tx}, P_{ti}, F_s\}$

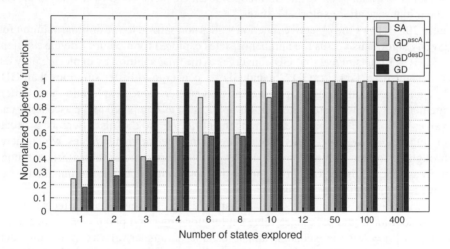

Figure 10.9   Objective function values normalized to the optimal solution for a varying number of states explored for SA and the greedy algorithms for a security/defense system where $\omega_l = 0.25$, $\omega_t = 0.35$, $\omega_r = 0.4$, and $|S| = 729$

quality solutions as GD^{desD} and GD^{desE} showing that ascending or descending parameter values exploration and parameter arrangements do not significantly impact the solution quality for this application for $|S| = 729$.

Results also indicate that the SA algorithm outperforms all greedy algorithms and converges to the optimal solution after exploring 400 states or 55% of the design space. Figure 10.9 also verifies the ability of our methodology to determine a good quality, near-optimal solution in

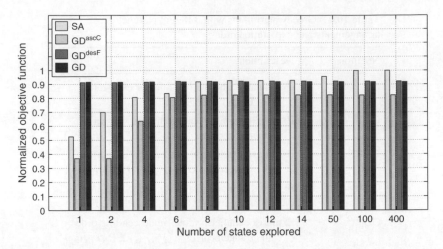

Figure 10.10 Objective function values normalized to the optimal solution for a varying number of states explored for SA and greedy algorithms for a security/defense system where $\omega_l = 0.25$, $\omega_t = 0.35$, $\omega_r = 0.4$, and $|S| = 31, 104$

one-shot that is within 1.4% of the optimal solution. GD achieves only a 1.8% improvement over the initial state after exploring 8 states.

Figure 10.10 shows the objective function values normalized to the optimal solution for SA and greedy algorithms versus the number of states explored for a security/defense system for $|S| = 31, 104$. Results reveal that GD converges to the final solution by exploring only 0.04% of the design space. GD^{desD}, GD^{desE}, and GD^{desF} converge to better solutions than GD^{ascA}, GD^{ascB}, and GD^{ascC} showing that descending parameter values exploration and parameter arrangements $\mathcal{D}$, $\mathcal{E}$, and $\mathcal{F}$ are better for this application as compared to the ascending parameter values exploration and parameter arrangements $\mathcal{A}$, $\mathcal{B}$, and $\mathcal{C}$. This difference is because a descending exploration order tends to select higher tunable parameter values, which increases the throughput considerably as compared to lower tunable parameter values. Since throughput has been assigned a higher weight factor for this application than the lifetime, better overall objective function values are attained.

Comparing Figs. 10.10 and 10.9 reveals that the design space size also affects the solution quality in addition to the parameter value exploration order and parameter arrangement. For example, for $|S| = 729$, the ascending and descending parameter values exploration order and parameter arrangement result in comparable quality solutions, whereas for $|S| = 31, 104$, the descending parameter values exploration order results in higher quality solutions. Again, the SA algorithm outperforms all greedy algorithms and converges to the optimal solution for $|S| = 31, 104$ after exploring 100 states or 0.3% of the design space. Figure 10.10 also verifies the ability of our methodology to determine a good quality, near-optimal solution in one-shot that is within 9% of the optimal solution. GD achieves only a 0.3% improvement over the initial state (one-shot solution) after exploring 11 states.

Results for a healthcare application for $|S| = 729$ reveal that GD converges to the final solution slightly faster than other greedy algorithms, exploring only 1% of the design space. The SA algorithm outperforms the greedy algorithm variants after exploring 400 states or 55% of the design space for $|S| = 729$, but the SA improvement over the greedy algorithm variants is insignificant as the greedy algorithm variants attain near-optimal solutions. Results indicate that the one-shot solution is within 2% of the optimal solution. GD achieves only a 2% improvement over the one-shot solution after exploring 8 states.

Results for a healthcare application for $|S| = 31,104$ reveal that GD converges to the final solution by exploring only 0.0257% of the design space. The SA algorithm outperforms all greedy algorithms and converges to the optimal solution after exploring 100 states (0.3% of the design space). The one-shot solution is within 1.5% of the optimal solution. GD achieves only a 0.2% improvement over the one-shot solution after exploring 8 states.

Figure 10.11 shows the objective function values normalized to the optimal solution versus the number of states explored for an ambient conditions monitoring application for $|S| = 729$. Results reveal that GD converges to the final solution slightly faster than other greedy algorithms, exploring only 1.1% of the design space. GD^{ascA}, GD^{ascB}, and GD^{ascC} converge to a higher quality solution than GD^{desD}, GD^{desE}, and GD^{desF} because the ascending exploration order tends to select lower tunable parameter values, which results in comparatively larger lifetime values as compared to higher tunable parameter values. This higher lifetime results in higher lifetime objective function values and thus higher overall objective function values. We observe that the greedy algorithm variants result in higher quality solutions after exploring more states than the one attained by GD since GD^{ascA}, GD^{ascB}, GD^{ascC}, and GD^{desF} attain the optimal solution for $|S| = 729$. This observation reveals that other arbitrary parameter arrangements and exploration orders may obtain better solutions than GD, but those arbitrary arrangements and exploration orders would not scale for different application domains with different weight factors and for different design space cardinalities. The SA algorithm outperforms GD^{desD}, GD^{desE}, and GD after exploring 400 states (55% of the design space). GD^{ascA}, GD^{ascB}, GD^{ascC}, and GD^{desF} attain optimal solutions. Our one-shot solution is within 8% of the optimal solution. GD achieves only a 2% improvement over the one-shot solution after exploring 8 states.

Results for an ambient conditions monitoring application for $|S| = 31,104$ indicate that GD converges to the optimal solution after exploring 13 states (0.04% of design space), with a 17%

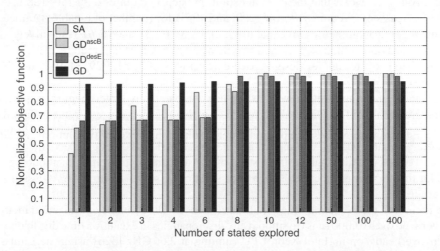

Figure 10.11 Objective function values normalized to the optimal solution for a varying number of states explored for SA and greedy algorithms for an ambient conditions monitoring application where $\omega_l = 0.4$, $\omega_t = 0.5$, $\omega_r = 0.1$, and $|S| = 729$

improvement over the one-shot solution. The one-shot solution is within 14% of the optimal solution. GD^{ascA}, GD^{ascB}, and GD^{ascC} converge to a better solution than GD^{desD}, GD^{desE}, and GD^{desF} for similar reasons as $|S| = 729$. The one-shot solution is within 14% of the optimal solution. SA converges to a near-optimal solution after exploring 400 states (1.3% of the design space).

The results for different application domains and design spaces verify that the one-shot mode provides a high quality solution that is within 8% of the optimal solution averaged over all application domains and design space cardinalities. These results also verify that improvements can be achieved over the one-shot solution during the improvement mode. The results indicate that GD may explore more states than other greedy algorithms if state exploration provides a noticeable improvement over the one-shot solution. The results also provide an insight into the convergence rates and reveal that even though the design space cardinality increases by 43×, both heuristic algorithms (greedy and SA) still explore only a small percentage of the design space and result in high-quality solutions. Furthermore, although SA outperforms the greedy algorithms after exploring a comparatively larger portion of the design space, GD still provides an optimal or near-optimal solution with significantly less design space exploration. These results advocate the use of GD as a design space exploration algorithm for constrained applications, whereas SA can be used for relatively less constrained applications. We point out that both GD and SA are online algorithms for dynamic optimization and are suitable for larger design spaces as compared to other stochastic algorithms, such as MDP-based algorithms, which are only suitable for restricted (comparatively smaller) design spaces [69].

10.4.2.4 Computational Complexity

We analyze the relative complexity of the algorithms by measuring their execution time and data memory requirements. We perform data memory analysis for each step of our dynamic optimization methodology. Our data memory analysis assumes an 8-bit processor for sensor nodes with integer data types requiring 2 B of storage and float data types requiring 4 B of storage. Analysis reveals that the one-shot solution (step 1) requires only 150, 188, 248, and 416 B, whereas step 2 requires 94, 140, 200, and 494 B for (number of tunable parameters N, number of application metrics m) equal to $(3, 2)$, $(3, 3)$, $(6, 3)$, and $(6, 6)$, respectively. GD in step 3 requires 458, 528, 574, 870, and 886 B, whereas SA in step 3 requires 514, 582, 624, 920, and 936 B of storage for design space cardinalities of 8, 81, 729, 31,104, and 46,656, respectively.

The data memory analysis shows that SA has comparatively larger memory requirements than the greedy algorithm. Our analysis reveals that the data memory requirements for all three steps of our dynamic optimization methodology increase linearly as the number of tunable parameters, tunable values, and application metrics, and thus the design space, increase. The analysis verifies that although all three steps of our dynamic optimization methodology have low data memory requirements, the one-shot solution in step 1 requires 361% less memory on average.

We measured the execution time for all three steps of our dynamic optimization methodology averaged over 10,000 runs (to smooth any discrepancies in execution time due to operating system overheads) on an Intel Xeon CPU running at 2.66 GHz [326] using the Linux/Unix time command [327]. We scaled these execution times to the Atmel ATmega1281 microcontroller [77] running at 8 MHz. Although scaling does not provide 100% accuracy for the microcontroller runtime because of different instruction set architectures and memory subsystems, scaling provides reasonable runtime estimates and enables relative comparisons. Results showed that steps 1 and 2 required 1.66 ms and 0.332 ms, respectively, both for $|S| = 729$ and $|S| = 31,104$. For step 3, we compared GD with SA. GD explored 10 states and required 0.887 ms and 1.33 ms on average to converge to the solution for $|S| = 729$ and $|S| = 31,104$, respectively. SA required 2.76 ms and 2.88 ms to explore the first 10 states (to provide a fair comparison with GD) for $|S| = 729$ and $|S| = 31,104$, respectively. The other greedy algorithms required comparatively more time than GD because they required more design state exploration to converge than GD; however, all the greedy algorithms required less execution time than SA.

To verify that our dynamic optimization methodology is lightweight, we compared the execution time results for all three steps of our dynamic optimization methodology with the exhaustive search. The exhaustive search required 29.526 ms and 2.765 s for $|S| = 729$ and $|S| = 31,104$, respectively, which gives speedups of 10× and 832×, respectively, for our dynamic optimization methodology. The execution time analysis reveals that all three steps of our dynamic optimization methodology require execution time on the order of milliseconds, and the one-shot solution requires 138% less execution time on average as compared to all three steps of the dynamic optimization methodology. Execution time savings attained by the one-shot solution as compared to the three steps of our dynamic optimization methodology are 73% and 186% for GD and SA, respectively, when $|S| = 729$, and are 100% and 138% for GD and SA, respectively, when $|S| = 31,104$. These results indicate that the design space cardinality affects the execution time linearly, and our dynamic optimization methodology's advantage increases as the design space cardinality increases. We verified our execution time analysis using the clock() function [328], which confirmed similar trends.

To further verify that our dynamic optimization methodology is lightweight, we calculate the energy consumption for the two modes of our methodology—the one-shot and the improvement modes with either a GD- or SA-based online algorithm. We calculate the energy consumption E^{dyn} for an Atmel ATmega1281 microcontroller [77] operating at $V_p = 2.7$ V and $F_p = 8$ MHz as $E^{dyn} = V_p \cdot I_p^a \cdot T_{exe}$ where I_p^a and T_{exe} denote the processor's active current and the execution time for the methodology's operating mode at (V_p, F_p), respectively (we observed similar trends for other processor voltage and frequency settings). We point out that we consider the execution time for exploring the first 10 states for both the GD- and SA-based online algorithms in our energy calculations as both the GD and SA algorithms attained near-optimal results after exploring 10 states both for $|S| = 729$ and $|S| = 31,104$. Table 10.5 summarizes the energy calculations for different modes of our dynamic optimization methodology as well as for the exhaustive search for $|S| = 729$ and $|S| = 31,104$. We assume that the sensor node's battery energy in our calculations is $E_b = 25,920$ J (which is computed using our application metrics estimation model). Results indicate that one-shot consumes 1679% and 166,510% less energy as compared to the exhaustive search for $|S| = 729$ and $|S| = 31,104$, respectively. Improvement mode using GD as the online algorithm consumes 926% and 83,135% less energy as compared to the exhaustive search for $|S| = 729$ and $|S| = 31,104$, respectively. Improvement mode using SA as the online algorithm consumes 521% and 56,656% less

Table 10.5 Energy consumption for the one-shot and the improvement mode for our dynamic optimization methodology

Mode	$T_{exe}(ms)$	$E_{dyn}(\mu J)$	B_f	R_l
One-shot	1.66	23.75	9.16×10^{-10}	1.1×10^{10}
$\mathcal{IM}_{\|S\|=729}^{GD}$	2.879	41.2	1.6×10^{-9}	629.13×10^6
$\mathcal{IM}_{\|S\|=729}^{SA}$	4.752	68	2.62×10^{-9}	381.2×10^6
$\mathcal{ES}_{\|S\|=729}$	29.526	422.52	1.63×10^{-10}	61.35×10^6
$\mathcal{IM}_{\|S\|=31104}^{GD}$	3.322	47.54	1.83×10^{-9}	545.22×10^6
$\mathcal{IM}_{\|S\|=31104}^{SA}$	4.872	69.72	2.7×10^{-9}	371.77×10^6
$\mathcal{ES}_{\|S\|=31104}$	2,765	39,570	1.53×10^{-6}	655×10^3

$\mathcal{IM}_{\|S\|=X}^{GD}$ and $\mathcal{IM}_{\|S\|=X}^{SA}$ denote the improvement mode using GD and SA as the online algorithms, respectively, for $|S| = X$ where $X = \{729, 31,104\}$. $\mathcal{ES}_{\|S\|=X}$ denotes the exhaustive search for $|S| = X$ where $X = \{729, 31,104\}$. B_f denotes the fraction of battery energy consumed in an operating mode and R_l denotes the maximum number of times (runs) our dynamic optimization methodology can be executed in a given mode depending on the sensor node's battery energy

energy as compared to the exhaustive search for $|S| = 729$ and $|S| = 31, 104$, respectively. Furthermore, our dynamic optimization methodology using GD as the online algorithm can be executed $545.22 \times 10^6 - 655 \times 10^3 = 544.6 \times 10^6$ more times than the exhaustive search and 173.45×10^6 more times than when using SA as the online algorithm for $|S| = 31, 104$. These results verify that our dynamic optimization methodology is lightweight and can be theoretically executed on the order of million times even on energy-constrained sensor nodes.

10.5 Chapter Summary

In this chapter, we proposed a lightweight dynamic optimization methodology for EWSNs, which provided a high-quality solution in one-shot using an intelligent initial tunable parameter value setting for highly constrained applications. We also proposed an online greedy optimization algorithm that leveraged intelligent design space exploration techniques to iteratively improve on the one-shot solution for less constrained applications. Results showed that our one-shot solution is near-optimal and within 8% of the optimal solution on average. Compared with simulating annealing (SA) and different greedy algorithm variations, results showed that the one-shot solution yielded improvements as high as 155% over other arbitrary initial parameter settings. Results indicated that our greedy algorithm converged to the optimal or near-optimal solution after exploring only 1% and 0.04% of the design space, whereas SA explored 55% and 1.3% of the design space for design space cardinalities of 729 and 31,104, respectively. Data memory and execution time analysis revealed that our one-shot solution (step 1) required 361% and 85% less data memory and execution time, respectively, when compared to using all the three steps of our dynamic optimization methodology. Furthermore, one-shot consumed 1679% and 166,510% less energy as compared to the exhaustive search for $|S| = 729$ and $|S| = 31, 104$, respectively. Improvement mode using GD as the online algorithm consumed 926% and 83,135% less energy as compared to the exhaustive search for $|S| = 729$ and $|S| = 31, 104$, respectively. Computational complexity along with the execution time, data memory analysis, and energy consumption confirmed that our methodology is lightweight and thus feasible for sensor nodes with limited resources.

11

Parallelized Benchmark-Driven Performance Evaluation of Symmetric Multiprocessors and Tiled Multicore Architectures for Parallel Embedded Systems*

As chip transistor counts increase, embedded system design has shifted from single-core to multicore and manycore architectures. A primary reason for this architecture reformation is that performance speedups are becoming more difficult to achieve by simply increasing the clock frequency of traditional single-core architectures because of limitations in power dissipation. This single-core to multicore paradigm shift in embedded systems has introduced parallel computing to the embedded domain, which was previously predominantly used in supercomputing only. Furthermore, with respect to the computing industry, this paradigm has led to the proliferation of diverse multicore architectures, which necessitates comparison and evaluation of these disparate architectures for different embedded domains (e.g., distributed, real time, reliability constrained).

Contemporary multicore architectures are not designed to deliver high performance for all embedded domains, but are instead designed to provide high performance for a subset of these domains. The precise evaluation of multicore architectures for a particular embedded domain requires executing complete applications prevalent in that domain. Despite the

---

*A portion of this chapter is copyrighted by IEEE. The definitive version appeared in: Arslan Munir, Ann Gordon-Ross, and Sanjay Ranka, Parallelized Benchmark-Driven Performance Evaluation for SMPs and Tiled Multi-core Architectures for Embedded Systems, in *Proc. of IEEE International Performance Computing and Communications Conference (IPCCC)*, Austin, Texas, December 2012. URL http://ieeexplore.ieee.org/xpl/articleDetails .jsp?arnumber=6407785. ©[2012] IEEE. Reprinted with permission from IEEE as we are the authors of this work.

Modeling and Optimization of Parallel and Distributed Embedded Systems, First Edition.
Arslan Munir, Ann Gordon-Ross and Sanjay Ranka.
© 2016 John Wiley & Sons, Ltd. Published 2016 by John Wiley & Sons, Ltd.

diversity of embedded domains, the critical application for many embedded domains (especially distributed embedded domains of which embedded wireless sensor networks (EWSNs) are a prominent example) is information fusion, which fuses/condenses the information from multiple sources. Furthermore, many other applications consist of various kernels, such as Gaussian elimination (GE) (which is used in network coding) and matrix multiplication (MM), which dominate the computation time [145]. An embedded domain's parallelized applications and kernels provide an effective way of evaluating multicore architectures for that embedded domain.

In this chapter, we evaluate two multicore architectures for embedded systems: symmetric multiprocessors (SMPs) and Tilera's tiled multicore architectures (TMAs). We consider SMPs because SMPs are ubiquitous and pervasive, which provides a standard/fair basis for comparing with other novel architectures, such as TMAs. We consider Tilera's TILEPro64 TMAs because of this architecture's innovative architectural features such as three-way issue superscalar tiles, on-chip mesh interconnect, and dynamic distributed cache (DDC) technology.

In some cases, such as with Tilera's TILEPro64, the multicore architecture directly dictates the high-level parallel language used, as some multicore architectures support proprietary parallel languages whose benchmarks are not available open source. Tilera provides a proprietary multicore development environment (MDE) ilib API [21]. Many SMPs are more flexible, such as the Intel-based SMP, which supports Open Multi-Processing (OpenMP). These differences in supported languages make *cross-architectural evaluation* challenging since the results may be affected by the parallel language's efficiency. However, our analysis provides insights into the attainable performance per watt from these two multicore architectures.

Our main contributions in this chapter are as follows:

- We evaluate SMPs and TMAs for multicore-based parallel embedded systems.
- We parallelize an information fusion application, a GE benchmark, an MM benchmark, and an embarrassingly parallel (EP) benchmark for SMPs and TMAs to compare and analyze the architectures' performance and performance per watt. This parallelized benchmark-driven evaluation provides deeper insights as compared to a theoretical quantitative approach.
- We provide a quantitative comparison between SMPs and TMAs based on various device metrics, such as computational density CD and memory subsystem bandwidth. This quantitative comparison provides a high-level evaluation of the computational capability of these architectures.

Our cross-architectural evaluation results reveal that TMAs outperform SMPs with respect to scalability and performance per watt for applications involving integer operations on data with little communication between processor cores (processor cores are also referred as *tiles* in TMAs). For applications requiring floating-point (FP) operations and frequent dependencies between computations, SMPs outperform TMAs with respect to scalability and performance per watt.

The remainder of this chapter is organized as follows. A review of related work is given in Section 11.1. Section 11.2 discusses the multicore architectures studied in this chapter along with the parallelized benchmarks for evaluating these architectures. Parallel computing metrics leveraged to evaluate the multicore architectures are described in Section 11.3. Performance evaluation results for the multicore architectures are presented in Section 11.4 and Section 11.5 concludes this chapter.

11.1 Related Work

In the area of parallelization of algorithms and performance analysis of SMPs, Brown and Sharapov [334] compared the performance and programmability of the Born calculation (a model used to study the interactions between a protein and surrounding water molecules) using both OpenMP and message passing interface (MPI). The authors observed that the OpenMP version's programmability and performance outperformed the MPI version; however, the scalability of the MPI version was superior to the OpenMP version. Sun and Zhu [335] investigated performance metrics, such as speedup, efficiency, and scalability, for shared memory systems. The authors identified the causes of superlinear speedups, such as cache size, parallel processing overhead reduction, and randomized algorithms for shared memory systems. Lively et al. [336] explored the energy consumption and execution time of different parallel implementations of scientific applications using MPI-only versus a hybrid of MPI and OpenMP. The results indicated that the hybrid MPI/OpenMP implementation resulted in shorter execution time and lower energy as compared to the MPI-only implementation. Our work differs from previous parallel programming and performance analysis work in that we compare parallel implementations of different benchmarks using OpenMP and Tilera's ilib proprietary API for two multicore architectures as opposed to comparing OpenMP with MPI, both of which are not proprietary, as in many previous works.

Bikshandi et al. [337] investigated the performance of TMAs and demonstrated that hierarchically tiled arrays yielded increased performance on parallelized benchmarks, such as MM and NASA advanced supercomputing (NAS) benchmarks, by improving the data locality. Zhu et al. [338] presented a performance study of OpenMP language constructs on the IBM Cyclops-64 (C64) architecture that integrated 160 processing cores on a single chip. The authors observed that the overhead of the OpenMP language constructs on the C64 architecture was at least one order of magnitude lower as compared to the previous work on conventional SMP systems.

Some previous work investigated multicore architectures for distributed embedded systems. Dogan et al. [39] evaluated a single- and multicore architecture for biomedical signal processing in wireless body sensor networks (WBSNs) where both energy efficiency and real-time processing are crucial design objectives. Results revealed that the multicore architecture consumed 66% less power than the single-core architecture for high biosignal computation workloads that averaged 50.1 mega operations per seconds (MOPS). However, the multicore architecture consumed 10.4% more power than the single-core architecture for relatively light computation workloads that averaged 681 kilo operations per second (KOPS). Kwok and Kwok [37] proposed FPGA-based multicore computing for batch processing of image data in distributed EWSNs. Results revealed that the speedup obtained by FPGA-based acceleration at 20 MHz for edge detection, an image processing technique, was 22× as compared to a 48 MHz MicroBlaze microprocessor. Our work differs from the Kwok's work in that we study the feasibility of two fixed logic multicore architecture paradigms, SMPs, and TMAs, instead of reconfigurable logic.

Various networking algorithms have been implemented on multicore architectures for investigating the architectures' feasibility for distributed embedded systems. Kim et al. [47] proposed and implemented a parallel network coding algorithm on the Cell Broadband Engine for demonstration purposes. Kulkarni et al. [41] evaluated computational intelligence algorithms for various tasks performed by distributed EWSNs, such as information fusion, energy-aware routing, scheduling, security, and localization. Our work differs from the previous work on architectural evaluation for distributed embedded systems in that we implement GE and EP benchmarks, which are used as kernels in many embedded domains (e.g., GE is used in the decoding part of network coding), as well as information fusion application for two multi-core architectures (SMPs and TMAs) amenable for distributed embedded systems. A research group at Purdue explored a parallel histogram-based particle filter for object tracking on sin-gle instruction multiple data (SIMD)-based smart cameras [339]. Our work differs from the previous work on filters in embedded systems in that we implement a moving average filter for reducing noise in sensed data as part of the information fusion application, which also serves as a performance evaluation benchmark for SMPs and TMAs.

Although there exists work for independent performance evaluation of SMPs and TMAs, to the best of our knowledge there is no previous work that cross-evaluates these architectures, which is the focus of our work. Furthermore, our work backs up experimental results with theoretical computation of performance metrics such as computational density and memory subsystem bandwidth for the two architectures.

11.2 Multicore Architectures and Benchmarks

Many applications require embedded systems to perform various compute-intensive tasks that often exceed the computing capability of traditional single-core embedded systems. In this section, we describe the multicore architectures along with the applications and/or kernels that we leverage to evaluate these architectures.

11.2.1 Multicore Architectures

11.2.1.1 Symmetric Multiprocessors

SMPs are the most pervasive and prevalent type of parallel architecture that provides a global physical address space and symmetric access to all of main memory from any processor core. Every processor has a private cache and all of the processors and memory modules attach to a shared interconnect, typically a shared bus [145]. In our evaluations, we study an Intel-based SMP, which is an eight-core SMP consisting of two chips containing 45 nm Intel Xeon E5430 quad-core processors [340] (henceforth, we denote the Intel-based SMP as $SMP^{2\times QuadXeon}$). The Xeon E5430 quad-core processor chip offers a maximum clock frequency of 2.66 GHz, integrates a 32 KB level one instruction (L1-I) and a 32 KB level one data (L1-D) cache per core, a 12 MB level two (L2) unified cache (a dual-core option with a 6 MB L2 cache is also available), and a 1333 MHz front-side bus (FSB). The Xeon E5430 leverages Intel's enhanced FSB running at 1333 MHz, which enables enhanced throughput between each of the processor cores [341].

11.2.1.2 Tiled Multicore Architectures

TMAs exploit massive on-chip resources by combining each processor core with a switch to create a modular element called a *tile*, which can be replicated to create a multicore archi-tecture with any number of tiles. TMAs contain a high-performance interconnection network that constrains interconnection wire length to be no longer than the tile width and a switch

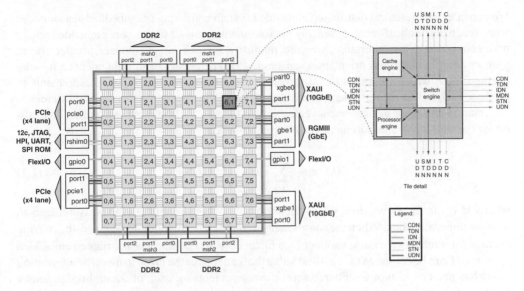

Figure 11.1　Tilera TILEPro64 processor [352]

(communication router) interconnects neighboring switches. Examples of TMAs include the Raw processor, Intel's Tera-Scale research processor, and Tilera's TILE64, TILEPro64, and TILE-Gx processor family [239, 342, 343]. In our evaluations, we study the TILEPro64 processor depicted in Fig. 11.1. The TILEPro64 processor features an 8×8 grid of sixty-four 90 nm tiles (cores) where each tile consists of a three-way very long instruction word (VLIW) pipelined processor capable of delivering up to 3 instructions/cycle, integrated L1 and L2 caches, and a nonblocking switch that integrates the tile into a power-efficient 31-Tbps on-chip interconnect mesh. Each tile has a 16-KB L1 cache (8-KB instruction cache and 8-KB data cache) and a 64-KB L2 cache, resulting in a total of 5 MB of on-chip cache with Tilera's *DDC* technology. Each tile can independently run a complete operating system or multiple tiles can be grouped together to run a multiprocessing operating system, such as SMP Linux [344].

11.2.2　Benchmark Applications and Kernels

11.2.2.1　Information Fusion

A crucial processing task in distributed embedded systems is information fusion. Distributed embedded systems, such as EWSNs, produce a large amount of data that must be processed, delivered, and assessed according to application objectives. Since the transmission bandwidth is often limited, information fusion condenses the sensed data and transmits only the selected, fused information to a base station node for further processing and/or evaluation by an operator. Information fusion is also used to reduce redundancy in the received data since the data gathered from neighboring sources/embedded nodes is typically highly correlated or redundant.

　　For our evaluations, we parallelize an information fusion application both for SMPs and TMAs to investigate the suitability of the two architectures for distributed embedded systems.

We consider a hierarchical distributed embedded system consisting of embedded sensor nodes where each cluster head receives sensing measurements from 10 single-core embedded sensor nodes equipped with temperature, pressure, humidity, acoustic, magnetometer, accelerometer, gyroscope, proximity, and orientation sensors [345]. The cluster head implements a moving average filter, which computes the arithmetic mean of a number of input measurements to produce each output measurement, to reduce random white noise from sensor measurements. Given an input sensor measurement vector $\mathbf{x} = (x(1), x(2), \ldots)$, the moving average filter estimates the true sensor measurement vector after noise removal $\mathbf{y} = (\hat{y}(1), \hat{y}(2), \ldots)$ as:

$$\hat{y}(k) = \frac{1}{M} \sum_{i=0}^{M-1} x(k-i), \forall\, k \geq M \tag{11.1}$$

where M is the filter's window, which dictates the number of input sensor measurements to fuse for noise reduction. When the sensor measurements have random white noise, the moving average filter reduces the noise variance by a factor of $\sqrt{M}$. For practical distributed embedded systems, M can be chosen as the smallest value that can reduce the noise to meet the application requirements. For each of the filtered sensor measurements for each of the embedded sensor nodes in the cluster, the cluster head calculates the minimum, maximum, and average of the sensed measurements. This information fusion application requires $100 \cdot N(3 + M)$ operations with complexity $\mathcal{O}(NM)$ where N denotes the number of sensor samples.

11.2.2.2 Gaussian Elimination

The GE kernel solves a system of linear equations and is used in many scientific applications, including the Linpack benchmark used for ranking supercomputers in the TOP500 list of the world's fastest computers [346, 347], and in distributed embedded systems. For example, the decoding algorithm for network coding uses a variant of GE (network coding is a coding technique to enhance network throughput in distributed embedded systems) [47]. The sequential runtime of the GE algorithm is $\mathcal{O}(n^3)$. Our GE kernel computes an upper triangularization of matrices and requires $(2/3) \cdot n^3 + (7/4) \cdot n^2 + (7/2) \cdot n$ FP operations, which includes the extra operations required to make the GE algorithm numerically stable.

11.2.2.3 Embarrassingly Parallel Benchmark

The EP benchmark is typically used to quantify the peak attainable performance of a parallel computer architecture. Our EP benchmark generates normally distributed random variates that are used in simulation of stochastic applications [348]. We leverage Box–Muller's algorithm, which requires $99n$ FP operations assuming that square root requires 15 FP operations, and logarithm, cosine, and sine each require 20 FP operations [349].

11.2.2.4 Matrix Multiplication

Since algorithms involving matrices and vectors are leveraged in various numerical and non-numerical applications [350], MM is one of the fundamental benchmarks used to evaluate different platforms. The sequential runtime for the conventional MM algorithm multiplying two $n \times n$ matrices is $\mathcal{O}(n^3)$ and requires $2n^3$ FP operations [350].

11.3 Parallel Computing Device Metrics

Parallel computing device metrics provide a means to compare different parallel architectures, and the most appropriate device metrics depends on the targeted application domain. For example, runtime (performance) may be an appropriate metric for comparing high-performance data servers, whereas performance per watt is a more appropriate metric for embedded systems that have a limited power budget. In this section, we characterize the metrics that we leverage in our study to compare parallel architectures.

Runtime: The *serial runtime* T_s of a program is the time elapsed between the beginning and end of the program on a sequential computer. The *parallel runtime* T_p is the time elapsed from the beginning of a program to the moment the last processor finishes execution.

Speedup: Speedup measures the performance gain achieved by parallelizing a given application/algorithm over the best sequential implementation of that application/algorithm. Speedup S is defined as T_s/T_p, which is the ratio of the serial runtime T_s of the best sequential algorithm for solving a problem to the time taken by the parallel algorithm T_p to solve the same problem on p processors. The speedup is ideal when the speedup is proportional to the number of processors used to solve a problem in parallel (i.e., $S = p$).

Efficiency: Efficiency measures the fraction of the time that a processor is usefully employed. Efficiency E is defined as S/p, which is the ratio of the speedup S to the number of processors p. An efficiency of one corresponds to the ideal speedup and implies good scalability.

Cost: Cost measures the sum of the time that each processor spends solving the problem. The cost C of solving a problem on a parallel system is defined as $T_p \cdot p$, which is the product of the parallel runtime T_p and the number of processors p used. A parallel computing system is *cost optimal* if the cost of solving a problem on a parallel computer is proportional to the execution time of the best known sequential algorithm on a single processor [350].

Scalability: Scalability of a parallel system measures the performance gain achieved by parallelizing as the problem size and the number of processors vary. Formally, scalability of a parallel system is a measure of the system's capacity to increase speedup in proportion to the number of processors. A scalable parallel system maintains a fixed efficiency as the number of processors and the problem size increase [350].

Computational Density: The computational density (CD) metric measures the computational performance of a device (parallel system). The CD for double precision FP (DPFP) operations can be given as [351]:

$$CD_{DPFP} = f \times \sum_i \frac{N_i}{CPI_i} \tag{11.2}$$

where f denotes the operating frequency of the device, N_i denotes the number of instructions of type i requiring FP computations that can be issued simultaneously, and CPI_i denotes the average number of cycles per instruction of type i.

Computational Density per Watt: The computational density per watt (CD/W) metric takes into account the power consumption of a device while quantifying performance. We propose a system-level power model to estimate the power consumption of multicore architectures that can be used in estimating the CD/W. Our power model considers both the active and idle modes' power consumptions. Given a multicore architecture with a total of N processor cores, the power consumption of the system with p active processor cores can be given as

$$P^p = p \cdot \frac{P_{\max}^{\text{active}}}{N} + (N - p) \cdot \frac{P_{\max}^{\text{idle}}}{N} \tag{11.3}$$

where $P_{\max}^{\text{active}}$ and $P_{\max}^{\text{idle}}$ denote the maximum active and idle modes' power consumptions, respectively. $P_{\max}^{\text{active}}/N$ and $P_{\max}^{\text{idle}}/N$ give the active and idle modes' power, respectively, per processor core and the associated switching and interconnection network circuitry. Our power model incorporates the power-saving features of state-of-the-art multicore architectures. Contemporary multicore architectures provide instructions to switch the processor cores and associated circuitry (switches, clock, interconnection network) not used in a computation to a low-power idle state. For example, a software-usable NAP instruction can be executed on a tile in the Tilera's TMAs to put the tile into a low-power IDLE mode [352, 353]. Similarly, Xeon 5400 processors provide an extended HALT state and Opteron processors provide a HALT mode, which are entered by executing the HLT instruction, to reduce power consumption by stopping the clock to internal sections of the processor. Other low-power processor modes are also available [341]. Investigation of a comprehensive power model for TMAs is the focus of our future work.

Memory-Sustainable Computational Density: Memory subsystem performance plays a crucial role in overall parallel embedded system performance, given the increasing disparity between the processor and memory speed improvements. The *internal memory bandwidth* (IMB) metric assesses on-chip memory performance by quantifying the number of operations that can be sustained by the computational cores for a given application. IMB can be given as (adapted from [351]):

$$\text{IMB} = \sum_i H_{c_i} \times \frac{N_{c_i} \times P_{c_i} \times W_{c_i} \times f_{c_i}}{8 \times \text{CPA}_{c_i}} \tag{11.4}$$

where H_{c_i} denotes the hit rate for a cache of type i; N_{c_i} denotes the number of caches of type i; P_{c_i}, W_{c_i}, f_{c_i}, and CPA_{c_i} denote the number of ports, memory width, operating frequency, and number of cycles per access for a cache of type i, respectively. IMB for each cache level and type is calculated separately and then summed to obtain the total IMB.

In parallel systems, external memory units supplement on-chip memory units. External memory units are farther from the computational cores as compared to the on-chip memory units; however, the external memory units' bandwidths impact the performance. The *external memory bandwidth* (EMB) metric assesses this EMB [354]. We define theoretical EMB as

$$\text{EMB}^{\text{th}} = \sum_i \frac{N_{m_i} \times W_{m_i} \times TR_{m_i}}{8} \tag{11.5}$$

where N_{m_i} denotes the number of memory modules of type i, and W_{m_i} and TR_{m_i} denote the memory interface width and transfer rate of a memory of type i, respectively. TR_{m_i} is typically a factor ($1–4\times$ depending on the memory technology) of the external memory clock rate. This theoretical EMB is typically not attainable in practice because of the delay involved in accessing external memory from a processor core; therefore, we define the *effective* external memory bandwidth, EMB^{eff} as

$$\text{EMB}^{\text{eff}} = \sum_i \frac{\text{EMB}^{\text{th}}_{m_i}}{\text{CPA}_{m_i}} \tag{11.6}$$

where $\text{EMB}^{\text{th}}_{m_i}$ and CPA_{m_i} denote the theoretical EMB and number of cycles per access for a memory of type i, respectively.

11.4   Results

The cross-architectural evaluation of SMPs and TMAs in terms of performance and performance per watt requires parallelization of benchmarks in two parallel languages: OpenMP for SMP and Tilera's MDE ilib API for TILEPro64 TMA. Performance per watt calculations leverage our power model (Eq. (12.3)) and we obtain the power consumption values for the SMPs and TMAs from the devices' respective datasheets. For example, the TILEPro64 has a maximum active and idle mode power consumption of 28 and 5 W, respectively [351, 355]. Intel's Xeon E5430 has a maximum power consumption of 80 W and a minimum power consumption of 16 W in an extended HALT state [340, 341].

In this section, we first present a quantitative comparison of SMPs and TMAs based on the device metrics characterized in Section 11.3. Then, we compare these architectures' metrics for our parallelized benchmarks. All results are obtained with the compiler optimization flag -O3 since our experiments showed that this optimization flag resulted in shorter execution times as compared to lower compiler optimization levels, such as -O2.

11.4.1   Quantitative Comparison of SMPs and TMAs

A quantitative comparison of multicore architectures provides a theoretical estimate of attainable performance from the architectures. Table 11.1 summarizes the quantitative comparison of SMPs and TMAs and reveals that the SMPs provide greater CD than the TMAs; however, the TMAs excel in internal memory subsystem performance in the last-level cache (LLC).

Table 11.1 provides lower and upper values for the theoretical CD and CD/W metrics. The upper CD values represent the absolute maximum CD when the superscalar processor cores in the multicore architectures issue, as well as retire, each clock cycle the maximum possible number of instructions, assuming that each FP instruction (operation) completes in one clock cycle. For example, the TILEPro64 and Xeon E5430 can simultaneously issue three integer instructions and four integer/FP instructions, respectively [341, 352]. The lower CD values indicate CD values that may be attainable for real workloads/benchmarks since the lower CD value is based on the actual number of cycles required for different FP operations. For example, we assume that the Xeon E5430 processor can perform 32- and 64-bit arithmetic and logic unit (ALU) instructions (e.g., add, subtract, rotate, shift) in 1 cycle, DPFP multiply in 4 cycles, and DPFP divide in 17 cycles. We point out that the lower CD value calculations in Table 11.1 are based on a fixed instruction mix (50% ALU, 35% multiply, and 15% divide), and different lower CD values can be obtained for different instruction mixes depending on a benchmark's/workload's particular characteristics. Since the TILEPro64 does not have FP

Table 11.1 Parallel computing device metrics for the multicore architectures (Intel's Xeon E5430 refers to the Xeon quad-core chip on SMP$^{2 \times QuadXeon}$)

Multicore platform	CD$_{DPFP}$ (GFLOPS)	CD/W (MFLOPS/W)	IMB$^{L1-I+L1-D}$ (GB/s)	IMB^{L2} (GB/s)	IMB^{L1+L2} (GB/s)	EMBth (GB/s)	EMB^{eff} (MB/s)
Intel's Xeon E5430	2.3–43	29–538	68–170	3–8	71–179	10.66 (per DDR2)	107
TILEPro64	0.4–18	14–643	89–222	8–28	97–249	25.6	324
SMP$^{2 \times QuadXeon}$	4.7–86	58–1076	136–340	6–16	142–358	170	1712

execution units nor does the official documentation mention FP performance, we calculate the CD values for the TILE64/TILEPro64 based on experimental estimates of cycles required to execute various FP operations.

The IMB and EMB calculations in Table 11.1 are based on Eqs. (11.4–11.6). The lower value for the IMB corresponds to typical low cache hit rates of L1-I (0.5), L1-D (0.3), and L2 (0.3) [179], whereas the upper value for the IMB corresponds to hit rates of 1 (or 100%).

11.4.2 Benchmark-Driven Results for SMPs

Table 11.2 depicts the increase in performance (throughput) in MOPS and performance per watt in MOPS/W for multicore SMP processors as compared to a single-core processor for the information fusion application for SMP$^{2 \times QuadXeon}$ when the number of fused samples $N = 3{,}000{,}000$, and the moving average filter's window $M = 40$. For example, an eight-core processor increases the information fusion application's throughput by $4.85 \times$ as compared to a single-core processor. The performance per watt results reveal that multiple cores execute the information fusion application more power efficiently as compared to a single-core processor. For example, a four-core processor attains a 49% better performance per watt than a single-core processor.

Table 11.3 depicts the performance and performance per watt results in MFLOPS and MFLOPS/W, respectively, for the GE benchmark for SMP$^{2 \times QuadXeon}$ when $(m, n) = (2000, 2000)$ where m is the number of linear equations and n is the number of variables

Table 11.2 Performance results for the information fusion application for SMP$^{2 \times QuadXeon}$ when $M = 40$

Problem size N	# of cores p	Execution time (s) T_p	Speedup $S = T_s/T_p$	Efficiency $E = S/p$	Cost $C = T_p \cdot p$	Performance (MOPS)	Performance per watt (MOPS/W)
3,000,000	1	12.02	1	1	12.02	1,073.2	22.36
3,000,000	2	7.87	1.53	0.76	15.74	1,639.14	25.61
3,000,000	4	4.03	2.98	0.74	16.12	3,201	33.34
3,000,000	6	2.89	4.2	0.7	17.34	4,463.67	34.87
3,000,000	8	2.48	4.85	0.61	19.84	5,201.6	32.51

Table 11.3 Performance results for the Gaussian elimination benchmark for SMP$^{2\times QuadXeon}$

Problem size (m, n)	# of cores p	Execution time (s) T_p	Speedup $S = T_s/T_p$	Efficiency $E = S/p$	Cost $C = T_p \cdot p$	Performance (MFLOPS)	Performance per watt (MFLOPS/W)
(2000, 2000)	1	8.05	1	1	8.05	663.35	13.82
(2000, 2000)	2	3.76	2.14	1.07	7.52	1420.21	22.2
(2000, 2000)	4	2.08	3.87	0.97	8.32	2567.31	26.74
(2000, 2000)	6	1.42	5.67	0.94	8.52	3760.56	29.38
(2000, 2000)	8	1.08	7.45	0.93	8.64	4944.44	30.9

Table 11.4 Performance results for the EP benchmark for SMP$^{2\times QuadXeon}$

Problem size n	# of cores p	Execution time (s) T_p	Speedup $S = T_s/T_p$	Efficiency $E = S/p$	Cost $C = T_p \cdot p$	Performance (MFLOPS)	Performance per watt (MFLOPS/W)
100,000,000	1	7.61	1	1	7.61	1,300.92	27.1
100,000,000	2	3.82	1.99	1	7.64	2,591.62	40.49
100,000,000	4	1.92	3.96	0.99	7.68	5,156.25	53.71
100,000,000	6	1.29	5.9	0.98	7.74	7,674.4	59.96
100,000,000	8	0.97	7.84	0.98	7.76	10,206.2	63.79

in the linear equation. Results show that the multicore processor speedups, as compared to the single-core processor, are proportional to the number of cores. For example, an eight-core processor increases the performance and performance per watt by 7.45× and 2.2×, respectively, as compared to a single-core processor.

Table 11.4 depicts the performance and performance per watt results in MFLOPS and MFLOPS/W, respectively, for the EP benchmark for SMP$^{2\times QuadXeon}$ when the number of random variates generated n is equal to 100,000,000. Results indicate that the SMP architecture delivers higher MFLOPS/W as the number of cores increases and the attained speedups are close to the ideal speedups. A comparison with Table 11.1 reveals that SMP$^{2\times QuadXeon}$ attains 96% of the theoretical lower CD values.

Table 11.5 depicts the performance and performance per watt results in MOPS and MOPS/W, respectively, for the integer MM benchmark for SMP$^{2\times QuadXeon}$ when $(m, n) = (1000, 1000)$ where m and n denote the number of rows and columns in the matrices, respectively. Results show that the multicore processor speedups, as compared to the single-core processor, are proportional to the number of cores. For example, an eight-core processor increases the performance and performance per watt by 7.3× and 2.2×, respectively, as compared to a single-core processor.

These results verify that embedded systems using an SMP-based multicore processor are more performance and power efficient as compared to embedded systems using a single-core processor.

Table 11.5   Performance results for the MM benchmark for SMP$^{2\times\text{QuadXeon}}$

Problem size (m, n)	# of cores p	Execution time (s) T_p	Speedup $S = T_s/T_p$	Efficiency $E = S/p$	Cost $C = T_p \cdot p$	Performance (MOPS)	Performance per watt (MOPS/W)
(1000, 1000)	1	4.89	1	1	4.89	409	8.52
(1000, 1000)	2	2.62	1.9	0.94	5.24	763.4	11.93
(1000, 1000)	4	1.29	3.8	0.95	5.16	1550.4	16.2
(1000, 1000)	6	0.89	5.5	0.92	5.34	2247.2	17.56
(1000, 1000)	8	0.67	7.3	0.91	5.36	2985.1	18.66

11.4.3   Benchmark-Driven Results for TMAs

Table 11.6 depicts the performance results for TMA-based multicore processors (TILEPro64) as compared to a single-core processor for the information fusion application when $N = 3,000,000$ and $M = 40$. Results indicate that the TMA-based multicore processor achieves ideal speedups, an efficiency of close to one, and nearly constant cost as the number of tiles increases indicating ideal scalability. For example, a TMA-based multicore processor with 50 tiles increases performance and performance per watt by 48.4× and 11.3×, respectively, as compared to a single TMA tile.

Table 11.7 depicts the performance results for the GE benchmark for the TILEPro64 when $(m, n) = (2000, 2000)$. Results show that the TMA-based multicore processor achieves less than ideal speedups, and that the efficiency decreases and the cost increases as p increases indicating poor scalability for the GE benchmark. The main reasons for poor scalability are excessive memory operations, dependency between the computations, and the core synchronization operations required by the GE benchmark. However, the TMA-based multicore processor still attains better performance and performance per watt than a single-core processor. For example, a TMA-based multicore processor with 56 tiles increases performance and performance per watt by 14× and 3×, respectively, as compared to a single TMA tile.

Table 11.6   Performance results for the information fusion application for the TILEPro64 when $M = 40$

Problem size N	# of tiles p	Execution time (s) T_p	Speedup $S = T_s/T_p$	Efficiency $E = S/p$	Cost $C = T_p \cdot p$	Performance (MOPS)	Performance per watt (MOPS/W)
3,000,000	1	70.65	1	1	70.65	182.6	34.07
3,000,000	2	35.05	2	1	70.1	368	64.33
3,000,000	4	17.18	4.1	1.02	68.72	750.87	116.6
3,000,000	6	11.48	6.2	1.03	68.9	1,123.69	156.94
3,000,000	8	8.9	7.94	0.99	71.2	1,449.44	183.94
3,000,000	10	6.79	10.4	1.04	67.9	1,899.85	221.17
3,000,000	50	1.46	48.4	0.97	73	8,835.62	384.66

Table 11.7 Performance results for the Gaussian elimination benchmark for the TILEPro64

Problem size (m, n)	# of tiles p	Execution time (s) T_p	Speedup $S = T_s/T_p$	Efficiency $E = S/p$	Cost $C = T_p \cdot p$	Performance (MFLOPS)	Performance per watt (MFLOPS/W)
(2000, 2000)	1	416.71	1	1	416.71	12.81	2.39
(2000, 2000)	2	372.35	1.12	0.56	744.7	14.34	2.51
(2000, 2000)	4	234.11	1.8	0.45	936.44	22.81	3.54
(2000, 2000)	6	181.23	2.3	0.38	1087.38	29.46	4.11
(2000, 2000)	8	145.51	2.86	0.36	1164.08	36.7	4.66
(2000, 2000)	16	84.45	4.9	0.31	1351.2	63.23	5.88
(2000, 2000)	28	52.25	7.98	0.28	1463	102.2	6.79
(2000, 2000)	44	36.26	11.49	0.26	1595.44	147.27	7.08
(2000, 2000)	56	29.72	14	0.25	1664.32	179.68	7.15

Table 11.8 Performance results for the EP benchmark for the TILEPro64

Problem size n	# of tiles p	Execution time (s) T_p	Speedup $S = T_s/T_p$	Efficiency $E = S/p$	Cost $C = T_p \cdot p$	Performance (MFLOPS)	Performance per watt (MFLOPS/W)
100,000,000	1	687.77	1	1	687.77	14.39	2.68
100,000,000	2	345.79	1.99	1	691.58	28.63	5
100,000,000	4	173.48	3.96	0.99	693.92	57.07	8.86
100,000,000	6	117.74	5.84	0.97	706.44	84.08	11.74
100,000,000	8	87.32	7.88	0.98	698.56	113.38	14.4
100,000,000	16	44.23	15.55	0.97	707.68	223.83	20.82
100,000,000	28	28.86	23.83	0.85	808.08	343.03	22.78
100,000,000	44	19.49	35.29	0.8	857.56	507.95	24.41
100,000,000	56	16.15	42.6	0.76	904.4	613	24.4

Table 11.8 depicts the performance results for the EP benchmark for the TILEPro64 when $n = 100,000,000$. Results show that the TMA-based multicore processor delivers higher performance and performance per watt as the number of tiles increases. For example, the TMA-based multicore processor with eight tiles increases performance and performance per watt by 7.9× and 5.4×, respectively, whereas with 56 tiles, the performance and performance per watt increase by 42.6× and 9.1×, respectively, as compared to a single TMA tile.

Similarly, performance results for the integer MM benchmark for the TILEPro64 reveals that the TMA-based multicore performance delivers higher performance and performance per watt as the number of tiles increases. For example, a TMA-based multicore processor with eight tiles increases performance and performance per watt by 5.6× and 3.8×, respectively, as compared to a single TMA tile. Results also reveal that the performance per watt suffers as the number of tiles increases because of nonideal scalability of the integer MM benchmark. The reason for this nonideal scalability is that our integer MM parallelization is based on the conventional MM algorithm and does not leverage cache blocking for high performance. Hence, excessive accesses to main memory and the load on the interconnection network accounts for nonideal scalability as the number of tiles increases. Attaining high performance from TMAs using MM as a case study is the focus of our future work [356].

Comparing the performance and performance per watt results for the information fusion application and EP benchmark reveals that TMAs deliver higher performance and performance per watt for benchmarks with integer operations as compared to the benchmarks with FP operations. For example, the increase in performance and performance per watt for integer operations as compared to FP operations is 13× on average for a TMA with eight tiles. This better performance and performance per watt for integer operations is because Tilera's TMAs do not contain dedicated FP units.

These results verify that an embedded system using TMAs as processing units is more performance and power efficient as compared to an embedded system using a single tile.

11.4.4 Comparison of SMPs and TMAs

To provide cross-architectural evaluation insights for SMPs and TMAs, we compare the performance per watt results based on our parallelized benchmarks for these architectures. These results indicate which of the two architectures is more suitable for particular types of embedded applications.

Figure 11.2 compares the performance per watt for the SMP$^{2 \times \text{QuadXeon}}$ and the TILEPro64 for a varying number of cores/tiles for the information fusion application and reveals that the TILEPro64 delivers higher performance per watt as compared to the SMP$^{2 \times \text{QuadXeon}}$. For example, when the number of cores/tiles is eight, the TILEPro64's performance per watt is 465.8% better than that of the SMPs. The reason for this better performance per watt for the TILEPro64 is that the information fusion application operates on the private data obtained from various sources, which is easily parallelized on the TILEPro64 using ilib API. This parallelization exploits data locality for enhanced performance for computing moving averages, minimum, maximum, and average of the sensed data. The exploitation of data locality enables

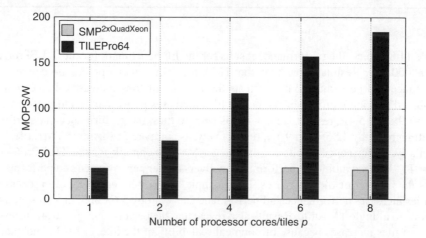

Figure 11.2 Performance per watt (MOPS/W) comparison between SMP$^{2 \times \text{QuadXeon}}$ and the TILEPro64 for the information fusion application when $N = 3,000,000$

fast access to private data, which leads to higher IMB (on-chip bandwidth between tiles and caches) and consequently higher MFLOPS and MFLOPS/W.

The SMP$^{2\times QuadXeon}$ attains comparatively lower performance than the TILEPro64 for the information fusion application due to two reasons: the SMP architecture is more suited for shared memory applications and the information fusion application is well suited for architectures that can better exploit data locality; and OpenMP-based parallel programming uses sections and parallel constructs, which requires sensed data to be shared by operating threads even if the data requires independent processing by each thread. While parallelizing the information fusion application for the SMP$^{2\times QuadXeon}$, we first tried using an independent copy of the sensed data (as with the TILEPro64) for each thread to maximize performance. This parallelization resulted in segmentation faults due to the extremely large memory requirements and required us to use shared memory for the sensed data since the current version of OpenMP provides no way of specifying private data for particular threads (although data can be declared private for all of the threads participating in a parallel computation). Therefore, the SMP's comparatively lower performance is partially due to the limitation of OpenMP, which does not allow the declaration of thread-specific private data (i.e., received data from the first source is private to the first thread only, whereas other threads have no information of this data; received data from the second source is private to the second thread only; and so on).

Figure 11.3 shows that the SMP$^{2\times QuadXeon}$ achieves higher MFLOPS/W than the TILEPro64 for the GE benchmark. For example, the SMP$^{2\times QuadXeon}$ achieves a 563% better performance per watt than the TILEPro64 when the number of cores/tiles is eight. The results also indicate that the SMP$^{2\times QuadXeon}$ exhibits better scalability and cost-efficiency than the TILEPro64. For example, the SMP$^{2\times QuadXeon}$'s cost-efficiency is 0.93 and the TILEPro64's cost-efficiency is 0.36 when the number of cores/tiles is eight. The GE benchmark requires excessive memory operations and communication and synchronization between processing cores, which favors the SMP-based shared memory architecture since the communication transforms to read and write operations in shared memory, and hence better performance per watt for the SMP$^{2\times QuadXeon}$ as compared to the TILEPro64. In TMAs, communication operations burden

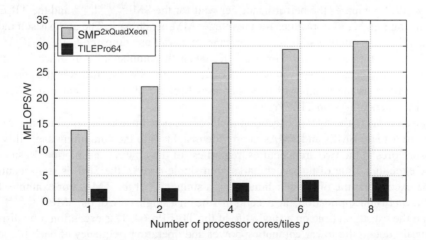

Figure 11.3 Performance per watt (MFLOPS/W) comparison between SMP$^{2\times QuadXeon}$ and the TILEPro64 for the Gaussian elimination benchmark when $(m, n) = (2000, 2000)$

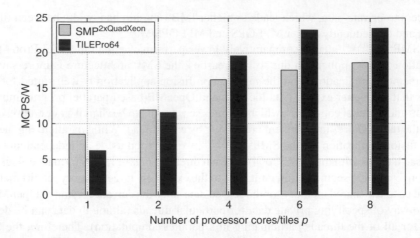

Figure 11.4 Performance per watt (MOPS/W) comparison between $\text{SMP}^{2\text{xQuadXeon}}$ and the TILEPro64 for the integer MM benchmark when $(m, n) = (1000, 1000)$

the on-chip interconnection network, especially when communicating large amounts of data. Furthermore, the higher memory bandwidth (both on-chip and external memory) for the $\text{SMP}^{2\text{xQuadXeon}}$ as compared to the TILEPro64 leads to higher memory-sustainable CD and thus enhanced performance for the GE benchmark, which requires frequent memory accesses.

For the EP benchmark, the $\text{SMP}^{2\text{xQuadXeon}}$ delivers higher MFLOPS/W than the TILEPro64 because the EP benchmark's execution time on the $\text{SMP}^{2\text{xQuadXeon}}$ is significantly less than the execution time on the TILEPro64 (detailed results are omitted for brevity). For example, the $\text{SMP}^{2\text{xQuadXeon}}$ achieves 4.4× better performance per watt than the TILEPro64 when the number of cores/tiles is equal to eight. The comparatively larger execution time on the TILEPro64 is due to the complex FP operations (e.g., square root, logarithm) in the EP benchmark, which require many cycles to execute on the integer execution units in the TILEPro64.

Figure 11.4 compares the performance per watt for the $\text{SMP}^{2\text{xQuadXeon}}$ and the TILEPro64 for a varying number of cores/tiles for the integer MM benchmark. The comparison indicates that the TILEPro64 delivers higher performance per watt as compared to the $\text{SMP}^{2\text{xQuadXeon}}$ for eight cores/tiles and fewer. For example, when the number of cores/tiles is eight, the TILEPro64's performance per watt is 26.3% better than the SMP's. However, the performance per watt suffers as the number of tiles increases because of the nonideal scalability of the integer MM benchmark on TILEPro64.

We also compare the overall execution time for the benchmarks (detailed results are omitted for brevity) for SMPs and TMAs to provide insights into the computing capability of the processor cores in the two architectures, regardless of the power consumption. Results show that the execution time of the benchmarks on a single core of the SMP is significantly less than the execution time of the benchmarks on a single tile of the TMA. For example, for the information fusion application, the execution time on a single core of the $\text{SMP}^{2\text{xQuadXeon}}$ is 6× less than the execution time on a single tile of the TILEPro64. This execution time difference is primarily due to the lower computing power and operating frequency of each tile and the TILEPro64's lack of FP execution units. Each tile on the TMA has a maximum clock frequency of 866 MHz as compared to the $\text{SMP}^{2\text{xQuadXeon}}$'s maximum clock frequency of 2.66 GHz. The better performance of a single core of the $SMP^{2xQuadXeon}$ as compared to a single tile of the TILEPro64 confirms the corollary of Amdahl's law that emphasizes the performance advantage of a powerful single core over multiple less powerful cores [357]. We point out that this execution time difference may be exacerbated for memory-intensive benchmarks because of the larger L2 cache on the $SMP^{2xQuadXeon}$ (12 MB) as compared to the TILEPro64 (5 MB on-chip cache with Tilera's DDC technology).

11.5 Chapter Summary

In this chapter, we compared the performance of SMPs and TMAs (focusing on the TILEPro64) based on a parallelized information fusion application, a Gaussian elimination (GE) benchmark, a matrix multiplication (MM) benchmark, and an embarrassingly parallel (EP) benchmark. Our results revealed that the SMPs outperform the TMAs in terms of overall execution time; however, TMAs can deliver comparable or better performance per watt. Specifically, results indicated that the TILEPro64 exhibited better scalability and attained better performance per watt than the SMPs for applications involving integer operations and for the applications that operate primarily on private data with little communication between operating cores by exploiting the data locality, such as in the information fusion application. The SMPs depicted better scalability and performance for benchmarks requiring excessive communication and synchronization operations between operating cores, such as in the GE benchmark. Results from the EP benchmark revealed that the SMPs provided higher peak floating-point performance per watt than the TMAs primarily because the studied TMAs did not have a dedicated floating-point unit.

Further evaluation of SMPs and TMAs for other benchmarks, such as a block matching kernel for image processing, video encoding and decoding, convolution, and fast Fourier transform (FFT) will be interesting because these benchmarks would provide insights into the architectures' suitability for other domains, such as signal processing. Development of a robust energy model for the SMPs and TMAs as well as extending the benchmark-driven evaluation to include field-programmable gate array (FPGA)-based multicore architectures will be an interesting research problem to explore.

12

High-Performance Optimizations on Tiled Manycore Embedded Systems: A Matrix Multiplication Case Study*

The scaling of complementary metal-oxide-semiconductor (CMOS) transistors into the nanometer regime unveils the possibility of integrating millions of transistors on a single chip. A major challenge for the computer industry is the efficient utilization of this ever-increasing number of on-chip transistors. Increasing clock frequency and single-core architectural innovations, such as deep pipelines, out-of-order execution, and prefetching, to exploit instruction-level parallelism (ILP) for enhancing single-thread performance yields diminishing returns as these innovations/techniques hit the *power wall* and the *ILP wall* [358]. Consequently, major segments of the computer industry conclude that future performance improvements must largely come from increasing the number of on-chip processor cores.

The transformation in the computer industry from single-core to multicore and subsequently manycore necessitates efficient exploitation of thread-level parallelism (TLP) for attaining high performance. The terms *manycore* and *massively multicore* are sometimes used to refer to multicore architectures with an especially high number of cores (tens or hundreds) [359, 360]. Manycore technologies aim to exploit concurrency, high computational density (CD), workload distribution, or a combination of these methods to attain high performance. The term *high performance* refers to attaining superior performance quantified in terms of mega operations per second (MOPS) or mega floating-point operations per second (MFLOPS)

*A portion of this chapter is copyrighted by Springer. The definitive version appeared in: Arslan Munir, Farinaz Koushanfar, Ann Gordon-Ross, and Sanjay Ranka, High-Performance Optimizations on Tiled Many-Core Embedded Systems: A Matrix Multiplication Case Study, *(Springer) The Journal of Supercomputing*, vol. 66, no. 1, pp. 431–487, October 2013. URL http://link.springer.com/article/10.1007%2Fs11227-013-0916-9. ©[2013] Springer. Reprinted with permission from Springer as we are the authors of this work.

from an architecture. A *tiled manycore architecture* (TMA) is an emerging trend in manycore architecture in which processor cores (known as *tiles* in a TMA) are arranged in a regular, grid-like manner and a network-on-chip (NoC) connects these tiles with each other and with input/output (I/O) devices. The increasing number of tiles in TMAs shifts the design focus from computation oriented to communication oriented, which makes a scalable NoC design imperative for TMAs.

TMAs are suitable for supercomputing and cloud computing [361] as well as embedded computing applications. Embedded system design is traditionally power-centric, but there has been a recent shift toward high-performance embedded computing because of the proliferation of compute-intensive embedded applications (e.g., networking, security, image processing). TMAs with massive computing resources on-chip and energy-saving features can be suitable for these high-performance embedded applications. Many TMAs (e.g., Tilera's TMAs [362]) offer low-power design features that allow idle tiles to be either clock gated (to save dynamic power) or power gated (to save static as well as dynamic power).

Although TMAs offer tremendous computational power, extracting this computational power is non-trivial because of two main challenges: (1) on-chip data communication becomes more expensive as the number of on-chip processing cores/tiles increases and (2) insufficient off-chip memory bandwidth limits the sustainable computational power. Overcoming these challenges requires manycore programmers to possess thorough knowledge of the underlying architecture. Without knowledge of the underlying TMAs' architectural features, programmers may experience performance degradation when migrating single-core software designs to TMAs [363]. John Hennessy, President of Stanford University, quotes on the challenge involved in attaining high performance from parallel computers [357]:

> " ... when we start talking about parallelism and ease of use of truly parallel computers, we're talking about a problem that's as hard as any that computer science has faced. ... I would be panicked if I were in industry."

The programming challenge in emerging TMAs is to exploit massive intrachip parallelism to obtain sustainable high performance. Many of these TMAs only support proprietary languages to exploit this intrachip parallelism, which increases the programming effort and the time required to parallelize applications, which includes the learning curve of proprietary languages. Support for widely accepted high-level programming models, such as Open Multi-Processing (OpenMP), would be beneficial for fast prototyping of applications on these TMAs. However, programming ease with high-level programming models comes at the expense of limited scalability for systems with a large number of processing elements. For example, language constructs in OpenMP can account for up to 12% of the total execution time, and developers are often advised to reduce the number of parallel regions to limit the impact of these overheads [364]. Nevertheless, quantifying the impact of existing and novel performance optimizations on TMAs would be beneficial for parallel programmers, aiming to attain sustainable high performance from TMAs.

Attaining high performance from TMAs is typically an *iterative process*. Even a good design requires running the application, measuring the application's performance, identifying bottlenecks and determining opportunities for improvement, modifying the application to achieve higher performance, and then re-measuring the application's performance. Obtaining high performance from TMAs requires determining how and where the execution time is being spent. Many times the bottleneck for attaining high performance is external memory latency or I/O throughput. Code optimizations and design decisions reflected in algorithmic-level changes can improve the performance by reducing external memory accesses. In cases where algorithmic-level changes and code optimizations fail to reduce the number of external memory accesses for an application, the attainable performance will be bounded by external memory bandwidth.

Previous works [365–368] discuss multicore architectures and performance of parallel applications; however, there has been limited discussion on high-performance optimization techniques that are applicable to TMAs. In this work, we focus on identifying key architecture and software optimizations to attain high performance from TMAs using Tilera's TILEPro64 and a dense matrix multiplication (MM) case study. Tilera's TMAs, to the best of our knowledge, are the first commercial TMA offering. Although dense MM algorithms have been studied extensively, optimizations on TMAs have not yet been explored in detail. We discuss performance optimizations on a single tile as well as platform considerations for parallel performance optimizations, such as cache locality, tile locality, translation look-aside buffer (TLB) locality, and memory balancing. Our main contributions are as follows:

- A discussion of the architectural features of contemporary TMAs.
- Identification and discussion of key architecture and software optimization techniques that are applicable to TMAs.
- Elaboration and experimental demonstration of various compiler optimization techniques for TMAs, including inlining, loop unrolling, software pipelining, and feedback-based optimizations.
- Experimental demonstration of performance and performance per watt advantages of algorithmic optimizations that exploit cache blocking, parallelization, and horizontal communication on Tilera's TILEPro64 with dense MM as a case study.
- Quantification of the peak attainable performance from Tilera's TILEPro64.

Although dense MM algorithms have been studied extensively, optimizations on TMAs have not yet been explored in detail. Our work contributions advance the state of the art since TMAs are a potential architectural choice for future manycore embedded systems. Considering the TILEPro64's suitability to networking, security, video processing, and wireless network domains [343, 359, 369], this study provides insights for signal processing, security, and networking experts that aim to leverage the TILEPro64 for applications acceleration in their respective domains.

We point out that many of the optimizations discussed in this chapter are also applicable to traditional central processing units (CPUs); however, our work investigates these optimizations on TMAs and quantifies the impact of these optimizations on TMAs. The authors believe that it is imperative to investigate traditional optimization techniques on emerging manycore architectures to make programmers aware of the impact of existing optimization techniques on these manycore architectures. Programming experience with TMAs reveals that the compiler for these emerging TMAs (e.g., TILEPro64) supports sophisticated feedback-based optimizations that are not commonly available for traditional multicore architectures. Results highlight the effectiveness of algorithmic choices, cache blocking, compiler optimizations, and horizontal communication in attaining high performance from TMAs.

The remainder of this chapter is organized as follows. A review of related work is given in Section 12.1. Section 12.2 gives an overview of architectural features of contemporary TMAs. Section 12.3 defines parallel computing metrics for TMAs and outlines the dense MM algorithms considered in our case study. Section 12.4 provides code snippets of our matrix multiplication algorithms for Tilera's TILEPro64. Performance optimizations for TMAs including platform optimizations and compiler-based optimizations are discussed in Section 12.5. Section 12.6 presents the performance optimization results for our MM case study on Tilera's TMAs, with a focus on the TILEPro64. Section 12.7 summarizes conclusions and insights obtained from this study.

12.1   Related Work

Previous work investigated performance analysis and optimization on multicore architectures. This section summarizes previous work related to performance analysis on multicore architectures, parallelized MM algorithms, cache blocking, and TMAs.

12.1.1   Performance Analysis and Optimization

In the area of performance analysis on parallel architectures, Brown and Sharapov [334] compared the performance and programmability of the Born calculation (a model used to study the interactions between a protein and surrounding water molecules) using both OpenMP and message passing interface (MPI). The authors observed that the OpenMP version's programmability and performance outperformed the MPI version; however, the scalability of the MPI version was superior to the OpenMP version. Sun and Zhu [335] investigated performance metrics, such as speedup, efficiency, and scalability, for shared memory systems. The authors identified the causes of superlinear speedups, such as cache size, parallel processing overhead reduction, and randomized algorithms for shared memory systems.

Some previous work explored performance optimizations. Cortesi [370] studied performance tuning of programs running on the Silicon Graphics' SN0 systems, including the Origin2000, Onyx2, and Origin200 multiprocessor systems. The author described the architectural features and memory management of SN0 systems that impacted performance. The author further discussed cache optimizations including array padding to avoid cache thrashing, loop fusion, and cache blocking. Although the work captured performance tuning for Silicon Graphics' multiprocessors, our work applies the performance optimization techniques to emerging TMAs.

12.1.2   Parallelized MM Algorithms

Krishnan and Nieplocha [371] described a new parallel algorithm for dense MM that had an efficiency equal to Cannon's algorithm for clusters and shared memory systems. The experimental results on clusters (IBM SP, Linux-Myrinet) and shared memory systems (SGI Altix, Cray X1) demonstrated the high performance of the proposed MM algorithm. The paper, however, did not compare the performance of the proposed algorithm with Cannon's algorithm. Our work implements both a blocked (B) MM algorithm and Cannon's algorithm to provide an insight into the attainable performance of the two algorithms on TMAs.

Lee et al. [372] generalized Cannon's algorithm for the case when the input matrices were block-cyclic distributed (blocks separated by a fixed stride in the column and row directions were assigned to the same processor) across a two-dimensional (2D) processor array with an arbitrary number of processors and toroidal mesh interconnections. Performance analysis revealed that the generalized Cannon's algorithm generated fewer page faults than the previously proposed algorithm Scalable Universal Matrix Multiplication Algorithm (SUMMA) [373] that utilized broadcast communication primitives for the MM algorithm. Experimental results on an Intel Paragon showed that the generalized Cannon's algorithm performed better than SUMMA when the blocks were larger than 65×65; however, the generalized Cannon's algorithm exhibited worse performance than SUMMA for smaller block sizes. Results indicated that SUMMA maintained the same performance for all block sizes.

Much research focuses on evaluating parallel performance optimizations using MM as a case study. Li et al. [374] optimized MM for NVIDIA's Tesla C1060 graphics processing unit (GPU) and were able to attain 60% of the GPU's theoretical peak performance (calculated from datasheets). To understand the impact of parallel algorithms on performance, More [375] implemented several versions of MM including simple, blocked, transposed, and Basic Linear Algebra Subroutine (BLAS) on an Intel Core Duo T2400 running at 1.83 GHz. Results revealed that carefully optimized MM implementations outperformed straightforward unoptimized implementations by orders of magnitude.

Higham [376] described FORTRAN-based level 3 BLAS (BLAS3) algorithms that were asymptotically faster than conventional versions. The author focused on Strassen's method for fast MM, which is practically useful for matrix dimensions greater than 100. Goto and Geijn [377] described the basic principles of a high-performance MM implementation that were used in the GotoBLAS library. The authors observed that the GotoBLAS MM attained near peak performance for various symmetric multiprocessor (SMP) architectures, such as Intel's Pentium 4, Intel's Itanium 2, and AMD's Opteron. We point out that BLAS algorithms are not available for existing TMAs, such as Tilera's TILE64/TILEPro64, nor do the existing TMAs' compilers support FORTRAN code fragments. Therefore, optimizations on TMAs can only be attained by parallelized algorithms tailored for TMAs, platform considerations, and compiler-based optimizations, which is the focus of this work.

12.1.3 Cache Blocking

Optimizations using cache blocking have been studied in the literature. Nishtala et al. [378] studied performance models of cache blocking for sparse matrix-vector multiply. The authors analyzed and verified the performance models on three processor architectures (Itenium 2, Pentium 3, and Power 4) and observed that while the performance models predicted performance and appropriate block sizes for some processors, none of the performance models were able to accurately predict performance and block sizes for all of the processor architectures. Our work takes an experimental approach to determine the best block size for cache blocking on TMAs.

Lam et al. [379] analyzed the performance of blocked code on machines with caches considering MM as a case study. By combining theory and experimentation, the work showed that blocking is effective generally for enhancing performance by reducing the memory access latency for caches; however, the magnitude of the performance benefit is highly sensitive to the problem size. The work focused only on blocking for single-core processor (DECstation 3100); however, our work analyzes blocking on multiple cores along with various compiler optimizations to attain high performance.

12.1.4   Tiled Manycore Architectures

TMAs have been studied in previous work. Wu et al. [367] described a tiled multicore stream architecture (TiSA) that consisted of multiple stream cores and an on-chip network to support stream transfers between tiles. In the stream programming model, which originated from the vector parallel model, an application is composed of a collection of data streams passing through a series of computation kernels running on stream cores. Stream cores were the basic computation units in TiSA, where the stream cores implemented stream processor architecture [380]. Each stream core had its own instruction controller, register file, and fully pipelined arithmetic and logic units (ALUs) that could perform one multiply–add operation per cycle. The authors implemented several benchmarks, such as MM, 3D-FFT, and StreamMD, on TiSA and were able to attain 358.9 GFLOPS for the MM benchmark. The paper, however, did not discuss high-performance optimizations for TiSA. Musoll [366] studied performance, power, and thermal behavior of TMAs executing flow-based packet workloads and proposed a load-balancing policy of assigning packets to tiles that minimized the communication latency. The emphasis of the work was, however, on load balancing and communication and not on performance optimization.

Vangal et al. [365] described the NoC architecture and Mattson et al. [368] described the instruction set, the programming environment, and their programming experience for Intel's TeraFLOPS research chip. The authors [365, 368] mapped several kernels, such as stencil, dense MM, spreadsheet, and 2D fast Fourier transform (FFT), to the TeraFLOPS chip. The authors were able to attain 1.0 TeraFLOPS (TFLOPS) (73.3% of theoretical peak attainable performance) for stencil, 0.51 TFLOPS (37.5% of theoretical peak attainable performance) for dense MM, 0.45 TFLOPS (33.2% of theoretical peak attainable performance) for spreadsheet, and 0.02 TFLOPS (2.73% of theoretical peak attainable performance) for 2D FFT. Results indicated that the experimentally attainable performance on the research chip was far less than the theoretical peak attainable performance. These previous works, however, provided little discussion for attaining high performance from the chip.

Zhu et al. [381] investigated the performance of OpenMP language constructs on IBM's Cyclops-64 (C64) manycore architecture based on microbenchmarks. The authors observed that the overhead of OpenMP on the C64 was less than conventional SMPs. Our work differs from Zhu et al.'s work in that we investigate high performance on the TILEPro64 manycore architecture using Tilera's ilib application programming interface (API), which is designed to attain high performance on Tilera's architectures since the TILEPro64 does not support OpenMP.

Cuvillo et al. [364] mapped the OpenMP parallel programming model to IBM's C64 architecture. To realize this mapping, the authors exploited optimizations, such as the memory aware runtime library that placed frequently used data structures in scratchpad (SP) memory and a barrier for collective synchronization that used C64 hardware support. The work, however, did not discuss techniques to obtain high performance from the C64. Garcia et al. [382] optimized MM for the C64 focusing on three optimizations: (1) balancing work distribution across threads; (2) minimal memory transfer and efficient register usage; and (3) architecture-specific optimizations, such as using special assembly functions for load and store operations. Their optimized MM implementation attained 55% of the C64's theoretical peak performance. Our work differs from [382] in that we discuss additional optimizations, such as algorithmic optimizations, cache blocking, horizontal communication, and compiler-based optimizations.

Yuan et al. [358] investigated key architectural mechanisms and software optimizations to attain high performance for a dense MM on the Godson-T manycore prototype processor. The authors focused on optimizing on-chip communication and memory accesses. Results on a cycle-accurate simulator revealed that the optimized MM could attain 97% (124.3 GFLOPS) of the Godson-T's theoretical peak performance due in part to the use of a BLAS-based MM sequential kernel. Although a BLAS-based kernel, in most cases, attains the best attainable performance, the absence of BLAS-based routines for existing TMAs required us to use other optimizations in our work. The development of BLAS routines for Tilera's TMAs can be an interesting avenue for future research. Furthermore, since the BLAS-based routines are applicable only to some linear algebra applications, study of other high-performance techniques is important for parallel programmers to attain high performance for algebraic as well as non-algebraic applications, which is the focus of our work.

Safari et al. [383] implemented a class of dense stereo vision algorithms on the TILEPro64 and were able to attain a performance of 30.45 frames/s for video graphics array (VGA) (640×480) images. The work demonstrated that emerging TMAs can achieve good performance in low-level image processing computations. Our work is complementary to that work and focuses on high-performance optimization techniques for TMAs.

In our prior work, we cross-evaluated two multicore architectural paradigms: SMPs and TMAs [384]. We based our evaluations on a parallelized information fusion application, Gaussian elimination, and an embarrassingly parallel benchmark. We compared and analyzed the performance of an Intel-based SMP and Tilera's TILEPro64 TMA. Results revealed that Tilera's TMAs were more suitable for applications with more TLP and little communication between the parallelized tasks (e.g., information fusion), whereas SMPs were more suitable for applications with floating-point (FP) computations and a large amount of communication between processor cores due to better exploitation of shared memory in SMPs than TMAs. Insights obtained for SMPs, however, were limited to eight processor cores, and the scalability of SMPs beyond eight processor cores was not investigated because of inexistence of an SMP platform with more than eight processor cores at the time of experimentation. Our current work differs from our previous work in that our current work does not cross-evaluate architectures, but rather focuses on attaining high performance from TMAs.

12.2 Tiled Manycore Architecture (TMA) Overview

A TMA is an emerging trend in manycore architecture that aims at exploiting massive on-chip resources furnished by recent advances in CMOS technology. TMAs combine each processor core with a switch/router to create a modular element called a *tile*, which can be replicated to create a manycore architecture with any number of tiles. The tiles are connected to an on-chip network, and the switch (router) in each tile interconnects with the neighboring tiles. Each tile may consist of one or more computing cores and a router, which includes logic responsible for routing and forwarding the packets based on the routing policy. Examples of TMAs include the Raw processor, Intel's TeraFLOPS research chip, IBM's C64, and Tilera's TILE64, TILE*Pro*64, and TILE-Gx processor family [239, 342, 343]. This section discusses three TMAs: Intel's TeraFLOPS research chip, IBM's C64, Tilera's TILEPro64, and Tilera's TILE64.

12.2.1   Intel's TeraFLOPS Research Chip

Intel's TeraFLOPS research chip contains 80 tiles arranged as an 8×10 2D mesh network that is designed to operate at a maximum frequency of 5.7 GHz. The 80-tile NoC architecture is implemented in 65 nm process technology and integrates a total of 100 million transistors on a $275 \, mm^2$ die. The tiled design approach permits designers to use smaller cores that can easily be replicated across the chip. A single-core chip of this size ($\approx$100 million transistors) would require twice as many designers and roughly twice the design time [385]. The TeraFLOPS research chip uses a 2D mesh because of the large number of tiles and requirements of high bisection bandwidth and low average latency between tiles. The 2D on-chip mesh network provides a bisection bandwidth in excess of 320 GB/s. Intel's TeraFLOPS leverages low-power mesochronous clock distribution that facilitates scalability, high integration, and single-chip realization of the TeraFLOPS processor.

Figure 12.1 shows one tile of Intel's TeraFLOPS research chip. Each tile consists of a processing engine (PE) connected to a 5-port router. The router in each tile connects to its four

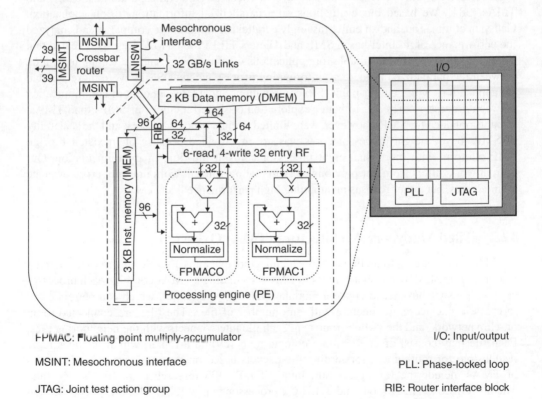

FPMAC: Floating point multiply-accumulator   I/O: Input/output

MSINT: Mesochronous interface   PLL: Phase-locked loop

JTAG: Joint test action group   RIB: Router interface block

Figure 12.1   Intel's TeraFLOPS research chip (adapted from [365])

neighbors and the local PE via point-to-point links that can deliver data at 20 GB/s. These links support mesochronous interfaces (MSINT) that can provide phase-tolerant communication across tiles and lightweight global clock distribution at the expense of synchronization latency [386]. The router forwards packets between the tiles and can support 16 GB/s over each port. The PE contains two independent nine-stage pipelined single-precision floating-point multiply-accumulator (FPMAC) units, 3-KB single cycle instruction memory, and 2-KB data memory. The PE operates on a 96-bit very long instruction word (VLIW) that can encode up to 8 operations/cycle. The 3 KB instruction memory can hold 256 96-bit VLIW instructions, and the 2 KB data memory can hold 512 single-precision FP numbers. The PE contains a 10-port (6 read and 4 write) register file that enables the PE to allow scheduling to both FPMACs, simultaneous loads and stores from the data memory, packet send/receive from the mesh network, program control, and dynamic sleep instructions. The packet encapsulation between the router and the PE is handled by a router interface block (RIB). The fully symmetric architecture of Intel's TeraFLOPS research chip permits any tile's PE to send (receive) instruction and data packets to (from) any other tile.

The programming model for Intel's TeraFLOPS research chip is based on *message passing*. Each tile runs its own program and the tiles exchange messages to share data and to coordinate execution between the tiles. The message passing model is anonymously one-sided wherein any tile can write into the instruction or data memory of any other tile including itself. The TeraFLOPS chip can handle both single program multiple data (SPMD) and multiple program multiple data (MPMD) applications.

Since Intel's TeraFLOPS is a research chip, the TeraFLOPS chip has a very modest software environment with no compiler or operating system [368]. The programs for the TeraFLOPS chip are assembly coded and hand optimized. The program instructions are laid out in the instruction memory, and the program is then launched simultaneously on all the tiles and progresses through the set of instructions in the program. The chip supports self-modifying code by sending new instructions as messages. The chip only supports single loop level with a single fixed stride (offset) across the memory. Nested loops require unrolling of the inner loops by hand. Hence, nested loops should be minimized or eliminated where possible. This modest software environment precludes the chip from full-scale application programming but is suitable for application kernels research.

The Intel's TeraFLOPS research chip implements fine-grained power management techniques to deliver power-efficient performance. The chip implements fine-grained clock gating and sleep transistor circuits to reduce active and standby leakage power, which can be controlled at chip, tile-slice/block, and individual tile levels depending on the workload. Approximately 90% of the FP units and 74% of each PE is sleep enabled [386]. The instruction set provides WAKE/NAP instructions that expose power management to the programmer, enabling the programmer to turn on/off the FP units depending on the application's requirements. The chip allows any tile to issue sleep packets to any other tile or wake up any other tile depending on the processing task demands.

Table 12.1 summarizes Intel's TeraFLOPS research chip's available voltage and frequency settings for adjusting the performance and power. Operation at higher voltage and frequency can result in performance improvements but at a significant associated power consumption cost. For example, increasing (voltage, frequency) from (0.95 V, 3.16 GHz) to (1.35 V, 5.7 GHz) increases the performance by 79% with an associated power consumption increase by 327%.

Table 12.1   Theoretical peak performance and power consumption of Intel's TeraFLOPS research chip [368, 385]

Frequency (GHz)	Voltage (V)	Performance (TFLOPS)	Power (W)
3.16	0.95	1.01	62
4.27	1.07	1.37	97
5.1	1.2	1.63	175
5.7	1.35	1.81	265

12.2.2   IBM's Cyclops-64 (C64)

IBM's C64 is a petaFLOPS supercomputer that is intended to serve as a dedicate compute engine for high-performance applications, such as molecular dynamics, to study protein folding or image processing for real-time medical procedures [364]. A C64 chip is attached to a host system over several Gigabit Ethernet links. The host system facilitates application software developers and end users of the chip by providing a familiar computing environment.

Figure 12.2 depicts IBM's C64 chip, which consists of 80 processors, each with two thread units (TUs), one 64-bit FP unit, and two static random-access memory (SRAM) banks of 32 KB each. Each TU is a 64-bit, single-issue, in-order, reduced instruction set computing

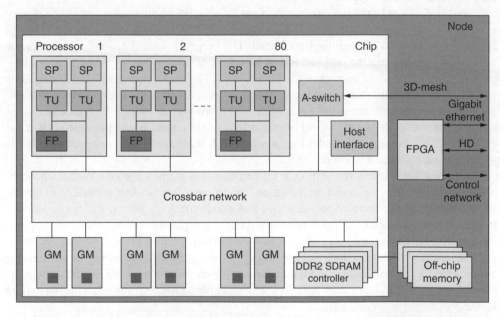

DDR2 SDRAM. Double data rate ? synchronous dynamic random-access memory
FPGA: Field-programmable gate array
SP: Scratchpad memory

GM: Global memory
TU: Thread unit
FP: Floating point unit

Figure 12.2   IBM Cyclops-64 chip (adapted from [364])

(RISC) processor that operates at a clock frequency of 500 MHz. The FP unit can issue one double precision FP multiply and add instruction per cycle for a total peak theoretical performance of 80 GFLOPS per chip when running at 500 MHz. A portion of each SRAM bank can be configured as scratchpad (SP) memory. The remaining portions of SRAM together form a global memory (GM) that is uniformly accessibly from all TUs. The C64 chip provides 32-KB instruction caches (not shown in Fig. 12.2) where each instruction cache is shared by five processors. The C64 chip has no data caches. The C64 on-chip resources (e.g., TUs, on-chip memory banks) are connected to a 96-port crossbar network, which provides a bandwidth of 4 GB/s per port and a total bandwidth of 384 GB/s in each direction. The C64 chip provides an interface to the off-chip double data rate 2 (DDR2) synchronous dynamic random-access memory (SDRAM) and bidirectional interchip routing ports.

A C64 chip has an explicit three-level memory hierarchy: SP memory, on-chip memory (SRAM), and off-chip memory (DRAM). The memory hierarchy is software-managed such that the programmer can control the data movement between different levels of memory hierarchy. Having a software-managed memory hierarchy without caches saves the die area that would be required for hardware cache controllers and over-sized caches. The software-managed memory hierarchy provides the potential to improve not only performance but also energy efficiency at the cost of relatively complex programming as compared to architectures with hardware-controlled caches.

The C64 instruction set architecture provides efficient support for thread-level execution, hardware barriers, and atomic in-memory operations. The C64 architecture provides no resource virtualization mechanisms [364] (i.e., execution is non-preemptive and there is no hardware virtual memory manager). Only one single application can be run on the C64 chip at a time and the C64 microkernel will not interrupt the application execution unless an exception occurs. Lack of a virtual memory manager allows the three-level memory hierarchy of the C64 chip to be visible to the programmer.

The C64 architecture is a general-purpose manycore architecture and energy efficiency was not a key design consideration [382]; therefore, there are no special features for energy savings. For example, the architecture does not allow processors to be turned off when unused nor can the clock rate to a set of processors or the whole chip be reduced.

12.2.3 Tilera's TILEPro64

Figure 12.3 depicts Tilera's TILEPro64 architecture. The TILEPro64 processor features an 8 × 8 grid of 64 tiles (cores) implemented in 90-nm process technology. The tiles are connected via multiple 2D mesh networks, designated as the iMesh interconnect by Tilera. The TILEPro64 integrates external memory and I/O interfaces on-chip that are connected to the tiles via the iMesh interconnect. Each tile shares an external off-chip global memory (also referred to as external memory henceforth), which consists of DRAM supported by four DDR2 memory controllers. Since Tilera's TMAs do not fall under the SMP architectural paradigm, a tile's access latency to external memory can be variable depending on the distance between the tile and external memory. Each tile can independently run a complete operating system or multiple tiles can be grouped together to run a multiprocessing operating system, such as SMP Linux [344]. Each tile contains a processor engine, a cache engine, and a switch engine [352].

The *processor engine* consists of a three-way VLIW pipelined processor with three instructions per bundle. Each tile has a program counter and is capable of issuing up to three

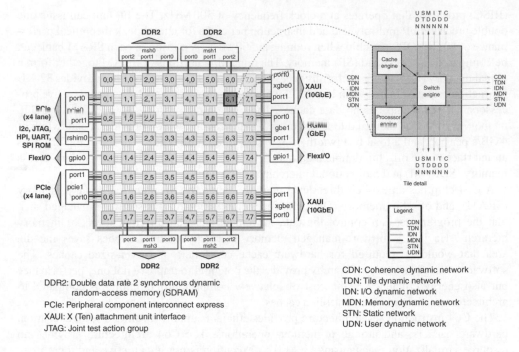

DDR2: Double data rate 2 synchronous dynamic
    random-access memory (SDRAM)
PCIe: Peripheral component interconnect express
XAUI: X (Ten) attachment unit interface
JTAG: Joint test action group

CDN: Coherence dynamic network
TDN: Tile dynamic network
IDN: I/O dynamic network
MDN: Memory dynamic network
STN: Static network
UDN: User dynamic network

Figure 12.3 Tilera's TILEPro64 processor (adapted from [352])

instructions per cycle. Compile-time scheduling of VLIW operations results in lower power consumption as compared to dynamically scheduled superscalar processors. The TILEPro64 includes special instructions to support commonly used operations in digital signal processing (DSP), encryption, network packet processing, and video processing, such as sum of absolute differences, hashing, and checksums.

The processor engine's VLIW architecture defines a 64-bit instruction bundle, which can specify either two or three instructions. The two-instruction $(X1, X0)$ bundle encoding is known as *X-mode* and the three-instruction bundle encoding $(Y2, Y1, Y0)$ is known as *Y-mode* where $X0 \in$ {arithmetic, compare, logical instructions, bit/byte instructions, multiply instructions} and $X1 \in$ {arithmetic, compare, logical instructions, control transfer instructions, memory management instructions}; $Y0 = X0, Y1 \in$ {arithmetic, compare, logical instructions}, and $Y2 \in$ {memory instructions}. The individual instructions are typical RISC instructions.

The three-way VLIW processor engine in each tile contain three computing pipelines: P0, P1, and P2. P0 executes all arithmetic and logical operations, bit and byte manipulation, and all multiply and fused multiply (multiply–add) instructions. P1 can execute all arithmetic and logical operations, control flow instructions, and special-purpose register reads and writes. P2 executes all memory operations including loads, stores, and test and set instructions. Both the X- and Y-modes can issue instructions in any of three pipelines (P0, P1, and P2). The Y-mode instruction issue uses all of the three pipelines simultaneously, whereas one of the pipelines remains in idle mode during X-mode instruction issue.

The *cache engine* contains the TLBs, caches, and a direct memory access (DMA) engine. Each tile has a 16 KB level one cache (8 KB instruction cache and 8 KB data cache) and a

64 KB level two cache, resulting in a total of 5.5 MB of on-chip cache with Tilera's *dynamic distributed cache (DDC)* technology. DDC provides a hardware-managed, cache-coherent approach to shared memory. DDC enables a tile to holistically view all of the tiles' on-chip caches as one large shared DDC. DDC increases on-chip cache access and reduces the off-chip memory bottleneck. Each tile also contains a 2D DMA engine that can be configured by the application programmer to move data between the tiles and between the level two cache and the main memory. Tilera's ilib API provides various functions that enable application programmers to perform background DMA operations. The DMA engine operates autonomously from the processor engine and issues DMA load and store operations during cycles in which the cache pipeline is not being used by the processor engine.

The cache subsystem is non-blocking and supports multiple concurrent outstanding memory operations. The cache subsystem supports *hit under miss* and *miss under miss*, and permits the loads and stores to different addresses to be reordered to achieve high bandwidth and to over-lap miss latencies, while ensuring that true memory dependencies are enforced. The processor engine does not stall on load or store cache misses and execution of subsequent instructions continues until the data requested by the cache miss is actually needed by another instruction.

The *switch engine* consists of six independent networks: one static network (STN) and five dynamic networks. The five dynamic networks are as follows: the I/O dynamic network (IDN), memory dynamic network (MDN), coherence dynamic network (CDN), tile dynamic network (TDN), and user dynamic network (UDN). The STN and the five dynamic networks constitute Tilera's iMesh interconnect and due to the mesh layout, each of the six networks intersects in every tile. The STN transfers scalar data between tiles with very low latency. The dynamic networks facilitate the switch engine by routing packet based data between tiles, tile caches, external memory, and I/O controllers. The dynamic networks leverage dimension-order routing—the x-direction first, and then the y-direction—until the packets reach the destination tile's switch engine. To reduce latency, packet routing is pipelined so that portions of the packet can be sent over a network link even before the remainder of the packet arrives at a switch. The IDN is used for data transfers between tiles and I/O devices and between I/O devices and memory. The MDN transfers data resulting from loads, stores, prefetches, cache misses, or DMAs between tiles and between tiles and external memory. The MDN has a direct hardware connection to the cache engine. The CDN carries cache coherence invalidation messages. The TDN supports data transfers between tiles and has a direct hardware connection to the cache engine.

Of the five dynamic networks, only the UDN is visible to the user, and therefore we elaborate on the UDN's functionalities. User-level APIs, such as ilib, are built on the UDN, which abstract the details of the underlying packetization, routing, transport, buffering, flow control, and deadlock avoidance in the network. The UDN supports low-latency communication using a packet-switched mesh network and can be used by applications to send messages between tiles. The UDN enables fine-grained stream programming and supports efficient streaming through a register-level first input first output (FIFO) interface and hardware-supported steering of distinct streams into separate FIFOs. The UDN-based stream data transfers have high bandwidth and have an overhead of only a few cycles.

The tile architecture provides a cache-coherent view of data memory to applications (i.e., a read by a thread or process at address A will return the value of the most recent write to address A). The hardware does not maintain coherence for the instruction memory but provides hardware cache coherence for I/O accesses.

Tilera's TILEPro64 supports 32-bit virtual memory addressing and can swap pages between the DRAM and the hard disk [361, 362]. The memory is byte addressable and can be accessed in units of 1, 2, and 4 B. Portions of the physical address space can be declared private or shared at the page granularity. Memory allocation requests by a tile (e.g., by using `malloc()`) allocate private memory to the tiles by default. When referencing private memory, a given virtual address on different tiles will reference different memory locations. Hence, the use of private memory enables efficient SIMD processing (i.e., the same code can be run on different tiles with each tile working on different data). The private memory is automatically cached in the on-chip caches when referenced by a tile. Shared memory allows multiple tiles to share instructions and data conveniently. A shared memory address on different tiles refers to the same global memory location.

Tiles in Tilera's TMAs can allocate shared memory using Tilera's multicore components (TMC) `cmem` API. Tilera's processor architecture provides flexibility of structuring shared memory as either distributed coherent cached or uncached shared memory. The uncached shared memory is allocated in uncached global shared memory, which can be accessed by an application using DMA. DMA operations copy uncached memory into the tiles' local caches. Using DMAs to create local private copies of data from uncached memory is suitable for coarse-grained data sharing where a process/tile wants to operate exclusively for some duration on a chunk of shared data before relinquishing control of that data to other processes/tiles. Tilera's processor architecture provides sequential consistency within a single thread of execution and relaxed memory consistency for the memory shared among multiple tiles. The architecture provides a memory fence instruction to force ordering when needed, as depicted in our parallel MM code scripts in Section 12.4.3 and Section 12.4.4.

Tilera's runtime software stack enables executing applications on the tile processor [387]. The runtime software stack includes an application layer, a supervisor layer, and a hypervisor layer. The *application layer* runs standard libraries, such as the C runtime library and Tilera's TMC library. The *supervisor layer*, which is composed of the Linux kernel, provides system calls for user-space applications and libraries. The supervisor layer also enables multiprocess applications and multithreaded processes to exploit multiple tiles for enhanced performance. The *hypervisor layer* abstracts the hardware details of Tilera's processors from the supervisor and manages communication between the tiles and between the tiles and the I/O controllers. Each tile runs a separate instance of the hypervisor.

Tilera's TMAs support energy-saving features. The tile processor implements clock gating for power-efficient operation. The architecture includes a software-usable `NAP` instruction that can put the tile in a low-power `IDLE` mode until a user-selectable external event, such an interrupt or packet arrival.

12.2.4   Tilera's TILE64

The architecture for Tilera's TILE64 is similar to the architecture for Tilera's TILEPro64 (Section 12.2.3) with a few differences. In this section, we highlight only the differences between the TILE64 and TILEPro64. Regarding interconnection network, the TILE64 has one STN and four dynamic networks (the CDN is not present in the TILE64) as compared to the TILEPro64's five dynamic networks. The addition of the CDN in the TILEPro64 increases the available network bandwidth. The TILEPro64 provides memory bandwidth that exceeds 205 Gbps as compared to 200 Gbps for the TILE64. The bisection bandwidth provided by the

TILEPro64 is 2660 Gbps as compared to 2217 Gbps for the TILE64. The TILEPro64 also implements additional instructions that are not present in the TILE64, which accelerate DSP applications that require saturating arithmetic and unaligned memory accesses [352, 353].

12.3 Parallel Computing Metrics and Matrix Multiplication (MM) Case Study

Parallel computing metrics quantify the performance and performance per watt of parallel architectures, such as TMAs, and enable architectural comparisons. The most appropriate metrics for a parallel architecture depends on the targeted application domain. For example, runtime performance is an appropriate metric for comparing high-performance systems, whereas performance per watt is a more appropriate metric for embedded systems that have a limited power budget. In this section, we characterize the parallel computing metrics for TMAs and briefly outline the dense MM algorithms that we consider for our case study.

12.3.1 Parallel Computing Metrics for TMAs

We discuss the following parallel computing metrics: runtime, speedup, efficiency, computational density, power, and performance per watt[1].

Runtime: The *serial runtime* T_s of a program is the time elapsed between the beginning and end of the program on a sequential computer. The *parallel runtime* T_p is the time elapsed from the beginning of a program to the moment the last processor finishes execution.

Speedup: Speedup measures the performance gain achieved by parallelizing a given application/algorithm over the best sequential implementation of that application/algorithm. Speedup S is defined as T_s/T_p, which is the ratio of the serial runtime T_s of the best sequential algorithm for solving a problem to the time taken by the parallel algorithm T_p to solve the same problem on p processors. The speedup is ideal when the speedup is proportional to the number of processors used to solve the problem in parallel (i.e., $S = p$).

Efficiency: Efficiency measures the fraction of the time that a processor is usefully employed. Efficiency E is defined as S/p, which is the ratio of the speedup S to the number of processors p. An efficiency of one corresponds to the ideal speedup and implies good scalability.

Computational Density/Peak Theoretical Performance: The computational density (CD) metric measures the peak theoretical performance of a parallel architecture. The CD for a TMA with p tiles can be given as

$$CD = p \times f \times \sum_i \frac{N_i}{CPI_i} \tag{12.1}$$

where f denotes the operating frequency, N_i denotes the number of instructions of type i requiring integer or FP computations that can be issued simultaneously, and CPI_i denotes the average number of cycles per instruction of type i. CD can be useful in estimating the peak theoretical performance of an architecture. For example, the CD for Tilera's TILEPro64 with each tile containing a 32-bit, 3-way issue VLIW processor and operating at 866 MHz can

---

[1] Portion of this section is reproduced here from Chapter 11 of this book for completeness.

be computed as: $CD^{TILEPro64} = 64 \times 866 \times 3$ MOPS $= 166,272$ MOPS $= 166.272$ GOPS. We point out that this is merely peak theoretical performance that cannot be attained for most real-world applications.

Power: Power consumption of a tile in a TMA is composed of a dynamic component and a static component. The dynamic power consumption depends on the supply voltage, clock frequency, capacitance, and the signal activity. The static power consumption mainly depends on the supply voltage, temperature, and capacitance [366]. The power consumption P of tile (both static and dynamic) can be divided into three components: the core's power P_{core}, the router's power P_{router}, and the interconnect power P_{net}:

$$P = P_{core} + P_{router} + P_{net} \tag{12.2}$$

The core's power is the power consumption in the tile's processor core. The router power is the power consumption in the tile's router, and the interconnect power is the power dissipated in the interconnection network due to traversal of messages/packets caused by the requests originating from that tile.

We propose a system-level power model to estimate the power consumption of TMAs that can be used in estimating the performance per watt. Our power model considers both the active and idle modes' power consumptions. Given a TMA with a total of N tiles, the power consumption of the TMA with p active tiles can be given as

$$P^p = p \cdot \frac{P_{max}^{active}}{N} + (N - p) \cdot \frac{P_{max}^{idle}}{N} \tag{12.3}$$

where P_{max}^{active} and P_{max}^{idle} denote the maximum active and idle modes' power consumptions, respectively. P_{max}^{active}/N and P_{max}^{idle}/N give the active and idle modes' power, respectively, per tile and associated switching and interconnection network circuitry (and can be determined by Eq. (12.2)). Our power model incorporates the power-saving features of state-of-the-art TMAs (e.g., Tilera's TILEPro64), which provide instructions to switch the processor cores and associated circuitry (switches, clock, interconnection network) not used in a computation to a low-power idle state. For example, a software-usable NAP instruction can be executed on a tile in Tilera's TMAs to put the tile into a low-power IDLE mode [352, 353]. Investigation of a comprehensive power model for TMAs is the focus of our future work.

Performance per Watt: The performance per watt metric takes into account the power consumption of a device while quantifying performance. For quantifying the performance per watt, we leverage our power model given by Eq. (12.3).

12.3.2 Matrix Multiplication (MM) Case Study

To demonstrate high-performance optimizations for TMAs, our work optimizes dense MM algorithms for Tilera's TMAs since MM is composed of operational patterns that are amenable for providing high performance. MM provides a wide range of insights since MM is a key building block in many scientific and engineering applications. The sequential runtime for the conventional MM algorithm multiplying two $n \times n$ matrices is $\mathcal{O}(n^3)$ and requires $2n^3$ operations [350]. To demonstrate high-performance optimizations, we implement the following variants of the MM algorithm: (1) non-blocked (NB) sequential algorithm; (2) blocked sequential algorithm; (3) parallelized blocked algorithm; and (4) blocked Cannon's algorithm.

The code for our MM algorithms' implementations on Tilera's TILEPro64 is presented in Section 12.4 and Interested readers can find further discussions on the MM algorithms in [350], which are not discussed in this chapter for brevity.

The original matrices for all of our MM algorithms reside in the shared memory. Our optimized blocked MM algorithm divides the matrices into sub-matrix blocks such that the sub-matrices fit in the caches for faster data access. Cannon's algorithm is a memory-efficient MM technique for parallel computers with toroidal mesh interconnections. The original Cannon's algorithm assumes that the input matrices are block distributed among the processors doing the computation for the MM algorithm [372]. Our case study implementation of Cannon's algorithm also divides the original matrices into sub-matrix blocks that fit in the caches; however, all of the participating tiles load the sub-matrix blocks from shared memory by appropriately calculating the indices.

12.4   Matrix Multiplication Algorithms' Code Snippets for Tilera's TILEPro64

This section provides code snippets of our matrix multiplication algorithms for Tilera's TILEPro64. The code snippets are presented selectively to provide an understanding of our algorithms, and some portions of the code are skipped for conciseness.

12.4.1   Serial Non-blocked Matrix Multiplication Algorithm

12.4.1.1   SerialNonBlockedMM.h

```
#ifndef MATRIXMULTIPLICATION_H_
#define MATRIXMULTIPLICATION_H_

#include <stdio.h>
#include <stdlib.h>
#include <time.h>
#include <sys/time.h>

#define     m    1024     // specify the dimension of matrices
#define     n    1024     // specify the dimension of matrices

void MatrixMultiplication(int *A, int *B, int *C);

#endif /* MATRIXMULTIPLICATION_H_ */
```

12.4.1.2   SerialNonBlockedMM.c

```
#include "SerialNonBlockedMM.h"

int main(int argc, char **argv)
{
```

```
int *A, *B, *C;
// pointers pointing to input matrices A and B and output matrix C

A = (int *) malloc (m * n * sizeof(int));
B = (int *) malloc (m * n * sizeof(int));
C = (int *) malloc (m * n * sizeof(int));

// initialize matrices

   :

MatrixMultiplication(A, B, C);

return 0;

} /* main function */

// integer matrix multiplication kernel
void MatrixMultiplication(int *A, int *B, int *C)
{
    int i, j, k;
    for (i = 0; i < n; i++)
    {
        for (j = 0; j < n; j++)
        {
            for (k = 0; k < n; k++)
            {
                C[i*n+j] = C[i*n+j] + (A[i*n+k] * B[k*n+j]);
            }
        }
    }
} /* MatrixMultiplication function */
```

12.4.2   Serial Blocked Matrix Multiplication Algorithm

12.4.2.1   SerialBlockedMM.h

```
#ifndef MATRIXMULTIPLICATION_H_
#define MATRIXMULTIPLICATION_H_

#include <stdio.h>
#include <stdlib.h>
#include <time.h>
#include <sys/time.h>

#define    m    1024    // specify the dimension of matrices
#define    n    1024    // specify the dimension of matrices
#define    bs   64      // block size for L2
#define    ssb  4       // block size for L1
```

```
void MatrixMultiplicationBlockedMain(int *A, int *B, int *C, int N);

void MatrixMultiplicationSubBlockedL2(int *A, int *B, int *C, int N);

void MatrixMultiplicationSubBlockedL1(int *A, int *B, int *C);

#endif /* MATRIXMULTIPLICATION_H_ */
```

12.4.2.2 SerialBlockedMM.c

```
#include "SerialBlockedMM.h"

int main(int argc, char **argv)
{
    int *A, *B, *C;

    // The algorithm tiles n x n original matrix in NxN sub-matrices
    int N = n/bs;

    A = (int *) malloc (m * n * sizeof(int));
    B = (int *) malloc (m * n * sizeof(int));
    C = (int *) malloc (m * n * sizeof(int));

    // initialize matrices

            ⋮

    MatrixMultiplicationBlockedMain(A, B, C, N);

    return 0;

} /* main function */

void MatrixMultiplicationBlockedMain(int *A, int *B, int *C, int N)
{
    int i, j, k;
    int tempbsn, tempibsn, tempjbs, tempC;
    tempbsn = bs * n;
    for (i = 0; i < N; i++)
    {
        tempibsn = i * tempbsn;
        for (j = 0; j < N; j++)
        {
            tempjbs = j*bs;
            tempC = tempibsn + tempjbs;

            for (k = 0; k < N; k++)
            {
```

```
                  MatrixMultiplicationSubBlockedL2(&A[tempibsn + k * bs],
                        &B[k * tempbsn + tempjbs], &C[tempC], N);
         }
      }
   }
} /* MatrixMultiplicationBlockedMain function */

void MatrixMultiplicationSubBlockedL2(int *A, int *B, int *C, int N)
{
   int i, j, k, M;
   int tempissbbsN, tempssbbsN, tempjssb, tempC;
   tempssbbsN = ssb * bs * N;
   M = bs/ssb;

   for (i = 0; i < M; i++)
   {
      tempissbbsN = i * tempssbbsN;

      for (j = 0; j < M; j++)
      {
         tempjssb = j * ssb;
         tempC = tempissbbsN + tempjssb;

         for (k = 0; k < M; k++)
         {
            MatrixMultiplicationSubBlockedL1(&A[tempissbbsN + k * ssb],
                        &B[k * tempssbbsN + tempjssb], &C[tempC]);
         }
      }
   }
} /* MatrixMultiplicationSubBlockedL2 function */

void MatrixMultiplicationSubBlockedL1(int *A, int *B, int *C)
{
   int i, j, k, temp;
   for (i = 0; i < ssb; i++)
   {
      for (j = 0; j < ssb; j++)
      {
         temp = 0;
         for (k = 0; k < ssb; k++)
         {
            temp += A[i*n+k] * B[k*n+j];
         }
         // storing the value of temp in C[i*n+j]
         C[i*n+j] += temp;
      }
   }
} /* MatrixMultiplicationSubBlockedL1 function */
```

12.4.3   Parallel Blocked Matrix Multiplication Algorithm

12.4.3.1   ParallelBlockedMM.h

```c
#ifndef MATRIXMULTIPLICATION_H_
#define MATRIXMULTIPLICATION_H_

#include <stdio.h>
#include <stdlib.h>
#include <ilib.h>        // Tilera's parallel API ilib
#include <tmc/cmem.h>
#include <time.h>
#include <sys/time.h>

#define      m     1024    // specify the dimension of matrices
#define      n     1024    // specify the dimension of matrices
#define      bs    64      // block size for L2
#define      ssb   4       // block size for L1
#define      NUM_TILES       16
#define      MASTER_RANK     0

// The implementation of the following functions is similar
// to the serial blocked MM
// algorithm and are skipped in the ParallelBlockedMM.c
// file for brevity
void MatrixMultiplicationSubBlockedL2(int *A, int *B, int *C,
int N);

void MatrixMultiplicationSubBlockedL1(int *A, int *B, int *C);

#endif /* MATRIXMULTIPLICATION_H_ */
```

12.4.3.2   ParallelBlockedMM.c

```c
#include "ParallelBlockedMM.h"

int main(int argc, char **argv)
{
    int *A, *B, *C;

    ilibStatus status;

    int processRank = 0;
    int N = n/bs;        // number of sub-blocks of main matrix of
                         // size n x n is equal to N^2;
                         // each NxN is of size bs x bs

    ilib_init();         // initializes ilib library state
```

```
// creating parallel processes
if (ilib_proc_go_parallel(NUM_TILES, NULL) != ILIB_SUCCESS)
    ilib_die("Failed to go parallel.");

processRank = ilib_group_rank(ILIB_GROUP_SIBLINGS);
// determining rank of processes

// Let process with rank 0 (root process) handle the
// initialization of matrices
if(processRank == 0)
{
    // process rank 0 (root process) allocates shared memory
    // for matrices A, B, and C
    tmc_cmem_init(0);
    A = (int *) tmc_cmem_malloc (m * n * sizeof(int));
    B = (int *) tmc_cmem_malloc (m * n * sizeof(int));
    C = (int *) tmc_cmem_malloc (m * n * sizeof(int));

    // initialize matrices

        ⋮


    // Performing memory fence to guarantee that the initialized
    // array values are visible to other processes
    ilib_mem_fence();
}

// broadcasts the shared memory addresses of A, B, and C
// from tile 0/process 0 to the other tiles
if(ilib_msg_broadcast(ILIB_GROUP_SIBLINGS, MASTER_RANK,
                    &A, sizeof(A), &status) != ILIB_SUCCESS)
    ilib_die("Failed to broadcast address of A");

if(ilib_msg_broadcast(ILIB_GROUP_SIBLINGS, MASTER_RANK,
                    &B, sizeof(B), &status) != ILIB_SUCCESS)
    ilib_die("Failed to broadcast address of B");

if(ilib_msg_broadcast(ILIB_GROUP_SIBLINGS, MASTER_RANK,
                    &C, sizeof(C), &status) != ILIB_SUCCESS)
    ilib_die("Failed to broadcast address of C");

// This barrier ensures that the broadcast of shared addresses
// is complete before further processing
ilib_msg_barrier(ILIB_GROUP_SIBLINGS);
for (i = 0; i < N; i++)
{
```

```
    for (j = 0; j < N; j++)
    {
        if(processRank == ((i + j)
        {
            for (k = 0; k < N; k++)
            {
                MatrixMultiplicationSubBlockedL2(&A[i * bs * n
                                                      + k * bs],
                        &B[k * bs * n + j * bs], &C[i * bs * n + j
                                                      * bs], N);
            }
        }
    }
}

// This barrier makes sure that all the processes have
// finished the assigned computations of matrix multiplication
ilib_msg_barrier(ILIB_GROUP_SIBLINGS);

// The process with rank 0 frees the allocated memory
if(processRank == 0)
{
    free(A);
    free(B);
    free(C);
}

ilib_finish();

return 0;

} /* main function */
```

12.4.4 *Parallel Blocked Cannon's Algorithm for Matrix Multiplication*

12.4.4.1 **ParallelBlockedCannonMM.h**

```
#ifndef MATRIXMULTIPLICATION_H_
#define MATRIXMULTIPLICATION_H_

#include <stdio.h>
#include <stdlib.h>
#include <ilib.h>          // Tilera's parallel API ilib
#include <tmc/cmem.h>
#include <time.h>
#include <sys/time.h>
```

```
#define     m     1024    // specify the dimension of matrices
#define     n     1024    // specify the dimension of matrices
#define     bs    64      // block size for L2
#define     ssb   4       // block size for L1
#define     NUM_TILES       16
#define     N               4        // equal to sqrt(NUM_TILES)
#define     MASTER_RANK     0

void MatrixMultiplicationSubBlockedL2(int *A, int *B, int *C, int L2B);

void MatrixMultiplicationSubBlockedL1(int *A, int *B, int *C);

#endif /* MATRIXMULTIPLICATION_H_ */
```

12.4.4.2   ParallelBlockedCannonMM.c

```
#include "ParallelBlockedCannonMM.h"

int main(int argc, char **argv)
{
    int r, c, s;        // loop variables for Cannon Rounds
    int loop;

    int *A, *B, *C;

    ilibStatus status;

    int processRank = 0;

    int pi, pj; // pi for i index of tile rank and pj for j index of
                // tile rank

    int CannonMatrix = bs * N;      // operates on this matrix size
                                    // in one Cannon Round
    int L2B = n/bs;
    int M = n/CannonMatrix;

    int Ai, Aj, Bi, Bj, Ci, Cj;     // (i,j) coordinates of blocks
    int As, Bs, Cs;                 // start indices of blocks

    int tempnbs = n*bs;
    int pipluspj= 0;

    ilib_init();

    // creating parallel processes
    if (ilib_proc_go_parallel(NUM_TILES, NULL) != ILIB_SUCCESS)
        ilib_die("Failed to go parallel.");
```

```
processRank = ilib_group_rank(ILIB_GROUP_SIBLINGS);

pi = processRank/N;
pj = processRank % N;
pipluspj = pi + pj;

// Let process with rank 0 (root process) handle the
// initialization of matrices
if(processRank == 0)
{
   // process rank 0 (root process) allocates shared memory
   // for matrices A, B, and C
   tmc_cmem_init(0);
   A = (int *) tmc_cmem_malloc (m * n * sizeof(int));
   B = (int *) tmc_cmem_malloc (m * n * sizeof(int));
   C = (int *) tmc_cmem_malloc (m * n * sizeof(int));

   // initialize matrices

        ⋮


   // Performing memory fence to guarantee that the initialized
   // array values are visible to other processes
   ilib_mem_fence();
}

// broadcasts the shared memory addresses of A, B, and C
// from tile 0/process 0 to the other tiles
if(ilib_msg_broadcast(ILIB_GROUP_SIBLINGS, MASTER_RANK,
                    &A, sizeof(A), &status) != ILIB_SUCCESS)
   ilib_die("Failed to broadcast address of A");

if(ilib_msg_broadcast(ILIB_GROUP_SIBLINGS, MASTER_RANK,
                    &B, sizeof(B), &status) != ILIB_SUCCESS)
   ilib_die("Failed to broadcast address of B");

if(ilib_msg_broadcast(ILIB_GROUP_SIBLINGS, MASTER_RANK,
                    &C, sizeof(C), &status) != ILIB_SUCCESS)
   ilib_die("Failed to broadcast address of C");

// This barrier ensures that the broadcast of shared addresses
// is complete before further processing
ilib_msg_barrier(ILIB_GROUP_SIBLINGS);

int temprN = 0, tempcN = 0, tempsN = 0;

for (r = 0; r < M; r++)
{
    temprN = r*N;
    for (c = 0; c < M; c++)
```

```
    {
        tempcN = c*N;
        for (s = 0; s < M; s++)
        {
            tempsN = s*N;
            Ai = temprN + pi;
            Aj = tempsN + (pipluspj) % N;
            Bi = tempsN + (pipluspj) % N;
            Bj = tempcN + pj;

            if(s == 0)
            {
                Ci = temprN + pi;
                Cj = tempcN + pj;
            }

            As = (Ai * tempnbs) + (Aj * bs);
            Bs = (Bi * tempnbs) + (Bj * bs);
            Cs = (Ci * tempnbs) + (Cj * bs);

            for (loop = 1; loop <= N; loop++)
            {
                // performs matrix multiplication on the local block
                MatrixMultiplicationSubBlockedL2(&A[As], &B[Bs],
                                                 &C[Cs], L2B);
                if (loop != N)
                {
                    Ai = temprN + pi;
                    Aj = tempsN + (pipluspj + loop) % N;
                    Bi = tempsN + (pipluspj + loop) % N;
                    Bj = tempcN + pj;
                    As = (Ai * tempnbs) + (Aj * bs);
                    Bs = (Bi * tempnbs) + (Bj * bs);
                }
            }
        }
    }
}

ilib_msg_barrier(ILIB_GROUP_SIBLINGS);

// The process with rank 0 frees the allocated memory
if(processRank == 0)
{
    free(A);
    free(B);
    free(C);
}

ilib_finish();
```

```
        return 0;

} /* main function */

void MatrixMultiplicationSubBlockedL2(int *A, int *B, int *C,
                                      int L2B)
{
    int i, j, k, L1B;   // L1B for L1 cache block size
    int tempissbbsL2B, tempssbbsL2B, tempjssb, tempC;
    tempssbbsL2B = ssb * bs * L2B;
    L1B = bs/ssb;

    for (i = 0; i < L1B; i++)
    {
        tempissbbsL2B = i * tempssbbsL2B;

        for (j = 0; j < L1B; j++)
        {
            tempjssb = j * ssb;
            tempC = tempissbbsL2B + tempjssb;

            for (k = 0; k < L1B; k++)
            {
                MatrixMultiplicationSubBlockedL1(&A[tempissbbsL2B +
                                                   k * ssb],
                                &B[k * tempssbbsL2B + tempjssb],
                                   &C[tempC]);
            }
        }
    }
} /* MatrixMultiplicationSubBlockedL2 function */

void MatrixMultiplicationSubBlockedL1(int *A, int *B, int *C)
{
    int i, j, k, temp, tempin;

    for (i = 0; i < ssb; i++)
    {
        tempin = i*n;
        for (j = 0; j < ssb; j++)
        {
            temp = 0;
            for (k = 0; k < ssb; k++)
            {
                temp += A[tempin+k] * B[k*n+j];
            }
            C[tempin+j] += temp;
        }
    }
} /* MatrixMultiplicationSubBlockedL1 function */
```

12.5   Performance Optimization on a Manycore Architecture

As with any other parallel architecture, the application performance while executing on a TMA depends on both the performance per tile and the scaling of the performance across multiple tiles. Hence, optimizations on a TMA require optimizing for a single tile as well as optimizing for multiple tiles, which results from the application decomposition into several parts for parallel execution. In order to fully exploit multiple-tile optimizations, parallel programming for a TMA requires programmers to have a more detailed understanding of the underlying architectural features as compared to the serial programming for a single-core architecture. This section presents performance optimizations on a single tile as well as platform considerations for parallel performance optimizations, such as chip locality, tile locality, cache locality, and memory balancing. This section also discusses compiler-based optimizations, such as scalar optimizations, function inlining, alias analysis, loop unrolling, loop-nest optimizations, software pipelining, and feedback-based optimizations.

12.5.1   Performance Optimization on a Single Tile

Performance optimizations on a single TMA tile requires effective use of the CPU and memory subsystem (including the caches and TLBs) as well as an optimized working set [388]. We point out that the effective use of aspects for a single tile is also important for parallel performance optimizations, thus to avoid redundancy with parallel performance optimizations (Section 12.5.2), this section only discusses the CPU, memory subsystem, and optimized working set.

12.5.1.1   CPU

Efficiently using the CPU for performance optimizations requires selecting efficient algorithms, compiler optimizations, and special-purpose instructions available on a TMA, such as sum of absolute differences, hashing, and checksums, depending on the application. The sequential code should be written to take advantage of ILP as much as possible. For fast access, frequently used variables should be directed as register-stored in the code when possible using the register keyword (in the C programming language).

12.5.1.2   Memory Subsystem

Efficiently using the memory subsystem, which comprises the cache subsystem and external memory, for performance optimizations aims at reducing the required external memory bandwidth. Since each level of the memory hierarchy is at least an order of magnitude faster than the next lower level (e.g., level one cache is faster than the level two cache), a fundamental guideline of good on chip memory management (e.g., caches/SP memory) that is equally applicable to TMAs is to fetch data from external memory, which has much larger latency than on-chip memory, only once, and use as many fetched words as possible before fetching the next data. The external memory bandwidth demand can be reduced in three ways: (1) maximizing the use of local caches (and SP memory if available) by keeping the code and data working sets small; (2) exploiting temporal locality by reusing recently accessed data; and (3) exploiting spatial locality by accessing nearby locations.

12.5.1.3 Working Set

An application's working set refers to the code and/or data currently (at any given instance) used by the application. For the best performance, the working set's code size should be kept small enough to fit in the instruction caches. Compiler performance optimizations, such as function inlining and loop unrolling, must take the instruction cache sizes into consideration, otherwise aggressive compiler optimizations may degrade performance due to increased code size. Similarly, the working set's data must be small enough to fit in the data caches, otherwise the program's performance will degrade due to excessive accesses to the external memory.

Blocking is a technique that enables the data's working set to fit in the on-chip caches. Blocking, which follows a divide-and-conquer paradigm, divides a problem into smaller subproblems such that the smaller subproblems fit in the on-chip caches. To enhance performance, blocking can be done in a nested manner taking into account both the level one and level two cache sizes. However, blocking adds complexity to the code. Cache blocking is advantageous when the benefits from the added locality due to cache blocking outweighs the cost of the additional overhead to access the data structure due to blocking. Furthermore, proper blocking granularity (block sizes) is not easy to determine theoretically (only an upper bound can be calculated in most cases), and the best blocking granularity for an algorithm is determined by experiments, as shown in Section 12.6.

12.5.2 Parallel Performance Optimizations

TMAs provide high computational density on-chip using multiple tiles, and a good understanding of parallel computing issues is necessary to fully leverage this computational density. Attaining high performance from a parallel architecture including TMAs requires efficient/balanced application decomposition as well as efficient use of hardware resources by exploiting architectural considerations such as chip locality, tile locality, cache locality, and memory balancing.

12.5.2.1 Application Decomposition

A TMA's parallel performance depends on an application's decomposition into several parts that can run in parallel. There are two types of application decomposition: data decomposition and functional decomposition. In *data decomposition*, the data that the application processes is divided into parts that can be processed in parallel. *Functional decomposition* separates subfunctions of an application and distributes the subfunctions across multiple tiles. Ideally, an application should be decomposed such that each of the participating tiles shares an equal amount of the processing load. The effectiveness of this decomposition, along with task mapping (how tasks/parts of an application are assigned to available tiles) and the communication mechanism, determines the *scalability* and attainable performance.

12.5.2.2   Chip Locality and Parallel Programming Paradigms

Chip locality refers to keeping communication, synchronization, and storage on-chip where possible. Different application programming paradigms exploit chip locality differently and, therefore, can affect the attained performance from a TMA. In *distributed memory programming*, the applications' decomposed components have private local memory and communicate explicitly with other components using message passing. Managing messages and explicitly distributing data structures in distributed memory programming can add considerable complexity to the software development. *Shared memory programming* uses shared memory objects to communicate with an application's decomposed components. Since sharing of data is not explicit as compared to the message passing, the accesses to these shared memory objects are indistinguishable from accesses to the local objects in the program source code and can only be determined by resolving the allocation point of memory and by use of specialized tools [388].

There are advantages of supporting distributed memory programming in TMAs. Although message passing requires explicitly managing data structures and adds complexity to the software development, the complexity is balanced by greater ease in avoiding race conditions when all data sharing is through explicit messages rather than through a shared address space [368]. Shared address space presents challenges to the programmers trying to attain high performance from a TMA. While a programmer can block data to fit into a cache or use prefetching to prepare a cache ahead of computation, programmers have little or no control over data eviction from the cache. Hence, software writing with predictable performance can be challenging, given that the state of the cache is difficult to control. Furthermore, it is difficult to assure in a shared address space that no unintended sharing is taking place, whereas a message passing architecture naturally supports isolation between modules since sharing can only occur through explicit exchange of messages. A TMA relying on the message passing paradigm can alleviate these issues at the cost of complex software development.

In practice, parallel applications aiming to attain high performance from a TMA may benefit from a hybrid of distributed and shared memory programming (supported by Tilera's TMAs) such that bulk data transfers are done explicitly using distributed memory programming, whereas more dynamic accesses use shared memory programming. Explicit communication as in message passing, enabled by ilib API in Tilera's TILE64/TILEPro64 that leverages UDN, exploits chip locality better as compared to using shared memory for communication via read and writes, which may spill data out of the caches into the external memory.

12.5.2.3   Tile Locality

Tile locality refers to accessing data locally or from nearby tiles' on-chip memory. In Tilera's TMAs, every fragment of code and data has a *home tile*, where the code/data can be cached. For the best performance, code and data accesses from the home tile should hit in the local cache. Code and data accesses from other (remote) tiles traverse the on-chip interconnect, which is faster than going to the external memory but slower than accessing a local cache. Tile locality is affected by cache coherence and thread migration.

Code and data accesses from caches in multicore/manycore architectures must ensure cache coherence, which can have an impact on performance. *Coherence* ensures that there is only one value for each memory location at any point in time. Some TMAs, such as the

TILE64, maintain coherence using *single-caching*, which restricts each memory location to be cacheable on only one tile at a time, requiring other tiles to access that location through the home tile where it is cached. For TMAs that maintain coherence via single-caching, tile locality can be exploited by caching data in the tiles that will most often access that data (these tiles become the home tile for that data). *Shared-default* programming styles, such as multithreading where global variables are shared across all threads, make tile locality difficult to achieve in single-caching architectures. Fortunately, some TMAs with single-caching (such as the TILE64) offer *neighborhood caching*, which exploits tile locality. Neighborhood caching enables data and code to be cached locally and spread across neighboring tiles to benefit from the large aggregate cache size of the neighboring tiles and minimizes off-chip memory references. Therefore, programmers should take advantage of tile locality by enabling neighborhood caching when using TMAs that support this functionality.

Some of Tilera's TMAs, such as the TILEPro64, implement a DDC technology (Section 12.2.3) that maintains coherence across multiple copies of cached data. DDC technology also leverages the *home tile* concept and directs all write updates and invalidates from other caches containing stale data after a write to the home tile. The TILEPro64 hardware distributes home tiles for memory regions at the cache line granularity. Each cache line's address is hashed where the hashing result determines which of the tiles to use as the home tile for that cache line. This hashing approach, referred to as *hash-for-home*, reduces potential hot spots when a particular region of memory is in heavy use and the home tile for that region of memory receives a disproportionate number of requests. On the TILEPro64, read-only data sections are cached using hash-for-home so that the cache lines are scattered across all of the hashing tiles. Additionally, the TILEPro64 caches read only data *non-inclusively*, which does not evict cache lines from the level two caches when a cache line is evicted from the level three cache on the home tile.

Tile locality is also affected by thread migration, which is an operating system's process management policy (handled by the supervisor layer in Tilera's processors (Section 12.2.3)) for moving threads/processes from one tile to another depending on the available resources. Thread migration is essentially a dynamic load-sharing policy that aims to ensure that there are no idle tiles when there are tasks waiting for execution on other tiles. Thread migration, which is enabled by default, can reduce performance in some cases due to context-switching overheads. To maintain the mapping between the home tile of frequently accessed data/code and the accessing threads/processes, threads/processes can be locked to tiles using *affinity*. This locking prevents threads/processes from unnecessarily sharing tiles and mitigates context-switching overheads, which can help in attaining high performance.

12.5.2.4 Cache Locality

A TMA generally consists of a large number of tiles, where each tile has a private processor and cache subsystem. Each tile is computationally less powerful and has small and low associativity caches; however, the aggregate cache size across all of the tiles is comparable to the cache size in high-end SMPs. Applications benefit from temporal and spatial locality, which in turn benefit from cache *associativity*. High associativity is important for exploiting cache locality because lower associativity caches suffer from conflicts (i.e., *cache thrashing* where multiple memory locations with temporal locality map to the same cache line, continually evicting each other), resulting in excess memory traffic.

Considering the significance of associativity for high performance, contemporary TMAs, which provide on-chip caches, offer a mix of cache associativities—from direct-mapped to fully-associative for different caches in the cache subsystem. For example, the TILEPro64 has direct-mapped level one instruction caches, two-way associative level one data caches, four-way associative unified level two caches, and fully-associative unified TLBs. To exploit temporal locality, memory accesses should be spread out so that the memory locations map to different cache lines over short spans of time. Instructions have natural spatial locality because when one instruction is executed, typically the next instruction is likely to execute as well, except for branches, which account for approximately 20–30% of the instructions [388]. Instructions also exhibit temporal locality, such as program loops or functions that are called repeatedly.

12.5.2.5 Translation Look-Aside Buffer (TLB) Locality

Most modern multicore architectures and some TMAs (e.g., Tilera's TMAs) use virtual memory so that the size of usable memory is not constrained by the size of the physical memory. Physical memory is typically partitioned into fixed-sized pages. *Page tables* map virtual addresses to physical addresses and keep track of whether a page resides in memory or the page's disk location. Page tables reside in memory, which adds additional memory access latency to perform virtual-to-physical address translations. To mitigate this additional latency, a small TLB stores information for the most recently used pages, acting as a cache for the page table. A TLB makes a virtual-to-physical address translation faster whenever the virtual address hits in the TLB. On a TLB miss, the page table is accessed and the translation is added to the TLB. Some recent architectures (e.g., Intel's Nehalem, Cortex-A15 MPCore [389]) use two-level TLBs to increase performance, under the same premise as two-level caches in processors.

In Tilera's TMAs, a TLB maps virtual address to physical addresses of the home tile at a virtual memory page size granularity. On most architectures, the page size is 64 KB by default, implying that the total amount of memory mapped by each TLB is small. Instruction and data TLBs are maintained separately (e.g., the TILEPro64 has an 8-entry instruction TLB and a 16-entry data TLB). TLB misses are handled effectively by hypervisor in approximately 100 cycles when the hypervisor's internal data structure contains the TLB entry. If the hypervisor's internal data structure does not contain the TLB entry, the hypervisor must access the page table entry, which can require 1000 cycles. The hypervisor stores TLB entries as a direct-mapped cache that holds approximately 1000 TLB entries. Tilera's TLBs support variable-sized pages with a minimum page size of 4 KB. To reduce TLB misses for applications referencing a wide span of code or data, programmers can use the *huge pages* or *large pages* option in Tilera's Linux kernel, where each TLB entry maps 16 MB of contiguous virtual memory as opposed to the default 64-KB page size. For example, hugepages=0,4,4,0 reserves 4 huge pages on memory controllers 1 and 2, and none on memory controllers 0 and 3 [387]. Although huge pages enable referencing a wide span of code or data, huge pages consume more physical memory and limit flexibility in mapping different pages with different cache properties.

An important difference between a cache miss and a TLB miss is that a cache miss does not necessarily stall the CPU [377]. A TLB miss causes the CPU to stall until the TLB has been updated with the new address. A small number of cache misses can be tolerated by algorithmic prefetching techniques as long as the data is read fast enough from the memory such that the data arrives at the CPU by the time the data is needed for computation. Prefetching can mask a cache miss, but not a TLB miss. Since TLB misses are more expensive than cache misses, minimizing TLB misses can enhance performance. Hence, programmers should use available options to adjust the mapping size of TLB entries (such as *huge pages* option in Tilera's TMAs) depending on the application size and the function call graph.

12.5.2.6 Memory Balancing

The overall memory bandwidth is maximized if external memory accesses are evenly balanced across the available memory controllers. High-order bits in the physical address select the memory controller, and the hypervisor maps virtual addresses to physical addresses to maximize the memory balance. For the TILEPro64, the programmer can view the chip as divided into 4 quadrants of 16 tiles where each tile maps memory to a memory controller adjacent to a quadrant. To achieve memory balancing, the TILEPro64 supports *memory striping*, which automatically spreads accesses across the available four memory controllers. The memory striping can be controlled by hypervisor's command: `options stripe_memory`. The `stripe_memory` option requests the hypervisor to configure the architecture to stripe memory accesses across all available memory controllers. Even with striped memory, the client supervisor and user programs see one unified physical address space rather than four separate address spaces. Striping is performed at a granularity of 8 KB (i.e., if physical address A is on controller N, physical address $A + 8192$ will be on controller $N + 1$, and so forth). By default, the hypervisor stripes memory if all memory controllers have an equal amount of memory. Hence, to achieve memory balancing and consequently high performance, parallel programmers for TMAs should enable memory striping if the parallelized application is to be run on a large number of tiles (greater than 16 for Tilera's TILE64 and TILEPro64).

12.5.2.7 On-Chip Mesh Interconnect

A parallel application's performance and scalability can be improved by reducing the load on the on-chip interconnect since the interconnect is shared by all of the tiles. If an algorithm's data flow is not carefully organized, excessive communication over the interconnect can become a performance bottleneck.

12.5.3 Compiler-Based Optimizations

Compiler-based optimizations remove artificial constraints imposed by a programmer and a programming language to improve efficiency and expose inherent parallelism. The primary benefits of compiler-based optimizations include faster execution time and typically smaller object code size. Compiler-based optimizations can speed up development time by reducing the time required for performance optimizations and letting the compiler optimizer improve low-level code quality. The compiler optimization options determine the optimization level applied to the program to be optimized. We point out that the compiler optimization options are compiler vendor specific. For example, Sun's Studio compiler provides five compiler optimization levels, -O1 to -O5, where each increasing level adds more optimization strategies for the compiler, with -O5 being the highest level [390]. The compiler optimization levels for Tilera's TMAs vary from -O0 to -O3. The -O0 option applies no optimizations and the -O3 option provides the highest level of aggressive compiler optimizations. The -Os optimization option optimizes the program for both size and performance. The -Os option applies -O2 optimizations except those optimizations that increase the program size. In this section, we discuss compiler-based optimizations for TMAs, focusing on the TILEPro64 compiler tile-cc/c++.

12.5.3.1   Scalar Optimizations

Scalar optimizations improve the execution time of a program using local and/or global optimizations. *Local optimizations* are applied to instructions within a basic block and do not leverage a holistic view of the function/program, such as considering data flow analysis to make optimization decisions. Local optimizations include constant propagation, copy propagation, common subexpression elimination, constant folding, operation folding, redundant load/store elimination, constant combining, strength reduction, and code reordering [391]. *Global optimizations* are applied among operations within the same function. Global optimizations include loop induction variable recognition and elimination, loop global variable migration, loop invariant code removal, and dead code removal [391]. Scalar optimizations are enabled at optimization level -O2 or above.

12.5.3.2   Function Inlining

An application's performance can benefit from function inlining because function inlining exposes more context to the scalar and loop-nest optimizers and eliminates the function call overheads, such as register saving and restoring, the call and return instructions, and so on. Function inlining can be user-directed and/or automatic. User-directed function inlining is performed at all optimization levels and can be specified by using the keyword inline or #pragma directives inline and noinline. We point out that the inline keyword is advisory, not mandatory (i.e., the keyword serves as a hint to the compiler to inline the function, but the function might or might not actually be inlined). The #pragma inline and the #pragma noinline directives instruct the compiler to inline or not inline, respectively, a function or set of functions. These #pragma directives can have next line, entire routine, or global scope. Automatic inlining is enabled by default at the -O3 optimization level, but restricts large increases in code size. Automatic inlining is also enabled by default at non-zero optimization levels below -O3, but function inlining is only allowed for functions that are not estimated to increase the code size. Too much inlining may degrade performance due to the code working set problem discussed in Section 12.5.1.3.

12.5.3.3   Alias Analysis

Memory aliases are caused when multiple pointers resolve to the same physical memory location. Compilers are conservative in optimization of memory references involving pointers because aliases can be difficult, or impossible, to detect at compile time. The compiler must conservatively assume that locations referenced by different pointers point to the same location, which limits the effectiveness of certain optimizations, such as instruction scheduling.

Programmers can assist the compiler with alias analysis by marking a pointer with the restrict keyword, which guarantees that the memory region referenced by that pointer is the only way to access that memory region over the lifetime of that pointer.

12.5.3.4 Loop Unrolling

Loop unrolling exposes more ILP, eliminates branches, amortizes loop overhead, and enables cross-loop-iteration optimizations, such as read/write elimination across the unrolled iterations. For example, loop unrolling can amortize loop overhead by replacing four loop counter increments $i+=1$ with one loop counter addition $i+=4$ if the loop unrolling factor is four. Loop unrolling can be performed if the loop to be unrolled satisfies the following conditions: the loop does not have internal cycles; the loop does not have an indirect branch that may jump back into the loop; the loop contains a single basic block; and the loop is a counter-based loop. Loop unrolling can be guided by placing a #pragma unroll n immediately before the loop where n is a constant specifying the loop unrolling factor. The pragma can be applied to both inner and non-inner loops. An n value of 0 or 1 directs the compiler not to unroll the loop. We point out that the unroll pragma is only processed if the optimization level is high enough (i.e., -O2 or -Os for inner loops, and -O3 for outer loops).

12.5.3.5 Loop-Nest Optimizations

A numerical program's execution time is mostly spent in loops. Loop-nest optimizations perform loop optimizations that can greatly increase performance by better exploiting caches and ILP. Loop-nest optimizations include loop interchange, cache blocking, outer loop unrolling, loop fusion, and loop fission. The order of loops in a nest can affect the number of cache misses, the number of instructions in the inner loop, and the compiler's ability to schedule an inner loop. Cache blocking and outer loop unrolling are closely related optimizations used to improve cache and register reuse. Loop fusion fuses multiple loop nests to improve cache behavior, to reduce the number of memory references, and to enable other optimizations, such as loop interchange and cache blocking. Loop fission, which is the opposite of loop fusion, distributes loops into multiple pieces. Loop fission is particularly useful in reducing register pressure in large inner loops. Loop fusion and fission can be enabled using #pragma fuse and #pragma fission, respectively. Loop-nest optimizations are enabled by default with -O3 optimization flag.

12.5.3.6 Code Generation Phase Optimizations

The compiler's code generator processes an input program in an intermediate representation format to produce an assembly file. A program is partitioned into basic blocks, such that a new basic block is started at each branch target and large blocks arbitrarily end after a certain number of operations/instructions. Code generation optimizations are not done at optimization level -O0. The code generator performs standard local optimizations on each basic block, such as copy propagation and dead code elimination, at optimization level -O1. The code generator performs global register allocation and various innermost loop optimizations at optimization levels -O2, -Os, and -O3.

12.5.3.7   Software Pipelining

Software pipelining is a type of out-of-order execution where reordering is done by the compiler instead of the processor. Software pipelining schedules innermost counting loops (i.e., loops with no other terminating conditions or conditional statements) such that the hardware pipeline remains full. Software pipelining can be enabled and disabled using #pragma swp and #pragma noswp, respectively.

12.5.3.8   Feedback-Based Optimizations

Feedback-based optimizations are an advanced compiler optimization technique that replaces a compiler's estimations with actual data collected at runtime using a specially instrumented executable. Collected data includes how many times a given loop executes and how often an if predicate is true. Feedback-based optimizations require compiling the program at least twice: the first compilation creates an instrumented executable and second compilation uses the information collected by the first executable to generate the optimized executable. Feedback-based optimizations help compilers with loop unrolling and other loop optimizations, in addition to determining frequently executed blocks of code, which can be used to guide code scheduling, layout, and register allocation decisions.

Figure 12.4 depicts the feedback mechanism's workflow. The main steps are as follows: (1) The source code/program is compiled and linked with the feedback collect option that creates an instrumented code that collects feedback data; (2) one or more training runs are performed on the instrumented executable with test inputs, also known as *training set*, to collect information about the program's typical behavior; (3) the compiler gathers information from the training run(s) in a raw feedback directory; (4) the compiler converts the contents of the raw feedback directory into a single feedback file, using the convert feedback option, suitable for use in the feedback optimization process; and (5) recompile and relink the source code with the feedback use option, which will optimize the executable using the feedback information generated previously. We point out that the same compiler optimization flag should be used for both the instrumented binary and the final optimized executable.

Feedback-based optimizations improve performance by leveraging both compiler and linker feedback. The compiler feedback improves code generation by recording various facts such as branch probabilities and executed loop counts. Based on the compiler feedback, the compiler rearranges code to straighten out likely code paths (e.g., remove branches) for more effective cache use. Linker feedback helps the compiler in selecting addresses for functions that reduce cache conflicts. During the creation of the instrumented executable, each instrumented function calls a runtime library that tracks the order in which the functions execute. For example, if a program executes function f_1, then function f_2, and then function f_1 again. The feedback mechanism identifies if f_1 and f_2 alias in the cache, in which case f_2 will evict f_1, causing cache misses when f_1 is executed again. The feedback mechanism selects non-aliasing addresses for f_1 and f_2 so that both of these functions can coexist in the cache at the same time given a sufficient cache size.

A modern compiler uses feedback-based optimizations as a hint for optimizations and not as a guarantee of what future program input will look like since the data is gathered using a training/synthetic input. Therefore, a compiler does not make assumptions based on feedback-based optimizations that may produce incorrect code for inputs different than the training input.

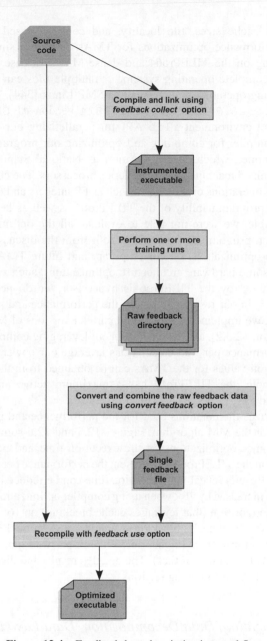

Figure 12.4 Feedback-based optimization workflow

12.6 Results

Attaining high performance and high performance per watt on TMAs is challenging mainly due to intricacies in parallel programming and parallel algorithms, complex hardware architecture, and scalability issues as the number of tiles increases. Some of the main factors influencing performance on TMAs include algorithmic choices, features of the underlying architecture, such as cache sizes, tile locality, and compiler-based optimizations. This section illustrates performance optimizations for TMAs, first on a single tile and then on multiple tiles, focusing on the TILEPro64 and dense MM as a case study. Each tile can independently run a complete operating system, or multiple tiles can be grouped together to run a multiprocessing operating system, such as SMP Linux [344]. The TILEPro64 runs Linux kernel 2.6.26.7-MDE-2.1.2.112814 version #1 SMP. We use Tilera's multicore development environment iLib API for parallelizing our MM algorithms and Tilera's tile-cc compiler for compiling and optimizing our programs. tile-cc is the cross-platform C compiler, which compiles American National Standards Institute(ANSI) standard C to an optimized machine code for Tilera's processors. The compiler also supports software emulation of operations on data types such as FP integers and 64-bit integers.

Due to the limited programmability of the TILEPro64 as well as keeping the number of experiments manageable, we were not able to evaluate all the optimizations discussed in Section 12.5. However, programmers can still benefit from the discussions in Section 12.5 for high-performance optimizations on contemporary and future TMAs that support these optimizations. Since some hardware architecture optimizations, such as memory balancing, are automatically enabled by the TILEPro64's hypervisor, we do not elaborate on these hardware optimizations in our results. To obtain the performance and performance per watt results in this section, we implemented serial and parallel versions of MM with and without cache blocking (Section 12.3.2), and with and without leveraging compiler optimizations on the TILEPro64. Performance per watt calculations leverage our power model in Eq. (12.3). The power consumption values for the TMAs can be obtained from the devices' respective datasheets. For example, the TILEPro64 has a maximum active and idle mode power consumption of 28 and 5 W, respectively [351, 355].

Table 12.2 summarizes the notations used for the performance and performance per watt optimization results for the MM algorithm. Figures 12.5 and 12.6 summarize the impact of various high-performance optimizations on the execution time and performance per watt, respectively, for MM on the TILEPro64. We present the performance per watt results in MOPS per watt (MOPS/W). Results reveal that execution time can be reduced by 152× and performance per watt can be increased by 76× when using compiler optimizations and parallelization of the optimized MM algorithm (that leverages cache blocking) on 16 tiles as compared to a naive MM algorithm (without cache blocking) as shown in Section 12.4.1) on a single tile without any compiler optimizations (higher performance per watt gains can be achieved by parallelization on a greater number of tiles). The detailed results and discussion of these optimizations are presented in the following sections.

12.6.1   Data Allocation, Data Decomposition, Data Layout, and Communication

Data allocation, data decomposition, data layout, and communication depend on the application and the architecture, and play an important role in attainable performance. This section discusses these aspects as well as the communication networks leveraged for communicating the data between the tiles and between the tiles and external memory for the MM algorithms implemented in this work.

Table 12.2 Performance and performance per watt optimization notations used in our MM case study

Notation	Description
b	Level two cache block size for the blocked MM algorithm
b'	Level one cache sub-block size for the blocked MM algorithm
$T_{\text{NB}}^{(p)}$	Execution time of the non-blocked MM algorithm on p tiles with no compiler optimization flag
$T_{\text{NB-O3}}^{(p)}$	Execution time of the non-blocked MM algorithm on p tiles with compiler optimization flag -O3
$T_{\text{B}}^{(p)}$	Execution time of the blocked MM algorithm on p tiles with no compiler optimization flag
$T_{\text{B-O3}}^{(p)}$	Execution time of the blocked MM algorithm on p tiles with compiler optimization flag -O3
$T_{\text{B-FBO}}^{(p)}$	Execution time of the blocked MM algorithm on p tiles with feedback-based optimizations
$\text{Perf}_{\text{NB}}^{(p)}$	Performance of the non-blocked MM algorithm on p tiles with no compiler optimization flag
$\text{Perf}_{\text{NB-O3}}^{(p)}$	Performance of the non-blocked MM algorithm on p tiles with compiler optimization flag -O3
$\text{Perf}_{\text{B}}^{(p)}$	Performance of the blocked MM algorithm on p tiles with no compiler optimization flag
$\text{Perf}_{\text{B-O3}}^{(p)}$	Performance of the blocked MM algorithm on p tiles with compiler optimization flag -O3
$\text{Perf}_{\text{B-FBO}}^{(p)}$	Performance of the blocked MM algorithm on p tiles with feedback-based optimizations
$\text{Perf/W}_{\text{NB}}^{(p)}$	Performance per watt of the non-blocked MM algorithm on p tiles with no compiler optimization flag
$\text{Perf/W}_{\text{NB-O3}}^{(p)}$	Performance per watt of the non-blocked MM algorithm on p tiles with compiler optimization flag -O3
$\text{Perf/W}_{\text{B}}^{(p)}$	Performance per watt of the blocked MM algorithm on p tiles with no compiler optimization flag
$\text{Perf/W}_{\text{B-O3}}^{(p)}$	Performance per watt of the blocked MM algorithm on p tiles with compiler optimization flag -O3
$\text{Perf/W}_{\text{B-FBO}}^{(p)}$	Performance per watt of the blocked MM algorithm on p tiles with feedback-based optimizations

For MM algorithms on a single tile, we allocate the data in external memory using the `malloc()` function. The data allocated using `malloc()` is only accessible to the tile allocating the data. For our parallel algorithms, we leverage Tilera's TMC `cmem` API for data allocation. We allocate the data in external memory and make the data shared for our parallel algorithms using the `tmc_cmem_malloc()` function, which maps the allocated shared memory at the same address on all the participating tiles/processes. Since our parallel MM algorithms operate on the same original matrices (A, B, and C), the data must be shared in the external memory. We point out that for parallel applications that can operate on their own private data, data can be declared private for each tile/process in the external memory. Our

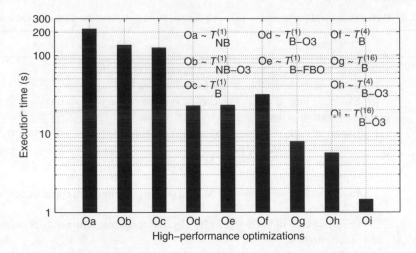

Figure 12.5 The impact of high-performance optimizations on the execution time of MM on the TILEPro64 ($\sim$ denotes corresponds to)

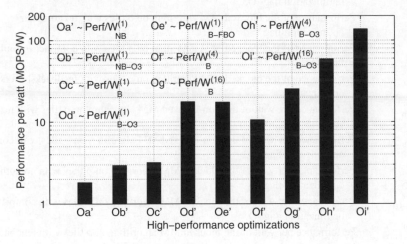

Figure 12.6 The impact of high-performance optimizations on the performance per watt of MM on the TILEPro64 ($\sim$ denotes corresponds to)

experiments with various benchmarks on the TILEPro64 indicate that parallel applications with private data can attain better performance on the TMA as compared to the applications using shared data [384].

For our blocked MM algorithms, data is decomposed into small blocks of the original matrices that reside in the shared memory. Each data access from the shared memory by a tile fits in the local cache of the operating tile. Communication is overlapped by computation in our blocked MM algorithms as the tiles start operating on the requested data as soon as the first requested data byte is available from the memory. All subsequent computations by a tile on a given block access the data from the tile's local cache without accessing external memory until the computation requires processing data not already present in the cache.

For our MM algorithms, the tiles access data from the external memory using MDN (Section 12.2.3), which transfers data resulting from loads, stores, prefetches, and cache misses. Cannon's MM algorithm that uses horizontal communication (communication between tiles) leverages MDN as well as TDN that supports data transfers between tiles. The CDN, which carries cache coherence invalidation messages, is leveraged by both our blocked parallel MM algorithm and Cannon's MM algorithm. ilib functions used in our algorithms (see Section 12.4.3 and Section 12.4.4 for code snippets) leverage UDN, which abstract the details of the underlying packetization, routing, transport, buffering, flow control, and deadlock avoidance in the network.

12.6.2   Performance Optimizations on a Single Tile

Single-tile performance optimizations are important to attaining high performance on a TMA. Blocking algorithms that take into account cache sizes can significantly improve performance; however, selection of the appropriate block size is important for attaining high performance. Furthermore, compiler optimization flags, such as -Os, -O2, or -O3, enable most of the compiler-based optimizations to attain high performance. Feedback-based optimizations can further enhance performance by eliminating the compiler's guesswork for certain optimizations, such as loop unrolling. This section highlights these performance optimizations on a single tile of the TILEPro64.

12.6.2.1   Algorithmic Optimizations and Compiler Optimizations

To evaluate the impact of algorithmic choices on performance and performance per watt, we implement a blocked integer MM algorithm considering the TILEPro64's cache sizes. We use an integer MM because the TILEPro64 does not have FP units, and software emulation of FP may not provide meaningful insights into the performance gains achieved by various performance optimizations.

The blocked MM algorithm divides the original MM into optimized smaller sub-MMs that leverage the cache hierarchy using nested blocking for level one and level two data cache sizes of 8 and 64 KB, respectively, for the TILE64/TILEPro64. All three sub-MMs (corresponding to matrices A, B, and C) must fit in the cache for blocking to be useful. The required memory size for the blocks should also incorporate the size of data types, which depends on the processor architecture and compiler (e.g., 4 B for integer data types for a 32-bit processor and 32-bit compiler). For the level two cache, we calculate the block size b as $4 \cdot 3 \cdot b^2 \leq 64$ KB, which gives $b \leq 74$. For a power of two block size, $b \leq 64$. There is no need for our algorithms to use block sizes that are powers of two; however, we use block sizes that are powers of two to keep the number of experiments manageable and still show scaling. We use the constant 3 in the block size calculation corresponding to the level two cache because all of the three blocks from matrices A, B, and C ($C = A \cdot B$) must fit in the cache simultaneously, and we use the constant 4 because the integer data type requires 4 B (32 bits) on the TILEPro64. Similar calculations for the block size corresponding to the level one cache b' gives $b' \leq 26$, or $b' \leq 16$, when considering the block size as a power of 2.

To illustrate the impact of the algorithmic choices and cache blocking on attainable performance and performance per watt, we compare the performance and performance per watt of

Table 12.3 Performance and performance per watt of a blocked (B) and a non-blocked (NB) MM algorithm on a single tile of the TILEPro64 for different matrix sizes n

n	$T^{(1)}_{NB-O3}$ (s)	$T^{(1)}_{B-O3}$ (s)	$T^{(1)}_{NB-O3}/T^{(1)}_{B-O3}$	$Perf^{(1)}_{NB-O3}$ (MOPS)	$Perf/W^{(1)}_{NB-O3}$ (MOPS/W)	$Perf^{(1)}_{B-O3}$ (MOPS)	$Perf/W^{(1)}_{B-O3}$ (MOPS/W)
1024	134.59	22.65	5.9	15.96	2.98	94.81	17.69
2048	2171.58	215.33	10	7.91	1.47	79.78	14.88

our blocked MM algorithm with a non-blocked MM algorithm. Table 12.3 depicts the performance and performance per watt of a blocked (B) and a non-blocked (NB) MM algorithm on a single tile using the compiler optimization level -O3 for two matrix sizes, $n = 1024$ and $n = 2048$, respectively, where n denotes the matrix dimensions of the square matrices A, B, and C. For the blocked MM algorithm, we select $b = 64$ and $b' = 4$, which satisfies the constraints on the calculated block sizes. The results indicate that the blocked MM algorithm provides 5.9× and 10× performance and performance per watt improvements over the non-blocked MM algorithm for $n = 1024$ and $n = 2048$, respectively. These results highlight the significance of carefully optimizing algorithms that are tailored for the underlying architectural specifications, such as the cache sizes, for attaining high performance and performance per watt from TMAs. The results also reveal that although compiler optimizations help both the blocked and non-blocked algorithms, compiler optimizations alone are not sufficient to achieve the maximum attainable performance (i.e., a non-blocked algorithm with aggressive compiler optimizations cannot attain the performance of a blocked optimized algorithm). We verified the results with other compiler optimization levels as well and present results show the best attainable performance from the compiler optimization levels.

Results in Table 12.3 highlight the effect of data sizes on the attainable performance per watt. For example, the attainable performance per watt for $n = 1024$ is 2× greater than that for $n = 2048$ for the non-blocked MM algorithm. Similarly, the attainable performance per watt for $n = 1024$ is 1.2× greater than that for $n = 2048$ for the blocked MM algorithm. This higher attainable performance per watt for smaller data sizes is due to the fact that smaller data sizes fit better in the cache and require lesser main memory requests to transfer data from main memory to the caches as compared to larger data sizes. We observe that even with large data sizes, the blocked MM algorithm helps in alleviating the performance per watt penalty for additional memory accesses. For example, the blocked MM algorithm reduces the performance per watt penalty due to additional memory accesses for $n = 2048$ over $n = 1024$ by 67% as compared to the non-blocked MM algorithm.

12.6.2.2 Evaluating Block Sizes and Compiler Optimizations

Table 12.4 shows the performance and performance per watt of the MM algorithm running on a single tile with and without compiler optimizations for different matrix sizes n, block sizes b, and sub-block sizes b'. The results reveal that as with traditional CPUs, block sizes are important in optimizing performance and performance per watt for a given TMA. Experiments indicate that block size calculations only give a constraint/upper bound (i.e., the maximum block size, for a given cache size), and the optimal block size for an algorithm can only be

Table 12.4 Performance of the blocked MM algorithm on a single tile of the TILEPro64 for different matrix sizes n, block sizes b, and sub-block sizes b'

n	b	b'	$T_B^{(1)}$ (s)	$T_{B-O3}^{(1)}$ (s)	$\mathrm{Perf}_B^{(1)}$ (MOPS)	$\mathrm{Perf/W}_B^{(1)}$ (MOPS/W)	$\mathrm{Perf}_{B-O3}^{(1)}$ (MOPS)	$\mathrm{Perf/W}_{B-O3}^{(1)}$ (MOPS/W)
	32	4	126.08	22.97	17.03	3.18	93.49	17.44
1024	64	4	125.71	22.65	17.08	3.19	94.81	17.69
	128	4	125.56	22.53	17.1	3.19	95.32	17.78
	32	8	107.77	19.63	19.9	3.71	109.4	20.4
1024	64	8	107.52	19.4	19.97	3.72	110.7	20.65
	128	8	107.42	19.3	19.99	3.73	111.27	20.76
	32	16	117.73	29	18.24	3.4	74.05	13.82
1024	64	16	117.6	28.86	18.26	3.4	74.41	13.88
	128	16	117.55	28.82	18.27	3.4	74.51	13.9
	32	4	1042.06	218.21	16.49	3.08	78.73	14.69
2048	64	4	1033.87	215.33	16.62	3.1	79.78	14.88
	128	4	1040.77	216.22	16.5	3.08	79.46	14.82
	32	8	1164.97	414.43	14.75	2.75	41.45	7.73
2048	64	8	1162.07	412.22	14.78	2.76	41.68	7.78
	128	8	1162.04	419.41	14.78	2.76	40.96	7.64
	32	16	1362.94	434.48	12.6	2.35	39.54	7.38
2048	64	16	1360.57	433.25	12.63	2.36	39.65	7.4
	128	16	1360.07	418.55	12.63	2.36	41.05	7.66

determined using a hit and try method (i.e., by selecting block sizes less than the maximum size obtained by the block size calculations, running the algorithm with each block size, measuring the performance, and then selecting the best block size based on the performance results). The results also reveal that compiler optimization level -O3 yields a significant improvement in execution time, performance, and performance per watt as compared to not using any compiler optimizations. For example, -O3 provides performance and performance per watt improvements of 5.6× and 4.8× for $n = 1024$ and $n = 2048$, respectively, when $b = 64$ and $b' = 4$. We also evaluated our blocked MM algorithm with other compiler optimization levels, such as -O2 and -Os; however, since -O3 yields the best performance, we present only results with -O3 for brevity.

The results in Table 12.4 depict that $b = 128$ and $b' = 8$ give the best results for $n = 1024$ and these sizes could be used for $n \leq 1024$; however, $b = 128$ and $b' = 8$ impose a 2× lower performance than $b = 64$ and $b' = 4$ for $n = 2048$. Hence, we apply further optimizations based on block and sub-block sizes of $b = 64$ and $b' = 4$, respectively.

12.6.2.3 Compiler Directives-Based Optimizations

Programmers can specify appropriate compiler directives to achieve performance improvements. In this section, we discuss the performance improvements attained by some of the compiler directives discussed in Section 12.5.3. We point out that not all of the available compiler directives are appropriate for a given program/application to attain high performance. A programmer needs to speculate which compiler directives can be beneficial and then apply these compiler directives selectively depending on the program's constructs. Hit and try can also be beneficial with some compiler directives, such as loop unrolling to determine the best loop unrolling value. Using appropriate compiler directives for attaining high performance requires programming experience as inappropriate use of compiler directives can deteriorate performance.

Table 12.5 depicts the impact of various compiler directives with the -O2 optimization level on the performance of the non-blocked MM algorithm on a single tile of the TILEPro64 for $n = 1024$. We point out that many compiler directives are enabled only at specific compiler optimization levels. Experiments reveal that the compiler directives presented in Table 12.5 have a negligible impact on performance with compiler optimization levels -O0 and -O1. Results indicate that compiler optimization directives with the -O2 flag can increase the performance by $1.8\times$ or by 77% as compared to not using any compiler directives. We also use hit and try to determine suitable parameters for compiler directives. For example, our experiments with #pragma unroll 2 does not give any performance improvement whereas #pragma unroll 4 increases the performance by 14% for the non-blocked MM algorithm. We also observe that not all the compiler directives result in performance improvement, (e.g., #pragma swp does not enhance performance for the non-blocked MM algorithm).

In Table 12.5, #pragma blocking size (n1,n2) directs the compiler that if the specified loop is involved in blocking of the primary or level one (secondary or level two) cache, then it will have the blocking size of $n1$ ($n2$). The specification of the blocking size for the secondary cache is optional; however, we observe that better performance results are attained if the blocking sizes for both primary and secondary caches are specified. We point out that this compiler blocking directive is loop-based and different from cache blocking sizes we calculated earlier for MM algorithms. If a blocking size of 0 is specified, then the loop is not split and the entire

Table 12.5 Compiler directives-based optimizations with compiler optimization level -O2 for the non-blocked MM algorithm

Compiler directives	$T^{(1)}_{\text{NB}-\text{O2}}(s)$
Without any compiler directives	136.32
#pragma inline here where call to MM kernel is made	121.43
#pragma inline here + #pragma blocking size (4,8) for outer MM loop	111.81
#pragma inline here + #pragma blocking size (4,8) for outer MM loop + #pragma blocking size (2,8) for inner MM loop	87.65
#pragma inline here + #pragma blocking size (4,8) for outer MM loop + #pragma blocking size (2,8) for inner MM loop + #pragma blocking size (2,8) for innermost MM loop	87.65
#pragma inline here + #pragma blocking size (4,8) for outer MM loop + #pragma blocking size (2,8) for inner MM loop + #pragma blocking size (2,8) for innermost MM loop + #pragma unroll 4	76.99
#pragma inline here + #pragma blocking size (4,8) for outer MM loop + #pragma blocking size (2,8) for inner MM loop + #pragma blocking size (2,8) for innermost MM loop + #pragma unroll 4 + #pragma swp	77.0

loop is inside the block. #pragma unroll (n) directs the compiler to add $(n - 1)$ copies of the inner loop body to the inner loop.

12.6.2.4 Feedback-Based Optimizations

Tables 12.6 and 12.7 depict performance and performance per watt, respectively, for the feedback-based optimizations applied to the blocked MM algorithm to investigate further performance and performance per watt enhancements on the TILEPro64. The results reveal that feedback-based optimizations do not improve performance and performance per watt for the TILEPro64 as compared to the when using compiler optimization level -O3. However, both the compiler optimization level -O3 and feedback-based optimization improve the performance and performance per watt by 5.5× and 4.8× for $n = 1024$ and $n = 2048$, respectively, for the blocked MM algorithm as compared to the blocked MM algorithm without any compiler optimizations.

To investigate whether feedback-based optimizations can be useful for TMAs other than the TILEPro64, we evaluated the TILE64. Tables 12.8 and 12.9 depict performance and

Table 12.6 Performance of the blocked MM algorithm on a single tile of the TILEPro64 using feedback-based optimizations for different matrix sizes n

n	b	b'	$T_{\mathrm{B}}^{(1)}$ (s)	$T_{\mathrm{B-O3}}^{(1)}$ (s)	$T_{\mathrm{B-FBO}}^{(1)}$ (s)	$\mathrm{Perf}_{\mathrm{B}}^{(1)}$ (MOPS)	$\mathrm{Perf}_{\mathrm{B-O3}}^{(1)}$ (MOPS)	$\mathrm{Perf}_{\mathrm{B-FBO}}^{(1)}$ (MOPS)
1024	64	4	125.71	22.65	22.96	17.08	94.81	93.53
2048	64	4	1033.87	215.33	214.73	16.62	79.78	80.0

Table 12.7 Performance per watt of the blocked MM algorithm on a single tile of the TILEPro64 using feedback-based optimizations for different matrix sizes n

n	b	b'	$\mathrm{Perf/W}_{\mathrm{B}}^{(1)}$ (MOPS/W)	$\mathrm{Perf/W}_{\mathrm{B-O3}}^{(1)}$ (MOPS/W)	$\mathrm{Perf/W}_{\mathrm{B-FBO}}^{(1)}$ (MOPS/W)
1024	64	4	3.19	17.69	17.45
2048	64	4	3.1	14.88	14.92

Table 12.8 Performance of the blocked MM algorithm on a single tile of the TILE64 using feedback-based optimizations for different matrix sizes n

n	b	b'	$T_{\mathrm{B}}^{(1)}$ (s)	$T_{\mathrm{B-O3}}^{(1)}$ (s)	$T_{\mathrm{B-FBO}}^{(1)}$ (s)	$\mathrm{Perf}_{\mathrm{B}}^{(1)}$ (MOPS)	$\mathrm{Perf}_{\mathrm{B-O3}}^{(1)}$ (MOPS)	$\mathrm{Perf}_{\mathrm{B-FBO}}^{(1)}$ (MOPS)
1024	64	4	130.18	28.98	22.96	16.5	74.1	93.53
2048	64	4	1109.08	307.34	214.71	15.49	55.9	80.01

Table 12.9 Performance per watt of the blocked MM algorithm
on a single tile of the TILE64 using feedback-based optimizations
for different matrix sizes n

n	b	b'	Perf/$W_B^{(1)}$ (MOPS/W)	Perf/$W_{B-O3}^{(1)}$ (MOPS/W)	Perf/$W_{B-FBO}^{(1)}$ (MOPS/W)
1024	64	4	3.08	13.82	17.45
2048	64	4	2.89	10.43	14.93

performance per watt results, respectively, for the feedback-based optimizations applied
to the blocked MM algorithm implemented on the TILE64 to provide comparison with
the corresponding results for the TILEPro64 (Tables 12.6 and 12.7). By using only compiler optimization flags, the better performance of the TILEPro64 over the TILE64 could
be attributed to slightly higher memory bandwidth of the TILEPro64 than the TILE64
(Section 12.2.4). The results for the TILE64 reveal that feedback-based optimizations can
improve the performance as compared to compiler optimization level -O3, which indicates
that there is room for improvement even after applying optimization level -O3. For example,
feedback-based optimizations provide 1.3× and 1.4× performance and performance per
watt improvements for $n = 1024$ and $n = 2048$, respectively, when $b = 64$ and $b' = 4$ for
the TILE64. These results indicate that the TILEPro64 can exploit compiler optimizations
better than the TILE64, which is why the TILEPro64 is able to attain performance close to
feedback-based optimizations only with the compiler optimization flags. Since a programmer
does not know in advance how much an architecture can exploit optimizations enabled by
compiler optimization flags, the programmer can leverage feedback-based optimizations,
when feasible, to provide further performance enhancements over the attainable performance
using only compiler optimization flags.

12.6.3 Parallel Performance Optimizations

Parallel performance optimizations are important to leverage the high computing density of
TMAs and require a parallel algorithm to be run on multiple tiles of a TMA. The parallel algorithm can either be a parallel version of a corresponding sequential algorithm or the parallel
algorithm can be designed from scratch considering a parallel architecture. Block size selection
for a parallel blocking algorithm is equally important as that for the serial blocking algorithm.
The block sizes selected from the single-tile optimization of a serial blocking algorithm may
be suitable for the parallel algorithm if the parallel blocking algorithm's design is such that
the decomposed algorithm running on a single tile is similar in structure to the corresponding
serial blocking algorithm. As with the optimizations on a single tile, compiler optimization
flags also help in attaining high performance from the parallel algorithm. Depending on the
data distribution, parallel algorithms that leverage TMA features, such as horizontal communication, can be useful for attaining high performance from the parallel algorithm. Additionally,
feedback-based optimizations are also beneficial in attaining parallel performance optimizations for TMAs. This section discusses these parallel performance optimizations focusing on
the TILEPro64.

12.6.3.1 Algorithmic Optimizations and Compiler Optimizations

We parallelize our blocked MM algorithm for the TILEPro64 to achieve performance enhancements via parallelization. Tables 12.10 and 12.11 depict the performance and performance per watt, respectively, of parallelized blocked MM algorithm running on four and 16 tiles, $p = 4$ and $p = 16$, respectively, for different block sizes b and sub-block sizes b' with and without compiler optimizations. The results reveal that compiler optimizations can greatly improve the performance and performance per watt of a parallelized blocked algorithm. For example, compiler optimization level -O3 yields 5.6× and 5.4× performance and performance per watt improvements when the blocked MM algorithm is executed on $p = 4$ and $p = 16$, respectively, when $n = 1024$, $b = 64$, and $b' = 4$. Similarly, compiler optimization level -O3 yields 5× and 4.8× performance and performance per watt improvements when the blocked MM algorithm is executed on $p = 4$ and $p = 16$, respectively, when $n = 2048$, $b = 64$, and $b' = 4$.

To quantify the parallel performance improvements, Table 12.12 also depicts the speedups attained by our parallelized blocked MM algorithm. We use the serial and parallel runtimes with compiler optimization level -O3 to calculate the speedups: $S^{(4)} = T_{O3}^{(1)}/T_{O3}^{(4)}$ and $S^{(16)} = T_{O3}^{(1)}/T_{O3}^{(16)}$ where $S^{(4)}$ and $S^{(16)}$ denote speedups for $p = 4$ and $p = 16$, respectively. The results reveal that the parallelized blocked MM algorithm attains ideal or close to ideal speedups for our selected block and sub-block sizes ($b = 64$ and $b' = 4$). The results also reveal that a poorly selected block and sub-block sizes can give results far from ideal. For example, using $b = 128$ and $b' = 8$ for $n = 1024$ gives $S^{(16)} = 7.8$, an efficiency of only 49%. We observe that the blocked MM algorithm can attain 8.4× and 8.2× better performance and performance per watt as compared to the non-blocked MM algorithm for $p = 4$ and $p = 16$, respectively, when $n = 1024$, $b = 64$, and $b' = 4$. Similarly, the performance and performance per watt improvements for the blocked MM algorithm over the non-blocked MM algorithm are 10.8× and 11.5× for $p = 4$ and $p = 16$, respectively, when $n = 2048$, $b = 64$, and $b' = 4$.

Results for the parallelized MM algorithm also verify that the attainable performance per watt for smaller data sizes is better than the attainable performance per watt for larger data sizes because smaller data sizes require fewer memory accesses as compared to larger data sizes. For example, the attainable performance per watt is 15% and 16% higher for $p = 4$ and $p = 16$, respectively, for $n = 1024$ as compared to that for $n = 2048$. We point out that ideal speedups may not be attainable with different kernels, such as comparison-based sorting and some real-world applications, because of frequent memory accesses, data sharing, load imbalance, and inherent overheads in parallelization, such as synchronization and data communication between tiles.

Table 12.12 also illustrates the impact of algorithmic choices on parallel performance and performance per watt by providing a comparison between parallelized blocked (B) and parallelized non-blocked (NB) MM algorithms. The results reveal that the parallelized blocked MM algorithm attains ideal or near-ideal speedups when block sizes are selected appropriately (e.g., ideal or near-ideal speedups are attained for $b = 64$ and $b' = 4$, whereas the attained speedups are far from ideal for inappropriate block sizes). Results indicate that with appropriate block size selection, the parallelized blocked MM algorithm provides better performance and performance per watt as compared to the non-blocked MM algorithm. For example, the parallelized blocked MM algorithm attains 743% and 717% better performance per watt than the parallelized non-blocked MM algorithm for $p = 4$ and $p = 16$, respectively, when $n = 1024$ ($b = 64$ and $b' = 4$ for the blocked MM algorithm).

Table 12.10 Performance of the parallelized blocked MM algorithm for a different number of tiles p for the TILEPro64 for different matrix sizes n, block sizes b, and sub-block sizes b'. $S^{(p)}$ denotes the speedup using p tiles

n	b	b'	$T_B^{(4)}$ (s)	$T_{B-O3}^{(4)}$ (s)	$S^{(4)}$	$T_B^{(16)}$ (s)	$T_{B-O3}^{(16)}$ (s)	$S^{(16)}$	$\mathrm{Perf}_B^{(4)}$ (MOPS)	$\mathrm{Perf}_{B-O3}^{(4)}$ (MOPS)	$\mathrm{Perf}_B^{(16)}$ (MOPS)	$\mathrm{Perf}_{B-O3}^{(16)}$ (MOPS)
1024	32	4	31.53	5.73	3.4	7.9	1.49	13.0	68.1	374.78	271.83	1441.26
	64	4	31.42	5.64	3.4	7.87	1.45	13.3	68.35	380.76	272.87	1481.02
	128	4	31.39	5.61	3.4	15.73	2.84	6.8	68.41	382.8	136.52	756.16
1024	32	8	26.94	4.88	4.0	6.75	1.25	15.4	79.7	440.06	318.14	1717.99
	64	8	26.86	4.82	4.0	6.73	1.22	15.8	79.95	445.54	319.09	1760.23
	128	8	26.85	4.79	4.0	13.48	2.46	7.8	79.98	448.33	159.31	872.96
1024	32	16	29.45	7.44	2.6	7.43	2.07	9.3	72.92	288.64	289.03	1037.4
	64	16	29.39	7.38	2.6	7.41	2.05	9.4	73.07	290.99	289.81	1047.55
	128	16	29.37	7.36	2.6	15.01	3.92	4.9	73.12	291.78	143.07	547.83
2048	32	4	258.72	52.65	4.0	64.82	13.8	15.6	66.4	326.3	265.04	1244.92
	64	4	257.59	51.84	4.0	64.56	13.49	16.0	66.69	331.4	266.11	1273.53
	128	4	257.93	52.05	4.0	64.73	13.6	15.8	66.61	330.06	265.41	1263.22
2048	32	8	287.14	107.33	2.0	72.7	30.57	7.0	59.83	160.06	236.31	561.98
	64	8	286.87	107.12	2.0	72.76	30.52	7.0	59.89	160.38	236.12	562.9
	128	8	286.88	107.13	2.0	72.8	30.53	7.0	59.88	160.36	235.99	562.72
2048	32	16	353.04	152.85	1.4	90.61	52.74	4.1	48.66	112.4	189.6	325.75
	64	16	352.47	150.57	1.4	90.4	51.57	4.2	48.74	114.1	190.04	333.14
	128	16	352.29	152.76	1.4	90.38	52.8	4.1	48.77	112.46	190.08	325.38

Table 12.11 Performance per watt of the parallelized blocked MM algorithm for a different number of tiles p for the TILEPro64 for different matrix sizes n, block sizes b, and sub-block sizes b'

n	b	b'	$\text{Perf}/\text{W}_{\text{B}}^{(4)}$ (MOPS/W)	$\text{Perf}/\text{W}_{\text{B-O3}}^{(4)}$ (MOPS/W)	$\text{Perf}/\text{W}_{\text{B}}^{(16)}$ (MOPS/W)	$\text{Perf}/\text{W}_{\text{B-O3}}^{(16)}$ (MOPS/W)
	32	4	10.57	58.2	25.29	134.07
1024	64	4	10.6	59.12	25.38	137.77
	128	4	10.62	59.44	12.7	70.34
	32	8	12.38	68.33	29.59	159.81
1024	64	8	12.41	69.18	29.68	163.74
	128	8	12.42	69.62	14.82	81.2
	32	16	11.32	44.82	26.89	96.5
1024	64	16	11.35	45.18	26.96	97.45
	128	16	11.35	45.3	13.31	50.96
	32	4	10.31	50.67	24.65	115.81
2048	64	4	10.36	51.46	24.75	118.47
	128	4	10.34	51.25	24.69	117.51
	32	8	9.29	24.85	21.98	52.28
2048	64	8	9.3	24.9	21.96	52.36
	128	8	9.3	24.9	21.95	52.35
	32	16	7.56	17.45	17.64	30.3
2048	64	16	7.57	17.72	17.68	30.99
	128	16	7.57	17.46	17.68	30.27

Table 12.12 Performance and performance per watt for a parallelized non-blocked (NB) and a parallelized blocked (B) MM algorithm for different number of tiles p for the TILEPro64 for different matrix sizes n. S_{B} denotes the speedup for the blocked MM algorithm

n	p	$T_{\text{NB-O3}}^{(p)}$ (s)	$T_{\text{B-O3}}^{(p)}$ (s)	S_{B}	$T_{\text{NB-O3}}^{(p)}/T_{\text{B-O3}}^{(p)}$	$\text{Perf}_{\text{NB-O3}}^{(p)}$ (MOPS)	$\text{Perf}/\text{W}_{\text{NB-O3}}^{(p)}$ (MOPS/W)	$\text{Perf}_{\text{B-O3}}^{(p)}$ (MOPS)	$\text{Perf}/\text{W}_{\text{B-O3}}^{(p)}$ (MOPS/W)
1024	4	47.55	5.64	4.0	8.4	45.16	7.01	380.76	59.12
1024	16	11.84	1.45	15.6	8.2	181.38	16.87	1481.02	137.77
2048	4	558.78	51.84	4.0	10.8	30.74	4.77	331.4	51.46
2048	16	154.64	13.49	16	11.5	111.1	10.33	1273.53	118.47

12.6.3.2 Horizontal Communication

Conventional interthread communication on shared memory can be inefficient due to the memory subsystem's limited bandwidth. Although all contemporary architectures provide vertical data communication (communication between different levels of the memory hierarchy), many TMAs (e.g., Tilera's TMAs) also support horizontal data communication (communication between different caches at the same level). Horizontal data communication provides efficient interthread communication by leveraging low on-chip communication latency and high on-chip bandwidth. To illustrate horizontal data communication for attaining high performance and performance per watt, we implement Cannon's MM algorithm [350] on the TILEPro64.

In Cannon's algorithm, only neighboring tiles communicate with each other using horizontal communication. Horizontal communication in Cannon's algorithm minimizes level two cache and main memory accesses, whereas communication with neighboring tiles minimizes the network contention [358]. We also use blocking with Cannon's algorithm so that the sub-matrix blocks fit in the caches. For Cannon's algorithm, we also experiment with separate temporary sub-matrices (D, E, F) to store the blocked sub-matrices to overlap communication and computation; however, we are able to attain similar performance without using temporary matrices because the memory footprint/size increases by using separate temporary matrices. Hence, we present results for Cannon's algorithm that does not use separate temporary sub-matrices.

Tables 12.13 and 12.14 depict the performance and performance per watt, respectively, of parallelized blocked Cannon's algorithm for MM running on $p = 4$ and $p = 16$ tiles for different block sizes b and b', with compiler optimization level -O3 and without compiler optimizations. The results reveal that Cannon's algorithm attains close to ideal speedups for appropriate block and sub-block sizes. We also observe superlinear speedup for $n = 2048$, $p = 4$, $b = 64$, and $b' = 4$. Superlinear speedups are achieved when a working set's data completely fits in the tiles' combined caches but was unable to fit in an individual tile's cache. The larger combined cache size, as well as the horizontal communication exploited by Cannon's algorithm, helps in attaining superlinear speedup for appropriate block and sub-block sizes. Results show that compiler optimizations can significantly enhance performance and performance per watt in addition to the horizontal communication leveraged in Cannon's algorithm. For example, compiler optimization level -O3 yields 5× and 4.8× improvements when Cannon's algorithm is executed on $p = 4$ and $p = 16$, respectively, when $n = 1024$, $b = 64$, and $b' = 4$. Similarly, compiler optimization level -O3 yields 4.5× and 4.2× improvements when the blocked Cannon's MM algorithm is executed on $p = 4$ and $p = 16$, respectively, when $n = 2048$, $b = 64$, and $b' = 4$.

Comparison of Tables 12.10 and 12.13 reveals that our parallelized blocked MM algorithm always attains equal or better performance than the parallelized blocked Cannon's algorithm on the TILEPro64 for our selected block and sub-block sizes $b = 64$ and $b' = 4$. One explanation for the blocked MM algorithm's better performance than Cannon's algorithm for optimal block and sub-block sizes could be that Cannon's algorithm stresses the on-chip network both for communication with external memory and for intertile communication, whereas the blocked MM algorithm uses the on-chip network only for communication with external memory.

12.6.3.3   Feedback-Based Optimizations

After observing that our parallelized blocked MM algorithm attains performance that is comparable to the blocked Cannon's algorithm, we investigate the impact of feedback-based optimizations on the performance of the parallelized blocked MM algorithm. Tables 12.15–12.17 depict the execution time, performance, and performance per watt, respectively, of our parallelized blocked MM algorithm with compiler optimization level -O3 and with feedback-based optimizations. Results reveal that feedback-based optimizations provide only a negligible performance improvement over compiler optimization level -O3

Table 12.13 Performance of a parallelized blocked Cannon's algorithm for MM for a different number of tiles p for the TILEPro64 for different matrix sizes n, block sizes b, and sub-block sizes b'

n	b	b'	$T_B^{(4)}$ (s)	$T_{B-O3}^{(4)}$ (s)	$S^{(4)}$	$T_B^{(16)}$ (s)	$T_{B-O3}^{(16)}$ (s)	$S^{(16)}$	$Perf_B^{(4)}$ (MOPS)	$Perf_{B-O3}^{(4)}$ (MOPS)	$Perf_B^{(16)}$ (MOPS)	$Perf_{B-O3}^{(16)}$ (MOPS)
1024	32	4	28.82	5.79	3.3	7.25	1.52	12.7	74.51	370.9	296.2	1412.8
	64	4	28.73	5.68	3.3	7.22	1.5	12.9	74.75	378.1	297.43	1431.6
	128	4	28.7	5.65	3.3	7.24	1.49	13.0	74.82	380.1	296.61	1441.3
1024	32	8	24.28	5	3.9	6.13	1.3	14.8	88.45	429.5	350.32	1651.91
	64	8	24.18	4.89	3.9	6.1	1.28	15.1	88.81	439.16	352.05	1677.72
	128	8	24.15	4.84	4.0	6.1	1.26	15.3	88.92	443.7	352.05	1704.35
1024	32	16	26.89	7.48	2.6	7.14	2.28	8.5	79.86	287.1	300.77	941.88
	64	16	27.03	7.47	2.6	7.1	2.26	8.5	79.45	287.48	302.46	950.21
	128	16	26.9	7.5	2.6	7	2.23	8.6	79.83	286.33	306.78	963.0
2048	32	4	238.64	52.79	4.0	60.33	14.36	15.0	72.0	325.44	284.76	1196.37
	64	4	236.42	52.1	4.1	60.1	14.11	15.3	72.67	329.75	285.85	1217.57
	128	4	237.09	53	4.0	60.04	14.55	14.8	72.46	324.15	286.14	1180.75
2048	32	8	264.62	106.98	2.0	70.23	30.83	7.0	64.92	160.59	244.62	557.24
	64	8	265.77	107.12	2.0	69.68	31.93	6.7	64.64	160.38	246.55	538.05
	128	8	266.05	107.84	2.0	69.87	32.27	6.7	64.57	159.31	245.88	532.38
2048	32	16	331.5	150.82	1.4	86.32	51.89	4.1	51.82	113.91	199.02	331.08
	64	16	331.04	150.82	1.4	86.06	52.15	4.1	51.9	113.91	199.63	329.43
	128	16	331.29	151.03	1.4	85.87	52.33	4.1	51.86	113.75	200.07	328.3

Table 12.14 Performance per watt of a parallelized blocked Cannon's algorithm for MM for a different number of tiles p for the TILEPro64 for different matrix sizes n, block sizes b, and sub-block sizes b'

n	b	b'	$\mathrm{Perf}/W_B^{(4)}$ (MOPS/W)	$\mathrm{Perf}/W_{B-O3}^{(4)}$ (MOPS/W)	$\mathrm{Perf}/W_B^{(16)}$ (MOPS/W)	$\mathrm{Perf}/W_{B-O3}^{(16)}$ (MOPS/W)
	32	4	11.57	57.59	27.55	131.42
1024	64	4	11.61	58.71	27.67	133.17
	128	4	11.62	59.02	27.59	134.07
	32	8	13.73	66.69	32.59	153.67
1024	64	8	13.79	68.19	32.75	156.1
	128	8	13.81	68.9	32.75	158.54
	32	16	12.4	44.58	27.98	87.62
1024	64	16	12.34	44.65	28.14	88.39
	128	16	12.4	44.46	28.54	89.58
	32	4	11.18	50.53	26.49	111.29
2048	64	4	11.28	51.2	26.59	113.26
	128	4	11.25	50.33	26.62	109.84
	32	8	10.08	24.94	22.76	51.84
2048	64	8	10.04	24.9	22.93	50.05
	128	8	10.03	24.74	22.87	49.52
	32	16	8.05	17.69	18.51	30.8
2048	64	16	8.06	17.69	18.57	30.64
	128	16	8.05	17.66	18.61	30.54

Table 12.15 Execution time of the parallelized blocked MM algorithm for a different number of tiles p for the TILEPro64 for different matrix sizes n

n	b	b'	$T_B^{(4)}$ (s)	$T_{B-O3}^{(4)}$ (s)	$T_{B-FBO}^{(4)}$ (s)	$T_B^{(16)}$ (s)	$T_{B-O3}^{(16)}$ (s)	$T_{B-FBO}^{(16)}$ (s)
1024	64	4	31.42	5.64	5.62	7.87	1.45	1.44
2048	64	4	257.59	51.84	50.73	64.56	13.49	13.23

Table 12.16 Performance of the parallelized blocked MM algorithm for a different number of tiles p for the TILEPro64 for different matrix sizes n

n	b	b'	$\mathrm{Perf}_B^{(4)}$ (MOPS)	$\mathrm{Perf}_{B-O3}^{(4)}$ (MOPS)	$\mathrm{Perf}_B^{(16)}$ (MOPS)	$\mathrm{Perf}_{B-O3}^{(16)}$ (MOPS)	$\mathrm{Perf}_{B-FBO}^{(4)}$ (MOPS)	$\mathrm{Perf}_{B-FBO}^{(16)}$ (MOPS)
1024	64	4	68.35	380.76	272.87	1481.02	382.11	1491.31
2048	64	4	66.69	331.4	266.11	1273.53	338.65	1298.55

Table 12.17 Performance per watt of the parallelized blocked MM algorithm for a different number of tiles p for the TILEPro64 for different matrix sizes n

n	b	b'	$\mathrm{Perf}/\mathrm{W}_{\mathrm{B}}^{(4)}$ (MOPS/W)	$\mathrm{Perf}/\mathrm{W}_{\mathrm{B-O3}}^{(4)}$ (MOPS/W)	$\mathrm{Perf}/\mathrm{W}_{\mathrm{B}}^{(16)}$ (MOPS/W)	$\mathrm{Perf}/\mathrm{W}_{\mathrm{B-O3}}^{(16)}$ (MOPS/W)	$\mathrm{Perf}/\mathrm{W}_{\mathrm{B-FBO}}^{(4)}$ (MOPS/W)	$\mathrm{Perf}/\mathrm{W}_{\mathrm{FBO}}^{(16)}$ (MOPS/W)
1024	64	4	10.61	59.12	25.38	137.77	59.33	138.73
2048	64	4	10.36	51.46	24.75	118.47	52.58	120.8

for the TILEPro64, which corroborates our findings for a single tile of the TILEPro64. These results indicate that compiler optimization level -O3 provides close to peak attainable performance for the TILEPro64 when proper load balancing and cache blocking is used.

12.6.3.4 Peak Attained Parallel Performance

Leveraging our algorithmic and compiler optimizations, we are able to attain peak performance of 7.2 GOPS for the MM algorithm running on $p = 57$ tiles of the TILEPro64. We also quantify the peak attainable performance for FP benchmarks on the TILEPro64. For FP performance benchmarking, we use an embarrassingly parallel benchmark that generated normally distributed random variates based on Box–Muller's algorithm. We are able to attain 618.4 MFLOPS for the embarrassingly parallel benchmark running on 57 tiles of the TILEPro64. We observe that the TILEPro64 delivers higher performance for benchmarks with integer operations as compared to the benchmarks with FP operations. For example, we were able to attain 11.6× better performance for integer benchmarks as compared to FP benchmarks while running the benchmarks on 57 tiles. The better performance and performance per watt for integer operations on the TILEPro64 are because Tilera's TMAs do not contain dedicated FP units. We point out that benchmarks could not be run on more than 57 tiles of the TILEPro64 as remaining tiles are reserved by the TILEPro64 for other purposes [21].

12.7 Chapter Summary

This work provides an overview of TMAs and discusses contemporary TMA chips, including Intel's TeraFLOPS research chip, IBM's C64, and Tilera's TILEPro64. Research on TMAs indicates that the TeraFLOPS research chip is suitable for kernel studies, whereas IBM's C64 and Tilera's TILEPro64 can run full-scale applications. Our work focuses on Tilera's TILEPro64 for demonstrating performance optimizations on TMAs. We highlight platform considerations for parallel performance optimizations, such as chip locality, cache locality, tile locality, TLB locality, and memory balancing. We elaborate on compiler-based optimizations for attaining high performance, such as function inlining, alias analysis, loop unrolling, loop-nest optimizations, software pipelining, and feedback-based optimizations.

To demonstrate high-performance optimizations on TMAs, we optimize dense matrix multiplication (MM) on Tilera's TILEPro64. Results verify that an algorithm must consider the underlying architectural features, such as the cache sizes, in order to maximize the performance attained from TMAs. For example, our blocked MM algorithm, which exploits cache blocking, provides 6× and 10× performance and performance per watt improvements over a non-blocked MM algorithm for $n = 1024$ and $n = 2048$, respectively (n denotes the matrix size). Results reveal that the performance advantage of blocking increases as the data size increases. Experiments verify that the best blocking granularity for an algorithm is determined by experiments, whereas calculations can only specify an upper bound for block sizes in most cases. We parallelize our blocked MM algorithm on multiple tiles to enhance performance by exploiting TLP. We are able to attain linear speedups using parallelization and proper load balancing on Tilera's TMAs. Experiments reveal that appropriate use of the cache subsystem (e.g., by blocking) also significantly improves attainable performance and performance per watt gains from parallelism. For example, the blocked MM algorithm attains 743% and 717% better performance per watt than the non-blocked MM algorithm for $p = 4$ and $p = 16$, respectively, when $n = 1024$ (p denotes number of tiles).

Experiments indicate that blocking and parallelization alone are not sufficient to achieve maximum attainable performance from TMAs, and compiler-based optimizations can provide tremendous enhancements in attainable performance and performance per watt. Results show that compiler optimization level -O3 yields 5.6× and 5.4× performance and performance per watt improvements when the blocked MM algorithm is executed on $p = 4$ and $p = 16$, respectively. Furthermore, as with traditional processors, appropriate use of compiler directives can enhance attainable performance from TMAs. For example, compiler optimization directives with optimization level -O2 can increase the performance by 1.8× (77%) as compared to not using any compiler directives for Tilera's TILEPro64. Experiments on the TILE64 and TILEPro64 suggest that advanced compiler optimization techniques, such as feedback-based optimizations, can improve performance on some TMAs, but cannot contribute much to the performance enhancements on other TMAs. For example, feedback-based optimizations provide 1.3× and 1.4× performance and performance per watt improvements for $n = 1024$ and $n = 2048$, respectively, for the TILE64, whereas negligible performance improvements are observed for the TILEPro64.

Results demonstrate that an algorithm exploiting horizontal communication, such as Cannon's algorithm, provides an effective means of attaining high performance on TMAs. However, our results reveal that our parallelized blocked MM algorithm, which is much simpler than Cannon's algorithm, is able to obtain comparable performance as that of Cannon's algorithm. Results suggest that optimized code that takes advantage of the memory hierarchy sizes via blocking can attain comparable performance to the algorithms that exploit horizontal communication on TMAs.

Leveraging our algorithmic and compiler optimizations, we are able to attain peak performance of 7.2 GOPS for the MM algorithm running on 57 tiles of the TILEPro64. We are able to attain 618.4 MFLOPS for an embarrassingly parallel FP benchmark running on 57 tiles of the TILEPro64.

Our programming experience with TMAs suggests that TMAs can deliver scalable performance per watt for applications with sufficient TLP. These application domains include, but are not limited to, networking, security, video processing, and wireless networks. In networking applications, packets of different flows have little or no dependencies among them, and thus enable exploitation of TLP to the fullest extent. An example of a security application exploiting available TLP effectively could be encryption of different data blocks in parallel on different tiles. Similarly, in image processing applications, different blocks of pixels can be operated in parallel on different tiles. TMAs in base stations for wireless networks can handle processing for different users on different tiles exploiting inherent TLP in the application. For all these application domains, the working set can be chosen to fit in the TMA's tiles' caches based on appropriate cache blocking. As demonstrated in our experiments, different compiler optimization flags as well as compiler directives (`pragmas`) can enhance the attainable performance and performance per watt for these applications. Furthermore, feedback-based optimizations, where feasible, can further enhance the attainable performance and performance per watt for these applications.

Research and programming experience with TMAs suggest some hardware/software optimizations. Research suggests that a portion of on-chip transistors should be used for on-die memory to provide sustainable high performance. Programming experience suggests that application programmers input need to be considered in the design of manycore chips as small easier to incorporate changes in the instruction set can potentially have a large impact on the chip programmability. For example, incorporation of `jump` instruction in Intel's TeraFLOPS research chip could have allowed addition of nested loops [368]. Research on TMAs reveals the scalability advantages of message passing architectures that allow data sharing through explicit messages rather than through a shared address space, which enables easy avoidance of race conditions. However, since software development with message passing alone can be complex, a TMA supporting both shared memory and message passing programming paradigm can benefit large-scale applications development. This hybrid messaging passing-shared memory programming paradigm would enable programmers to take advantage of the two programming paradigms' features depending on the application structure and decomposition.

13

Conclusions

In this book, we presented novel methods for modeling and optimization of parallel and distributed embedded systems. We illustrated our modeling and optimization of distributed embedded systems using our research and experimental evaluation, which focused on distributed embedded wireless sensor networks (EWSNs). Specifically, we developed and tested our dynamic optimization methodologies on an embedded senor node's tunable parameter value settings for EWSNs and modeled application metrics, such as lifetime and reliability. We demonstrated our modeling and optimization methods for parallel embedded systems using our research on multicore-based parallel embedded systems.

Chapter 1 introduced the modeling and optimization of embedded systems and further discussed various diverse embedded system application domains including cyber-physical systems (CPSs), space, medical, and automotive. The chapter presented an overview of modeling, modeling objectives, and various modeling paradigms.

Chapter 2 presented our proposed architecture for heterogeneous hierarchical multicore embedded wireless sensor networks (MCEWSNs). The increased computation power afforded by multicore embedded sensor nodes benefits a myriad of compute-intensive tasks, such as information fusion, encryption, network coding, and software-defined radio, which are prevalent in many application domains. MCEWSNs are especially beneficial for wireless sensor networking application domains, such as wireless video sensor networks, wireless multimedia sensor networks, satellite-based sensor networks, space shuttle sensor networks, aerial–terrestrial hybrid sensor networks, and fault-tolerant sensor networks. Both academia and industry have recognized the MCEWSN's potential benefits and have undertaken several initiatives to develop multicore embedded sensor nodes, such as InstraNode, satellite-based sensor node, and smart camera mote. The chapter elaborated on these endeavors.

Chapter 3 proposed an application metric estimation model to estimate high-level metrics, such as lifetime, throughput, and reliability from an embedded sensor node's parameters. This estimation model's main purpose is to assist dynamic optimization methodologies in comparing different operating states. Our application metric estimation model provided a prototype model for application metric estimation, which can be easily extended to other application metrics.

Chapter 4 provided a comprehensive research on modeling and analysis of fault detection and tolerance in EWSNs. To elucidate fault detection in EWSNs, we presented a taxonomy for fault diagnosis in EWSNs. Using ns−2, we simulated several prominent fault detection algorithms to evaluate the algorithms' accuracies and false alarm rates. We developed comprehensive Markov models that hierarchically encompassed the individual sensor nodes, WSN clusters, and the overall WSN. Our models characterized WSN reliability and mean time to failure (MTTF) for different sensor failure probabilities, and can assist WSN designers in achieving closer application requirement adherence by evaluating the reliability and MTTF in the pre-deployment phase.

Chapter 5 detailed our development of closed product-form queueing network models for performance evaluation of multicore embedded architectures for different workload characteristics. The performance evaluation results indicated that shared last-level cache (LLC) architectures provide better cache response times and MFLOPS/W as compared to private LLC architectures, regardless of the specific cache miss rate, especially as the number of cores increases. The results also revealed that shared LLCs have some disadvantages, such as being more susceptible to causing main memory response time bottlenecks for large cache miss rates as compared to the private LLCs. However, results indicated that these bottlenecks can be mitigated using a hybrid combination of private and shared LLCs (i.e., sharing LLCs by only a subset of cores, rather than all cores). The trade-offs for this hybrid LLC architecture is increased power consumption as compared to shared LLCs, and comparatively less MFLOPS/W. The performance per watt and performance per unit area results for the multicore embedded architectures revealed that shared LLC multicore architectures become more area and power efficient as compared to private LLC architectures as the number of cores increases.

Chapter 6 explored optimization strategies for distributed EWSNs at various design levels to meet disparate application requirements. To aid in easy design incorporation, we discussed commercial off-the-shelf (COTS) embedded sensor node components and the components' associated tunable parameter value settings that can be specialized to provide component-level optimizations. We explored data link-level and network-level optimization strategies focusing on medium access control (MAC) and routing protocols, respectively. The MAC protocols presented targeted load balancing, throughput, and energy optimizations, and the routing protocols focused on query dissemination, real-time data delivery, and network topology. We illustrated sensor node operating system (OS)-level optimizations, such as power management and fault tolerance, using state-of-the-art sensor node OSs. Finally, we described dynamic optimizations, such as dynamic voltage and frequency scaling (DVFS) and dynamic network reprogramming.

Chapter 7 gave a holistic survey of high-performance energy-efficient parallel embedded computing (HPEPEC) techniques that enable meeting diverse embedded application requirements. We presented novel architectural approaches for core layout (e.g., heterogeneous chip multiprocessors (CMPs), tiled multicore architectures (TMAs), 3D multicore architectures), memory design (e.g., cache partitioning, cooperative caching), interconnection networks (e.g., 2D mesh, hypercube), and reduction techniques (e.g., leakage current reduction, peak power reduction), which enhance performance and reduce energy consumption in parallel embedded systems. We discussed hardware-assisted middleware techniques, such as DVFS, advanced configuration and power interface (ACPI), threading techniques (hyper-threading, helper threading, and speculative threading), dynamic thermal management (DTM), and various low-power gating techniques for performance and energy optimizations of parallel embedded systems. We also considered software approaches, such as task scheduling, task migration, and load balancing, to improve the attainable parallel performance and power efficiency. Finally, we discussed some prominent multicore-based parallel processors, emphasized these processors' HPEPEC features, and concluded with HPEPEC research challenges and future research directions.

Chapter 8 focused on our proposed EWSN-based application-oriented dynamic optimization methodology using Markov decision processes (MDPs). Our MDP-based optimal policy tuned sensor node processor voltage, frequency, and sensing frequency in accordance with application requirements during a sensor node's lifetime. Our methodology was highly adaptive to changing application requirements and determined a new MDP-based policy whenever these requirements changed, which may also reflect changing environmental stimuli. We compared our MDP-based policy with four fixed-heuristic policies and concluded that our proposed MDP-based policy outperformed each heuristic policy for all sensor node lifetimes, state transition costs, and application metric weight factors. We also provided implementation guidelines to assist embedded system designer in designing and architecting appropriate sensor nodes given application requirements.

Although our MDP-based methodology presented in Chapter 8 provided a sound foundation for high-quality sensor node parameter tuning with respect to diverse application requirements, this methodology was only a first step toward holistic EWSN dynamic optimization. Since our initially proposed MDP-based methodology required high computational and memory resources for large design spaces and necessitated a high-performance base station/sink node to compute the optimal operating state for large design spaces, much research was left to architect a less computational complex methodology. The original methodology had to determine operating states at the base station, and then these states were communicated to the other sensor nodes. Given the constrained resources of individual sensor nodes, these high resource requirements made the MDP-based methodology infeasible for autonomous dynamic optimization of large design spaces and individual nodes.

Chapter 9 extended this initial work on sensor node parameter tuning discussed in Chapter 8 and proposed lightweight online greedy and simulated annealing algorithms that are suitable for dynamic optimizations of distributed, resource-constrained EWSNs. As compared to prior work, our refined methodology considered an extensive embedded sensor node design space, which allowed embedded sensor nodes to more closely adhere to diverse application requirements. Our experimental results revealed that our online algorithms were lightweight; required little computational, memory, and energy resources; and thus are amenable to sensor nodes with highly constrained resources and energy budgets. Furthermore, our online algorithms could perform in situ parameter tuning to adapt to changing environmental stimuli to meet application requirements.

Chapter 10 proposed an EWSN's lightweight dynamic optimization methodology that provided high-quality solutions in one-shot using intelligent initial tunable parameter value settings for highly constrained application domains. To improve on the one-shot solution for less constrained application domains, we proposed an additional online greedy optimization algorithm that leveraged intelligent design space exploration techniques to iteratively improve on the one-shot solution. Results showed the near-optimality of our one-shot solution, which was within 8% of the optimal solution on average. Results indicated that our greedy algorithm converged to the optimal or near-optimal solution after exploring only 1% and 0.04% of the design space, whereas SA explored 55% and 1.3% of the design space for design space cardinalities of 729 and 31,104, respectively. Data memory and execution time analysis revealed that one-shot solution required 361% and 85% less data memory and execution time, respectively, as compared to using all the three steps required by our dynamic optimization methodology. Furthermore, the one-shot methodology consumed 1679% and 166,510% less energy as compared to an exhaustive search for $|S| = 729$ and $|S| = 31,104$, respectively. The improvement mode using a greedy online algorithm consumed 926% and 83,135% less energy as compared to the exhaustive search for $|S| = 729$ and $|S| = 31,104$, respectively. Computational complexity analysis coupled with the execution time, data memory analysis, and energy consumption confirmed that our methodology was in fact lightweight and thus feasible for limited-resource sensor nodes.

Chapter 11 compared the performance of symmetric multiprocessors (SMPs) and TMAs with respect to a parallelized information fusion application, Gaussian elimination (GE), and embarrassingly parallel (EP) benchmarks. We provided a quantitative comparison of these architectures using various device metric calculations, including computational density (CD), computational density per watt (CD/W), internal memory bandwidth (IMB), and external memory bandwidth (EMB). Although a quantitative comparison provides a high-level evaluation of the architectures' computational capabilities, our evaluations provided deeper insights considering parallelized benchmark-driven evaluation. Our results revealed that the SMPs outperform the TMAs in terms of overall execution time; however, TMAs can deliver comparable or better performance per watt. Specifically, our results indicated that the TILEPro64 exhibited better scalability and attained better performance per watt as compared to SMPs for applications consisting of integer operations and those that operate primarily on private data with little communication between operating cores by exploiting the data locality, such as information fusion application. The SMPs depicted better scalability and performance for benchmarks that required extensive inter-core communication and synchronization operations, such as the GE benchmark. Results from the EP benchmark revealed that the SMPs provided higher peak floating point performance per watt as compared to the TMAs primarily because the TMAs we studied did not contain dedicated floating-point unit.

Chapter 12 provided an overview of TMAs and evaluated several contemporary TMA chips, such as Intel's TeraFLOPS research chip, IBM's C64, and Tilera's TILEPro64. Our analysis focused on Tilera's TILEPro64 to demonstrate TMA performance optimizations. We highlighted platform considerations for parallel performance optimizations, such as chip locality, cache locality, tile locality, translation look-aside buffer locality, and memory balancing. We also investigated compiler-based optimizations for attaining high performance, such as function inlining, alias analysis, loop unrolling, loop nest optimizations, software pipelining, and feedback-based optimizations.

To demonstrate the TMAs high-performance optimization capabilities, we optimized a dense matrix multiplication (MM) application for Tilera's TILEPro64, and results indicated that blocking and parallelization alone are not sufficient to achieve maximum TMA performance. Compiler-based optimizations were required to provide tremendous enhancements in attainable performance and performance per watt. Results demonstrated that an algorithm exploiting horizontal communication, such as Cannon's algorithm, provided an effective means of attaining high performance on TMAs.

Future Research Directions: System optimizations have always played a key role in meeting design goals, such as reducing the system's power/energy consumption. Given the relative simplicity of past systems (e.g., single core, few tunable parameters, small design spaces), determining the best parameter configuration was reasonably accomplished via directly evaluating different configurations during runtime and selecting the configuration that most closely adhered to the desired design goals. However, increasing system complexity (e.g., manycore systems result in explosively large design spaces) makes this direct evaluation infeasible, even with highly efficient design space exploration heuristics. This complexity, coupled with the fact that much prior work has shown that maximum design goal adherence requires per-application and/or per-application execution phase parameter turning, necessitates ultra-fast configuration selection/determination mechanisms in order to successfully integrate optimization into future systems.

In order to enable future optimizations in highly complex system with a myriad of tunable parameters and parameter values, and considering massively manycore systems (e.g., hundreds to thousands of cores), physical design space exploration must be replaced with fast, analytical, predictive mechanisms. In this book, we have presented several methods that intend to bridge the complexity gap between modern and future systems, providing high-level modeling and predictive optimization methods. However, these methods are only a small step toward sustaining optimizations in future massively complex systems, and there is an urgent need to progress the optimization methods, underlying evaluation frameworks and modeling techniques in order to sustain the progression of system complexity. We summarize some of these challenges as follows:

- Since the cache hierarchy is a key system resource with large impacts on power/energy consumption, performance, and chip area, large optimization impacts are possible via cache hierarchy specialization for specific application/phase requirements. Even though there is a large number of cache simulators and evaluation frameworks, each offering different coverage, accuracy, and simulation speed, a specially designed, accurate, fast cache simulator for an arbitrary cache hierarchy for a system with an arbitrary number of cores and intercore communication is still needed.
- In the massively manycore era, accurately capturing intercore communication, dependencies, interactions, synchronizations will play an enormous role in cross-core system optimizations. The main challenge will be in capturing the dynamic and timing-dependent behavior for simulations of out-of-order processors and multithreaded/multicore architectures.
- Given the vast number of tunable parameters, it will be important to clearly delineate independent and dependent parameters, since independent parameters can be explored in isolation, whereas dependent parameters must be explored together, which vastly increase the design space. In order to minimize the design space, it will be necessary to decouple this parameter interference and clearly categorize independent and dependent parameters. Furthermore, even for dependent parameters, the level of dependence must be quantified with respect to the desired design constraints, such that even if parameters are dependent, and if those parameters have a small affect on the design constraints, those parameters can be classified as independent to reduce the design space and tuning complexity.
- Runtime parameter tuning is essential for future systems since runtime tuning can dynamically react to changing execution patterns, application requirements, application phases, and so on. Existing runtime tuning and phase change detection techniques introduce hardware overhead, can be intrusive to normal system execution, and are not geared toward massively complex, manycore systems. Reducing the impact of parameter tuning and phase change detection on energy consumption is critical.

References

[1] Marwedel, P. (2010) Embedded and Cyber-Physical Systems in a Nutshell, in *Design Automation Conference (DAC) Knowledge Center Article*. http://www.dac.com/front_end+topics.aspx? article=58&topic=1.

[2] Edwards, S., Lavagno, L., Lee, E., and Sangiovanni-Vincentelli, A. (1997) Design of Embedded Systems: Formal Models, Validation, and Synthesis. *Proceedings of the IEEE*, **85** (3), 366–390.

[3] Wolf, M. (2014) *High-Performance Embedded Computing: Applications in Cyber-Physical Systems and Mobile Computing*, Elsevier Morgan Kaufmann.

[4] Wang, S. and Riccardo, B. (2001) Reactive Speed Control in Temperature-Constrained Real-Time Systems, in *Proceedings of Euromicro Conference on Real-Time Systems*, Yokohama, Japan, pp. 239–244.

[5] Dally, W., Balfour, J., Black-Shaffer, D., Chen, J., Harting, R., Parikh, V., Park, J., and Sheffield, D. (2008) Efficient Embedded Computing. *IEEE Computer*, **41** (7), 27–32.

[6] Balfour, J. (2010) Efficient Embedded Computing. *Ph.D. Thesis*, EE Department, Stanford University.

[7] Gepner, P., Fraser, D., Kowalik, M., and Tylman, R. (2009) New Multi-Core Intel Xeon Processors Help Design Energy Efficient Solution for High Performance Computing, in *Proceedings of IMCSIT*, Mragowo, Poland.

[8] Crowley, P., Franklin, M., Buhler, J., and Chamberlain, R. (2006) Impact of CMP Design on High-Performance Embedded Computing, in *Proceedings of HPEC Workshop*, Lexington, Massachusetts.

[9] Lee, E. (2006) Cyber-Physical Systems—Are Computing Foundations Adequate? in *NSF Workshop on Cyber-Physical Systems: Research Motivations, Techniques and Roadmap (Position Paper)*, Austin, Texas.

[10] Starr, G., Wersinger, J., Chapman, R., Riggs, L., Nelson, V., Klingelhoeffer, J., and Stroud, C. (2009) Application of Embedded Systems in Low Earth Orbit for Measurement of Ionospheric Anomalies, in *Proceedings of International Conference on Embedded Systems & Applications (ESA'09)*, Las Vegas, Nevada.

[11] Samson, J., Ramos, J., George, A., Patel, M., and Some, R. (2006) Technology Validation: NMP ST8 Dependable Multiprocessor Project, in *Proceedings of IEEE Aerospace Conference*, Big Sky, Montana.

[12] Intel (2010) Advantech Puts Intel Architecture at the Heart of LiDCO's Advanced Cardiovascular Monitoring System, in *White Paper*. http://download.intel.com/design/embedded/medical/323210 .pdf.

Modeling and Optimization of Parallel and Distributed Embedded Systems, First Edition.
Arslan Munir, Ann Gordon-Ross and Sanjay Ranka.
© 2016 John Wiley & Sons, Ltd. Published 2016 by John Wiley & Sons, Ltd.

[13] Reunert, M. (2007) High Performance Embedded Systems for Medical Imaging, in *Intel's White Paper*. ftp://download.intel.com/design/embedded/medical-solutions/basoct07p9.pdf.

[14] Intel (2011) Intel Technology Helps Medical Specialists More Quickly Reach—and Treat—Patients in Remote Areas, in *White Paper*. http://download.intel.com/embedded/applications/medical/325447.pdf.

[15] Muller-Glaser, K., Frick, G., Sax, E., and Kuhl, M. (2004) Multiparadigm Modeling in Embedded Systems Design. *IEEE Transactions on Control Systems Technology*, **12** (2), 279–292.

[16] Sangiovanni-Vincentelli, A. and Natale, M. (2007) Embedded System Design for Automotive Applications. *IEEE Computer*, **40** (10), 42–51.

[17] Milojicic, D. (2000) Trend Wars: Embedded Systems. *IEEE Concurrency*, **8** (4), 80–90.

[18] Kornaros, G. (2010) *Multi-Core Embedded Systems*, Taylor and Francis Group, CRC Press.

[19] Gonzales, C. and Wang, H. (2011) White Paper: Thermal Design Considerations for Embedded Applications. http://download.intel.com/design/intarch/papers/321055.pdf.

[20] Knight, J.C. (2002) *Software Challenges in Aviation Systems*, Springer-Verlag, Berlin/Heidelberg.

[21] TILERA (2009) Tilera Multicore Development Environment: iLib API Reference Manual, in *Tilera Official Documentation*.

[22] Young, W., Boebert, W., and Kain, R. (1985) Proving a Computer System Secure. *Scientific Honeyweller*, **6** (2), 18–27.

[23] Munir, A. and Gordon-Ross, A. (2012) An MDP-based Dynamic Optimization Methodology for Wireless Sensor Networks. *IEEE Transactions on Parallel and Distributed Systems (TPDS)*, **23** (4), 616–625.

[24] Zhao, J. and Govindan, R. (2003) Understanding Packet Delivery Performance in Dense Wireless Sensor Networks, in *Proceedings of ACM SenSys*, Los Angeles, California.

[25] Myers, C. (2011) Modeling and Verification of Cyber-Physical Systems, in *Design Automation Summer School*, University of Utah. http://www.lems.brown.edu/~iris/dass11/Myers-DASS.pdf.

[26] OMG (2011) Unified Modeling Language, in *Object Management Group Standard*. http://www.uml.org/.

[27] Xie, Y. and Hung, W.L. (2006) Temperature-Aware Task Allocation and Scheduling for Embedded Multiprocessor Systems-on-Chip (MPSoC) Design. *Journal of VLSI Signal Processing Systems*, **45** (3), 177–189.

[28] Murali, S., Mutapcic, A., Atienza, D., Gupta, R., Boyd, S., and De Micheli, G. (2007) Temperature-Aware Processor Frequency Assignment for MPSoCs Using Convex Optimization, in *Proceedings of IEEE/ACM International Conference on Hardware/Software Codesign and System Synthesis (CODES+ISSS)*, Salzburg, Austria, pp. 111–116.

[29] Ebi, T., Kramer, D., Karl, W., and Henkel, J. (2011) Economic Learning for Thermal-Aware Power Budgeting in Many-Core Architectures, in *Proceedings of IEEE/ACM International Conference on Hardware/Software Codesign and System Synthesis (CODES+ISSS)*, Taipei, Taiwan, pp. 189–196.

[30] Jian-Jia, C., Shengquan, W., and Lothar, T. (2009) Proactive Speed Scheduling for Real-Time Tasks Under Thermal Constraints, in *Proceedings of IEEE Real-Time and Embedded Technology and Applications Symposium (RTAS)*, San Francisco, California, pp. 141–150.

[31] Wang, S. and Bettati, R. (2008) Reactive Speed Control in Temperature-Constrained Real-Time Systems. *Real-Time Systems*, **39** (1-3), 73–95.

[32] Vahid, F. and Givargis, T. (2002) *Embedded System Design: A Unified Hardware/Software Introduction*, John Wiley and Sons, Inc.

[33] Akyildiz, I.F., Melodia, T., and Chowdhury, K.R. (2008) Wireless Multimedia Sensor Networks: Applications and Testbeds. *Proceedings of the IEEE*, **96** (10), 1588–1605.

[34] Akyildiz, I.F., Su, W., Sankarasubramaniam, Y., and Cayirci, E. (2002) Wireless Sensor Networks: A Survey. *Elsevier Computer Networks*, **38** (4), 393–422.

[35] Liu, Y. and Das, S.K. (2006) Information-Intensive Wireless Sensor Networks: Potential and Challenges. *IEEE Communications Magazine*, **44** (11), 142–147.

[36] Rockwell (2011) Rockwell Automation. www.rockwellautomation.com.

[37] Kwok, T.T.O. and Kwok, Y.K. (2006) Computation and Energy Efficient Image Processing in Wireless Sensor Networks Based on Reconfigurable Computing, in *Proceedings of the International Conference on Parallel Processing Workshops (ICPPW)*, Columbus, Ohio.

[38] Kleihorst, R., Schueler, B., Danilin, A., and Heijligers, M. (2006) Smart Camera Mote with High Performance Vision System, in *Proceedings of the Workshop on Distributed Smart Cameras (DSC)*, Boulder, Colorado.

[39] Dogan, A.Y., Atienza, D., Burg, A., Loi, I., and Benini, L. (2011) Power/Performance Exploration of Single-Core and Multi-core Processor Approaches for Biomedical Signal Processing, in *Proceedings of the Workshop on Power and Timing Modeling, Optimization and Simulation (PATMOS)*, Madrid, Spain.

[40] Rajagopalan, R. and Varshney, P. (2006) Data-Aggregation Techniques in Sensor Networks: A Survey. *IEEE Communications Surveys & Tutorials*, **8** (4), 48–63.

[41] Kulkarni, R., Forster, A., and Venayagamoorthy, G. (2011) Computational Intelligence in Wireless Sensor Networks: A Survey. *IEEE Communications Surveys & Tutorials*, **13** (1), 68–96.

[42] Kak, A. (2011) Parallel Histogram-based Particle Filter for Object Tracking on SIMD-based Smart Cameras, in *Purdue Robot Vision Lab*, Purdue University, West Lafayette, Indiana. https://engineering.purdue.edu/RVL/Research/SIMD_PF/index.html.

[43] MEMSIC (2011) Imote2 Hardware Bundle for Wireless Sensor Networks. www.memsic.com.

[44] Munir, A. and Gordon-Ross, A. (2010) Optimization approaches in wireless sensor networks, in *Sustainable Wireless Sensor Networks* (eds W. Seah and Y.K. Tan), InTech. http://www.intechopen.com/articles/show/title/optimization-approaches-in-wireless-sensor-networks.

[45] Nakamura, E.F., Loureiro, A.A., and Frery, A.C. (2007) Information Fusion for Wireless Sensor Networks: Methods, Models, and Classifications. *ACM Computing Surveys*, **39** (3), Article 9.

[46] Bedworith, M. and O'Brien, J. (2000) The Omnibus Model: A New Model for Data Fusion? *IEEE Aerospace and Electronic Systems Magazine*, **15** (4), 30–36.

[47] Kim, D., Park, K., and Ro, W. (2011) Network Coding on Heterogeneous Multi-Core Processors for Wireless Sensor Networks. *Sensors*, **11** (8), 7908–7933.

[48] Murthy, G.R. (2010) Control, Communication and Computing Units: Converged Architectures. *International Journal of Computer Applications*, **1** (4), 49–54.

[49] Li, W., Arslan, T., Han, J., Erdogan, A.T., El-Rayis, A., Haridas, N., and Yang, E. (2009) Energy Efficiency Enhancement in Satellite Based WSN through Collaboration and Self-Organized Mobility, in *Proceedings of the IEEE Aerospace Conference*, Big Sky, Montana.

[50] Vladimirova, T., Bridges, C., Prassinos, G., Wu, X., Sidibeh, K., Barnhart, D., Jallad, A.H., Paul, J., Lappas, V., Baker, A., Maynard, K., and Magness, R. (2007) Characterizing Wireless Sensor Motes for Space Applications, in *Proceedings of the NASA/ESA Conference on Adaptive Hardware and Systems (AHS)*, Edinburgh, UK.

[51] Lappas, V., Prassinos, G., Baker, A., and Magness, R. (2006) Wireless Sensor Motes for Small Satellite Applications. *IEEE Antennas and Propagation Magazine*, **48** (5), 175–179.

[52] Champaigne, K. (2005) Wireless Sensor Systems for Near-term Space Shuttle Missions, in *Proceedings of the Conference & Exposition on Structural Dynamics (IMAC)*. http://sem.org/Proceedings/ConferencePapers-Paper.cfm?ConfPapersPaperID=23262.

[53] Hamdi, M., Boudriga, N., and Obaidat, M. (2008) Bandwidth-Effective Design of a Satellite-Based Hybrid Wireless Sensor Network for Mobile Target Detection and Tracking. *IEEE Systems Journal*, **2** (1), 74–82.

[54] Ye, W., Silva, F., DeSchon, A., and Bhatt, S. (2008) Architecture of a Satellite-Based Sensor Network for Environmental Observation, in *Proceedings of the Earth Science Technology Conference (ESTC)*, Adelphi, Maryland.

[55] Park, C., Xie, Q., and Chou, P. (2005) InstraNode: Dual-Microcontroller Based Sensor Node for Real-Time Structural Health Monitoring, in *Proceedings of the IEEE Communications Society*

Conference on Sensor and Ad Hoc Communications and Networks (SECON), Santa Clara, California.

[56] Etchison, J., Skelton, G., Pang, Q., and Hulitt, T. (2010) *Mobile Intelligent Sensor Network Used for Data Processing*, Jackson State University, Jackson, Mississippi. http://www.iiis.org/CDs2010/CD2010SCI/SCI_2010/PapersPdf/SA874PZ.pdf.

[57] Vladimirova, T., Bridges, C., Paul, J., Malik, S., and Sweeting, M. (2009) Space-based Wireless Sensor Networks: Design Issues, in *Proceedings of the IEEE Aerospace Conference*, Big Sky, Montana.

[58] Aeroflex (2011) Leon3 Processor. http://www.gaisler.com/cms/index.php?option=com_content&task=view&id=13&Itemid=53.

[59] Ohara, S., Suzuki, M., Saruwatari, S., and Morikawa, H. (2008) A Prototype of a Multi-Core Wireless Sensor Node for Reducing Power Consumption, in *Proceedings of the International Symposium on Applications and the Internet (SAINT)*, Turku, Finland.

[60] TinyOS (2013) TinyOS. http://www.tinyos.net/.

[61] MANTIS (2013) MANTIS—MultimodAl NeTworks of In-situ Sensors. http://mantisos.org/index/tiki-index.php.html.

[62] Sankaranarayanan, A.C., Studer, C., and Baraniuk, R.G. (2012) CS-MUVI: Video Compressive Sensing for Spatial-Multiplexing Cameras, in *Proceedings of the IEEE International Conference on Computational Photography (ICCP)*, Seattle, Washington.

[63] LYTRO (2013) LYTRO—Light Field Camera. http://www.lytro.com/camera/.

[64] Kinect (2013) Kinect. http://en.wikipedia.org/wiki/Kinect.

[65] Calhoun, B.H. and Brooks, D. (2010) Can Subthreshold and Near-Threshold Circuits Go Mainstream? *IEEE Micro*, **30** (4), 80–85.

[66] Seo, S., Dreslinski, R.G., Woh, M., Chakrabarti, C., Mahlke, S., and Mudge, T. (2010) Diet SODA: A Power-Efficient Processor for Digital Cameras, in *Proceedings of International Symposium on Low Power Electronics and Design (ISLPED)*, Austin, Texas.

[67] Seo, S., Dreslinski, R.G., Woh, M., Park, Y., Chakrabarti, C., Mahlke, S., Blaauw, D., and Mudge, T. (2012) Process Variation in Near-Threshold Wide SIMD Architectures, in *Proceedings of Design Automation Conference (DAC)*, San Francisco, California.

[68] Zhang, W., Fossum, J.G., Mathew, L., and Du, Y. (2005) Physical Insights Regarding Design and Performance of Independent-Gate FinFETs. *IEEE Transactions on Electronic Devices (T-ED)*, **52** (10), 2198–2206.

[69] Munir, A. and Gordon-Ross, A. (2009) An MDP-based Application Oriented Optimal Policy for Wireless Sensor Networks, in *Proceedings of the International Conference on Hardware/Software Codesign and System Synthesis (CODES+ISSS)*, ACM, Grenoble, France, pp. 183–192.

[70] Sha, K. and Shi, W. (2005) Modeling the Lifetime of Wireless Sensor Networks. *Sensor Letters*, **3**, 126–135.

[71] Jung, D., Teixeira, T., Barton-Sweeney, A., and Savvides, A. (2007) Model-based Design Exploration of Wireless Sensor Node Lifetimes, in *Proceedings of the ACM 4th European conference on Wireless sensor networks (EWSN'07)*, Delft, The Netherlands.

[72] Jung, D., Teixeira, T., and Savvides, A. (2009) Sensor Node Lifetime Analysis: Models and Tools. *ACM Transactions on Sensor Networks (TOSN)*, **5** (1), 1–33.

[73] Munir, A., Gordon-Ross, A., Lysecky, S., and Lysecky, R. (2010) A One-Shot Dynamic Optimization Methodology for Wireless Sensor Networks, in *Proceedings IARIA IEEE International Conference on Mobile Ubiquitous Computing, Systems, Services and Technologies (UBICOMM)*, Florence, Italy.

[74] Nguyen, H., Forster, A., Puccinelli, D., and Giordano, S. (2011) Sensor Node Lifetime: An Experimental Study, in *Proceedings of IEEE International Conference on Pervasive Computing and Communications (PerCom'11)*, Seattle, Washington.

[75] Crossbow (2010) MTS/MDA Sensor Board Users Manual, in *Crossbow Technology, Inc.*, San Jose, California. http://www.xbow.com/support/Support_pdf_files/MTS-MDA_Series_Users_Manual.pdf.

[76] Sensirion (2010) Datasheet SHT1x (SHT10, SHT11, SHT15) Humidity and Temperature Sensor, in *SENSIRION - The Sensor Company*, Staefa, Switzerland. http://www.sensirion.com/en/pdf/product_information/Datasheet-humidity-sensor-SHT1x.pdf.

[77] Atmel (2010) ATMEL ATmega1281 Microcontroller with 256K Bytes In-System Programmable Flash, in *ATMEL Corporation*, San Jose, California. http://www.atmel.com/dyn/resources/prod_documents/2549S.pdf.

[78] Atmel (2010) ATMEL AT86RF230 Low Power 2.4 GHz Transceiver for ZigBee, IEEE 802.15.4, 6LoWPAN, RF4CE and ISM Applications, in *ATMEL Corporation*, San Jose, California. http://www.atmel.com/dyn/resources/prod_documents/doc5131.pdf.

[79] Friis, H. (1946) A Note on a Simple Transmission Formula. *Proceedings of the IRE*, **34**, 254.

[80] Crossbow (2010) Crossbow IRIS Datasheet, in *Crossbow Technology, Inc.*, San Jose, California. http://www.xbow.com/Products/Product_pdf_files/Wireless_pdf/IRIS_Datasheet.pdf.

[81] Akyildiz, I., Su, W., Sankarasubramaniam, Y., and Cayirci, E. (2002) Wireless Sensor Networks: A Survey. *Elsevier Computer Networks*, **38** (4), 393–422.

[82] Winkler, M., Tuchs, K.D., Hughes, K., and Barclay, G. (2008) Theoretical and Practical Aspects of Military Wireless Sensor Networks. *Journal of Telecommunications and Information Technology*, **2**, 37–45.

[83] Jiang, M., Guo, Z., Hong, F., Ma, Y., and Luo, H. (2009) OceanSense: A Practical Wireless Sensor Network on the Surface of the Sea, in *Proceedings of IEEE International Conference on Pervasive Computing and Communications (PerCom)*, Galveston, Texas.

[84] Werner-Allen, G., Lorincz, K., Welsh, M., Marcillo, O., Johnson, J., Ruiz, M., and Lees, J. (2006) Deploying a Wireless Sensor Network on an Active Volcano. *IEEE Internet Computing*, **10** (2), 18–25.

[85] Yifan, K. and Peng, J. (2008) Development of Data Video Base Station in Water Environment Monitoring Oriented Wireless Sensor Networks, in *Proceedings of IEEE ICESS*, Washington, DC.

[86] Mainwaring, A., Culler, D., Polastre, J., Szewczyk, R., and Anderson J. (2002) Wireless Sensor Networks for Habitat Monitoring, in *Proceedings of ACM WSNA*, Atlanta, Georgia.

[87] NASA (2011) NASA Kennedy Space Center: NASA Orbiter Fleet. http://www.nasa.gov/centers/kennedy/shuttleoperations/orbiters/orbitersdis.html.

[88] Moustapha, A. and Selmic, R. (2007) Wireless Sensor Network Modeling Using Modified Recurrent Neural Networks: Application to Fault Detection, in *Proceedings of IEEE ICNSC*, London, UK.

[89] Bredin, J., Demaine, E., Hajiaghayi, M., and Rus, D. (2010) Deploying Sensor Networks With Guaranteed Fault Tolerance. *IEEE/ACM Transactions on Networking*, **18** (1), 216–228.

[90] Chen, J., Kher, S., and Somani, A. (2006) Distributed Fault Detection of Wireless Sensor Networks, in *ACM DIWANS*, Los Angeles, California.

[91] Ding, M., Chen, D., Xing, K., and Cheng, X. (2005) Localized Fault-Tolerant Event Boundary Detection in Sensor Networks, in *Proceedings of IEEE INFOCOM*, Miami, Florida.

[92] Koren, I. and Krishna, M. (2007) *Fault-Tolerant Systems*, Morgan Kaufmann Publishers.

[93] Sharma, A., Golubchik, L., and Govindan, R. (2007) On the Prevalence of Sensor Faults in Real-World Deployments, in *Proceedings of IEEE Communications Society Conference on Sensor, Mesh and Ad Hoc Communications and Networks (SECON)*, San Diego, California.

[94] Koushanfar, F., Potkonjak, M., and Sangiovanni-Vincentelli, A. (2002) Fault Tolerance Techniques for Wireless Ad Hoc Sensor Networks, in *Proceedings of IEEE Sensors*, Orlando, Florida.

[95] Hopkins, A., Smith, T.B., and Lala, J. (1978) FTMP - A Highly Reliable Fault-Tolerant Multiprocessor for Aircraft. *Proceedings of the IEEE*, **66** (10), 1221–1239.

[96] Wensley, J., Lamport, L., Goldberg, J., Green, M., Levitt, N., Melliar-Smith, P., Shostak, R., and Weinstock, C. (1978) SIFT: Design and Analysis of a Fault-Tolerant Computer for Aircraft Control. *Proceedings of the IEEE*, **66** (10), 1240–1255.

[97] Avizienis, A. (1985) The N-Version Approach to Fault-Tolerant Software. *IEEE Transactions on Software Engineering*, **11** (12), 1491–1501.

[98] Somani, A. and Vaidya, N. (1997) Understanding Fault Tolerance and Reliability. *IEEE Computer*, **30** (4), 45–50.

[99] Sklaroff, J. (1976) Redundancy Management Technique for Space Shuttle Computers. *IBM Journal of Research and Development*, **20** (1), 20–28.

[100] Avizienis, A. and Laprie, J. (1986) Dependable Computing: From Concepts to Design Diversity. *Proceedings of the IEEE*, **74** (5), 629–638.

[101] ns2 (2014) The Network Simulator—ns-2. http://www.isi.edu/nsnam/ns/.

[102] Jiang, P. (2009) A New Method for Node Fault Detection in Wireless Sensor Networks. *Sensors*, **9** (2), 1282–1294.

[103] Jian-Liang, G., Yong-Jun, X., and Xiao-Wei, L. (2007) Weighted-Median based Distributed Fault Detection for Wireless Sensor Networks. *Journal of Software*, **18** (5), 1208–1217.

[104] Lee, M. and Choi, Y. (2008) Fault Detection of Wireless Sensor Networks. *Elsevier Computer Communications*, **31** (14), 3469–3475.

[105] Khilar, P. and Mahapatra, S. (2007) Intermittent Fault Diagnosis in Wireless Sensor Networks, in *Proceedings of IEEE ICIT*, Rourkela, India.

[106] Krishnamachari, B. and Iyengar, S. (2004) Distributed Bayesian Algorithms for Fault-Tolerant Event Region Detection in Wireless Sensor Networks. *IEEE Transactions on Computers*, **53** (3), 241–250.

[107] Wu, J., Duh, D., Wang, T., and Chang, L. (2007) On-Line Sensor Fault Detection Based on Majority Voting in Wireless Sensor Networks, in *Proceedings of 24th Workshop on Combinatorial Mathematics and Computation Theory (ALGO)*, Eilat, Israel.

[108] Lo, C., Lynch, J.P., and Liu, M. (2013) Distributed Reference-Free Fault Detection Method for Autonomous Wireless Sensor Networks. *IEEE Sensors Journal*, **13** (5), 2009–2019.

[109] Miao, X., Liu, K., He, Y., Papadias, D., Ma, Q., and Liu, Y. (2013) Agnostic Diagnosis: Discovering Silent Failures in Wireless Sensor Networks. *IEEE Transactions on Wireless Communications*, **12** (12), 6067–6075.

[110] Bhargava, A. and Raghuvanshi, A. (2013) Anomaly Detection in Wireless Sensor Networks using S-Transform in Combination with SVM, in *Proceedings of 5th International Conference on Computational Intelligence and Communication Networks (CICN)*, pp. 111–116.

[111] Salem, O., Guerassimov, A., Mehaoua, A., Marcus, A., and Furht, B. (2013) Sensor Fault and Patient Anomaly Detection and Classification in Medical Wireless Sensor Networks, in *Proceedings of IEEE International Conference on Communications (ICC)*, pp. 4373–4378.

[112] Clouqueur, T., Saluja, K., and Ramanathan, P. (2004) Fault Tolerance in Collaborative Sensor Networks for Target Detection. *IEEE Transactions on Computers*, **53** (3), 320–333.

[113] Chiang, M., Zilic, Z., Chenard, J., and Radecka, K. (2004) Architectures of Increased Availability Wireless Sensor Network Nodes, in *Proceedings of IEEE ITC*, Washington, DC.

[114] Krasniewski, M., Varadharajan, P., Rabeler, B., Bagchi, S., and Hu, Y.C. (2005) TIBFIT: Trust Index Based Fault Tolerance for Arbitrary Data Faults in Sensor Networks, in *Proceedings of IEEE International Conference on Dependable Systems and Networks (DSN)*, pp. 672–681.

[115] Sun, Y., Luo, H., and Das, S.K. (2012) A Trust-Based Framework for Fault-Tolerant Data Aggregation in Wireless Multimedia Sensor Networks. *IEEE Transactions on Dependable and Secure Computing*, **9** (6), 785–797.

[116] Zhang, W., Xue, G., and Misra, S. (2007) Fault-Tolerant Relay Node Placement in Wireless Sensor Networks: Problems and Algorithms, in *Proceedings of IEEE INFOCOM*, Anchorage, Alaska.

[117] Han, X., Cao, X., Lloyd, E., and Shen, C.C. (2010) Fault-Tolerant Relay Node Placement in Heterogeneous Wireless Sensor Networks. *IEEE Transactions on Mobile Computing*, **9** (5), 643–656.

[118] Baldi, M., Chiaraluce, F., and Zanaj, E. (2009) Fault Tolerance in Sensor Networks: Performance Comparison of Some Gossip Algorithms, in *IEEE WISES*, Ancona, Italy.

[119] Sen, A., Shen, B., Zhou, L., and Hao, B. (2006) Fault-Tolerance in Sensor Networks: A New Evaluation Metric, in *Proceedings of IEEE INFOCOM*, Barcelona, Catalunya, Spain.

[120] Alwan, H. and Agarwal, A. (2009) A Survey on Fault Tolerant Routing Techniques in Wireless Sensor Networks, in *Proceedings of IEEE SENSORCOMM*, Athens, Greece.

[121] Souza, L. (2007) FT-CoWiseNets: A Fault Tolerance Framework for Wireless Sensor Networks, in *Proceedings of IEEE SENSORCOMM*, Valencia, Spain.

[122] Cai, W., Jin, X., Zhang, Y., Chen, K., and Tang, J. (2006) Research on Reliability Model of Large-Scale Wireless Sensor Networks, in *Proceedings of IEEE WiCOM*, Wuhan, China.

[123] Zhu, J. and Papavassiliou, S. (2003) On the Connectivity Modeling and the Tradeoffs between Reliability and Energy Efficiency in Large Scale Wireless Sensor Networks, in *Proceedings of IEEE WCNC*, New Orleans, Louisiana.

[124] Vasar, C., Prostean, O., Filip, I., Robu, R., and Popescu, D. (2009) Markov Models for Wireless Sensor Network Reliability, in *Proceedings of IEEE ICCP*, Cluj-Napoca, Romania.

[125] Xing, L. and Michel, H. (2006) Integrated Modeling for Wireless Sensor Networks Reliability and Security, in *Proceedings of IEEE/ACM RAMS*, Newport Beach, California.

[126] Kannan, R. and Iyengar, S. (2004) Game-Theoretic Models for Reliable Path-Length and Energy-Constrained Routing With Data Aggregation in Wireless Sensor Networks. *IEEE Journal on Selected Areas in Communications (JSAC)*, **22** (6), 1141–1150.

[127] Mukhopadhyay, S., Schurgers, C., Panigrahi, D., and Dey, S. (2009) Model-Based Techniques for Data Reliability in Wireless Sensor Networks. *IEEE Transactions on Mobile Computing*, **8** (4), 528–543.

[128] Ni, K., Ramanathan, N., Chehade, M., Balzano, L., Nair, S., Zahedi, S., Pottie, G., Hansen, M., Srivastava, M., and Kohler, E. (2009) Sensor Network Data Fault Types. *ACM Transactions on Sensor Networks*, **5** (3).

[129] Mahapatro, A. and Khilar, M.P. (2013) Fault Diagnosis in Wireless Sensor Networks: A Survey. *IEEE Communications Surveys & Tutorials*, **15** (4), 2000–2026.

[130] Munir, A. and Gordon-Ross, A. (2011) Markov Modeling of Fault-Tolerant Wireless Sensor Networks, in *Proceedings of IEEE International Conference on Computer Communication Networks (ICCCN)*, Maui, Hawaii.

[131] Johnson, N., Kotz, S., and Balakrishnan, N. (1994) *Continuous Univariate Distributions*, John Wiley & Sons, Inc.

[132] NIST (2011) Engineering Statistics Handbook: Exponential Distribution. http://www.itl.nist.gov/div898/handbook/apr/section1/apr161.htm.

[133] Wikipedia (2014) ns (simulator). http://en.wikipedia.org/wiki/Ns_(simulator).

[134] Intel (2009) Intel-Berkeley Research Lab. http://db.csail.mit.edu/labdata/labdata.html.

[135] Sahner, R., Trivedi, K., and Puliafito, A. (1996) *Performance and Reliability Analysis of Computer Systems: An Example-Based Approach Using the SHARPE Software Package*, Kluwer Academic Publishers.

[136] SHARPE (2014) The SHARPE Tool & the Interface (GUI). http://people.ee.duke.edu/chirel/IRISA/sharpeGui.html.

[137] Munir, A. and Gordon-Ross, A. (2009) An MDP-based Application Oriented Optimal Policy for Wireless Sensor Networks, in *Proceedings of IEEE/ACM CODES+ISSS*, Grenoble, France.

[138] Du, X. and Chen, H.H. (2008) Security in Wireless Sensor Networks. *IEEE Wireless Communications*, **15** (4), 60–66.

[139] Sichitiu, M.L. and Veerarittiphan, C. (2003) Simple, Accurate Time Synchronization for Wireless Sensor Networks, in *Proceedings of IEEE Wireless Communications and Networking (WCNC)*, New Orleans, Louisiana.

[140] Ganeriwal, S., Kumar, R., and Srivastava, M. (2003) Timing-Sync Protocol for Sensor Networks, in *Proceedings of 1st International Conference on Embedded Networked Sensor Systems (SenSys)*, Los Angeles, California, pp. 138–149.

[141] Sun, B., Osborne, L., Xiao, Y., and Guizani, S. (2007) Intrusion Detection Techniques in Mobile Ad Hoc and Wireless Sensor Networks. *IEEE Wireless Communications*, **14** (5), 56–63.

[142] Munir, A., Gordon-Ross, A., and Ranka, S. (2014) Multi-core Embedded Wireless Sensor Networks: Architecture and Applications. *IEEE Transactions on Parallel and Distributed Systems*, **25** (6), 1553–1562.

[143] Balfour, J. (2010) Efficient Embedded Computing. *Ph.D. Thesis*, Department of Electrical Engineering, Stanford University.

[144] Fedorova, A., Blagodurov, S., and Zhuravlev, S. (2010) Managing Contention for Shared Resources on Multicore Processors. *Communications of the ACM*, **53** (2), 49–57.

[145] Culler, D., Singh, J., and Gupta, A. (1999) *Parallel Computer Architecture: A Hardware/Software Approach*, Morgan Kaufmann Publishers, Inc.

[146] Savage, J. and Zubair, M. (2008) A Unified Model for Multicore Architectures, in *Proceedings of ACM International Forum on Next-generation Multicore/Manycore Technologies (IFMT)*, Cairo, Egypt.

[147] Jain, R. (1991) *The Art of Computer Systems Performance Analysis: Techniques for Experimental Design, Measurement, Simulation, and Modeling*, Wiley.

[148] Flynn, M.J. (1995) *Computer Architecture: Pipelined and Parallel Processor Design*, Jones & Bartlett Learning.

[149] Sorin, D.J., Pai, V.S., Adve, S.V., Vernon, M.K., and Wood, D.A. (1998) Analytic Evaluation of Shared-Memory Systems with ILP Processors, in *Proceedings of the 25th Annual International Symposium on Computer Architecture (ISCA'98)*, Barcelona, Spain.

[150] İpek, E., McKee, S.A., Supinski, B., Schulz, M., and Caruana, R. (2006) Efficiently Exploring Architectural Design Spaces via Predictive Modeling, in *Proceedings of the 12th International Conference on Architectural Support for Programming Languages and Operating Systems (ASPLOS-XII)*, San Jose, California.

[151] Chandra, D., Guo, F., Kim, S., and Solihin, Y. (2005) Predicting Inter-Thread Cache Contention on a Chip Multi-Processor Architecture, in *Proceedings of the 11th International Symposium on High-Performance Computer Architecture (HPCA-11)*, San Francisco, California.

[152] Chen, X.E. and Aamodt, T.M. (2011) Modeling Cache Contention and Throughput of Multiprogrammed Manycore Processors. *IEEE Transactions on Computers*, (99).

[153] Samari, N. and Schneider, G. (1980) A Queueing Theory-Based Analytic Model of a Distributed Computer Network. *IEEE Transactions on Computers*, **C-29** (11), 994–1001.

[154] Kleinrock, L. (1976) *Queueing Systems, Volume II: Computer Applications*, Wiley-Interscience.

[155] Mainkar, V. and Trivedi, K. (1991) Performance Modeling Using SHARPE, in *Proceedings of the Eighth Symposium on Reliability in Electronics (RELECTRONIC)*, Budapest, Hungary.

[156] Willick, D.L. and Eager, D.L. (1990) An Analytic Model of Multistage Interconnection Networks, in *Proceedings of the ACM SIGMETRICS Conference on Measurement and Modeling of Computer Systems*, Boulder, Colorado.

[157] Nussbaum, S. and Smith, J.E. (2001) Modeling Superscalar Processors via Statistical Simulation, in *Proceedings of the 2001 International Conference on Parallel Architectures and Compilation Techniques (PACT)*, Barcelona, Spain.

[158] Karkhanis, T.S. and Smith, J.E. (2004) A First-Order Superscalar Processor Model, in *Proceedings of the 31st Annual International Symposium on Computer Architecture (ISCA'04)*, Munchen, Germany.

[159] Wunderlich, R.E., Wenisch, T.F., Falsafi, B., and Hoe, J.C. (2003) SMARTS: Accelerating Microarchitecture Simulation via Rigorous Statistical Sampling, in *Proceedings of the 30th Annual International Symposium on Computer Architecture (ISCA)*, San Diego, California.

[160] Kumar, R., Tullsen, D., Jouppi, N., and Ranganathan, P. (2005) Heterogeneous Chip Multiprocessors. *IEEE Computer*, **38** (11), 32–38.

[161] Sabry, M., Ruggiero, M., and Valle, P. (2010) Performance and Energy Trade-offs Analysis of L2 On-chip Cache Architectures for Embedded MPSoCs, in *Proceedings of IEEE/ACM Great Lakes Symposium on VLSI (GLSVLSI)*, Providence, Rhode Island, USA.

[162] Benítez, D., Moure, J., Rexachs, D., and Luque, E. (2007) Adaptive L2 Cache for Chip Multiprocessors, in *Proceedings of ACM International European Conference on Parallel and Distributed Computing (Euro-Par)*, Rennes, France.

[163] Ruggiero, J. (2008) Measuring Cache and Memory Latency and CPU to Memory Bandwidth. *Intel White Paper*, pp. 1–14.

[164] Medhi, J. (2003) *Stochastic Models in Queueing Theory*, Academic Press, An imprint of Elsevier Science.

[165] Intel (2011) Dual-Core Intel Xeon Processors LV and ULV for Embedded Computing. ftp://download.intel.com/design/intarch/prodbref/31578602.pdf.

[166] Kwon, O., Bahn, H., and Koh, K. (2008) FARS: A Page Replacement Algorithm for NAND Flash Memory Based Embedded Systems, in *Proceedings of IEEE CIT*, Sydney, Australia.

[167] Shi, L., Xue, C.J., Hu, J., Tseng, W.C., Zhou, X., and Sha, E.H.-M. (2010) Write Activity Reduction on Flash Main Memory via Smart Victim Cache, in *Proceedings of ACM GLSVLSI*, Providence, Rhode Island, USA.

[168] Reiser, M. and Lavenberg, S. (1980) Mean Value Analysis of Closed Multi-chain Queueing Networks. *Journal of ACM*, **27** (2), 313–322.

[169] Sevcik, K. and Mitrani, I. (1981) The Distribution of Queueing Network States at Input and Output Instants. *Journal of ACM*, **28** (2), 358–371.

[170] Woo, S., Ohara, M., Torrie, E., Singh, J., and Gupta, A. (1995) The SPLASH-2 Programs: Characterization and Methodological Considerations, in *Proceedings of ACM ISCA*, Santa Margherita Ligure, Italy.

[171] Bienia, C., Kumar, S., and Li, K. (2008) PARSEC vs. SPLASH-2: A Quantitative Comparison of Two Multithreaded Benchmark Suites on Chip-Multiprocessors, in *Proceedings of the IEEE International Symposium on Workload Characterization (IISWC)*, Seattle, Washington.

[172] SESC (2011) SESC: SuperESCalar Simulator. http://iacoma.cs.uiuc.edu/paulsack/sescdoc/.

[173] CHREC (2011) NSF Center for High-Performance Reconfigurable Computing. http://www.chrec.org/.

[174] ARM7TDMI (2010) ATMEL Embedded RISC Microcontroller Core: ARM7TDMI. http://www.atmel.com/.

[175] ARM7TDMI (2010) ARM7TDMI Data Sheet. http://www.atmel.com/.

[176] TILERA (2009) Tile Processor Architecture Overview, in *TILERA Official Documentation, Copyright 2006-2009 Tilera Corporation*.

[177] Yang, L., Dick, R., Lekatsas, H., and Chakradhar, S. (2010) Online Memory Compression for Embedded Systems. *ACM Transactions on Embedded Computing Systems (TECS)*, **9** (3), 27:1–27:30.

[178] Freescale (2011) Cache Latencies of the PowerPC MPC7451. http://cache.freescale.com/files/32bit/doc/app_note/AN2180.pdf.

[179] Min, R., Jone, W.B., and Hu, Y. (2004) Location Cache: A Low-Power L2 Cache System, in *Proceedings of ACM International Symposium on Low Power Electronics and Design (ISLPED)*, Newport Beach, California.

[180] Chen, Y., Li, E., Li, J., and Zhang, Y. (2007) Accelerating Video Feature Extractions in CBVIR on Multi-core Systems. *Intel Technology Journal*, **11** (4), 349–360.

[181] Jain, P. (2008) Software-assisted Cache Mechanisms for Embedded Systems. Ph.D. Thesis, Department of Electrical Engineering and Computer Science, Massachusetts Institute of Technology.

[182] CACTI (2010) An Integrated Cache and Memory Access Time, Cycle Time, Area, Leakage, and Dynamic Power Model. http://www.hpl.hp.com/research/cacti/.

[183] ITRS (2011) International Technology Roadmap for Semiconductors. http://www.itrs.net/.

[184] ARM (2011) ARM7 Thumb Family. http://saluc.engr.uconn.edu/refs/processors/arm/arm7_family.pdf.

[185] Brooks, D. and Martonosi, M. (2000) Value-based Clock Gating and Operation Packing: Dynamic Strategies for Improving Processor Power and Performance. *ACM Transactions on Computer Systems*, **18** (2), 89–126.

[186] Hamed, H., El-Atawy, A., and Ehab, A.S. (2006) On Dynamic Optimization of Packet Matching in High-Speed Firewalls. *IEEE Journal on Selected Areas in Communications*, **24** (10), 1817–1830.

[187] Hazelwood, K. and Smith, M. (2006) Managing Bounded Code Caches in Dynamic Binary Optimization Systems. *ACM Transactions on Architecture and Code Optimization*, **3** (3), 263–294.

[188] Hu, S., Valluri, M., and John, L. (2006) Effective Management of Multiple Configurable Units using Dynamic Optimization. *ACM Transactions on Architecture and Code Optimization*, **3** (4), 477–501.

[189] Mahalik, N. (2007) *Sensor Networks and Configuration: Fundamentals, Standards, Platforms, and Applications*, Springer-Verlag.

[190] Karl, H. and Willig, A. (2005) *Protocols and Architectures for Wireless Sensor Networks*, John Wiley & Sons, Inc.

[191] StrongARM (2011) Intel StrongARM SA-1110 Microprocessor. http://bwrc.eecs.berkeley.edu/research/pico_radio/test_bed/hardware/documentation/arm/sa1110briefdatasheet.pdf.

[192] ATMEL (2010) ATMEL ATmega128L 8-bit Microcontroller Datasheet, in *ATMEL Corporation*, San Jose, California. http://www.atmel.com/dyn/resources/prod_documents/doc2467.pdf.

[193] Rappaport, T.S. (1996) *Wireless Communications, Principles and Practice*, Prentice-Hall.

[194] Abramson, N. (1985) Development of the ALOHANET. *IEEE Transactions on Information Theory*, **31** (2), 119–123.

[195] IEEE Standards (1999), Wireless LAN Medium Access Control (MAC) and Physical Layer (PHY) Specification, IEEE Std 802.11-1999 edition: LAN MAN Standards Committee of the IEEE Computer Society.

[196] Sohraby, K., Minoli, D., and Znati, T. (2007) *Wireless Sensor Networks: Technology, Protocols, and Applications*, John Wiley & Sons, Inc.

[197] Chandrakasan, A., Amirtharajah, R., Cho, S., Konduri, J., Kulik, J., Rabiner, W., and Wang, A. (1999) Design Considerations for Distributed Microsensor Systems, in *Proceedings of IEEE Custom Integrated Circuits Conference (CICC)*, San Diego, California.

[198] Rajendran, V., Obraczka, K., and Garcia-Luna-Aceves, J. (2003) Energy-efficient Collision-free Medium Access Control for Wireless Sensor Networks, in *Proceedings of International Conference on Embedded Networked Sensor Systems (SenSys)'03*, ACM, Los Angeles, California.

[199] Polastre, J., Hill, J., and Culler, D. (2004) Versatile Low Power Media Access for Wireless Sensor Networks, in *Proceedings of International Conference on Embedded Networked Sensor Systems (SenSys)'04*, ACM, Baltimore, Maryland.

[200] Rhee, I., Warrier, A., Aia, M., and Min, J. (2005) Z-MAC: A Hybrid MAC for Wireless Sensor Networks, in *Proceedings of International Conference on Embedded Networked Sensor Systems (SenSys)'05*, ACM, San Diego, California.

[201] Ye, W., Heidemann, J., and Estrin, D. (2002) An Energy-Efficient MAC protocol for Wireless Sensor Networks, in *Proceedings of INFOCOM'02*, IEEE, New York, New York.

[202] Bao, L. and Garcia-Luna-Aceves, J. (2001) A New Approach to Channel Access Scheduling for Ad Hoc Networks, in *Proceedings of MobiCom'01*, ACM, Rome, Italy.

[203] Raghavendra, C., Sivalingam, K., and Znati, T. (2004) *Wireless Sensor Networks*, Kluwer Academic Publishers.

[204] Stojmenović, I. (2005) *Handbook of Sensor Networks: Algorithms and Architectures*, John Wiley & Sons, Inc.

[205] Van Dam, T. and Langendoen, K. (2003) An Adaptive Energy-Efficient MAC Protocol for Wireless Sensor Networks, in *Proceedings of International Conference on Embedded Networked Sensor Systems (SenSys)'03*, ACM, Los Angeles, California.

[206] Singh, S. and Raghavendra, C.S. (1998) PAMAS - Power Aware Multi-Access protocol with Signaling for ad hoc networks. *ACM Sigcomm Computer Communication Review*, **28** (3), 5–26.

[207] Culler, D., Hill, J., Horton, M., Pister, K., Szewczyk, R., and Woo, A. (2002) MICA: The Commercialization of Microsensor Motes, in *Sensor Magazine*. http://www.sensorsmag.com/articles/0402/40/.

[208] Ye, W., Heidemann, J., and Estrin, D. (2004) Medium Access Control with Coordinated Adaptive Sleeping for Wireless Sensor Networks. *IEEE/ACM Transactions on Networking*, **12** (3), 493–506.

[209] Varga, A. (2001) The OMNeT++ discrete event simulation system, in *Proceedings of European Simulation Multiconference (ESM)'01*, Prague, Czech Republic.

[210] EYES (2010) Energy Efficient Sensor Networks. http://www.eyes.eu.org/sensnet.htm.

[211] Coffin, D., Hook, D., McGarry, S., and Kolek, S. (2000) Declarative Ad-hoc Sensor Networking, in *SPIE Integrated Command Environments*.

[212] Intanagonwiwat, C., Govindan, R., Estrin, D., Heidemann, J., and Silva, F. (2003) Directed Diffusion for Wireless Sensor Networking. *IEEE/ACM Transactions on Networking*, **11** (1), 2–16.

[213] Poor, R. (2010) Gradient Routing in Ad Hoc Networks. http://www.media.mit.edu/pia/Research/ESP/texts/poorieeepaper.pdf.

[214] Ye, F., Zhong, G., Lu, S., and Zhang, L. (2005) GRAdient Broadcast: A Robust Data Delivery Protocol for Large Scale Sensor Networks. *ACM Wireless Networks (WINET)*, **11** (3), 285–298.

[215] Shah, R. and Rabaey, J. (2002) Energy Aware Routing for Low Energy Ad Hoc Sensor Networks, in *Proceedings of Wireless Communications and Networking Conference (WCNC)*, IEEE, Orlando, Florida.

[216] Lu, C., Blum, B., Abdelzaher, T., Stankovic, J., and He, T. (2002) RAP: A Real-Time Communication Architecture for Large-Scale Wireless Sensor Networks, in *Real-Time and Embedded Technology and Applications Symposium (RTAS)'02*, San Jose, California.

[217] He, T., Stankovic, J., Lu, C., and Abdelzaher, T. (2003) SPEED: A Stateless Protocol for Real-time Communication in Sensor Networks, in *Proceedings of International Conference on Distributed Computing Systems (ICDCS)'03*, IEEE, Providence, Rhode Island.

[218] Heinzelman, W., Chandrakasan, A., and Balakrishnan, H. (2000) Energy-Efficient Communication Protocols for Wireless Microsensor Networks, in *Hawaiian International Conference on System Sciences*.

[219] Kulik, J., Heinzelman, W., and Balakrishnan, H. (2002) Negotiation-Based Protocols for Disseminating Information in Wireless Sensor Networks. *ACM Wireless Networks (WINET)*, **8** (2/3), 169–185.

[220] TinyOS (2010) http://www.tinyos.net/.

[221] Akhmetshina, E., Gburzynski, P., and Vizeacoumar, F. (2002) PicOS: A Tiny Operating System for Extremely Small Embedded Platforms, in *Proceedings of Conference on Embedded Systems and Applications (ESA)'02*, Las Vegas, Nevada, pp. 116–122.

[222] Sinha, A. and Chandrakasan, A. (2001) Operating System and Algorithmic Techniques for Energy Scalable Wireless Sensor Networks, in *Proceedings of International Conference on Mobile Data Management*, Hong Kong, pp. 199–209.

[223] Barr, R., Bicket, J.C., Dantas, D.S., Du, B., Danny Kim, T.W., Zhou, B., and Sirer, E.G. (2002) On the Need for System-Level Support for Ad Hoc and Sensor Networks. *ACM SIGOPS Operating Systems Review*, **36** (2), 1–5.

[224] Abrach, H., Bhatti, S., Carlson, J., Dai, H., Rose, J., Sheth, A., Shucker, B., Deng, J., and Han, R. (2003) MANTIS: System Support for Multimodal Networks of In-Situ Sensors, in *Proceedings of Workshop on Wireless Sensor Networks and Applications (WSNA)'03*, San Diego, California, pp. 50–59.

[225] Min, R., Furrer, T., and Chandrakasan, A. (2000) Dynamic Voltage Scaling Techniques for Distributed Microsensor Networks, in *Proceedings of the Workshop on VLSI (WVLSI)*, IEEE, Orlando, Florida, pp. 43–46.

[226] Yuan, L. and Qu, G. (2002) Design Space Exploration for Energy-Efficient Secure Sensor Network, in *Proceedings of the International Conference on Application-Specific Systems, Architectures, and Processors (ASAP)*, IEEE, San Jose, California, pp. 88–97.

[227] Kogekar, S., Neema, S., Eames, B., Koutsoukos, X., Ledeczi, A., and Maroti, M. (2004) Constraint-Guided Dynamic Reconfiguration in Sensor Networks, in *Proceedings of the 3rd International Symposium on Information Processing in Sensor Networks (IPSN)*, ACM, Berkeley, California, pp. 379–387.

[228] Hwang, K. (1987) Advanced Parallel Processing with Supercomputer Architectures. *Proceedings of the IEEE*, **75** (10), 1348–1379.

[229] Klietz, A., Malevsky, A., and Chin-Purcell, K. (1994) Mix-and-match High Performance Computing. *IEEE Potentials*, **13** (3), 6–10.

[230] Pulleyblank, W. (2004) How to Build a Supercomputer. *IEEE Review*, **50** (1), 48–52.

[231] Bokhari, S. and Saltz, J. (2010) Exploring the Performance of Massively Multithreaded Architectures. *Concurrency and Computation: Practice & Experience*, **22** (5), 588–616.

[232] Feng, W.C. and Cameron, K. (2007) The Green500 List: Encouraging Sustainable Supercomputing. *IEEE Computer*, **40** (12), 38–44.

[233] Top500 (2014) Top 500 Supercomputer Sites. http://www.top500.org/.

[234] Green500 (2011) Ranking the World's Most Energy-Efficient Supercomputers. http://www.green500.org/.

[235] Ahmad, I. and Ranka, S. (2011) *Handbook of Energy-Aware and Green Computing*, Taylor and Francis Group, CRC Press.

[236] Kumar, R., Tullsen, D., Ranganathan, P., Jouppi, N., and Farkas, K. (2004) Single-ISA Heterogeneous Multi-Core Architectures for Multithreaded Workload Performance, in *Proceedings of IEEE ISCA*, Munich, Germany.

[237] Kumar, R., Tullsen, D., and Jouppi, N. (2006) Core Architecture Optimization for Heterogeneous Chip Multiprocessors, in *Proceedings of ACM International Conference on Parallel Architectures and Compilation Techniques (PACT)*, Seattle, Washington.

[238] Kumar, R., Jouppi, N., and Tullsen, D. (2004) Conjoined-core Chip Multiprocessing, in *Proceedings of IEEE/ACM MICRO-37*, Portland, Oregon.

[239] Keckler, S., Olukotun, K., and Hofstee, H. (2009) *Multicore Processors and Systems*, Springer-Verlag.

[240] Puttaswamy, K. and Loh, G. (2007) Thermal Herding: Microarchitecture Techniques for Controlling Hotspots in High-Performance 3D-Integrated Processors, in *Proceedings of IEEE HPCA*, Phoenix, Arizona.

[241] Pande, P., Ganguly, A., Belzer, B., Nojeh, A., and Ivanov, A. (2008) Novel Interconnect Infrastructures for Massive Multicore Chips - An Overview, in *Proceedings of IEEE ISCAS*, Seattle, Washington.

[242] Narayanan, S., Sartori, J., Kumar, R., and Jones, D. (2010) Scalable Stochastic Processors, in *Proceedings of IEEE/ACM DATE*, Dresden, Germany.

[243] Hill, M. (2010) Transactional Memory, in *Synthesis Lectures on Computer Architecture*. http://www.morganclaypool.com/toc/cac/1/1.

[244] Guan, N., Stigge, M., Yi, W., and Yu, G. (2009) Cache-Aware Scheduling and Analysis for Multicores, in *Proceedings of ACM EMSOFT*, Grenoble, France.

[245] Fide, S. (2008) *Architectural Optimizations in Multi-Core Processors*, VDM Verlag.

[246] Chang, J. and Sohi, G. (2006) Cooperative Caching for Chip Multiprocessors, in *Proceedings of ACM ISCA*, Boston, Massachusetts.

[247] Flautner, K., Kim, N., Martin, S., Blaauw, D., and Mudge, T. (2002) Drowsy Caches: Simple Techniques for Reducing Leakage Power, in *Proceedings of IEEE/ACM ISCA*, Anchorage, Alaska.

[248] Lee, S.B., Tam, S.W., Pefkianakis, I., Lu, S.L., Chang, M., Guo, C., Reinman, G., Peng, C., Naik, M., Zhang, L., and Cong, J. (2009) A Scalable Micro Wireless Interconnect Structure for CMPs, in *Proceedings of ACM MobiCom*, Beijing, China.

[249] Shacham, A., Bergman, K., and Carloni, L. (2008) Photonic Networks-on-Chip for Future Generations of Chip Multiprocessors. *IEEE Transactions on Computers*, **57** (9), 1246–1260.

[250] Pande, P., Ganguly, A., Chang, K., and Teuscher, C. (2009) Hybrid Wireless Network on Chip: A New Paradigm in Multi-Core Design, in *Proceedings of IEEE NoCArc*, New York, New York.

[251] Kontorinis, V., Shayan, A., Tullsen, D., and Kumar, R. (2009) Reducing Peak Power with a Table-Driven Adaptive Processor Core, in *Proceedings of IEEE/ACM MICRO-42*, New York, New York.

[252] Donald, J. and Martonosi, M. (2006) Techniques for Multicore Thermal Management: Classification and New Exploration, in *Proceedings of IEEE ISCA*, Boston, Massachusetts.

[253] Jayaseelan, R. and Mitra, T. (2009) A Hybrid Local-Global Approach for Multi-Core Thermal Management, in *Proceedings of IEEE/ACM ICCAD*, San Jose, California.

[254] Park, J., Shin, D., Chang, N., and Pedram, M. (2010) Accurate Modeling and Calculation of Delay and Energy Overheads of Dynamic Voltage Scaling in Modern High-Performance Microprocessors, in *Proceedings of ACM/IEEE ISLPED*, Austin, Texas.

[255] ACPI (2011) Advanced Configuration and Power Interface. http://www.acpi.info/.

[256] Lee, J. and Kim, N. (2009) Optimizing Throughput of Power- and Thermal-Constrained Multicore Processors Using DVFS and Per-Core Power-Gating, in *Proceedings of IEEE/ACM DAC*, San Francisco, California.

[257] Freescale (2009) Green Embedded Computing and the MPC8536E PowerQUICC III Processor. http://www.freescale.com/files/32bit/doc/white_paper/MPC8536EWP.pdf.

[258] Ge, R., Feng, X., Song, S., Chang, H.C., Li, D., and Cameron, K. (2010) PowerPack: Energy Profiling and Analysis of High-Performance Systems and Applications. *IEEE Transactions on Parallel and Distributed Systems*, **21** (5), 658–671.

[259] Hoffmann, H., Sidiroglou, S., Carbin, M., Misailovic, S., Agarwal, A., and Rinard, M. (2011) Dynamic Knobs for Responsive Power-Aware Computing, in Proceedings of ACM International Conference on Architectural Support for Programming Languages and Operating Systems (ASPLOS), Newport Beach, California, March, 199–212.

[260] Baek, W. and Chilimbi, T. (2010) Green: A Framework for Supporting Energy-Conscious Programming using Controlled Approximation, in *Proceedings of ACM SIGPLAN PLDI*, Toronto, Ontario, Canada.

[261] Zhou, X., Yang, J., Chrobak, M., and Zhang, Y. (2010) Performance-aware Thermal Management via Task Scheduling. *ACM Transactions on Architecture and Code Optimization (TACO)*, **7** (1), 5:1–5:31.

[262] Jacobs, A., George, A., and Cieslewski, G. (2009) Reconfigurable Fault Tolerance: A Framework for Environmentally Adaptive Fault Mitigation in Space, in *Proceedings of IEEE FPL*, Prague, Czech Republic.

[263] Sloan, J. and Kumar, R. (2009) Towards Scalable Reliability Frameworks for Error Prone CMPs, in *Proceedings of ACM CASES*, Grenoble, France.

[264] Poulsen, D. and Yew, P.C. (1994) Data Prefetching and Data Forwarding in Shared Memory Multiprocessors, in *Proceedings of IEEE ICPP*, North Carolina State University, North Carolina.

[265] Yan, L., Hu, W., Chen, T., and Huang, Z. (2008) Hardware Assistant Scheduling for Synergistic Core Tasks on Embedded Heterogeneous Multi-core System. *Journal of Information & Computational Science*, **5** (6), 2369–2373.

[266] Chaparro, P., Gonzalez, J., Magklis, G., Cai, Q., and Gonzalez, A. (2007) Understanding the Thermal Implications of Multicore Architectures. *IEEE Transactions on Parallel and Distributed Systems*, **18** (8), 1055–1065.

[267] Suo, G. and Yang, X.J. (2009) Balancing Parallel Applications on Multi-core Processors Based on Cache Partitioning, in *Proceedings of IEEE ISPA*, Chendu and JiuZhai Valley, China.

[268] Jeon, H., Lee, W., and Chung, S. (2010) Load Unbalancing Strategy for Multi-Core Embedded Processors. *IEEE Transactions on Computers*, **59** (10), 1434–1440.

[269] ARM (2011) ARM11 MPCore Processor Technical Reference Manual. http://infocenter.arm.com/help/topic/com.arm.doc.ddi0360e/DDI0360E_arm11_mpcore_r1p0_trm.pdf.

[270] Hirata, K. and Goodacre, J. (2007) ARM MPCore: The Streamlined and Scalable ARM11 Processor Core, in *Proceedings of IEEE ASP-DAC*, Yokohama, Japan.

[271] ARM (2011) White Paper: The ARM Cortex-A9 Processors. http://www.arm.com/files/pdf/ARMCortexA-9Processors.pdf.

[272] ARM (2011) Cortex-A9 MPCore Technical Reference Manual. http://infocenter.arm.com/help/topic/com.arm.doc.ddi0407f/DDI0407F_cortex_a9_r2p2_mpcore_trm.pdf.

[273] Freescale (2011) MPC8572E PowerQUICC III Processor. http://www.freescale.com/files/netcomm/doc/fact_sheet/MPC8572FS.pdf.

[274] Freescale (2011) MPC8572E PowerQUICC III Integrated Processor Hardware Specifications. http://cache.freescale.com/files/32bit/doc/data_sheet/MPC8572EEC.pdf.

[275] TILERA (2011) Manycore without Boundaries: TILEPro64 Processor. http://www.tilera.com/products/processors/TILEPRO64.

[276] TILERA (2011) Manycore without Boundaries: TILE-Gx Processor Family. http://www.tilera.com/products/processors/TILE-Gx_Family.

[277] AMD (2011) AMD Cool'n'Quiet Technology. http://www.amd.com/us/products/technologies/cool-n-quiet/Pages/cool-n-quiet.aspx.

[278] Intel (2011) High-Performance Energy-Efficient Processors for Embedded Market Segments. http://www.intel.com/design/embedded/downloads/315336.pdf.

[279] Intel (2011) Intel Core 2 Duo Processor Maximizing Dual-Core Performance Efficiency. ftp://download.intel.com/products/processor/core2duo/mobile_prod_brief.pdf.

[280] Intel (2011) Intel Xeon Processor LV 5148. http://ark.intel.com/Product.aspx?id=27223.

[281] Intel (2011) Intel Microarchitecture Codename Sandy Bridge. http://www.intel.com/technology/architecture-silicon/2ndgen/index.htm.

[282] Intel (2011) Intel's 'Sandy Bridge' Core processors. http://techreport.com/articles.x/20188.

[283] Intel (2011) Intel Turbo Boost Technology 2.0. http://www.intel.com/technology/turboboost/.

[284] NVIDIA (2011) NVIDIA Tesla C1060 Computing Processor. http://www.nvidia.com/object/product_tesla_c1060_us.html.

[285] NVIDIA (2011) NVIDIA Tesla Personal Supercomputer. http://www.nvidia.com/docs/IO/43395/NV_DS_Tesla_PSC_US_Mar09_LowRes.pdf.

[286] NVIDIA (2011) NVIDIA PowerMizer Technology. http://www.nvidia.com/object/feature_powermizer.html.

[287] NVIDIA (2011) NVIDIA Tesla C2050/C2070 GPU Computing Processor. http://www.nvidia.com/object/product_tesla_C2050_C2070_us.html.

[288] Berg, T. (2009) Maintaining I/O Data Coherence in Embedded Multicore Systems. *IEEE Micro*, **29** (3), 10–19.

[289] Bournoutian, G. and Orailoglu, A. (2008) Miss Reduction in Embedded Processors through Dynamic, Power-Friendly Cache Design, in *Proceedings of IEEE/ACM DAC*, Anaheim, California.

[290] SeaMicro (2011) The SM10000 Family. http://www.seamicro.com/.

[291] AMAX (2011) High Performance Computing: ClusterMax SuperG Tesla GPGPU HPC Solutions. http://www.amax.com/hpc/productdetail.asp?product_id=superg.

[292] Koka, P., McCracken, M., Schwetman, H., Zheng, X., Ho, R., and Krishnamoorthy, A. (2010) Silicon-photonic Network Architectures for Scalable, Power-efficient Multi-chip systems, in *Proceedings of ACM/IEEE ISCA*, Saint-Malo, France.

[293] Asghari, M. and Krishnamoorthy, A. (2011) Silicon Photonics: Energy-efficient Communication. *Nature Photonics*, **5**, 268–270.

[294] Lee, C.W., Yun, S.R.N., Yu, C.G., Park, J.T., and Colinge, J.P. (2007) Device Design Guidelines for Nano-scale MuGFETs. *Elsevier Solid-State Electronics*, **51** (3), 505–510.

[295] Collange, S., Defour, D., and Tisserand, A. (2009) Power Consumption of GPUs from a Software Perspective, in *Proceedings of ACM ICCS*, Baton Rouge, Louisiana.

[296] Horton, M. (2004) Commercial Wireless Sensor Networks: Status, Issues and Challenges, in *Proceedings of IEEE SECON: Keynote Presentation*, Santa Clara, California.

[297] Greene, K. (2006) Sensor Networks for Dummies. *Technology Review (published by MIT)*.

[298] Seong, C.Y. and Widrow, B. (2001) Neural Dynamic Optimization for Control Systems. *IEEE Transactions on Systems, Man, and Cybernetics*, **31** (4), 482–489.

[299] Stevens-Navarro, E., Lin, Y., and Wong, V. (2008) An MDP-based Vertical Handoff Decision Algorithm for Heterogeneous Wireless Networks. *IEEE Transactions on Vehicular Technology*, **57** (2), 1243–1254.

[300] Sridharan, S. and Lysecky, S. (2008) A First Step Towards Dynamic Profiling of Sensor-Based Systems, in *Proceedings of the Conference on Sensor, Mesh and Ad Hoc Communications and Networks (SECON)*, IEEE, San Francisco, California, pp. 600–602.

[301] Tilak, S., Abu-Ghazaleh, N., and Heinzelman, W. (2002) Infrastructure Tradeoffs for Sensor Networks, in *Proceedings of the 1st ACM International Workshop on Wireless Sensor Networks and Applications*, Atlanta, Georgia.

[302] Kadayif, I. and Kandemir, M. (2004) Tuning In-Sensor Data Filtering to Reduce Energy Consumption in Wireless Sensor Networks, in *Proceedings of ACM DATE*, Paris, France.

[303] Marrón, P., Lachenmann, A., Minder, D., Hähner, J., Rothermel, K., and Becker, C. (2004) Adaptation and Cross-Layer Issues in Sensor Networks, in *Proceedings of IEEE ISSNIP*, December.

[304] Vecchio, A. (2008) Adaptability in Wireless Sensor Networks, in *Proceedings of IEEE ICECS*, September.

[305] ITA (2010) International Technology Alliance in Network and Information Science. http://www.usukita.org/.

[306] Pillai, P. and Shin, K. (2001) Real-Time Dynamic Voltage Scaling for Low-Power Embedded Operating Systems, in *Proceedings of ACM SOSP*, Banff, Alberta, Canada.

[307] Childers, B., Tang, H., and Melhem, R. (2001) Adapting Processor Supply Voltage to Instruction-Level Parallelism, in *Proceedings of Koolchips Workshop, in conjunction with MICRO-33*, Monterey, California.

[308] Liu, D. and Svensson, C. (1993) Trading Speed for Low Power by Choice of Supply and Threshold Voltages. *IEEE Journal of Solid-State Circuits*, **28** (1), 10–17.

[309] Burd, T., Pering, T., Stratakos, A., and Brodersen, R. (2000) A Dynamic Voltage Scaled Microprocessor System. *IEEE Journal of Solid-State Circuits*, **35** (11), 1571–1580.

[310] Lysecky, S. and Vahid, F. (2006) Automated Application-Specific Tuning of Parameterized Sensor-Based Embedded System Building Blocks, in *Proceedings of the International Conference on Ubiquitous Computing (UbiComp)*, Orange County, California, pp. 507–524.

[311] Verma, R. (2008) Automated Application Specific Sensor Network Node Tuning for Non-Expert Application Developers. Master's Thesis, Department of Electrical and Computer Engineering, University of Arizona.

[312] Munir, A., Gordon-Ross, A., Lysecky, S., and Lysecky, R. (2010) A Lightweight Dynamic Optimization Methodology for Wireless Sensor Networks, in Proceedings of IEEE International Conference on Wireless and Mobile Computing, Networking and Communications (WiMob), Niagara Falls, Canada, October 2010.

[313] Puterman, M. (2005) *Markov Decision Processes: Discrete Stochastic Dynamic Programming*, John Wiley & Sons, Inc.

[314] Lane, T. (2011) MDP Policy Iteration Lecture. http://www.cs.unm.edu/terran/.

[315] Dutta, P., Grimmer, M., Arora, A., Bibyk, S., and Culler, D. (2005) Design of a Wireless Sensor Network Platform for Detecting Rare, Random, and Ephemeral Events, in *Proceedings of ACM IPSN*, Los Angeles, California.

[316] Munir, A., Gordon-Ross, A., Lysecky, S., and Lysecky, R. (2010) A Lightweight Dynamic Optimization Methodology for Wireless Sensor Networks, in *Proceedings of IEEE WiMob*.

[317] Yu, F. and Krishnamurthy, V. (2007) Optimal Joint Session Admission Control in Integrated WLAN and CDMA Cellular Networks with Vertical Handoff. *IEEE Transactions on Mobile Computing*, **6** (1), 126–139.

[318] Chadès, I., Cros, M., Garcia, F., and Sabbadin, R. (2005) Markov Decision Process (MDP) Toolbox v2.0 for MATLAB, in *INRA Toulouse*, INRA, France. http://www.inra.fr/internet/Departements/MIA/T/MDPtoolbox/.

[319] Dutta, P. and Culler, D. (2005) System Software Techniques for Low-Power Operation in Wireless Sensor Networks, in *Proceedings of IEEE/ACM ICCAD*, San Jose, California.

[320] Honeywell (2009) Honeywell 1- and 2- Axis Magnetic Sensors HMC1001/1002, and HMC1021/1022 Datasheet, in *Honeywell International Inc.*, Morristown, New Jersey. http://www.ssec.honeywell.com/magnetic/datasheets/hmc1001-2_1021-2.pdf.

[321] DPOP (2010) Dynamic Profiling and Optimization (DPOP) for Sensor Networks. http://www.ece.arizona.edu/dpop/.

[322] Huber, M.F., Kuwertz, A., Sawo, F., and Hanebeck, U.D. (2009) Distributed Greedy Sensor Scheduling for Model-based Reconstruction of Space-Time Continuous Physical Phenomenon, in *Proceedings of the International Conference on Information Fusion (FUSION)*, IEEE, Seattle, Washington, pp. 102–109.

[323] Xu, L. and Oja, E. (1990) Improved Simulated Annealing, Boltzmann Machine, and Attributed Graph Matching, in *Proceedings of the EURASIP Workshop on Neural Networks*, Springer-Verlag, pp. 151–160.

[324] Kirkpatrick, S., Gelatt, C., and Vecchi, M. (1983) Optimization by Simulated Annealing. *Science*, **220** (4598), 671–680.

[325] Ben-Ameur, W. (2004) Computing the Initial Temperature of Simulated Annealing. *Computational Optimization and Applications*, **29** (3), 369–385.

[326] Xeon (2010) Intel Xeon Processor E5430. http://processorfinder.intel.com/details.aspx?sSpec=SLANU.

[327] Linux (2010) Linux Man Pages. http://linux.die.net/man/.

[328] cplusplus.com. (2010) C++ Reference Library, in *cplusplus.com*. http://cplusplus.com/reference/clibrary/ctime/clock/.

[329] Gordon-Ross, A., Vahid, F., and Dutt, N. (2009) Fast Configurable-Cache Tuning With a Unified Second-Level Cache. *IEEE Transactions on Very Large Scale Integration (VLSI) Systems*, **17** (1), 80–91.

[330] Zhang, C., Vahid, F., and Lysecky, R. (2004) A Self-Tuning Cache Architecture for Embedded Systems. *ACM Transactions on Embedded Computing Systems*, **3** (2), 407–425.

[331] Shenoy, A., Hiner, J., Lysecky, S., Lysecky, R., and Gordon-Ross, A. (2010) Evaluation of Dynamic Profiling Methodologies for Optimization of Sensor Networks. *IEEE Embedded Systems Letters*, **2** (1), 10–13.

[332] Wang, X., Ma, J., and Wang, S. (2006) Collaborative Deployment Optimization and Dynamic Power Management in Wireless Sensor Networks, in *Proceedings of the International Conference on Grid and Cooperative Computing (GCC)*, IEEE, Changsha, Hunan, China, pp. 121–128.

[333] Ning, X. and Cassandras, C. (2008) Optimal Dynamic Sleep Time Control in Wireless Sensor Networks, in *Proceedings of the Conference on Decision and Control (CDC)*, IEEE, Cancun, Mexico, pp. 2332–2337.

[334] Brown, R. and Sharapov, I. (2008) *Performance and Programmability Comparison Between OpenMP and MPI Implementations of a Molecular Modeling Application, Lecture Notes in Computer Science*, Vol. **4315**, Springer-Verlag, pp. 349–360.

[335] Sun, X. and Zhu, J. (1995) Performance Considerations of Shared Virtual Memory Machines. *IEEE Transactions on Parallel and Distributed Systems (TPDS)*, **6** (11), 1185–1194.

[336] Lively, C., Wu, X., Taylor, V., Moore, S., Chang, H.C., and Cameron, K. (2011) Energy and Performance Characteristics of Different Parallel Implementations of Scientific Applications on Multicore Systems. *International Journal of High Performance Computing Applications*.

[337] Bikshandi, G., Guo, J., Hoeflinger, D., Almasiy, G., Fraguelaz, B., Garzaran, M., Padua, D., and von Prauny, C. (2006) Programming for Parallelism and Locality with Hierarchically Tiled Arrays, in *Proceedings of the ACM SIGPLAN Symposium on Principles and Practice of Parallel Programming (PPoPP)*, Manhattan, New York City, New York.

[338] Zhu, W., Cuvillo, J., and Gao, G. (2008) Performance Characteristics of OpenMP Language Constructs on a Many-core-on-a-chip Architecture, in *Proceedings of the 2005 and 2006 International Conference on OpenMP Shared Memory Parallel Programming*, Springer-Verlag, Berlin, Heidelberg, IWOMP'05/IWOMP'06, pp. 230–241. http://portal.acm.org/citation.cfm?id=1892830.1892855.

[339] Kak, A. (2012) Parallel Histogram-based Particle Filter for Object Tracking on SIMD-based Smart Cameras, in *Purdue Robot Vision Lab*, Purdue University, West Lafayette, Indiana. https://engineering.purdue.edu/RVL/Research/SIMD_PF/index.html.

[340] Intel (2012) Intel Xeon Processor E5430. http://ark.intel.com/Product.aspx?id=33081.

[341] Intel (2008) Quad-Core Intel Xeon Processor 5400 Series Datasheet. http://www.intel.com/assets/PDF/datasheet/318589.pdf.

[342] TILERA (2012) Manycore without Boundaries: TILE64 Processor. http://www.tilera.com/products/processors/TILE64.

[343] TILERA (2012) Manycore without Boundaries: TILEPro64 Processor. http://www.tilera.com/products/processors/TILEPRO64.

[344] IBM (2012) Linux and Symmetric Multiprocessing. http://www.ibm.com/developerworks/library/l-linux-smp/.

[345] Android (2012) SensorEvent. http://developer.android.com/reference/android/hardware/SensorEvent.html.

[346] Top500 (2012) Top 500 Supercomputer Sites. http://www.top500.org/.

[347] LINPACK (2012) LINPACK Benchmarks. http://en.wikipedia.org/wiki/LINPACK.

[348] NPB (2012) NASA Advanced Supercomputing (NAS) Parallel Benchmarks. http://www.nas.nasa.gov/Resources/Software/npb.html.

[349] JavaDoc (2012) Class Flops: Counting floating point operations. http://ai.stanford.edu/paskin/slam/javadoc/javaslam/util/Flops.html.

[350] Kumar, V., Grama, A., Gupta, A., and Karypis, G. (1994) *Introduction to Parallel Computing*, The Benjamin/Cummings Publishing Company, Inc.

[351] Williams, J., Massie, C., George, A., Richardson, J., Gosrani, K., and Lam, H. (2010) Characterization of Fixed and Reconfigurable Multi-Core Devices for Application Acceleration. *ACM Transactions on Reconfigurable Technology and Systems*, **3** (4), 19:1–19:29.

[352] TILERA (2009) Tile Processor Architecture Overview for the TILEPro Series, in *Tilera Official Documentation*.

[353] TILERA (2009) Tile Processor Architecture Overview, in *Tilera Official Documentation*.

[354] Richardson, J., Fingulin, S., Raghunathan, D., Massie, C., George, A., and Lam, H. (2010) Comparative Analysis of HPC and Accelerator Devices: Computation, Memory, I/O, and Power, in *Proceedings of the IEEE Workshop on HPRCTA*, New Orleans, Louisiana.

[355] TILERA (2010) TILEmPower Appliance User's Guide, in *Tilera Official Documentation*.

[356] Munir, A., Koushanfar, F., Gordon-Ross, A., and Ranka, S. (2013) High-Performance Optimizations on Tiled Many-Core Embedded Systems: A Matrix Multiplication Case Study. *Journal of Supercomputing*, **66** (1), 431–487.

[357] Asanovic, K., Bodik, R., Demmel, J., Keaveny, T., Keutzer, K., Kubiatowicz, J., Morgan, N., Patterson, David Sen, K., Wawrzynek, J., Wessel, D., and Yelick, K. (2009) A View of the Parallel Computing Landscape. *Communications of the ACM*, **52** (10).

[358] Yuan, N., Zhou, Y., Tan, G., Zhang, J., and Fan, D. (2009) High Performance Matrix Multiplication on Many Cores, in *Proceedings of the 15th International Euro-Par Conference on Parallel Processing (Euro-Par'09)*, Delft, The Netherlands.

[359] MAXIMUMPC (2007) Fast Forward: Multicore vs. Manycore. http://www.maximumpc.com/article/fast_forward_multicore_vs_manycore.

[360] Wikipedia (2013) Multi-core processor. http://en.wikipedia.org/wiki/Manycore.

[361] Tilera (2013) Tilera Cloud Computing. http://www.tilera.com/solutions/cloud_computing.

[362] Tilera (2013) Tilera TILEmpower Platform. http://www.tilera.com/sites/default/files/productbriefs/TILEProEmpower_PB021_v4.pdf.

[363] Levy, M. and Conte, T. (2009) Embedded Multicore Processors and Systems. *IEEE Micro*, **29** (3), 7–9.

[364] Cuvillo, J.d., Zhu, W., and Gao, G.R. (2006) Landing OpenMP on Cyclops-64: An Efficient Mapping of OpenMP to a Many-Core System-on-a-Chip, in *Proceedings of ACM 3rd conference on Computing frontiers (CF)*, Ischia, Italy.

[365] Vangal, S.R., Howard, J., Ruhl, G., Dighe, S., Wilson, H., Tschanz, J., Finan, D., Singh, A., Jacob, T., Jain, S., Erraguntla, V., Roberts, C., Hoskote, Y., Borkar, N., and Borkar, S. (2008) An 80-Tile Sub-100-W TeraFLOPS Processor in 65-nm CMOS. *IEEE Journal of Solid-State Circuits*, **43** (1), 29–41.

[366] Musoll, E. (2010) A Cost-Effective Load-Balancing Policy for Tile-Based, Massive Multi-Core Packet Processors. *ACM Transactions on Embedded Computing Systems*, **9** (3).

[367] Wu, N., Yang, Q., Wen, M., He, Y., Ren, J., Guan, M., and Zhang, C. (2011) Tiled Multi-Core Stream Architecture. *Transactions on High-Performance Embedded Architectures and Compilers IV (HiPEAC IV)*, **4**, 274–293.

[368] Mattson, T.G., Wijngaart, R.V.d., and Frumkin, M. (2008) Programming the Intel 80-core network-on-a-chip Terascale Processor, in *Proceedings of IEEE/ACM conference on Supercomputing (SC)*, Austin, Texas.

[369] Crowell, T. (2011) Will 2011 mark the beginning of manycore? http://talbottcrowell.wordpress.com/2011/01/01/manycore/.

[370] Cortesi, D. (1998) Origin2000 and Onyx2 Performance Tuning and Optimization Guide. http://techpubs.sgi.com/library/dynaweb_docs/0640/SGI_Developer/books/OrOn2_PfTune/sgi_html/index.html.

[371] Krishnan, M. and Nieplocha, J. (2004) SRUMMA: A Matrix Multiplication Algorithm Suitable for Clusters and Scalable Shared Memory Systems, in *Proceedings of the International Parallel and Distributed Processing Symposium (IPDPS)*, Santa Fe, New Mexico.

[372] Lee, H.J., Robertson, J.P., and Fortes, J. (1997) Generalized Cannon's Algorithm for Parallel Matrix Multiplication, in *Proceedings of the ACM International Conference on Supercomputing (ICS)*, Vienna, Austria, pp. 44–51.

[373] van de Geijn, R.A. and Watts, J. (1995) SUMMA: Scalable universal matrix multiplication algorithm, *Tech. Rep.*, University of Texas at Austin. http://www.ncstrl.org:8900/ncstrl/servlet/search?formname=detail&id=oai%3Ancstrlh%3Autexas_cs%3AUTEXAS_CS%2F%2FCS-TR-95-13.

[374] Li, J., Ranka, S., and Sahni, S. (2012) Gpu matrix multiplication, in *Handbook on Multicore Computing* (ed. S. Rajasekaran), CRC Press.

[375] More, A. (2008) A Case Study on High Performance Matrix Multiplication. mm-matrixmultiplicationtool.googlecode.com/files/mm.pdf.

[376] Higham, N. (1990) Exploiting Fast Matrix Multiplication Within the Level 3 BLAS. *ACM Transactions on Mathematical Software*, **16** (4), 352–368.

[377] Goto, K. and Geijn, R. (2008) Anatomy of High-Performance Matrix Multiplication. *ACM Transactions on Mathematical Software*, **34** (3).

[378] Nishtala, R., Vuduc, R.W., Demmel, J.W., and Yelick, K.A. (2004) Performance modeling and analysis of cache blocking in sparse matrix vector multiply, *Tech. Rep. UCB/CSD-04-1335*, EECS Department, University of California, Berkeley. http://www.eecs.berkeley.edu/Pubs/TechRpts/2004/5535.html.

[379] Lam, M.D., Rothberg, E.E., and Wolf, M.E. (1991) The Cache Performance and Optimizations of Blocked Algorithms, in *Proceedings of the fourth ACM International Conference on Architectural*

Support for Programming Languages and Operating Systems (ASPLOS), Santa Clara, California, pp. 63–74.

[380] Rixner, S. (2002) *Stream Processor Architecture*, Kluwer Academic Publishers.

[381] Zhu, W., Cuvillo, J.d., and Gao, G.R. (2005) Performance Characteristics of OpenMP Language Constructs on a Many-core-on-a-chip Architecture, in *Proceedings of the 2005 and 2006 International Conference on OpenMP Shared Memory Parallel Programming (IWOMP'05/IWOMP'06)*, Eugene, Oregon.

[382] Garcia, E., Venetis, I., Khan, R., and Gao, G. (2010) Optimized Dense Matrix Multiplication on a Many-Core Architecture, in *Proceedings of the ACM Euro-Par conference on Parallel processing*.

[383] Safari, S., Fijany, A., Diotalevi, F., and Hosseini, F. (2012) Highly Parallel and Fast Implementation of Stereo Vision Algorithms on MIMD Many-Core Tilera Architecture, in *Proceedings of the IEEE Aerospace Conference*, Boston, Massachusetts, pp. 1–11.

[384] Munir, A., Gordon-Ross, A., and Ranka, S. (2012) Parallelized benchmark-driven performance evaluation of SMPs and tiled multi-core architectures for embedded systems, in *Proceedings of IEEE International Performance Computing and Communications Conference (IPCCC)*, Austin, Texas.

[385] Intel (2013) Intel's Teraflops Research Chip. http://download.intel.com/pressroom/kits/Teraflops/Teraflops_Research_Chip_Overview.pdf.

[386] Hoskote, Y., Vangal, S., Singh, A., Borkar, N., and Borkar, S. (2007) A 5-GHz Mesh Interconnect for a TeraFLOPS Processor. *IEEE Micro*, **27** (5), 51–61.

[387] TILERA (2010) Multicore Development Environment System Programmer's Guide, in *Tilera Official Documentation*.

[388] TILERA (2010) Multicore Development Environment Optimization Guide, in *Tilera Official Documentation*.

[389] ARM (2012) Cortex-A15 MPCore: Technical Reference Manual. http://infocenter.arm.com/help/topic/com.arm.doc.ddi0438e/DDI0438E_cortex_a15_r3p0_trm.pdf.

[390] Oracle (2013) Sun Studio 12: Fortran Programming Guide. http://docs.oracle.com/cd/E19205-01/819-5262/aeuic/index.html.

[391] Mahlke, S., Warter, N., Chen, W., Chang, P., and Hwu, W.m. (1991) The Effect of Compiler Optimizations on Available Parallelism in Scalar Programs, in *Proceedings of 20th Annual IEEE International Conference on Parallel Processing (ICPP)*, Austin, Texas.

Index

Modeling and Optimization of Parallel and Distributed Embedded Systems, First Edition.
Arslan Munir, Ann Gordon-Ross and Sanjay Ranka.
© 2016 John Wiley & Sons, Ltd. Published 2016 by John Wiley & Sons, Ltd.